Sea Nomads of Southeast Asia

Sea Nomads of Southeast Asia

From the Past to the Present

Edited by
Bérénice Bellina, Roger Blench and
Jean-Christophe Galipaud

NUS PRESS
SINGAPORE

© Bérénice Bellina, Roger Blench and Jean-Christophe Galipaud

Published by:

NUS Press
National University of Singapore
AS3-01-02, 3 Arts Link
Singapore 117569

Fax: (65) 6774-0652
E-mail: nusbooks@nus.edu.sg
Website: http://nuspress.nus.edu.sg

ISBN 978-981-325-125-0 (paper)

First edition 2021
Reprint 2022

All rights reserved. This book, or parts thereof, may not be reproduced in any form or by any means, electronic or mechanical, including photocopying, recording or any information storage and retrieval system now known or to be invented, without written permission from the Publisher.

National Library Board, Singapore Cataloguing in Publication Data

Name(s): Bellina, Bérénice, editor. | Blench, R., editor. | Galipaud, Jean-Christophe, editor.
Title: Sea nomads of Southeast Asia : from the past to the present / edited by Bérénice Bellina, Roger Blench and Jean-Christophe Galipaud.
Description: Singapore : NUS Press, [2021] | Includes index.
Identifier(s): OCN 1164382426 | ISBN 978-981-3251-25-0 (paperback)
Subject(s): LCSH: Nomads--Southeast Asia--History. | Bajau (Southeast Asian people)--History. | Seafaring life--Southeast Asia--History. | Southeast
Classification: DDC 305.9069180959--dc23

Cover image: Tukang Besi and Buton, 2011. Photograph courtesy of Lance Nolde.

Typeset by: Ogma Solutions Pvt Ltd
Printed by: Markono Print Media Pte Ltd

Contents

List of Illustrations		vii
Acknowledgements		xv

1. Sea Nomadism from the Past to the Present
   Bérénice Bellina, Roger Blench and Jean-Christophe Galipaud — 1

2. Communities of Practice in a Maritime World: Shared Shell Technology and Obsidian Exchange in the Lesser Sunda Islands, Wallacea
   Sue O'Connor, Christian Reepmeyer, Mahirta, Michelle C. Langley and Elena Piotto — 28

3. Late Pleistocene to Mid-Holocene Maritime Exchange Networks in Island Southeast Asia
   David Bulbeck — 51

4. Southeast Asian Early Maritime Silk Road Trading Polities' Hinterland and the Sea Nomads of the Isthmus of Kra
   Bérénice Bellina, Aude Favereau and Laure Dussubieux — 102

5. The Orang Suku Laut: Movement, Maps and Mapping
   Cynthia Chou — 142

6. The Linguistic Background to Southeast Asian Sea Nomadism
   Roger Blench — 157

7. A Genomic Perspective of the Origin and Dispersal of the Bajau Sea Nomads in Indonesia
   Pradiptajati Kusuma, Nicolas Brucato, Murray Cox, Chandra Nuraini, Thierry Letellier, Philippe Grangé, Herawati Sudoyo and François-Xavier Ricaut — 177

8. Ship Construction and Navigation in the Early South China Seas
   Roger Blench — 198

9. 'The Muscles and Sinews of the Kingdom': The Sama Bajau in Early Modern Eastern Indonesia
   Lance Nolde — 214

10. Nomads in the Interstices of History
    Jacques Ivanoff 236

11. Ethno-archaeological Evidence of 'Resilience' Underlying the Subsistence Strategy of the Maritime-adapted Inhabitants of the Andaman Sea
    Ayesha Pamela Rogers and Richard Engelhardt 254

12. Sea People, Coastal Territories and Cultural Interactions: Tetun Terik and Bunak in the Suai District on the South Coast of Timor-Leste
    Jean-Christophe Galipaud, Dominique Guillaud, Rebecca Kinaston and Brunna Crespi 282

13. The Bajau Diaspora: Origin and Transformation
    Charles Illouz and Chandra Nuraini 301

14. Maritime Diaspora and Creolisation: A Genealogy of the Sama Bajau in Insular Southeast Asia
    Nagatsu Kazufumi 323

List of Contributors 358
Index 364

List of Illustrations

Figures

1.1	Houseboats in Banjarmasin (southeast Borneo) carry trade goods up and down the rivers from the coast to the interior.	14
1.2	Hoklo (Hok-ló 福佬) are coastal fishing and trading groups along the coast of southeast China.	15
1.3	The Royal Palace of Gowa (South Sulawesi).	19
2.1	J-shaped fish hooks from A) Lene Hara Cave Timor and B) Tron Bon Lei B shelter Alor. The shaft in the Tron Bon Lei B hook has been extrapolated as shown by the dotted line.	31
2.2	Examples of marine shell beads recovered from Timor-Leste.	32
2.3	Example of the ethnographic items decorated with Nassarius shell beads from Timor-Leste and Papua New Guinea.	34
2.4	Stratigraphic section drawing from Tron Bon Lei Square B showing distribution of radiocarbon dates down the profile and position of fish hooks associated with burial in Layer 11.	38
2.5	Concentric rotating hooks from Tron Bon Lei B Layer 11, Alor.	39
2.6	Examples of marine shell beads recovered from Tron Bon Lei B shelter, Alor.	40
2.7	Total number of stone artefacts, obsidian artefacts and bone fragments by layer at Tron Bon Lei B (left). Distribution of obsidian artefacts from Tron Bon Lei B by stratigraphic layer shown as a percentage of all obsidian artefacts analysed by pXRF (right).	42
4.1	Some of the goods characterising the 'Late Prehistoric South China Sea style'.	109
4.2	Local and exogenous ceramics found on sites of the Isthmus of Kra.	112
4.3	Bracelet fragments (left), lapidary glass beads (right) from Khao Sek and Khao Sam Kaeo, early period.	118

viii *List of Illustrations*

4.4	Local Sa Huynh-Kalanay related types of ceramics found in the Kra Isthmus in the Thai-Malay Peninsula.	121
4.5	Glass material from Ban Na Hyan.	124
6.1	The Samalic languages.	160
6.2	Orang Laut settlement in Riau.	161
6.3	Schematic model of trade mosaic in the trans-Isthmian region.	171
7.1	Geographic distribution of Bajau communities in Island Southeast Asia (dark grey) and the Kendari population in south-western Sulawesi (star).	179
7.2	Phylogenetic analysis with fineSTRUCTURE showing that the Kendari Bajau (Sulawesi) cluster with populations from Sumba (eastern Indonesia), the Philippines and North Borneo.	186
7.3a	Multidimensional scaling (MDS) plot showing F_{ST} values between Indonesian and Malagasy populations based on mtDNA haplogroup frequencies. Western Indonesian populations are shown by triangles; eastern Indonesian populations are shown by circles.	187
7.3b	Multidimensional scaling (MDS) plot showing F_{ST} values between Indonesian and Malagasy populations based on Y-chromosome haplogroup frequencies. Western Indonesian populations are shown by triangles; eastern Indonesian populations are shown by circles.	188
7.4	TreeMix analysis on autosomal genome-wide SNP data showing migration nodes from Papua New Guinea Highlander and South Asian groups to the Kendari Bajau population, with migration weights of 13% and 9%, respectively.	191
7.5	Shared Identity-By-Descent (IBD) fragments between pairs of individuals in Southeast Asia, using nine filtering thresholds representing old connections (20 cM) to recent connections (80 cM).	192
8.1	Schematic evolution of boat types in the South China Seas.	201
8.2	High-keel boats of the Yami on Lanyu Island.	201
8.3	Toraja funerary monument, Waseput.	203
8.4	Sailing raft, Borobudur.	205
8.5	Coastal craft, Borobudur.	205
8.6	Large trading ship, Borobudur.	206
8.7	Siamese ship in Japanese scroll.	206
8.8	Star chart, Marshall Islands.	207

8.9	Astro-navigation chart of the South China Sea.	209
8.10	The Selden map of China and Southeast Asia, ca. 1620.	210
10.1	First photographed encounter between the Moken and British government officers in colonial Burma.	238
10.2	For the Moken, harpooning turtles symbolises harpooning women, an act of cultural anthropophagy, as well as their refusal of literacy, as script is believed to have been written on the shells of turtles, the consumption of which deprived them of this opportunity.	241
10.3	A Moken flotilla of more than 40 boats, representing about 40 nuclear families, hiding from the military underneath foliage.	242
10.4	Ritually consumed turtles are offered to the ancestors by sacred men. This symbolic act of social anthropophagy (as turtles represent women) enables the Moken to retain their collective memory of and refocus on their relationship with the world and the myths that determine the specificities of their social space.	243
10.5	Despite all the threats that could potentially lead to the disappearance of nomads and their traditions, the Moken are resilient and still know how to build the *kabang*, a marvel of naval technology, and know where to flee if oppression were to become unbearable.	247
10.6	The Moklen keep traces of past and external influences, illustrated here by an authentic version of the *Manora* (a well-known theatrical performance in Thailand) performed around a shamanic trance intended to invoke the spirits of the earth and to call upon the divinities to 'repair' what has been destroyed (here, the land devastated by tin mines).	248
10.7	Moken extracting tin from the river in Ko Ra (southern Thailand).	251
11.1	View of Chaw Lay Sea Gypsies of Phuket, southern Thailand; tying up a boat in the bay.	256
11.2	Cultural mapping of the Chaw Lay living within the Phuket area.	258
11.3	Detailed mapping of the elements of a maritime adapted settlement, including the contents and location of discard middens.	259

11.4	View of 'dermabrasion' of the area underneath a stilted house at Phap Pha—a base camp abandoned more than 100 years ago—to examine fine vertical and horizontal detail.	260
11.5	The landscape which the Chaw Lay inhabit is characterised by long stretches of sandy beach broken by estuarine areas of mangrove and mud-flat, rocky outcrops and off-shore island groups.	263
11.6	Access to and harvesting of shellfish is the essential feature of the traditional economic adaptation of all Chaw Lay communities. As a result, bulky and highly visible shell debris is the main archaeological marker of their use of a site.	265
11.7	Tools used by the Chaw Lay are characteristically few in number and easily movable, as they suit a lifestyle where numerous possessions would be a burden. Items are multi-purpose, light and easy to transport, made of wood, coconut, bamboo, stone and other materials easily available from the local environment.	267
11.8	Among the few functional specialists in a Chaw Lay community are those self-identified individuals who have knowledge of spirit matters and can lead ritual activities. They function at ceremonies such as Loy Rua, the biannual gathering with the ancestors immediately before and after annual dispersal at the end of the monsoon season.	268
11.9	Diagram illustrating the Adaptive Cycle which models the interaction and function of traits of resilience.	270
11.10	View of a base camp evolved to supply central points and rainy season gathering nodes, reflecting the conservation phase (k) of the Adaptive Cycle.	272
11.11	Extending the construction of houses into the intertidal by building on stilts in an attempt to increase carrying capacity at a base camp under stress.	273
11.12	A woman processing fish at Sapam on a village-wide secondary deposition of subsistence refuse.	275
11.13	View of Rawai illustrating the blanketing layer of occupation filling up what were formerly open, clean communal spaces.	275
11.14	Rawai base camp – a constricted settlement under severe stress, where over recent decades site space has become so spatially packed that there is no option for expansion, resulting in the blurring or loss of the characteristic Chaw Lay sense of differentiation of space and functional grouping.	279

13.1	Sama Bajau in all Austronesian languages.	303
13.2	Tree diagram of Sama Bajau languages.	304
14.1	An aerial view of Sapeken Island taken by satellite image.	308

Maps

1.1	Approximate distribution of sea nomad groups in Southeast Asia.	13
2.1	Location map showing Lesser Sunda Islands (lower map) and location of archaeological sites discussed in the text (upper map).	30
3.1	Southeast Asian sites with anatomically modern human habitation by 30,000 BP.	52
3.2	Southeast Asian sites with 17,000–15,000 BP human habitation, with and without ground-stone tools.	64
3.3	Southeast Asian sites with 30,000–28,000 BP human habitation, with and without rock art.	65
3.4	Southeast Asian sites with 14,000–11,000 BP human habitation, with and without bone tools.	67
3.5	Southeast Asian sites with 10,000–7500 BP human habitation, with and without bone points.	68
3.6	Southeast Asian sites with 12,000–10,000 BP human habitation, with and without shell fish hooks.	69
3.7	Southeast Asian sites with 12,000–10,000 BP human habitation, with and without shell ornaments.	70
3.8	Southeast Asian sites with 7000–5000 BP human habitation, with and without marine shell ornaments.	71
3.9	Southeast Asian sites with 9000–7000 BP human habitation, with and without marine shell adzes.	72
3.10	Southeast Asian sites with 9000–6000 BP human habitation, with and without marine shell scrapers.	73
3.11	Southeast Asian sites with 11,000–10,000 BP flexed and fractional burials.	74
3.12	Mortuary disposals in sites with 4000–3000 BP human habitation in Southeast Asia.	75
3.13	Southeast Asian sites with 11,000–9000 BP human habitation, with and without obsidian.	77
3.14	Southeast Asian sites with 8000–7000 BP human habitation, with and without translocated fauna.	78
3.15	Southeast Asian sites with 5000–4000 BP human habitation, with and without translocated fauna.	79

xii List of Illustrations

3.16	Lithics characterisation of sites with 6000–5000 BP human habitation in Southeast Asia.	82
3.17	Pottery characterisation of sites with 4500–3500 BP human habitation in Southeast Asia.	83
4.1	Sites surveyed and/or excavated by the French-Thai Archaeological Mission.	108
4.2	Maps showing the location of sites and types of industries analysed for each site.	113
5.1	Orang Suku Laut Map.	144
6.1	Linguistic subgroups of the Bajau.	168
10.1	Distribution of the main Austronesian sea nomad groups of the Malay Peninsula.	240
11.1	The main base camps discussed showing their locations in the network, evolving towards entrophy through a series of seasonal fluctuations in size and population density.	277
12.1	The area of Suai on the southwest coast of East Timor with localisation of names cited in the chapter.	283
13.1	Overview of locations of Bajau groups over their dispersal area.	306
13.2	Wuring, a Bajau village near Maumere in Flores.	308
14.1	Southeast Asian Maritime World and the two Focused Regions.	324
14.2	Selected sites of intensive and extensive fieldworks the author conducted from 1994 to 2015.	326
14.3	Distribution of the Bajau population in 2000. Population by province in the Philippines, by *daerah* (district) in Malaysia, and by *kabupaten* (regency) in Indonesia.	329
14.4	Distribution of the Bajau.	330
14.5	Distribution and cluster of the Bajau in Indonesia, 2000.	334
14.6	Sapeken and the maritime networks of the Bajau.	348

Tables

3.1	Numerical identification of sources used for the distribution maps.	55
3.2	Sources by distribution map.	57
3.3	Summary of Liang Bua Sector IV identifications (number of individual specimens) relevant to this contribution, from Van den Burgh et al. (2009: Fig. 2, Appendix A). Note: Deepest porcupine, civet and macaque remains all occur in spit 16 or spit 17.	63

3.4	Southeast Asia osseous artefacts 16,000 BP and older.	66
3.5	Fourth millennium BP ISEA dates for domesticates also found in Lapita sites.	80
3.6	Summary of proposed Pleistocene maritime exchange networks (approximate chronological order).	85
3.7	Summary of proposed Holocene maritime exchange networks (approximate chronological order).	86
3.8	Correspondences between mtDNA haplogroup dispersals and archaeologically attested maritime interaction axes.	86
4.1	Sites and analysed material by the authors in the Isthmus of Kra.	114
6.1	Linguistic affiliation of sea nomad populations.	158
6.2	Sailfish in Moken/Moklen.	164
6.3	Big-eye scad in Moken/Moklen.	164
6.4	Lake/ocean in Moklen.	164
6.5	Gill net in Moken/Moklen.	165
6.6	Hearth on boat in Moken/Moklen.	165
6.7	Fishtrap in Moken/Moklen.	165
6.8	Bracelet in Moken/Moklen.	165
6.9	Vezo fish names and their corresponding Malayopolynesian etymologies.	166
7.1	Frequency of Bajau haplogroups for mtDNA (left) and the Y chromosome (right).	184
7.2	Admixture sources showing the percentage of admixture for each population of interest with dates in generations and years before present (YBP). Bootstrap 95% confidence intervals are given in parentheses.	194
14.1	Population change in Kangean and Sapeken (1896–2000).	350

Acknowledgements

The editors would like to acknowledge the referees who took time to comment on each chapter on what were sometimes complex issues as well as the two anonymous referees who reviewed the complete manuscript. Their comments and suggestions were greatly valued.

The editors also wish to thank the following departments for supporting the publication of this book: the CNRS department Prétech (UMR7055, Nanterre) and the IRD/Muséum National d'Histoire Naturelle UMR PALOC (UMR208). At the UMR208, we wish to thank Mrs Laurence Billault for drawing and redrawing the maps used in this book.

1

Sea Nomadism from the Past to the Present

Bérénice Bellina, Roger Blench and Jean-Christophe Galipaud

INTRODUCTION

Today along the coasts and off the islands of Southeast Asia are populations who have acquired or retained a marine nomadic lifestyle, a way of living that can be traced back into prehistory. Nomadism as a term covers a large array of situations and ways of mobility (and control of mobility). As a category it is opposed to sedentism or sedentariness, but in fact the two qualities should be seen as complementary. Terrestrial nomadism is common in Island Southeast Asia (ISEA), among the Orang Asli in Malaysia, and the Suku Anak Dalam in Sumatra, for example, and in most cases describes populations with a history of foraging activities. They have a complementary relationship with the sedentary world, from where they often claim to come. Sea nomads also share a complementary, but less easily defined, relationship with sedentism. The majority of these marine nomads are not landless people and they recognise themselves within a land- and seascape, a territory consisting of small islets, sandbanks or mangroves where they operate and where they bury their dead (cf. McNiven 2003). The sea is for them a resource landscape as well as a 'spiritual landscape' visited and controlled by spirits:

> For the sea people in general, the seascape remains the source of knowledge for survival in their environment and a living history of their past. Each of the islands provides not only shelter and sustenance, but represents a group specific storehouse of information for present and future generations. Inhabiting an island claimed by an Orang Laut group, or preventing that group from visiting its islands, is tantamount to denying the Orang Laut access to their ancestors, their history, and their source of knowledge. These form the building blocks of their ethnic identity and distinguish them from others (Andaya 2008: 200).

This territory must be considered at different scales, from the island that a group traditionally exploits or relies upon, to the regional seascape of connected families and at an even larger scale with the sea territory known to long-distance sailors.

Historically, sea nomads generated great wealth by providing maritime commodities to facilitate trade, forming a naval force to secure and protect sea lanes that were vital to the development of maritime Southeast Asia, and serving as 'integrating information-carriers' connecting subsidiary chiefs with a developing peasantry.

These roles were paramount to the larger-scale implementation of increasingly centralised polities that shaped and developed maritime Southeast Asia (Benjamin 1986: 16; Hoogervorst 2012). Paradoxically, as modern states emerged, the sea nomads became progressively marginalised and impoverished, as happened on the mainland also with the forest dwellers. It has reached the point that they are now defined as being on the margins of 'otherness' by the culturally and politically dominant populations of the region (Chou 2006: 2; 2010: 40–58; Illouz et al. this volume).

From guardians of the sea-lanes to pirates, merchants or explorers, sea nomads have embraced a multiplicity of roles during their history. It is therefore important to keep in mind the diversity and flexibility of this sea nomad world.

THE SUPPOSED 'INVISIBILITY' OF SEA NOMADS

Sea nomads have been part of the economic and political landscape of Southeast Asia for millennia. Several overviews have been published, as well as ethnographic and historical monographs on individual groups. These include White (1922), Sather (1997, 1999), Andaya (1975), Chou (2003, 2010), Benjamin and Chou (2002) and others. But so far there have been few attempts to trace the evolution of sea nomadism in the archaeological record or to make use of modern genetics in understanding these trajectories. There has been a certain bias against these communities because of their supposed 'archaeological invisibility'. For archaeologists, it was taken for granted that the sea nomads left no traces; that they were invisible (Sopher 1977). Only a few discussions raised the possibility that they played a role in the past and offered to identify their traces (Engelhardt and Roger 1998; Chen 2002; Bulbeck 2008; Noury and Galipaud 2011; Bellina et al. 2012). Part of the subtext of this book is to suggest this is far from the situation. As such it is the first book providing historical, archaeological and genetic data in the attempt to explore sea nomads' *longue-durée* historical trajectory as well as their role in regional historical developments. Several essays in this book explore means to trace sea nomads in archaeological assemblages and other historical sources, and to uncover what may have been their contribution in regional socio-political landscapes, past and present.

Books have so far dealt with only one of each main group; none so far has brought them all together. Many books deal with later historical data and only very few go beyond the medieval period. The present book moves from the prehistoric period before the emergence of the earliest trade-related polities in the South China Sea to the near present. As highlighted by both Bulbeck and

O'Connor et al. (this volume), as early as the late Pleistocene and early Holocene, inter-island exchange networks and the movements of scarce materials confirm the importance of mastering of the sea.

The other aspect of this evolution is environmentally determined and relates to a specialisation in exploiting specific ecological niches. The availability of scarce resources potentially valued as luxury goods may have played a determining role in laying the ground for an exchange network to supply these goods. In the recent past, sea nomads were key players in developing such networks in ISEA. There is compelling evidence that there were also sea and river nomads in adjacent areas, such as coastal China (Chen 2002; Blench this volume: Chapter 6), and rather more speculative evidence of activity in the Ryukyus and the Bay of Bengal (Mahdi 2016); those must inevitably have also been involved in the trans-regional networks.

The focus of previous books has been mainly anthropological, sociological and linguistic or dealing with policy issues. Hence there was space for a *longue-durée* approach to sea nomadism and its links with the political and economic landscapes with which it was intertwined. This chimes well with a refocusing of historical narratives, to look beyond centralised societies and written scripts.

The origin of the chapters in this book partly stems from two panels convened by the editors. The most recent was entitled 'Towards an ethno-archaeological framework for sea nomads in Southeast Asia?' and was convened by B. Bellina, R.M. Blench and J.-C. Galipaud at the 15th International Conference of the European Association of Southeast Asian Archaeologists in July 2015.[1] The earlier one was entitled 'What recent archaeological, anthropological, historical and linguistic data tell us about the role of Southeast Asian populations in Indian Ocean maritime transfers' organised by B. Bellina, R.M. Blench and F.-X. Ricaut at the Indo-Pacific Prehistoric Archaeology Congress in Siem Reap in January 2014. To ensure that the final book contained a more complete conspectus of issues concerning sea nomads, and to include unpublished data from recent excavations and archaeological reconstructions, several new chapters were commissioned. The editors would like to thank the referees who took time to comment on what were sometimes complex issues.

A MULTIFACETED DEFINITION OF 'SEA NOMADS'

There is no simple definition of sea nomadism. This is because sea nomads have embraced a multiplicity of roles during their history and were always flexible, developing relationships with regional powers of different nature. It is also difficult to provide a definition of sea nomadism because a great diversity of economic and political organisations characterise them. Sea nomadism is a characteristic lifeway in island and coastal Southeast Asia today. Each group's territory encompasses well-defined zones of land and sea which is exploited and where rituals are performed (Chou this volume; Ivanoff this volume). Sea nomads have developed an adaptation that has been qualified as 'semi-sedentary' (Hoogervorst 2012). They differ from fishermen who are sedentary and whose economy relies exclusively on sea exploitation. Sea nomadism can be defined by the suite of subsistence strategies of populations based on the exchange of patchy maritime resources, staples and trade goods. It exists because these resources can only be exploited by fishermen willing to move and conduct opportunistic trade; moving goods between isolated ports and along non-standard routes, often by smuggling or at least extra-legal activities. Because sea nomads spend a larger proportion of their time at sea, they have developed a rudimentary material culture (Hoogervorst 2012).

Other aspects of sea nomadism which should be emphasised are diversity, routes, subsistence strategies, trade goods and modes of interaction with land peoples and with larger trading networks. Sea nomads were not necessarily traders of subsistence goods; much of their trade may have been in luxuries, such as feathers and other items, which do not preserve in the archaeological record. They are characterised by a mastery of the sea and complex mental mapping of maritime routes (Chou this volume). They exploit well-defined areas of their 'seascape' for subsistence and for trade with sedentary communities (Chou 2010; Andaya 2008: 180). Because of the very diverse resources sea nomads exploit for trade as well as their interactions with regional states, it has been argued that 'boat nomadism' should be considered in the light of its particular historical and ecological contexts (Sather 2006), with the caveat that the level of information on the different Southeast Asian sea nomads' past activities is highly uneven. As an illustration, the Urak Lawoi and Moken/Moklen—located in the northern part of the Strait of Malacca—have been less studied than the Orang Laut further south and the Sama Bajau further east in ISEA. Regarding the Orang Laut, this is because they were actively socially and economically involved with Malay trading polities and thus appear in literary sources as well as modern ethnographies (Andaya 2008). Nowadays, sea nomads are all marginalised people treated with disdain by both the traditional states, the colonial-era authorities (Skeat and Blagden 1906) and modern nation-states (Illouz and Nuraini this volume; Chou this volume), and in recent times, much wasted energy has been put into making them settle.[2]

Diversity also characterises sea nomad group size, economic importance and socio-political organisation. These differences vary between the major groups of Moken, Orang Laut and Sama Bajau but also within them such as in the case of the Bajau (Sandbukt 1983, 1984; Nolde this volume; Chou 2010). (Please note: Over time Bajau has been spelled in various ways and different spellings including Bajauw and Bajo are used interchangeably to respect older sources.) Nowadays, Bajau live on scattered shoreline and island settlements, often in the vicinity of the agrarian groups they interact with. In the past, they were one of the different specialised groups that composed the historical Sulu State of the Philippines. The Sulu State structure was pyramidal, based on personal allegiances and alliances which aimed to control trade. Whilst some stayed mostly at sea, constituting seamen who applied their skills to navigation, boat construction, craft activities (smiths, potters) or inter-island trade, others were involved in raids against passing ships and coastal settlements for the benefit of a port-entrepôt leader. The Sama sea nomads lived in bands and provided their partners—port-entrepôt leaders—sea products for trade, such as sea cucumbers, pearls and dry fish. They moved with their family on board and exchanged with other families when anchoring at the same moorage site seasonally (Sather 2006). Originally, the Sama would have been a sea-oriented group with a knowledge of the land who experienced a dissimilation process when trade on the Maritime Silk Road increased from the tenth century. They then moved and settled in different zones: some established ports, others settled in bays in the mangroves and others on land. Some would have established networks of trading colonies on the coastlines of the islands and river mouths to control the local river trade, like at the mouth of the Agusan River in Mindanao. In these places, they would have married local land-based wives; some stayed there, others returned to Sulu, establishing the trading community of Jolo which became a major trading centre (Sather 2006: 260–1). Amongst the Sama, sea nomad communities emerged out of a common coastal population, originally shoreline foragers, who would have become 'increasingly specialised and trade-dependent with the rise of maritime states, a development to which their presence itself almost certainly contributed' (Sather 2006: 263).

As for the Orang Laut, their tasks in relation to the state were varied and contributed to shaping subgroups. Some were engaged in the port-entrepôt ruler's navy, where they would fight with spears provided to them and serve as rowers. They could also patrol and guard sea lanes for the land-based leader they decided to be affiliated to, activities labelled as piracy by Dutch observers; arguably, they were privateers. The Orang Laut were also engaged in economic activities on land. Their horticultural activities were concerned with sago, coconut trees and pepper; they collected specific woods like eagle and lacquer-wood, ebony, rattan and construction timbers. They could also be involved in craft activities such as gold panning, working iron to produce weapons for the ruler, making pots, weaving palm-leaves mats for roofing and sails, producing coconut oil, etc. (Pelras 1972; Sather 2006; Andaya 2008; Nolde this volume). The earliest mention of sea nomads is in Arab and Chinese sources predating the sixteenth century, and they are described as cruel pirates who dominated the maritime world (Ferrand 1913).

Their mastery of the sea and their capacity to integrate widely-dispersed communities via a complex network of exchange and communication is indeed an essential trait characterising sea nomads. Blench (this volume: Chapter 8) discusses our understanding of the maritime archaeology of the South China

Sea with particular reference to ship construction techniques, the growth of navigational expertise and development of cartography. Anthropologists and historians have thus considered that sea nomads have been long-standing political and cultural actors in the South China Sea. But since when? How far back can we go?

The forms of sea nomadism present in Southeast Asia today are almost certainly linked with the rise of trading states or trading polities (Benjamin 2002; Bellina et al. this volume). This is confirmed by the linguistic evidence, which links sea nomads to well-established languages such as Malay, and not marginal forager languages (Blench this volume: Chapter 6). Sea nomads depend on such states as buyers for fish and other aquatic resources as well as carrying their trade goods from one region to another. The first evidence for early trading polities in the maritime Southeast Asia qualifying for incipient city-state is around 400 BCE (Bellina, ed. 2017; Bellina 2017, 2018). The rise of Srivijaya (seventh century CE) presumably provided much greater stimulus. In this way the nomads were able to acquire key technologies, including iron tools and improved boat-building techniques to extend the range and diversity of their commercial activities. The earliest references show that there was already a political and economic association between the Orang Laut and a Malay trading polity during Srivijayan's thalassocracy (seventh–thirteenth century CE) (Chou 2010; Hall 2011; Andaya 2008). Although evidence is tenuous, Andaya (2008: 192) also believes that mutually profitable relationships are attested in the 'Hikayat Merong Mahawangsa' (or 'Kedah Annals', a Malay literary account of the history of Kedah) between the Urak Lawoi and the leaders of the different port-entrepôts of the Kedah region (northwest part of Malaysia, bordering Thailand and encompassing the Langkawi archipelago). He supposes that mutually beneficial cooperation between the Moken and peninsular trading polities further north may have existed as well. This cooperation may have involved promoting the use of trans-peninsular routes, at the exit of some of which port-polities were located. The 'Sejarah Melayu' annals describe how the Orang Laut and the refugee Prince of Palembang Sri Tri Buana, also known as Parameswara, contributed to the founding of Malacca in about 1400 CE. The Orang Laut, located at the mouth of River Bertam (Malacca River), suggested to Prince Parameswara that he establish an entrepôt there because it would secure a market for the products they collected and legitimise their activities. In the sixteenth century book by Portuguese merchant and diplomat Tomé Pires, *Suma Oriental*, the Orang Laut are recorded as recommending this location because they found it suitable for a large Malayu town where the Malay could exploit big areas for rice fields, gardens and cattle/livestock. The clear contrast between their respective lifeways and economic specialisations made the relations between trading rulers and sea nomads mutually beneficial. These clear-cut identity boundaries probably also helped to maintain freedom and independence (Hall 2011; Andaya 2008: 198; Chou 2010).

What about the more distant past, where there are no written sources? For earlier periods, we have little idea of sea nomadism's antiquity or how its societies can be characterised archaeologically. Very few archaeologists have tackled these issues, but some types of evidence could point towards sea nomads' existence. Three main stages of development can be identified and are outlined below. They are further discussed in the volume.

1. *Palaeolithic evidence of movement between islands.* Hominims may have crossed to Luzon as early as 700,000 BP, while modern humans reached Australia by 65,000 BP—part of which included sea transit. Evidence for movement between islands in the Ryukyus goes back to 35,000 BP (Fujita et al. 2016) and in the Talaud Islands 20,000 BP. There is archaeological and genetic evidence for long-distance circulations between the mainland and ISEA in the early Holocene (Bulbeck 2008, this volume; Soares et al. 2016; Brandão et al. 2016).

2. *Maritime expansion associated with the Austronesian expansion, the so-called 'fisher-foragers'* (Bulbeck 2008). For example, the Lapita expansion has been tentatively attributed to sea nomads (Galipaud 2015; Galipaud et al. this volume). For Sather, coastal adaptation along with the development of navigational skills and inter-island trade were critical elements to Austronesian-speakers' expansion after 4000 BCE (Sather 2006). In ISEA, Bellwood (2007) associates the Austronesian speakers' diaspora with farmers' migrations. On the other hand, many researchers now argue that Austronesian speakers were actually opportunistic maritime forager-traders who acquired cultural traits from amongst the various coastal groups they encountered. Many researchers also believe that these forager-traders were then responsible for disseminating cultural similarities between various groups and that these common traits were later thought to be typical of Austronesian speakers (Blench 2012). The social motivations for these long-distance interactions favouring alliances and shared ideational themes—materialised in decorated pottery styles and shell and obsidian goods—is also emphasised. Instead of a homogenised process of neolithisation, archaeologists now portray multiple histories reflecting the diversity of peoples who practised heterogeneous strategies that cannot simply be categorised under either forager or farmer. These economically heterogeneous groups seemed to have developed interdependent interactions early on (Bulbeck 2008; Solheim, Bulbeck and Flavel 2006; Oppenheimer and Richards 2001; Spriggs 2011; Higham et al. 2011). Amongst archaeologists, it is this ability to connect groups and to disseminate cultural traits, a role more closely associated with the Austronesian forager-traders, which is most often highlighted. Chen (2002) believed that many coastal shell midden sites on low terraces alongside estuaries in the coastal regions of southeast China and

Taiwan—at Ch'in-Kuei-Shan (Jinguishan) (6000–4000 BCE) and at P'u-pien (Pubian) (2500–1500 BCE)—were remains left by coastal Yue, which he interpreted as being ancient Austronesian sea nomads. All were small and briefly occupied, possibly seasonally, and revealed shell gathering and fishing practices but no agriculture. Chen thought that the Yue would have helped diffuse material culture amongst these coastal communities. Another coastal site, Bukit Tengkorak in Sabah, occupied during the first millennium BCE by foragers was associated with the precursors of sea nomads. This association was made because these foragers combined long-distance exchange with marine, river and coastal forest exploitation (Bellwood 1989) and they produced the portable pottery hearths traditionally linked to the maritime Sama Bajau (Sather 2006).

3. *Early trade.* The circulation of nephrite in particular argues that trade, especially between the mainland and western ISEA, was well-established by 3000 BP (Hung et al. 2007). This is due to extensive sea voyages probably carried out by small, highly mobile groups, whose travels and cross-cultural interactions can be followed through some ceramics (Favereau and Bellina in press). In eastern ISEA, Galipaud considers that ancient, highly mobile groups involved in inter-island exchanges could represent sea nomadism; they would be responsible for bringing social complexity, diffusing cultural models, techniques and material culture such as Dong Son drums during the early centuries CE (Galipaud 2015). In the upper Thai-Malay Peninsula decorated pots found in caves offshore, and showing parallels to pots in the Philippines, were interpreted as possible funerary deposits associated with mobile groups moving between the Philippines and the peninsula (Bellina, Epinal and Favereau 2012). From the fourth century BCE, Favereau (2015) observed further evidence of centuries of cross-fertilising exchanges between the Isthmus of Kra and the Philippines. In parallel, some nephrite from Taiwan—and possibly from other sources in the Philippines—was being imported as raw material into various places in Vietnam and the Isthmus of Kra (Hung et al. 2007). Once there, local workshops manufactured nephrite and other imported stones in a pan-regional style (Bellina 2014). However, there is as yet no evidence for direct Taiwanese involvement in South China Sea networks. This could suggest that raw material was collected and exchanged by mobile intermediaries, possibly from the Philippines (Favereau and Bellina in press). Referring to a slightly later period in the Malaysian part of the peninsula, Bulbeck (2004, 2014) suggested that the offshore islands of Pulau Kelumpang near the mouth of Kuala Selinsing may correspond to a camp of sea nomads during the early centuries CE. Leong interpreted the site as a 'feeder point'—one of the local supply centres serving South Kedah entrepôts (1990). At Kuala

Selinsing, groups were living in the vicinity of major historical port-cities, sharing some of their material culture with the latter, in particular prestige items such as stone and glass beads. However, Bulbeck observes that they seem not to have adopted Indic religious traits. He interprets these non-Indianised maritime groups of Pulau Kelumpang as the precursors of 'sea gypsies'. They were producing stone beads (rock crystal and cornelian), which signalled this community's prosperity and its likely involvement in trade, at least insofar as they were able to obtain the raw material for what was small scale production (Bellina 2001). However, they depended on mainland populations for rice and meat. For the historical period, written sources account for the close association between some of these groups and trading polities whilst remaining on their periphery (Andaya 2008).

To summarise, sea nomads were probably originally coastal forager-traders, characterised by their adaptive capacities. They were thus enmeshed in symbiotic specialised networks. In the context of increasing trade and the rise of trading states, they may have taken advantage of their knowledge of the sea and the connections they established through their networks to become intermediaries facilitating trade over long-distances. They would have been key cultural agents facilitating diffusion amongst those various groups.

An area that is so far little explored is the link between the forest hunter-gatherers and sea nomads. Andaya (2008) refers to river estuaries where Orang Laut and Orang Asli met for exchanges. Chou (this volume) notes that the sea nomads Orang Suku Laut sailed along rivers of eastern Sumatra to the South China Sea. Other interactions along rivers are relevant in the case of the sandalwood trade (Galipaud et al. this volume). Interactions in the forest for products collected or exploited inland are also relevant (Bellina et al. this volume).

SEEKING ARCHAEOLOGICAL HORIZONS

One motivation for this book was to suggest a trajectory for sea nomads' origin, to try to find the means to detect them within broad historical processes and in particular to determine their input into models of the rise and persistence of complex polities. Of course, these aims sounded ambitious, if not a pure fantasy, to many archaeologists. It is true that archaeologists aiming to unravel sea nomads' past activities face several major obstacles. The first one arises from the fact that sea nomad lifeways as known today develop a rudimentary material culture which does not preserve. However, if sea nomads today are poor and marginalised by nation-states, this was not the case in the past. Many chapters in this book demonstrate that they were economically and politically-valued partners of regional trading polities. Also, as mentioned before, some sea nomads took part in craft activities such as ceramics and metal working and were therefore actively involved in producing artefacts for archaeologists to recover. Evidently, to relate those craft activities to sea nomads securely is difficult. In particular, it might be hard to distinguish a sea nomad involved in craft activities from an itinerant artisan. Nonetheless, even if it may appear daunting, it is argued here that it is possible to detect them through minute regional archaeological work. Only such work can potentially provide discrete hints to their possible presence or action (Bellina et al. this volume). Another difficulty comes from the absence of ethno-historical work focused on ancient sea nomads' material culture that would inform us, for instance, on their material culture associated with their everyday life and funerary practices (excluding boat techniques). Engelhardt and Rogers' ethnoarchaeological project (1998) was the first attempt to establish an archaeological framework to analyse sea nomads' settlement remains based upon those left by Chaw Lay, along and off the southwestern coast of Thailand. Those sites were used temporarily as camps or longer-term as base settlements until the exploitation of the econiche was exhausted. The two researchers show how restricted archaeological remains can be and emphasise the great flexibility those groups developed to exploit their environment (Rogers and Engelhardt this volume). Though in contact with land-based groups and nation-states, those sea nomads are today economically marginalised and their activities produce no wealth. Their capacity to obtain or produce archaeologically more visible material culture that would preserve better such as metal, stone or ceramic artefacts, may thus be more limited. As noted above, nowadays this remark is also valid for many other sea nomads. This observation shows some of the limits of ethnoarchaeological research conducted to characterise the means to detect sea nomads' past activities and lifeways.

Bearing in mind those restrictions, and without excluding other sources of information (linguistic, historic, genetic, ethnographic), how can we track sea nomads in the archaeological record?

If sea nomadism is to be detected archaeologically, it can only be by combining different categories of evidence: (1) material, (2) locational/spatial and (3) physical/biological.

The first category is the material one. A difficulty arises from the fact that, apart from the emblematic Bajau portable stove, it is taken for granted that there is apparently no distinctive sea nomad material culture. As suggested in the chapter by Bellina et al., this was probably not the case. They may have shared much of their material culture with their immediate land-based neighbours as well as with those coming from the foreign traders they dealt with. A combination of marine-related material culture is associated with valued goods imported or locally-made (potentially for them) such as some of the ceramics in the Isthmus of Kra (Bellina et al. this volume). These early sea nomads of the Isthmus of Kra were exhibiting their extensive connections and promoted their intermediary role on those networks for which they became key actors. The movement of rare materials through extensive networks may also reflect the activities of sea nomads (Bellina et al. this volume). To be able to differentiate sea nomads' material culture from their land-based neighbours thus implies a minute region-focused archaeological programme. Only such work can provide data to draw the necessary 'complex, multi-ethnic social landscapes' (Junker and Smith 2017) where sea nomads can be detected in the archaeological assemblage (Bellina et al. this volume).

Nomadic sea life relies heavily on the mastering of boat construction technologies and navigation and specific artefacts might be associated with these technologies (tools, portable stoves). Sea nomads used a wide variety of trading ships, but these are rarely characterised in the monographs of social scientists. Valuable monographs on coastal shipping, such as Holbrook and Suriya (2000), who described the types of boats seen along the coast of Thailand, can provide clues to older methods of ship construction.

Similarly, the architecture of coastal dwellings—houses on piles along the coasts or on exposed reef flats, known ethnographically among the Bajau for instance—may be also attributed to sea nomads. Galipaud suggests that coastal or island cemeteries with marine-oriented grave goods such as shells or coral and a diversity of urn burials scattered throughout the region could in some instances attest to a regionally shared nomadic treatment of the dead. These similarities may be the results of sea nomads' interactions (Galipaud et al. 2016).

The second indicator is geographical. Sea nomads adapted to a maritime environment tend to settle their seasonal camps on offshore islands or reefs in rich coastal environments (estuaries, mangroves) and we can seek older settlements in these zones. Their presence at estuaries can be detected due to their role as intermediaries in the upstream–downstream exchanges and between those and port-polities as shown in the Isthmus of Kra (Bellina et al. this volume).

A third category is biological evidence. One could think of specific pathologies associated with a life at sea and a marine-dominated diet, as in the case of the Teouma cemetery in Vanuatu (Buckley et al. 2014). Genetics could provide one line of evidence of detection in the future, as demonstrated with Kusuma et al.'s research (this volume).

The search for sea nomadic evidence in archaeological contexts will require focused excavations on coastal and offshore islands in Southeast Asia. Much more thought should be dedicated to methodological issues and to try to detect sea nomadism from the past. Attempts described above and in this book only represent preliminary ones.

WHERE ARE SEA NOMADS CURRENTLY FOUND?

DISTRIBUTION

Sea nomads correspond extremely well to pastoralists in land contexts, except that pastoralists own their mobile resource (i.e., livestock). Sea nomads exist in an ambiguous relationship with more settled land and maritime populations, both feared and depended upon. As far as we know, there are three areas in coastal and ISEA where sea nomads are active today: the Mergui archipelago, west off Thailand/Myanmar, where the Moken/Moklen/Urak Lawoi live; between Riau and Sumatra, where the Orang Laut operate; and in the large area between northeast Borneo, the Sulu Archipelago and northwest Papua, where the various Samal populations are found. However, there are scattered reports of Orang Laut in other parts of Indonesia, as might be expected. The chapter by Nagatsu plots out the communities listed in censuses as Samal or related peoples.

Map 1.1 shows the approximate distribution of these language groups, with the caveat that highly mobile people can touch many islands outside their normal zone of migration.

ARE EXISTING POPULATIONS RELATED?

Are these populations related? The languages they speak belong to different sub-groups of Austronesian. The Moken/Moklen languages are related to each other and ultimately to the Malayic group. The Riau Orang Laut/Orang Sawang speak at least two dialects of Malay (Sekak and Bintan Orang Laut Malay). The Samal speak a cluster of related languages, interestingly not related to the Philippines group of Austronesian, but to Borneo languages. There are Samalic languages, Yakan and Abaknon, spoken by farming populations in the Philippines, presumably sea nomads who have returned to the land. This suggests these are local adaptations to a foraging lifestyle and not relics of some ancient nomadic culture spread over the region.

It was suggested earlier that the Austronesian expansion was characterised by forager-traders, rather than agriculturalist seeking new land to cultivate. Could its whole early phase be interpreted as underlain by subsistence strategy typical of sea nomads? This is probably an exaggeration; the early Austronesians were quite diverse—with traders, pirates and migrant colonists—who rapidly moved inland when they encountered new territories, such as the Philippines or Borneo. The lack of diverse languages among today's sea nomads argues strongly that the present pattern is quite recent and does not reflect this early diaspora.

OTHER TYPES OF AQUATIC NOMADISM IN SOUTHEAST ASIA

A question which is not fully answered is whether we should regard the highly mobile trading peoples operating on the southeast China sea coast as nomads. Peoples such as the Tanka definitely do not follow the fish, but some still live on their boats and pursue a trading lifestyle up to the present. There are also river nomads, operating on the great inland rivers of Borneo. At Banjarmasin, many of these permanent houseboats carry trade goods up and down the river. Apart from sea nomads, very large islands such as Borneo create opportunities for a

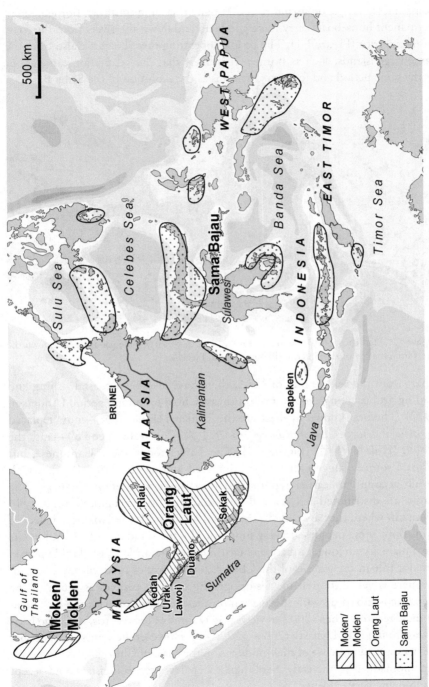

Map 1.1 Approximate distribution of sea nomad groups in Southeast Asia.

comparable lifestyle on inland rivers. At Banjarmasin in southeast Borneo, many permanent houseboats carry trade goods up and down the rivers from the coast to the interior (Figure 1.1). The peoples operating these boats are also from the same large islands, such as Borneo. It is likely that this adaptation came about at the same period and for similar reasons as the evolution of the Sama Bajau.

Figure 1.1 Houseboats in Banjarmasin (southeast Borneo) carry trade goods up and down the rivers from the coast to the interior (Photo credit: R. Blench).

Apart from the sea peoples of ISEA, there have also been coastal fishing and trading groups along the coast of southeast China for a long period (Anderson 1972). The best known of these are the Tanka (Danjiā 蜑家)—now replaced in official sources by *shuǐshàng rén* 水上人 ('on-water people')—and the Hoklo (Hok-ló 福佬) (Figure 1.2). The Tanka today speak Cantonese, but historic sources suggest that they originated among the Mien (Yao), which would account for earlier reports that they spoke a different language. The Tanka are distributed across a wide area and are also a recognised minority in Vietnam, where they are called *Dàn*. The Hoklo speak the Hokkien dialect of Min. Both these peoples are very numerous by the standards of ISEA, but the great majority no longer practise a maritime lifestyle. Indeed, the Hoklo played a major role in the genesis of the Chinese population of modern-day Taiwan.

There is very little reliable historiography of these peoples as much of the literature is mixed up with speculation on their relationship with the Ba Yue in Chinese records. Chen (2002) reviews briefly some of the records, which go back at least to the Han Dynasty (206 BCE–220 CE). However, he wants to argue that the widespread presence of shell-middens on the coast of China allows us to push back nomadism to the early Neolithic, a view few archaeologists would accept without ancillary evidence.

Figure 1.2 Hoklo (Hok-ló 福佬) are coastal fishing and trading groups along the coast of southeast China (Photo credit: R. Blench).

Their languages do not provide significant clues today. Nonetheless, a minority still operates from houseboats, and are still fully engaged in a maritime lifestyle in the modern era. Modernised fisheries have largely displaced their role as fishermen, but trading is clearly an effective substitute. To what extent their network was entirely separate from the ISEA sea peoples remains an open question. However, the inhabiting of Taiwan is clearly associated with thriving cross-straits traffic in raw materials and an energetic regional network, so it would not be unreasonable to push back this type of subsistence to an early period (Blench in press).

In the southwest of Madagascar, the Vezo people are semi-nomadic fisherpeople who have a lifestyle similar to many Bajau groups. They set off for long-term circuits of the reefs, setting up camp on sandbanks, living on boats and exchanging fish for staples. Interestingly, their fishing terms are quite different from standard Malagasy. Is it possible these represent a distinct migration from the Bajau area who have brought the subsistence strategy and then have switched to Malagasy (like other parallel migrations to Madagascar)?

REVIEW OF SOURCES

WHEN WAS THE EXISTENCE OF SEA NOMADS FIRST NOTED?

The earliest Portuguese sources refer to the Celates or Orang Selat. These peoples were sea nomads in the Strait of Malacca and the Riau-Lingga Archipelago, and are included in the *Suma Oriental* of Tomé Pires, based on observations in 1512–15 (Pires 1944). The earliest European sources for sea nomads are those in Spanish which focus on the Sulu Seas.[3] The *Historia de las islas de Mindanao, Joló y sus adyacentes* (Combés 1667) is a description of the culture and ethnography of the Sulu area by the Jesuit priest, Francisco Combés (1620–65). Barros

(1496–1570) did not visit the region directly but reviewed the historical and oral sources available for the early sixteenth century (Barros 1553). The missionary François Valentijn (travelling between 1724–26) compiled Portuguese reports on the eastern Bajau at the end of the seventeenth century. The English captain and explorer Thomas Forrest (1780, 1792) describes the Bajau at the close of the eighteenth century.

From the early nineteenth to the early twentieth century, the study of sea nomads was mostly carried out by colonial administrators. Findlayson and Raffles (1826) described the sea nomads as a 'lower class of Malays'. Skeat and Blagden (1906) compiled a two-volume compendium of Malayan ethnography, where they describe the Orang Suku Laut as primitive forest nomads of the interior of Batam Island and the 'Orang Laut, Sambimba' as possessing no boats and fearing water. This seems somewhat surprising, but in the light of research by Ivanoff (this volume) it is possible to see where this idea arises. The account by White (1922) is far more sympathetic and provides a valuable ethnographic picture of the Moken at this period.

BRIEF OVERVIEW OF RESEARCH ON SEA NOMADS

Earlier descriptions of sea nomads tended to be marginalising or patronising and not based on much direct enquiry. Modern sea nomad research can probably be said to begin with Sopher's (1965) literature review that merges all sea nomad communities into a single entity, which is far from the actual situation. Later accounts, which tend to emerge from fieldwork-oriented anthropology, describe individual communities in much greater detail and focus on their specificity. Sather (1997) is predominantly an account of the Sabah community with whom he worked, but his final section begins by splitting the sea nomads into different groups and considers the questions this book has tried to address, namely: the origin of sea nomadism, its definition, whether all maritime exchange systems can somehow be subsumed under this label and other questions. The publications of Jacques Ivanoff (1997, this volume) focus on social and ritual systems, but also discuss technical factors, such as boat construction, in more detail. Cynthia Chou (2003, 2010) has focused on the Orang Laut, particularly their social life, and their understanding of territory and borders. Historians have taken a rather different approach, focusing on the abundant documentation of the last few centuries. Andaya (1975) includes extensive material on the sea nomad culture in his historical study of Johor, Malaysia. Nolde (2014, this volume) has explored the history of the Bajau of eastern Indonesia.

SUMMARIES OF CONTRIBUTIONS

The ordering of the chapters in this book is broadly chronological. We begin with the early evidence for inter-island exchange, which may go back as far as 40,000 BP.

O'Connor and her co-authors, drawing on field data from their research in East Timor and the nearby island of Alor, look at evidence for shared cultural practices during the Pleistocene and the early Holocene. They discuss the likelihood that such practices were maintained by maritime interaction and exchange of materials, objects or ideas, and review archaeological evidence for the use of marine resources and inter-island transport of scarce items such as obsidian. In Timor and the nearby island of Alor, beads of *Oliva* spp. and beads and pendants of *Nautilus* sp. shells occur in most of the coastal Timor-Leste sites, from the earliest human presence around 40,000 years ago to the present. Obsidian flakes from an unknown source are also present at most sites. Some of these items have been directly dated to the terminal Pleistocene/early Holocene. In all these sites, shell ornaments and hooks retain traces of red ochre. Such shared craft production in different islands suggests to the authors shared personal adornments and/or craft production that were remarkably stable through time and could reflect social or family networks. The existence of such networks at an early stage in the prehistory of those islands is also attested by the presence of obsidian in most of these early sites.

The study of long-distance exchange networks within ISEA and between ISEA and Mainland Southeast Asia (MSEA), leads David Bulbeck to infer a long history of maritime exchange in ISEA, which intensified during the Neolithic. His analysis goes back to the late Pleistocene/early Holocene period during which distant connections were established, followed by localised networks within Wallacea. During the early to mid-Holocene, the network expanded in ISEA to include the Sunda shelf islands, MSEA and Taiwan, where Neolithic material culture was well-established. These exchanges allowed the introduction of Neolithic traits from MSEA into western ISEA and from Taiwan into eastern ISEA. Bulbeck relates this to the origins of the Bajau, although this book takes the view these particular groups are of later origin.

Based on research conducted by the French-Thai Archaeological Mission in the Upper Thai-Malay Peninsula, Bellina and colleagues raise the possibility that in the Kra Isthmus, socio-economic specialisation probably began with late Neolithic long-distance exchange, and accelerated from the fourth to third century BCE, with the rise of the Maritime Silk Road. There is archaeological evidence for increasing social, economic and cultural differentiation and cooperation between the different groups participating in local and long-distance networks. Soon after the emergence of port-cities, some coastal groups displayed behaviour that could be later identified amongst historical sea nomads. Settled at river mouths, they may have played an intermediary role between upstream groups and regional early port-of-trade and long-distance traders. They developed a common material culture distinct both from the people established in ports and those inland. This research is the first to suggest that sea nomads emerged with the first Maritime Silk Road polities and their presence can be traced archaeologically: ancient sea nomads developed a material culture that can be characterised through a sustained regional archaeological programme.

Cynthia Chou discusses the Orang Suku Laut representation of maritime cultural space. The sea is a world occupied and inhabited by the Orang Suku Laut who make it their own territory. These capacities, associated with their movement patterns, have played a key role in linking groups and in shaping regional cultures in ISEA.

The chapter by Roger Blench covers the languages spoken by the sea nomads. It is noteworthy that they fall into three groups, all Austronesian: the Samalic languages; Moken/Moklen, which is related to Malayic; and the Orang Laut cluster, which is closely related to Malay. None of the languages are in any way archaic and none have been shown to retain subsistence vocabulary from presumed substrate populations. This is an important element in the broader argument that the sea nomads as seen today are related to the growth of the major trading empires, not a relic of the more ancient fisher-forager systems. Blench also raises the possibility that the Vezo of Madagascar are transformed migrants from ISEA.

The Bajau represent the largest sea nomad community in ISEA, located in several coastal communities in Indonesia (east Borneo, Sulawesi, the Lesser Sunda Islands and the Maluku Islands), Philippines and Malaysia. However, their genetic history is unknown and deserves to be investigated to better understand their genetic structure, origin, admixture with regional groups, and their broader biological influence across ISEA. In their study, Kusuma and colleagues summarise genetic analyses performed on 27 Bajau individuals from the Kendari region of south-eastern Sulawesi. They studied maternal (mitochondrial DNA) and paternal (Y chromosome) lineages, and genome-wide data of this sea nomad group. These data were compared to a large dataset of over 2,000 individuals using a combination of lineage-specific, SNP-based and haplotype-based analyses. They show the complexity of the genomic profile of the Kendari Bajau community and provide some hypotheses regarding its origin, pattern of admixture and potential dispersal route.

The second chapter by Blench explores the sources of evidence for the growth of shipbuilding techniques in the South China Seas, as well as the development of navigational techniques and early cartography. Maritime archaeology remains a major primary source and new finds of all sizes of ship are reported yearly. Recent finds, often packed with trade goods, provide important clues to the nature of inter-island trade. Textual and iconographic sources are also important, although the richest material, in Chinese languages, all refers to a comparatively late period. The recently republished title by Boxer provides a wealth of new material on Spanish explorations in the region. Finally, the chapter draws attention to early maps, in particular the remarkable Selden map (ca. 1620), which may be the first surviving complete regional map.

The chapter by Nolde focuses on the early modern period, in particular the role of the Bajau in South Sulawesi, where they played an important role in mediating the interminable conflicts between the numerous small polities. Nolde argues the Bajau played a major role in the rise of Gowa-Talloq in the sixteenth and seventeenth centuries and the expansion of its trade networks to Eastern Indonesia. It was conquered by the Dutch East India Company (VOC) and its Bugis allies in 1669 and declined massively in subsequent years. However, in parallel, the Papuq Sama Bajau polity arose, led apparently by a charismatic leader in South Sulawesi, and persisted for nearly a century until the settlements on Flores were destroyed. Nolde focuses on the *Lemo bajo lontaraq* manuscript, a unique example of a historical chronicle relating to sea nomads. The usual pattern is for sea nomads to form unstructured, acephalous groups with little in the way of social hierarchy, but Nolde reminds us that occasionally opposing trends can be observed.

Figure 1.3 The Royal Palace of Gowa (South Sulawesi) (Photo credit: R. Blench).

Ivanoff relates the Moken to what Scott (2009) has defined as a 'Zomia', a libertarian group living on the periphery of nation-states but interacting with them. He thus argues that the ethnography of the Moken can provide an insight into the 'historical' corpus both of the dominant group (nation-state) and themselves. This knowledge can help archaeologists set up event sequences, to define groups' identity and relations with historical sites. The Moken have an in-depth knowledge of their environment and territory. Their management of past remains and their interaction in a history emerging out of their rituals and oral sources can help clarify how such societies can contribute to our understanding of past cultural behaviours.

Engelhardt and Rogers interpret aspects of the maritime adapted resilience of the strandloping Chaw Lay[4]—the 'sea gypsies' of Phuket on the Andaman coast of Thailand—to address questions such as: What would a pattern of cultural resilience look like in archaeological deposits in sand and mud that characterise insular and coastal sites? What is the archaeologically retrievable evidence of tangible adaptations to ensure resilience and intangible acts which bind the community and pass on knowledge and values in an 'equitable' and sustainable way?

Galipaud and colleagues develop an archaeo-geographical perspective on the recent history of coastal communities in eastern Indonesia. They put forward hypotheses on the potential impact and consequences of sea nomad influence on local cultures in and beyond the inter-island trading networks over the last millennium. Their work draws on recent research in the southern part of East Timor in the Tetun-Terik linguistic area, around Suai. The contemporary proximity and mutual cultural assimilation between Austronesian-speaking Tetun-Terik and non-Austronesian Bunak, possibly originating in the ancient honey and sandalwood trade in the Wehali Kingdom, attest to interactions in historical times. They explore complex interchanges between maritime newcomers and inland settlers, initiated by trade and exchange over time, leading to a hierarchical society that has retained both languages but adapted their cultural content. Such an example of a successful cultural integration leading to new coastal polities could exemplify the processes of integration of newcomers over time in the islands and give clues to the potential role of sea nomads in the rapid spread of Austronesian-speaking populations in ISEA some 3,000 years ago.

Using information from long-term ethnographic research on the Sama Bajau in the Indonesian archipelago, Illouz and Nuraini describe the characteristics and specificity of the Bajau diaspora. Their approach combines linguistics and history. They discuss the position of the language within the Malayo-Polynesian languages, geographical research to describe the settlement patterns of today's Bajau communities and history to discuss two alternative scenarios of dispersal from two potential 'proto-Bajau' homelands. From this synthesis emerges an outline of Sama Bajau movements over time, which highlights the navigational skills and adaptability of these groups. Coming from the Barito River area in southeast Borneo, the Bajau migrated to the Sulu Archipelago around 800 CE, under pressure from the Srivijaya Empire. Partly assimilated to the Tausug, who gradually dominated the Sulu Archipelago from 1300 CE onwards, they exploited maritime resources and became heavily involved in maritime trade. After the introduction of Islam and the restructuring of trade in the region, some groups returned to Borneo and Sulawesi while others migrated further south and east, and later to the Lesser Sunda Islands, in search of marine species. In late colonial times their involvement in trading became greatly reduced and since the 1970s governments have been encouraging them to settle.

The study by Nagatsu has two parts: a geographical study of the distribution of sea nomad communities in eastern Indonesia and some more detailed, personal case studies based on the island of Sapeken, which illuminate the question of ethnicity. The detailed maps accompanying this chapter are compiled from many years' fieldwork and provide a fairly comprehensive overview of an elusive phenomenon—the size and location of Bajau communities—from the southern Philippines to the Aru Islands, south of New Guinea. The island of Sapeken, described in the second part of the chapter, retains its function as a trade entrepot, and more remarkably, the dominant language is Bajau, not Indonesian, even though the island is multi-ethnic. Nagatsu argues that because of the rich trading opportunities, Mandar, Javanese and even Chinese found it to their advantage to switch language and even identity. The case studies present some narratives illustrating this process. Sapeken is a remarkable example of a community where the Bajau identity has triumphed, rather than being marginalised, as in most other places in ISEA.

CONCLUDING REMARKS AND FUTURE PROSPECTS

This book helps to place the emergence of sea nomadism within a long (pre)historic sequence. This sequence began with the late Pleistocene-early Holocene networks that witnessed the development of a community of culture (Bulbeck this volume; O'Connor this volume). It was then followed from the mid-late Holocene by the Austronesian expansion, associated with opportunistic maritime forager-traders who acquired cultural traits from their land-based neighbours (Bulbeck 2008). The turning of the first millennium BCE/CE witnessed the co-emergence of Maritime Silk Road early trading polities and sea nomads, as described by historical sources (Bellina et al. this volume). From then on, sea nomads were key to trading polities; facilitating trade, locating new sources of goods for trade, exploring and guarding maritime routes and possibly new locations for settlements (Galipaud et al. this volume; Nolde this volume). Forming an autonomous part of trading polities' hinterland, sea nomads were probably more often crucial for the rise, maintenance, and perhaps, the decline of those polities than is suspected on the basis of written sources. Today, sea nomads are marginalised by nation-states and 'treated with disdain' by their land-based neighbours (Chou 2010).

This book shows for the first time that multi-disciplinary research provides the means to detect sea nomads' input into major (pre)historic processes. Such an initiative has been called for by an authoritative historian on the subject, B.W. Andaya (2019), and this is the archaeological response after five years of intense discussion and deliberation (Andaya 2019). As described in the case of the Bajau, their polycentric structure (Nolde this volume) and their 'accommodative ethnic identity' (Nagatsu this volume) made sea nomads especially flexible, reactive and efficient partners on maritime networks. Given these characteristics, there is still a much research, both empirical (minute regional archaeological programmes) and methodological, to be carried out to fully characterise them archaeologically (Bellina et al. this volume) and to track their social evolution and the extent of their movements. Finally, the research presented in this book provides avenues of evidence that should be pursued and enriched to keep investigating sea nomads in other places in Southeast Asia where their presence is not suspected (as the Isthmus of Kra early nomads example shows) or associated with many other polities. A large part of Southeast Asian history may need to be rewritten to take sea nomads into account. We hope this book will encourage archaeologists, historians, ethnographers, geographers, linguists and geneticists to follow up these methodological reflections and to work together to provide a history for the ancestors of a large proportion of current Southeast Asian populations.

NOTES

[1] See: http://www.nomadit.co.uk/euraseaa/euraseaa15/panels.php5?PanelID=3542.

[2] The parallel with land-based pastoralism is apparent here.

[3] This section adapted from an online review by Cynthia Chou: <https://kyotoreview.org/book-review/research-trends-on-southeast-asian-sea-nomads/>.

[4] The Chaw Lay have paradoxically benefited from the COVID-19 pandemic, as tourism and construction are currently on hold in their fishing grounds, with the consequence that catches are much increased.

REFERENCES

Andaya, Barbara Watson. 2019. 'Recording the Past of "Peoples without History": Southeast Asia's Sea Nomads.' *Asian Review* 32 (1): 5–33.

Andaya, Leonard Y. 1975. *The Kingdom of Johor, 1641–1728*. Kuala Lumpur: Oxford University Press.

———. 2008. 'Leaves of the Same Tree: Trade and Ethnicity in the Straits of Melaka.' In *The Orang Laut and the Malay*, ed. L. Andaya, 173–201. Honolulu: University of Hawai'i Press.

Anderson, Eugene Newton. 1972. *Essays on South China's Boat People*. Taipei: Orient Cultural Service.

Barros, João de. 1553. *Da Asia. Dos Feitos que os Portuguezes fizeram no descubrimento e conquista dos mares e terras do Oriente. Segunda Década* [Of Asia. The deeds of the Portuguese in the discovery and conquest of the seas and lands of the Orient. Second Decade]. Lisbon: Germão Galherde.

Bellina, B. 2001. 'Témoinages archéologiques d'échanges entre l'Inde et l'Asie du Sud-Est: morphologie, morphométrie et techniques de fabrication des perles en agate et en cornaline.' Thèse de Doctorat, Sorbonne Nouvelle, Paris.

———. 2014. 'Maritime Silk Roads' Ornament Industries: Socio-Political Practices and Cultural Transfers in the South China Sea.' *Cambridge Archaeological Journal* 24 (3): 345–77.

———. 2017. 'Khao Sam Kaeo: A Cosmopolitan Port-city or City-state in the South China Sea?' In *Khao Sam Kaeo: An Early Port-city Between the Indian Ocean and the South China Sea*, ed. B. Bellina, 621–61. Mémoires Archéologiques 28. Paris: Ecole française d'Extrême-Orient.

———. 2018. 'Development of Maritime Trade Polities and Diffusion of the "South China Sea Sphere of Interaction Pan-Regional Culture": The Khao Sek Excavations and Industries' Studies Contribution.' *Archaeological Research in Asia* 13: 1–12.

Bellina, Bérénice, ed. 2017. *Khao Sam Kaeo: An Early Port-city Between the Indian Ocean and the South China Sea*. Mémoires Archéologiques 28. Paris: Ecole française d'Extrême-Orient.

Bellina, Bérénice, Epinal, Guillaume, and Favereau, Aude. 2012. 'Caractérisation préliminaire des poteries marqueurs d'échanges en mer de Chine méridionale à la fin de la préhistoire.' *Archipel* 84: 7–33.

Bellina, Bérénice, Aude Favereau, and Laure Dussubieux. This volume. 'Southeast Asian Early Maritime Silk Road Trading Polities' Hinterland and the Sea Nomads of the Isthmus of Kra.' In *Sea Nomads of Southeast Asia: From the Past to the Present*, ed. B. Bellina, R. Blench, and J.-C. Galipaud. Singapore: NUS Press.

Bellwood, P. 1989. 'Archaeological investigation at Bukit Tengkorak and Segurong, southeastern Sabah.' *Bulletin of the Indo-Pacific Prehistory Association* 9: 122–62.

———. 2007. *Prehistory of the Indo-Malaysian archipelago*. ANU E Press, The Australian National University.

Benjamin, Geoffrey. 1986. 'Achievements and Gaps in Orang Asli Research.' *Akademika* 35 (1): 7–46.

Benjamin, Geoffrey and Cynthia Chou, eds. 2002. *Tribal Communities in the Malay World: Historical, Cultural and Social Perspectives*. Leiden and Singapore: International Institute for Asian Studies and Institute of Southeast Asian Studies.

Blench, Roger Marsh. 2012. 'Almost Everything You Believed about the Austronesians isn't True.' In *Crossing Borders: Selected Papers from the 13th International Conference of the European Association of Southeast Asian Archaeologists*, Volume 1, ed. M.L. Tjoa-Bonatz, A. Reinecke, and D. Bonatz, 128–48. Singapore: NUS Press.

———. This volume. 'The Linguistic Background to Southeast Asian Sea Nomadism.' In *Sea Nomads of Southeast Asia: From the Past to the Present*, ed. B. Bellina, R. Blench, and J.-C. Galipaud. Singapore: NUS Press.

———. In press. 'Restructuring our Understanding of the South China Sea Interaction Sphere: The Evidence from Multiple Disciplines.' In *Taiwan Maritime Landscapes from Neolithic to Early Modern Times: Cross-Regional Perspectives*, ed. P. Calanca and F. Muyard. Taiwan: Academica Sinica.

Brandão, A. et al. 2016. 'Quantifying the Legacy of the Chinese Neolithic on the Maternal Genetic Heritage of Taiwan and Island Southeast Asia.' *Human Genetics* 135 (4): 363–76.

Bulbeck, D. 2004. 'Indigenous traditions and exogenous influences in the early history of Peninsular Malaysia.' In *Southeast Asia: From Prehistory to History*, ed. I. Glover and P. Bellwood, 314–36. London: RoutledgeCurzon.

———. 2008. 'An Integrated Perspective on the Austronesian Diaspora. The Switch from Cereal Agriculture to Maritime Foraging in the Colonisation of Island Southeast Asia.' *Australian Archaeology* 67: 31–51.

———. 2014. 'The Chronometric Holocene Archaeological Record of the Southern Thai-Malay Peninsula.' *International Journal of Asia-Pacific Studies* 10 (1): 111–62.

———. This volume. 'Late Pleistocene to Mid-Holocene Maritime Exchange Networks in Island Southeast Asia.' In *Sea Nomads of Southeast Asia: From the Past to the Present*, ed. B. Bellina, R. Blench, and J.-C. Galipaud. Singapore: NUS Press.

Buckley, Hallie et al. 2014. 'Scurvy in a tropical paradise? Evaluating the possibility of infant and adult vitamin C deficiency in the Lapita skeletal sample of Teouma, Vanuatu, Pacific islands.' *International Journal of Paleopathology* 5: 72–85.

Chen, Jonas Chung-yu. 2002. 'Sea Nomads in Prehistory on the Southeast Coast of China.' *Bulletin of the Indo-Pacific Prehistory Association* 22: 51–4.

Chou, Cynthia. 2003. *Indonesian Sea Nomads: Money, Magic, and Fear of the Orang Suku Laut*. Leiden, London and New York: International Institute for Asian Studies and RoutledgeCurzon.

———. 2006. 'Research Trends on Southeast Asian Sea-nomads.' In *States, People, and Borders in Southeast Asia*. Kyoto Review of Southeast Asia, issue 7. Kyoto University: Center for Southeast Asian Studies.

———. 2010. *The Orang Suku Laut of Riau, Indonesia: The Inalienable Gift of Territory*. The Modern Anthropology of Southeast Asia. London; New York: Routledge.

———. This volume. 'The Orang Suku Laut: Movement, Maps and Mapping.' In *Sea Nomads of Southeast Asia: From the Past to the Present*, ed. B. Bellina, R. Blench, and J.-C. Galipaud. Singapore: NUS Press.

Combes, Francisco. [1667] 1897. *Historia de las Islas de Mindanao, Joló y sus Adyacentes*. [History of the Mindanao Islands, Jolo and Nearby]. Madrid: Retana W.E. and P. Pastells.

Engelhardt, Richard A. and Pamela R. Rogers. 1998. 'The Ethno-archaeology of Southeast Asian Coastal Sites: A Model for the Deposition and Recovery of Archaeological Material.' *Journal of the Siam Society* 86: 131–59.

Favereau, Aude. 2015. *Interactions et Modalités des Échanges en Mer de Chine Méridionale (500 Avant Notre Ère – 200 de Notre Ère): Approche Technologique des Assemblages Céramiques*. Muséum national d'histoire Naturelle.

Favereau, Aude and Bérénice Bellina. In press. 'Philippines and the Late Prehistoric South China Sea Sphere of Exchange: Linking Taiwan and the Upper Thai-Malay Peninsula.' In *Taiwan Maritime Landscapes from Neolithic to Early Modern Times*, ed. P. Calanca, Liu Yi-ch'ang, and F. Muyard. Paris, Taipei: EFEO, Institute of History and Philology, Academia Sinica.

Ferrand, Gabriel. 1913. *Relations de Voyages et Textes* Géographiques *Arabes, Persans et Turks Relatifs à l'Extrême-Orient du VIIIe Siècles*. 2 vols. Paris: Ernst Leroux.

Forrest, Thomas. 1780. *A Voyage to New Guinea, and the Moluccas from Balambangan*. 2nd ed. London: G. Scott.

———. 1792. *A Voyage from Calcutta to the Mergui Archipelago, Lying on the East Side of the Bay of Bengal*. London: G. Scott.

Fujita, Masaki, Shinji Yamasaki, Chiaki Katagiri, Itsuro Oshiro, Katsuhiro Sano, Taiji Kurozumi, Hiroshi Sugawara, Dai Kunikita, Hiroyuki Matsuzaki, Akihiro Kano, Tomoyo Okumura, Tomomi Sone, Hikaru Fujita, Satoshi Kobayashi, Toru Naruse, Megumi Kondo, Shuji Matsu'ura, Gen Suwa, and Yousuke Kaifu. 2016. 'Advanced Maritime Adaptation in the Western Pacific Coastal Region Extends Back to 35,000–30,000 Years Before Present.' *Proceedings of the National Academy of Sciences* 113: 11184–9.

Galipaud, Jean-Christophe. 2015. 'Réseaux Néolithiques, Nomades Marins et Marchands dans les Petites Îles de la Sonde.' *Archipel* 90: 49–74.

Galipaud Jean-Christophe et al. 2016. 'The Pain Haka burial ground on Flores: Indonesian evidence for a shared Neolithic belief system in Southeast Asia.' *Antiquity* 90 (354): 1505–21.

Galipaud, Jean-Christophe, Dominique Guillaud, Rebecca Kinaston, and Brunna Crespi. This volume. 'Sea People, Coastal Territories and Cultural Interactions: Tetun Terik and Bunak in the Suai District on the South Coast of Timor-Leste.' In *Sea Nomads of Southeast Asia: From the Past to the Present*, ed. B. Bellina, R. Blench, and J.-C. Galipaud. Singapore: NUS Press.

Hall, Kennneth. 2011. *A History of Early Southeast Asia: Maritime Trade and Societal Development c. 100–1500*. Lanham, MD: Rowman & Littlefield Publishers.

Higham, Charles F.W., Xie Guangmao, and Lin Qiang. 2011. 'The Prehistory of a Friction Zone: First Farmers and Hunters-gatherers in Southeast Asia.' *Antiquity* 11 (85): 529–43.

Holbrook, Manob R.D. and Manob Suriya. 2000. *Blue Book of Coastal Vessels Thailand*. Bangkok: White Lotus Press.

Hoogervorst, Thomas G. 2012. 'Ethnicity and Aquatic Lifestyles: Exploring Southeast Asia's Past and Present Seascapes.' *Water History* 4 (3): 245–65.

Hsiao-Chun Hung, Yoshi Iizuka, Peter Bellwood, Nguyen Kim Dung, Bérénice Bellina, Praon Silapanth, Bong Dizon, Ray Santiago, Ipoi Datan, and John Manton. 2007. 'Ancient Jades Map 3000 Years of Prehistoric Exchange in Southeast Asia.' *Proceedings of the National Academy of Sciences* 104 (50): 19745–50.

Illouz, Charles and Chandra Nuraini. This volume. 'The Bajau Diaspora: Origin and Transformation.' In *Sea Nomads of Southeast Asia: From the Past to the Present*, ed. B. Bellina, R. Blench, and J.-C. Galipaud. Singapore: NUS Press.

Ivanoff, Jacques. 1997. *Moken: Sea Gypsies of the Andaman Sea Post-war Chronicles*. Bangkok: White Lotus.

———. This volume. 'Nomads in the Interstices of History.' In *Sea Nomads of Southeast Asia: From the Past to the Present*, ed. B. Bellina, R. Blench, and J.-C. Galipaud. Singapore: NUS Press.

Junker, L. and Smith, L.M. 2017. 'Farmer and Forager Interactions in Southeast Asia.' In *Handbook of East and Southeast Asian Archaeology*, ed. J. Habu, P.V. Lape, and J.W. Olsen, 619–32. New York: Springer.

Kinaston, Rebecca and Hallie Buckley. 2013. 'The Stable Isotope Analysis of Prehistoric Human Diet in the Pacific Islands with an Emphasis on Lapita.' In *Pacific Archaeology: Documenting the Past 50,000 Years*, ed. G. Summerhayes and H. Buckley, 91–107. Otago: University of Otago Press.

Kusuma, Pradiptajati, Nicolas Brucato, Murray Cox, Chandra Nuraini, Thierry Letellier, Philippe Grangé, Herawati Sudoyo, and François-Xavier Ricaut. This volume. 'A Genomic Perspective of the Origin and Dispersal of the Bajaw Sea Nomads in Indonesia.' In *Sea Nomads of Southeast Asia: From the Past to the Present*, ed. B. Bellina, R. Blench, and J.-C. Galipaud. Singapore: NUS Press.

Leong, Sau Heng. 1990. *Collecting centres, feeder points and entrepots in the Malay Peninsula, c. 1000 B.C.–A.D. 1400*. National University of Singapore.

McNiven, Ian. 2003. 'Saltwater People: Spiritscapes, Maritime Rituals and the Archaeology of Australian Indigenous Seascapes.' *World Archaeology* 35 (3): 329–49.

Mahdi, Waruno. 2016. 'Origins of Southeast Asian Shipping and Maritime Communication across the Indian Ocean.' In *Early Exchange between Africa and the Wider Indian Ocean World*, ed. G. Campbell, 25–49. Cham, Switzerland: Palgrave Macmillan.

Nagatsu, Kazufumi. This volume. 'Maritime Diaspora and Creolisation: A Genealogy of the Sama-Bajaw in Insular Southeast Asia.' In *Sea Nomads of Southeast Asia: From the Past to the Present*, ed. B. Bellina, R. Blench, and J.-C. Galipaud. Singapore: NUS Press.

Nolde, Lance. 2014. 'Changing Tides: A History of Power, Trade, and Transformation among the Sama Bajo Sea Peoples of Eastern Indonesia in the Early Modern Period.' PhD dissertation. University of Hawai'i at Manoa.

———. This volume. '"The Muscles and Sinews of the Kingdom": The Sama Bajo in Early Modern Eastern Indonesia.' In *Sea Nomads of Southeast Asia: From the Past to the Present*, ed. B. Bellina, R. Blench, and J.-C. Galipaud. Singapore: NUS Press.

Noury, Arnaud and Jean-Christophe Galipaud. 2011. *Les Lapita, nomades du Pacifique*. Marseille: IRD Editions.

O'Connor, Sue, Christian Reepmeyer, Mahirta, Michelle C. Langley, and Elena Piotto. This volume. 'Communities of Practice in a Maritime World: Shared Shell Technology and Obsidian Exchange in the Lesser Sunda Islands, Wallacea.' In *Sea Nomads of Southeast Asia: From the Past to the Present*, ed. B. Bellina, R. Blench, and J.-C. Galipaud. Singapore: NUS Press.

Oppenheimer, Stephen and Martin Richards. 2001. 'Fast Trains, Slow Boats, and the Ancestry of the Polynesian Islanders.' *Science Progress* 84 (3): 157–81.

Pelras, Christian. 1972. 'Notes sur Quelques Populations Aquatiques de l'Archipel Nusantarien.' *Archipel* 3: 133–68.

Pires, Tomé. 1944. *Suma Oriental: An Account of the East from the Red Sea to Japan, Written in Melaka 1512–1515*. 2 vols. Translated by A. Cortesão. London: Hakluyt Society.

Rogers, Ayesha P. and Richard Engelhardt. This volume. 'Ethno-archaeological Evidence of "Resilience" Underlying the Subsistence Strategy of the Maritime-adapted Inhabitants of the Andaman Sea.' In *Sea Nomads of Southeast Asia: From the Past to the Present*, ed. B. Bellina, R. Blench, and J.-C. Galipaud. Singapore: NUS Press.

Reepmeyer, Christian, Matthew Spriggs, Anggraeni, Peter Lape, Lee Neri, Wilfredo P. Ronquillo, Truman Simanjuntak, Glen Summerhayes, Daud Tanudirjo, and Archie Tiauzoni. 2011. 'Obsidian Sources and Distribution Systems in Island Southeast Asia: New Results and Implications from Geochemical Research using LA-ICPMS.' *Journal of Archaeological Science* 38 (11): 2995–3005.

Sandbukt, Øyvind. 1983. 'Duano Littoral Fishing: Adaptive Strategies within a Money Economy.' PhD thesis. University of Cambridge.

———. 1984. 'The Sea Nomads of Southeast Asia: New Perspectives on Ancient Traditions.' *Annual Newsletter of the Scandinavian Institute of Asian Studies* 17: 3–13.

Sather, Clifford A. 1997. *The Bajau Laut: Adaptation, History, and Fate in a Maritime Fishing Society of South-eastern Sabah*. Kuala Lumpur: Oxford University Press.

———. 1999. *The Orang Laut*. Academy of Social Sciences (AKASS) Heritage Paper Series, Occasional Paper No. 5. Penang: Academy of Social Sciences.

———. 2006. 'Sea Nomads and Rainforest Hunter-gatherers: Foraging Adaptations in the Indo-Malaysian Archipelago.' In *The Austronesians: Historical and Comparative Perspectives*, ed. P. Bellwood, J.J. Fox, and D. Tryon, 245–83. Canberra: ANU E Press.

Scott, James C. 2009. *The Art of Not Being Governed: An Anarchist History of Upland Southeast Asia*. New Haven: Yale University Press.

Skeat, Walter William and Charles Otto Blagden. 1906. *Pagan Races of the Malay Peninsula*. 2 vols. London: Macmillan & Co. Ltd.

Soares, Pedro A., Jean Alain Trejaut, Teresa Rito, Bruno Cavadas, Catherine Hill, Ken Eng, and Maru Mormina. 2016. 'Resolving the Ancestry of Austronesian-speaking Populations.' *Human Genetics* 135: 309–26.

Solheim, Wilhelm G., David Bulbeck, and Ambika Flavel. 2006. *Archaeology and Culture in Southeast Asia: Unraveling the Nusantao*. Diliman, Quezon City: University of the Philippines Press.

Sopher, David. 1977. *The Sea Nomads: A Study of the Maritime Boat People of Southeast Asia*. Singapore: National Museum Publication.

Spriggs, Matthew. 2011. 'Archaeology and the Austronesian Expansion: Where Are We Now?' *Antiquity* 85 (328): 510–28.

Valentijn, François. 1724–26. *Oud en Nieuw Oost-Indiën, Vervattendeeen Naaukeurigeen Uitvoerige Verhandelinge van Nederlands Mogenthevd in die Gewesten in vyfdeelen* [Old and New East Indies. Containing an Accurate and Detailed Record of Progress of Dutch Potential in those Regions]. Dordrecht-Amsterdam.

White, Walter Grainge. 1922. *The Sea Gypsies of Malaya: An Account of the Nomadic Mawken People of the Mergui Archipelago with a Description of their Ways of Living, Customs, Habits, Boats, Occupations*. London: Seeley, Service & Co.

2

Communities of Practice in a Maritime World: Shared Shell Technology and Obsidian Exchange in the Lesser Sunda Islands, Wallacea

Sue O'Connor, Christian Reepmeyer, Mahirta, Michelle C. Langley and Elena Piotto

INTRODUCTION

Shell ornaments and tools have been reported in both Mainland and Island Southeast Asia (MSEA; ISEA). They are two of the hallmarks of the Austronesian diaspora throughout ISEA and into the Pacific, and have thus been thought to have a predominantly Neolithic temporal distribution (Bellwood 1997). While some detailed studies have been undertaken of shell artefacts in Lapita assemblages (Szabó 2010), there have been few comparable studies of the range of ISEA shell artefacts and manufacturing methods outside of Sarawak, the Philippines and Timor-Leste. Shell beads have occasionally been found in pre-ceramic contexts in Indonesia (Mahirta 2003; Mahirta et al. 2004) but until recently there has been no direct dating to establish whether they were the same age as the dated levels of deposit surrounding them or displaced from higher in the profile, as often happens with small objects in loose sandy deposits (O'Connor et al. 2002).

Fish hooks are a significant category of shell technology in the ISEA and wider Pacific region. The majority of prehistoric fish hooks from around the world derive from Holocene contexts owing to the drowning of Pleistocene coastal sites by post glacial sea-level rise. Currently, the oldest known hooks are a pair made from single pieces of shell, found recently on Okinawa Island, Japan, dating to ~23,000 cal. BP (Fujita et al. 2016). Of a comparable age is the hook from Jerimalai Cave in Timor-Leste, found in a deposit dated between 23,000 and 16,000 cal. BP (O'Connor et al. 2011).

Hooks are generally rare in archaeological sites in ISEA, leading Bellwood (1997: 235) to propose that they were a technological adaptation confined mainly to Oceania, while noting that bait hooks made from shell were occasionally found in Neolithic contexts in Taiwan and Timor. Glover (1986: 117, Plate 32c) recovered a circular rotating hook made of *Rochia nilotica* (synonyms *Trochus niloticus* and *Tectus niloticus*) in his excavation at Bui Ceri Uato (BCU) rockshelter in the Baucau region of Timor-Leste, which based on its provenance and associated artefacts was believed to date to ca. 4000 BP. A larger, incomplete hook made of the same shell taxa was also found at BCU and seems to be part of a J-shaped jabbing hook (Glover 1986: 117). In Island Melanesia, and elsewhere in Oceania, definite examples of fish hooks are found in Neolithic or later contexts (Kirch 1985; Szabó and Summerhayes 2002: 95).

Intensive archaeological research has been carried out in Timor-Leste since 2000 and in 2014 a number of sites were excavated in Timor's neighbouring island, Alor, which revealed commonalities in the range of material cultural items used by the coastal communities on both islands (Figure 2.1). Here we describe the assemblages from the excavated sites focusing on shell-made fish hooks, personal decorative items and obsidian stone artefacts. We present evidence that the stone artefacts found on both islands were made of obsidian from the same source location and examine whether the similarities in the shell decorative items and fish hooks result from direct exchange of objects or ideas between island communities, or alternatively, whether similarities in form, material choice and manufacturing methods might be constrained by the intended purpose of the object, that is, its function.

SHELL FISH HOOKS, BEADS AND PENDANTS FROM TIMOR-LESTE

An intensive excavation programme in Timor-Leste since 2000 has shown that fish hooks, shell beads and other decorative shell artefacts occur in caves and shelters along the northern coastline and direct AMS dating has confirmed that they occur in Pleistocene contexts (O'Connor 2010; Langley and O'Connor 2015, 2016; Langley et al. 2016). A single-piece fish hook made of *Rochia nilotica*—identified by the physical attributions of the shell in comparison with reference specimens—was found at Jerimalai shelter (now renamed Asitau Kuru) in levels between 23,000 and 16,000 cal. BP (O'Connor et al. 2011) (Map 2.1). At nearby Lene Hara Cave a complete hook also made of *Rochia nilotica* was AMS dated to ca. 10,500 cal. BP (9741±60, NZA 17000) and was in good stratigraphic agreement with the radiocarbon dates from overlying and underlying units, thus demonstrating conclusively that it was not manufactured from old shell (O'Connor and Veth 2005) (Figure 2.2).

Shell beads are found in all the Timor-Leste sites. They include two distinct types:

1. Those made of whole gastropod shells of *Oliva* spp. (Figure 2.2D and 2.2E) and *Nassarius* spp. (Figure 2.2 A–C) (Langley and O'Connor 2015, 2016); and

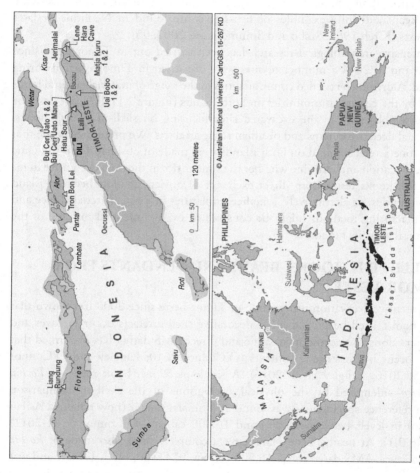

Map 2.1 Location map showing Lesser Sunda Islands (lower map) and location of archaeological sites discussed in the text (upper map).

2. Those elsewhere called 'disc beads', made of flat tabs of shell removed from the body of *Nautilus pompilius* (O'Connor 2010: 222; Langley et al. 2016) (Figure 2.2 F–J).

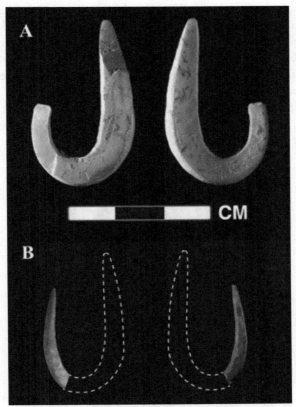

Figure 2.1 J-shaped fish hooks from (A) Lene Hara Cave Timor and (B) Tron Bon Lei B shelter Alor. The shaft in the Tron Bon Lei B hook has been extrapolated as shown by the dotted line [modified from O'Connor and Veth (2005: Figure 5) and O'Connor et al. (2017: Figure 8)].

These archaeological beads were identified through comparison with ethnographic examples, experimental replication, and the presence of recognised traces of manufacture and use wear (e.g., d'Errico et al. 2005; Stiner et al. 2013; Vanhaeren et al. 2013; Cristiani et al. 2014). Examples of *Oliva* and *Nautilus* beads and fragments with manufacturing traces occur in the lowest excavated units and have been directly dated using the AMS radiocarbon method demonstrating that they were made from the time of the initial occupation of the sites (O'Connor 2010; Langley and O'Connor 2016; Langley et al. 2016).

Because of the potential for recrystallisation of shell leading to erroneously old radiocarbon dates if unrecognised, shell samples, including shell artefacts, were tested for recrystallisation prior to dating. To identify whether recrystallisation had occurred, x-ray diffraction (XRD) was used to detect whether calcite was present. Samples were only dated where calcite was not detected (Siroquant™ was used to quantify the calcite content. The detection limit is 0.3% calcite). Charcoal dates have been calibrated against IntCal13 and shell dates against Marine13 (Reimer et al. 2013) in OxCal v.4.2 (Ramsay 2009). A local ΔR has not been established for Timor-Leste or Alor and thus has not been applied to the calibrated shell dates.

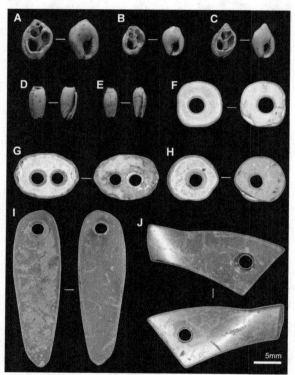

Figure 2.2 Examples of marine shell beads recovered from Timor-Leste. (A–C) *Nassarius* shell appliqués from Jerimalai; (A) SQ B, EU 13, (B) SQ B, EU 14, (C) SQ B EU 26; (D–E) *Oliva* shell beads from Jerimalai; (D) SQ A, EU 32, (E) SQ A, EU 44; (F) *Nautilus* disc bead from Lene Hara, SQ F, EU 23; (G) Double-holed *Nautilus* bead from MK2 D, EU 35; (H) *Nautilus* disc bead from MK2 D, EU 24 with a direct AMS radiocarbon age of 4490±40 BP (OZG896); (I) *Nautilus* pendant or fishing lure from Jerimalai B EU 29; (J) *Nautilus* pendant or fishing lure from MK2 EU 31 with a direct AMS radiocarbon age of 9190±50 BP (OZG899) (Photos credit: M.C. Langley and S. O'Connor).

NASSARIUS BEADS

Nassarius beads first appear about 6000 cal. BP in the Timor-Leste sites (Langley and O'Connor 2015). Two species of *Nassarius* (*Nassarius pullus* and *Nassarius globosus*) are present in the studied assemblages (Figure 2.2). A detailed study of the manufacturing and wear patterns on the *Nassarius* beads has shown that they were manufactured in a standardised way, characterised by the removal of the dorsum. Several of the beads exhibit tool marks consistent with the use of a lithic edge to achieve this alteration, such as irregular striations and small chattermarks. The wear and polish on the beads show that they were used as appliqués (Langley and O'Connor 2015) (Figure 2.2). They were likely used to decorate items that were worn such as head bands, belts or bags, or on craft pieces such as wall hangings for houses (Figure 2.3).

NAUTILUS BEADS AND PENDANTS

Nautilus beads and fragments exhibiting traces of manufacturing are found in the basal levels of Jerimalai where they are dated by association to about 42,000 cal. BP (Langley et al. 2016). A *Nautilus* bead at Matja Kuru 2 (MK2) from EU 31 was directly dated to 10,155–9801 cal. BP (9190±50, OZG 899) (O'Connor 2010: 228).

The large creamy-white and orange-brown patterned shells of *Nautilus pompilius* have a nacreous interior. Some of the items made on this species show clear striations across one or both faces. Experimental studies undertaken by one of the authors (M.C. Langley) indicate that these traces result from the use of a fine to medium-grained abrasive—such as ochre or sand—to remove the outer, creamy prismatic layer to expose the inner lustrous nacre. Finished beads and tear-dropped shaped pieces also display traces of grinding along the edge of the circumference as a result of shaping (Langley et al. 2016).

Examination of the round disc beads and tear-drop shaped *Nautilus* artefacts with single asymmetrically-placed drilled perforations, found that the perforation was primarily drilled from one face of the artefact; however, in some cases the perforation was drilled from both faces. In the case of the tear-dropped shaped pieces, the perforations show localised wear indicating that they were suspended as pendants (Langley et al. 2016). It is possible that the oblong *Nautilus* beads with double perforations may have been sewn onto bark cloth headbands or belts, or used to decorate other fibre items in the same way as the *Nassarius* beads described above (O'Connor 2010; Langley et al. 2016) (Figure 2.2G).

OLIVA BEADS

Large numbers of *Oliva* spp. beads occur in most of the coastal Timor-Leste sites with more than 480 identified thus far from Jerimalai, Lene Hara, Matja Kuru 1 (MK1) and MK2. These artefacts appear in the earliest layers of human occupation and continue throughout the sequence into the most recent levels. One *Oliva* shell bead in Jerimalai Pit B EU 56 returned an age of 38,246–36,136 cal. BP (33,294±380, ANU-48106) (Langley and O'Connor 2016). The shells were modified by removing the apex in order to create a perforation through the length of the shell (Figure 2.2). The wear patterns observed on these beads indicate that they were worn as a string (Langley and O'Connor 2016).

A persistent feature of all the Timor-Leste decorative items is the presence of red pigment (hematite) on the surface, in the natural crenulations, or caked

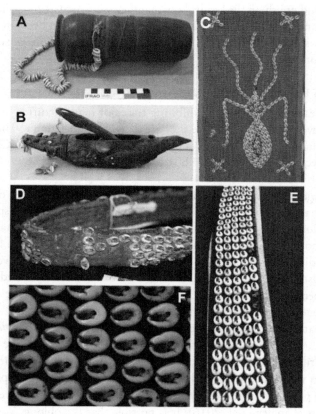

Figure 2.3 Example of the ethnographic items decorated with *Nassarius* shell beads from Timor-Leste and Papua New Guinea. (A and B) Timorese musical instrument with *Nassarius* shell inlay, included with the kind permission of the Basel Museum, Basel, (B) New Guinea musical instrument with *Nassarius* shell inlay, private collection, (C) Wall hanging composed of *Nassarius* shell appliqués, Australian National University collection, (D) Timorese headband with *Nassarius* appliqués (Australian Museum, Sydney); (E and F) *Nassarius* shell appliquéd war/raid belt from Timor-Leste (no. 71.1959.26.67). Images included with the kind permission of the Musée du Quai Branly-Jacques Chirac (Photos credit: S. O'Connor and M.C. Langley).

within the drilled perforations (Langley and O'Connor 2015, 2016; Langley et al. 2016). The pigment may have been applied to the string or the backing material to which the bead was threaded or sewn, as can be seen on objects in ethnographic collections. Alternatively, they could have been worn against a body which was painted with red pigment. The application of ochre to the backing material—either fabric or skin—would have created a striking contrast between the white beads and the background (e.g., Figure 2.3D).

SHELL DECORATIVE ITEMS FROM OTHER ISLANDS IN THE LESSER SUNDA ISLANDS GROUP

Shell ornaments have also been reported from Roti to the west of Timor (Mahirta 2003; Mahirta et al. 2004). Mahirta and colleagues (2004: 373) reported that 'flat shell beads' with a single perforation were found at Pia Hudale Cave, which were said to be like those found by Glover at BCU. A second type—a perforated shell pendant in the shape of a fish—was also found there (Mahirta et al. 2004: 373). The photos of the Pia Hudale bead suggest it is made of *Nautilus*. Although no dating of the shell beads was undertaken, Pia Hudale is a Pleistocene-aged site with layers 1 and 2, from which the shell ornaments derive, dating to 12,920–10,403 cal. BP (10,440±500, ANU-11102) and 13,112–12,553 cal. BP (11,290±150, ANU-10912) respectively. Beads were also reported at Lua Meko and Lua Manggetek in Roti in pre-ceramic layers (Mahirta 2003: 80, 89–90, 102). *Oliva* and *Dentalium* are the only species mentioned but the photographs of the 'round' beads (Mahirta 2003: 102, Figure 5.14; a–e, i, k, l) and 'pointed' bead (Figure 5.14; f) indicate that they are made of *Nautilus*. Finally, Van Heekeren (1972: 146) describes a 'lozenge-shaped pendant' from Liang Rundung, Flores which is also likely made of *Nautilus* and similar to the pendants in Roti and Timor-Leste.

OBSIDIAN ARTEFACTS FROM SITES IN TIMOR-LESTE

Volcanic glass artefacts have been recovered from sites in widely spaced coastal locations across Timor-Leste. Glover (1986) recovered volcanic glass artefacts from all four of his excavated sites on the Baucau Plateau. The extremely small unretouched pieces made up less than 1% of the flaked stone in the assemblages (Glover 1986: 56). Significantly, he did not recover any obsidian artefacts from his higher altitude inland excavations at Uai Bobo 1 and 2 in Venilale (Glover 1986: 132–3). Subsequently, archaeological investigation at another Baucau Plateau shelter—Bui Ceri Uato Mane (BCUM)—and at four cave and shelter sites at the eastern extreme of Timor-Leste—MK1, MK2, Jerimalai and Lene Hara—have also produced volcanic glass artefacts (Ambrose et al. 2009).

Geochemical finger-printing of obsidian artefacts from BCU and the more recent excavations in BCUM, MK1 and MK2 using Laser Ablation ICP-MS (LA-ICP-MS) found that there were two sources represented in the artefact assemblages (Groups A and B). One group was identified as low grade pitchstone (Group B) confined exclusively to the Baucau sites and could be matched with a local identified source in the same region (Ambrose et al. 2009). The second group (Group A) were made of high silicate obsidian and occurred in all four widely spaced Timor-Leste sites, but no source could be identified. Despite the small size of the artefacts and their low frequency in the lithic assemblages Ambrose and colleagues (2009: 614) concluded that the most parsimonious explanation was that the Group A artefacts also came from a local, unknown source in Timor-Leste.

Ten obsidian stone artefacts were recovered from Jerimalai shelter at the eastern end of Timor-Leste during excavations carried out in 2005. These were analysed in a separate study using SEM-EDXA and LA-ICP-MS (Reepmeyer et al. 2011). The geochemical characterisation of the Jerimalai obsidian artefacts indicated that they originated from the same obsidian outcrop as the high silicate obsidian artefacts (Group A) in the previous study. However, this later study came to a different conclusion regarding the likely source location. It reasoned that this high-grade obsidian might have been a valued lithic raw material and the small size of the artefacts, coupled with their rarity in assemblages, suggested long-distance transportation. The lack of artefacts made of this obsidian in inland sites in Timor-Leste, together with the general geology of Timor, made it highly unlikely that the source was located inland on the island. Thus, the authors concluded that the high silica obsidian was unlikely to be from a source in Timor (Reepmeyer et al. 2011: 89).

All of the obsidian artefacts in Timor-Leste made of obsidian from the high silica source were found in layers dating from the terminal Pleistocene about 15,000 cal. BP through to the late Holocene (Reepmeyer et al. 2019). Although it was originally believed that one obsidian flake in Jerimalai was derived from an older Pleistocene occupation unit, this provenance was later discovered to a data entry error (Shipton et al. 2020: 531). A recent analysis of obsidian artefacts from the Hatu Sour and Laili sites in central Timor-Leste using pXRF has identified the same high-grade obsidian and extended its known distribution within Timor-Leste (Reepmeyer et al. 2016: 28). Again, this third study shows that obsidian artefacts occur in very low numbers, are small in size, and have a terminal Pleistocene to late Holocene distribution. For example, in Laili Cave where the excavated deposits date back to 44–42,000 cal. BP, only two obsidian flakes were found, and these were in EU 4 which dates to ~12,000 cal. BP (O'Connor et al. 2017). In Hatu Sour, which has an archaeological sequence spanning the Holocene, 35 obsidian artefacts were found throughout (Brockwell et al. 2016; Reepmeyer et al. 2016).

EXCAVATIONS IN ALOR ISLAND 2014

In 2014, excavations carried out in a shelter site on the south coast of Alor Island, Tron Bon Lei (TBL) Pit B (Map 2.1), also uncovered shell fish hooks' shell beads, and obsidian artefacts in pre-Neolithic contexts. The 2014 excavation comprised a single 1 m² test pit excavated to bedrock at about 3.2 m depth below the site surface (Figure 2.3). A clearly defined sequence comprising 13 stratigraphic layers was identified. Radiocarbon dating indicates that the shelter saw three main phases of occupation:

(1) late Holocene (~ 3500 cal. BP);
(2) terminal Pleistocene-early Holocene (around 12,000 to 7500 cal. BP); and
(3) late Pleistocene (ca. 21,000–18,000 cal. BP) (Samper Carro et al. 2016) (Figure 2.4).

The uppermost excavation units contained a small number of earthenware sherds. Stone artefacts manufactured from basalt, obsidian and chert, and abundant shellfish and faunal remains occurred throughout the deposit, but were less abundant in the uppermost pottery bearing units. The faunal assemblage was dominated by marine resources. This single test pit produced over 28,000 fish bones as well as a small amount of marine turtle bone (Chelonioidea) (Samper Carro et al. 2016). The non-marine fauna found comprised of small mammals, reptiles and birds and was very sparse, making up 0.6% of the total faunal assemblage (Number of Identified Specimens or NISP). The Tron Bon Lei B fish hooks' shell beads, and obsidian are remarkably similar to those found in Timor-Leste.

SHELL FISH HOOKS AND BEADS FROM ALOR

The TBL B fish hooks include four single piece concentric hooks and a fragment from a J-shaped hook interred with a burial (O'Connor et al. 2017) and dated to ca. 11,200 cal. BP (Figures 2.1 and 2.5). An AMS radiocarbon date of 11,300–11,130 cal. BP (10,230±30 BP, S-ANU-41825) was obtained on one of the rotating hooks (Figure 2.5 Hook C). The dated hook is not made of 'old shell' as the date is consistent with other dates from the burial and the chronology of the surrounding units (O'Connor et al. 2017). The upper part of the layer that the hooks were buried within, Layer 11, has an AMS radiocarbon age of ca. 10,245–10,110 cal. BP (9340±35, S-ANU-40128) and charcoal from directly beneath the burial is dated to 12,545–12,115 cal. BP (10,445±50, S-ANU 40124). Thus, the date on the hook is in agreement with the dates from the stratigraphy (Figure 2.4).

Aside from the choice of shell taxa as raw material, the Alor and Timor-Leste hooks have additional common features. The circular rotating hooks from TBL B in Alor look remarkably similar to the hook from BCU illustrated by Glover

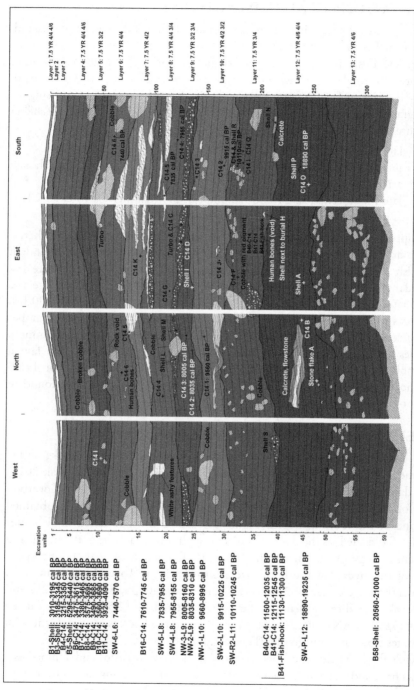

Figure 2.4 Stratigraphic section drawing from Tron Bon Lei Square B showing distribution of radiocarbon dates down the profile and position of fish hooks associated with burial in Layer 11 [from O'Connor et al. (2017: Figure 5)].

(1986: 117 Plate 32c). They are almost circular with the shaft being only slightly longer than the point and a narrow gape (Figure 2.5). All are thickest and widest at the bend, midway between the shank and the hook and all lack any notch or other augmentation of the shaft for line attachment (O'Connor et al. 2017). The broken single-piece hook in TBL B is also very similar in form and size to the jabbing hook from Lene Hara Pit F, which is about the same age. Again, neither have a notch for line attachment (O'Connor and Veth 2005).

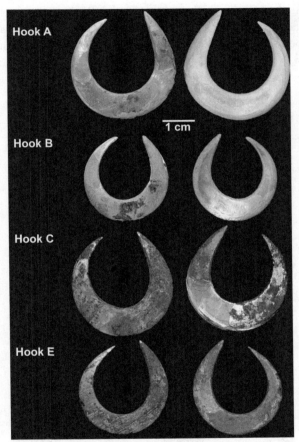

Figure 2.5 Concentric rotating hooks from Tron Bon Lei B Layer 11, Alor [from O'Connor et al. (2017: Figure 7)].

In the Tron Bon Lei B site, shell beads were found only in Pit B, in which organic materials were well preserved. Pit B contained the same range of shell beads as found in the Timor-Leste sites: *Nassarius* and *Oliva* beads and single and double holed *Nautilus pompilius* beads with drilled perforations (Figure 2.6). *Nautilus* beads were most numerous and were found throughout (Figure 2.6A–F, H, I).

The earliest beads in TBL are made of *Nautilus* and have two symmetrically placed holes. They first appear in EU 43, Layer 12 and are thus bracketed by dates of ~19,000 and ~12,000 cal. BP (Figure 2.4). These are indistinguishable from the double-holed *Nautilus* beads found in Timor-Leste (Glover 1986: 117 Plate 32d; O'Connor 2010) (Figure 2.2G) in terms of form, size and manufacturing evidence. Like examples from Timor-Leste some of the *Nautilus* beads from Alor retain the creamy external layer of the shell. Like the Timor-Leste examples, the Alor beads also show evidence of use in association with ochre or ochred surfaces—resulting in patterned distribution of ochre traces on the bead surfaces. For example, the *Nautilus* bead in Figure 2.6B has ochre caked around the perforation, suggesting it was applied to the string on which the bead was threaded.

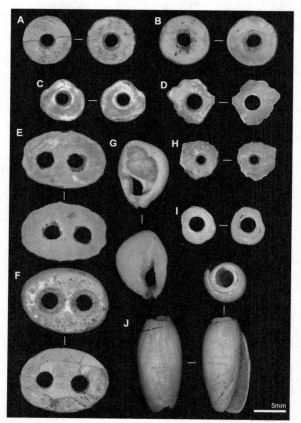

Figure 2.6 Examples of marine shell beads recovered from Tron Bon Lei B shelter, Alor. A–D, H, I: *Nautilus* disc beads (A) EU 12, (B) EU 11, (C) EU 7, (D) EU 31, (H) EU 31, (I) EU 18. E and F: Double-holed *Nautilus* beads (E) EU 43, (F) EU 37. (G) *Nassarius* appliqué from EU 12. (J) *Oliva* shell bead EU 12 (Photos credit: E. Piotto).

OBSIDIAN STONE ARTEFACTS FROM TBL SITE ALOR

Obsidian artefacts from TBL B in Alor were geochemically analysed by pXRF (Reepmeyer et al. 2016). The study showed an unambiguous separation of three different source locations: Groups 1, 2 and 3 (Figure 2.7). Two sources, Groups 2 and 3, dominate the assemblage numerically and probably indicate use of a local volcanic formation. There are three subgroups in Group 3 with some geochemical variation but all are likely to derive from the same source location. The third identified source Group 1 (Figure 2.7) matches the high silica obsidian artefacts identified in Timor-Leste (Group A in Ambrose et al. 2009; Reepmeyer et al. 2011). Like the Timor-Leste obsidian assemblages, the Alor obsidian flakes and cores are distinguished by their extremely small size and lack of retouch. While artefacts made of obsidian occur in TBL B Layer 13, the earliest occupation level at the shelter dating from the Last Glacial Maximum 21,000 years ago, Group 1 obsidians are not represented here, making their first appearance in Layer 12, which is dated to the terminal Pleistocene ca. 12,000 cal. BP (Figures 2.3 and 2.6). The small size of the Group 1 artefacts, the lack of unworked nodules and their late appearance in the assemblage suggest that it is unlikely that Group 1 obsidian comes from a local source in Alor. It is probable that Group 1 artefacts are from neither Timor nor Alor but from an as yet unexplored island on the Sunda Arc. Although no source has been found so far, the distribution of Group 1 obsidian shows that there was an interaction sphere connecting widely spaced sites in Timor-Leste as well as in Alor. These islands were never connected during the period of human inhabitation and the transportation of obsidian necessitates maritime interaction between islands in the Lesser Sundas—beginning in the terminal Pleistocene ca. 12,000 years ago and continuing into the late Holocene.

DISCUSSION

The shell artefact assemblages from the Lesser Sunda Islands of Timor, Alor, Flores and Roti are remarkably similar. With hundreds of molluscan taxa available from the rock platforms, reefs and sand flats along these island coastlines—and found in abundance as food refuse in the archaeological deposits in Timor-Leste, Alor and Roti—it would seem more than coincidental that the same three taxa were consistently selected to make the same forms of personal decorations. Further, these artefacts exhibit extraordinary continuity through time.

Artefacts made of shell were originally identified as one of the type-markers of the Austronesian tool kit (Bellwood 1997: 219–35). While we do not dispute that a range of shell artefacts are associated with Austronesian migration out of Taiwan and into the Pacific, it is important to recognise that a distinctly different range of shell ornaments are present in the islands of the Lesser Sundas representing a different shell working tradition which dates back to the

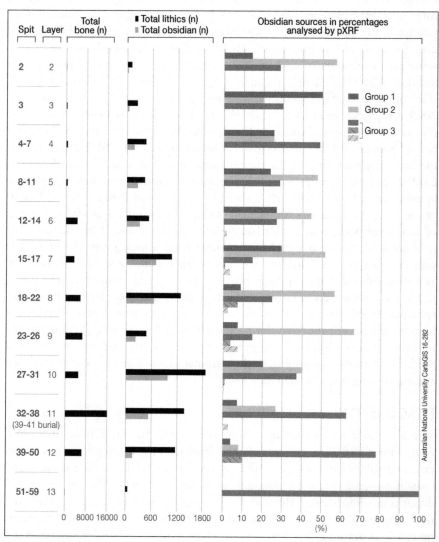

Figure 2.7 Total number of stone artefacts, obsidian artefacts and bone fragments by layer at Tron Bon Lei B (left). Distribution of obsidian artefacts from Tron Bon Lei B by stratigraphic layer shown as a percentage of all obsidian artefacts analysed by pXRF (right).

Pleistocene. There is little overlap between the shell artefact assemblages from Timor, Alor and Roti and those from Taiwan, the Philippines and the Lapita sites of the western Pacific. Significantly, the cave and shelter assemblages in Timor-Leste, Alor and Roti largely lack the distinctive perforated *Conus* rings, *Tridacna* rings and bi-perforated units found in Neolithic or later contexts in the Philippines and the Lapita sites of Oceania[1] (Szabó 2004: 261–2; Szabó 2010: 116–18). Other taxa used for artefact production in Lapita sites but not recorded as utilised at all in Timor, Alor or Flores are the pearl oysters *Pinctada maxima* and *P. margaritifera*, and the thorny oyster *Spondylus* (Kirch 1985; Szabó and Summerhayes 2002; Szabó 2007) and *Turbo* (Szabó 2007). The pearl oysters and thorny oyster do not appear in the mollusc shell assemblages in Timor or Alor and so may not have been an option for use, however *Turbo marmoratus*, *T. argyrostomus* and *T. setosus* do occur but were apparently not selected. Sites in the Philippines and Palawan have *Nassarius* beads manufactured in the same manner as those from Timor-Leste (Szabó 2004: 256–7; Szabó and Ramirez 2009), but the Timor examples occur far earlier in time. *Oliva* beads have been identified in the Niah Caves and Lobang Hangus in Sarawak but not prior to the Metal Age, where they seem to be predominantly in mortuary contexts (Szabó et al. 2013). Sites in Taiwan, northern Luzon, Micronesia, and near and remote Oceania contain shell fish hooks but these are confined to Neolithic or later contexts (Bellwood 1997: 235; Szabó 2007; Carson 2013), whereas in Timor-Leste and Alor, fish hooks are found from the terminal Pleistocene and are clearly an innovation designed to exploit the rich maritime resources in the Wallacean islands, which were depauperate in terrestrial fauna (O'Connor and Aplin 2007; O'Connor 2015; Samper Carro et al. 2016). Perhaps the Austronesian shell working tradition travelled east from the Philippines into the Marianas Islands and Island Melanesia but not south into Sulawesi and the Lesser Sundas (e.g., Carson 2013; Carson et al. 2013).

We might also consider the similarities of the Timor-Leste/Alor fish hooks in terms of communities of practice, and the impact of style against function. There are two distinct attributes which a worked artefact embodies: 'functional' attributes, dictated by the raw material from which the artefact is made or the purpose it must meet; and 'stylistic' attributes, which are the product of choices selected from among a variety of possible solutions by the artisan (e.g., Sackett 1973). Style allows material culture to be tracked spatially and temporally and can be used to examine the volume and diversity of information flow within and between groups in a social network (e.g., Wobst 1977; Conkey 1980; Gamble 1980, 1982; Bahn 1982; Jochim 1983; Wiessner 1983, 1984, 1985; Barton et al. 1994; Vanhaeren and d'Errico 2006).

Functional attributes for the single piece J-shaped hooks and concentric rotating hooks differ in accordance with the different marine environments and weather conditions in which they are primarily used, their mechanical properties, or the way in which they operate when the fish takes the hook (Reinman 1970; Allen 1996). Concentric hooks, with their short shaft and narrow gape, are suited for fishing in deep water and/or in windy conditions where tension cannot be maintained on the line (Reinman 1970: 188–9; Johannes 1981: 113–14). Historically, they were also used in shallow water where coral heads were likely to cause an open gaped jabbing hook to snag (Johannes 1981: 116). When the fish takes the hook and swims away, the concentric hook rotates and the fish effectively hooks itself. J-shaped hooks are used in a variety of weather and water conditions but rely on the line being jerked when the fish bites in order to set the hook (Allen 1996: 108). The form of these two hooks is thus strongly controlled by their function.

The concentric rotating hooks from Alor and Timor are remarkably similar and might be interpreted as a clear-cut case of style diffusion were it not for the fact that they are near identical to concentric rotating hooks found in Japan (Fujita et al. 2016), Arabia (Santini 1987: Fig. 10), along the California coast and islands (Hoover 1973; Greenwood 1978; Rick et al. 2002), in the islands of Baja California, Mexico (Fujita 2014), Chile (Llagostera 1992) and Ecuador (Meggers and Evans 1962). Indeed, the technological parallels between the concentric rotating hooks on the American coast and those in Polynesia have in the past been argued to result from migration or diffusion (e.g., Heyerdahl 1952: 698–700; Reinman 1967: 187). The appearance of almost identical hooks in Alor Island, Indonesia and Timor-Leste dated to the terminal Pleistocene and their absence in MSEA and other parts of ISEA at this early date refuted any suggestion of diffusion as the cause of the appearance of these hooks in such widely spaced areas of the world. Rather, they can be seen as a form which arose independently in different parts of the world to meet particular functional requirements under similar ecological conditions (see Allen 1996). One-piece fish hooks made of *Rochia nilotica* are common in Lapita sites in the Bismarcks (Szabó and Summerhayes 2002) and in Tikopia in the southeast Solomon Islands (Kirch and Yen 1982). However, elsewhere in Oceania a variety of other shell species were used for hook manufacture including *Turbo marmoratus*, *T. argyrostomus* and *T. setosus*, and the pearl shell *Pinctada* spp. and abalone (*Haliotis* sp.) (Szabó 2010: 121). All of these shell species occur in the shell assemblages of Timor-Leste and Alor and thus the consistent choice of *Rochia nilotica* for fish hook manufacture may be seen as a stylistic choice, in that it is independent of raw material availability, and one which is shared between these island communities.

Also to be avoided in assessing interaction spheres in prehistory is what has been called elsewhere 'the ambiguity of "similarity"' (Szabó and O'Connor 2004). This is where the mere presence of 'shell ornaments' in sites widely separated in time and space is deemed sufficient to demarcate an interaction sphere (e.g., Bulbeck 2008). Use of broad terms such as 'shell beads' or 'shell ornaments' makes it possible to infer similarities in assemblages when in fact the types of artefacts made, the shells selected as raw material and the production techniques evince no relationship at all.

A small number of artefacts made of obsidian have been found in cave and shelter assemblages in coastal locations throughout Timor-Leste (Ambrose et al. 2009; Reepmeyer et al. 2011). These artefacts have been shown to be made of material from the same volcanic source locality as obsidian artefacts in the Alor site of Tron Bon Lei. The obsidian artefacts occur in low numbers in both Timor and Alor and are uniformly small in size. In the Alor site of Tron Bon Lei, and in Timor-Leste, obsidian artefacts are confined to the terminal Pleistocene and Holocene levels. Importantly, while obsidian is found in the lowest levels of the TBL site dated to between 19,000 and 21,000 cal. BP these earlier assemblages do not include any artefacts made from Group 1 obsidian. Unfortunately, the source is unknown so far, but it is unlikely that it will be located on either Alor or Timor-Leste. One of the nearby volcanic islands seems more likely with obsidian beginning to be moved throughout the Lesser Sunda Islands sometime after about 15,000 years ago. Other raw materials such as fine-grained basalt and chert were available for flaked artifacts and these are abundant in the site. The use of the tiny obsidian flakes is unclear. Perhaps the widespread use of Group 1 obsidian signals shared values or bonds between coastal communities who were able to receive it from across the sea; thus operating beyond the functional level of the material. In this respect it is interesting to note that Group 1 obsidian, with such a widespread distribution in coastal locations on Timor-Leste, does not occur at all in the inland sites of Uai Bobo 1 and 2 despite large lithic assemblage sizes (Glover 1986). This distribution of material, it might be suggested, could be a material reflection of social or familial networks maintained between coastal groups in adjacent islands communities, and the lack of such networks between the coastal and inland communities within the same island.

CONCLUSION

Migration, diffusion and the timing and phasing of cultural transmissions between islands have been dominant and controversial themes in the archaeology of ISEA (Bellwood 1997; Szabó and O'Connor 2004; O'Connor 2006, 2015; Bulbeck 2008; Blench 2012). However, finding firm evidence for migration or diffusion in the archaeological record is problematic and arguments made for cultural links or interaction spheres between regions are often based on superficial classifications of artefact type which may be merely coincidental or due to convergence, as seems to be the case with the fish hooks. However, comparisons of the shell decorative items in the archaeological sites in Timor, Alor and Roti suggest that these communities shared norms of personal adornment and/or craft production which were remarkably stable through time in terms of the items made, choice of shell taxa, the methods of manufacture and the accompanying use of hematite. This may have been maintained by the exchange of value items and/or craft goods through familial ties or marriage exchange.

Geochemical fingerprinting provides a unique opportunity to investigate movement of raw materials and artefacts and has confirmed that Alor and Timor-Leste were connected in an interaction network, receiving obsidian from the same source location over a time span of at least 12,000 years, although the source location for the obsidian is currently unknown. Identifying the source location will assist us to understand the extent of, and fluctuations in, the maritime network in the Lesser Sunda Islands and should be a priority for the future.

ACKNOWLEDGEMENTS

The fieldwork for this project was funded by an ARC Laureate grant to O'Connor (FL120100156) and the paper was written and revised with support from the ARC Centre of Excellence for Australian Biodiversity and Heritage, College of Asia and the Pacific, The Australian National University, Canberra (CE170100015). Permission for the research in Indonesia was granted by RISTEK, Foreign Research Permit ([1304]/FRP/SM/V/2014) and in Timor-Leste by Mrs Cecilia Assis, Secretaria de Estado Arte e Cultura. We would also like to thank the landowners of the Tutuala and Poros communities in Timor-Leste and the Lerabain community in Alor for access to the sites. Students from Universitas Gadjah Mada, Yogyakarta and The Australian National University, and Mr Putu Yuda from Balai Arkeologi Bali are thanked for their assistance in the field.

NOTE

[1] Glover (1986: 152, 184–5) does report finding two fragments of *Rochia nilotica* (synonyms *Trochus niloticus* and *Tectus niloticus*) shell rings in his excavation at Uai Bobo 1.

REFERENCES

Allen, Melinda S. 1996. 'Style and Function in East Polynesian Fish-hooks.' *Antiquity* 70 (267): 97–116.

Ambrose, Wal, Melinda Allen, Sue O'Connor, Matthew Spriggs, Oliveira Nuno, and Chistian Reepmeyer. 2009. 'Possible Obsidian Sources for Artifacts from Timor: Narrowing the Options Using Chemical Data.' *Journal of Archaeological Science* 36: 607–15.

Bahn, Paul G. 1982. 'Inter-site and inter-regional links during the Upper Palaeolithic: The Pyrenean evidence.' *Journal of Archaeology* 1 (3): 247–68.

Barton, C. Michael, G.A. Clark, and Allison Cohen. 1994. 'Art as Information: Explaining Upper Palaeolithic Art in Western Europe.' *World Archaeology* 26: 186–207.

Bellwood, Peter. 1997. *Prehistory of the Indo-Malaysian Archipelago*. Revised edition. Honolulu: University of Hawai'i Press.

Blench, Roger. 2012. 'Almost Everything you Believed about the Austronesians Isn't True.' In *Crossing Borders: Selected Papers from the 13th International Conference of the European Association of Southeast Asian Archaeologists*, Volume 1, ed. M.L. Tjoa-Bonatz, A. Reinecke, and D. Bonatz, 128–48. Singapore: NUS Press.

Brockwell, Sally, Sue O'Connor, Mirani Litster, and Richard C. Willan. 2016. 'New Insights into Holocene Economies and Environments of Central East Timor: Analysis of the Molluscan Assemblage at the Rockshelter Site of Hatu Sour.' *Northern Territory Naturalist* 27: 2–12.

Bulbeck, David. 2008. 'An Integrated Perspective on the Austronesian Diaspora: The Switch from Cereal Agriculture to Maritime Foraging in the Colonisation of Island Southeast Asia.' *Australian Archaeology* 67: 31–51.

Carson, Mike. 2013. 'Austronesian Migrations and Developments in Micronesia.' *Journal of Austronesian Studies* 4 (1): 25–50.

Carson, Mike, Hsiao-chun Hung, Summerhayes Glen, and Peter Bellwood. 2013. 'The Pottery Trail from Southeast Asia to Remote Oceania.' *The Journal of Island and Coastal Archaeology* 8(1): 17–36.

Conkey, Margaret W. 1980. 'The Identification of Prehistoric Hunter-gatherer Aggregation: The Case of Altamira.' *Current Anthropology* 21: 609–30.

Cristiani, Emanuela, Rebecca Farbstein, and Preston Miracle. 2014. 'Ornamental Traditions in the Eastern Adriatic: The Upper Palaeolithic and Mesolithic Personal Adornments from Vela Spila (Croatia).' *Journal of Anthropological Archaeology* 36: 21–31.

d'Errico, Fracesco, Christopher Henshilwood, Marian Vanhaeren, and Karen Van Niekerk. 2005. 'Nassarius Kraussianus Shell Beads from Blombos Cave: Evidence for Symbolic Behaviour in the Middle Stone Age.' *Journal of Human Evolution* 48: 3–24.

Fujita, Harumi. 2014. 'Early Holocene Pearl Oyster Circular Fishhooks and Ornaments on Espíritu Santo Island, Baja California Sur.' *Monographs of the Western North American Naturalist* 7 (1): 129–34.

Fujita, Masaki, Shinji Yamasaki, Chiaki Katagiri, Itsuro Oshiro, Katsuhiro Sano, Taiji Kurozumi, Hiroshi Sugawara, Dai Kunikita, Hiroyuki Matsuzaki, Akihiro Kano, Tomoyo Okumura, Tomomi Sone, Hikaru Fujita, Satoshi Kobayashi, Toru Naruse, Megumi Kondo, Shuji Matsu'ura, Gen Suwa, and Yousuke Kaifu. 2016. 'Advanced Maritime Adaptation in the Western Pacific Coastal Region Extends Back to 35,000–30,000 Years Before Present.' *Proceedings of the National Academy of Sciences* 113: 11184–89.

Gamble, Clive. 1980. 'Information exchange in the Palaeolithic.' *Nature* 283: 522–3.

———. 1982. 'Interaction and Alliance in Palaeolithic Society.' *Man* 17 (1): 92–107.

Glover, Ian C. 1986. *Archaeology in Eastern Timor, 1966–67*. Terra Australis 11. Canberra: Department of Prehistory, Research School of Pacific Studies, Australian National University.

Greenwood, Roberta S. 1978. 'Obispeño and Purisimeño Chumash.' In *Handbook of North American Indians*, ed. R. Heizer, 520–3. Volume 8: California. Washington: Smithsonian Institution.

Heyerdahl, Thor. 1952. *American Indians in the Pacific*. London: George Allen and Unwin.

Hoover, Robert. 1973. *Chumash Fishing Equipment. San Diego Museum of Man Ethnic Technology*, note 9. Salinas: Coyote Press.

Jochim, Michael A. 1983. 'Palaeolithic Art in Ecological Perspective.' In *Hunter-Gatherer Economy in Prehistory: A European Perspective*, ed. G. Bailey, 212–19. Cambridge: Cambridge University Press.

Johannes, Robert Earle. 1981. *Words of the Lagoon: Fishing and Marine Lore in the Palau District of Micronesia.* Berkeley: University of California Press.

Kirch, Patrick Vinton. 1985. *Feathered Gods and Fishhooks: An Introduction to Hawaiian Archaeology and Prehistory.* Honolulu: University of Hawai'i Press.

Kirch, Patrick Vinton and D.E. Yen 1982. *Tikopia: The Prehistory and Ecology of a Polynesian Outlier.* Honolulu: Bishop Museum.

Langley, Michelle C. and Sue O'Connor. 2015. '6,500-year-old Nassarius Shell Appliqués in Timor-Leste: Technological and Use Wear Analyses.' *Journal of Archaeological Science* 62: 175–92.

———. 2016. 'An Enduring Shell Artefact Tradition from Timor-Leste: Oliva Bead Production from the Pleistocene to Late Holocene at Jerimalai, Lene Hara, and Matja Kuru 1 and 2.' *PLOS ONE* 11(8): e0161071.

Langley, Michelle C., Sue O'Connor, and Elena Piotto. 2016. '42,000-year-old Worked and Pigment-stained Nautilus Shell from Jerimalai (Timor-Leste): Evidence for an Early Coastal Adaptation in ISEA.' *Journal of Human Evolution* 97: 1–16.

Llagostera, Agustín. 1992. 'Early Occupations and the Emergence of Fisherman on the Pacific Coast of South America.' *Andean Past* 3: 87–109.

Mahirta. 2003. 'Human Occupation on Roti and Sawu Islands, Nusa Tenggara Timur.' Unpublished PhD dissertation. Department of Archaeology and Anthropology, Australian National University, Canberra.

Mahirta, Ken Aplin, David Bulbeck, Walter Boles, and Peter Bellwood. 2004. 'Pia Hudale Rockshelter: A Terminal Pleistocene Occupation Site on Roti Island, Nusa Tenggara Timor, Indonesia.' In *Quaternary Research in Indonesia. Modern Quaternary Research in Southeast Asia*, Vol. 18, ed. S.G. Keates and J. M. Pasveer, 361–94. Leiden: A.A. Balkema.

Meggers, Betty J. and Clifford Evans. 1962. 'The Machalilla Culture: An Early Formative Complex on the Ecuadorian Coast.' *American Antiquity* 28 (2): 186–92.

O'Connor, Sue. 2006. 'Unpacking the Island Southeast Asian Neolithic Cultural Package, and Finding Local Complexity.' In *Uncovering Southeast Asia's Past: Selected Papers from the Tenth Biennial Conference of the European Association of Southeast Asian Archaeologists*, ed. E.A. Bacus, I.C. Glover, and V.C. Pigott, 74–87. Singapore: NUS Press.

———. 2010. 'Continuity in Shell Artefact Production in Holocene East Timor.' In *50 Years of Archaeology in Southeast Asia: Essays in Honour of Ian Glover*, ed. B. Bellina, E.A. Bacus, T. O. Pryce, and J. Wisseman Christie, 218–33. Bangkok: River Books.

———. 2015. 'Crossing the Wallace Line: The Maritime Skills of the Earliest Colonists in the Wallacean Archipelago.' In *The Emergence and Diversity of Modern Human Behavior in Palaeolithic Asia*, ed. Y. Kaifu, M. Izuho, T. Goebel, H. Sato, and A. Ono, 214–24. Texas: Texas A&M University Press.

O'Connor, Sue, Matthew Spriggs, and Peter Veth. 2002. 'Direct Dating of Shell Beads from Lene Hara Cave, East Timor.' *Australian Archaeology* 55: 18–21.

O'Connor, Sue and Peter Veth. 2005. 'Early Holocene Shell Fish Hooks from Lene Hara Cave, East Timor Establish Complex Fishing Technology was in use in Island Southeast Asia Five Thousand Years before Austronesian Settlement.' *Antiquity* 79: 1–8.

O'Connor, Sue and Ken Aplin. 2007. 'A Matter of Balance: An Overview of Pleistocene Occupation History and the Impact of the Last Glacial Phase in East Timor and the Aru Islands, Eastern Indonesia.' *Archaeology in Oceania* 42: 82–90.

O'Connor, Sue, Rintaro Ono, and Christopher Clarkson. 2011. 'Pelagic Fishing at 42,000 Years Before the Present and the Maritime Skills of Modern Humans.' *Science* 334: 1117–21.

O'Connor, Sue, Anthony Barham, Kenneth Aplin, and Tim Maloney. 2017. 'Cave Stratigraphies and Cave Breccias: Implications for Sediment Accumulation and Removal Models and Interpreting the Record of Human Occupation.' *Journal of Archaeological Science* 77: 143–59.

Ramsey, Bronk C. 2009. 'Bayesian Analysis of Radiocarbon Dates.' *Radiocarbon* 51 (1): 337–60.

Reepmeyer, Christian, Sue O'Connor, and Sally Brockwell. 2011. 'Long-term Obsidian Use in East Timor: Provenancing Lithic Artefacts from the Jerimalai Cave.' *Archaeology in Oceania* 46: 85–90.

Reepmeyer, Christian, Sue O'Connor, Mahirta, Tim Maloney, and Shimona Kealy. 2016. 'Late Pleistocene/Early Holocene Maritime Interaction in Southeastern Indonesia – Timor Leste.' *Journal of Archaeological Science* 76: 21–30.

Reepmeyer, Christian, Sue O'Connor, Mahirta, Shimona Kealy, and Tim Maloney. 2019. 'Kisar, a small island participant in an extensive maritime obsidian network in the Wallacean Archipelago.' *Archaeological Research in Asia* 19: 100139.

Reimer, Paula J., Edouard Bard, Alex Bayliss, Warren Beck, Paul G. Blackwell, Christopher Bronk Ramsey, Caitlin E. Buck, Hai Cheng, R. Lawrence Edwards, Michael Friedrich, Pieter M. Grootes, Thomas P. Guilderson, Haflidi Haflidason, Irka Hajdas, Christine Hatte, Timothy J. Heaton, Dirk L. Hoffmann, Alan G. Hogg, Konrad A. Hughen, K. Felix Kaiser, Bernd Kromer, Sturt W. Manning, Mu Niu, Ron W. Reimer, David A. Richards, E. Marian Scott, John R. Southon, Richard A. Staff, Christian S.M. Turney, and Johannes van der Plicht. 2013. 'IntCal13 and Marine13 Radiocarbon Age Calibration Curves 0–50,000 Years cal bp.' *Radiocarbon* 55 (4): 1869–87.

Reinman, Fred M. 1967. 'Fishing: An Aspect of Oceanic Economy: An Archaeological Approach.' *Fieldiana: Anthropology* 56 (2): 95–208.

———. 1970. 'Fishhook Variability: Implications for the History and Distribution of Fishing Gear in Oceania.' In *Studies in Oceanic Culture History*, ed. R. Green and M. Kelly, 47–60. Honolulu: Department of Anthropology, Bishop Museum.

Rick, Torben C., Rene Vellanoweth, Jon M. Erlandson, and Douglas Kennett. 2002. 'On the Antiquity of the Single-piece Shell Fishhook: AMS Radiocarbon Evidence for the Southern California Coast.' *Journal of Archaeological Science* 29: 933–42.

Sackett, James R. 1973. 'Style, Function and Artifact Variability in Palaeolithic Assemblages.' In *The Explanation of Culture Change*, ed. C. Renfrew, 317–25. Pittsburgh: University of Pittsburgh Press.

Samper Carro, Sofia, Sue O'Connor, Julien Louys, Stuart Hawkins, and Mahirta. 2016. 'Human Maritime Subsistence Strategies in the Lesser Sunda Islands During the Terminal Pleistocene-Early Holocene: New Evidence from Alor, Indonesia.' *Quaternary International* 416: 64–79.

Santini, Geraldina. 1987. 'Site RH-10 at Qurum and a Preliminary Analysis of its Cemetery: An Essay in Stratigraphic Discontinuity.' In *Proceedings of the Seminar for Arabian Studies* 17: 179–98.

Shipton, Ceri, Sue O'Connor, Christian Reepmeyer, Shimona Kealy, and Nathan Jankowski. 2020. 'Shell Adzes, Exotic Obsidian, and Inter-Island Voyaging in the Early and Middle Holocene of Wallacea.' *The Journal of Island and Coastal Archaeology* 15 (4): 525–46.

Stiner, Mary C., Steven L. Kuhn, and Erksin Güleç. 2013. 'Early Upper Palaeolithic Shells Beads at Üçağizili Cave I (Turkey): Technology and the Socioeconomic Context of Ornament Life-histories.' *Journal of Human Evolution* 64: 380–98.

Szabó, Katherine. 2004. 'Technique and Practice: Shell-Working in the Western Pacific and Island Southeast Asia.' Unpublished PhD dissertation. Department of Archaeology and Natural History, Australian National University, Canberra.

———. 2007. 'An Assessment of Shell Fishhooks of the Lapita Cultural Complex.' In *Vastly Ingenious: The Archaeology of Pacific Material Culture in Honour of Janet Davidson*, ed. A. Anderson, K. Green, and F. Leach, 227–41. Dunedin: Otago University Press.

———. 2010. 'Shell Artefacts and Shell-working within the Lapita Cultural Complex.' *Journal of Pacific Archaeology* 1 (2): 115–27.

Szabó, Katherine and Glen Summerhayes. 2002. 'Worked Shell Artefacts – New Data from Early Lapita.' In *Fifty Years in the Field. Essays in Honour and Celebration of Richard Shutler Jr's Archaeological Career*, ed. S. Bedford, C. Sand, and D. Burley, 91–100. Auckland: New Zealand Archaeological Association Monograph 25.

Szabó, Katherine and Sue O'Connor. 2004. 'Migration and Complexity in Holocene Island Southeast Asia.' *World Archaeology* 36 (4): 621–8 (Special issue edited by Peter Rowley Conwy, Debates in World Archaeology).

Szabó, Katherine and Hazel Ramirez. 2009. 'Worked Shell from Leta Leta Cave, Palawan, Philippines.' *Archaeology in Oceania* 44: 150–9.

Szabó, Katherine, Franca Cole, Lindsay Lloyd-Smith, Graham Barker, Chris Hunt, Philip Piper, and Chris Doherty. 2013. 'The "Metal Age" at the Niah Caves, c. 2000–500 Years Ago.' In *Rainforest Foraging and Farming in Island Southeast Asia*, ed. G. Barker, 299–340. Cambridge: McDonald Institute Monographs.

van Heekeren, H.R. 1972. *The Stone Age of Indonesia*. The Hague: Martinus Nijhoff.

Vanhaeren, Marian and Francesco d'Errico. 2006. 'Aurignacian Ethno-linguistic Geography of Europe Revealed by Personal Ornaments.' *Journal of Archaeological Science* 33: 1105–28.

Vanhaeren, Marian, Francesco d'Errico, Karen Loise Van Niekerk, Christopher Stuart Henshilwood, and Rudolph M. Erasmus. 2013. 'Thinking Strings: Additional Evidence for Personal Ornament Use in the Middle Stone Age at Blombos Cave, South Africa.' *Journal of Human Evolution* 64: 500–17.

Wiessner, Polly. 1983. 'Style and Social Information in Kalahari San Projectile Points.' *American Antiquity* 48: 253–76.

———. 1984. 'Reconsidering the Behavioral Basis for Style: A Case Study Among the Kalahari San.' *Journal of Anthropological Archaeology* 3 (3): 190–234.

———. 1985. 'Style or Isochrestic Variation? A Reply to Sackett.' *American Antiquity* 50 (1): 160–6.

Wobst, Martin H. 1977. 'Stylistic Behavior and Information Exchange.' In *For the Director: Research Essays in Honor of James B. Griffin*, ed. Charles E. Cleland, 317–42. Ann Arbor: Museum of Anthropology, University of Michigan.

3

Late Pleistocene to Mid-Holocene Maritime Exchange Networks in Island Southeast Asia

David Bulbeck

INTRODUCTION

The purpose of this chapter is to investigate archaeological evidence for maritime interactions associated with anatomically modern humans (AMH) in Island Southeast Asia (ISEA). As discussed by Bulbeck and Marwick (in press), archaic hominins had crossed ISEA seas to reach Sulawesi and Flores, and probably Luzon and Timor, but Southeast Asian sites dating to ~45,000 BP and later (calendrical rather than radiocarbon years) can be confidently identified with AMH (Map 3.1). Kealy and colleagues explain well the importance of maritime interconnections for early AMH in ISEA (Kealy et al. 2017). Connections between inter-visible islands not only fostered colonisation of Sahulland (Australia/New Guinea) by ~50,000 BP but also, as exemplified by Liang Sarru in the Talaud Islands, allowed the intermittent Pleistocene occupation of remote, marginal islands from which colonists could withdraw when conditions on marginal islands deteriorated. One particular inter-connection proposed by Soares et al. (2008) is a dispersal of populations across eastern and central ISEA during the Pleistocene-Holocene transition in response to rising sea-levels. A later interconnection, which has potential implications for the immediate origins of ISEA's sea nomads, is the movement of Malayo-Polynesian speakers from Taiwan into ISEA—a movement which many scholars (e.g., Bellwood 1997) would view as a large-scale migration responsible for introducing the Neolithic across ISEA.

The AMH maritime interactions of relevance for ISEA prehistory could be as localised as connections between adjacent islands and as wide-ranging as migrations that may have enveloped much of ISEA. To accommodate such diversity, this chapter uses the term 'axis' to refer to apparent maritime interactions without prejudging their nature. Most definitions of this term refer to pivotal lines but there are also definitions that focus on the term's formative connotations, such as that found in the Oxford English Dictionary: 'An agreement or alliance between two or more countries that forms a centre for an eventual larger grouping of nations' (https://en.oxforddictionaries.com/definition/axis). In adapting this definition to the topic of prehistoric maritime interaction, the following criteria are central:

- material cultural traits of a restricted distribution that crosses open sea, suggesting that the trait is not generic but that its shared presence at two or more sites reflects open-sea cultural interaction;
- a well-defined time range (the more tightly defined, the better) to increase confidence that the sharing of traits reflects cultural interaction rather than independent development; and
- a basis for future growth.

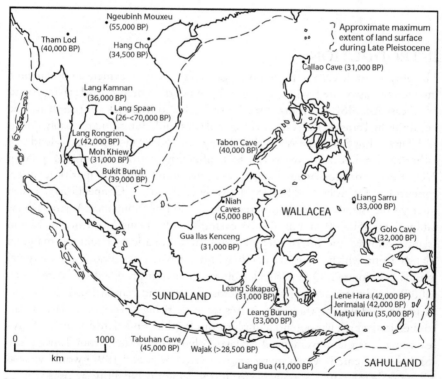

Map 3.1 Southeast Asian sites with anatomically modern human habitation by 30,000 BP.

The traits referred to here can be as broad as technologies or as specific as styles, and may also extend to dated evidence from sites of exploited resources distributed beyond their natural range (implying human translocation). Some examples of where technologies, traditions, styles and exploited resources have been used by other scholars to infer ISEA maritime interaction are presented below.

TECHNOLOGIES

Rabett (2005) proposed that terminal Pleistocene dispersal of bone-tool technology across much of Southeast Asia reflected widespread maritime interactions that assisted cultural adaptation to the restructured coastal environments. Similarly, Solheim (2006) posited shell working as a technology that reflected initial Holocene connections between eastern ISEA and Melanesia.

TRADITIONS

Bellwood (1997: 222) allowed for the possibility that the tradition of shell adzes documented in northern Maluku between the terminal Pleistocene and mid-Holocene may have been the source for the shell adzes dated to a mid-Holocene context at Duyong Cave in the Philippines.

STYLES

Bellwood (1997: 196–7) suggested a connection between the stylistically similar stone points with hollowed bases from Gua Lawa in Java and Toalean sites in Sulawesi.

EXPLOITED RESOURCES

Bellwood (1997: 188) proposed inter-island translocation to explain the early to mid-Holocene appearance of two marsupial species at North Maluku sites. He also noted the long-distance exchange of New Britain obsidian, indicated by its appearance in the Neolithic levels of Gua Tengkorak in Sabah (Bellwood 1997: 224), which ties in with the frequent use of geochemical sourcing of valuable stone in archaeology to trace prehistoric exchange networks (Renfrew and Bahn 2000: 371–8).

While these proposals were accompanied by maps showing the location of the referenced sites, none of them explicitly presented the distribution maps time-honoured in archaeology (e.g., Hodder and Orton 1976) for marking out the zone of occurrence of relevant cultural traits. This was first attempted by Bulbeck (2008) who also extended the approach by searching for any traits that might reflect maritime interaction. The study led to the inference of a long history of maritime exchange in ISEA leading up to the intensification of these maritime networks during the Neolithic, and a greater predication of the ISEA Neolithic on intensified maritime exchange than any associated spread of farming. Responses have ranged from blatant dismissal as 'supposition' (Bellwood 2011: S369) through partial acceptance (e.g., Spriggs 2010) to the constructive development of one or more of the issues raised in the 2008 paper (e.g., Blench 2012; Plutniak et al. 2014; O'Connor 2015; Piper 2016). As Bulbeck (2008) was a pilot study, and reliant on a very partial if rapidly growing database of archaeological documentation, the opportunity presented here to test previously proposed inferences was welcomed.

A valuable improvement to the approach was suggested to the author by François-Xavier Ricaut after the presentation at the 'Sea Nomad' session at the 15th International Conference of the European Association of Southeast Asian Archaeologists (Paris, 2015). He observed that demarcating maritime zones of a trait's presence is predicated on the trait's absence at sites outside of the inferred maritime distribution, which should be investigated and mapped. This advice was not only theoretically sound but also of practical value in promoting a thorough review of the relevant archaeological literature, often coming upon previously unknown trait presences. On the down side, this thorough approach has demanded a huge amount of time both in terms of consulting references, including those pertaining to the adjacent landmass of Mainland Southeast Asia (MSEA), and preparing graphical presentation of the site-based absences as well as the presences.

One potentially relevant topic placed outside the scope of this study is the role of domesticated plants, for several reasons. First, as Bellwood (2011: S372) notes: 'Caves in marginal agricultural terrain such as Niah are of questionable relevance for any discussion of agricultural origins in Island Southeast Asia. Real data on agricultural prehistory are likely to come from waterlogged alluvial and coastal sites….' The absence of pre-Iron Age archaeological sites in ISEA that meet this specification clashes with the focus of the present study on Neolithic and earlier site-based archaeology. Second, the bulk of the discourse on which crops may have been introduced to ISEA either before or during the Neolithic incorporates an abundance of evidence from historical linguistics, the present day distribution of potential progenitors, and archaeological evidence outside of ISEA (e.g., Bellwood 2011; Denham 2011; Blench 2012; Fuller and Castillo 2015). There is such a diversity of informed opinion here that a full review (rather than the passing coverage in Bulbeck 2008) would be mandatory to attempt to square the presented evidence with the archaeological data that are available for ISEA, creating a major distraction from this paper's focus on maritime interactions. Third, the hundreds of hours of work devoted to the documentation presented here have made scope extension a practical impossibility. Fortunately, Donohue and Denham (2010), Barker and Richards (2013) and O'Connor (2015) provide recent overviews of the topic, which the interested reader can consult.

MATERIALS AND METHODS

The materials utilised in this study are the publications, research theses and conference presentations to which the author had access up to mid-2016, and which present data on the dated occurrence (up to 3000 BP) of items of material culture in Southeast Asian archaeological sites. Sources in English dominate the literature which could be accessed, excluding much of the relevant literature in Southeast Asian languages except where it is covered by secondary sources in English. Notwithstanding this limitation, a very large number of sources were consulted. The most useful provide detailed and wide-ranging information on dated site contents—for instance, Rabett (2012), which also includes a useful appendix of dates associated with AMH occupation and their calibrated equivalent where appropriate. Nonetheless, many sources with a narrower focus provide critical additional information for investigating and documenting a particular point of enquiry. The sources necessary for documenting the information presented here are enumerated in alphabetical order in Table 3.1, and their assigned numbers are listed for each of the maps in Table 3.2.

Table 3.1 Numerical identification of sources used for the distribution maps.

1: Aeutrakulvit et al. 2012.
2: Allard 2001.
3: Anggraeni 2012.
4: Anggraeni et al. 2014.
5: Aplin et al. 2016.
6: Arifin 2004.
7: Azis et al. 2016.
8: Barton et al. 2013.
9: Bayard 1996–7.
10: Bay-Peterson 1987.
11: Bellwood 1978.
12: Bellwood 1998a.
13: Bellwood 1998b.
14: Bellwood 1997.
15: Bellwood 2001.
16: Bellwood et al. 1998.
17: Bellwood et al. 2013.
18: Bonatz 2009.
19: Bulbeck 2003.
20: Bulbeck 2004a.
21: Bulbeck 2004b.
22: Bulbeck 2004c.
23: Bulbeck 2004d.
24: Bulbeck 2005.
25: Bulbeck 2011.
26: Bulbeck 2014.
27: Bulbeck 2016.
28: Chazine 2005.
29: Chazine and Ferrié 2008.

30: Chia 2007.
31: Chia et al. 2005.
32: Cooling 2012.
33: Conrad 2015.
34: Datan and Bellwood 1991.
35: Demeter 2006.
36: Détroit 2002.
37: Edwards-McKinnon 1990.
38: Fage 2009.
39: Fakhri 2016.
40: Fauzi 2016.
41: Foo 2010.
42: Forestier 2007.
43: Forestier et al. 2005.
44: Forestier et al. 2015.
45: Fox 1970.
46: Fox 1978.
47: Glover 1976.
48: Glover 1986.
49: Grenet et al. 2016.
50: Guillaud et al. 2006.
51: Ha Van Tan 1997.
52: Hiep and Huffer 2015.
53: Higham 1989.
54: Higham 1996.
55: Higham 2006.
56: Higham and Kijngam 2011.
57: Higham and Thosarat 2014.
58: Hiscock 2005.

(cont'd overleaf)

Table 3.1 *(cont'd)*

59: Hung 2008.
60: Hung and Carson 2014.
61: Hutterer 1974.
62: Lampert et al. 2002.
63: Langley and O'Connor 2016.
64: Langley et al. 2016.
65: Lara et al. 2016.
66: Lloyd-Smith et al. 2016.
67: Lu 2011.
68: Mahirta 2003.
69: Mahirta 2009.
70: Mahirta et al. 2004.
71: Majid et al. 1998.
72: Marwick 2007.
73: Marwick 2013.
74: Matthews 1966.
75: Mijares 2002.
76: Mijares 2006.
77: Mijares 2007.
78: Miksic 1980.
79: Moore et al. 2009.
80: Morley et al. 2016.
81: Morwood et al. 2007.
82: Neri et al. 2015.
83: Nguyen et al. 2004.
84: Nguyen et al. 2011.
85: Noerwidi 2011/12.
86: O'Connor 2015.
87: O'Connor and Bulbeck 2014.
88: O'Connor et al. 2005a.
89: O'Connor et al. 2005b.
90: O'Connor et al. 2014b.
91: O'Connor et al. this volume.
92: Ogawa 2004.
93: Oktaviana et al. 2016.
94: Oliveira 2008.
95: Ono et al. 2010.
96: Ono et al. 2015.
97: O'Reilly and Shewan 2016.
98: Oxenham et al. 2015.
99: Oxenham et al. 2016.
100: Pasveer 2004.
101: Pasveer 2005.
102: Pasveer and Bellwood 2004.
103: Patole-Edouamba et al. 2015.
104: Pawlik et al. 2014a.
105: Pawlik et al. 2014b.
106: Pawlik et al. 2015.
107: Paz et al. 2012.
108: Peterson 1974.
109: Pigott and Natapintu 1996–97.
110: Piper 2016.
111: Piper et al. 2014.
112: Plutniak et al. 2014.
113: Prasetyo 2002a.
114: Prasetyo 2002b.
115: Rabett 2007.
116: Rabett 2012.
117: Rabett and Piper 2012.
118: Rabett et al. 2013.
119: Reepmeyer et al. 2011.
120: Reynolds 1989.
121: Samper Carro et al. 2015.
122: Sarjeant 2014.
123: Shelach-Levi 2015.
124: Shoocongdej 2000.
125: Shoocongdej 2006.
126: Simanjuntak 2002.
127: Simanjuntak and Asikin 2004.
128: Simanjuntak and Prasetyo 2002.
129: Simanjuntak et al. 2006.
130: Simanjuntak et al. 2015.
131: Simons and Bulbeck 2004.
132: Solheim et al. 1979.
133: Sophady et al. 2015.
134: Spriggs 2003.

Table 3.1 *(cont'd)*

135: Spriggs et al. 2011.
136: Srisuchat and Srisuchat 1992.
137: Storm 1995.
138: Storm et al. 2013.
139: Suryatman et al. 2016.
140: Szabó et al. 2004.
141: Szabó et al. 2007.
142: Szabó and Ramirez 2009.
143: Tanudirjo 2001.
144: Tayles et al. 2015.
145: Thiel 1990.
146: Tilley and Oxenham 2016.
147: Tin Htut Aung et al. 2015.
148: Tsang 2005.
149: U Aung Thaw 1971.
150: Valentin et al. 2015.
151: Van den Bergh et al. 2009.
152: Van Heekeren 1972.
153: Van Vlack 2014.
154: Wiradnyana and Setiawan 2011.
155: Yi et al. 2008.
156: Zeitoun et al. 2012.
157: Zhang 2000.

Table 3.2 Sources by distribution map.

Map	Sites (Reference)
1	Ngeubhinh Mouxeu (156); Hang Cho (155); Tham Lod (73); Lang Kamnan, Lang Rongrien, Moh Khiew 1, Bukit Bunuh, Callao Cave, Niah Caves, Leang Sakapao 1, Leang Burung 2, Golo (116); Laang Spean (133); Tabon (104); Gua Ilas Kenceng (38); Tabuhan Cave (130); Wajak (138); Liang Bua (80); Liang Sarru (96); Lene Hara, Jerimalai, Matja Kuru 2 (87).
2	Mai Da Dieu, Xom Trai, Xom Tre, Tham Huong, Hang Cho, Hang Trong, Gua Balambangang, Uai Bobo 2 (116); Tham Lod (125); Lang Kamnan (124); Laang Spean (133); Gua Sagu (71); Gua Harimau (40); Tabon (104); Hagop Bilo (12); Niah Caves (8); Liang Abu (49); Lubang Payau (6); Gua Tabuhan, Gua Braholo (87); Song Keplek (42); Gua Talimbue (139); Lua Meko (69); Jerimalai, Matja Kuru 1 (63); Daeo 2 (16); Toé Cave (100); Liang Lemdubu, Liang Nabulei Lisa (58).
3	Hang Cho (155); Tham Lod (73); Lang Kamnan (124); Laang Spean (133); Callao Cave, Tabon, Golo (116); Niah Caves (8); Gua Ilas Kenceng, Leang Sakapao 1, Gua Jing, Leang Barugayya 1, Leang Lompoa, Leang Burung 2, Lene Hara (93); Liang Bua (80); Gua Braholo (87); Song Keplek (42); Matja Kuru 2 (63); Liang Lemdubu (89).
4	Hang Cho (155); Mai Da Dieu, Con Moong, Hang Boi, Spirit Cave, Padah-lin, Khao Talu, Lang Kamnan, Lang Rongrien, Moh Khiew 1, Gua Gunung Runtuh, Gua Sagu, Gua Tenggek, Tianko Panjang, Musang Cave, Ille Cave, Tabon, Gua Balambangang, Niah Caves (116); Hang Pong 1, Sung Sam (53); Tam Hang (103); Tam Ongbah (152); Laang Spean (44); Moh Khiew 2 (1); Khao Toh Chong (153); La Sawang, Gua Peraling, Gua Chawas (33); Bubog 1, Gua Braholo, Song Terus, Song Keplek, Song Gupuh (110); Sohoton 1 (61); Hagop Bilo (12); Liang Abu (49); Kimanis, Lubang Payau (6); Gua Talimbue (5); Liang Bua (151); Tron Bon Lei (121); Lua Meko, Pia Hudale (68); Uai Bobo 2 (48); Jerimalai, Matja Kuru 1 (63); Golo (102); Toé Cave (100); Liang Nabulei Lisa (101).

(cont'd overleaf)

Table 3.2 (cont'd)

Map	Sites (Reference)
5	Bo Nam, Hang Dang, Cai Beo, Steep Cliff Cave (53); Pho Binh Gia, Cau Giat (35/74); Hang Cho (155); Mai Da Dieu, Hang Trong, Khao Talu, Lang Rongrien, Moh Khiew 1, Sakai Cave, Gua Gunung Runtuh, Gua Cha, Ille Cave, Lipuun Point Caves, Balobok, Niah Caves, Gua Lawa, Song Gupuh, Paso, Ulu Leang 1, Lie Siri, Uai Bobo 2 (116); Spirit Cave (72); Ban Rai, Ment Cave, La Sawang, Thung Nong Nien, Gua Teluk Kelawar, Gua Peraling, Gua Chawas (33); Padah-lin (149); Laang Spean (44); Moh Khiew 2 (1); Khao Toh Chong (153); Gua Singa, Gua Kajang, Gua Teluk Kelawar B, Gua Batu Tukang, Gua Bukit Taat (25); Sukajadi Pasar (37); Tögi Ndrawa (43); Gua Pandan (129); Musang Cave (145); Agop Atas (12); Liang Abu (49); Kimanis (6); Gua Pawon (85); Song Terus (110); Song Keplek (117); Liang Sarru (96); Gua Talimbue (5); Liang Bua (151); Tron Bon Lei (121); Lua Munggeta (68); Bui Ceri Uato, Bui Ceri Uato Mane (94); Lene Hara (63); Tanjung Pinang (16); Wetef, Golo (102); Kria Cave (100); Liang Nabulei Lisa (101).
6	Hang Cho (155); Mai Da Dieu, Con Moong, Hang Boi, Spirit Cave, Lang Kamnan, Khao Talu, Lang Rongrien, Moh Khiew 1, Gua Gunung Runtuh, Tianko Panjang, Ille Cave, Tabon, Gua Balambangan, Niah Caves, Song Gupuh, Gua Braholo, Golo (116); Hang Pong 1, Sung Sam (53); Ban Rai, La Sawang, Gua Peraling, Gua Chawas (33); Tam Hang (103); Padah-lin (149); Tam Ongbah (152); Laang Spean (44); Moh Khiew 2 (1); Khao Toh Chong (153); Gua Sagu, Gua Tenggek (71); Tögi Ndrawa (43); Musang Cave (145); Sohoton 1 (61); Agop Atas, Agop Sarapad, Hagop Bilo (12); Liang Abu (49); Kimanis, Lubang Payau (6); Gua Pawon (85); Song Keplek (42); Gua Talimbue (90); Liang Bua (151); Tron Bon Lei (121); Lua Meko, Pia Hudale (68); Uai Bobo 2 (86); Jerimalai, Lene Hara, Matja Kuru 1 and 2 (63); Toé Cave (100); Liang Lemdubu (89); Liang Nabulei Lisa (88).
7	Hang Cho (155); Mai Da Dieu, Con Moong, Hang Boi, Spirit Cave, Lang Kamnan, Khao Talu, Lang Rongrien, Moh Khiew 1, Gua Gunung Runtuh, Tianko Panjang, Ille Cave, Tabon, Gua Balambangan, Niah Caves, Song Gupuh, Gua Braholo, Golo (116); Hang Pong 1, Sung Sam (53); Ban Rai, La Sawang, Gua Peraling, Gua Chawas (33); Tam Hang (103); Padah-lin (149); Tam Ongbah (152); Laang Spean (44); Moh Khiew 2 (1); Khao Toh Chong (153); Gua Sagu, Gua Tenggek (71); Tögi Ndrawa (43); Musang Cave (145); Sohoton 1 (61); Agop Atas, Agop Sarapad, Hagop Bilo (12); Liang Abu (49); Kimanis, Lubang Payau (6); Gua Pawon (85); Song Keplek (42); Gua Talimbue (90); Liang Bua (151); Tron Bon Lei (121); Lua Meko (68); Pia Hudale, Uai Bobo 2, Matja Kuru 2 (86); Jerimalai, Lene Hara, Matja Kuru 1 (63); Toé Cave (100); Liang Lemdubu (89); Liang Nabulei Lisa (88).
8	Lang Cuom (35/83); Ha Lung, Cai Beo, Quynh Van, Spirit Cave, Banyan Valley Cave, Steep Cliff Cave (53); Ban Thuy, Con Co Ngua, Da But, Go Trung, Lang Cong (52); Ban Rai (73); Bau Du (51); Lang Kamnan (124); Khao Talu, Moh Khiew 1, Sakai Cave, Gua Cha, Ille Cave, Niah Caves (116); Ment Cave (33); Laang Spean (44); Khao Khi Chan (136); Tham Sua, Gua Bukit Taat (26); Moh Khiew 2 (1); Khao Toh Chong (153); Gua Singa, Gua Kajang, Gua Teluk Kelawar, Gua Batu Tukang, Gua Chawas, Gua Peraling, Sebarang Perak (19); Guar Kepah (41); Gua Sagu (71); Tögi Ndrawa (43); Gua Pandan (129); Leodivico Capina (134); Pasqua (92); Nagsabaran (59); Minori Cave (75); Callao Cave, Laurente Cave, Dalan Serkot Cave (77); Dimolit (108); Bubog 1 (106); Bagumbayan (10);

Table 3.2 *(cont'd)*

Map	Sites (Reference)
	Duyong (45); Balobok (132); Bukit Tengkorak (30); Liang Abu, Liang Jon (49); Kimanis, Lubang Payau (6); Gua Peturon (127); Gua Braholo, Song Keplek (113/126); Song Gupuh (81); Leang Tahuna, Leang Tuwo Mane'e, Liang Manaf (143); Kamassi, Minanga Sipakko (3); Gua Talimbue, Gua Mo'o hono, Gua Sambagoala (90); Bola Batu, Ulu Leang 1, Leang Burung 1, Leang Pattae, Panganreang Tudea (21); Liang Bua (151); Tron Bon Lei (121); Lua Meko, Lie Madira (68); Lie Siri, Bui Ceri Uato, Uai Bobo 1 and 2 (48); Bui Ceri Uato Mane (94); Jerimalai, Lene Hara, Matja Kuru 1 and 2 (63); Tanjung Pinang, Daeo 2, Siti Nasifah, Um Kapat Papo (16); Golo (141); Toé Cave, Kria Cave (100); Liang Nabulei Lisa (88).
9	Bo Nam, Hang Dang, Ha Lung, Spirit Cave, Steep Cliff Cave (53); Pho Binh Gia, Cau Giat (35/74); Hang Cho (155); Mai Da Dieu, Khao Talu, Lang Rongrien, Moh Khiew 1, Sakai Cave, Gua Gunung Runtuh, Gua Cha, Niah Caves, Paso (116); Sáo Cave (52); Ban Rai, Ment Cave, Thung Nong Nien (33); Padah-lin (149); Lang Kamnan (124); Laang Spean (44); Khao Khi Chan (136); Moh Khiew 2 (1); Khao Toh Chong (153); Gua Singa, Gua Kajang, Gua Teluk Kelawar, Gua Teluk Kelawar B, Gua Batu Tukang, Gua Chawas, Gua Peraling, Gua Bukit Taat (26); Gua Sagu (71); Sukajadi Pasar (37); Tögi Ndrawa (43); Gua Pandan (129); Leodivico Capina (134); Minori Cave (75/104); Dalan Serkot Cave (77); Bubog 1, Ille Cave, Duyong, Balobok, Liang Manaf (110); Agop Atas (13); Liang Abu, Liang Jon (49); Kimanis, Lubang Payau (6); Gua Peturon, Song Keplek (127); Gua Braholo (113); Song Gupuh (81); Leang Tahuna (143); Liang Sarru (95); Kamassi (3); Gua Talimbue, Gua Mo'o hono, Gua Sambagoala (90); Bola Batu, Ulu Leang 1, Leang Burung 1, Leang Pattae, Panganreang Tudea (21); Liang Bua (151); Tron Bon Lei (121); Lua Meko, Lua Munggeta (68); Lie Siri, Uai Bobo 2 (48); Bui Ceri Uato (48/94); Bui Ceri Uato Mane (94); Lene Hara, Matja Kuru 1 and 2 (63); Jerimalai (64); Tanjung Pinang, Daeo 2, Golo (16); Toé Cave, Kria Cave (100); Liang Nabulei Lisa (88).
10	Bo Nam, Hang Dang, Ha Lung, Cai Beo, Spirit Cave, Steep Cliff Cave (53); Pho Binh Gia, Cau Giat (35/74); Lang Cuom (35/83); Hang Cho (155); Mai Da Dieu, Khao Talu, Lang Rongrien, Moh Khiew 1, Sakai Cave, Gua Gunung Runtuh, Gua Cha, Ille Cave, Niah Caves, Paso (116); Da But, Sáo Cave (52); Ban Rai, Ment Cave, Thung Nong Nien (33); Padah-lin (149); Lang Kamnan (124); Laang Spean (44); Khao Khi Chan (136); Moh Khiew 2 (1); Khao Toh Chong (153); Gua Singa, Gua Kajang, Gua Teluk Kelawar, Gua Teluk Kelawar B, Gua Batu Tukang, Gua Chawas, Gua Peraling, Gua Bukit Taat (26); Guar Kepah (41); Sebarang Perak (25); Gua Sagu (71); Sukajadi Pasar, Gua Pandan (37/78/129); Tögi Ndrawa (43); Leodivico Capina (134); Minori Cave (75/104); Callao Cave, Laurente Cave, Dalan Serkot Cave (77); Bubog 1 (110); Bagumbayan (10); Lipuun Point caves, Balobok (132); Agop Atas (13); Bukit Tengkorak (30); Liang Abu, Liang Jon (49); Kimanis, Lubang Payau (6); Gua Peturon, Song Keplek (127); Gua Braholo (113); Song Gupuh (81); Leang Tahuna, Liang Manaf (143); Liang Sarru (95); Kamassi (3); Gua Talimbue, Gua Mo'o hono, Gua Sambagoala (90); Bola Batu, Ulu Leang 1, Leang Burung 1, Leang Pattae, Panganreang Tudea (21); Liang Bua (151); Tron Bon Lei (121); Lua Meko, Lua Munggeta, Lie Madira (68); Lie Siri, Uai Bobo 2 (48); Bui Ceri Uato (48/94); Bui Ceri Uato Mane (94); Lene Hara, Matja Kuru 1 and 2 (63); Jerimalai (64); Tanjung Pinang, Daeo 2, Um Kapat Papo (16); Golo (141); Toé Cave, Kria Cave (100); Liang Nabulei Lisa (88).

(cont'd overleaf)

Table 3.2 *(cont'd)*

Map	Sites (Reference)
11	Bo Lum, Sung Sam, Tham Hoi (53); Hang Cho, Niah Caves (110); Mai Da Dieu, (35/116); Con Moong, Hang Boi, Spirit Cave, Khao Talu, Gua Gunung Runtuh, Tianko Panjang, Gua Balambangang, Song Gupuh, Golo (116); Sao Cave (52); Ban Rai, Tam Hang (144); Padah-lin (149); Tam Ongbah (152); Lang Kamnan (124); Laang Spean (44); Lang Rongrien, Moh Khiew 1, Gua Chawas, Gua Peraling, Gua Tenggek (25); Moh Khiew 2 (1); Khao Toh Chong (153); La Sawang (33); Musang Cave (145); Sohoton 1 (61); Ille Cave (65); Tabon, Gua Braholo, Song Terus (36); Agop Atas, Agop Sarapad (12); Liang Abu (49); Kimanis, Lubang Payau (6); Gua Pawon, Song Keplek (85); Gua Talimbue (5); Liang Bua (151); Tron Bon Lei (121); Pia Hudale (70); Uai Bobo 2 (48); Jerimalai, Lene Hara, Matja Kuru 2 (63); Toé Cave (20); Liang Nabulei Lisa (24); Liang Lemdubu (89).
12	Dadunzi (55); Fuchuanling, Youyugang, Yinzhou, Xiantouling, Yuanzhou, Houshanwan (67); Shixia, Sham Wan (2); Ling-Ding, You-Xian-Fang, Niuchouzi, Tao-Zi-Yuan (150); Peinan (15); Torongan Cave, Reranium Cave, Sunget, Savidug Dune (17); Phung Nguyen, Lung Hoa (54); Ha Long (83); Man Bac (146); Spirit Cave (62); Banyan Valley Cave, Long Thanh (53); Phu Lon Pottery Flats (109); Non Pa Wai, Ban Chiang, Non Nok Tha, Ban Lum Khao, Non Mok La, Ban Tha Kae, Ban Kao, Khok Phanom Di, Nong Nor, Lang Rongrien, Gua Harimau (25); Non Kao Noi, Ban Non Wat (56); Koh Ta Meas (97); Laang Spean (133); An Son (122); Co Gao Su, Long Giang, Rach Nui (98); Khao Sam Kaeo, Pak Om, Gua Chawas, Gua Batu Tukang, Gua Chawas, Gua Cha, Jenderam Hilir, Gua Sagu (26); Loyang Mendale (154); Tögi Ndrawa (43); Bukit Arat (18); Pondok Selabe 1 (129); Benua Keling Lama (50); Nagsabaran (99); Irigayen, Gaerlan (92); Pamittan, Magapit, Dalan Serkot, Callao Cave, Emme Cave (76); Pintu Cave, Dimolit (108); Leta Leta (142); Pasimbahan (107); Bukit Tengkorak (30); Melanta Tutup (31); Niah Caves (66); Liang Jon, Liang Kaung, Nangabalang, Jambu Hilir (112); Gua Sireh (34); Gua Lawa (127); Gua Braholo (36); Song Keplek (85); Hoekgrot, Gua Kecil (137); Leang Tahuna, Leang Tuwo Mane'e (143); Mansiri (7); Kamassi, Minanga Sipakko (3); Gua Talimbue, Gua Mo'o hono, Gua Sambagoala (90); Mallawa (22); Ulu Leang 1, Leang Burung 1 (23); Liang Bua (79); Tron Bon Lei (121); Lie Siri, Bui Ceri Uato, Uai Bobo 1 and 2 (48); Bui Ceri Uato Mane (94); Lene Hara, Matja Kuru 1 (86); Tanjung Pinang, Golo, Bawuwansi, Uattamdi (16).
13	Bo Lum, Sung Sam, Tham Hoi, Tham Hai, Hang Chua (53); Hang Cho (155); Mai Da Dieu, Con Moong, Hang Boi, Lang Kamnan, Khao Talu, Lang Rongrien, Moh Khiew 1, Gua Gunung Runtuh, Tabon, Gua Balambangang, Song Gupuh, Gua Braholo, Ulu Leang 1, Uai Bobo 2 (116); Sao Cave (52); Tam Hang (103); Spirit Cave, Ban Rai (73); Padah-lin (149); Tam Ongbah (152); Laang Spean (44); Moh Khiew 2 (1); Khao Toh Chong (153); La Sawang (33); Gua Chawas, Gua Peraling (19); Gua Tenggek (71); Tögi Ndrawa (43); Tianko Panjang, Gua Pawon, Paso (135); Musang Cave (145); Sohoton 1 (61); Bubog 1, Ille Cave (82); Agop Atas, Agop Sarapad (12); Niah Caves (118); Liang Abu (49); Kimanis, Lubang Payau (6); Song Keplek (42); Liang Sarru (96); Gua Talimbue (139); Liang Bua (79); Lua Meko, Pia Hudale (69); Tron Bon Lei, Matja Kuru (91); Jerimalai, Bui Ceri Uato, Bui Ceri Uato Mane (119); Bawuwansi, Golo (16); Toé Cave (100); Liang Lemdubu, Liang Nabulei Lisa (58).

Table 3.2 *(cont'd)*

Map	Sites (Reference)
14	Lang Cuom (35/83); Bo Nam, Hang Dang, Spirit Cave, Steep Cliff Cave (53); Hang Cho (155); Ban Rai, Khao Talu, Ment Cave, Sakai Cave, Gua Teluk Kelawar, Gua Chawas (33); Padah-lin (149); Laang Spean (44); Moh Khiew 1, Ille Cave, Lipuun Point caves, Balobok, Niah Caves, Gua Lawa, Song Gupuh (116); Moh Khiew 2 (1); Khao Toh Chong (153); Gua Singa, Gua Gunung Runtuh, Gua Kajang, Gua Teluk Kelawar B, Gua Cha, Gua Peraling (19); Gua Batu Tukang, Gua Bukit Taat (26); Tögi Ndrawa (43); Sukajadi Pasar (37); Gua Pandan (129); Agop Atas (12); Liang Abu (49); Kimanis (6); Gua Pawon (85); Gua Braholo (126); Song Keplek (42); Paso (14/116); Gua Talimbue (5); Ulu Leang 1 (47); Liang Bua (151); Tron Bon Lei (121); Lua Munggeta (68); Lie Siri, Bui Ceri Uato, Uai Bobo 2 (48); Bui Ceri Uato Mane (94); Lene Hara (63); Tanjung Pinang, Golo, Um Kapat Papo (16); Toé Cave, Kria Cave (100); Liang Nabulei Lisa (88).
15	Nanguanlidong (60); Lo Gach (83); Cai Beo, Banyan Valley Cave (53); Co Cave (52); Da But (52/83); Quynh Van (53/83); Moebyae Cave (147); Bau Du (51); Ment Cave, Khao Talu, Moh Khiew 1 and 2 (33); Laang Spean (44); Nong Nor (57); Khao Khi Chan, Buang Baeb (136); Khao Toh Chong (153); Gua Batu Tukang, Gua Teluk Kelawar, Gua Ngaum, Gua Chawas (19/33); Gua Cha (115); Sukajadi Pasar (37); Tögi Ndrawa (43); Pondok Selabe 1 (129); Gua Harimau (40); Nagsabaran (111); Miguel Supnet (134); Pasqua (92); Rabel Cave (77); Pintu Cave, Dimolit (108); Bubog 1 (105); Bagumbayan (10); Ille Cave (65); Pasimbahan (107); Guri Cave (46); Talikod (132); Liang Jon (29/49); Gua Sireh (34); Kimanis, Lubang Payau (6); Gua Braholo, Song Keplek (127/128); Song Gupuh (81); Leang Tahuna, Leang Tuwo Mane'e (143); Gua Talimbue, Gua Mo'o hono (90); Gua Sambangoala (39); Ulu Leang 1, Leang Burung 1, Batu Ejaya 1 (131); Liang Bua (151); Lie Siri, Bui Ceri Uato, Uai Bobo 1 and 2 (48); Bui Ceri Uato Mane (94); Jerimalai, Matja Kuru 1 and 2 (63); Lene Hara (86); Tanjung Pinang, Golo, Siti Nasifah, Um Kapat Papo (16); Kria Cave (100).
16	Dingsishan, Xiantouling (123); Shixia, Sham Wan (2); Ta Pen Keng sites on Penghu Islands and Taiwan (148); Baxiandong cave sites (157); Lo Gach, Go Trung, Quynh Van (83); Con Co Ngua (52); Banyan Valley Cave, Steep Cliff Cave, Ment Cave, Khao Talu (72); Moebyae Cave (147); Bau Du (51); Laang Spean (44); Khao Khi Chan (120); Khao Toh Chong (153); Moh Khiew 1, Gua Singa, Gua Ngaum, Gua Teluk Kelawar, Gua Teluk Kelawar B, Gua Batu Tukang, Gua Chawas, Gua Peraling, Gua Cha, Gua Bukit Taat (25); Guar Kepah (41); Sukajadi Pasar (78); Tögi Ndrawa (43); Pondok Selabe 1 (129); Gua Harimau (40); Minori Cave (75); Dimolit (108); Bubog 1 (105); Ille Cave (140); Duyong (45); Talikod (132); Niah Caves (118); Liang Abu, Liang Jon (49); Kimanis, Lubang Payau (6); Gua Peturon (127); Gua Braholo (126); Song Keplek (42); Song Gupuh (81); Leang Tahuna, Leang Tuwo Mane'e (143); Minanga Sipakko (3); Gua Talimbue (139); Gua Mo'o hono, Gua Sambagoala (90); Ulu Leang 1, Leang Burung 1 (21); Liang Bua (79/151); Lua Meko, Lie Madira (69); Lie Siri, Bui Ceri Uato, Uai Bobo 1 and 2 (48); Bui Ceri Uato Mane (94); Hata Sour, Lene Hara, Jerimalai (32); Tanjung Pinang, Sitti Nasifah, Um Kapat Papo, Golo (16); Toé Cave, Kria Cave (100).

(cont'd overleaf)

Table 3.2 *(cont'd)*

Map	Sites (Reference)
17	Baiyangcun, Dadunzi, Phung Nguyen culture sites, Non Kao Noi (55); Fuchuanling, Shixia, Youyugang, Yinzhou, Xiantouling, Yuanzhou, Guye, Houshanwan (67); Xuntangpu culture sites, Hongmaogang culture sites, Niamatou culture sites, Fushan culture sites, Nangaulani, Nanguanlidong, Niuchouzi culture sites (60); Torongan Cave (17); Lo Gach, Cai Beo, Bau Tro (83); Man Bac (84); Banyan Valley Cave, Ban Chiang, Long Thanh, Khok Phanom Di, Laang Spean (53); Phu Lon Pottery Flats, Non Pa Wai (109); Non Kao Noi, Ban Non Wat (56); Non Nok Tha (9); Ban Kao (11); Nong Nor (57); An Son (122); Khao Khi Chan (136); Moh Khiew 1 (27); Gua Harimau, Gua Batu Tukang, Jenderam Hilir (30); Gua Ngaum, Gua Chawas, Gua Cha, Gua Bukit Taat (19); Loyang Mendale (154); Tögi Ndrawa (43); Bukit Arat (18); Pondok Selabe 1 (129); Benua Keling Lama (50); Pamittan, Magapit, Nagsabaran, Andarayan, Dalan Serkot, Callao Cave, Emme Cave (76); Pintu Cave, Dimolit (108); Bubog 1 (106); Pasimbahan (107); Talikod (132); Gua Tengkorak (28); Gua Sireh (34); Gua Braholo (114); Song Keplek (85); Hoekgrot (137); Leang Tahuna, Leang Tuwo Mane'e (143); Kamassi, Minanga Sipakko (4); Gua Talimbue, Gua Mo'o hono, Gua Sambagoala (90); Ulu Leang 1, Leang Burung 1, Mallawa (22); Liang Bua (151); Tron Bon Lei (121); Lie Siri, Bui Ceri Uato, Uai Bobo 1 and 2 (48); Bui Ceri Uato Mane (94); Lene Hara, Matja Kuru 1 (86); Tanjung Pinang, Golo, Bawuwansi (16).

The methodology involved investigation of proposals for evidence of maritime interaction that affected ISEA, not only those in Bulbeck (2008) but also other published proposals. Translocation of exploited resources (as described in the Introduction) was regarded as the most diagnostic evidence, followed successively by sharing of style and tradition, with shared technology the least diagnostic. Only cases with potentially related cultural items dating to the same time frame are presented, with the time frame limited to the smallest possible interval, because cultural sharing should be registered by archaeologically instantaneous presence at the connected sites. In particular, the chronologically earliest instances are presented, because later instances could well represent separate continuations of the material culture subsequent to its sharing. Information on archaeological context (where available) is not considered central to the investigation, because sharing of material culture need not imply its same use or ideational connotations at the sites concerned.

The analysis treats the data on an 'as is' basis, to avoid confusing caution in archaeological interpretation with the imposition of a predetermined view. For instance, based on their faunal identifications from Liang Bua in Flores (Table 3.3), Van den Bergh et al. (2009) somewhat controversially date the appearance of the Sulawesi warty pig (*Sus celebensis*) to around 7000 BP, and the appearance of porcupines, civets, macaques and the domesticated *S. scrofa* pig to around 4000 BP. These estimates are accepted here as the best available on the current data, even though it would be possible that the seven *S. celebensis* fragments stratigraphically beneath the 6400 BP date could have been vertically displaced downward from the 4000–6400 BP spits that have a larger number of *S. celebensis* specimens.

Table 3.3 Summary of Liang Bua Sector IV identifications (number of individual specimens) relevant to this contribution, from Van den Burgh et al. (2009: Fig. 2, Appendix A). Note: Deepest porcupine, civet and macaque remains all occur in spit 16 or spit 17.

Spits	Marine shell	Porcu-pine	Civet	Macaque	Suid (*Sus scrofa cum S. celebensis*)	Suid (*S. celebensis*)	Human remains
1–17 (pottery, 3600 BP date spit 16)	12	80	31	43	213	0	18
18–25 (pre-pottery, 6400 BP date spit 24)	2	0	0	0	0	23	31
26–30 (pre-pottery)	0	0	0	0	0	7	146
31–35 (pre-pottery, dates of 10,200 BP and 11,300 BP)	0	0	0	0	0	0	4

Also, the assumption of continual occupancy of a site from its oldest to its youngest dating is avoided; where there appear to have been occupancy gaps, as at Lang Rongrien and Liang Sarru (Bulbeck and Marwick, in press), the site is deemed irrelevant to recognising archaeological presences or absences during these gap periods. However, the 'absences' may include some cases where the relevant data are simply unavailable in the consulted documentation, whether or not the investigated phenomena had been encountered at a given site, or where taphonomic factors (such as non-preservation of organic remains) may have negatively impacted a site's archaeological record. Future research can be expected to unearth additional relevant data from sources which could not be accessed or through excavation of 'sister sites' with more favourable taphonomic conditions than those where absences were recorded due to non-preservation.

The inferences drawn from the axes mapped in this chapter can be regarded as hypotheses for future empirical testing. Additional data in the future could lead to:
- straightforward confirmation, if any additional presences fall within the mapped axis;
- extended confirmation, if any additional presences enlarge the mapped axis but retain the evidence for maritime interaction;
- re-dated confirmation, if there are additional presences that point to an earlier dating for the inferred maritime exchange of the material culture under investigation; and
- refutation, if there are additional presences that obviate maritime exchange as a likely explanation for shared, diagnostic material culture.

An example of where additional research can refute a proposed maritime interconnection is provided by terminal Pleistocene stone tools with ground edges and/or surfaces. Being aware only of their occurrence in North Vietnam sites and at the Niah Caves in Borneo, and notwthstanding Borneo's connection by land to MSEA at the time, Bulbeck (2008) suggested they may reflect a maritime link across the South China Sea. But in fact, the documentation by Majid et al. (1998) of grinding slabs at Gua Sagu in the Malay Peninsula, and more recently of ground-edge pestles at Gua Harimau in Sumatra (Fauzi 2016), dating to the same millennia as the earliest ground-edge tools recorded from North Vietnam and Niah, points to terrestrial interaction as a more parsimonious explanation for any technological diffusion that may have been involved (Map 3.2).

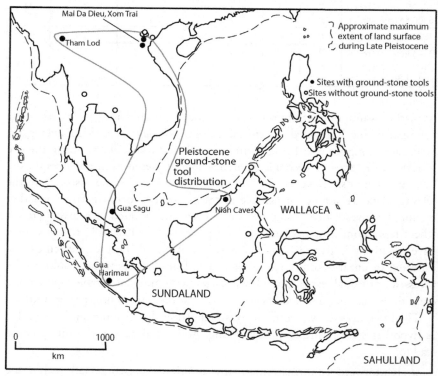

Map 3.2 Southeast Asian sites with 17,000–15,000 BP human habitation, with and without ground-stone tools.

PLEISTOCENE ROCK ART

Rock art is of similar antiquity to the oldest AMH habitation deposits in ISEA, as shown by minimum direct dates of around 40–18,000 BP on animal paintings and hand stencils in several Maros caves (without Pleistocene habitation deposits) in southwest Sulawesi. The circa 30,000 BP examples coincide chronologically with the onset of habitation (abandoned by 20,000 BP) at two further southwest Sulawesi sites with hand stencils: Leang Sakapao 1 and Leang Burung 2. A dating of circa 30,000 BP also applies to red pigment from a piece of rock fall at Lene Hara in Timor-Leste, and to the onset of habitation at Gua Ilas Kenceng (East Kalimantan) whose abundant hand stencils include an example with a minimum direct date of around 10,000 BP (Oktaviana et al. 2016). Accordingly, Map 3.3 links southwest Sulawesi, Timor-Leste and East Kalimantan into a 'Pleistocene rock art axis', beyond which there is as yet no evidence for rock art in ISEA of comparable antiquity.

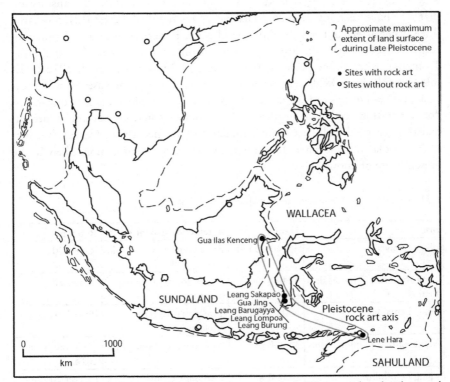

Map 3.3 Southeast Asian sites with 30,000–28,000 BP human habitation, with and without rock art.

Rich, widespread bodies of rock art, which include images of large mammals and hand stencils with 'narrowed fingers' resulting from a second application of pigment, occur across both southern Sulawesi and East Kalimantan (Oktaviana et al. 2016). Accordingly, they appear to be related artistic traditions, with circa 30,000 BP the best currently available estimate for the onset of the maritime interaction that was apparently involved. On the other hand, the mooted connection between Sulawesi and Timor-Leste is less well attested; although they were connected by a chain of inter-visible islands (Kealy et al. 2017), these latter islands are yet to be documented for rock art of potentially Pleistocene antiquity.

EARLY OSSEOUS ARTEFACTS

Rabett (2012), Rabett and Piper (2012) and Piper (2016) extend the earlier research by Rabett (2005) into Southeast Asia's early osseous (bone and teeth) artefacts. These date back to around 45,000 BP but, until 16,000 BP, they are few and far apart both geographically and chronologically (Table 3.4). Most were recovered from Sundaland/MSEA sites and so any cultural transmission that may have been involved could have been overland (Rabett 2012). Similarly, three other artefacts from the Aru Islands, which were then part of Sahulland, could reflect overland cultural influence from southern Australia (including Tasmania) where bone points date back to 35,000 BP (Allen et al. 2016). The sole example from Wallacea, a circa 34,000 BP bone point base from Timor-Leste, is also Timor's only bone artefact older than the mid-Holocene on current documentation (e.g., Glover 1986). This artefact could conceivably represent maritime cultural influence from Sahulland or Borneo (Niah Caves), but it is such an isolated occurrence that independent development is more likely in the present state of knowledge.

Table 3.4 Southeast Asia osseous artefacts 16,000 BP and older.

Site	Date(s)	Artefact classification	Reference
Niah, Sarawak	45–40,000 BP	Bone point, worked tusk, bone spatula	Rabett 2012
Lang Rongrien, Thai-Malay Peninsula	42,000 BP	Antler groove-and-snap fragment	Rabett 2012
Song Terus, Java	>30,000 BP	Two potential bone artefacts	Piper 2016
Matja Kuru 2, Timor-Leste	34,000 BP	Base to hafted bone point	O'Connor et al. 2014a
Liang Lemdubu, Aru	26,000 BP	Two bone points	Pasveer 2005
Xom Trai, North Vietnam	22–19,000 BP	Miscellaneous bone artefacts	Piper 2016
Liang Lemdubu, Aru	16,000 BP	Worked bone shaft	Pasveer 2005

Rabett and Piper (2012) draw attention to the proliferation of bone-tool technology across Southeast Asia during the terminal Pleistocene and early Holocene, and conclude that prehistoric maritime interaction was probably involved in the transmission of innovations across the region. Their appraisal is supported by distribution maps for these two intervals (Maps 3.4 and 3.5). At around 15,000 BP, bone point production resumed at the Niah Caves (Rabett and Piper 2012), which may be the source for the 14–11,000 BP bone points documented for East Kalimantan, North Vietnam and the Arus. The validity of this 'Pleistocene bone point axis' would imply introduction of bone points to Sulawesi by the Pleistocene/Holocene junction, as confirmed by their early Holocene presence at three widely distributed Sulawesi sites (unless attributable to initial Holocene influence from Borneo). A second, 14–11,000 BP maritime axis is suggested by the earliest appearance of bone artefacts at Sabah and in the Philippines at opposing ends of the Sulu Sea. Further expansion of the associated maritime interactions is suggested by the early Holocene appearance of bone points in the Philippines and North Maluku, as part of an 'early Holocene bone point axis' covering Wallacea from Sulawesi northwards (Map 3.5).

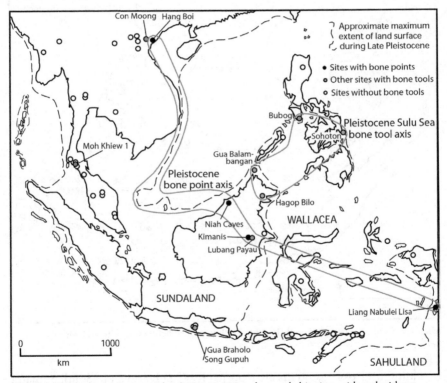

Map 3.4 Southeast Asian sites with 14,000–11,000 BP human habitation, with and without bone tools.

Map 3.5 presents a minimalist appraisal of the maritime cultural influence related to the spread of bone tool technology during the early Holocene. Such an influence may have been responsible for the early Holocene appearance of bone tools at Song Terus and Song Gupuh in Java and at Kria Cave in Western Papua. These possibilities have been excluded from Map 3.5 because overland extension of bone point technology during the terminal Pleistocene would have an equally feasible explanatory force: respectively, a Sundaland extension from Borneo to Java; and a Sahulland extension from the Aru Islands to Western Papua. Also, note that North Vietnam had a vigorous bone-tool industry during the early Holocene but shortcomings in documentation—such as poor description of the bone tools' morphology, poor documentation of which particular sites had bone artefacts, and the lack of dates for the bone-tool rich site of Da Phuc (Rabett 2012)—prevent this fact from being reflected in Map 3.5.

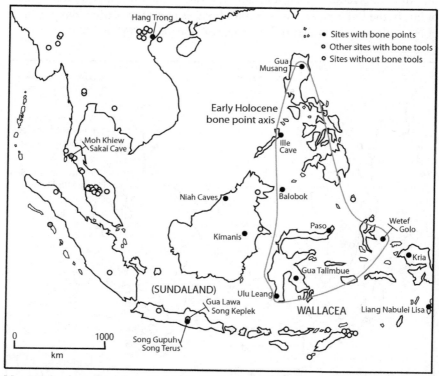

Map 3.5 Southeast Asian sites with 10,000–7500 BP human habitation, with and without bone points.

In addition, 11 osseous points are reported for Gua Harimau in South Sumatra but their stratigraphic position and likely antiquity (as with all of the faunal remains) are not provided (Ansyori and Rokhus 2016). Similarly, punches and spatulae of bone and deer antler are reported for the Nias Island site of Tögi Ndrawa but without any indication of their chronological status within the site's terminal Pleistocene to late Holocene deposits (Forestier et al. 2005).

WORKED MARINE SHELL

Marine shell was utilised as a raw material from early years at coastal locations in ISEA. For instance, very early shell ornaments date back to around 40,000 BP at Jerimalai in Timor-Leste and the tradition continued there until recent centuries (Langley and O'Connor 2016). Similarly, utilitarian artefacts made from marine shell are reported in Golo Cave dating back to around 30,000 BP (Szabó et al. 2007). Several shell fish hooks at Jerimalai may date to between 23,000 and 16,000 BP based on their stratigraphic position (O'Connor 2015) and shell adzes from Golo Cave are associated with dates reaching back to 13,000 BP (Bellwood et al. 1998). However, current available evidence for maritime exchange of shell-working traditions (proposed by Bulbeck 2008) dates to later times.

The oldest directly dated shell fish hook in Timor-Leste is from Lene Hara, with an uncalibrated date of 9741±60 BP (Langley and O'Connor 2016), very close to the uncalibrated direct date of 10,230±30 BP from Tron Bon Lei in Alor (Samper Carro et al. 2015). These are the two dates focused on in suggesting a terminal Pleistocene shell fish hook axis in Nusatenggara (Map 3.6).

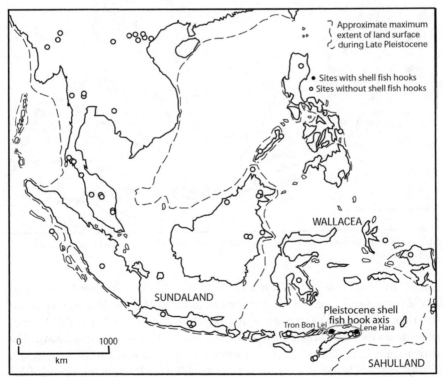

Map 3.6 Southeast Asian sites with 12,000–10,000 BP human habitation, with and without shell fish hooks.

Beads of olive shell and other marine shells date to 12,000–10,000 BP on Rote as well as Timor-Leste (Map 3.7). Notwithstanding the propinquity of these two islands, a land connection between them rarely if ever existed during the period of AMH occupation of ISEA (Kealy et al. 2017), and definitely not at the Pleistocene/Holocene transition when any cultural contact would have required crossing a small sea gap. Pierced Neritidae shells from Hang Boi probably dating to this same interval (Rabett 2012, 238–9) are likely to reflect an independent development in view of the distance (without intermediaries) involved.

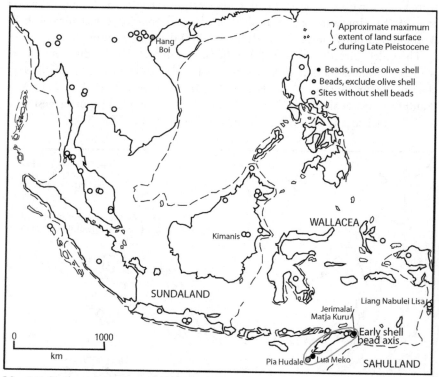

Map 3.7 Southeast Asian sites with 12,000–10,000 BP human habitation, with and without shell ornaments.

Later expansion of the Timor/Rote shell bead axis within ISEA is possibly reflected in the recovery of a pierced Terebra shell from Liang Nabulei Nisa dating to just less than 10,000 BP (O'Connor et al. 2005a) and some barely modified cowry shells from the Pleistocene/Holocene transition at Kimanis (Arifin 2004). The early to mid-Holocene occurrence of further cowry ornaments at Kimanis (Arifin 2004), and simple shell ornaments at Song Keplek, Gua Braholo (Prasetyo 2002a) and Liang Bua (Van den Bergh et al. 2009), points to consolidation and further expansion of this preceramic tradition of shell ornaments in ISEA (Map 3.8). This tradition may have been the source for the Conus ornaments associated with a circa 5000 BP burial from Duyong Cave in Palawan (Fox 1970), although another possible source is North Vietnam where some sites also have marine shell ornaments dated to the same time frame.

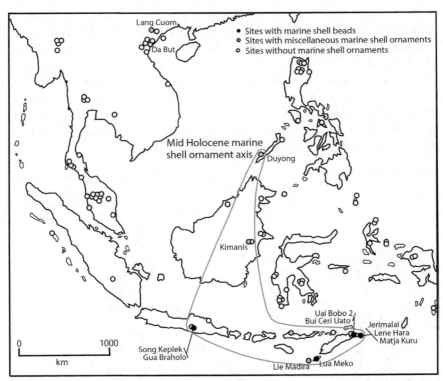

Map 3.8 Southeast Asian sites with 7000–5000 BP human habitation, with and without marine shell ornaments.

A distinct tradition of shell ornaments, based on armlets, spacer beads and disc beads (mainly Trochus and Nautilus), is dated to 3500 BP or later from sites in the Batanes (Bellwood and Dizon 2013), Luzon, Sabah (Bellwood 1997), Palawan (Szabó and Ramirez 2009), Java (Prasetyo 2002a: 187–8), Flores (Galipaud et al. 2016), Timor-Leste (Glover 1986; O'Connor 2015), Talaud Islands (Tanudirjo 2001), and the Pacific in association with Lapita pottery (Bellwood 1978). While there are certainly strong grounds for associating this tradition with the southward expansion of Malayo-Polynesian speakers from a homeland in or near Taiwan, it should not be confused or conflated with the older ISEA axis illustrated in Map 3.8 (Spriggs 2010).

Turning to the topic of marine shell adzes, we note that direct dates on Tridacna adzes if unsupported by other stratigraphically anchored dates are to be avoided, as these adzes could have been made on fossil shell (Tanudirjo 2001). This cautious approach removes certain specimens from contention, for instance, the surface finds of a Tridacna adze from Timor-Leste directly dated to the early Holocene (Piper 2016). This approach nonetheless allows for the recognition of marine shell adzes at Golo Cave in the Moluccas through to 8000 BP, and a distribution that extended as far east as the Pamwak site on Manus and as far north as Bubog 1 on Mindoro by 7000 BP (Piper 2016). Other early Holocene dates for ISEA marine shell adzes allow recognition of an 'early Holocene marine shell adze axis' bridging the Sulu and Halmahera Seas (Map 3.9). This tradition of valuing shell adzes appears to have expanded during the mid-Holocene as reflected by Tridacna adzes interred with a preceramic flexed burial at Duyong Cave in Palawan (in keeping with the suggestion by Bellwood 1997: 222), the recovery of a Tridacna adze from the upper pre-pottery layers of Leang Tahuna (Tanudirjo 2011), and a Tridacna adze directly dated to around 5000 BP from the Sepik region in Papua New Guinea (Piper 2016).

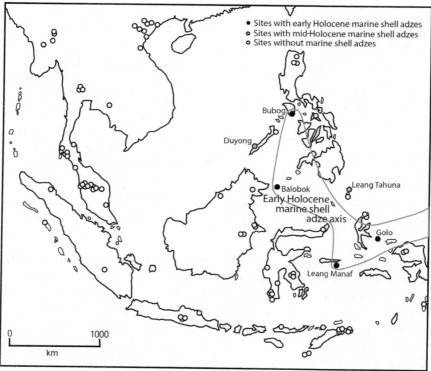

Map 3.9 Southeast Asian sites with 9000–7000 BP human habitation, with and without marine shell adzes.

The early to mid-Holocene (9–6000 BP) witnessed the widespread use of marine shell for scrapers across south-western ISEA, but not reported for many other areas even in assemblages characterised by large quantities of marine shell.

Unifacially worked marine shell scrapers are also described by Simanjuntak and colleagues (2006) as a common feature of the Hoabinhian shell mounds of northeast Sumatra. Unfortunately, no Sumatra shell mounds have been dated, with the exception of Sukajadi Pasar in field studies by Miksic (1980) and Edwards-McKinnon (1990), but which did not allow the authors to examine the contents of the shell mound closely. On balance, it would be reasonable to extend the 'early Holocene marine shell scraper axis' to include Sumatra's Hoabinhian shell mounds, with Sukajadi Pasar singled out as the dated example of these sites (Map 3.10).

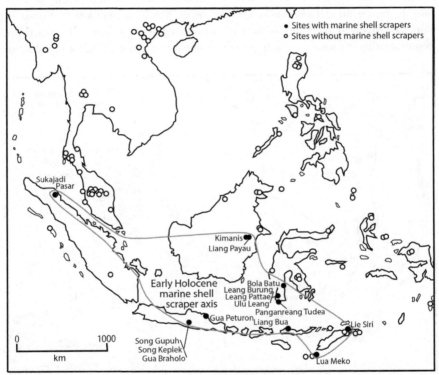

Map 3.10 Southeast Asian sites with 9000–6000 BP human habitation, with and without marine shell scrapers.

A wide interval of 3,000 years is allowed for the 'early Holocene marine shell scraper axis' because the scrapers are dated broadly rather than tightly (and none have been directly dated). It may be hypothesised that the initial extent of the axis was smaller, and expanded as the mid-Holocene approached—a hypothesis to be tested when tighter date estimates become available. It is also of relevance that Bellwood (2011: S374) recognised the production of marine shell scrapers as a pre-Neolithic technology that was bequeathed to the Neolithic occupants of ISEA.

MORTUARY PRACTICES

Piper (2016) draws attention to the appearance of prescribed mortuary practices, specifically flexed inhumations and cremations, as a marker of increased social complexity at the Pleistocene/Holocene transition. More specifically, this interval reveals a dichotomy between Sundaland and Wallacea burials (Map 3.11). A number of Sundaland/MSEA sites, from North Vietnam to Java and Sarawak, include flexed inhumations dated to 11–10,000 BP. Flexed inhumations date back to circa 16,000 BP at Tam Hang in Laos (Piper 2016) and 14,000 BP at Tham Lod in Thailand (Shoocongdej 2006) and Gua Braholo in Java (Détroit 2002: 174), so there would have been ample time for overland transmission of this practice during the terminal Pleistocene. On the other hand, contemporary burials in Wallacea involved fragmentary human remains ('fractional burials'), sometimes demonstrating crematory reduction of the original bones as at Ille Cave in Palawan.

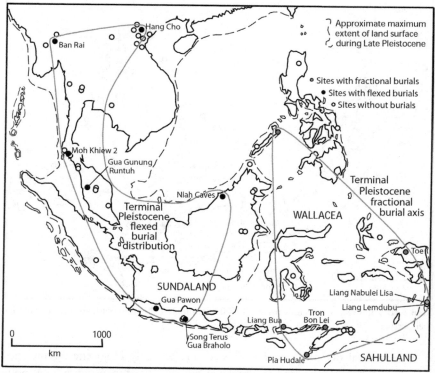

Map 3.11 Southeast Asian sites with 11,000–10,000 BP flexed and fractional burials.

A small number of secondary, cremated burials of early Holocene age are reported for Niah's West Mouth (Lloyd-Smith 2012) and these could well represent short-range, maritime cultural influence from Palawan. Indeed, there may well have been two-way exchange, because preceramic flexed burials are reported for Palawan at the Tabon Caves (Fox 1970) and Sa'gung Rockshelter (Kress 2004), probably reflecting Holocene cultural transmission from Borneo, where the Niah Cave cemeteries show continuation of this burial mode until mid-Holocene times (Piper 2016). However, south and east of Palawan, fractional burials persisted as the burial mode across Wallacea until the Neolithic (e.g., Bulbeck 2004a), whereas flexed burials were the dominant mid-Holocene burial mode across western Southeast Asia, including Java, Sumatra, Peninsular Malaysia and North Vietnam (e.g., Bulbeck 2011; Piper 2016).

Two new mortuary practices appeared in ISEA during the Neolithic (fourth millennium BP): extended inhumations and mortuary disposals in jars. However, they need not have resulted in blanket replacement of earlier mortuary practices, as at the Niah Caves where they were practised alongside flexed inhumations and fractional burials (Lloyd-Smith and Cole 2010). Pit burials recorded for southern China and North Vietnam add to the diversity of burial practices in Southeast Asia and the subtropics to the immediate north at the time (Map 3.12).

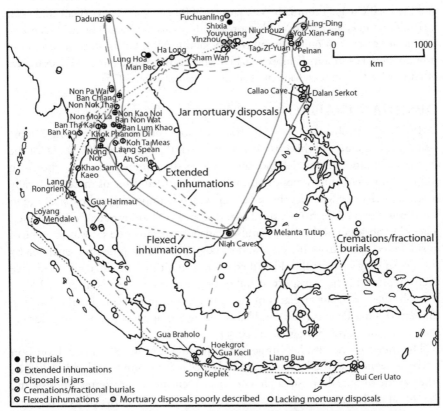

Map 3.12 Mortuary disposals in sites with 4000–3000 BP human habitation in Southeast Asia and its north.

Flexed inhumations had the least extensive distribution, ranging from the Niah Caves and Lang Rongrien in the south to Man Bac (North Vietnam) in the north, and expressed as a minority practice wherever in evidence. They evidently represent a retention of the widespread Sundaland tradition of flexed burials. Cremations/fractional burials in contrast had a very widespread distribution, to the degree that they would no longer qualify as culturally diagnostic during the fourth millennium BP.

The practice of Neolithic extended inhumations can be reasonably sourced to MSEA, the geographic centre of distribution and the location where most of the mortuary disposals were extended burials. While they were present in Taiwan, here they appear to have been an offshoot from northern MSEA. Certainly, southern MSEA (including the Thai-Malay Peninsula) would be more parsimonious than Taiwan as the source for extended inhumations by 3000 BP at the Niah Caves and Song Keplek (Java). Taiwan on the other hand would be the likely source for the mortuary disposals in jars recorded for Dalan Serkot Cave (Luzon) and the Niah Caves before 3000 BP (Map 3.12), and other sites in ISEA (e.g., Pain Haka in Flores) and the Pacific (e.g., Teouma in Vanuatu) at 3000 BP or soon after (Galipaud et al. 2016; Valentin et al. 2015). While mortuary disposals in jars are also in evidence as a minority practice at quite a number of Neolithic MSEA sites, these involved the primary burial of infants (Bulbeck 2011), whereas the Taiwan and ISEA examples often involved secondary disposal of adults (Valentin et al. 2015).

OBSIDIAN TRAFFIC

In ISEA, use of obsidian may date back to more than 40,000 years in Timor-Leste, but the source of this obsidian is unknown (Spriggs et al. 2011). As for the terminal Pleistocene/initial Holocene levels of the Timor-Leste sites shown in Map 3.13, two distinct types of obsidian are identified. One of these is a locally sourced pitchstone, whereas the other was evidently imported to these sites and to Tron Bon Lei on Alor from a third island source (O'Connor et al. this volume). The other obsidian of the same age also transported across the sea was the type of obsidian recovered from Ille Cave and Bubog 1, two Philippine sites separated by sea. Depending on its still unidentified source, maritime exchange may well have been involved in the transport of the obsidian to both sites (Neri et al. 2015). The obsidian used for artefacts of comparable antiquity from Tianko Panjang (Sumatra), Gua Pawon (Java) and Paso (Sulawesi) appears to have been locally sourced in each case (Spriggs et al. 2011).

The traffic in the obsidian imported to Jerimalai, Matja Kuru and Tron Bon Lei became more active during the mid-Holocene (O'Connor et al. this volume), whereas the Bubog/Ille obsidian has not been identified from contexts postdating the initial Holocene, presumably because the source was drowned by rising sea-levels (Neri et al. 2015). Traffic in obsidian does not appear to have been a major feature of the Southeast Asia pre-Neolithic, although artefacts of obsidian imported from an unknown source have been reported in the mid-Holocene levels at Bukit Tengkorak in Sabah (Spriggs et al. 2011).

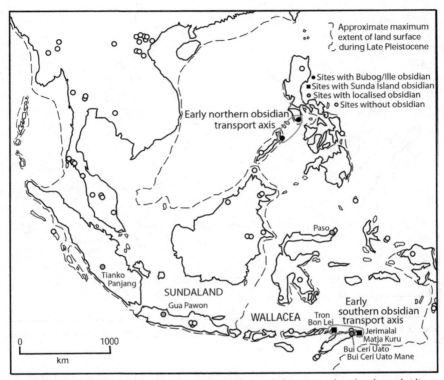

Map 3.13 Southeast Asian sites with 11,000–9000 BP human habitation, with and without obsidian.

FAUNAL TRANSLOCATION

One of the proposals for early Holocene inter-island faunal exchange (Map 3.14) involves the appearance of the Dorcopsis wallaby at Um Kapat Papo and Golo in the northern Moluccas at about 8000 BP, quite possibly from Misool Island which lies off the West Papua coast. The wallaby's range extended to Sitti Nasifah on Halmahera by the fifth millennium BP, coincidentally with the appearance of bandicoots (Map 3.15). The appearance of wallabies in Halmahera during the mid-Holocene may well reflect translocation within the northern Moluccas, but bandicoots are unrecorded at other northern Molucca sites and so may have been introduced directly from New Guinea (Bellwood et al. 1998). Subsequent expansion of the translocated marsupial axis to Timor-Leste during the fourth millennium BP is indicated by a direct dating of about 3200 BP for a cuscus tooth from Matja Kuru 2 (O'Connor 2015) as well as cuscus remains at Uai Bobo 2 in contexts dated to about 4000 BP (Glover 1986).

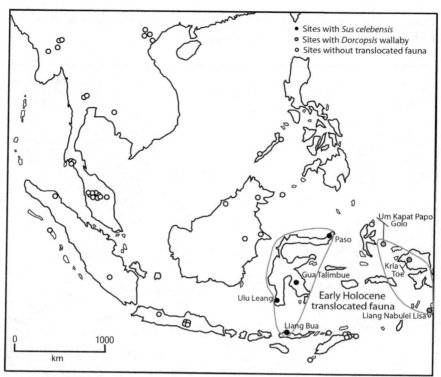

Map 3.14 Southeast Asian sites with 8000–7000 BP human habitation, with and without translocated fauna.

The second proposed case of early Holocene inter-island faunal exchange is the Sulawesi warty hog (Sus celebensis) at Liang Bua in Flores dated to around 7000 BP (Table 3.3). Bellwood (1978: 74–5) even allowed for the possibility that Sus celebensis had been domesticated in prehistoric times, while Simons and Bulbeck (2004: 177) argued that the species' high representation in the mid- to late-Holocene faunal identifications of the Sulawesi Maros karsts suggests a commensal relationship with the local 'Toalean' inhabitants. Interestingly, Piper and colleagues (2014) contend that the remains of the Eurasian wild boar Sus scrofa at Nagsabaran in North Luzon, one of which is directly dated to 4500–4200 BP, represents a species that was domesticated or at least managed by the local inhabitants. However, their support for this claim appears to be restricted to the fact that the 'Lanyu clade' of domesticated pig (as genetically identified) has a current distribution across the Philippines and Taiwan. Thus, while Taiwan was almost certainly the source of the Nagsabaran S. scrofa, it may have originally been introduced as a non-domesticate, which would be more in line with the oldest dates of about 3200 BP for the presumably domesticated S. scrofa on the Batanes, lying between Taiwan and northern Luzon (Piper et al. 2013).

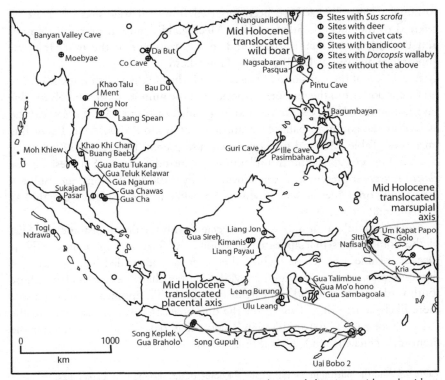

Map 3.15 Southeast Asian sites with 5000–4000 BP human habitation, with and without translocated fauna.

A more southerly pulse of placental translocation dating to 5000–4000 BP involved deer at Ulu Leang 1 in the Maros karsts and civets at Uai Bobo 2 (Map 3.15). The deer species found today in Sulawesi is *Cervus timorensis* with its origins in Java, and so this would presumably be the applicable identification for any archaeological deer remains in Sulawesi (Simons 1997). Deer identifications are not frequent in Sulawesi sites but in South Sulawesi they do include identifications by D.A. Hooijer from the mid to late-Holocene site of Leang Balisao, and identifications by Simons from a mid-Holocene context at Leang Burung 1, a mid to late-Holocene context at Batu Ejaya 1, and late-Holocene contexts at Leang Burung 1, Leang Karassak and Batu Ejaya 2 (Simons and Bulbeck 2004). On balance, this suggests a continuous presence of deer in South Sulawesi from the mid-Holocene (as represented in the Leang Burung 1 excavated trench with its almost entirely mid-Holocene deposit) through to recent times.

The civet species found today in Timor-Leste is the common palm civet *Paradoxurus hermaphroditus*, found widely across eastern Indonesia following its dispersal from Java or another western Indonesian source (Monk et al. 1997).

Although civet remains have been reported from Sulawesi sites, they are all referred to the endemic Sulawesi civet Macrogalidia musschenbroekii (Simons and Bulbeck 2004; Fakhri 2016) and so are irrelevant to the mid-Holocene appearance of civets at Uai Bobo 2 in Timor-Leste.

Expansion of the translocated placental axis during the fourth millennium BP is evident both from the number of species and the number of sites involved. The Java porcupine (*Hystrix javanica*) and long-tailed macaque (*Macaca fascicularis*) as well as the common palm civet appeared at around 4000 BP at Liang Bua on Flores (Table 3.3), and macaques were also present by circa 4000 BP at Uai Bobo 2 (Glover 1986). Fourth millennium BP introductions to Sulawesi include *Rattus tanezumi* present at Leang Burung 1 by 3500 BP (Simons and Bulbeck 2004) and porcupines present at Minanga Sipakko in West Sulawesi by 3000 BP (Simanjuntak et al. 2008).

The fourth millennium BP is also associated with the first appearance in ISEA of the domesticates that appeared at around 3000 BP at Lapita sites in Near Oceania (Table 3.5). These include the genetically identified 'Pacific clade' of domestic pigs, with their origins in MSEA, rather than the Lanyu clade whose southward distribution did not extend beyond the Philippines. MSEA is also a more likely source than Taiwan for the dog breed that was transported to the Pacific (Greig et al. 2016) although Taiwan may have been the source for the prehistoric chickens of Oceania (Storey 2016).

Table 3.5 Fourth millennium BP ISEA dates for domesticates also found in Lapita sites.

Site	Presumed 'Pacific clade' *S. scrofa*	Dog	Chicken	Reference
Callao Cave, northern Luzon	0	~3350 BP (associated date)	0	Piper et al. 2013
Pasimbahan Cave, Palawan	0	~3600 BP (associated date)	0	Ochoa et al. 2014
Niah Caves, Borneo	~3200 BP (direct bone dating)	0	0	Piper et al. 2009
Minanga Sipakko, Sulawesi	~3500 BP (associated date)	~3000 BP (associated date)	0	Anggraeni et al. 2014
Uattamdi, northern Moluccas	~3300 BP (associated date)	~3300 BP (associated date)	0	Bellwood et al. 1998
Liang Bua, Flores	~3500 BP	0	0	Table 3
Matja Kuru 2, Timor-Leste	0	~3050 BP (direct bone dating)	0	Greig et al. 2016
Pulau Ay 1, Bandas	~3100 BP (associated date)	0	~3100 BP (associated date)	Lape 2000

MID-HOLOCENE EXCHANGE NETWORKS INVOLVING NEOLITHIC ELEMENTS

To bring Neolithic material technology into consideration, we extend our geographic scope to the north, to southern China and Taiwan where the Neolithic was established earlier than in Southeast Asia. That said, the same issues arise as are debated for Southeast Asia on the degree of association between early Neolithic material culture and an agricultural subsistence: southern China is discussed by Lu (2011) and Taiwan is discussed by Hung and Carson (2014).

On the topic of pre-Neolithic Holocene stone artefacts, conventional wisdom invokes 'Hoabinhian' industries based on flaked cobbles across MSEA/ Sumatra (e.g., Bulbeck 2011), and similar cobble-based industries in southern China (Shelach-Levi 2015) and Taiwan (Hung and Carson 2014). In contrast, industries based on detaching small flakes from cores with distinct striking platforms are well known for their predominance across ISEA, extending into New Guinea (e.g., Bellwood 1978, 1997). This MSEA/ISEA distinction is somewhat oversimplified as shown by the occurrence of mid-Holocene cobble-based industries at the Niah Caves in Sarawak, Bubog 1 in the Philippines and various northern Moluccan sites (Map 3.16).

A technological focus on Neolithic, polished stone tools appear to have expanded during the mid-Holocene, overland as far south as Khao Toh Chong in the Thai-Malay Peninsula (Van Vlack 2014) and across the seas to Taiwan (Tsang 2005). Around 5,000 years ago a polished stone adze was interred with a flexed burial at Duyong Cave on Palawan, presumably imported from MSEA (North Vietnam) or Taiwan. Dispersal across ISEA of the technology to manufacture Neolithic polished stone tools experienced considerable delay, reaching the Batanes Islands in the far northern Philippines at around 4000 BP, the Karama River sites in West Sulawesi by 3500 BP (Anggraeni et al. 2014), the Niah Caves in Sarawak (Lloyd-Smith et al. 2016) and Gua Uattamdi in the northern Moluccas by 3000 BP (Bellwood et al. 1998), but an apparently later date (or not at all) across much of ISEA.

Importantly, there would appear to have been two mid-Holocene maritime extensions—into locations with cobble-based industry—of the technology of detaching small flakes from cores equipped with striking platforms. The first was a northern extension from Luzon represented by the 5–6000 BP Baxiandong cave sites in Taiwan (Bulbeck 2008), and the second was a south-western extension into southern Sumatra at around 5000 BP represented by the distinction between the small flakes at Pondok Selabe I and the earlier Hoabinhian lithics at Gua Pandan (Simanjuntak et al. 2006; see also Fauzi 2016).

Specific contact between southwest Sulawesi and Java is perhaps suggested by the finds of obsidian arrowheads with hollowed bases, and microliths with bipolar trimming along their backs, at various open-air sites on the Bandung

Plateau in West Java (Forestier 2007). However, while these are certainly the signature stone-tool types of the Toalean of southwest Sulawesi, dated to around 8000–3500 BP (Bulbeck 2004b), the spatial association of the Bandung Plateau examples with polished stone adzes would suggest a dating post-3500 BP.

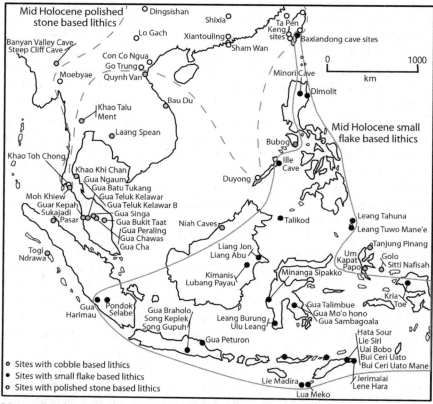

Map 3.16 Lithics characterisation of sites with 6000–5000 BP human habitation in Southeast Asia and its north.

Our review of maritime interaction finally turns to the topic of pottery, focusing on the 4500–3500 BP interval to cover the oldest pottery reported for ISEA. Important background here includes the diffusion of predominantly cordmarked pottery across southern China and North Vietnam by around 7000 BP, with further southward extension into the northern Thai-Malay Peninsula by around 6500 BP and eastward extension into Taiwan by 6000 BP. Cordmarked pottery was also evidently present at Gua Sireh in Sarawak by 4500 BP, some 500–1000 years older than any other securely dated pottery in ISEA. However, by 4500–3500 BP, other pottery traditions were making their mark on the local material culture (Map 3.17). One case involves the red-slipped pottery widespread across

Taiwan except the Nangaulani and Nanguanlidong sites where cordmarked pottery still prevailed (Hung and Carson 2014). A second case involves the 'geometric incised and impressed' pottery of Yunnan origins with an influence that infiltrated south into MSEA (Higham 2006).

Anderson (2005) grouped the Gua Sireh pottery with other ISEA Neolithic assemblages characterised by cordmarked and related paddle-impressed ware into a 'Neolithic I' horizon of MSEA (Thai-Malay Peninsula) origins. The justification for this argument is clear from Map 3.17, which demonstrates the predominance of cordmarked cum paddle-impressed pottery across southern MSEA, which is moreover the closest potential source not only for Gua Sireh but also for the two 'Neolithic I' assemblages in northern Sumatra that predate 3500 BP. By 3000 BP, predominantly paddle-impressed pottery assemblages extended from Sumatra and Java (Guillaud et al. 2006) to the Niah Caves in Sarawak (Lloyd-Smith and Cole 2010) and sites in Palawan (Mijares 2006).

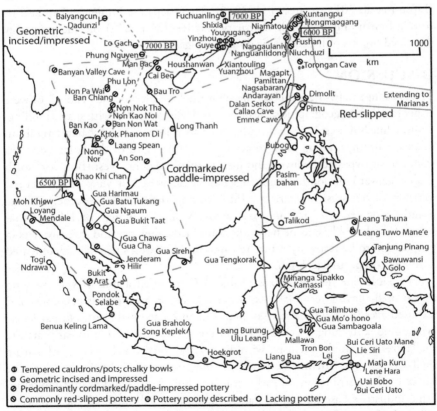

Map 3.17 Pottery characterisation of sites with 4500–3500 BP human habitation in Southeast Asia and its north.

Red-slipped pottery, which characterises Anderson's (2005) 'Neolithic II' had, on the other hand, commenced its dispersal into ISEA as far south as Sulawesi and its eastward dispersal into the Marianas by 3500 BP (Map 3.17). Subsequent dispersals of red-slipped pottery by 3000 BP include Bukit Tengkorak in Sabah (Chia 2007), Uattamdi in the northern Moluccas (Bellwood et al. 1998) and Lapita sites of the Bismarck Archipelago in Papua New Guinea (e.g., Spriggs 2003).

The dispersal of red-slipped pottery can be confidently identified with the movement of early Malayo-Polynesian speakers into eastern ISEA and the Pacific. However, in the case of western ISEA, while the ethnographically spoken languages are also Malayo-Polynesian, recent studies in historical linguistics have identified here an Austroasiatic substratum of MSEA origins (e.g., Blench 2012). Studies in human genetics have also revealed separate genetic influences from MSEA and Taiwan on recent ISEA inhabitants, with the MSEA influence more pronounced in the west and the Taiwan influence more prominent in the east (Lipson et al. 2014; Soares et al. 2016). These separate influences can also be seen in fourth millennium BP mortuary practices (Map 3.12) and the previously discussed origins of ISEA/Pacific domestic pigs.

DISCUSSION

The exchange networks proposed here for the Late Pleistocene (Table 3.6) were either localised in geographic scale or involved lengthy strikes with sparse infilling. Thus, while Sulawesi is linked to adjacent East Kalimantan by a shared tradition of cave paintings dating back to around 30,000 BP, all of the latter networks excluded or bypassed Sulawesi and instead involved zones west (Borneo), north (Sulu/Palawan) or south (Nusatenggara) of Sulawesi. In view of the central location of Sulawesi in maritime ISEA during the Late Pleistocene, and the island's long tentacles reaching out across Wallacea, it may be inferred that none of the Late Pleistocene networks combined coherence and extensiveness (a proposition to be tested by future research into Sulawesi's patchily documented Late Pleistocene archaeology).

The Holocene maritime axes (Table 3.7) included a mix of wide-ranging axes (usually having terminal Pleistocene origins, or Neolithic associations) and localised axes (notably the translocated suid and marsupial axes). No particular geographic patterning is evident. For instance, the distribution of early marine shell adzes is mutually exclusive with the distributions (which overlap) of marine shell scrapers and ornaments. However, these two sets of distributions are cut across by the distributions of early Holocene bone points and of mid-Holocene lithic industries based on small flakes. In summary, throughout the Holocene (to about 3500 BP) there appears to have been a loose network of inter-island connections across ISEA, with further Moluccas↔New Guinea, Taiwan↔Luzon and Borneo↔MSEA connections.

Table 3.6 Summary of proposed Pleistocene maritime exchange networks (approximate chronological order).

Exchanged item	Locations involved	Subsequent growth	Comment
Cave painting	South Sulawesi/ East Kalimantan	Extensions across Sulawesi and Kalimantan	Possible extension to Timor-Leste
Bone points	North Vietnam–Borneo-Aru	Holocene extension across Wallacea north of Lesser Sundas	Overland connection between North Vietnam and Borneo
Other bone tools	Sulu Sea coastlines	Part of above	
Shell fish hooks	Timor/Alor	None documented	Neolithic dating for fish hooks elsewhere
Shell beads	Timor/Rote	Java/Borneo/Palawan (Holocene)	
Fractional burials	Palawan/ Nusatenggara	Borneo by initial Holocene	Subsequent westward Holocene expansion
Obsidian traffic	Timor/Alor and Palawan/Mindoro	More intensive obsidian use in Timor and Alor during Holocene	Palawan/Mindoro obsidian source probably drowned by Holocene sea-level rises

This chapter's definition of 'axis' included subsequent growth, as documented archaeologically for most of the proposed axes. The four instances lacking evidence for subsequent growth include one that was itself the outcome of earlier growth (mid-Holocene marine shell ornaments) and three that indicate pre-Neolithic maritime exchange with crystal clarity (Timor/Alor shell fish hooks, Palawan/Mindoro obsidian, and the translocation of *Sus celebensis* to Flores). Thus, these instances certainly substantiate the case for a long-standing, loose network of maritime connections across ISEA.

The present findings are in broad agreement with the conclusion by Soares et al. (2008) of substantial population dispersals within ISEA during the terminal Pleistocene to early Holocene. Not only is there agreement on the general concept of cross-sea interactions but also the four mitochondrial DNA haplotypes, which are recognised as having expanded, correspond in their antiquity and geographic concentration (Soares et al. 2008: Fig. 3) to particular maritime interaction axes (Table 3.8). This last point may help explain why Soares and collagues' E1 and E2 spatial distributions overlap and interconnect but do not coincide: they trace communication channels between interacting communities, including many separated by sea, rather than population flight driven by sea-level rise. The advantages of open community contact would have included exposure to novel technologies and importation of exotic resources of potentially local benefit, as well as social connections to assist outbreeding and periodic, small-scale transmigration.

Table 3.7 Summary of proposed Holocene maritime exchange networks (approximate chronological order).

Exchanged item	Locations involved	Subsequent growth	Comment
Bone points	Sulawesi–North Moluccas–Philippines	Sumatra at some point	Widespread east of Sumatra by early Holocene
Marine shell adzes	Sulu/Molucca Seas to Manus	Extension to Palawan	
Marine shell scrapers	Timor/Kalimantan/ Java/ Sumatra	Widespread distribution	Distribution includes Sulawesi
Marsupial translocation	New Guinea to Northern Moluccas	Further species/ islands	
Sulawesi warty pig	Sulawesi to Flores	None documented	Possible hybridisation with domestic Sus scrofa
Marine shell ornaments	Timor/Java/Borneo/ Palawan	None documented	Different tradition from Neolithic shell ornaments
Small flake based lithics	Philippines to Taiwan and Java to south Sumatra	Toalean artefacts in Neolithic Java	Distribution includes Sulawesi
Java-based placentals	Java/Sulawesi/Timor	Continuing translocations into historical times	
Lanyu clade Sus scrofa	Taiwan to Luzon	Distribution across Philippines	Pacific clade of pigs elsewhere in ISEA
Pottery styles	MSEA to Sarawak and Taiwan to Philippines	Both expanded south after 3500 BP	Suspected language group associations

Table 3.8 Correspondences between mtDNA haplogroup dispersals (Soares et al. 2008) and archaeologically attested maritime interaction axes.

mtDNA haplogroup	Approximate estimated founder age (with 1 standard error range)	Corresponding maritime axis
E1a	11,000 BP (7–15,000 BP)	Early Holocene bone points (Map 3.5)
E1b	7000 BP (5–9000 BP)	Early Holocene marine shell scrapers (Map 3.10)
E2a	7500 BP (5500–9500 BP)	Pleistocene-Holocene transition fractional burials (Map 3.11 plus related discussion)
E2b	5000 BP (2–8000 BP)	Mid-Holocene Taiwan-Luzon interactions (Maps 3.15 and 3.16)

The model proposed here does not necessitate the pre-Neolithic existence in ISEA of sailing technology or specialist Nusantao 'boat-people', as famously argued by Solheim (2006). The general outlines are similar, including the correspondence of ISEA to Solheim's 'Western Lobe', and the present analysis adduces specifically dated interactions whereas Solheim's examples mostly relied on conjectural age estimates. However, to apply the principle of parsimony, paddle-craft connections between coastal communities within two-way inter-visibility may be sufficient to explain the available evidence.

On the topic of Neolithic elements, these were widespread across southern China by 5000 BP and had been transmitted into MSEA to the south and Taiwan to the east, but they had minimal impact on ISEA for a further millennium and, in most places, considerably longer. The subsequent intrusion of Neolithic influences into ISEA apparently had two sources: MSEA, affecting western ISEA as far east as Sarawak; and Taiwan, affecting eastern ISEA, before these influences linked up with the pre-Neolithic ISEA inter-island network.

CONCLUSION

Thanks to the more rigorous methodology suggested to the author by Ricaut, a constructive revision of the maritime networks proposed by Bulbeck (2008) is now available. The first phase, of Late Pleistocene antiquity, involved distant connections or, approaching the Holocene transition, localised networks within Wallacea (Table 3.6). During the early to mid-Holocene (Table 3.7), network consolidation and/or expansion occurred in ISEA, a region that now included the Sunda shelf islands. By the mid-Holocene, the connections had reached MSEA and Taiwan where Neolithic material culture was well established, leading to the introduction of Neolithic elements from MSEA into western ISEA and from Taiwan into eastern ISEA. At this stage, contact having been made with the previously established ISEA maritime routes, Neolithic influences dispersed irregularly across ISEA during the period 3500–2500 BP.

Building on this perspective, we may suggest that the Taiwan-based thrust was associated with advanced sailing technology, as witnessed by early Neolithic forays into western Pacific islands. Since the Taiwan-based thrust can be identified with Malayo-Polynesian speakers, we would also have a mechanism for the spread of Malayo-Polynesian across western ISEA where, apparently, Austroasiatic languages had previously been established (cf. Blench 2012). The mechanism in question, sailing and advanced watercraft, would have enhanced the inter-island connections which were a lifeblood of ISEA community life.

The Taiwan-based thrust was also the likely source for the Bajau sea gypsies of Southeast Asia. Supporting archaeological evidence comes from the ceramic stoves at Bukit Tengkorak in Sabah, similar to those used ethnographically by the Bajau (Bellwood 1997), and the siting of Lapita sites in the Bismarck Archipelago at offshore and littoral locations (Bellwood 1978). Without caricaturising the Bajau as 'living fossils' of the Malayo-Polynesian expansion across ISEA, it would appear reasonable to propose that the range of Malayo-Polynesian lifestyles included adaptations that were ancestral to the Bajau in a generic sense.

ACKNOWLEDGEMENTS

The comments from two anonymous referees, and the editors' advice on dealing with these comments, have stimulated the author to improve on the originally submitted draft of this chapter. As noted in the text, François-Xavier Ricaut's words of advice have been of great benefit.

REFERENCES

Aeutrakulvit, Prasit, Hubert Forestier, Chaowalit Khaokhiew, and Valéry Zeitoun. 2012. 'New Excavation at Moh Khiew Site, Southern Thailand.' In *Crossing Borders: Selected Papers from the 13th International Conference of the European Association of Southeast Asian Archaeologists*. Volume 1, ed. M.L. Tjoa-Bonatz, A. Reinecke, and D. Bonatz, 60–70. Singapore: NUS Press.

Allard, Francis. 2001. 'Southeast China Late Neolithic.' In *Encyclopedia of Prehistory Volume 3: East Asia and Oceania*, ed. P. Peregrine, and M. Ember, 312–28. New York: Kluwer Academic/Plenum Publishers.

Allen, Harry, Michelle C. Langley, and Paul S.C. Taçon 2016. 'Bone Projectile Points in Prehistoric Australia: Evidence from Archaeologically Recovered Implements, Ethnography, and Rock Art.' In *Osseous Projectile Weaponry*, ed. M.C. Langley, 209–18. New York: Springer.

Anderson, Atholl. 2005. 'Crossing the Luzon Strait: Archaeological Chronology in the Batanes Islands, Philippines and the Regional Sequence of Neolithic Dispersal.' *Journal of Austronesian Studies* 1: 25–44.

Anggraeni. 2012. 'The Austronesian Migration Hypothesis as Seen from Prehistoric Settlements on the Karama River, Mamuju, West Sulawesi.' Unpublished PhD thesis. Canberra: The Australian National University.

Anggraeni, Truman Simanjuntak, Peter Bellwood, and Philip Piper. 2014. 'Neolithic Foundations in the Karama River, West Sulawesi, Indonesia.' *Antiquity* 88: 740–56.

Ansyori, M. Mirza and Rokhus D. Awe. 2016. 'Traces of Fauna Utilization at Harimau Cave Site.' In *Harimau Cave and the Long Journey of OKU Civilization*, ed. T. Simanuntak, 212–25. Yogyakarta: University of Gadjah Mada Press.

Aplin, Kenneth, Sue O'Connor, Philip Piper, David Bulbeck, Ben Marwick, Emma St. Pierre, and Fadhila Aziz. 2016. 'The Walandawe Tradition from Southeast Sulawesi and Osseous Artifact Traditions in Island Southeast Asia.' In *Osseous Projectile Weaponry*, ed. M.C. Langley, 189–208. New York: Springer.

Arifin, Karina. 2004. 'Early Human Occupation of the East Kalimantan Rainforest (the Upper Birang River Region, Berau).' Unpublished PhD dissertation. Canberra: The Australian National University.

Azis, Nazrullah, Christian Reepmeyer, Geoffrey Clark, Daud A. Tanudirjo, and Sriwigati. 2016. *Mansiri: A New Dentate-stamped Pottery Site in Northern Sulawesi*. Presentation at 'The Archaeology of Sulawesi – An Update' symposium, Makassar, Indonesia, 31 January–3 February 2016.

Barker, Graeme and Martin B. Richards. 2013. 'Foraging–farming Transitions in Island Southeast Asia.' *Journal of Archaeological Theory and Method* 20: 256–80.

Barton, Huw, Graeme Barker, David Gilbertson, Chris Hunt, Lisa Kealhofer, Helen Lewis, Victor Paz, Philip Piper, Ryan J. Rabett, Tim Reynolds, and Katherina Szabó. 2013. 'Late Pleistocene Foragers, c. 35,000–11,500 Years Ago.' In *Rainforest Foraging and Farming in Island Southeast Asia*, ed. G. Barker, 173–215. Cambridge: McDonald Institute for Archaeological Research.

Bayard, Donn. 1996–97. 'Bones of Contention: The Non Nok Tha Burials and the Chronology and Context of Early Southeast Asian Bronze.' In *Ancient Chinese and Southeast Asian Bronze Age Cultures, Vol. II*, ed. F.D. Bulbeck and N. Barnard, 889–940. Taipei: SMC Publishing.

Bay-Peterson, Jan. 1987. 'Excavations at Bagumbayan, Masbate, Central Philippines: An Economic Analysis.' *Asian Perspectives* 25: 67–98.

Bellwood, Peter. 1978. *Man's Conquest of the Pacific*. Sydney: Collins.

———. 1988a. 'The Baturong and Madai Flaked Stone Industries.' In *Archaeological Research in South-eastern Sabah*, ed. P. Bellwood, 155–72. Sabah Museum Monograph 2. Kota Kinabalu: Sabah Museum and State Archives.

———. 1988b. 'Molluscan Remains in the Baturong and Madai Caves.' In *Archaeological Research in South-eastern Sabah*, ed. P. Bellwood, 132–41. Sabah Museum Monograph 2. Kota Kinabalu: Sabah Museum and State Archives.

———. 1997. *Prehistory of the Indo-Malaysian Archipelago*. Revised edition. Honolulu: University Hawai'i Press.

———. 2001. 'Southeast Asia Neolithic and Early Bronze.' In *Encyclopedia of Prehistory Volume 3: East Asia and Oceania*, ed. P. Peregrine and M. Ember, 287–306. New York: Kluwer Academic/Plenum Publishers.

———. 2011. 'Holocene Population History in the Pacific Region as a Model for Worldwide Food Producer Dispersals.' *Current Anthropology* 52, supplement 4: S363–78.

Bellwood, Peter and Eusobio Dizon. 2013. 'Other Portable Artefacts from the Batanes Sites.' In *4000 Years of Migration and Cultural Exchange: The Archaeology of the Batanes Islands, northern Philippines*, ed. P. Bellwood and E. Dizon, 123–48. Canberra: Australian National University E-Press.

Bellwood, Peter, Gunadi Nitihaminoto, Geoffrey Irwin, Agus Waluyo, and Daud Aris Tanudirjo. 1998. '35,000 Years of Prehistory in the Northern Moluccas.' In *Bird's Head Approaches: Irian Jaya Studies—A Programme for Interdisciplinary Research*, ed. G.-J. Bartstra, 233–75. Rotterdam: A.A. Balkema.

Bellwood, Peter, Eusobio Dizon, and Alexandra de Leon. 2013. 'The Batanes Pottery Sequence, 2500 BC to Recent.' In *4000 Years of Migration and Cultural Exchange: The Archaeology of the Batanes Islands, Northern Philippines*, ed. P. Bellwood and E. Dizon, 77–113. Canberra: Australian National University E-Press.

Blench, Roger. 2012. 'Almost Everything You Believed About the Austronesians isn't True.' In *Crossing Borders: Selected Papers from the 13th International Conference of the European Association of Southeast Asian Archaeologists*, Volume 1, ed. M.L. Tjoa-Bonatz, A. Reinecke, and D. Bonatz, 122–42. Singapore: NUS Press.

Bonatz, Dominik. 2009. 'The Neolithic in the Highlands of Sumatra: Problems of Definition.' In *From Distant Tales: Archaeology and Ethnohistory in the Highlands of Sumatra*, ed. D. Bonatz, J. Miksic, J.D. Neidel, and M.L. Tjoa-Bonatz, 43–74. Newcastle upon Tyne: Cambridge Scholars Publishing.

Bulbeck, David. 2003. 'Hunter-gatherer Occupation of the Malay Peninsula from the Ice Age to the Iron Age.' In *The Archaeology of Tropical Rain Forests*, ed. J. Mercader, 119–60. New Brunswick: Rutgers University Press.

———. 2004a. 'Appendix 1: Human Remains from Kria Cave and Toé Cave, Papua, Indonesia.' In *The Djief Hunters: 26,000 Years of Rainforest Exploitation on the Bird's Head of Papua, Indonesia*, ed. J.M. Pasveer, 379–98. Modern Quaternary Research in Southeast Asia 17. Leiden: A.A. Balkema.

———. 2004b. 'Divided in Space, United in Time: The Holocene Prehistory of South Sulawesi.' In *Quaternary Research in Indonesia*, ed. S.G. Keates and J.M. Pasveer, 129–66. Modern Quaternary Research in Southeast Asia 18. Leiden: A.A. Balkema.

———. 2004c. 'An Archaeological Perspective on the Diversification of the Languages of the South Sulawesi Stock.' In *Austronesian in Sulawesi*, ed. Truman Simanjutak, 185–212. Jakarta: Center for Prehistoric and Austronesian Studies.

———. 2004d. 'South Sulawesi in the Corridor of Island Populations along East Asia's Pacific Rim.' In *Quaternary Research in Indonesia*, ed. S.G. Keates and J.M. Pasveer, 221–58. Modern Quaternary Research in Southeast Asia 18. Leiden: A.A. Balkema.

———. 2005. 'Human Remains from Liang Nabulei Lisa.' In *The Archaeology of the Aru Islands, Eastern Indonesia*, ed. S. O'Connor, M. Spriggs, and P. Veth, 163–70. Terra Australis 22. Canberra: The Australian National University, Pandanus Books.

———. 2008. 'An Integrated Perspective on the Austronesian Diaspora: The Switch from Cereal Agriculture to Maritime Foraging in the Colonisation of Island Southeast Asia.' *Australian Archaeology* 67: 31–51.

———. 2011. 'Biological and Cultural Evolution in the Population and Culture History of Malaya's Anatomically Modern Inhabitants.' In *Dynamics of Human Diversity: The Case of Mainland Southeast Asia*, ed. N. Enfield, 207–55. Pacific Linguistics 627. Canberra: The Australian National University.

———. 2014. 'The Chronometric Holocene Archaeological Record of the Southern Thai-Malay Peninsula.' *International Journal of Asia-Pacific Studies* 10: 109–60.

———. 2016. 'The Neolithic Gap in the Southern Thai-Malay Peninsula and its Implications for Orang Asli Prehistory.' In *Malaysia's Original People: Past, Present and Future of the Orang Asli*, ed. K. Endicott, 123–52. Singapore: NUS Press.

Bulbeck, David and Ben Marwick. In press. 'Stone Industries of Mainland and Island Southeast Asia.' In *The Oxford Handbook of Southeast Asian Archaeology*, ed. C.F.W. Higham and N.C. Kim. New York: Oxford University Press.

Chazine, Jean-Marie. 2005. 'Rock Art, Burials, and Habitiation: Caves in East Kalimantan.' *Asian Perspectives* 44: 219–30.

Chazine, Jean-Marie and Jean-George Ferrié. 2008. 'Recent Archaeological Discoveries in East Kalimantan, Indonesia.' *Bulletin of the Indo-Pacific Prehistory Association* 28: 16–22.

Chia, Stephen. 2007. 'Scientific Studies of Prehistoric Pottery in Malaysia.' In *Archaeological Heritage in Malaysia*, ed. M. Saidin and S. Chia, 81–95. Penang: Universiti Sains Malaysia, Centre for Archaeological Research.

Chia, Stephen, Arif Johan, and Hirofumi Matsumura. 2005. 'Dental Characteristics of Prehistoric Human Teeth from Melanta Tutup, Semporna, Sabah.' In *The Perak Man and other Prehistoric Skeletons of Malaysia*, ed. Z. Majid, 239–51. Penang: Universiti Sains Malaysia.

Conrad, Cyler. 2015. 'Archaeozoology in Mainland Southeast Asia: Changing Methodology and Pleistocene to Holocene Forager Subsistence Patterns in Thailand and Peninsular Malaysia.' *Open Quaternary* 1 (7): 1–23.

Cooing, Samantha. 2012. 'Investigations of Site Use through the Analysis of the Lithic Assemblage from the Site of Hata Sour, East Timor.' Unpublished MA thesis. Canberra: The Australian National University.

Datan, Ipoi, and Peter Bellwood. 1991. 'Recent Research at Gua Sireh (Serian) and Lubang Angin (Gunung Mulu National Park), Sarawak.' *Bulletin of the Indo-Pacific Prehistory Association* 10: 386–405.

Demeter, Fabrice. 2006. 'New Perspectives on the Peopling of Southeast and East Asia During the Late Upper Pleistocene.' In *Bioarchaeology of Southeast Asia*, ed. M. Oxenham and N. Tayles, 112–33. Cambridge: Cambridge University Press.

Denham, Tim. 2011. 'Early Agriculture and Plant Domestication in New Guinea and Island Southeast Asia.' *Current Anthropology* 52, supplement 4: S379–S395.

Détroit, Florent. 2002. 'Origine et évolution des Homo sapiens en Asie du Sud-Est: Descriptions et analyses morphométriques de nouveaux fossiles.' Unpublished PhD thesis. Paris: Muséum National d'Histoire Naturelle.

Donohue, Mark and Tim Denham. 2010. 'Farming and Language in Island Southeast Asia: Reframing Austronesian History.' *Current Anthropology* 51 (2): 223–56.

Edwards-McKinnon, Edward. 1990. 'The Hoabinhian in the Wampu/Lau Biang Valley of Northeastern Sumatra: An Update.' *Bulletin of the Indo-Pacific Prehistory Association* 10: 132–42.

Fage, Luc-Henri. 2009. 'De Gua Masri à Ilas Kenceng.' In *Bornéo: La Mémoire de Grottes*, ed. L.-H. Fage and J.-M. Chazine, 55–69. Lyon: Fage Éditions.

Fakhri. 2016. *Fauna of Sambangoala Cave Sites*. Presentation at 'The Archaeology of Sulawesi – An Update' symposium, Makassar, Indonesia, 31 January–3 February 2016.

Fauzi, Mohammad Ruly. 2016. 'The Characterization of Stone Tool Types and Technology from Harimau Cave.' In *Harimau Cave and the Long Journey of OKU Civilization*, ed. T. Simanuntak, 184–211. Yogyakarta: University of Gadjah Mada Press.

Foo Shu Tieng. 2010. 'Hoabinhian Rocks: An Examination of Guar Kepah Artifacts from the Heritage Conservation Centre in Jurong.' MA thesis. National University of Singapore.

Forestier, Hubert. 2007. *Ribuan Gunung, Ribuan Alat Batu: Prasejarah Song Keplek, Gunung Sewu, Jawa Timur*. Jakarta: Kepustakaan Populer Gramedia.

Forestier, Hubert, Truman Simanjuntak, Dominique Guillaud, Dubel Driwantoro, Ketut Wiradnyanya, Darwin Siregar, Rokus Due Awe, and Budiman. 2005. 'Le Site de Tögi Ndrawa, Île de Nias, Sumatra Nord: Les Premières Traces d'une Occupation Hoabinhienne en Grotte en Indonésie.' *Comptes Rendus Palévol* 4: 727–33.

Forestier, Hubert, Heng Sophady, Simon Puaud, Vincenzo Celiberti, Stéphane Frère, Valéry Zeitoun, Cécile Mourer-Chauviré, Roland Mourer, Than Heng, and Laurence Billault. 2015. 'The Hoabinhian from Laang Spean Cave in its Stratigraphic, Chronological, Typo-technological and Environmental Context (Cambodia, Battambang Province).' *Journal of Archaeological Science*: Reports 3: 194–206.

Fox, Robert B. 1970. *The Tabon Caves*. Manila: National Museum Monograph 1.

———. 1978. 'The Philippine Paleolithic.' In *Early Paleolithic in South and East Asia*, ed. F. Ikawa-Smith, 59–85. Berlin: De Gruyter Mouton.

Fuller, Dorian Q. and Cristina Castillo Cobo. 2015. 'Bananas: The Spread of a Tropical Forest Fruit as an Agricultural Staple.' In *The Oxford Handbook of the Archaeology of Diet*, ed. J. Lee-Thorp and M.A. Katzenburg, 1–26. Oxford: Oxford University Press.

Galipaud, Jean-Christophe, Rebecca Kinnaston, Sian Halcrow, Aimee Foster, Nathaniel Harris, Truman Simanjuntak, Jonathon Javelle, and Hallie Buckley. 2016. 'The Pain Haka burial ground on Flores: Indonesian evidence for a shared Neolithic belief system in Southeast Asia.' *Antiquity* 90: 1505–21.

Glover, Ian C. 1976. 'Ulu Leang Cave, Maros: A Preliminary Sequence of Post-Pleistocene Cultural Development in South Sulawesi.' *Archipel* 11: 113–54.

———. 1986. *Archaeology in Eastern Timor, 1966–67*. Terra Australis 11. Canberra: The Australian National University, Department of Prehistory.

Grenet, Michel, Josette Sarel, Ruly Fauzy, Adhi Agus Oktaviana, Bambang Sugiyanto, Jean-Marie Chazine, and François-Xavier Ricaut. 2016. 'New Insights on the Late Pleistocene–Holocene Lithic Industry in East Kalimantan) Borneo: The Contribution of Three Rock Shelter Sites in the Karstic Area of the Mangkalihat Peninsula.' *Quaternary International* 416: 126–50.

Greig, Karen, Richard Walter, and Elisabeth A. Matisoo-Smith. 2016. 'Dogs and People in Southeast Asia and the Pacific.' In *The Routledge Handbook of Bioarchaeology in Southeast Asia and the Pacific Island*, ed. M. Oxenham and H.R. Buckley, 462–82. London: Routledge.

Guillaud, Dominique, Hubert Forestier, Romsan Achman, and Bagyo Prasetyo. 2006. 'Bab 2 – Sebuah Pendekatan Arkeogeografis untuk Mengetengahkan Zaman Protosejarah.' In *Menyelesuri Sungai, Merunut Waktu: Penelitian Arkeologi di Sumetara Selatan*, ed. D. Guillaud, 35–47. Jakarta: Pusat Penelitian dan Perkembangan Arkeologi Nasional.

Ha Van Tan. 1997. 'The Hoabinhian and Before.' *Bulletin of the Indo-Pacific Prehistory Association* 16: 35–41.

Hiep, Trin Hoang and Damien Huffer. 2015. 'The Đa Bút Period in Northern Vietnam: Current Knowledge and Future Directions.' *Journal of Indo-Pacific Archaeology* 35: 36–47.

Higham, Charles. 1989. *The Archaeology of Mainland Southeast Asia from 10,000 B.C. to the Fall of Angkor*. Cambridge: Cambridge University Press.

———. 1996. *The Bronze Age of Southeast Asia*. Cambridge: Cambridge University Press.

———. 2006. 'Crossing National Boundaries: Southern China and Southeast Asia in Prehistory.' In *Uncovering Southeast Asia's Past*, ed. E.A. Bacus, I.C. Glover, and V.C. Pigott, 13–21. Singapore: NUS Press.

Higham, Charles F.W. and Amphan Kijngam, eds. 2011. *The Origins of Civilization of Angkor. Volume IV. The Excavation of Ban Non Wat: The Neolithic Occupation*. Bangkok: The Thai Fine Arts Department.

Higham, Charles F.W. and Rachanie Thosarat, eds. 2014. *The Excavation of Nong Nor: A Prehistoric Site in Central Thailand*. Oxford: Oxbow Books.

Hiscock, Peter. 2005. 'Artefacts on Aru: Evaluating the Technological Sequences.' In *The Archaeology of the Aru Islands, Eastern Indonesia*, ed. S. O'Connor, M. Spriggs, and P. Veth, 205–34. Terra Australis 22. Canberra: The Australian National University, Pandanus Books.

Hodder, Ian and Clive Orton. 1976. *Spatial Analysis in Archaeology*. Cambridge: Cambridge University Press.

Hung, Hsiao-chun. 2008. 'Migration and Cultural Interaction in Southern Coastal China, Taiwan and the Northern Philippines, 3000 BC to AD 100: The Early History of the Austronesian-Speaking Populations.' Unpublished PhD thesis. Canberra: The Australian National University.

Hung, Hsiao-chun and Mike T. Carson. 2014. 'Foragers, Fishers and Farmers: Origins of the Taiwanese Neolithic.' *Antiquity* 88: 1115–31.

Hutterer, Karl L. 1974. 'The Evolution of Philippine Lowland Societies.' *Mankind* 9 (4): 287–99.

Kealy, Shimona, Julien Louys, and Sue O'Connor. 2017. 'Reconstructing Palaeogeography and Inter-island Visibility in the Wallacean Archipelago During the Likely Period of Sahul Colonization, 65–45,000 Years Ago.' *Archaeological Prospection* 24: 259–72.

Kress, Jonathan H. 2004. 'The Necrology of Sa'gung Rockshelter and its Place in Philippine Prehistory.' In *Southeast Asian Archaeology: Wilhelm G. Solheim II Festschrift*, ed. V. Paz, 239–75. Quezon City: University of Philippines Press.

Lampert, Cynthia D., Ian C. Glover, Robert Ernest Mortimer Hedges, Carl P. Heron, Tom Higham, Bern Stern, Rasmi Shoocongdej, and Gertrude B. Thompson. 2002. 'Dating Resin Coating on Pottery: The Spirit Cave Early Ceramic Dates Revised.' *Antiquity* 77: 126–33.

Langley, Michelle C. and Sue O'Connor. 2016. 'An Enduring Shell Artefact Tradition from Timor-Leste: Oliva Bead Production from the Pleistocene to Late Holocene at Jerimalai, Lene Hara, and Matja Kuru 1 and 2.' *PLOS ONE* 11 (8): e0161071.

Langley, Michelle C., Sue O'Connor, and Elena Piotto. 2016. '42,000-year-old Worked and Pigment-stained Nautilus Shell from Jerimalai (Timor-Leste): Evidence for an Early Coastal Adaptation in ISEA.' *Journal of Human Evolution* 79: 1–16.

Lape, Peter. 2000. 'Contact and Conflict in the Banda Islands, Eastern Indonesia, 11th–17th Centuries AD.' Unpublished PhD thesis. Providence, Rhode Island: Brown University.

Lara, Myra, Helen Lewis, Victor Paz, and Wilfredo Ronquillo. 2016. 'Implications of Pathological Changes in Cremated Human Remains from Palawan, Philippines, for Island Southeast Asian archaeology.' In *The Routledge Handbook of Bioarchaeology in Southeast Asia and the Pacific Island*, ed. M. Oxenham and H.R. Buckley, 339–59. London: Routledge.

Lipson, Mark, Po-Ru Loh, Nick Patterson, Priya Moorjani, Ying-Chin Ko, Mark Stoneking, Bonnie Berger, and David Reich. 2014. 'Reconstructing Austronesian Population History in Island Southeast Asia.' *Nature Communications* 5, 4689.

Lloyd-Smith, Lindsay. 2012. 'Early Holocene Burial Practice at Niah Cave, Sarawak.' *Journal of Indo-Pacific Archaeology* 32: 54–69.

Lloyd-Smith, Lindsay and Franca Cole. 2010. 'The Jar-burial Tradition in the West Mouth of Niah Cave, Sarawak.' In *50 Years of Archaeology in Southeast Asia: Essays in Honour of Ian Glover*, ed. B. Bellina, E.A. Bacus, T.O. Pryce, and J. Wisseman Christie, 114–27. Bangkok: River Books.

Lloyd-Smith, Lindsay, John Krigbaum, and Benjamin Valentine. 2016. 'Social Affiliation, Settlement Pattern Histories and Subsistence Change in Neolithic Borneo.' In *The Routledge Handbook of Bioarchaeology in Southeast Asia and the Pacific Island*, ed. M. Oxenham and H.R. Buckley, 257–88. London: Routledge.

Lu, Tracey L.-D. 2011. 'Coexistence in Prehistoric Guangdong, South China.' In *Co-existence and Cultural Transmission in East Asia*, ed. N. Matsumoto, H. Bessho, and M. Tomii, 4–18. Walnut Creek, California: Left Coast Press.

Mahirta. 2003. 'Human Occupation on Rote and Sawu Islands, Nusa Tenggara Timur.' Unpublished PhD dissertation. Canberra: The Australian National University.

———. 2009. 'Stone Technology and the Chronology of Human Occupation on Rote, Sawu and Timor, Nusa Tenggara Timur, Indonesia.' *Bulletin of the Indo-Pacific Prehistory Association* 29: 101–8.

Mahirta, Kenneth Aplin, David Bulbeck, Walter E. Boles, and Peter Bellwood. 2004. 'Pia Hudale Rockshelter: A Terminal Pleistocene Occupation Site on Roti Island, Nusa Tenggara Timur, Indonesia.' In *Modern Quaternary Research in Indonesia*, ed. S.G. Keates and J.M. Pasveer, 361–94. Modern Quaternary Research in Southeast Asia 18. Leiden: A.A. Balkema.

Majid, Zuraina, Ang Bee Haut, and Jeffrei Ignatius. 1998. 'Late Pleistocene-Holocene Sites in Pahang: Excavations of Gua Sagu and Gua Tenggek.' *Malaysia Museums Journal* 34: 65–116.

Marwick, Ben. 2007. 'Approaches to Flaked Stone Artefact Technology in Thailand: A Historical Review.' *Silkaporn University International Journal* 7: 48–88.

———. 2013. 'Multiple Optima in Hoabinhian Flaked Stone Artefact Palaeoeconomics and Palaeoecology at Two Archaeological Sites in Northwest Thailand.' *Journal of Anthropological Archaeology* 32: 553–64.

Matthews, John. 1966. 'A Review of the "Hoabinhian" in Indochina.' *Asian Perspectives* 9: 86–95.

Mijares, Armand Salvador B. 2002. *The Minori Cave Expedient Lithic Technology*. Quezon City: University of Philippines Press.

———. 2006. 'Lowland-upland Interaction: The 3500–1500 BP Ceramic Evidence from the Peñablanca Cave Sites, Northeastern Luzon, Philippines.' In *Uncovering Southeast Asia's Past*, ed. E.A. Bacus, I.C. Glover, and V.C. Pigott, 360–78. Singapore: NUS Press.

———. 2007. *Unearthing Prehistory: The Archaeology of Northeastern Luzon, Philippine Islands*. Oxford: BAR International Series 1613.

Miksic, John. 1980. 'Classical Archaeology in Sumatra.' *Indonesia* 30: 43–66.

Monk, Kathryn A., Yance de Fretes, and Gayatri Reksodiharjo-Lilley. 1997. *The Ecology of Nusa Tenggara and Maluku*. Singapore: Periplus Editions.

Moore, Mark W., Thomas Sutikna, Jatmiko, Mike J. Morwood, and Adam Brumm. 2009. 'Continuities in Stone Flaking Technology at Liang Bua, Flores, Indonesia.' *Journal of Human Evolution* 57: 503–26.

Morley, Mike W., Paul Goldberg, Thomas Sutnika, Matthew W. Tocheri, Linda C. Prinsloo, Jatmiko, E Wahyu Saptomo, Sri Wasisto, and Richard G. Roberts. 2016. 'Initial Micromorphological Results from Liang Bua, Flores (Indonesia): Site Formation Processes and Hominin Activities at the Type Locality of Homo Floresiensis.' *Journal of Archaeological Science* 77: 125–42.

Morwood, Mike J., Thomas Sutikna, E. Wahyu Saptomo, Kira E. Westaway, Jatmiko, Rokus Awe Due, Mark W. Moore, Dwi Yani Yuniawati, P. Hadi, Jian-xin Zhao, Chris S. Turney, Keith Fifield, , Harry Allen, and R.P. Soejono. 2007. 'Climate, People and Faunal

Succession on Java, Indonesia: Evidence from Song Gupuh.' *Journal of Archaeological Science* 35: 1776–89.

Neri, Lee Anthony M., Alfred Pawlik, Christian Reepmeyer, Armand Salvador B. Mijares, and Victor J. Paz. 2015. 'Mobility of Early Islanders in the Philippines During the Terminal Pleistocene/early Holocene Boundary: PXRF-analysis of Obsidian Artefacts.' *Journal of Archaeological Science* 61: 149–57.

Nguyen Khac Su, Pham Minh Huyen, and Tong Trung Tin. 2004. 'Northern Vietnam from the Neolithic to the Han Period.' In *Southeast Asia from Prehistory to History*, ed. I. Glover and P. Bellwood, 177–208. London: Routledge.

Nguyen Kim Dung, Mariko Yamagata, Shinya Watanabe, and Peter Bellwood. 2011. Appendix 2. 'The Man Bac Burial Pottery – An Illustrated Corpus of the Whole Vessels from the Burials in Cultural Unit II.' In *Man Bac: The Excavation of a Neolithic Site in Northern Vietnam*, ed. M.F. Oxenham, H. Matsumura, and Nguyen Kim Dung, 169–85. Canberra: ANU E-Press.

Noerwidi, Sofwan. 2011/12. 'The Significance of the Holocene Human Skeleton Song Keplek 5 in the History of Human Colonization of Java: A Comprehensive Morphological and Morphometric Study.' Unpublished MA thesis. Paris: Muséum National d'Histoire Naturelle.

Ochoa, Janine, Victor Paz, Helen Lewis, Jane Carlos, Emil Robles, Noel Amano, Maria Rebecca Ferreras, Myra Lara, Benjamin Vallejo Jr., Gretchen Velarde, Sarah Agatha Villaluz, Wilfredo Ronquillo, and Wilhelm Solheim II. 2014. 'The Archaeology and Palaeobiological Record of Pasimbahan-Magsanib Site, Northern Palawan, Philippines.' *Philippine Science Letters* 7 (1): 22–36.

O'Connor, Sue. 2015. 'Rethinking the Neolithic in Island Southeast Asia, with Particular Reference to the Archaeology of Timor-Leste and Sulawesi.' *Archipel* 90: 15–47.

O'Connor, Sue and David Bulbeck. 2014. 'Homo Sapiens Societies in Indonesia and Southeastern Asia.' In *Oxford Handbook of the Archaeology and Anthropology of Hunter-Gatherers*, ed. V. Cummings, P. Jordan, and M. Zvelebil, 346–67. Oxford: Oxford University Press.

O'Connor, Sue, Kenneth Aplin, Juliette Pasveer, and Geoff Hope. 2005a. 'Liang Nabulei Lisa: A Late Pleistocene and Holocene Sequence from the Aru Islands.' In *The Archaeology of the Aru Islands, Eastern Indonesia*, ed. S. O'Connor, M. Spriggs, and P. Veth, 125–61. Terra Australis 22. Canberra: The Australian National University, Pandanus Books.

O'Connor, Sue, Kenneth Aplin, Katherina Szabó, Juliette Pasveer, Peter Veth, and Matthew Spriggs. 2005b. 'Liang Lemdubu: A Pleistocene Cave Site in the Aru Islands.' In *The Archaeology of the Aru Islands, Eastern Indonesia*, ed. S. O'Connor, M. Spriggs, and P. Veth, 171–204. Terra Australis 22. Canberra: The Australian National University, Pandanus Books.

O'Connor, Sue, Gail Robertson, and Kenneth Aplin. 2014a. 'Are Osseous Artefacts a Window to Perishable Material Culture? Implications of an Unusually Complex Bone Tool from the Late Pleistocene of East Timor.' *Journal of Human Evolution* 67: 108–19.

O'Connor, Sue, Fadhila A. Aziz, Ben Marwick, Jack Fenner, Bagyo Prasetyo, David Bulbeck, Tim Maloney, Emma St. Pierre, Rose Whitau, Unggull P. Wibowo, Budianto Hakim, Ambra Calo, Husni Fakhri, Hasanuddin Muhammad, Adhi Agus Oktaviana, Dyas Prastinintyas, Fredeliza Z. Campos, and Philip J. Piper. 2014b. *Final Report on the Project "The Archaeology of Sulawesi: A Strategic Island for Understanding Modern Human*

Colonization and Interactions Across our Region". Canberra: The Australian National University.

O'Connor, Sue, Christian Reepmeyer, Mahirta, Michelle C. Langley, and Elena Piotto. This volume. "Communities of Practice in a Maritime World: Shared Shell Technology and Obsidian Exchange in the Lesser Sunda Islands, Wallacea". In *Sea Nomads of Southeast Asia: From the Past to the Present*, ed. B. Bellina, R. Blench, and J.-C. Galipaud. Singapore: NUS Press.

Ogawa, Hidefumi. 2004. 'Chronological Context of Non-decorated Black Pottery from Lallo Shell Middens, Cagayan Province, Philippines.' In *Southeast Asian Archaeology: Wilhelm G. Solheim II Festschrift*, ed. V. Paz, 184–208. Quezon City: University of Philippines Press.

Oktaviana, Adhi Agus, David Bulbeck, Sue O'Connor, Budianto Hakim, Wibowo Suryatman, Prasetyo Unggul, Emma St Pierre, and Fakhri. 2016. 'Hand Stencils with and without Narrowed Fingers at Two New Rock Art Sites in Sulawesi.' *Rock Art Research* 33 (1): 32–48.

Oliveira, Nuno V. 2008. 'Subsistence Archaeology: Food Production and the Agricultural Transition in East Timor.' Unpublished PhD thesis. Canberra: The Australian National University.

Ono, Rintaro, Sontoso Soegondho, and Minoru Yoneda. 2010. 'Changing Marine Exploitation During Late Pleistocene in Northern Wallacea: Shell Remains from Leang Sarru Rockshelter in Talaud Islands.' *Asian Perspectives* 48: 318–41.

Ono, Rintaro, Naoki Nakajima, Hiroe Nishizawa, Sakunosuke Oda, and Santoso Soegondho. 2015. 'Maritime Migration and Lithic Assemblage on the Talaud Islands in Northern Wallacea During the Late Pleistocene to the Early Holocene.' In *Emergence and Diversity of Modern Human Behavior in Paleolithic Asia*, ed. Y. Kaifu, M. Izuho, T. Goeble, H. Sato, and A. Ono, 201–13. College Station: Texas A&M University Press.

O'Reilly, Dougald and Louise Shewan. 2016. 'Prehistoric Mortuary Traditions in Cambodia.' In *The Routledge Handbook of Bioarchaeology in Southeast Asia and the Pacific Island*, ed. M. Oxenham, and H.R. Buckley, 45–67. Canberra: ANU E-Press.

Oxenham, Marc F., Philip Piper, Peter Bellwood, Chi Hoang Bui, Khanh Trung Kien Nguyen, Quoc Manh Nguyen, Fredeliza Campos, Cristina Castillo, Rachel Wood, Carmen Sarjeant, Noel Amano, Anna Willis, and Jasminda Ceron. 2015. 'Emergence and Diversification of the Neolithic in Southern Vietnam: Insights from Coastal Rach Nui.' *The Journal of Island and Pacific Archaeology* 10 (3): 309–38.

Oxenham, Marc, Anna Willis, Hsiao-chun Hung, Ruth Page, and Hirofumi Matsumura. 2016. 'Dealing with Death in Late Neolithic to Metal Period Nagsabaran, the Philippines.' In *The Routledge Handbook of Bioarchaeology in Southeast Asia and the Pacific Island*, ed. M. Oxenham and H.R. Buckley, 311–38. Canberra: ANU E-Press.

Pasveer, Juliette M. 2004. 'The Djief Hunters: 26,000 Years of Rainforest Exploitation on the Bird's Head of Papua, Indonesia.' *Modern Quaternary Research in Southeast Asia* 17. Leiden: A.A. Balkema.

———. 2005. 'Bone Artefacts from Liang Lemdubu and Liang Nabulei Lisa, Aru Islands.' In *The Archaeology of the Aru Islands, Eastern Indonesia*, ed. S. O'Connor, M. Spriggs, and P. Veth, 235–54. Terra Australis 22. Canberra: The Australian National University, Pandanus Books.

Pasveer, Juliette M. and Peter Bellwood. 2004. 'Prehistoric Bone Artefacts from the Northern Moluccas, Indonesia.' In *Quaternary Research in Indonesia*, ed. S.G. Keates and J.M. Pasveer, 301–59. Modern Quaternary Research in Southeast Asia 18. Leiden: A.A. Balkema.

Patole-Edoumba, Elise, Philippe Duringer, Pascale Richardin, Laura Shackelford, Anne-Marie Bacon, Thongsa Sayavongkhamdy, Jean-Luc Ponche, and Fabrice Demeter. 2015. 'Evolution of the Hoabinhian Techno-complex of Tam Hang Rock Shelter in Northeastern Laos.' *Archaeological Discovery* 3: 140–57.

Pawlik, Alfred F., Philip J. Piper, and Armand Salvador Mijares. 2014a. 'Modern Humans in the Philippines: Colonization, Subsistence and New Insights into Behavioural Complexity.' In *Southern Asia, Australia, and the Search for Human Origins*, ed. R. Dennell and M. Porr, 135–47. Cambridge: Cambridge University Press.

Pawlik, Alfred F., Philip J. Piper, Maria Grace Pamela G. Faylona, Sabino G. Padilla Jr., Jane Carlos, Armand Salvador Mijares, Benjamin Vallejo Jr., Marian Reyes, Noel Amano, Thomas Ingicco, and Martin Porr. 2014b. 'Adaptation and Foraging from the Terminal Pleistocene to the Early Holocene: Excavation at Bubog on Ilin Island, Philippines.' *Journal of Field Archaeology* 39: 230–47.

Pawlik, Alfred F., Philip J. Piper, Rachel E. Wood, Kristine Kate A. Lim, Maria Grace Pamela G. Faylona, Armand Salvador B. Mijares, and Martin Porr. 2015. 'Shell Tool Technology in Island Southeast Asia: An Early Middle Holocene Tridacna Adze from Ilin Island, Mindoro, Philippines.' *Antiquity* 89: 292–308.

Paz, Victor, Wilfredo Ronquillo, Helen Lewis, Emil Robles, Vito Hernandez, Jane Carlos, Andrea Malaya Ragragio, Myra Lara, Noel Amano, Shawn O'Donnell, Caterine Manalo, Michael Herera, Janine Ochoa, Darko Stojanovski, and Wilhelm Solheim II. 2012. 'The Palawan Island Palaeohistoric Research Project: Report on the 2012 Season.' Quezon City: University of the Philippines Archaeological Studies Program.

Peterson, Warren. 1974. 'Summary Report of Two Archaeological Sites from North-eastern Luzon.' *Archaeology and Physical Anthropology in Oceania* 9: 26–35.

Pigott, Vince C. and Suraphol Natapintu. 1996–97. 'Investigating the Origins of Metal Use in Prehistoric Thailand.' In *Ancient Chinese and Southeast Asian Bronze Age Cultures* Vol II, ed. F.D. Bulbeck and N. Barnard, 787–808. Taipei: SMC Publishing Inc.

Piper, Philip J. 2016. 'Human Cultural, Technological and Adaptive Changes from the End of the Pleistocene to the Mid-Holocene in Southeast Asia.' In *The Routledge Handbook of Bioarchaeology in Southeast Asia and the Pacific Island*, ed. M. Oxenham and H.R. Buckley, 24–44. London: Routledge.

Piper, Philip J., Hsiao-chun Hung, Fredeliza Z. Campos, Peter Bellwood, and Ray Santiago. 2009. 'A 4000-year-old Introduction of Domestic Pigs into the Philippine Archipelago: Implications for Understanding Routes of Human Migration Through Island Southeast Asia and Wallacea.' *Antiquity* 83: 687–95.

Piper, Philip J., Noel Amano Jr., Shawna Hsiu-Ying Yang, and Terry O'Connor. 2013. 'The Terrestrial Vertebrate Remains.' In *4000 Years of Migration and Cultural Exchange: The Archaeology of the Batanes Islands, Northern Philippines*, ed. P. Bellwood and E. Dizon, 169–99. Canberra: ANU E-Press.

Piper, Philip J., Fredeliza Z. Campos, and Hsiao-chun Hung. 2014. 'A Study of the Animal Bones Recovered from Pits 9 and 10 at the Site of Nagsabaran in Northern Luzon, Philippines.' *Hukay* 14: 47–90.

Plutniak, Sebastien, Adhi Agus Oktaviana, Bambang Sugiyanto, Jean-Marie Chazine, and François-Xavier Ricaut. 2014. 'New Ceramic Data from East Kalimantan: The Cord-marked and Red-slipped Sherds of Liang Abu's Layer 2 and Kalimantan's Pottery Chronology.' *Journal of Pacific Archaeology* 5: 90–9.

Prasetyo, Bagyo. 2002a. 'The Bone Industry.' In *Gunung Sewu in Prehistoric Times*, ed. T. Simanjuntak, 181–94. Yogyakarta: Gadjah Mada University Press.

———. 2002b. 'The Neolithic of Gunung Sewu: From Caves to Open Sites.' In *Gunung Sewu in Prehistoric Times*, ed. T. Simanjuntak, 206–14. Yogyakarta: Gadjah Mada University Press.

Rabett, Ryan J. 2005. 'The Early Exploitation of Southeast Asian Mangroves: Bone Technology from Caves and Open Sites.' *Asian Perspectives* 44: 154–79.

———. 2007. 'Vertebrate Faunal Remains from Gua Cha, Kelantan: New Material Found in Association with Recently Re-discovered Human Remains from the 1954 Sieveking Excavation.' In *Archaeological Heritage in Malaysia*, ed. M. Saidin and S. Chia, 61–72. Penang: Universiti Sains Malaysia Centre for Archaeological Research.

———. 2012. *Human Adaptation in the Asian Palaeolithic*. Cambridge: Cambridge University Press.

Rabett, Ryan J. and Philip J. Piper. 2012. 'The Emergence of Bone Technologies at the End of the Pleistocene in Southeast Asia: Regional and Evolutionary Implications.' *Cambridge Archaeological Journal* 22: 37–56.

Rabett, Ryan J., Graeme Barker, Huw Barton, Chris Hunt, Lindsay Lloyd-Smith, Victor Paz, Philip J. Piper, Ratnasiri Premathilake, Garry Rushworth, Mark Stephens, and Katherine Szabó. 2013. 'Landscape Transformations and Human Responses c. 11,500–c. 4500 Years Ago.' In *Rainforest Foraging and Farming in Island Southeast Asia*, ed. G. Barker, 217–53. Cambridge: McDonald Institute for Archaeological Research.

Reepmeyer, Christian, Sue O'Connor, and Sally Brockwell. 2011. 'Long-term Obsidian Use at the Jerimalai Rock Shelter in East Timor.' *Archaeology in Oceania* 46: 85–90.

Renfrew, Colin and Paul Bahn. 2000. *Archaeology: Theories Methods and Practice*. 2nd ed. London: Thames & Hudson.

Reynolds, Tim. 1989. 'Techno-typology in Thailand: A Case Study of Tham Khao Khi Chan.' *Bulletin of the Indo-Pacific Prehistory Association* 9: 33–43.

Samper Carro, Sofía C., Sue O'Connor, Julien Louys, Stuart Hawkins, and Mahirta Mahirta. 2015. 'Human Maritime Subsistence Strategies in the Lesser Sunda Islands During the Terminal Pleistocene–early Holocene: New Evidence from Alor, Indonesia.' *Quaternary International* 416: 64–79.

Sarjeant, Carmen. 2014. 'Contextualising the Neolithic Occupation of Southern Vietnam: The Role of Ceramics and Potters at An Son.' Terra Australis 42. Canberra: Australian National University E-Press.

Shelach-Levi, Gideon. 2015. *The Archaeology of Early China from Prehistory to the Han Dynasty*. Cambridge: Cambridge University Press.

Shoocongdej, Rasmi. 2000. 'Forager Mobility Organization in Seasonal Tropical Environments of Western Thailand.' *World Archaeology* 32: 14–40.

———. 2006. 'Late Pleistocene Activities at the Tham Lod Rockshelter in Highland Pang Mapha, Mae Hong Son Province, Northwestern Thailand.' In *Uncovering Southeast Asia's Past*, ed. A. Bacus, I.C. Glover, and V.C. Pigott, 22–37. Singapore: NUS Press.

Simanjuntak, Truman. 2002. 'Braholo Cave, an Ideal Settlement Site in Western Gunung Sewu.' In *Gunung Sewu in Prehistoric Times*, ed. T. Simanjuntak, 119–27. Yogyakarta: Gadjah Mada University Press.

Simanjuntak, Truman and Inda Nurani Asikin. 2004. 'Early Holocene Human Settlement in Eastern Java.' *Bulletin of the Indo-Pacific Prehistory Association* 24: 13–19.

Simanjuntak, Truman and Bagyo Prasetyo. 2002. 'Subsistence of the Cave Dwellers.' In *Gunung Sewu in Prehistoric Times*, ed. T. Simanjuntak, 147–58. Yogyakarta: Gadjah Mada University Press.

Simanjuntak, Truman, Hubert Forestier, Dubel Driwantoro, Jatmiko, and Darwin Sinegar. 2006. 'Bab 1 – Daerah Kaki Gunung Berbagai Tahap Zaman Batu.' In *Menyelesuri Sungai, Merunut Waktu: Penelitian Arkeologi di Sumetara Selatan*, ed. D. Guillaud, 21–33. Jakarta: Pusat Penelitian dan Perkembangan Arkeologi Nasional.

Simanjuntak, Truman, Mike J. Morwood, Fatika S. Intan, I. Mahmud, Kevin Grant, N. Somba, Bernadetta Akw, and D.W. Utomo. 2008. 'Minanga Sipakko and the Neolithic of the Karama River.' In *Austronesian in Sulawesi*, ed. T. Simanjuntak, 57–76. Jakarta: Center for Prehistoric and Austronesian Studies.

Simanjuntak, Truman, François Sémah, and Anne-Marie Sémah. 2015. 'Tracking Evidence for Modern Human Behavior in Paleolithic Indonesia.' In *Emergence and Diversity of Modern Human Behavior in Paleolithic Asia*, ed. Y. Kaifu, M. Izuho, T. Goebel, H. Sato, and A. Ono, 158–70. College Station: Texas A&M University Press.

Simons, Alison. 1997. 'The Whole Hog. The Indigenous Response to the Introduction of Farming to South Sulawesi: A Faunal Analysis.' Unpublished BA (Hons) thesis. Perth: University of Western Australia, Centre for Archaeology.

Simons, Alison and David Bulbeck. 2004. 'Late Quaternary Faunal Successions in South Sulawesi.' In *Quaternary Research in Indonesia*, ed. S.G. Keates and J.M. Pasveer, 167–89. Modern Quaternary Research in Southeast Asia 18. Leiden: A.A. Balkema.

Soares, Pedro, Jean-Alain Trejaut, Jun-Hun Loo, Catherine Hill, Maru Mormina, Chien-Lang Lee, Yao-Ming Chen, Georgi Hudjashov, Peter Forster, Vincent Macaulay, David Bulbeck, Stephen Oppenheimer, Marie Li, and Martin B. Richards. 2008. 'Climate Change and Post-Glacial Human Dispersals in Southeast Asia.' *Molecular Biology and Evolution* 25 (6): 1209–18.

Soares, Pedro, Jean-Alain Trejaut, Teresa Rito, Bruno Cavadas, Catherine Hill, Ken Khong Eng, Maru Mormina, Adreia Brandão, Ross M. Fraser, Tse-Yi Wang, Jun-Hun Loo, Christopher Snell, Tsang-Ming Ko, Antonio Amorim, Maria Pala, Vincent Macaulay, David Bulbeck, James F. Wilson, Leonor Gusmão, Luisa Pereira, Stephen Oppenheimer, Marie Lin, and Martin B. Richards. 2016. 'Resolving the Ancestry of Austronesian-speaking Populations.' *Human Genetics* 135: 309–26.

Solheim, Wilhelm G. II. 2006. *Archaeology and Culture in Southeast Asia: Unraveling the Nusantao*. Diliman, Quezon City: The University of the Philippines Press.

Solheim, Wilhelm G. II, Avelino M. Legaspi, and Jaime S. Neri. 1979. *Archaeological Survey in Southeastern Mindanao*. Monograph No. 8. Manila: National Museum of the Philippines.

Sophady, Heng, Hubert Forestier, Valéry Zeitoun, Simon Puaud, Stéphane Frère, Vincenzo Celiberti, Kira Westaway, Roland Mourer, Cécile Mourer-Chauviré, Heng Than, Laurence Billault, and Srun Tech. 2016. 'Laang Spean Cave (Battambang Province): A Tale of Occupation in Cambodia from the Late Upper Pleistocene to Holocene.' *Quaternary International* 416: 165–76.

Spriggs, Matthew. 2003. 'Chronology of the Neolithic Transition in Island Southeast Asia and the Western Pacific: A View from 2003.' *The Review of Archaeology* 24 (2): 57–80.

———. 2010. 'Archaeology and the Austronesian Expansion: Where Are We Now?' *Antiquity* 85: 510–28.

Spriggs, Matthew, Christian Reepmeyer, Anggraeni, Peter Lape, Lee Neri, Wilfredo P. Ronquillo, Truman Simanjuntak, Glenn Summerhayes, Daud Tanudirjo, and Archie Tiauzon. 2011. 'Obsidian Sources and Distribution Systems in Island Southeast Asia: A Review of Previous Research.' *Journal of Archaeological Science* 38: 2873–81.

Srisuchat, Tharapong and Amara Srisuchat. 1992. *Archaeological Analysis No. 1: An Application of Technology and Science in Archaeological Work in Thailand*. Bangkok: Division of Fine Arts, Archaeology Division.

Storey, Alice. 2016. 'Scratching Out a Living: Chickens in Ancient Pacific Economies.' In *The Routledge Handbook of Bioarchaeology in Southeast Asia and the Pacific Island*, ed. M. Oxenham and H.R. Buckley, 483–50. London: Routledge.

Storm, Paul. 1995. 'The Evolutionary Significance of the Wajak Skulls.' *Scripta Geologica* 110. Leiden: National Natuurhistorisch Museum.

Storm, Paul, Rachel Wood, Chris Stringer, Antonis Bartsiokas, John de Vos, Maxime Aubert, Les Kinsley, and Rainer Grün. 2013. 'U-series and Radiocarbon Analyses of Human and Faunal Remains from Wajak, Indonesia.' *Journal of Human Evolution* 64: 356–65.

Suryatman, Suryatman, Sue O'Connor, David Bulbeck, Ben Marwick, Adhi Agus Oktaviana, Wibowo, Unggul Prasetyo. 2016. 'Teknologi Litik di Situs Talimbue, Sulawesi Tenggara: Teknologi Berlanjut Dari Masa Pleistosen Akhir Hingga Holosen.' AMERTA *Jurnal Penelitian dan Pengambangan Arkeologi* 34 (2): 81–98.

Szabó, Katherine and Hazel Ramirez. 2009. 'Worked Shell from Leta Leta Cave, Palawan, Philippines.' *Archaeology in Oceania* 44: 150–9.

Szabó, Katherine, Marie Clare Swete Kelly, and Antonio Peñaloso. 2004. 'Preliminary Results from Excavations in the Eastern Mouth of Ille Cave, Northern Palawan.' In *Southeast Asian Archaeology: Wilhelm G. Solheim II Festschrift*, ed. V. Paz, 209–24. Quezon City: University of Philippines Press.

Szabó, Katherine, Adam Brumm, and Peter Bellwood. 2007. 'Shell Artefact Production at 32,000–28,000 BP in Island Southeast Asia: Thinking Across Media?' *Current Anthropology* 48 (5): 701–23.

Tanudirjo, Daud. 2001. 'Islands in Between: Prehistory of the Northeastern Indonesian Archipelago.' Unpublished PhD dissertation. Canberra: The Australian National University.

Tayles, Nancy, Sian E. Halcrow, Thongsa Sayavongkhamdy, and Viengkeo Souksavatdy. 2015. 'A Prehistoric Flexed Burial from Pha Phen, Middle Mekong Valley, Laos: Its Context in Southeast Asia.' *Anthropological Science* 123: 1–12.

Thiel, Barbara. 1990. 'Excavations at Musang Cave, Northeast Luzon, Philippines.' *Asian Perspectives* 28: 229–64.

Tilley, Lorna and Marc Oxenham. 2016. 'Reflections on Life and Times in Neolithic Vietnam.' In *The Routledge Handbook of Bioarchaeology in Southeast Asia and the Pacific Island*, ed. M. Oxenham and H.R. Buckley, 95–109. Canberra: Australian National University E-Press.

Tin Htut Aung, Ben Marwick, and Conrad Cyler. 2015. 'Palaeolithic Zooarchaeology in Myanmar: A Review and Future Prospects.' *Journal of Indo-Pacific Archaeology* 39: 50–6.

Tsang, Cheng-Hwa. 2005. 'Recent Discoveries of the Tap'enkeng Culture in Taiwan: Implications for the Problem of Austronesian Origins.' In *Perspectives in the Phylogeny of East Asian Languages*, ed. L. Sagart, R.M. Blench, and A. Sanchas-Mazas, 63–73. London: Curzon Press.

U Aung Thaw. 1971. 'The "Neolithic" Culture of the Padah-lin Caves.' *Asian Perspectives* 14: 123–33.

Valentin, Frédérique, Jeong-in Choi, Hsiuman Lin, S. Bedford, and Matthew Spriggs. 2015. 'Three-thousand-year-old Jar Burials at the Teouma Cemetery (Vanuatu): A Southeast Asian–Lapita Connection?' In *The Lapita Cultural Complex in Time and Space: Expansion Routes, Chronologies and Typologies*, ed. C. Sand, S. Chiu, and N. Hogg, 81–101. Noumea: Institut d'archéologie de la Nouvelle-Calédonie et du Pacifique.

Van den Bergh, Gerrit D., Hanneke Meijer, Rokhus Awe Due, Michael J. Morwood, Katherina Szabó, Lars W. van den Hoeke Ostende, Thomas Sutikna, Wahyu E Saptomo, Philip J. Piper, and Keith M. Dobney. 2009. 'The Liang Bua Faunal Remains: A 95 k. yr. sequence from Flores, East Indonesia.' *Journal of Human Evolution* 57: 527–37.

Van Heekeren, Hanna R. 1972. *The Stone Age of Indonesia*. 2nd revised ed. The Hague: Martinus Nijhoff.

Van Vlack, Hannah G. 2014. 'Forager Subsistence Regimes in the Thai-Malay Peninsula: An Environmental Archaeological Case Study of Khao Toh Chong Rockshelter, Krabi.' Unpublished MA dissertation. San Jose, CA: San José State University.

Wiradnyana, Ketut and Taufiqurrahman Setiawan. 2011. *Gayo Merangkat Identitas*. Jakarta: Yayasan Pustaka Obor Indonesia.

Yi, Seonbok, June-Jeong Lee, Seongnam Kim, Yongwook Yoo, and D. Kim. 2008. 'New Data on the Hoabinhian: Investigations at Hang Cho Cave, Northern Vietnam.' *Bulletin of the Indo-Pacific Prehistory Association* 28: 73–80.

Zeitoun, Valéry, Hubert Forestier, Alain Pierret, Chantalpilith Chiemsisouraj, Mien Lorvankham, Amthilor Latthagnot, Tammalay Chanthamoungkhon, and Sèngpeth Norkhamsomphou. 2012. 'Multi-millennial Occupation in Northwestern Laos: Preliminary Results of Excavations at the Ngeubhinh Mouxeu Rock-shelter.' *Comptes Rendus Palevol* 11: 305–13.

Zhang, Senshui. 2000. 'The Epipalaeolithic in China.' *Journal of East Asian Archaeology* 2: 51–66.

4

Southeast Asian Early Maritime Silk Road Trading Polities' Hinterland and the Sea Nomads of the Isthmus of Kra

Bérénice Bellina, Aude Favereau and Laure Dussubieux

INTRODUCTION

BACKGROUND—GENERAL ISSUES

When, how and why does cultural differentiation take place? Which environmental, social, demographic and economic factors are at play? These questions are perhaps even more pertinent when dealing with mobile or semi-sedentary and forager or semi-agriculturalist groups living on the margins of centralised polities. Anthropologists and archaeologists have long abandoned the evolutionist postulate that the social organisation of foragers (hunter-gatherers) represented a stage preceding state societies. On the contrary, they now often argue that foragers or nomadic groups form part of regional states' political economies and that there are no states without those highly adaptive groups that academics often label 'peripheral', 'marginal' or 'minorities' (Possehl 2002; Ivanoff 2015). Forager or nomadic lifeways are viewed as complementary adaptations to those of complex societies. Groups were rarely truly isolated and their interdependent relationships mostly developed with different socially and economically-organised groups, in particular with traders (Morrison 2002) and/or with agriculturalists (Junker 2002; Junker and Smith 2017). In South and Southeast Asia, these symbiotic relationships would represent an adaptive strategy, allowing groups to thrive in a politically and economically changing world and in a diversified ecological environment (Morrison and Junker 2002). The environmental diversity that characterises Southeast Asia, as well as its physically fragmented nature in the case of Island Southeast Asia (ISEA), are important ecological constraints put on food production. These are interpreted as important factors that contributed to social diversity and interactions between different economically specialised groups, lowland rice farmers, upland swidden-farmers and forest foragers. There, as well as in southern India (Kerala in particular), the forest foragers' role in collecting goods for trading states is an external factor often put forward to explain this adaptation (Dunn 1975; Headland et al. 1989).

In Southeast Asia, the pressures lowland regional states exerted over neighbouring groups, such as 'corvées' (forced or required labour), war, slave raids and plunder, are often cited to explain groups' voluntary marginalisation. Scott's anarchist model pushed this logic further: the states' repelling action was a core agent for various farming groups' sociogenesis in the refuge zone of 'Zomia', a large mountainous zone spanning from northern South and Southeast Asia (Scott 2009). Several anthropologists have found this heuristic value of Scott's libertarian framework useful to rethink ethnicity, relationships between nomadic and sedentary groups as well as those between states and minorities. The concept has also been de-territorialised and applied elsewhere in Southeast Asia to other peripheral groups who resisted states' norms but stayed within the ethno-national border finding adaptations, niches or 'interstices' (Winichakul 2003) as is the case with the sea nomads of Thailand (Moklen) and Myanmar (Moken) (Ivanoff 2015; this volume; Bourdier et al. 2015; Ferrari 2015). Nomads or foragers are clearly analysed as a facet of the state political structure. Benjamin's (2002) theory suggests that in the Malay world marginal groups emerged in parallel with centralised powers, but to this external factor he associates an internal process of dissimilation between the different socio-economically organised groups. There, terrestrial and maritime minorities (what he calls 'tribal') would result from their choice to live on the margins of centralised polities to avoid 'the imposition of a hierarchically organized, supralocal, state apparatus' (2002: 9). It would also be a choice that ensured their respective independence and gave value to their specialisation. Alternatively, ethnographic and historical sources clearly demonstrate that several of these marginal groups were also crucial for the emergence of some trading polities and their maintenance, in particular the Orang Laut and Sama Bajau (Benjamin 2002; Chou 2010, this volume; Nolde this volume; Sather 2006).

This chapter addresses cultural adaptations in the Kra Isthmus in conjunction with the rise of centralised trading powers from the fourth century BCE in this region that was key to the early Maritime Silk Road. This chapter argues that the emergence of 'minorities'—of which the 'sea nomads' are a part—went along with economic specialisation and cooperation between different groups participating in local and long-distance networks. In Southeast Asia, fairly recent research showed that the earliest incipient states emerged during the Iron Age by the late fifth and early fourth century BCE (Kim 2013; Bellina 2017, 2018a; Stark 2015). Their hinterland remained to be studied. This chapter wishes to define the earliest trading powers' hinterland based on original data obtained through a region-scale research conducted there over more than a decade and on ethnographic parallels.[1] Various groups in the Isthmus of Kra belonging to the forest or the maritime spaces were thus characterised. Amongst the latter, we trace what we consider to be the first evidence for 'sea nomads'. There, soon after the rise of lowland trading polities, some coastal groups different both from lowland coastal and inland groups arrive and become visible in the archaeological records. They settled at river mouths at the termini of transpeninsular routes. Transpeninsular routes are a series of passages using river valleys and tracks (mountains up to 2,000 m height in the northern part of the peninsula) crossing different environments (marine, estuarine, plains and forests) that connected the Bay of Bengal and the South China Sea (Bellina et al. 2014; Bellina 2018a). These early sea nomads played an intermediary role between upstream forest groups and the occupants of early multi-ethnic ports-of-trade, and traders from afar. They developed a common material culture. Their culture is distinct both from the urban and upland populations with whom they interacted but nevertheless with some shared elements. These features taken independently cannot by themselves be taken as indicative of these groups. It is the combination, the sum of these elements altogether, that signal the group. This contradicts the assumption that, because these highly mobile groups were spending a large proportion of their time at sea, they did not develop a material culture and hence were invisible to archaeologists. An important implication of this discovery is that an archaeology of sea nomadism can be developed, along with a long-term history of these groups. By unravelling the presence of these groups, this study supports Benjamin's (2002) framework that in the Malay world 'tribal' groups—be they forest, estuarine or sea nomads—emerged in response to regional centralised trading polities. It also supports historians' work emphasising the long-lasting and close partnership between sea nomads and Southeast Asian states (Andaya 2019; Andaya 2008; Nolde this volume). Finally, it also highlights for the first time the key role that these 'marginal' groups and sea nomads in particular may have played in the development of the Maritime Silk Road, their associated centralised trading polities and regional cultural transfers.

BACKGROUND OF CULTURAL EVOLUTION IN THE UPPER THAI-MALAY PENINSULA DURING THE LATE PREHISTORIC PERIOD

In the Thai-Malay Peninsula, groups experienced cultural differentiation from the mid-Holocene (White 2011); a process that some connect to the Neolithic and the establishment of regional exchange networks (Higham et al. 2011). In Mainland Southeast Asia (MSEA), the dispersion of new lifestyles associated with the Neolithic has traditionally been linked to the migration of Neolithic populations or to contacts between them and local groups of scattered hunter-gatherers. The oldest evidence for rice cultivation is found at the coastal site of Khok Phanom Di in Thailand in the Gulf of Siam. The community there kept exploiting the resources from the mangrove and practising vegeculture (possible exploitation of taro and yam, banana, etc.), whilst rice was obtained first by exchange and at a later stage by their own agricultural efforts (Higham and Thosarat 2012). Recent excavation of Rach Nui in southern Vietnam showed that rather than an abrupt transition, coastal groups shifted gradually from a hunter-gatherer lifestyle to an agrarian one. The inhabitants were mainly hunter-gatherers who exploited the mangroves and surrounding swamps, and practised a mixed economy that combined traditional exploitation of the environment, vegeculture and rice cultivation (Castillo et al. 2017).

In the Thai-Malay Peninsula, both the issues of the transition/adaptation to the Neolithic lifestyle and cultural differentiation are hazy. The link between the two is also debated. The peninsula today presents a palimpsest of groups of different origins and social and economic organisations. South Asian, Chinese and Malays result from economic migrations that occurred over several centuries (plantations, mine exploitations, etc.). Other groups considered indigenous or aboriginal, called Orang Asli, today occupy the southern part of the peninsula. For the latter, Benjamin describes a social pattern characterised by three organisations that relate to three modes of environmental exploitation (Benjamin 2002). First, egalitarian groups of low-density nomadic hunting-and-gathering foragers. This characterises the Semang who are found in the northern part of Peninsular Malaysia and who exploit their surrounding environment. Second, groups of medium-density egalitarian semi-sedentary swidden-farmers. They also trade with outsiders and the state although they remain autonomous from it. This is the 'Senoi' group represented by Temiars and upland Semais in the central parts of the Peninsula. Finally, a 'Malayic' group combines farming or fishing with collecting forest or marine products for trade with outsiders. Many groups with variations to these can be found including the Orang Laut who are sea nomads. However, they all have in common collecting for trade.

There used to be two main frameworks to explain this 'layer-cake' palaeosociology in Peninsular Malaysia. First, that of successive waves of migrants who had already differentiated elsewhere in MSEA, who maintained their difference and pushed earlier established groups like the Orang Asli further in refuge zones (Bellwood 2007). The arrival of Austroasiatic-speaking farmers would have pushed older indigenous groups further inland. In this scenario, there is a link between the tripartite social patterning described above and the successive waves of migrants. In particular, Bellwood (2007) linked waves of Austroasiatic-speaking farmers coming down the peninsula from further north to the 'Ban Khao culture' (after the name of the eponymous site in the west-central province of Kanchanaburi). These would be epitomised by ceramics with a tripod shape, pedestalled pots, finely polished adzes, barkcloth beaters and extended burials. However, no clear open-air settlement of Ban Khao culture provided robust data to confirm this farming transition. A second hypothesis based on archaeological, genetic and linguistic evidence posits a common cultural matrix with a local differentiation based on lifestyle complementarity and distinct cultures between the groups described above (Benjamin 1987, 2002). These differing traditions were maintained even if some gene flow occurred between those groups and between some of them and ISEA groups (Indonesian) through occasional coupling (Fix 2002). The importance of the Neolithic in this model on cultural differentiation is still unclear. Benjamin clearly establishes links between the social pattern and the 'long-established presence in the region of three main modes of environmental appropriation: foraging (nomadic hunting-and-gathering), horticulture (semi sedentary swidden-farming), and collecting (the gathering of natural products for trade with outsiders). He also believes that the collecting for trade 'would have intensified around 2,000 years ago, when Chinese, Indian, and West Asian interests had led to the exploitation by tribal "fetchers" of the region's lac, wood-oil, camphor, and minerals' (2002: 10). This suggests an earlier differentiation that would have increased along with the intensification of trade during the early centuries CE. Fix's position on whether this goes back to the Neolithic or to an early stage of trade is not clear.

Bulbeck clearly supports the idea that groups differentiated during the Neolithic. He also called for a reassessment of the supposed link of the Ban Kao culture to the Neolithic (Bulbeck 2011). First, he divides the Neolithic in two phases. There would be an early Neolithic phase by the mid-Holocene during which arboriculture developed but not agriculture, as indicated by phytoliths and populations moving to Malaya bringing the N9a6a haplogroup (Hill et al. 2006). Artefacts including cord marked pottery and lightly polished cobble tools show similarities between the Da But culture of North Vietnam and what can be observed at Gua Kepah in Malaysia and in southern Thailand sites (Bulbeck 2011). The second phase by 2000 BCE purportedly took place with the arrival of proto-Aslian language speakers (Austro-Asiatic speakers)—the Orang Asli groups who nowadays practise horticulture in Malaysia—from the Mekong delta region. They are ancestors of the Senoi and introduced the F1a1a haplogroup in association with extended burials, pedestalled pots and slash-and-burn agriculture including rice alongside other crops. Bulbeck believes that the differentiation between Orang Asli would have been catalysed by competition for land during this second phase. In addition, he also disconnects the tripod complex from the arrival of proto-Aslian speakers from further north and instead relates it to a point of origin that could well be the Isthmus of Kra. There, tripods appear older and in larger numbers than in the Kanchanaburi province. Moreover, tripods as well as pedestalled pots and polished adzes were found earlier in the peninsula than in Kanchanaburi; the latter was the source (Bulbeck 2014).

In the peninsula, in general, the period from the turn of the second millennium to the mid first millennium BCE is still very poorly documented. Inland, the French-Thai Archaeological Mission found evidence dating to this period in Tham Nam Lot in the Khao Thalu relief (Nasak district, Chumphon province) (Map 4.1). There in 2012, the mission excavated a series of caves located in a hill hosting two natural underground tunnels through which the River Sawi flows, constituting part of a secondary transpeninsular network. A few test pits opened near the entrance of this tunnel revealed a sequence of use from the Neolithic onward. The use was characterised by ceramics made by a pottery-producing group. The quantity of ceramics increased through time, suggesting a growing frequentation of this transhipment zone from the first millennium BCE. The pits also yielded bronze axes in a style comparable with some excavated in northeastern Thailand and were produced with ores likely imported from the source of Xepon in Laos (Pryce, personal communication). This sum of evidence indicates the involvement of the peninsula in extensive exchange networks from that time. Those point towards the extension of regional exchange networks within which the peninsula was engaged. The presence of sea shells used as ornaments in funerary deposits in caves inland indicates movements to the coast. This is not a great surprise given the short distance between the two coasts in this part of the peninsula, at places equating to 40–50 kilometres. Similar types of shells were used for funerary practices in burials across ISEA and thus attest to the extension of the networks in MSEA and ISEA by 1000 BCE and the existence of similar cultural practices throughout the maritime region. Indeed, there is increasing evidence that extensive links within the South China Sea took place during the second millennium BCE. They may be the key to the initiation of common practices and cultural affinities there visible from the first millennium BCE (Bulbeck 2008). These may account for the ease with which populations were able to circulate and the speed with which they were exchanging the goods and ideas of the Iron Age by 500 BCE. The causal incentive for these second millennium BCE movements is not totally clear (Spriggs 2011). Some view Bellwood's Austronesian-speakers 'farmer demographic' expansion as the precedent underpinning Iron Age ease of connectivity in a predominantly Austronesian speaking South China Sea (Hung and Bellwood 2010; Hung et al. 2013). Alternatively, for Bulbeck, population movements may be accounted for by 'fisher-foragers' having both mobility and capacity to interact and exchange with various groups including settled vegeculturalists (Blench 2012; Bulbeck 2008). Solheim's 'Nusantao Maritime Trading and Communication Network' (NMTCM) portrays a multidirectional inter-ethnic network which sustained interactions that produced cultural similarities, with Malay as the lingua franca (Solheim et al. 2006). The overall picture is that interactions in the South China Sea transformed mutual cultural and linguistic influences on a range of coastal populations and that those second to early first millennium interactions laid the ground for a prehistoric cultural matrix and shared cultural repertoire.

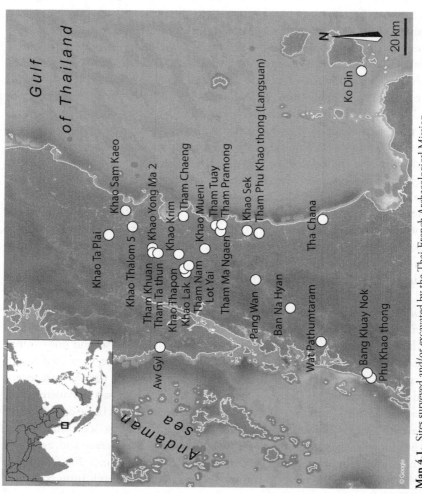

Map 4.1. Sites surveyed and/or excavated by the Thai-French Archaeological Mission (Source: A. Favereau).

By the fourth century BCE, the material culture of coastal groups bordering the South China Sea, and in particular the Gulf of Siam, appeared to share many similarities. Bellina labelled this pan-regional style 'Late Prehistoric South China Sea style' (2018a). In the Isthmus of Kra, the late fifth/early fourth century BCE coincides with the insertion of the region in the 'Maritime Silk Road' and the development of trading polities in the lowlands at a short distance from the coast and along a river leading to it (discussed below). There, South Asian and East Asian-related materials were identified. This 'Late Prehistoric South China Sea style' includes similar stone (siliceous stones and nephrite), glass (drawn and lapidary) and gold ornaments, Dong Son bronze drums, Indian-inspired decorated bronze bowls, and the so-called 'Sa Huynh-Kalanay' inspired ('SHK-inspired') ceramics (Figure 4.1). This is the crucial period that the French-Thai Archaeological Mission has been focusing on—main results are synthesised below.

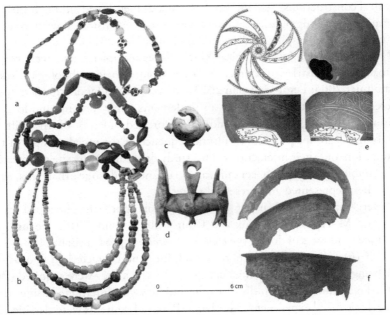

Figure 4.1 Some of the goods characterising the 'Late Prehistoric South China Sea style' (Source: B. Bellina).

METHODS AND MATERIALS (CORPUS OF REMAINS)

Methods

In the field, the French-Thai Archaeological Mission carries out extensive regional survey and excavation programmes. This approach is the only one providing data to draw a 'complex, multi-ethnic social landscapes' picture (Junker and Smith

2017). Projects often focus on a single site, a cave or a cemetery and only very few investigate settlements where the archaeological record is tenuous due to tropical conditions. A few projects have studied second millennium historical kingdoms or states' hinterland such as in the Philippines where forager-farmers' trade involved the exchange of agricultural foodstuffs and lowland utilitarian or status-conferring manufactured goods (metal implements, pottery, stone, glass and shell ornaments) with tropical forest products (meat, honey, resin, birds, spices, etc.) (Junker 1999; 2002; Junker and Smith 2017). In MSEA, another project focused on the Angkor state exchanges with the Kuay groups who were iron-producers and forest products collectors (Pryce et al. 2014; Hendrickson et al. 2017). Other studies tackled the upland-lowland exchange networks of Iron Age trading polities in Central Vietnam (Phuong 2010) and late first to early second millennium Malaysia (Allen 1991) and Indonesia (Miksic 1979; Manguin 2009); but evidence of the upland groups was very limited (Junker and Smith 2017) and beyond merchants, maritime groups were not integrated into historical constructions. Seldom were sea nomads mentioned although their role in relation to trading polities is known thanks to a few historical written sources and modern ethnographic studies (Andaya 2008; Hall 2011).

The French-Thai Archaeological Mission's team implements a technological approach for industries to characterise each group's socio-technological system (Lemonnier 2004; Leroi-Gourhan 2013, 2014). The spatial distribution among different types of sites (caves, open-air settlements, relay stations) and locations (coastal, mangrove, offshore islands and forested inland) of the different technological groups provides a cultural sequence of the social groups, of their organisation and their interactions. This study draws upon the site's excavations and technological analysis of ceramics and glass and hard stone ornaments, which are the best represented and preserved materials.

Pottery was analysed using a technological approach developed by V. Roux and M.-A. Courty (Roux and Courty 2007; Roux 2016). Focusing on techniques and ways of doing, the *chaîne opératoire* approach (Balfet 1991; Roux 2010, 2016) defined technical pottery traditions and characterised know-hows, these being representative of the social group in which they were acquired (Roux 2016). Traces and features indicative of techniques were interpreted using ethno-archaeological and experimental databases. Pottery fragments were classified first based on techniques, then based on fabrics. Within each group, pottery shapes and decorations were examined.

Glass was studied combining descriptive information and compositions obtained using laser ablation—inductively coupled plasma—mass spectrometry (LA-ICP-MS). The analytical work was conducted at the Field Museum with an Analytik Jena and then (after 2015) a Thermo ICAP Q ICP-MS connected to a New Wave UP213 laser for direct introduction of solid samples. The protocol of analysis was described in detail in Dussubieux and Bellina (2017). It is important to emphasise that this approach is virtually non-destructive, leaving traces invisible to the naked eye, while being extremely sensitive with limits of detection in the range of the ppm or below depending on the elements.

The hard stone technological analysis is based on a frame of reference elaborated in an ethnoarchaeological study carried out in the Cambay workshops (Roux 2000). This frame of references made possible the characterisation of every stage of the *chaîne opératoire*, from the extraction, heating and knapping (Pelegrin 2000) to the operation of final polishing (D'Errico et al. 2000) and the quality of the product (hence the artisan's skill) (Bellina 2007, 2014).

Corpus of remains

Ceramics: Ceramic assemblages from 18 sites dated between 500 BCE–500 CE and located in the Thai-Malay Peninsula have been analysed, representing nearly 24,000 fragments (including those studied by Bouvet (Bouvet 2017a, 2017b, 2017c) at Khao Sam Kaeo (KSK). Pottery sherds have been classified into six pottery traditions and many subgroups (Favereau 2015). Two of these traditions have been interpreted as locally produced. Among each group of locally-produced ceramics, a minority of sherds display specific decorated motifs that relate to the so-called 'Sa Huynh-Kalanay' style. These locally-produced SHK-inspired ceramics come from 16 sites, including three ports-of-trade (KSK, Khao Sek (KK) and Tha Chana) and 13 caves (Tham Phu Khao Thong, Tham Tuay, Tham Chaeng, Khao Krim, Ko Din, Tham Ma Ngaen, Tham Ta Thun, Tham Kuan, Khao Lak, Khao Ta Plai, Khao Thalom 5, Khao Yong Ma 2 and Tham Ma Yang) (Table 4.1).[2] In total, 420 locally produced Sa Huynh-Kalanay-inspired fragments have been analysed. Furthermore, ceramics belonging to three different traditions found in the Thai-Malay Peninsula have been interpreted as imported. One tradition is likely to come from the Philippines (Kalanay-related pottery), one from China (Han dynasty-related fragments) and one from India (Fine Wares). Another tradition identified in the peninsula gathers together paddled and impressed fragments (Figure 4.2) but its origin is still uncertain. The artefacts from the other industries studied here do not necessarily come from the same sites, but because of looting, which in some cases did not allow us to access the pottery, we cannot be certain (e.g., Khao Mueni, an important site for glass and stone materials).

Glass: As far as glass is concerned, the upper Thai-Malay Peninsula can be considered as a region fairly well studied compared to other Southeast Asian areas. For this chapter, 12 sites were considered. Their different layouts, functions and types of location with the number of glass samples available for LA-ICP-MS study can be found in Table 4.1.

Whereas several thousand glass artefacts were extracted from two locations, KSK and KK, the 10 other sites investigated here yielded only 348 catalogued

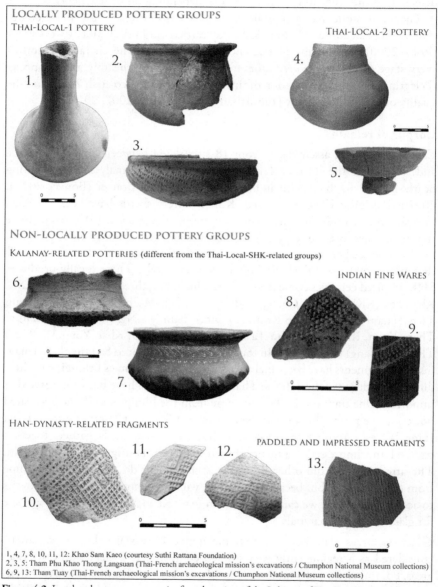

Figure 4.2 Local and exogenous ceramics found on sites of the Isthmus of Kra (Source: A. Favereau).

glass artefacts. KSK and KK showed indisputable evidence for beads and bracelet manufacturing (Dussubieux and Bellina 2017, 2018). Glass from two close by inland transhipment sites along the River Langsuan was studied. At the other sites consisting of caves and rockshelters, beads and more rarely bracelets were mostly associated with burials. At Ban Na Hyan glass waste and melted clusters of beads along lapidary beads and a glass vessel fragment were found. Generally, the vast majority of the beads were drawn monochrome beads.

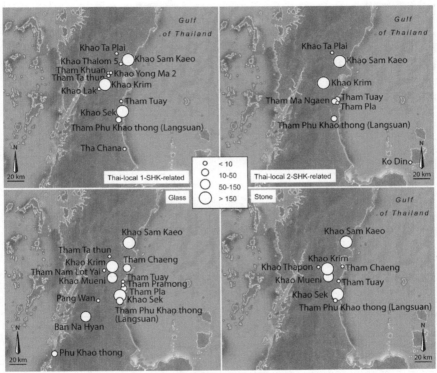

Map 4.2 Maps showing the location of sites and types of industries analysed for each site (Source: A. Favereau).

Stone: The stone assemblage used for this study include 725 stone beads (Table 4.1). Attention was mainly given to KSK (435 pieces) and KK (sampling: 191 pieces) workshops. The characterisation of these beads was essential to trace their distribution within the peninsula and abroad, and hence to reconstruct the social, economic and political structure of these trading polities. A detailed presentation of the *chaîne opératoire* and technological groups for those two manufacturing centres is published elsewhere (Bellina 2014; Bellina 2018b). More than 83 beads from sites in the provinces of Chumphon and Ranong other than the production sites were analysed. Found in funerary deposits in caves distributed

Table 4.1 Sites and analysed material by the authors in the Isthmus of Kra.

SITE	TYPE OF SITE	FUNCTION	LOCATION	THAI-LOCAL-1-SHK-RELATED	THAI-LOCAL-2-SHK-RELATED	STONE ORNAMENT	TYPE OF STONE ORNAMENT	GLASS SAMPLES RECORDED	GLASS SAMPLES ANALYSED WITH LA-ICP-MS	TYPE OF GLASS SAMPLE
Khao Sam Kaeo (KSK)	Open-air port-settlement	Port-of-trade	Lowland coastal	152	2	435	Beads, pendants, production wastes	2701	162	Drawn lapidary beads, bracelets wastes
Khao Sek (KK)	Open air port-settlement	Port-of-trade	Lowland coastal	77 highly fragmented (MNI=1)		171	Beads, pendants, production wastes	157	45	
Tha Chana	Open air port-settlement	Port-of-trade	Lowland coastal	8						
Ko Din	Cave	Funerary	offshore		1					
Tham Phu Khao Thong Langsuan	Cave	Funerary	Lowland coastal	46	43	1	Pendant	12	4	
Tham Pramong	Cave	Funerary	Lowland coastal			4	Beads			
Tham Tuay	Cave	Funerary	Coastal/estuarine	9	34	1	Bead	6	6	Drawn beads
Tham Chaeng	Cave	Funerary	Coastal/estuarine			1	Bead	66	5	Drawn beads
Tham Phla	Cave	Funerary	Coastal/estuarine					13	1	Drawn beads
Ban Na Hyan	Open air	Transhipment/feeding point	inland					18	18	Drawn and lapidary beads, cluster of melted beads, bracelets wastes Glass beads, wastes and cluster of melted beads
Pang Wan/Pang Thaw	Open air	Transhipment/feeding point	inland					7	7	Drawn beads
Nasak Lot Yai/Tham Nam Lot	Cave	Funerary/transhipment	inland					1	1	Drawn beads
Khao Krim	Cave	Funerary	Inland	1	2	3		26	5	Drawn beads
Tham Ma Ngaen	Cave	Funerary	Inland		22					
Tham Ta Thun	Cave	Funerary	Inland	2		18	Beads	4	1	Drawn beads
Khao Ta Plai	Cave	Funerary	Inland	8	3					
Khao Thalom 5	Cave	Funerary	Inland	1						
Khao Yong Ma 2	Cave	Funerary	Inland	3	1					
Tham Ma Yang	Cave	Funerary	Inland	1						
Tham Khuan	Cave	Funerary	Inland	3						
Khao Lak	Cave	Funerary	Inland	1						
Khao Mueni	Cave	Funerary/ritual site	Inland			49	Beads	195	13	Drawn beads bangles
Khao Thapon	Cave	Funerary/ritual site	Inland			18	Beads			
Tham Khao Krok	Cave	Funerary/ritual site	Inland			1	Bead			
Tham Tasak	Cave	Funerary/ritual site	Inland			3	Beads			
Total				312	108	725		3206	268	

across a large territory, they are all finished products. Unfortunately, looting activities make it difficult to estimate what may have been their importance. A few come from our excavations (one at Tham Tuay and one Tham Phu Khao Thong) and 81 were studied in villagers' collections with eight from coastal caves (Tham Pramon, Tham Chaeng, and others. See Table 4.1) and 74 from inland caves (Khao Mueni, Khao Krim, Tham Thapon, and others. See Table 4.1).

RESULTS—SYNTHESIS ON THE CULTURAL PROFILES AND SOCIO-ECONOMIC ORGANISATION DURING THE LAST CENTURIES BCE

The spatial distribution of the different technological groups of materials draws a picture of a dynamic socio-economic landscape evolving though time between two main stages. The early regional networks, originating by the first part of the first millennium BCE, strengthened, allowing the development of regional ports-of-trade such as KSK from the early fourth century BCE. During the later period, perhaps from the third century to the first century BCE, activity on the exchange network is shown to increase. Local and exogenous groups belonging to different environments now appear economically and culturally better defined and working in concert. Found among these exogenous groups are those we interpret as early sea nomads.

Earliest riverine ports-of-trade and its immediate hinterland—centripetal dynamic—fourth century BCE

During this early phase, the rise of ports-of-trade and already developed complex urban and political models are evidenced. Ports-of-trade concentrate the largest range of imports and develop culturally hybrid industries. They redistribute their culturally hybrid products—characterised by a pan-regional style—at a regional level. At this period, the involvement of surrounding local groups only appears discreetly in the archaeological records. In ports-of-trade and in the caves around, these lowland groups' material culture reveals a well-grounded maritime orientation towards the Bay of Bengal and more strongly (i.e., currently supported by more archaeological evidence) towards the South China Sea.

The ports-of-trade

During the very late fifth century or the early fourth century BCE, local ports-of-trade acting as regional economic and cultural centres emerged, such as at KSK (Bellina 2017) and potentially at Tha Chana (unfortunately, not subjected to controlled excavations). They were likely preceded by more discrete small coastal trading nodes: as we have seen, there is evidence for early first century BCE regional networks linking this part of the peninsula with other sites in MSEA and ISEA. This is further supported by the material culture style in ports-of-trade and more discreetly in surrounding sites (funerary deposits in caves) which reveals longer-established links with other coastal groups. The local repertoire integrates traits shared by other coastal communities along the South China Sea (Bellina 2018a).

Ports of trade arose on barely elevated hills along rivers a few kilometres from the sea (less than 10 kilometres). They are currently represented by KSK (Bellina 2017), KK (Bellina 2018a) and Tha Chana on the eastern coast and by the complex of Ban Kluay Nok and Phu Khao Thong (Bellina et al. 2014) on the west coast—although this group of sites is less well dated. Survey and excavations on the Myanmar side of the peninsula have begun to uncover more of these sites. The ports-of-trade show signs of early urbanism and in the specific case of KSK, a cosmopolitan character with compounds hosting foreign communities such as South Asian, North Vietnamese or Chinese, different Southeast Asian groups of merchants and skilled craftsmen. The political structure emerging from comparative study of KSK and KK is that of a confederation of hierarchically specialised and complementary small city-states. These developed highly skilled and culturally hybrid industries that fed different levels of the networks and played a role in rulers' political and economic strategy within the confederation and between the city-states and their hinterland (Bellina 2018a). These fourth century BCE ports-of-trade drained imports from various South and Southeast Asian regions. They also manufactured goods that they distributed locally and regionally. Their workshops fed other smaller and affiliated specialised sites such as the port-of-trade of KK (Bellina 2018a, 2018b; Dussubieux and Bellina 2018; Favereau 2018) and local networks. In the larger port-settlements such as KSK and probably Tha Chana too, the broadest variety of ceramic, glass and stone types—local, local with foreign characteristics and imports—was concentrated.

For ceramics, all pottery groups identified in the peninsula were found in ports-of-trade: local types, local types with Indian-inspired traits or South China Sea traits and imported types (Bouvet 2017a, b; Favereau et al. 2017, 2018; Péronnet and Srikanlaya 2017). Earthenware burial jars drawing links with the Philippines and Vietnam were also discovered. These were first identified by Bouvet (2017c) at KSK and named Black and Red Jars. They were later recognised at KK and Tha Chana. They are rare in the peninsula (about 50 jars in total in the current state of research). In the Philippines, similar jars were found on the island of Masbate (see Bay-Petersen 1982 and 1982–83: 266, Fig. 3) and also reported on Palawan and Samar islands (Hutterer 1969; Fox 1970; Bay-Petersen 1982: 80). In Vietnam, such jars differ from those of the Sa Huynh culture. In the cemetery of Hoa Diem in Khanh Hoa province for instance, jars similar to the Black and Red Jars from Thailand were used for funerary purposes (see Yamagata 2012: 125, Fig. 52). Given their distribution and their scarcity, they seem to be associated with small groups of people involved in the South China Sea networks.

During this early stage, glass and stone industries were hybrid: they produced local goods with foreign raw materials and technologies in the pan-regional style. The pattern of distribution of glass and stone ornaments is less clear, a situation resulting from the more limited amount recovered in context due to looting activities. As for pottery, KSK and KK implemented the same hybrid productions. They combined the same foreign elements occurring at the same stages of a similar *chaîne opératoire*. Both used South Asian raw materials and techniques that they associated to a regional style characteristic of the 'early late prehistoric South China Sea style' (Bellina 2018b; Dussubieux and Bellina 2017). In addition to similarities in the sites' configuration, the parallels in their industries supports the hypothesis that they were closely linked and part of the same political confederated entity (Bellina 2018a). During this early phase, glasswork mainly consists of faceted beads produced at KSK and KK with South Asian techniques traditionally used to work stones and bracelets. Raw material from northeastern India was imported and worked in KK and KSK's workshops to manufacture lapidary glass beads, glass bracelets and minute red draw beads.

Lapidary glass beads and bracelets have not yet been found within the peninsula but they appear more clearly distributed regionally as part of this set of objects in the 'early late prehistoric South China Sea style' (Figure 4.3). Lapidary glass beads were found in Thailand at Ban Chiang and at Ban Don Ta Phet. Bracelets were found at Ban Don Ta Phet in Thailand; at the Mimotien site in Cambodia; at certain Sa Huynh-related sites in Vietnam such as Giong Ca Vo, Phu Hoa, and Go Ma Voi; possibly in the Oc Eo area in Vietnam; and in the Tabon Caves in the Philippines (Chamber B in Manunggul Cave, Palawan Island). Minute red beads with a similar northeastern Indian composition were present at Ban Don Ta Phet, Giong Ca Vo and sites of the Samon Valley in central Myanmar. Those sites belong to an Iron Age network that encompasses the Bay of Bengal and the South China Sea. In contrast, the recovery of these productions at a local level is still limited. As per lapidary glass, so far, it has only been unearthed at the cave of Phu Khao Thong Langsuan (Bellina et al. 2014 unpublished report) located in the lowland area about 5 kilometres from KK. The production may have been predominantly oriented towards regional networks around the South China Sea including Ban Don Ta Phet in west-central Thailand, Giong Ca Vo in southern Vietnam and the Tabon Cave in The Philippines (Lankton et al. 2008).

Similar to glass ornaments, the pattern of distribution for stone ornament production within the peninsula is sketchy due to looting. At this early stage, workshops in ports-of-trade were producing stone ornaments made of raw material likely imported from South Asia and, like the glass beads, worked with South Asian skilled techniques in the regional 'early late prehistoric South China Sea style'. Very similar ornaments were uncovered at Ban Don Ta Phet in Thailand, at Sa Huynh-related sites such as Giong Ca Vo and in the Tabon caves in the Philippines (Bellina 2014). These stone productions are found within the two port-settlements and in defined zones at KSK.

The bronze industry in these ports is also hybrid. However, as opposed to glass and stone, the raw material is most likely local. The Ranong area along the western coast of the Kra Isthmus is renowned for its sources of tin which were exploited historically and up to the present. KSK and KK provided evidence again for a hybrid industry combining local tin and Indian technologies to produce high-tin bronze ingots likely aimed at exportation (Pryce and Bellina 2018; Pryce et al. 2017). Lead isotope analysis has established links between the high-tin bronze alloy used for bowls found at Ban Don Tha Phet (west central Thailand), KSK and KK and an ingot from Tilpi in West Bengal (Pryce et al. 2014).

Figure 4.3 Bracelet fragments (left), lapidary glass beads (right) from Khao Sek and Khao Sam Kaeo, early period (Source: B. Bellina).

Port-of-trade's immediate hinterland (surrounding)

The local populations of villagers lying in the vicinity were until now only visible through neighbouring caves, some of which yielded funerary deposits. No open-air sites have been found. The villagers used the manufactured goods in funerary contexts, which have been found in caves at Tham Phu Khao Thong Langsuan located near KK (French-Thai excavations in 2014, hereafter PKTL), Khao Krim, Khao Lak, Tham Phla, Tham Tuay, and at the caves of Khao Ta Plai, Khao Thalom 5, Tham Khuan and Khao Yong Ma Cave 2. In terms of material culture, the influence of the ports-of-trade and their exchanges with local groups is well-evidenced by the main local pottery tradition named 'Thai-

Local-1' (Figure 4.3) identified in the peninsula. Thai-Local-1 products have been found on sites both coastal and inland. Within this tradition, which represents 60.7% of the pottery sherds under study, a small proportion (~1.2%) displays decorations showing SHK influences. These ceramics share a few stylistic traits that can be found in various sites along the South China Sea: some of the pots are decorated with incisions, often filled with impressions and/or red painting, creating SHK-inspired geometric designs. The more frequent and relevant patterns for this group are spirals, rectangles, triangles and waves. Patterns are usually repeated either by interlocking or by forming a frieze and can be combined (i.e., interlocking triangles or alternating triangles and spirals for instance). Such designs are identified on several vessels from other sites located along the South China Sea, for example, they can be found at sites in central and southern Vietnam, central Philippines (chiefly the Visayas and Palawan) and Indonesia (Sulawesi and Borneo) (see for instance Balbaligo 2016; Bellina et al. 2012; Favereau and Bellina 2016; Dizon 2003; Lewis et al. 2011; Reinecke et al. 2002; Solheim et al. 2006; Yamagata 2012). The main local SHK-related group (Thai-Local-1-SHK-related) was distributed both to ports such as KSK and Tha Chana in specific domestic contexts and a few caves spread over a large territory. Because of its specific distribution—specifically at KSK—and its rarity (see contexts in KSK, e.g. Favereau 2015), this type of ceramic might be 'prestigious'. It is likely that these pots were produced upon order. Strong links between KSK and its immediate hinterland are attested by the presence of this Thai-Local-1-SHK-related group (Figure 4.3) but also and more clearly with the distribution of its variants ('Thai-Local-1-SHK-related&impressed-with-shell'). Besides KSK, the latter has so far only been recovered from caves, coastal or inland: Khao Ta Plai, Khao Thalom 5, Tham Ma Yang, Khao Yong Ma 2, Tham Khuan and Tham Phu Khao Thong Langsuan. They evidence the central role of KSK because they are systematically present and more numerous there. All pottery groups and subgroups identified at Tham Phu Khao Thong Langsuan are present at KSK and Tha Chana, but absent at KK, although KK is located in the immediate vicinity of Tham Phu Khao Thong Langsuan. This contributes to the argument that there is a marked hierarchy within this confederation. KSK and perhaps Tha Chana exert a stronger influence in the region despite the fact that other ports-of-trade are located in their neighbourhood.

Locally-made hybrid stone ornaments may well have been distributed locally also. Iron Age inhumations in the neighbouring caves and rockshelters often yield stone and glass jewellery, many of which could come from the regional industrial ports. The only object found in context dating of this early period was excavated at Tham Phu Khao Thong Langsuan in 2014. It is a small carnelian pendant of a singular morphology, part of one of the funerary deposits in this cave radiocarbon dated of the fourth–third century BCE (WK 39004: 2338±25 BP; SacA47091: 2205±30 BP; SacA47092: 2210±30 BP). Given the unique morphology and the skill involved, it is conceivable that the pendant was made to order in one of the two contemporary workshops of KSK or the neighbouring port of KK. Burials in this cave yielded several fragments of high-tin bronze bowls, one of which was definitely decorated with a central knob, looking very similar to the bronze vessels at Ban Don Ta Phet (Kanchanaburi) and at KSK. At KK, working evidence for high-tin bronze was uncovered (see below).

Though still tenuous, these manufactured goods suggest links between regional ports themselves and with their immediate hinterland. How extensive and intensive these links were is difficult to appreciate given the material's scarcity. In any case, we know that such exchanges took place. One possibility is that they occurred for the exchange of agricultural products. Rice and millet constituted the agricultural base at KSK and potentially at KK too, though evidence is sparse in the latter. This agricultural base could support local and transient merchants or artisans (Castillo 2017). Other indirect evidence for links with the hinterland lies in the material found along transpeninsular routes and local tin exploitation. Transpeninsular routes passing by the Kraburi/Ta Thapao and the Langsuan river systems were already used. Indian raw materials (stone for ornaments and raw glass) and other long-distance trade-related materials (imported Indian Fine Ware, Dong Son drums from southern China or northern Vietnam) have been uncovered on sites along these routes, such as at Ban Na Hyan in the middle of the peninsula along the Langsuan river system (Chumphon) or in ports at their ends (Bellina et al. 2014; Bellina 2017).

The results of this first period can be summarised as follows: long-distance networks and ports-of-trade were already well-developed by the fourth century BCE, likely relying on formerly established nodes. Local populations around those fluvial ports-of-trade appear linked with them, exchanging manufactured material against various goods, many of which did not preserve. Tenuous indirect evidence suggests that they may have been involved providing agricultural, forest and mineral products, tin in particular. Foreign traders and craftsmen also lived in ports-of-trade. The latter probably produced goods for local rulers to build their prestige but also to seal alliances with surrounding populations who supplied their local ports' marketplaces with goods for regional trade.

The later period: Upstream-downstream and inland networks and more groups involved—culturally/economically better defined and cooperating

Ports-of-trade

During this later period, more ports-of-trade emerged: Phu Khao Thong and Ban Kluay Nok on the western coast in Thailand and possibly Aw Gyi in southern Myanmar. Many more foreign groups and imports are found there, some indicating links with the Western world. This is probably the period when

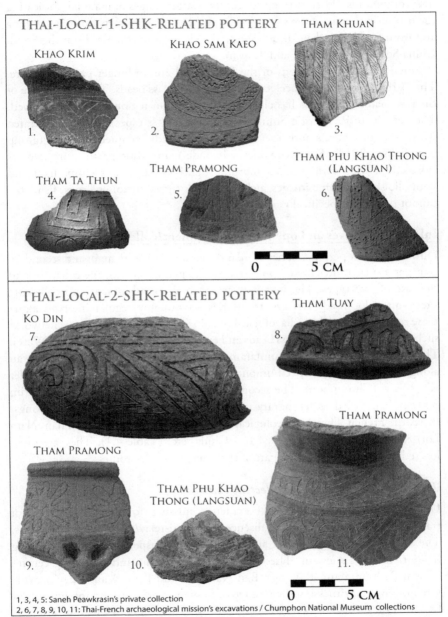

Figure 4.4 Local Sa Huynh-Kalanay related types of ceramics found in the Kra Isthmus in the Thai-Malay Peninsula (Source: A. Favereau).

KSK extended further north and new surrounding walls were built around the new compounds. Ports-of-trade concentrate larger ranges of materials indicating the presence of many more social groups. In the latter, imports from Han China and from South Asia have been found, as well as more material from the South China Sea, the Philippines and Taiwan.

Some of the hybrid goods of the first period are no longer produced there. This is the case of glass bracelets and of lapidary glass beads. The provenance of the raw material for glass has changed too. The pan-regional style has evolved. The 'later Late Prehistoric South China Sea style' is especially well illustrated with stone ornaments and now includes more Indic adapted material (group 3 in Bellina 2014). Stone ornaments include many widespread morphologies alongside a wide variety of zoomorphic figurines, structures (stupa-like) and symbolic shapes. Some images such as lions or tigers, tortoises, frogs, fish, etc., cannot be related specifically to Indic imagery.

Inland sites: Caves and open-air transhipment/collecting centres

During this later period, a series of inland sites located along main and secondary transpeninsular routes linked one coast of the peninsula with the other. Inland sites are of two types. The first type are open-air transhipment and collecting sites—often localised at rivers' tributaries—at roughly regular intervals along these routes. They yield archaeological remains related to long-distance networks such as Dong Son drums, glass beads and exogenous ceramic (Indian Fine Ware). These sites include Wat Pathumtaram (Ranong), Ban Na Hyan and Pangwan along the River Langsuan (Chumphon) and Tham Nam Lot along the smaller River Sawi (Chumphon). The second type are caves located in the Tenasserim central chain, used as temporary camps and for funerary practices. Amongst these, the French-Thai Archaeological Mission investigated caves at Tham Nam Lot, Khao Krim, Khao Mueni, Khao Chula, etc. (Table 4.1). They are often located along rivers which are part of the transpeninsular routes.

Transhipment places and collecting centres

Until recently, amongst crucial evidence missing to support the use of transpeninsular routes was the absence of inland-relay/transhipment stations. The first ones were evidenced along the major transpeninsular route linking Kraburi to KK/Langsuan. These are the transhipment and collecting centres of Wat Pathumtaram (Ranong), Ban Na Hyan and Pang Wan. They provide foreign imports witnessing the passage of foreign merchants and foreign goods. In terms of glass, Ban Na Hyan is puzzling as it yielded a range of artefacts considerably more diverse than those found at other sites inland. Blocks of glass, clusters of melted glass beads and drawn and lapidary beads were found at the site (Figure 4.5). Is that a sign that glass beads were manufactured at this location? This cannot be excluded. Was Ban Na Hyan just a point of transit to other sites that would have used the raw glass and recycled the melted beads? The type of glass that was found there, places Ban Na Hyan in the same type of network than the sites dating from the third century BC–third century AD period. However, the type of material seems to indicate a more complex organisation at this site compared to the others. The absence of excavations there and the extent of the lootings may prevent any in-depth study or the possibility to interpret the economic and political significance of this site and the glass work that took place there.

The site of Pang Wan (about 30 kilometres east from Ban Na Hyan) contrasts with Ban Na Hyan as glass artefacts only appear in the form of small translucent turquoise and dark blue beads showing much less diversity. The beads found were associated with a Dong Son drum recovered after the collapse of the Langsuan riverbank during a monsoon season. The lack of diversity probably reflects the sampling opportunities at a looted site whose beads are kept in private collections, rather than the reality of the past. The compositions of the glass artefacts at Pang Wan that are potash are similar to the compositions found at Ban Na Hyan, suggesting that the two sites belong to the same network of relay stations and operated around the same period despite different status or functions. As a matter of fact, Ban Na Hyan may have taken advantage of its privileged position along what was then an important transpeninsular route and may have grown in importance so greatly that a glass workshop may have arisen. There are historical examples in Sumatra of thriving inland secondary and tertiary exchange centres that grew economically powerful (Andaya and Andaya 2015: 193).

Merchants crossing the peninsula were likely assisted by local groups who had a good knowledge of their environment. This knowledge was crucial in a hostile environment through which circulation could not be improvised, both on land along tracks or on rivers whose course and water level varied quickly, greatly and dramatically and which implied using multiple means of transport (Jacq-Hergoualc'h 2002). This leads us to question the respective role of each group in this network. Who were the groups familiar with this difficult and changing environment who assisted foreign merchants and transportation of the goods? Were the people collecting goods from the forest the same people who were engaged in assisting travellers and goods circulation? It is hard to answer this question at this stage but it is likely that groups from the interior did so. What material culture tells us is that foreign influence appears rather limited inland. Though looted, burials found there along major or secondary fluvial systems yielded important quantities of hard stone and glass ornaments that may well have been produced in regional ports-of-trade. Stone beads appeared rather simple and did not seem Indic or South China Sea influenced. They were made in various materials, some imported and others possibly of local origin. To sum up, they do not compare with those found in ports-of-trade. These burials never seemed to include long-distance imported material—such as the

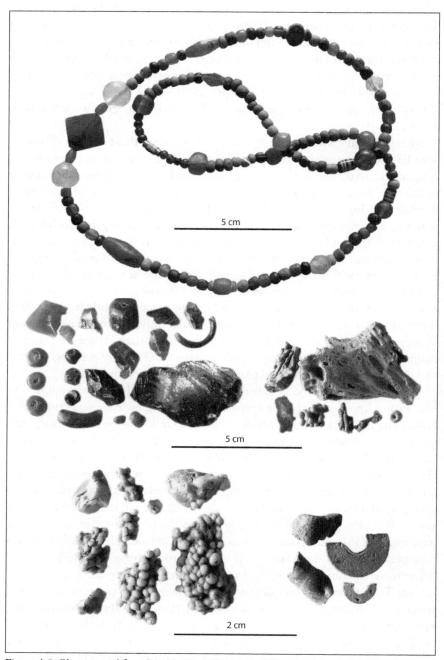

Figure 4.5 Glass material from Ban Na Hyan (Source: B. Bellina).

Indian Fine Ware, the Han Chinese imports, or Dong Son drums—amongst funerary deposits in caves inland. Those imports were encountered in the transhipment/collecting places only where traders were stopping. Were inland groups taking forest goods they collected to local collecting/transhipment sites only, thus limiting their exposure to foreign traders/travellers? It seems unlikely. More plausibly, inland groups may have signalled their distinct socio-economic specialisation through their material culture. These inland groups would have taken those forest goods at the river mouth. From there coastal/estuarine groups acting as middlemen could have taken the material on to the regional city-port. One cannot exclude that some downstream groups at the river mouth may also have become specialised as middlemen gathering and redistributing goods from inland transhipment/collecting centres to regional ports. The latter could also have acted as guides for foreigners crossing the peninsula and joining inter-regional ports. This is discussed in the following section.

Inland caves

The inland sites include cave sites such as Khao Krim and Khao Muni along the River Langsuan and transhipment and collecting open-air sites along tributaries such as Pangwan and Ban Na Hyan, located along the River Langsuan leading to the port of KK. This river system is part of the transpeninsular network. Archaeological remains in inland sites are sparse due to numerous disturbances. Nevertheless, they show the appearance of a new tradition of local pottery with organic temper (Thai-Local-2), which co-exists with the mineral-tempered traditional production (the tradition Thai-Local-1).

Estuarine, coastal and offshore caves

From this period, exogenous groups settled in the peninsula. The local pottery tradition Thai-Local-2 ceramic signals the arrival of foreign groups with closer connections with the South China Sea and the Philippines in particular. The Thai-Local-2-SHK-related pottery (Figure 4.3) may correspond to pottery used by some of those groups who locally settled at river mouths to command the upstream-downstream trade and that we interpret as early sea nomads. The privileged relation between estuarine, coastal and offshore caves mean that the groups that produced and acquired Thai-Local-2-SHK-related pottery were more influential in these areas that were strategic locations both between ports-of-trade and the upstream-downstream/transpeninsular networks. It shows their involvement both into inter-regional networks and in local upstream-downstream exchange networks. These groups located at estuaries played an intermediary role redistributing goods between upstream inland sites and regional ports, although inland groups may also have come downstream to exchange.

Their activities are currently only attested by supposed funerary deposits found in estuarine, coastal and offshore caves. Funerary contexts are clearly attested at

Tham Tuay and Tham Phu Khao Thong Langsuan. Other caves are said to have been used for funerary purposes by our informants (villagers) who found human remains/bones associated. Among these caves, only Tham Tuay and Tham Chaeng yielded Black and Red Jars as well as imported pottery material the same as at ports-of-trade, such as Indian Fine Wares and Han Chinese wares.

Thai-Local-2-SHK-related is a sub group of the local pottery tradition Thai-Local-2, which represents a small number of vessels (~0.5%) decorated with SHK-inspired designs. Thai-Local-2-SHK-related pottery are systematically present at Tham Tuay, Tham Phla, Tham Ma Ngaen, Tham Phu Khao Thong Langsuan and on the island of Ko Din. However, they remain rare (less than 100 pots). They are very similar from one site to the next: manufacturing traces are identical; finishing is carefully made; decorative techniques include incision, painting, shaving and impressions, and decorative patterns are clearly different from what is found in the sites of the interior, the ports-of-trade and the other cave sites. Motifs associated with the SHK style include incised interlocking spirals or triangles, scalloped decorations shaved on carinations, incised geometric motives often combined with red and yellow paintings, and patterns impressed with the edge of a shell. Other motifs—not diagnostic of the SHK lexicon but still evoking the SHK style—consist of floral and animal designs. The contours are incised and then filled up with reddish and yellow paintings. Such designs do not appear on any other site in the peninsula. These motives, specific to these caves, attest to the use and reinterpretation of the SHK style repertoire.

The Thai-Local-2-SHK-related wares are interpreted as being produced upon order. Such occasional productions are almost exclusively found in coastal caves (95% to 98% of the pots); very rare in ports-of-trade such as KSK and Tha Chana and absent at KK. Indeed, outside of these caves, only a few Thai-Local-2-SHK-related pottery were identified at KSK: two at the interior cave of Khao Krim and one at Tha Chana and these do not display any floral or animal-like decorations. The decorative style found on the pots in the coastal caves is absolutely unique and distinct from what is found in ports and inland caves. The distribution of these specific decorated pottery indicates privileged links between coastal caves at the mouth of the Rivers Tako and Langsuan and caves offshore like Ko Din, all of them sharing comparable patterns.

The groups we interpret as sea nomads who were using these coastal caves seem to have been in recurrent contact with the Philippines. Comparative studies of SHK-related pottery from the Thai-Malay Peninsula and from the Philippines reveals that a style circulated and developed through time as a result of prolonged and repeated interactions between Thailand and the Philippines, suggesting round trips between the two areas and synchronised developments (Favereau 2015; Favereau and Bellina in press). Circulations involved groups of people, presumably from the central Philippines as the earlier dates from the Philippines suggests. These individuals may have come to the Thai-Malay

Peninsula around 500/400 BCE and represented by the pottery group Thai-Local-2-SHK-related.

Contrary to Thai-Local-2-SHK-related pottery, which is rare, pottery classified within the tradition Thai-Local-2 was found in larger quantities on ports-of-trade such as KSK and KK.

Estuarine, coastal and offshore caves links with inland caves: Upstream–downstream

Some artefacts now clearly evidence upstream-downstream exchange and special connections between a few estuarine, coastal and offshore caves and inland caves upstream. This is the case for Tham Tuay at the River Tako estuary and Tham Chaeng at the River Sawi mouth on one hand, and for Khao Krim and Khao Muni, two inland caves upstream along the River Sawi on the other. These two river systems belong to what can be labelled a secondary network, that is, used by local groups and only perhaps occasionally by traders. The coastal caves of Tham Tuay and Tham Chaeng may be interpreted as regional collecting sites that supplied local ports' marketplaces with inland products, as they are directly located at the rivers' mouths, between the major ports of Tha Chana, KK and KSK. They may have redistributed products collected inland to the regional major ports acting as international marketplaces such as KSK and Tha Chana, but also have been more directly involved in regional maritime networks, as the presence of foreign imports may suggest. The pottery at Tham Tuay and Tham Chaeng includes imported Indian Fine Wares and Han ceramics, which are usually found in ports-of-trade like KSK and Tha Chana (albeit excluding KK).

Glass too supports the hypothesis of connections between estuarine coastal groups and the latter and upstream groups. For this later period, a certain number of sites yielded material with a Southeast Asian/Southern Chinese composition. The presence of this glass but the absence of northeastern Indian glass is typical of this period. Such a glass type was found at a number of sites: Tham Chaeng, Tham Pla, Khao Krim, Pang Wan, Ban Nai Hyan and Khao Muni, which would support upstream–downstream connections. Tham Tuay can be associated chronologically to this group of sites despite the presence of two opaque green beads of South Asian northeastern composition. The colour of these artefacts does not correspond to the colour of very early northeastern Indian glass and might have been brought to the site by a network different from the early one that was identified for earlier periods.

It is important to note that the glass material at all those sites is not uniform, albeit with more similarities between certain sites and more disparities between others. The Southeast Asian/Southern Chinese compositions of the glass found at Tham Chaeng and Tham Tuay are similar but this Southeast Asia/Southern Chinese glass subtype is fairly common. Tham Chaeng only yielded turquoise blue beads, while the range of colours for Khao Krim is limited to dark blue and turquoise blue. Khao Krim and Tham Chaeng have in common the presence of high alumina Southeast Asian/Southern Chinese glass that is absent at Tham Tuay and fairly rare in general.

Drawing a pattern of distribution of hard stone material beyond port-settlements is currently a difficult task. The corpus available is uneven: the vast majority corresponds to ornaments from the production sites and their settlements, KSK and KK. Similar styles can also be sparsely found inland in the cave of Khao Muni. However, a preliminary analysis of the material from other sites, now in private collections, suggests that most of it was imported from production sites other than KSK and KK. Very few coastal caves escaped looters and most of the Tham Chaeng material has been spread across various private collections. The site has yielded a Dong Son drum, a high-tin bronze bowl and a nephrite *lingling-o*. One of the three caves at Tham Tuay was excavated by the French-Thai Archaeological Mission and yielded an iron dagger, a small banded agate flat bead along with local SHK-related ceramic and glass beads.

To summarise, in the course of this second period, a larger number of the local groups and others who came to the peninsula both from South Asia and South China Sea became actively involved in exchange. The local groups appeared more culturally and economically defined and distinct than they previously had been. Other groups we interpret as newcomers played an important role in the networks. Amongst those are groups identified in ports-of-trade and along the coast near river mouths and in caves on offshore islands. They were groups sharing a similar outward orientation, having close links with the South China Sea and the Philippines in particular. Those evidenced at coastal locations and estuaries may have specialised as intermediaries, probably based on their knowledge both of riverine and maritime networks. We argue that those may correspond to early sea nomads. They cooperated with inland groups who collected and supplied goods to relay to transhipment stations along primary and secondary transpeninsular routes. At this stage, it is unclear whether coastal/estuarine groups served as guides for merchants and transporters for goods across the peninsula or whether this was done exclusively by inland groups.

DISCUSSION

The spatial distribution of the archaeological materials analysed indicates a chain of cooperation between groups whose lifeways and cultures seemed to diverge significantly in conjunction with the expansion of Maritime Silk Road activities by the fourth century BCE and the development of regional centralised trading polities. This would bring support to Benjamin's and Fix's hypotheses according to which local groups developed complementary lifeways from a common matrix as a profitable strategy (Benjamin 1987; Fix 2002). This chain of collaborations shows parallels with ethnohistorical accounts: the first circle involves inland "Orang Asli" and "Orang Laut" established in the lower portion of the transpeninsular routes; the second engages estuarine groups and traders settled in regional port-entrepôts. During the historical period, oral traditions and texts attest that sea nomads such as the Urak Lawoik of Lanta Island off the Kedah coast in Malaysia (the Kalah of Arab sources) were located in the vicinity of trading polities that developed there and that they cooperated with them. They were also at the mouth of transpeninsular routes and/or along the coast of the Malacca Strait. Besides the Urak Lawoik, Andaya (2008) also hypothesises that mutually beneficial cooperation probably existed between the Moken and trading polities further in the northern part of the Strait of Malacca. It is conceivable that such cooperation may have involved encouraging traders to use the transpeninsular route that the port-of-trade 'controlled' and to which the coastal/estuary group may have been affiliated. Sea peoples' languages bear evidence of their close relationship with dominant regional languages, thus attesting long-established symbiotic relations between them and regional trading polities (Blench this volume: Chapter 6).

In addition to internal dissimilation, cultural diversity visible in the Isthmus of Kra was also fashioned by interactions and interbreeding with foreign traders coming from the western and the eastern horizons: amongst the former, South Asians. There is evidence of South Asian contribution to the genomes of modern MSEA and ISEA populations beginning from the fourth century BC, that is, the period during which Maritime Silk Road activities developed and their presence is identified in ports such as in KSK, their compound being located on Hill 3 (Mörseburg et al. 2016). Furthermore, in the Thai-Malay Peninsula, gene flow is attested between indigenous groups and the island world and Oceania (Fix 2002). Linguistic data also point to the presence and close ties developed through recurring interactions and possible mixing with groups closely linked with the Philippines. These are foreign groups we propose to link with Thai-Local-2 ceramic present in ports-of-trade and with the Thai-Local-2-SHK-related pottery found in coastal/estuarine and neighbouring islands caves. We interpret the Thai-Local-2-SHK-related pottery as ceramics used by those amongst these foreign groups who specialised as sea nomads. These groups and close links with the Philippines are further evidenced by ornaments, glass, stone and gold analysed by the archaeological mission. Sea nomads may have married those in other groups to build political and economic alliances. Some could have settled and taken local wives as frequently happens with traders. Marriage would have been advantageous for the exchange relationships, which clearly helped maintain links between the Philippines and the peninsula. This hypothesis would support Benjamin's hypothesis based on his analysis of lexical elements where traces of very early forms of Austronesian would suggest direct contact between the Philippines and the Thai-Malay Peninsula prior to the later Malay expansion from Sumatra (Benjamin 1987: 130–1). Further south in the peninsula, biological data show that gene flow also took place linking local groups with some from Oceania

(Fix 2002). Mating with central Philippines traders could explain these close links. It has been hypothesised elsewhere that these small groups in connection with the Philippines may have been involved with inter-island exchanges and in particular nephrite from sources in Taiwan and elsewhere (Favereau and Bellina in press). Historical sources attest that marriage with the dominant land groups was widespread at least in the modern period. Orang Laut found it strategic to marry local entrepôt rulers' family members to strengthen their trading partnership (Andaya 2008: 189). These practices are also attested amongst the Bajau by ethnographic, genetic and linguistic studies. In the case of the Bajau, they predominantly married local neighbouring land groups, than other groups of Bajau, but also the dominant trading partners. This intermixing may have been the case all throughout history (Kusuma et al. 2017). In Timor too, there is evidence for a mutually beneficial intermix between inland resource-procuring (sandalwood) group, the Bunaq, and the coastal dwellers who organised its trade, the Tetun, probable former sea nomads (Galipaud et al. this volume).

In the Kra Isthmus during the late prehistoric period, groups along the coast and estuaries not only became economic and cultural intermediaries between the different foreign and local groups but also key actors in the political landscape. This is well reflected in their material culture that at the same time shared common trends, was distinct from other groups (inland and from trading communities in port-of-trade), but included some of the elements from these groups they interacted with. It is by combining this set material culture made of a combination of trade-related items with their spatial distribution limited to river mouths and islands which, we believe, can signal the presence of these groups. Perhaps because much of the evidence comes from burials, their material culture currently mainly consists of what is interpreted as honorific or prestigious artefacts; some made in port workshops, perhaps made especially for them, as in the case of ornaments and perhaps too of the Thai-Local-2-SHK-related pottery that they used for funerary practices. Their assemblage also included some of the imports found in these ports and along transpeninsular routes such as the Indian Fine Ware and Han ceramic. Port-of-trade leaders and sea nomads shared prestigious goods such as beads, which reflects the close and mutually beneficial links established between them. These goods can be compared to the honorific titles the port-of-trade rulers gave them, which legitimised sea nomads' activity and valued their specialised skills. There is perhaps a bias as much of the material dealt with which comes from funerary deposits. So far, no mundane or organic material associated to these groups has been recovered, hence limiting evidence to potentially valued artefacts. Burial practices took place in coastal/estuarine or offshore caves located on elevated peaks, which possibly served as landmarks for passing ships. These practices are also attested amongst historical Orang Laut. Besides constituting landmarks, they were considered to be the home of powerful spirits. Very few ethnohistorical or ethnographic sources provide accounts of the different sea nomads' funerary practices. White describes the Moken's habits of placing the body either on a stick or in the deceased's boat on a dedicated remote island, a sort of cemetery island (White 1922). Hogan accounts that in the 1970s, the Urak Lawoi of southern Thailand and the Moken were burying their dead in a burial ground near the coastal village but that before, the dead were buried in caves and coastal caves (Hogan 1972: 217). Andaya refers to the use of islands and caves in islands by Orang Laut (2008).

Their material culture also reflects their pivotal role as intermediaries dealing with inter-island exchanges—or what can be called 'feeder trade' (Blench this volume: Chapter 6)—linking the populations scattered across the numerous islands and carrying sparse resources (Nolde this volume; Galipaud et al. this volume). This role is perhaps comparable to the intermediaries carrying nephrite raw material that Favereau and Bellina proposes to trace between Taiwan, the Philippines and the Kra Isthmus (Favereau and Bellina in press). A similar hypothesis, involving maritime- and trade-oriented people, has also been raised by Hung and Chao (2016) to explain the movements of raw materials, technologies and ideas in Taiwan, based on comparisons with an historically documented group, i.e. the Basay people (Hung and Chao 2016: 1547). This was made possible thanks to their mastering of navigational techniques and boat constructions (Blench this volume: Chapter 8) and their ability to map maritime spaces into territories engaging all human groups' movements and connections (Chou this volume). This trading linkage between scattered groups may be the result of a network based on 'kinship-infused cultural-economic units' comparable to that described of the Orang Laut (Chou this volume) or the Sama trading colonies (Sather 2006).

The full range of services the sea nomads provided to the port-of-trade cannot be determined at this stage. It is however likely that they obtained their goods by providing services such as helping with the upstream/downstream collection and redistribution of goods, and perhaps guiding traders along the perilous transpeninsular tracks. Whether they patrolled and guarded sea lanes for the port's ruler, like the historical Orang Laut, or travelled in extensive zones to trade or find new routes cannot be determined. However, what appears plausible is that they encouraged foreign traders to use the transpeninsular routes for the benefit of the port-entrepôt ruler they were associated with. In doing so, they would have been key actors in the success of the trading polity, in their rise and decline. As described in Galipaud et al. (this volume), current sociopolitical configuration in Timor probably owes much to ancient sea nomads' involvement in organising trade and raising entrepôts. Settled along the coast, they would have structured trade organising resource procurement by developing mutually profitable relationships with inland groups. In Timor they would be directly linked to the Wehali Kingdom, which literature refers to as 'a complex confederation of Timorese political domains which played an important role in sandalwood trade' from the fifteenth to the seventeenth century (Galipaud et al. this volume).

The narrowest part of the Kra Isthmus (currently covering Ranong and Chumphon provinces) became economically and politically less important by the mid first millennium CE. Many parts of this region show no signs of activity or even occupation until very recently. It is likely that the decline of the local ports-of-trade entailed the departure of these groups, either further south where trade was thriving by the mid first millennium CE such as Chaiya and Satinpra, or further north (around the Mergui-Prachuap Khiri Khan route). They may have followed the port-entrepôt ruler they were affiliated to, such as the Orang Dalam who left the Malay Peninsula with their ruler to the Riau Islands (Andaya 2008: 183). As with the founding of Malacca, sea nomads could have helped their defeated leader establish another port-of-trade elsewhere, further north or south. Alternatively, they may simply have changed to a more discrete local maritime lifestyle or land-based lifestyle. Such is the case of the Moklen of the Phuket area, coastal dwellers who practice some agriculture (Ivanoff this volume). Such may also have been the case of some farming groups in the Philippines like the Yakan, Mapun and Inabaknon that speak Samalic languages, who may correspond to settled sea nomads. This is most likely what happened to the Tetun in Timor who became farmers once the local entrepôt and trade in sandalwood collapsed (Galipaud et al. this volume). In any case, in the region, even if some of the groups who specialised as sea nomads stayed and settled, their material culture would hardly be distinguishable from other land-based coastal groups whose material culture is very discrete.

CONCLUSION

To conclude, it can be conceived that estuarine, coastal and island groups of the Kra Isthmus laid the foundation of the historical sea nomads, especially those present further south at the entrances of the Malacca Strait, which became the favoured route by the first centuries CE. Their roots go back far into a long-established tradition of highly adaptive and mobile forager-traders found in the South China Sea and whose activities pioneered later trade routes (Bulbeck 2008). Like other 'marginal' groups in the region, they would have formed in response to trade and to the emergence of early centralised trading polities with which they interacted. It may be considered that the distinctive socio-economic groups emerged in and off the peninsula because they found it profitable to do so in the context of increasing inter-regional trade with the Maritime Silk Road. In the Kra Isthmus, these foreign groups had close links with the Philippines. They came to settle and likely intermarried there to take advantage of the Maritime Silk Road and the transpeninsular routes using river systems that were then used.

Based on archaeological evidence, the emergence of ancient sea nomads can be considered a dual response to emerging trading polities that developed in the peninsula first. On the one hand, they seem to maintain a self-protective and independent position possibly to counteract regional polities' raids, and social (such as hierarchy) and economic constraints (such as corvées). In this perspective, they maintained a lifestyle that was different but complementary to that of the groups present in multi-ethnic trading polities. On the other hand, they seem to have had close ties, possibly through alliances to maintain profitable trading relationships—perhaps with intermarriage. As intermediaries they operated on the local and regional levels, potentially thanks to networks of trading colonies such as the Sama. In doing so, they secured and legitimised their role and became key economic and political actors for trading polities. This dual relationship is reflected in their material culture, which is distinct from the land-based trading groups but at the same time shares elements with them. Their ability to link distant groups and to disseminate cultural traits is undeniable. In this perspective, what remains to be explored much further is the role they played as cultural vectors. This role remains to be elucidated in the Bay of Bengal, at the opposite side of the transpeninsular routes that they might have crossed themselves. There, they would have preceded the Bajau, who later pushed further west, helping traders/merchants to make their way in the Indian Ocean to reach Madagascar, perhaps even playing a role in the settlement of Madagascar (Kusuma et al. 2015, 2017). If this research has succeeded in beginning to uncover some of the socio-political contributions sea nomads made in the late prehistoric South China Sea, it is evident that the majority of their role remains to be unravelled, both through time and extending to the Bay of Bengal and beyond.

ACKNOWLEDGEMENTS

We wish to express our sincere gratitude to Silpakorn University, in particular Dr Rasmi Shoocongdej and Dr Chawalit Khaokhiew, as well as the Fine Arts Department, in particular the 14th Fine Arts office in Nakhon Si Thammarat and its Archaeology Division, including Anat Bamrungwong (director of the 14th Fine Arts office), Phanuwat Ueasaman (head of the Archaeology Division of the 14th Fine Arts office), Pongdhan Sampaongern (former head of Archaeology Division of the 14th Fine Arts office), Sarat Chlawsuntisakul, Chakrit Sittirit and Apirat Chehlao (who planned and surveyed in the Chumphon area), the Chumphon National Museum, the National Science Museum (in particular Cholawit Thongcharoenchaikit), the Suthi Rattana Foundation (in particular Bunchar Pongpanich) and Saneh Peawkrasin, for kindly providing us opportunities to analyse archaeological materials from Peninsular Thailand. We are also grateful for the thoughtful comments and constructive suggestions from

Catherine Perlès, David Bulbeck, Roger Blench, Thomas Oliver Pryce and Jean-Christophe Galipaud that were made on earlier versions of this chapter. We extend our thanks to Prof. Carla Sinopoli for allowing Aude Favereau to examine Philippine earthenware from the Guthe collection kept in the Museum of Anthropology (Michigan University). We also acknowledge Sachipan Srikanlaya, Jutinach Bowonsachoti, all members of the French-Thai Archaeological Mission, the Fyssen Foundation and the Archaeological Studies Program (University of the Philippines). The French-Thai Archaeological Mission has received financial support from the French Ministry of Foreign Affairs (and its excavation division) and the National Centre for Scientific Research (CNRS).

NOTES

[1] The picture drawn here is based on excavations and survey conducted in the Isthmus of Kra by the French-Thai Archaeological Mission since 2005. This mission is supported by the French Ministry of Foreign Affairs and by the National Centre for Scientific Research. It is a collaboration with Silpakorn University and the Fine Arts department. Amongst the mission's research themes are the co-evolution of populations and of their environment in relation to long-distance maritime exchange networks and the role they played in trade and cultural productions in Asia. The project pays special attention to the various social, economic and political evolutions these interacting populations experienced in relation to regional and inter-regional maritime exchanges.

[2] KSK, KK, Tha Chana, Tham Phu Khao Thong, Tham Tuay, Tham Chaeng, Khao Krim, Ko Din, Tham Ma Ngaen, Tham Ta Thun, Tham Kuan and Khao Lak were excavated and/or surveyed by the French-Thai Archaeological Mission (Table 4.1). Khao Ta Plai, Khao Thalom 5, Khao Yong Ma 2 and Tham Ma Yang were investigated by the Archaeology Department in Nakhon Si Thammarat.

REFERENCES

Allen, Jane. 1991. 'Trade and Site Distribution in Early Historic-period Kedah: Geoarchaeological, Historic, and Locational Evidence.' In *Indo-Pacific Prehistory 1990* Vol. 1, ed. P. Bellwood, 307–19. Canberra.

Andaya, Barbara Watson. 2019. 'Recording the Past of "Peoples Without History": Southeast Asia's Sea Nomads.' *Asian Review* 32 (1): 5–33.

Andaya, Barbara Watson and Leonard Y. Andaya. 2015. *A History of Early Modern Southeast Asia, 1400–1830*. Cambridge, New York: Cambridge University Press.

Andaya, Leonard, Y. 2008. 'Leaves of the Same Tree: Trade and Ethnicity in the Straits of Melaka.' In *The Orang Laut and the Malay*, 173–201. Honolulu: University of Hawai'i Press.

Balbaligo, Yvette. 2015. 'Ceramics and Social Practices at Ille Cave, Philippines.' Doctoral thesis. London: University College London.

———. 2016. 'Ceramics and Social Practices at Ille Cave, Philippines.' PhD thesis, London: The Institute of Archaeology, University College of London.

Balfet, Hélène, ed. 1991. *Observer L'action Technique: Des Chaînes Opératoires, pour quoi Faire?* Paris: Editions du CNRS.

Bay-Petersen, J. 1982. 'Textile Impressions on Iron Age Pottery in Masbate, Philippines.' *Quarterly of Culture and Society*, no. 10: 261–8.

Bellina, Bérénice. 2007. *Cultural Exchange between India and Southeast Asia. Production and Distribution of Hard Stone Ornaments (VI c. BC– VI c. AD)*. Paris: Editions de la Maison des Sciences de l'Homme, participation de l'Ecole Française d'Extrême-Orient et d'Epistèmes.

———. 2014. 'Maritime Silk Roads' Ornament Industries: Socio-Political Practices and Cultural Transfers in the South China Sea.' *Cambridge Archaeological Journal* 24 (3): 345–77.

———. 2018a. 'Development of Maritime Trade Polities and Diffusion of the "South China Sea Sphere of Interaction Pan-Regional Culture": The Khao Sek Excavations and Industries' Studies Contribution.' *Archaeological Research in Asia* 13: 1–12.

———. 2018b. 'Khao Sek Hard-stone Industry: An Insight into Early Port-polities Structure and Regional Material Culture.' *Archaeological Research in Asia* 13: 13–24.

Bellina, Bérénice, ed. 2017. *Khao Sam Kaeo: An Early Port-city between the Indian Ocean and the South China Sea*. Mémoires Archéologiques 28. Paris: Ecole française d'Extrême-Orient.

Bellina, Bérénice, Guillaume Epinal, and Aude Favereau. 2012. 'Caractérisation Préliminaire des Poteries Marqueurs d'échanges en mer de Chine Méridionale à la Fin de la Préhistoire.' *Archipel* 84: 7–33.

Bellina, Bérénice, Praon Silapanth, Boonyarit Chaisuwan, Cholawit Thongcharoenchaikit, Jane Allen, Vincent Bernard, Brigitt Borell, Phaedra Bouvet, Cristina Castillo, Laure Dussubieux, Julie Malakie LaClair, Sachipan Srikanlaya, Sophie Peronnet, and Thomas Oliver Pryce. 2014. 'The Development of Coastal Polities in the Upper Thai-Malay Peninsula.' In *Before Siam: Essays in Art and Archaeology*, ed. P. Murphy and N. Revire, 69–89. Bangkok: River Books.

Bellina, Bérénice, Cholawit Thongcharoenchaikit, and Sachipan Srikanlaya. 2014. 'Thai-French Archaeological Mission in the Thai-Malay Peninsula. Report of the Four Year Program 2011-2014.' Report for the National Research Council of Thailand and the FAD. Paris: Thai-French Archaeological Mission in the Thai-Malay Peninsula.

———. 2007. *Prehistory of the Indo-Malaysian Archipelago*. Canberra: ANU Press.

Benjamin, Geoffrey. 1987. 'Ethnohistorical Perspectives on Kelantan's Prehistory.' In *Kelantan Zaman Awal: Kajian Arkeologi Dan Sejarah Di Malaysia*, ed. Nik Hassan Shuhaimi Bin Nik Abd Rahman, 108–53. Kota Bharu, Kelantan: Muzium Negeri Kelantan.

———. 2002. 'On Being Tribal in the Malay World.' In *Tribal Communities in the Malay World: Historical, Cultural and Social Perspectives*, ed. B. Geoffrey and C. Chou, 7–76. Singapore: ISEAS / IIAS.

Blench, Roger. 2012. 'Almost Everything You Believed about the Austronesians Isn't True.' In *Crossing Borders: Selected Papers from the 13th International Conference of the European Association of Southeast Asian Archaeologists*, Volume 1, ed. M.L. Tjoa-Bonatz, A. Reinecke, and D. Bonatz, 128–48. Singapore: NUS Press.

———. This volume, Chapter 6. 'The Linguistic Background to Southeast Asian Sea Nomadism.' In *Sea Nomads of Southeast Asia: From the Past to the Present*, ed. B. Bellina, R. Blench, and J.-C. Galipaud. Singapore: NUS Press.

———. This volume, Chapter 8. 'Ship Construction and Navigation in the Early South China Seas.' In *Sea Nomads of Southeast Asia: From the Past to the Present*, ed. B. Bellina, R. Blench, and J.-C. Galipaud. Singapore: NUS Press.

Bourdier, Frédéric, Maxime Boutry, Jacques Ivanoff, and Olivier Ferrari. 2015. *From Padi States to Commercial States: Reflections on Identity and the Social Construction of Space in the Borderlands of Cambodia, Vietnam, Thailand and Myanmar*. Global Asia 3. Amsterdam: Amsterdam University Press.

Bouvet, Phaedra. 2017a. 'Indian Fine Wares.' In *Khao Sam Kaeo: An Early Port-city between the Indian Ocean and the South China Sea*, ed. B. Bellina, 281–309. Mémoires Archéologiques 28. Paris: Ecole française d'Extrême-Orient.

———. 2017b. 'Local and Regional Pottery Traditions.' In *Khao Sam Kaeo: An Early Port-city between the Indian Ocean and the South China Sea*, ed. B. Bellina, 231–80. Mémoires Archéologiques 28. Paris: Ecole française d'Extrême-Orient.

———.2017c. 'Lustrous Black and Red Wares.' In *Khao Sam Kaeo: An Early Port-city between the Indian Ocean and the South China Sea*, ed. B. Bellina, 309–43. Mémoires Archéologiques 28. Paris: Ecole française d'Extrême-Orient.

———. 2008. 'An Integrated Perspective on the Austronesian Diaspora. The Switch from Cereal Agriculture to Maritime Foraging in the Colonisation of Island Southeast Asia.' *Australian Archaeology* 67: 31–51.

Bulbeck, David. 2011. 'Biological and Cultural Evolution in the Population and Culture History of Homo Sapiens in Malaya.' In *Dynamics of Human Diversity: The Case of Mainland Southeast Asia*, ed. N.J. Enfield, 207–55. Pacific Linguistics. Canberra: The Australian National University.

———. 2014. 'The Chronometric Holocene Archaeological Record of the Southern Thai-Malay Peninsula.' *International Journal of Asia-Pacific Studies* 10 (1): 111–62.

Castillo, Cristina Cobo. 2017. 'Archaeobotany, Evidence of Exchange Networks and Agricultural Practices.' In *Khao Sam Kaeo: An Early Port-city between the Indian Ocean and the South China Sea*, ed. B. Bellina, 71–124. Mémoires Archéologiques 28. Paris: Ecole française d'Extrême-Orient.

Castillo, Cristina Cobo, Dorian K. Fuller, Philip J. Piper, Peter Bellwood, and Marc Oxenham. 2017. 'Hunter-gatherer Specialization in the Late Neolithic of Southern Vietnam – The Case of Rach Nui.' *Quaternary International* 489: 1–17.

Chou, Cynthia. 2010. *The Orang Suku Laut of Riau, Indonesia: The Inalienable Gift of Territory*. London, New York: Routledge, The Modern Anthropology of Southeast Asia.

———. This volume. 'The Orang Suku Laut: Movement, Maps and Mapping.' In *Sea Nomads of Southeast Asia: From the Past to the Present*, ed. B. Bellina, R. Blench, and J.-C. Galipaud. Singapore: NUS Press.

D'Errico, Francesco, Valentine Roux, and Yveline Dumond. 2000. 'Identification des Techniques de Finition des Perles en Calcédoine par l'analyse Microscopique et Rugosimétrique.' In *Cornalines de l'Inde. Des Pratiques Techniques de Cambay aux Technosystèmes de l'Indus*, ed. V. Roux, 97–169. Paris: Editions de la Maison des Sciences de L'Homme.

Dizon, Eusobio. 2003. 'Anthropomorphic Pottery from Ayub Cave, Piñol, Maitum Saranggani Province, Mindanao.' In *Earthenware in Southeast Asia: Proceedings of the Singapore Symposium on Premodern Southeast Asian Earthenwares*, ed. J.N. Miksic, 52–68. Singapore: NUS Press.

Dunn, Frederik. 1975. 'Rain-forest Collectors and Traders: A Study of Resource Utilization in Modern and Ancient Malaya.' *Monographs of the Malaysian Branch of the Royal Asiatic Society* 5.

Dussubieux, Laure and Bérénice Bellina. 2017. 'Glass from an Early Southeast Asian Producing and Trading Centre.' In *Khao Sam Kaeo: An Early Port-city between the Indian Ocean and the South China Sea*, ed. B. Bellina, 547–55. Mémoires Archéologiques 28. Paris: Ecole française d'Extrême-Orient.

———. 2018. 'Glass Ornament Production and Trade Polities in the Upper-Thai Peninsula during the Early Iron Age.' *Archaeological Research in Asia* 13: 25–36.

Favereau, Aude. 2015. 'Interactions et Modalités des Échanges en Mer de Chine Méridionale (500 Avant Notre Ère – 200 de Notre Ère): Approche technologique des assemblages Céramiques.' Thèse de doctorat. Muséum National d'Histoire Naturelle.

———. 2018. 'The Analysis of Khao Sek Pottery: Insight into the Circulations and the Politico-Economic Context of the Thai-Malay Peninsula during the Second Half of the 1st Millenium BC.' *Archaeological Research in Asia* 13: 37–49.

Favereau, Aude and Bérénice Bellina. 2016. 'Thai-Malay Peninsula and South China Sea Networks (500 BC–AD 200), Based on a Reappraisal of "Sa Huynh-Kalanay"-Related Ceramics.' *Quaternary International* 416: 219–27.

———. In press. 'Reviewing the Connections Between the Upper Thai-Malay Peninsula and the Philippines During the Late Prehistoric Period (500 BC–AD 500).' In *Taiwan Maritime Landscapes from Neolithic to Early Modern Times*, ed. P. Calanca, Liu Yi-ch'ang, and F. Muyard. Paris, Taipei: EFEO, Institute of History and Philology, Academia Sinica.

Ferrari, Olivier. 2015. 'Borders and Cultural Creativity. The Case of the Chao Lay, the Sea Gypsies of Southern Thailand.' In *From Padi States to Commercial States: Reflections on Identity and the Social Construction Space in the Borderlands of Cambodia, Vietnam, Thailand and Myanmar*, ed. F. Bourdier, J. Ivanoff, M. Boutry, and O. Ferrari, 119–40. Global Asia 3. Amsterdam: IIAS.

Fix, Alan. 2002. 'Foragers, Farmers, and Traders in the Malayan Peninsula: Origins of Cultural and Biological Diversity.' In *Economic Specialisation and Inter-ethnic Trade between Foragers and Farmers in the Prehispanic Philippines*, ed. K.D. Morrisson and L.L. Junker, 185–202. Cambridge: Cambridge University Press.

Fox, Robert Bradford. 1970. *The Tabon Caves: Archaeological Explorations and Excavations on Palawan Island, Philippines*. Manila: National Museum Publication.

Galipaud, Jean-Christophe, Dominique Guillaud, Rebecca Kinaston, and Brunna Crespi. This volume. 'Sea People, Coastal Territories and Cultural Interactions: Tetun Terik and Bunak in the Suai District on the South Coast of Timor-Leste.' In *Sea Nomads of Southeast Asia: From the Past to the Present*, ed. B. Bellina, R. Blench, and J.-C. Galipaud. Singapore: NUS Press.

Hall, Kenneth. 2011. *A History of Early Southeast Asia: Maritime Trade and Societal Sevelopment c. 100–1500*. Lanham, Maryland: Rowman and Littlefield Press.

Headland, Thomas N., Lawrence A. Reid, M.G. Bicchieri, Charles. A. Bishop, Robert Blust, Nicholas E. Flanders, Peter. M. Gardner, Karl L. Hutterer, Arkadiusz Marciniak, Robert F. Schroeder, and Stefan Seitz. 1989. 'Hunter-gatherers and their Neighbors from Prehistory to the Present [and Comments and Replies].' *Current Anthropology* 30 (1): 43–66.

Hendrickson, Mitch, Stépahnie Leroy, Quan Hua, Kaseka Phon, and Vuthy Voeun. 2017. 'Smelting in the Shadow of the Iron Mountain: Preliminary Field Investigation of the Industrial Landscape around Phnom Dek, Cambodia (Ninth to Twentieth Centuries A.D.).' *Asian Perspectives* 56 (1): 55–91.

Higham, Charles F.W. and Rachanie Thosarat. 2012. *Early Thailand from Prehistory to Sukhothai.* Bangkok: River Books.

Higham, Charles F.W., Xie Guangmao, and Lin Qiang. 2011. 'The Prehistory of a Friction Zone: First Farmers and Hunters-gatherers in Southeast Asia.' *Antiquity* 11 (85): 529–43.

Hill, Catherine, Pedro Soares, Maru Mormina, Vincent Macaulay, William Meehan, James Blackburn, Douglas Clarke, Joseph Maripa Raja, Patimah Ismail, David Bulbeck, Stephen Oppenheimer, and Martin Richards. 2006. 'Phylogeography and Ethnogenesis of Aboriginal Southeast Asians.' *Molecular Biology and Evolution* 23 (12): 2480–91.

Hogan, David W. 1972. *Men of the Sea: Coastal Tribes of South Thailand's West Coast.* Bangkok: Siam Society.

Hung, Hsiao-Chun and Peter Bellwood. 2010. 'Movement of Raw Materials and Manufactured Goods Across the South China Sea After 500 BCE: From Taiwan to Thailand, and Back.' In *50 Years of Archaeology in Southeast Asia. Essays in Honour of Ian Glover*, ed. B. Bellina, E.A. Bacus, T.O. Pryce, and J.W. Christie, 234–45. Thailand: Bangkok River Books.

Hung, Hsiao-Chun and Chin-yung Chao. 2016. 'Taiwan's Early Metal Age and Southeast Asian Trading Systems.' *Antiquity* 90 (354): 1537–51. https://doi.org/10.15184/aqy.2016.184.

Hung, Hsiao-Chun, Yoshiyuki Iizuka, Peter Bellwood, Kim Dung Nguyen, Bérénice Bellina, Praon Silapanth, Eusobio Dizon, Raya Santiago, I. Datan, and Jonathan H. Manton. 2007. 'Ancient Jades Map 3,000 Years of Prehistoric Exchange in Southeast Asia.' *Proceedings of the National Academy of Sciences* 104 (50): 19745–50.

Hutterer, Karl. 1969. 'Preliminary Report on Archaeological Field Work in Southwestern Samar Leyte.' *Samar Studies* 3: 37–56.

Ivanoff, Jacques. 2015. 'The "Interstices": A History of Migration and Ethnicity.' In *From Padi States to Commercial States: Reflections on Identity and the Social Construction Space in the Borderlands of Cambodia, Vietnam, Thailand and Myanmar*, ed. F. Bourdier, J. Ivanoff, M. Boutry, and O. Ferrari, 83–118. Amsterdam: IIAS. Global Asia 3.

———. This volume. 'Nomads in the Interstices of History.' In *Sea Nomads of Southeast Asia: From the Past to the Present*, ed. B. Bellina, R. Blench, and J.-C. Galipaud. Singapore: NUS Press.

Jacq-Hergoualc'h, Michel. 2002. *The Malay Peninsula: Crossroads of the Maritime Silk Road (100 BC–1300 AD).* Handbook of Oriental Studies. Section 3 Southeast Asia, Vol. 13. Handbuch Der Orientalistik. Leiden; Boston: Brill.

Junker, Laura Lee. 1999. *Raiding, Trading, and Feasting: The Political Economy of Philippine Chiefdoms.* Honolulu: University of Hawai'i Press.

———. 2002. 'Economic Specialisation and Inter-ethnic Trade between Foragers and Farmers in the Prehispanic Philippines.' In *Forager-traders in South and Southeast Asia*, ed. K.D. Morrisson, and L.L. Junker, 203–41. Cambridge: Cambridge University Press.

Junker, Laura Lee, and Larissa M. Smith. 2017. 'Farmer and Forager Interactions in Southeast Asia.' In *Handbook of East and Southeast Asian Archaeology*, ed. J. Habu, P.V. Lape, and J.W. Olsen, 619–32. New York: Springer.

Kim, Nam C. 2013. 'Lasting Monuments and Durable Institutions: Labor, Urbanism, and Statehood in Northern Vietnam and Beyond.' *Journal of Archaeological Research* 21 (3): 217–67.

Kusuma, Pradiptajati, Murray P. Cox, Denis Pierron, Harilanto Razafindrazaka, Nicolas Brucato, Laure Tonasso, Helene Loa Suryadi, Thierry Letellier, Herawati Sudoyo, and François-Xavier Ricaut. 2015. 'Mitochondrial DNA and the Y Chromosome Suggest the Settlement of Madagascar by Indonesian Sea Nomad Populations.' *BMC Genomics* 16: 191.

Kusuma, Pradiptajati, Nicolas Brucato, Murray P. Cox, Thierry Letellier, Abdul Manan, Chandra Nuraini, Philippe Grangé, Herawati Sudoyo and François-Xavier Ricaut. 2017. 'The Last Sea Nomads of the Indonesian Archipelago: Genomic Origins and Dispersal.' *European Journal of Human Genetics* 25 (8): 1004–10.

Lankton, James, Laure Dussubieux, and Bernard Gratuze. 2008. 'Glass from Khao Sam Kaeo: Transferred Technology for an Early Southeast Asian Exchange Network.' *Bulletin de l'Ecole Française d'Extrême-Orient* 93: 317–51.

Lemonnier, Pierre. 2004. 'Mythiques Chaînes Opératoires.' *Techniques et Culture*: 43–4.

Leroi-Gourhan, André. 2013. *L'homme et la Matière: Évolution et Techniques*. Numérisation et impr. Sciences d'aujourd'hui 1. Paris: éd. Albin Michel.

———. 2014. *Le geste et la parole. 2: La mémoire et les rythmes*. Repr. Sciences d'aujourd'hui. Paris: éd. Albin Michel.

Manguin, Pierre-Yves. 2009. 'Southeast Sumatra in Protohistoric and Srivijaya Times: Upstream-downstream Relations and the Settlement of the Peneplain.' In *From Distant Tales: Archaeology and Ethnohistory in the Highlands of Sumatra*, ed. D. Bonatz, J. Miksic, J.D. Neidel, and M.L. Tjoa-Bonatz, 434–84. Newcastle upon Tyne: Cambridge Scholars Publishing.

Miksic, John N. 1979. 'Archaeology, Trade and Society in Northeast Sumatra.' Thesis presented to the Faculty of the Graduate School of Cornell University.

Morrison, Kathleen D. 2002. 'Pepper in the Hills: Upland-lowland Exchange and the Intensification of Spice Trade.' In *Forager-Trader in South and Southeast Asia: Long Term Histories*, ed. K.D. Morrison and L.L. Junker, 105–28. Cambridge: Cambridge University Press.

Morrison, Kathleen D. and Laura Lee Junker, eds. 2002. *Forager-Traders in South and Southeast Asia: Long-Term Histories*. Cambridge: Cambridge University Press.

Mörseburg, Alexander, Luca Pagani, François-Xavier Ricaut, Bryndis Yngvadottir, Eadaoin Harney, Cristina Castillo, Tom Hoogervorst, Kusuma Pradiptajati, Nicolas Brucato, Alexia Cardona, Denis Pierron, Thierry Letellier, Joseph Wee, Syafiq Abdullah, Mait Metspalu, and Toomas Kivisild. 2016. 'Multi-layered Population Structure in Island Southeast Asians.' *European Journal of Human Genetics* 24: 1605–11.

Nolde, Lance. This volume. '"The Muscles and Sinews of the Kingdom": The Sama Bajo in Early Modern Eastern Indonesia.' In *Sea Nomads of Southeast Asia: From the Past to the Present*, ed. B. Bellina, R. Blench, and J.-C. Galipaud. Singapore: NUS Press.

Lewis, Helen, Victor Paz, Emil Robles, Vito Hernandez, Andrea Malaya M. Ragragio, Shawn O'Donnell, Kathryn Ann Manalo, Michael James Herrera, and Janine Ochoa. 2011. *Palawan Island Palaeohistoric Research Project: Report on the 2011 El Nido Field Season*. Archaeological Studies Program, University of the Philippines and National Museum of the Philippines.

Pelegrin, Jacques. 2000. 'Technique et Méthodes de Taille Pratiquées à Cambay.' In *Cornalines de l'Inde. Des Pratiques Techniques de Cambay aux Techno-systèmes de l'Indus*, ed. V. Roux, 55–93. Paris: Editions de la Maison des Sciences de l'Homme.

Perronet, Sophie and Srikanlaya Sachipan. 2017. 'The Han Ceramics.' In *Khao Sam Kaeo: An Early Port-City between the Indian Ocean and the South China Sea*, ed. Bellina, Bérénice, 393–421. Mémoires Archéologiques 28. Paris: Ecole française d'Extrême-Orient.

Possehl, Gregory L. 2002. 'Harrappans and Hunters: Economic Interaction and Specialization in Prehistoric India.' In *Forager-Trader in South and Southeast Asia: Long Term Histories*, ed. K.D. Morrison and L.L. Junker, 62–76. Cambridge: Cambridge University Press.

Pryce, Thomas Oliver, Sandrine Baron, Bérénice Bellina, Peter Bellwood, Nigel Chang, Pranab Chattopadhyay, Eusobio Dizon, Ian C.Glover, Elizabeth Hamilton, Charles F.W. Higham, Aung Aung Kyaw, Vin Laychour, Surapol Natapintu, Viet Nguyen, Jean-Pierre Pautreau, Ernst Pernicka, Vincent C. Pigott, Mark Pollard, Christophe Pottier, Andreas Reinecke, Thongsa Sayavongkhamdy, Viengkeo Souksavatdy, Joyce White 2014. 'More Questions than Answers: The Southeast Asian Lead Isotope Project 2009–2012.' *Journal of Archaeological Science* 42: 273–94.

Pryce, Thomas Oliver, Mercedes Murillo-Barroso, Lynn Biggs, Marcos Martinon-Torres, and Bérénice Bellina. 2017. 'The Metallurgical Industries.' In *Khao Sam Kaeo: An Early Port-City between the Indian Ocean and the South China Sea*, ed. Bellina, Bérénice, 501–46. Mémoires Archéologiques 28. Paris: Ecole française d'Extrême-Orient.

Pryce, Thomas Oliver and Bérénice Bellina. 2018. 'High-Tin Bronze Bowls and Copper Drums: Non-Ferrous Archaeometallurgical Evidence for Khao Sek's Involvement and Role in Regional Exchange Systems.' *Archaeological Research in Asia* 13 (March): 50–8. https://doi.org/10.1016/j.ara.2017.07.002.

Reinecke, Andreas, Chiueu Nguyen, and Lam Thi My Dzung. 2002. *Go Ma Voi: The New Discoveries of Sa Huynh Culture*. Cologne: Linden soft.

Roux, Valentine, ed. 2000. *Cornaline de l'Inde: Des Pratiques Techniques de Cambay aux Ttechno-systèmes de l'Indus*. Paris: Éditions de la Maison des Sciences de l'homme.

Roux, Valentine. 2010. 'Lecture Anthropologique des Assemblages Céramiques. Fondements et Mise en œuvre de l'Analyse Technologique.' *Les Nouvelles de l'Archéologie* 119: 4–9.

———. 2016. *Des Céramiques et des Hommes: Décoder les Assemblages Archéologiques*. Nanterre: Presses Universitaires de Paris Ouest.

Roux, Valentine and Marie-Agnès Courty. 2007. 'Analyse Techno-Pétrographique Céramique et Interprétation Fonctionnelle des Sites: Un Exemple d'Application dans le Levant Sud Chalcolithique.' In *Recherches en Archéométrie: la Mesure du Passé*, ed. A. Bain, J. Chabot, and M. Mousette, 153–67. Oxford: British Archaeological Reports International Series 1700.

Sather, Clifford. 2006. 'Sea Nomads and Rainforest Hunter-gatherers: Foraging Adaptations in the Indo-Malaysian Archipelago.' In *The Austronesians: Historical and Comparative Perspectives*, ed. P. Bellwood, J.J. Fox, and D. Tryon, 245–83. Canberra: ANU E-Press.

Scott, James C. 2009. *The Art of Not Being Governed: An Anarchist History of Upland Southeast Asia*. Yale Agrarian Studies Series. New Haven, CT: Yale University Press.

Solheim, Wilhelm G., David Bulbeck, and Ambika Flavel. 2006. *Archaeology and Culture in Southeast Asia: Unraveling the Nusantao*. Diliman, Quezon City: University of the Philippines Press.

Spriggs, Matthew. 2011. 'Archaeology and the Austronesian Expansion: Where Are We Now?' *Antiquity* 85 (328): 510–28.

Tran Ky Phuong. 2010. 'Interactions between Uplands and Lowlands through the "riverine Exchange Network" of Central Vietnam – A Case Study in the Thu Bon River Valley.' In *50 Years of Archaeology in Southeast Asia. Essays in Honour of Ian Glover*, ed. Bérénice Bellina, Elisabeth A. Bacus, Thomas Oliver Pryce, and Jan Wisseman Christie, 207–15. Bangkok: River Books.

Stark, Miriam T. 2015. 'Southeast Asian Urbanism: From Early City to classical State.' In *The Cambridge World History*, ed. N. Yoffee, 74–93. Cambridge: Cambridge University Press.

White, Joyce C. 2011. 'Emergence of Cultural Diversity in Mainland Southeast Asia: A View from Prehistory.' *Dynamics of Human Diversity*, Pacific Linguistics: 9–46.

White, Walter G. 1922. *The Sea Gypsies of Malaya. An Account of the Nomadic Mawken People of the Mergui Archipelago with a Description of their Ways of Living, Customs, Habits, Boats, Occupations*. London: Seeley, Service & Co.

Winichakul, Thongchai. 2003. 'Writing at the Interstices: Southeast Asian Historians and Post-National Histories in Southeast Asia.' In *New Terrains in Southeast Asian History*, ed. Abu Talib Ahmad and Tan Liok, 3–29. Athens: Ohio University Press.

Yamagata, Mariko. 2012. *The Excavation of Hoa Diem in Central Vietnam*. Showa Women's University Institute of International Culture Bulletin. Showa Women's University Institute.

5

The Orang Suku Laut: Movement, Maps and Mapping

Cynthia Chou

Can the sea be considered as a territory of its own for human groups? The ethnography of the Orang Suku Laut (literally, 'Tribal People of the Sea') provides a good starting point for this discussion. In writings about them, they have also been called 'sea nomads' (Sopher 1977) or simply, 'Orang Laut' (sea people). In this chapter, the term 'Orang Suku Laut' is used in preference to 'Orang Laut' because the latter term of reference is known to include congeries of coastal dwelling Malays and other sea-dwelling populations too.

The Orang Suku Laut consist of variously named groups. Located principally at the gateways to the Straits of Malacca and at the southern tip of the Malay Peninsula extending all the way into the Riau-Lingga Archipelago of Indonesia, they also row along the rivers of eastern Sumatra into the South China Sea. Because of their deep understanding of the confluences of movements in the maritime world, they played a central role in shaping the regional culture. They possessed the knowledge and techniques to lay the building blocks for the emergence of maritime societies in Island Southeast Asia (ISEA) and Oceania. They were also pivotal in establishing the region's international linkages. Today, they continue to play these important roles, yet the Orang Suku Laut are an overlooked population. Neglect in comprehending how they perceive movements in the making of the maritime world has resulted in the erroneous belief that they merely sail helter-skelter across the seas in the region. Common beliefs hold them to be aimless wanderers without a compass and therefore lost in their surroundings.

This chapter examines Orang Suku Laut spatial imaginings of the maritime cultural landscape and their interaction with it. They may not be able to record their location according to contemporary cartographic conventions of coordinates, but they nonetheless know where they are, where they have come from and where they are moving to. Central to this is the question, 'What part can flexible movement patterns play in understanding long-term histories and time-depth patterns of adaptions to provide an understanding of regional culture?'

The ethnography of the Orang Suku Laut reveals the sea to be a world that is occupied and inhabited. It is not just a vast expanse of boundless space. Through their stories of how they see and think about their movements—and movements of the waves, winds, sun, moon and stars—as well as global movements, they demonstrate to us how they have mapped maritime spaces into territories for human groups. Their ways of knowing have emerged as a culture of mapping the region.

THE ORANG SUKU LAUT

For centuries, the sea has been home to the Orang Suku Laut. It is a gift and an inalienable ancestral estate from their ancestors (Chou 2010). Presently though, their existence at sea is being threatened. Perennial tensions exist between them and state policy makers of Indonesia and Singapore. The policy makers are imposing centrally managed plans of directed change to permanently settle them on land. These efforts of sedentarisation are to arrange the mariners in ways that would re-orient them to become law-abiding citizens of nation-states. Such negative top-down perspectives of the Orang Suku Laut have also worked upon many land-based communities to view them as a backward and marginalised people.

It is uncertain if the Orang Suku Laut of today are the direct descendants of the early 'oceanic nomads' (Sather 1995: 238) in the prehistory of the Indo-Malaysian region. Nonetheless, what is clear is that the early nomadic seafarers were not subjected to a depressed status. Instead, as historical archives indicate, it was they—or a population following the same way of life—in the prehistory of the Indo-Malaysian region who gained mastery of the seas, bridged the barrier between land and sea and had the knowledge to realise this cultural variety to its full potential (Urry 1981: 7).[1]

Geographically, the region is dotted with thousands of islands. At the end of the Pleistocene when ocean levels rose, the sea impeded wider integration.[2] To integrate the region, marine innovation was crucial (Urry 1981: 4). It was none other than the oceanic nomads, those able to control the seas, who integrated communities as well as regions. To achieve this, they mapped out a complex network of communication in addition to networks of raiding and exchange relations based on their knowledge of the confluence movements in the maritime world. These were also the very skills that subsequently led them to performing a significant role in Malay political history.

The Orang Suku Laut were tangential in forming the earliest historical states in the region. They provided the naval prowess and communicative links on which the hegemony of successive Malay states were based in an area of relatively sparse population (Andaya 2010: 173–201). Moreover, their seafaring activities supported large-scale integration of the increasingly centralised polities that

Map 5.1 Orang Suku Laut Map.

shaped and developed the political and cultural landscape of the Malay World (Benjamin 2002: 45).

Trade, exchanges of ideas and socio-cultural diversity in the region flourished based upon the seafarers' functioning structures of communication and integration of the maritime world (Urry 1981: 7). Due to their abilities to attract trade, their superior skills cum knowledge in locating mother-of-pearl from the shell of the sea turtle (hawksbill turtle or *eretmocheslys imbricata*), edible seaweed and sea cucumbers that were much needed for the China trade, they were undoubtedly vital to the development of international trade in the Malay World (Andaya 1997: 487). As demand for such maritime products increased, so did their skills in procuring these products in places unreachable by others.

Until the mid-twentieth century, the mariners' mobile seafaring lifestyle and knowledge of the waters were highly valued by the power-holders of the early Malay states of the western Malay region and by various sultanates that arose in coastal Borneo, southern Philippines and eastern Indonesia. Trade and various micro-polities in the region flourished because the mariners secured and guarded crucial sea-lanes to generate trading wealth for the sustenance of land-based communities. In addition, they protected and led ships calling at ports of the Malay sultans to a safe docking. On bad weather days, they navigated the ships to sheltered anchorage places and fresh water sources (Andaya 1997: 487). For those who strayed from calling at the ports of the Malay rulers, the mariners punished them mercilessly (Andaya 1975: 51). At the behest of Malay lords, the mariners would also dutifully raid incoming ships to garner supplies for trade essential for the success of the Malay entrepôt (Andaya 2010: 181).

As skilled seafarers who were always on the move to places with resources as well as to obtain resources, their form of subsistence pointedly contributed to the development of many human societies. They were so highly valued by the Malay rulers that they were accorded the status 'maritime subjects *par excellence*' (Wolters 1975: 10) and granted possession of 'the seas and what floated on them by hereditary feudal right from the Sultan of Johor' (Trocki 1979: 56).

The current marginal status of the Orang Suku Laut is one that has been culturally and politically construed through shifts in political rule and their attendant social ideologies in the region. Pressures to eradicate their seafaring lifestyle began with the dominance of European colonialists in the region. Labelled criminals by the colonial masters, the latter assumed the 'sacred obligation' to restore a 'moral condition' (Logan 1849: 466) of the mariners.

The legacy of the European colonialists' stance on the seafarers has endured. Present-day state administrators echo colonial policies to permanently settle them on land. Some Orang Suku Laut have moved ashore, but others continue with their seafaring and highly mobile lifestyle. Nonetheless, they all distinguish themselves by identification with the sea itself. They speak of themselves as 'Orang Suku Laut' ('Tribal People of the Sea') rather than *orang darat* (land people) or even any other kind of sea people. As the sea is for them an inalienable gift from their ancestors, it means that their occupancy of it cannot be separated, removed or alienated from them. They possess an identity that is capable of being carried anywhere in the vast maritime world and they continue to map the region according to wherever—however far—their navigational skills take them. Local inhabitants of the region acknowledge them as the *orang asli* (indigenous peoples); that is to say, the 'true', 'genuine', or 'real' inhabitants of the archipelagos and attribute them to having mapped the sea as a territory for human groups (Chou 2005).

MOVEMENT AND MAPPING THE MARITIME WORLD

What is a map? 'A map' as described by the International Cartographic Association is 'a representation normally to scale and on a flat medium, of a selection of material or abstract features on, or in relation to, the surface of the Earth or of a celestial body' (Robinson and Petchenik 1976: 17). Simply put, contemporary cartographic maps are oftentimes regarded as sophisticated and clean-cut 'representation[s] of things in space' (Robinson and Petchenik 1976: 15). Such are the ideas that have come to dominate current definitions of maps.

Yet, it is noteworthy that the most valued maps by collectors are the ones richly illustrated with drawings of the different kinds of journeys that people have undertaken to places and the variety of populations, flora and fauna as well as sea- cum land-forms that they have encountered. Indubitably, the value of these maps lie in the stories they narrate and the appreciation of being able to see the active plus constructive processes that accorded meanings to experiences in creating these maps. The stories provide an invaluable medium to learn about other life forms by affording them a context to be understood through the lived experiences of others (Garro and Mattingly 2000: 1).

Various attempts have been made to jettison the ethnographic experiences that shape contemporary cartographic maps (Certeau 1984: 120–1; Turnbull 1996: 62). Be that as it may, it is important to remember that maps took root as drawings of spatial representation to encapsulate 'sense data' (Ingold 2000: 234) that were generated through movements across oceans and land masses. The point of the matter is that all maps—including cognitive maps—are made through journeys to acquire knowledge of environments. Maps can never be void of the praxes and perceptions of their makers and users (Chou 2006b). A map is but 'a totalising stage on which elements of diverse origin are brought together to form a tableau of a "stage" of geographical knowledge' (Certeau 1984: 121).

At the heart of mapping is knowledge (Chou 2006a). A prerequisite in mapping the sea or land masses into territories for human groups is possessing the required knowledge about the dynamic continuums of actions, thoughts and things that exist and move in that space. That is to say, it is about unfurling the field of relations through immersing the actor–perceiver within a given environment context. In this manner, maps are a composite of histories of movements.

Movements necessitate the updating of maps too. In what is called 'process cartography', mapping is considered an open-ended and continuous activity that is 'always leading to the next instance of mapping the next map' (Rundstrom 1993: 21). The task of updating maps requires nothing less than 'a complex cognitive skill' (Oatley 1977: 537); it stretches beyond computational techniques for the reason that environments are complex terrains. Movements continually contour their change in shape and character. Updating of maps therefore requires knowing the histories of movements and being able to respond to what is happening in the environment.

Places in maps come to life through stories of lived experiences of movements. Through movements too, particular parts of an environment are interlinked to form a network with other parts (Chou 2010: 70–4). It has been said that 'places always open up to disclose other places within them ... while from within any particular place one can always look outwards to find oneself within some much larger expanse' (Malpas 1999: 170–1). A place is but a temporal series of movements. It reveals a myriad of human thoughts and actions that people have carried with them as they move from point to point or from island to island even as they go about their daily errands. In the words of Ingold:

> [E]very place holds within it memories of previous arrivals and departures, as well as expectations of how one may reach it, or reach other places from it. Thus, do places enfold the passage of time; they are neither of the past, present or future but all three rolled into one. Endlessly generated through the comings and goings of their inhabitants, they figure not as locations in space but as specific cortices in a current of movement, of innumerable journeys actually made (2000: 237–8).

Places have been compared to knots: where people meet in places, their lives become tied up with one another (Ingold 2007: 80). There can be no better environment than the sea to afford the scope for movements that are essential for the life and growth of places and territories. Lives are lived in, through, around, to and from places or territories. Via movements, places are connected. Even more important, movements are the conduits of life that encapsulate the most fundamental mode of being in the world. At every territory and place, through movements that give rise to them, relations to all others enfold. Knowledge is accrued through observations made while in movement.

THE SEA: A TERRITORY OF ITS OWN FOR HUMAN GROUPS

Insights into the formation of the sea for human groups are best exemplified in the ethnography of the Orang Suku Laut. Their stories lucidly tell of the different confluences of movements that have mapped the maritime world.

MOVEMENTS AND THE FORMATION OF A NETWORK OF INTER-RELATED TERRITORIES

Movement is central to the identity of the Orang Suku Laut. It is an ongoing process of self-renewal and development. As mariners, they are continually and actively engaging with the sea for their sustenance. As they traverse the waters, it is necessary for them to pause to fish, to obtain drinking water, to rest and to take shelter from choppy waters.

'Place' as explicated by Tuan (1977: 6), 'is pause; and that each pause in movement makes it possible for location to be transformed into place'. How pause becomes a part of mapping the maritime world is clearly narrated by the Orang Suku Laut. Stories of the histories of their islands as told by Bari, an Orang Suku Laut man from Senang[3] and Joya, an Orang Suku Laut woman of Dapur Enam, provide just two examples of how places emerge.

Bari

> I am head of the Orang Suku Laut [on Senang island]. Yang Cik bin Lang was head before me ... He rowed from Singkep. [S]o did I ... Yang Cik bin Lang came here to fish and rest. That was how he started Senang island. Other families followed after that ... [They] report their movements to me. They tell me when they are leaving this place or when they are returning.

Joya

> [My] ancestry is from Dapur Enam. My grandfather Umur lived in a boat. He was the first to move into Dapur Enam. He would return to live in his boat whenever he needed to fish for food. My father, Awang Ketah, was the first to settle in Dapur Enam. When the weather is bad and when the sea is choppy, one can feel very dizzy in a boat. Hence, my father decided to move to land ... All the houses in Dapur Enam belong to my father's children. My father feels that it would be a pity if he should ever have to leave our territory ... We have many family graves in Dapur Enam. Although my father has moved to land ... From time to time, he returns to live in his boat ... So do we ... We sail to be with our families and to fish.[4]

Places that emerge embody a range of Orang Suku Laut knowledge and their lived experiences. Their life and genealogy are but a sum of their movements. As Joya's story points out, their journeys map a network of inter-related territories and life spaces. Different Orang Suku Laut groups speak of possessing different networks of kin-based territories. These networks altogether have brought a region into existence. This regional seascape of connected families has in turn been vitally important in the development of international trade that has provided much revenue for the region.

Places and territories are collectively owned by the seafarers. Their collective title-deeds are certified by their stories detailing how they founded these places.

Confirmation of the validity of their stories are provided by other Orang Suku Laut groups and non-Orang Suku Laut in the area.

Notably, the network of inter-related territories mapped by the seafarers reflects an intricate matrix of inter-related kinship-infused cultural-economic units. That is to say, this network translates into spheres of resource sites that spawn sustenance (Chou 2013: 61). They can choose areas to sail to and stay for a while or areas to return to. Usually, as explained by Meen who is head of the Orang Suku Laut Teluk Nipah island group, their decisions are oriented to areas that would be best for them to eke out a living:

> We go where there is food. After a few days if the place runs out of food, we have to move again to look for food. Life as a fisherperson can be difficult. If we want to stay stationary in a village for long, we still have to be able to catch fish ... if you want to eat fish, you have to be prepared to always be on the move. If you just want to eat rice, then you can be sedentary.

Different groups of Orang Suku Laut have different networks of inter-related territories. This arrangement parcels out resources to each group so that they are able to obtain the best harvest for each and every season. Their movement from place to place also means that they are never concentrated in any one place long enough to endanger utilisation of the areas' resources. This arrangement facilitates population dispersal and evenly spreads resource consumption over a wide area, consequently generating the aquatic unity of a very vast expanse of maritime space. This network of kin-related territories links the seafarers in space and time.

The network of kinship-infused cultural-economic units have also been crucial in establishing international trading linkages. As in earlier times, trading relations with the Chinese constitute one of the most important sources of revenue for the region. Chinese *thau-ke* (bosses) in the Malay world who are the main middlemen in present day international trade rely heavily on the Orang Suku Laut. From them, supplies of jellyfish, sea turtles, sea cucumbers, sharksfin and agar-agar (a jelly-like susbtance obtained from red algae) are obtained for the international Asian market. As explained by Tekong, an Orang Suku Laut man from Nanga Island, only they know how to gather jellyfish without being stung:

> When you first came, we were not too interested in gathering jellyfish because people around here do not eat it. However, the Chinese *thau-ke* were asking if we could supply them with jellyfish. The Chinese know how to cook it and consider it a delicacy. Now, we gather jellyfish for the *thau-ke*. It is a profitable trade. All other fisherpeople here do not deal with jellyfish for fear of being stung. They lack the knowledge of how to prevent this from happening. If you get stung, it is not only very painful but it could also endanger your life.

To supply jellyfish for the international market, the seafarers utilise their network of inter-related kinship cultural-economic units. As an exemplification of how one such network operates can be observed in the Riau archipelago. Mariners from the islands of Tiang Wang Kang, Setengah, Air Linga, Nanga and Belakang Padang belong to one network. In the waters of Riau, jellyfish is more abundant during the dry season of March to November. Within this period, there appears to be a greater profusion of jellyfish in the waters surrounding Nanga Island. Usually, a number of Orang Suku Laut families from the other related islands—particularly those from Tiang Wang Kang island—sail to Nanga Island to join the gathering of jellyfish. The catch is sold to the *thau-ke* and exported to the Pasir Panjang Wholesale Centre in Singapore, an important node in the Singapore food chain supply as well as a distribution centre for the wider international market. When the season changes to that of the *comek* (a variety of cuttlefish) or monsoon rains, the mariners from Nanga Island often move to Tiang Wang Kang. Here, they not only gather cuttlefish, but also work in the mangrove and charcoal industry. The charcoal kilns owned by the Orang Suku Laut in Tiang Wang Kang are an important global supplier of charcoal. A common sight at the Orang Suku Laut charcoal producing areas are the Maersk international Danish shipping containers waiting to be loaded for the export market.

Occasionally, the seafarers opt to bring their maritime products directly to Singapore to secure better profits. Each network of kinship-infused cultural-economic units has established relations with different *thau-ke* at the wholesale centre, but sailing to Singapore is not without problems. Firstly, it necessitates stops at different points to obtain fresh water: navigating within the network of inter-related territories ensures the availability of resources to meet their basic needs. Secondly, authorities in Singapore only permit Orang Suku Laut men to step ashore at the wholesale centre. Even though women and children have also gathered these maritime products, they are obliged to stay behind as the men sail the last stretch into Singapore. Once again, they look to their network of inter-related territories to determine a place closest to the border where women and children can be left to wait for the men to return. For those in the aforementioned network of inter-related territories comprising Tiang Wang Kang, Setengah, Air Linga, Nanga and Belakang Padang, the waiting area is usually at the island of Belakang Padang. Other male kin at the island that they have stopped at might step in to help sail the last stretch into Singapore. In this network of kinship-infused cultural-economic units, kinspeople also exchange information on how best to negotiate with the maritime authorities to facilitate this international crossing. Information is also shared on how certain maritime products—including the lucrative but endangered sea turtle—might be smuggled into the international wholesale centre.

MOVEMENTS OF THE WAVES, WINDS, SUN, MOON AND STARS

The ethnography of the Orang Suku Laut also shows that they have had to make constant sailing adjustments to map the maritime world. With their deep knowledge of the waters, they are aware that the seas can only be mapped in relation to movements of the waves, winds, sun, moon and stars. Their stories, as illustrated in the excerpts below, explicate how maritime areas for human groups begin under the guiding movements of these changing constellations and horizons. As Latib, an Orang Suku Laut man at Teluk Nipah Island elaborated:

> We are so used to knowing how and where best to sail because we have been seafarers for our entire lives. As an example, movements in tides guide us. We look to see if the tides are high or low, which direction are currents flowing … We look at the winds too. Right now, because of the west winds, we stay here on the island of Korek. If it is east winds, we know then that we will move in the direction towards Wan Island. We relate to the movements in the tides, currents and winds and sail to look for places in this way … There are different kinds of winds that we have to know to guide us … east, south, west.

Meen also offered the following explanation:

> There are four seasons in a year. Each season is divided into about three months. It is now the season of west winds. After this, it will be the season of the north winds. After that, we will have the seasons of the south and east winds. Within each season, we can break it down further. In each season, the currents move in from different places. The sun and moon also rise and set differently. We sail in directions by relating to these movements.

The Orang Suku Laut's knowledge and mapping of their water spaces undergoes continuous formation as they move. Moving is knowing, and in the same way, knowing is about engaging with movements.

From the perspective of the Orang Suku Laut, even the first breath of human life can only be mapped in the maritime world via an attentive engagement of the self with movements in the environment. In the course of my fieldwork, I witnessed the birth of a child by Ramrah of the Teluk Nipah island Orang Suku Laut community (Chou 2016: 272–3). When Ramrah's amniotic fluid burst and her contractions began, she was lying on the floor of the inner room of her house. It was a house that stood on stilts over the sea. While the women from the community gathered by her side, the men congregated to drink alcohol in the outer room. Among the reasons for the men to be there was the need to look out for the time of *air pasang belum* (when the sea level is rising).

Halfway through Ramrah giving birth, the men in the outer room called out that movements in the tides had changed. It was almost '*tukar pasang*' (change in the tide). The tide was rising and they had to move into action to quickly '*putar*' (rotate, turn) Ramrah to reposition her to align her with the changing seascape. She was lifted and turned to lie in another position. She had been lying in a position whereby her head was pointing backwards to the door of her house. Now, she was moved in a clockwise direction so that the back of her head no longer pointed towards the entrance of the door. Instead, she now lay diagonally across the room with the back of her head pointed towards a wall and her feet towards the opposite wall. Ramrah had to be repositioned to be in harmony with the rising tide, otherwise she would not be able to give birth. As Meen, her stepfather elucidated:

> If it were a doctor, if they place you in one direction to give birth, it would definitely be in that position. However, it is not the same for [us]. We have to look at the sea and the direction of the house in the sea. The woman giving birth has to be placed in accordance with the tide of the sea. If the direction is bad, the woman will not give birth. We have to look at the sea, and then the direction of the house to see if the woman would or would not be able to give birth.

Guided also by the confluences of movements of the waves, winds, sun, moon and stars, the mariners procure the knowledge to map new places and new lives to populate the maritime world.

A WORLD OF MOVEMENTS

Orang Suku Laut stories also map movements that position the sea as a territory for diverse human groups at the global level. As acutely observed by Scott (2009: 16), 'the principle' behind the making of regions in each case is 'water' and that 'especially if it is calm, [it] joins people'. From the perspective of the Orang Suku Laut, the sea is a territory for all kinds of human groups both at local and global levels.

Orang Suku Laut stories chronicle how through history, global movements motivated by purposes of war, international trade, or proselytisation have all resulted in the sea becoming an important territory for diverse human groups. Examples of stories of this kind include those narrated by Ceco, an Orang Suku Laut man from Nanga Island and by Buntot, an Orang Suku Laut woman from the island of Teluk Nipah. They both explain how movements by global groups such as the Japanese and Dutch, in their pursuits of war and wanting to monopolise international trade, have attempted to territorialise the maritime world.

Ceco

> The Dutch, Japanese, Portuguese, Malay kings and now multi-national corporations; they have all journeyed here to try to set up new territories and places in our waters. They come and go all the time, wanting to stake claims to all sorts of areas for themselves. During the Dutch period, life was difficult. Then it was the Japanese. During the Dutch period, we were already born. We were still very young ... as young as my daughter, Liah. We were also here during the Japanese Occupation. There were many Japanese in Galang during that period ... There were so many of them ... [so that] we had to sail away from them. They were in Tanjung Malang, Dapur Enam ... they lived there. They were also in Galang ... *aiyoh* [oh dear!] ... it is like what people say ... we are Orang Laut and we go here and there. The Japanese were like that too, they moved here and there all over the sea ... We as Orang Suku Laut sailed the seas so much ... so we know everything. If you talk about the Japanese, we can still remember that period. We

were very young children then ... My mother knew the history of every place ... Our ancestors told us stories about the history of all who came and who went ... They knew so much and described everything in great detail ... We could travel all over the place in the past without a passport. We went into [what is now] Singapore and Malaysia. The immigration in Pasir Panjang [in Singapore] is very recent. We used to go into Singapore bringing turtles and charcoal. We used to accompany our father.

Buntot

[The Japanese] entered Korek island ... by water to get here ... very close-by. I cannot remember the exact year, but they also attacked Singapore. Life was extremely difficult during the Japanese Occupation ... We wanted them to leave ... [During] the era of the Dutch and the Republic of Indonesia, nothing much happened. It was better during the era of the Dutch ... The Portuguese did not come at all.

The world of movements that the Orang Suku Laut speak of as they explain the mapping of the maritime world continues to this very day. Presently, their stories describe how multi- and transnational investors in collaboration with various states are attempting to rearrange the maritime world into a global estate of productive space for resource modification and ownership (Chou 2010: 120–1).

From the perspective of the seafarers, this world of movements has offered another level of connection too. It has connected their local maritime places and territories to wider global territories, and by extension to global realms of modernity. Examples of this are their stories of how Christian missionaries from far away foreign lands have journeyed by sea to link their local maritime territories to the global Roman Catholic church. To show what they mean, some Orang Suku Laut have even produced pictures of the pope to emphasise their international links.

As groups of people from all over the world journey in and out of the maritime world, the sea has become 'an area concatenated by peregrinations between the places it connects' (Casey 1996: 24). The sea has the power to provide orientation to other spaces whereas for example, the Vatican is situated and to be incorporated with other cultures and social experiences. The sea is irrefutably the key to forming connections with peoples, places and communities far beyond. Often, such connections offer significant points of socio-cultural, religious and aesthetic references. To state it concisely, the sea is an important site for self-reflexive engagement. It gives rhythm, movement and context to experience the unique modality of human experience.

CONCLUSION

With every additional story of the confluence movements that the Orang Suku Laut tell, their map of the sea as a territory for human groups grows. The stories detailing how they map the maritime world reveal to us that lives at sea are never necessarily fixed at specific points. Instead, the essence of a map lies entirely in the confluence of movements, intersections and routes journeyed (Ingold 2000: 240).

In the words of Ingold:

> [T]he world of our experience is a world suspended in movement, that is continually coming into being as we—through our own movement—contribute to its formation. In the cartographic world, by contrast, all is still and silent. There is neither sunlight nor moonlight; there is no variation of light or shade, no clouds, no shadows or reflections. The wind does not blow, neither disturbing the trees nor whipping water into waves. No bird flies in the sky, or sing in the woods; forests and pastures devoid of animal life; houses and streets are empty of people and traffic. To dismiss all this—to suggest that what is excluded in the cartographic reduction amounts, in Monmonier's words, a 'fog of detail' (2000: 242).

Insights can be gained from the Orang Suku Laut's deep knowledge of the cultural context of the maritime world; from them we can comprehend the confluence of movements that spin the threads of life that make the sea a territory of its own for human groups. For them, the sea has always been home.

NOTES

[1] In a correspondence with Geoffrey Benjamin (3 to 18 September 2017) concerning the presence of secondary tribalisation in the region, he cautions against assuming the present-day populations of Orang Suku Laut to be 'direct descendants of essentially unchanged earlier populations [of oceanic nomads], *unless there is specific evidence to that effect*'. One of the reasons 'is that certain ways of life are always available for rediscovery or borrowing if a population feels they want to move out of the mainstream'. Another reason 'is the difficulty of demonstrating the continued unaltered identity of any one tribal population through time—not just because it is difficult, but also because it may not even be the case, and would depend on projecting present-day arrangements back into the past' (see also Benjamin 2002: 19).

[2] The Pleistocene Epoch began about 2.6 million years ago and lasted until about 11,700 years ago.

[3] This is Senang, the island in the Indonesian Riau archipelago and not the Senang Island in Singapore.

[4] No definite rules abound for how the Orang Suku Laut mark their graves. Several ways are in use. Fruit trees might be planted at the gravesite, Islamic looking gravestones may be placed (flat ones for females and rounded ones for males), Christian like crosses or specially built small sheds to shelter the graves may be erected: these are just a few examples of how graves are marked. Food offerings are placed at the gravesites. Each grave has at least one Orang Suku Laut descendant caring for it. When the deceased in the grave is hungry, it will appear in a dream to its caregiver who will be responsible for feeding it. Caregivers are also responsible for remembering the grave's location.

REFERENCES

Andaya, Barbara. 1997. 'Recreating a Vision: Daratan and Kepulauan in Historical Context.' In *Riau in Transition*, ed. C. Chou and Will Derks. *Bijdragen Tot de Taal-, Land-en Volkenkunde* 53 (4e): 483–508.

Andaya, Leonard. 1975. *The Kingdom of Johor 1641–1728: Economic and Political Developments.* Kuala Lumpur: Oxford University Press.

———. 2010. *Leaves of the Same Tree: Trade and Ethnicity in the Straits of Melaka.* Singapore: NUS Press.

Benjamin, Geoffrey. 2002. 'On Being Tribal in the Malay World.' In *Tribal Communities in the Malay World: Historical, Cultural and Social Perspectives*, ed. G. Benjamin and C. Chou, 7–76. Leiden and Singapore: International Institute for Asian Studies and Institute of Southeast Asian Studies.

Casey, Edward S. 1996. 'How to Get from Space to Place in a Fairly Short Stretch of Time: Phenomenological Prolegomena.' In *Senses of Place*, ed. S. Feld and K. H. Basso, 13–52. Santa Fe, New Mexico: School of American Research Press.

Certeau, Michel de. 1984. *The Practice of Everyday Life.* Berkeley, California: University of California Press.

Chou, Cynthia. 2005. 'Southeast Asia through an Inverted Telescope: Maritime Perspectives on a Borderless Region.' In *Locating Southeast Asia: Geographies of Knowledge and Politics of Space*, ed. P.H. Kratoska, R. Raben, and H. Schulte Nordholt, 234–49. Singapore and Athens: NUS Press and Ohio University Press.

———. 2006a. 'Borders and Multiple Realities: The Orang Suku Laut of Riau, Indonesia.' In *Centering the Margin: Agency and Narrative in Southeast Asian Boderlands*, ed. A. Horstmann and L. Reed Wadley, 111–34. New York and Oxford: Berghahn Books.

———. 2006b. 'Multiple Realities of the Growth Triangle: Mapping Knowledge and the Politics of Mapping.' *Asia Pacific Viewpoint* 47 (2): 41–56.

———. 2010. *The Orang Suku Laut of Riau, Indonesia: The Inalienable Gift of Territory.* London and New York: Routledge Taylor and Francis Group.

———. 2013. 'Space, Movement and Place: The Sea Nomads.' In *The Sea, Identity and History: From the Bay of Bengal to the South China Sea*, ed. S. Chandra and H. Prabha Ray, 41–66. New Delhi: Manohar.

———. 2016. 'The Water World of the Orang Suku Laut in Southeast Asia.' *TRaNS: Trans-Regional and National Studies of Southeast Asia* 4 (2): 265–82.

Garro, Linda C. and Cheryl Mattingly. 2000. 'Narrative as Construct and Construction.' In *Narrative and the Cultural Construction of Illness and Healing*, ed. Cheryl Mattingly and Linda C. Garro. Berkeley, Los Angeles and London: University of California Press.

Ingold, Tim. 2000. *The Perception of the Environment: Essays in Livelihood, Dwelling and Skill.* London and New York: Routledge.

———. 2007. *Lines: A Brief History.* London: Routledge.

Logan, James. 1849. 'Malay Amoks and Piracies: What Can We Do to Abolish Them?' *Journal of the Indian Archipelago and Eastern Asia* 3: 436–67.

Malpas, Jeff E. 1999. *Places and Experience: A Philosophical Topography.* Cambridge: Cambridge University Press.

Oatley, Keith G. 1977. 'Inference, Navigation and Cognitive Maps.' In *Thinking: Readings in Cognitive Science*, ed. P.N. Johnson-Laird and P. Cathcart Wason, 537–47. Cambridge: Cambridge University Press.

Robinson, Arthur H. and Barbara Bartz Petchenik. 1976. *The Nature of Maps: Essays Towards Understanding Maps and Mapping*. Chicago: University of Chicago Press.

Rundstrom, Robert A. 1993. 'The Role of Ethics, Mapping, and the Meaning of Place in Relations between Indians and Whites in the United States.' *Cartographica* 30: 21–8.

Sather, Clifford. 1995. 'Sea Nomads and Rainforest Hunters-gatherers: Foraging Adaptations in the Indo-Malaysian Archipelago.' In *The Austronesians: Historical and Comparative Perspectives*, ed. Peter Bellwood, James J. Fox, and Darrell Tryon, 229–68. Canberra: Australian National University, Department of Anthropology, Research School of Pacific and Asian Studies Publication.

Scott, James C. 2009. *The Art of Not Being Governed: An Anarchist History of Upland Southeast Asia*. New Haven and London: Yale University Press.

Sopher, David E. 1977. *The Sea Nomads: A Study of the Maritime Boat People of Southeast Asia*. Singapore: National Museum Publication.

Trocki, Carl A. 1979. *Prince of Pirates: The Temenggongs and the Development of Johor and Singapore, 1784–1885*. Singapore: NUS Press.

Turnbull, David. 1996. 'Constructing Knowledge Spaces and Locating Sites of Resistance in the Modern Cartographic Transformation.' In *Social Cartography: Mapping Ways of Seeing Social and Education Change*, ed. R. G. Paulston, 53–79. New York: Garland.

Tuan, Yi-Fu. 1977. *Space and Place: The Perspective of Experience*. Minneapolis and London: University of Minnesota Press.

Urry, James. 1981. 'A View from the West: Inland, Lowland and Islands in Indonesian Prehistory.' Unpublished paper presented at the 51st ANZAAS Congress, Brisbane.

Wolters, Oliver W. 1975. *The Fall of Srivijaya in Malay History*. Kuala Lumpur: Oxford University Press.

6

The Linguistic Background to Southeast Asian Sea Nomadism

Roger Blench

INTRODUCTION

Sea nomadism is a unique and characteristic subsistence strategy in Island Southeast Asia (ISEA) reflecting a confluence of sophisticated maritime technology and resources scattered across thousands of islands (Yesner 1980). Nomadic pastoralism on land is a response to patchy and ephemeral grazing resources. In the same way, sea nomads can respond to mobile maritime resources and a changing market and exchange environment, which requires the flexible transport of goods. We do not know if the practice of sea nomadism in ISEA evolved once or many times. There are archaeological reasons for thinking inter-island movement of resources may be as old as 20,000 years in the region in the Talaud Islands (Ono et al. 2010). Blench (in press) has termed this the 'South China Sea Interaction Sphere' to try and capture the intensity of commercial interaction over millennia and the exchange of goods, languages and cultural practice (see also Acri et al. 2017). An important clue to the origins of sea nomad populations in the Southeast Asian region is the languages they speak.

This chapter presents an overview of what is known about these languages and what historical conclusions can be drawn from this. It focuses in particular on Samalic, both because it is the most widespread and internally ramified of the three major subsets, and because it is implicated in one of the most striking migrations of ISEA peoples, the colonisation of Madagascar. Although there is now a fair amount of descriptive materials on the languages of sea nomads, so far there has been only very limited ethnolinguistic analysis. For example, we do not know whether some of the specialised technologies, such as techniques of fishing and fish preservation, have distinctive terminologies, or simply borrow from major languages.

Two further issues are highlighted in the classification of maritime peoples; the inclusion of the Tanka (Dànjiā 蜑家), and other coastal traders of the coast of China, and the inland river boatmen who traverse the river systems in the interior of Borneo. This chapter also suggests that the Vezo, a people on the coast of southern Madagascar who practise extensive maritime migrations may well have resulted from a separate movement, distinct from the Barito/Malay ships which are the principal source of the dominant Malagasy language. Whatever the antiquity of the subsistence practices, sea peoples' languages turn out to be in a close relationship with dominant regional languages such as Malay and not marginal speech forms with substrates of hard to identify lexicon (although Duano constitutes a partial exception). This suggests that the present groups evolved in symbiosis with the great trading cultures of the region and are not the inheritors of a tradition descending from the pre-metal age.

THE BROAD PICTURE

The languages of the sea nomads in ISEA fall into three major groups: Samalic or Sama Bajau, the Orang Laut between eastern Sumatra and the Riau Islands, and the Moken/Moklen complex of the Andaman Sea, west of Thailand and Myanmar (Sopher 1977). These languages are all Austronesian and part of the broad category of western Malayo-Polynesian, which includes most of ISEA. Table 6.1 summarises the linguistic affiliations of sea nomad populations. See Bellina et al. this volume, Chapter 1: Map 1.1 for the approximate distribution of these groups.

Table 6.1 Linguistic affiliation of sea nomad populations.

Category	Location	Linguistic classification
Samalic	Scattered from Sulu throughout eastern Indonesia	Subgroup of Greater Barito
Orang Laut	Between the Riau Islands and the east coast of Sumatra	Malay dialects
Urak Lawoi	Andaman Sea, west of Thailand	Malay dialect
Moken/Moklen	Andaman Sea, west of Thailand	Malayic or parallel branch
Vezo	Southern Madagascar	Malagasy, part of Greater Barito

Austronesian originated in Taiwan more than 5,000 years ago, but Malayo-Polynesian is a somewhat unsatisfactory subgroup; it has not proven possible to subgroup it further as it divides into a complex parallel array. This may reflect a pattern of 'explosive dispersal' of early Austronesian languages out of Taiwan—something which is also reflected in the archaeology (Spriggs 2011; Blench 2012, 2016).

Malayic, however, is a much smaller grouping, consisting of languages that spread out with the Malay trading empire, generally identified with the expansion of Srivijaya in the sixth to seventh century (cf. Adelaar 1992 for a linguistic characterisation). The causes of this expansion remain controversial, but increased access to improved maritime technology was clearly a factor. The fact that the languages of sea nomads are all associated with a relatively small area of ISEA, southeast Borneo and the adjacent waters, is clearly significant.

THE SAMALIC [BAJAU] LANGUAGES

The Samal (Sama Bajau) peoples speak a cluster of related Austronesian languages, now generally referred to as Samalic. Although the majority of these are in the Philippines, they are not closely related to the Philippines group of Austronesian but to Borneo languages, in particular the Greater Barito group (Blust 2005). Figure 6.1 shows a schematic tree of the relationships between the Samalic languages. However, the Sama Bajau peoples are highly fragmented and those in the sea between northeast Borneo and the Sulu Archipelago speak languages related in complex, overlapping chains (Mead and Lee 2007).

Their languages are relatively well described in overviews by Pallesen (1985) and Mead and Lee (2007). They are also covered in detailed studies of individual languages such as Verheijen (1986) (Sunda dialects), Akamine (2003) (Sinama), Collins and Collins (2001) (Mapun), Behrens (2002) (Yakan), Brainard and Behrens (2002) (Yakan) and Miller (2007) (West Coast Bajau). The Sama Bajau are well-known for their lengthy epic recitations and these have been described in some detail in Zacot (1978) and Nuraini-Grangé (2008). Ethnographic descriptions are also quite abundant, although not all are reliable (see Nimmo 1972; Sather 1975; Allison 1984).

Despite their strong presence in the Philippines today, the affiliation of Samalic strongly points to a Borneo origin. Pallesen (1985) argued that their genesis may have been as late as the fifteenth century, although the internal diversity of Samalic seems to point to an earlier date. It is striking that some Samalic languages are spoken by farming populations in the southern Philippines (Yakan, Mapun and Inabaknon) and it is likely these are settled sea nomads rather than indigenous farmers whose relatives took to the ocean.

It is likely that the genesis of the Samalic peoples is connected with the growth of maritime activity in the area between southeast Kalimantan and Sulawesi and thus with the rise of Srivijaya. We know that the voyages which crossed the Indian Ocean and brought about the genesis of Malagasy originated in the same area, and it is likely that the explosion of Samalic reflects the spread of new types of boats (Blench 2018). Of equal importance is the 'feeder' trade: pioneering new sea routes, discovering sources of raw materials and manufactured goods and building links with fragmented populations around the shores of the numerous islands. The Samal—and elsewhere the Orang Laut—functioned as the antennae of the great Malay trading ships and the two cultures existed in symbiosis. So while it is likely that some form of maritime nomadism existed prior to the rise of the Samal, it was wholly displaced by a modernised combination of foraging and trading over the last millennium.

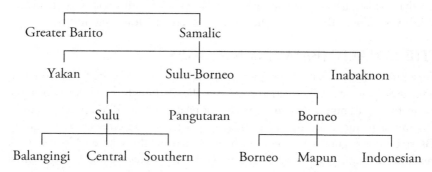

Figure 6.1 The Samalic languages (Source: adapted from Pallesen [1985]).

THE ORANG LAUT LANGUAGES

The Orang Laut languages are spoken in the region between the Riau Islands and the west coast of Myanmar, taking in the diverse communities on islands south of Singapore.

Although the first record of one of these languages was published in the early nineteenth century (Smith et al. 1814), the literature is extremely patchy. Skeat and Ridley (1900) represent the first description of these languages, while Anderbeck (2012) represents a comprehensive overview of the materials on the languages of the 'Sea Tribes'. He divides these languages into four major subgroups, broadly defined by geography: Kedah, Duano, Riau and Sekak. His conclusion is that all the records of the Orang Laut languages form a defined subgroup of Malayic, except Duano, which shows some intriguing anomalies.

The Riau Orang Laut/Orang Sawang live on the Riau Islands and across to the Straits of Singapore and the east coast of Sumatra (Figure 6.2). They have been divided into as many as 45 groups (Chou 2010: 26) although this is an ethnographic classification, not a linguistic one. The review by Anderbeck (2012) of the scattered linguistic data concludes that the Riau speak a Malayic language, very close to Peninsular Malay and that there is no evidence of a substrate (cf. also Suwardi 1993). It is therefore most likely that the Riau developed together with the rise of the Malay trading empire and did not inherit anything from a prior sea nomad culture.

Kedah is the dialect cluster spoken by the Urak Lawoi who live south of the Moken/Moklen and are often grouped with them. However, linguistic data indicates that their genetic affiliation is with Malayic and shows little influence from

Figure 6.2 Orang Laut settlement in Riau (Source: Creative Commons).

Austroasiatic (Saengmani 1979; Hogan and Pattemore 1988; Steinhauer 2008; Robert 2010). Ethnographically, they have been little studied and the lengthiest piece is hardly more than an account of a visit by tourists (Granbom 2007).

The Duano language (dup) is spoken by approximately 17,500 people, mostly in the coastal region of Riau and Jambi provinces of Sumatra, but a few on the opposite coast in Johor, Malaysia. Other names for the Duano include Orang Kuala (people of the estuaries) and Desin Dola (people of the sea). The first record of Duano is Schot (1884) and a short unidentified wordlist is included in Skeat and Blagden (1906). Kähler (1946a, 1946b) recorded some hard to interpret material from Rangsang Island. Seidlitz (2007) wrote a phonology of Duano based on material from both sides of the Straits. Yusof (2006) is an account of language obsolescence among the Duano and Kanak. Sandbukt (1983) is one of the few ethnographic studies of the Duano, focusing on the adaptation of subsistence fisheries to a market economy. Anderbeck (2012) has reviewed this literature and points to the exceptional nature of Duano, which does not share a number of sound changes characteristic of Malayic, as well as having an exceptional proportion of its lexicon from an unknown source. A possible hypothesis to explain this is that the Duano were originally one of the Orang Asli groups of the region, speaking either a now lost but archaic Austronesian language or something else perhaps affiliated to Aslian. Their language has gradually become relexified from Malay, but retains some of its previous phonology and lexicon.

Anderbeck (2012: 274) also highlights the intriguing problem of Jakun, a Malayic language spoken by one of the Orang Asli groups in Johor. The Jakun are not sea people, at least today, but their language shows common innovations with some of the Orang Laut lects. Earlier records of Jakun (in Skeat and Blagden 1906) show a much greater admixture of Aslian (i.e. Austroasiatic) lexicon and it seems credible that the Jakun were originally an Aslian group, which has become progressively Malayised over the centuries.

The Sekak group of dialects include those spoken on the islands of Bangka and Belitung (Loncong) (Nothofer 1994). Of these, the Bangka language is much better described than Loncong. Bangka is the subject of several ethnographic publications, including Anonymous (1862), Hagen (1908), Smedal (1989) and Chou (2003) as well as two linguistic studies (Kähler 1960, 1966; Smedal 1987). By contrast Loncong features only in two much older Dutch-language publications (Ecoma Verstege 1877; Riedel 1881). The Sekak group is severely endangered with as few as 600 speakers, according to Anderbeck (2012).

THE ANDAMAN SEA LANGUAGES

Two languages are spoken by the maritime peoples of the Andaman Sea, the 'Sea Gypsies'. Moklen and Moken are related to one another and ultimately to the Malayic group, either as a member of it or as a parallel branch of western Malayo-polynesian (WMP) (Chantanakomes 1980; Makboon 1981; Larish 1999, 2005). The Moken/Moklen have been the subject of considerable ethnographic research (Anderson 1890; White 1922; Ivanoff 1997; Larish 1999). Although their lives are based on seagoing vessels, they are not wide-ranging traders like the other groups described here, but are confined to a relatively small area, exchanging maritime produce for necessary items. Indeed, somewhat surprisingly, the Moklen are sedentary seashore dwellers and land-based hunting plays a significant role in their subsistence.

Chinese records frequently refer to the Kunlun (崑崙), the 'sea people' found around ISEA. The problem is that these references are highly inconsistent and are often mixed with descriptions of Africans brought to east Asia via the slave trade (Wilensky 2002). References to dark skin may simply reflect weather exposure, but it is worth noting that the Negritos, the prior Austromelanesian inhabitants of the region, would have been far more numerous in the Malay Peninsula at this period and may well have also played a role in the sea trade (see above discussion of the Jakun). Nonetheless, as Wheatley (1961: 283) observes, Kunlun is probably best understood as 'a succession of peoples ranging from Malays around the coasts of the Peninsula to Chams along the shores of Indo-China'.

Estimating the time at which the Moken/Moklen broke from the Malayic stem is far more difficult and Larish (1999) discusses this issue at length. He points out that Moken/Moklen has been heavily influenced by Austroasiatic languages (and more recently, Thai). Moken/Moklen has many changes in common with the Chamic languages of Vietnam and this may point to the split of these two languages from Chamic at around the same period, namely some 2,000 years ago. Indeed, he goes further to suggest that the Cham-speakers themselves were originally sea nomads who then settled. This is not impossible, but would be entirely speculative. Larish assigns the Moken/Moklen split to a much later period, somewhere after the thirteenth century.

Another aspect of understanding the relationship of Moken/Moklen to the broader Austronesian world is their technical vocabulary. The external cognates of Moken/Moklen in relation to fisheries present an intriguing contrast. Because these groups have moved into an entirely new zoogeographic area, the fish fauna is largely unfamiliar or only related to Indo-Pacific species at the genus level. Larish (1999) has a very extensive dataset on both fish names and other fisheries terminology such as traps. Curiously, Blust has not incorporated the Moken/Moklen data into the Austronesian Comparative Dictionary (ACD) comparative sets, despite the thesis in which they are presented being compiled in Hawai'i.

An exploration of this terminology shows that very few fish names are retained from Proto-Malayopolynesian (PMP), whereas many are borrowed from Thai or calqued (i.e. the Thai name is literally translated in Moken/Moklen). The following tables take the Moken/Moklen names given in Larish (1999) and

164 Roger Blench

compare them with the reconstructions in the ACD and other data, where available. One of the rare fish names that reflect PMP is the name for the sailfish (*Istiophorus* spp.) as shown in Table 6.2.

Table 6.2 Sailfish in Moken/Moklen.

Language	Form	Gloss
Moken/Moklen	*l/nayan	*Istiophorus gradius*
Proto-Austronesian	*layaR	sail
Fijian	saku layar	sawfish

This word has a rather tangled history, since the Proto-Austronesian (PAN) reconstruction is for 'sail' and yet the forms for 'sailfish, swordfish' seem to reflect a prior form such as the Fijian, which by the later period is applied to any large predatory species, including the swordfish.

Another intriguing case is the big-eye scad, *Selar crumenophthalmus*, which is found throughout the region. The ACD gives this as PMP although only three forms support a reconstruction at this level. However, the Thai forms also closely resemble the Austronesian and are etymologisable, suggesting this may be an early borrowing into Austronesian. The Moken/Moklen is probably not a direct cognate of the Austronesian forms but a calque from the Thai (Table 6.3).

By contrast Tables 6.4 to 6.7 show the Moken/Moklen reflexes of mainstream Austronesian lexemes to do with the sea and fisheries, which seem to be inherited entirely regularly.

Table 6.3 Big-eye scad in Moken/Moklen.

Language	Form	Gloss
Moken/Moklen	ma^{32}.ta:ʔ^{44} ʔa^{32}daʔ^{343}	big-eye scad lit. 'eye big'
PMP	*qatulay	*Trachurops crumenophthalmus*
Samal	tulay	*Selar crumenophthalmus*
Thai	pla ta: lɔ:	big-eye scad lit. 'fish eye big'

Table 6.4 Lake/ocean in Moklen.

Language	Form	Gloss
Moklen	taʔaw	ocean
PAN	*danaw	lake
PMP	*danaw	lake
Proto-Chamic	*danau	lake
Malay	danaw	lake

Table 6.5 Gill net in Moken/Moklen.

Language	Form	Gloss
Moken/Moklen	*pukat	gill net
PMP	*puket	dragnet
Malay	*pukat	driftnet

Table 6.6 Hearth on boat in Moken/Moklen.

Language	Form	Gloss
Moken/Moklen	*dapan	fireplace in boat
PMP	*dapuR	hearth
Malay	dapur	kitchen
Acehnese	dapu	kitchen

Table 6.7 Fishtrap in Moken/Moklen.

Language	Form	Gloss
Moken/Moklen	*bubəy	fishtrap
PAN	*bubu	conical bamboo basket trap for fish
Kavalan	bubu	fishtrap
Malay	bubu	fishtrap

Clues to some of the trade goods the Moken/Moklen may have handled are to be found in words such 'bracelet/brass' (Table 6.8).

Table 6.8 Bracelet in Moken/Moklen.

Language	Form	Gloss
Moken/Moklen	*gila:ŋ/ŋila:ŋ	bracelet/brass
Acehnese	geleŋ	bracelet
Proto-Chamic	*ko:ŋ	bracelet/brass/copper
Proto-Katuic	*kɔŋ	bracelet ~ brass
Proto-Bahnaric	*kɔɔŋ	bracelet

This word has no reconstruction in Austronesian and it appears these brass goods must have been traded in the region between the Austroasiatic speakers on the mainland, the Chamic speakers and eventually the Moken/Moklen.

THE VEZO HYPOTHESIS

The Vezo people live on the south coast of Madagascar and practice seasonal migration in search of fish (Koechlin 1975; Astuti 1995; Sanders 2005). The Vezo spend many months a year at sea, living on sandbanks and fishing. Dahl (1988) argued for a link between the Vezo and the Sama Bajau languages, indeed that the name 'Vezo' was a phonological transformation of Bajau. There is no direct linguistic evidence in basic vocabulary for a connection between Vezo and Bajau, however, it is very striking that Vezo marine fish names are very different from other Malagasy names, although they resemble those of their neighbours, the Antanosy (Bauchot and Bianchi 1984; Poirot 2011). Given that Vezo is generally close linguistically to Merina, this is quite surprising and may point to a distinct origin for their fishing culture. To approach this, Table 6.9 presents a brief list of Vezo fish names and their likely origins in ISEA languages.

Table 6.9. Vezo fish names and their corresponding Malayopolynesian etymologies.

Vezo	English	Latin	Commentary
akio foty	requiem shark	*Carcharhinus* sp.	Almost all Austronesian languages have lost the initial velar, which is retained only in Agutaynen *kiw*, Komodo *kiu*.
aloalo	barracuda	*Sphyraena barracuda*	Also other *Sphyraena* spp. The reduplicated form could be a direct Malay borrowing: *ikan alu alu*. *Sphyraena obtusata* (same species is known to the Vezo).
fay andema	stingray	*Dasyatis* sp.	cf. Borneo languages, e.g., Bintulu, Melanau *pai* WMP **pariH*
gepo	herring	*Herklotsichthys* sp.	cf. Gela *kepo*, *Herklotsichthys quadrimaculatus*, fourspot herring. Ross et al. (2011) reconstruct POc **kepʷa* Clupeidae, but this suggests that the form goes higher in the Austronesian tree and this species is the referent.
hatoka tendro	torpedo scad	*Megalaspis cordyla*	cf. PMP **qatulay* a fish: the big-eyed scad *Trachurops crumenophthalmus* Samal *tulay* scad-like fish: *Selar crumenophthalmus*. This is one of the rare examples, where Vezo connects directly with Samal. Other cognates are (curiously) in Oceanic and Chamorro.
lamera, lamahira	moray eel	*Echidna* spp.	POc has **maraya* for 'eel' but typical attestations are Raga *marea* (generic eel). Micronesian languages such as Carolinian *(li) mware-mwar*, 'white or yellow eel with black banded stripes', have a li- prefix denoting (at least in Puluwatese) 'bird, fish, eels'. Could the la- prefixes in Vezo reflect this?

Table 6.9. cont'd

Vezo	English	Latin	Commentary
lovo hara	marbled grouper	*Epinephelus polypheakadion*	cf. Longgu ɣ*ulava* 'Cephalopholis argus, peacock rock cod' Teop *rovu* 'rock cod generic'
talantala	small-spotted pompano	*Trachinotus bailloni*	Pompanos are usually *Alectis* spp. *Talatala* is usually for the queenfish, *Scomberoides commersonnianus*, or the needlescaled queenfish, *Scomberoides tol*. ACD has PWMP *talaŋtalaŋ for horse mackerel although given the vague definition in the sources, this could be a wide variety of spp.
varavara	blackspot snapper	*Lutjanus fulviflammus*	Hebert (1964) notes the Vezo name and compares with Malay *babaran*, poisson à ecailles.
vavana	sawfish		cf. Malay *bambanan*
voavoa	Indo-pacific tarpon	*Megalops cyprinoides*	Bauchot and Bianchi 1984 gives *bekapoka*. Possibly WMP *bulanbulan* which certainly looks cognate with *bokalana*.

It certainly would not be unreasonable to imagine the Bajau, following the route pioneered by the Malay ships, reaching Madagascar independently. However, this hypothesis needs more positive linguistic evidence before it can be accepted uncritically.

SHOULD WE INCLUDE RIVER NOMADS?

Apart from sea nomads, very large islands such as Borneo create opportunities for a comparable lifestyle on inland rivers. At Banjarmasin in southeast Borneo, many permanent houseboats carry trade goods up and down the rivers from the coast to the interior. The peoples operating these boats are also from the same Greater Barito group as the Samalic languages and the Barito who are the core population of Madagascar. It is likely that this adaptation came about at the same period and for similar reasons as the evolution of the Sama Bajau.

BOAT PEOPLE ALONG THE COAST OF CHINA

Apart from the sea peoples of ISEA, there have also been coastal fishing and trading groups along the coast of southeast China for a long period (Anderson 1972). The best known of these are the Tanka (Dànjiā 蜑家)—now replaced in official sources by *shuǐshàng rén* 水上人 ('on-water people')—and the Hoklo (Hok-ló 福佬). The Tanka today speak Cantonese, but historic sources suggest that they originated among the Mien (Yao), which would account for earlier reports that they spoke a quite different language. The Tanka are distributed across a wide area and are also a recognised minority in Vietnam, where they are

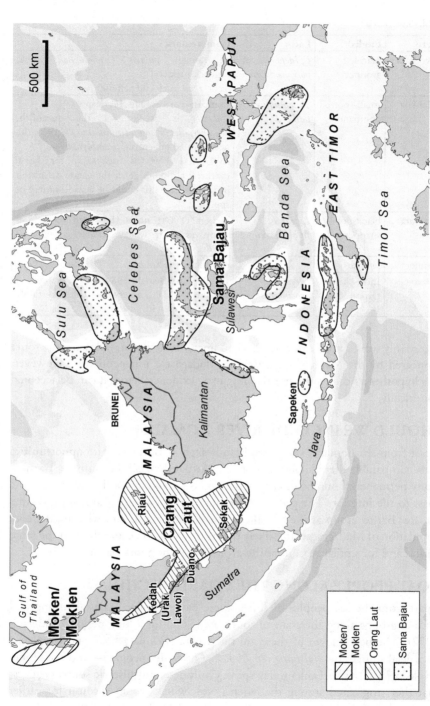

Map 6.1 Linguistic subgroups of the Bajau.

called Dàn. The Hoklo speak the Hokkien dialect of Min. Both these peoples are very numerous by the standards of ISEA, but the great majority no longer practise a maritime lifestyle. Indeed, the Hoklo played a major role in the genesis of the Chinese population of modern-day Taiwan.

There is very little reliable historiography of these peoples, as much of the literature is mixed up with speculation on their relationship with the Ba Yue of Chinese records. Chen (2002) briefly reviews some of the records, which go back at least to the Han Dynasty (206 BCE–220 CE). However, he argues that the widespread presence of shell-middens on the coast of China allows us to push back nomadism to the early Neolithic; a view few archaeologists would accept without ancillary evidence.

The languages of the Chinese boat people do not provide significant clues today. Nonetheless, a minority still operate from houseboats and are still fully engaged in a maritime lifestyle. Modernised fisheries have largely displaced their role as fishermen, but trading is clearly an effective substitute. To what extent their network was entirely separate from the ISEA sea peoples remains an open question, however the peopling of Taiwan is clearly associated with a thriving cross-straits traffic in raw materials and an energetic regional network, so it would not be unreasonable to push back this type of subsistence to an early period (Blench in press).

HISTORICAL INTERPRETATION

The first conclusion that can be drawn from this review of the ISEA sea nomad languages is that none of them are in any way unusual in terms of genetic affiliation. All the languages are part of mainstream subgroups of Austronesian, Malayic or Greater Barito. This strongly suggests that, unlike marginal foragers in other parts of the world, the evolution of sea nomad society is tied to historical events over the last 2,000 years. How can this be interpreted in the light of long-term archaeological evidence for intensive traffic between islands in the region and regional exchange networks?

The answer may be that technological and mercantile innovation was a force sufficiently powerful to completely replace the more informal, dispersed and linguistically diverse networks that previously existed. We know that Malayic spreads out from Borneo and that trading networks developed rapidly. It has been suggested above that the Samalic languages reflect an expansion from the same area, probably using the same type of boats and feeding local trade items into the Malay network. This almost certainly was initiated with the growth of the Srivijaya trading empire from the sixth to seventh century onwards. The evolution of mercantile sea-traders did not end with the Samal. Later groups such as the Buginese and Makassarese of Sulawesi (who probably originated as a distinct identity in the sixteenth century) also serviced the commercial networks, although they remained more obviously land-based.

Very intriguing is the possibility that the relationship between the shore hunter-gatherers, the sea nomads and long-distance merchants played a role in the evolution of the trans-Isthmian trade (Blench 2017a, 2017b). The movement of Indian Ocean goods to the South China Sea can be shortened considerably by making use of land routes across the Isthmus of Kra. Archaeological excavation has focused on the narrowest point, illustrated by the excavations at Khao San Kheo (Bellina and Silapanth 2006a; Bellina-Pryce and Silapanth 2006b; Bellina 2017). However, in a complex region such as this, there would probably be many strategies both to cross and circumnavigate the Isthmus. Larish (1999) has proposed that the Moken/Moklen evolved as facilitators of the trans-Isthmian trade. He says:

> Various lines of evidence support the possibility that the Moken/Moklen represent a remnant population of a once larger and more widely distributed—possibly trans-Isthmian—PMM ancestral population. The PMM may have established on the early Peninsular politico-cultural zones ... or were possibly vassals to one of the ethnolinguistic groups that dominated these areas. Most importantly, present-day speakers of Moken and Moklen are found distributed at the coastal endpoints of four separate trans-Isthmian routeways.

The evidence from the Jakun and the Duano allow us to expand this hypothesis. Prior to the expansion of Malayic, the region must have been occupied by a complex mosaic of fishing peoples, sea traders and land-based foragers. As the potential for long-distance trade expanded, demand for food and forest products, as well as labour and construction, allowed these groups to develop more specialised and formalised niches. The Orang Asli foragers and fishers supplied the local produce and the Orang Laut facilitated local movement of goods and services, feeding the long-distance trade. The model is schematically represented in Figure 6.3.

Over time, the constant interaction with Malay culture gradually relexified these divergent speech communities until they 'became' Malay, with their language only containing scattered pointers to their original speech community.

The peopling of Madagascar also occurs during this significant period, apparently in Malay-captained ships with Barito-speaking crews (Blench 2010). The Malagasy language also contains a significant Sulawesi component (Blench 2018), arguing for interaction across the islands—something which appears to be confirmed in the genetics (Kusuma et al. this volume). The possibility that the Vezo resulted from an independent migration of a Samalic group using a route already pioneered should be considered.

Less well documented are the river nomads of Borneo and the 'sea peoples' of the coast of China. There is reason to believe the Borneo peoples spring from the same upsurge of mercantile innovation as their seagoing cousins. However, the Chinese groups seem to have limited interaction with the ISEA networks and presumably have a quite different origin. Today they speak no unusual

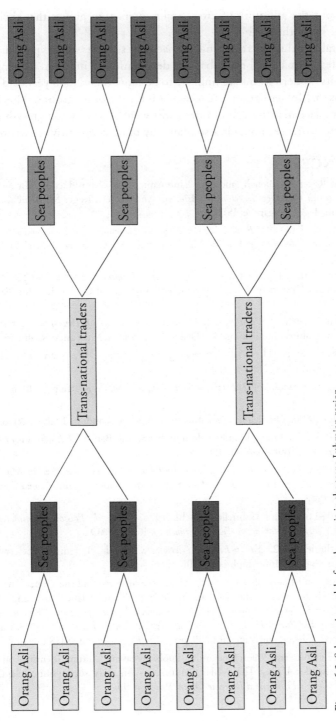

Figure 6.3 Schematic model of trade mosaic in the trans-Isthmian region.

languages, but the antiquity of cross-straits interaction argues that their roots may well lie far in the past.

The overall conclusion is that while archaeology suggests some type of maritime nomadic lifestyle may well reach back to deep antiquity in ISEA, language data shows that its modern forms are unlikely to be more than 2,000 years old (in the case of Moken/Moklen) and more recent still for the other groups. This in turn suggests a replacement model; old networks were erased by the growth of new and similarly earlier sea nomads assimilated by more competitive newcomers.

REFERENCES

Acri, Andrea, Roger M. Blench, and Alix Landmann. 2017. 'Introduction.' In *Spirits and Ships: Cultural Exchanges in Monsoon Asia*, ed. Andrea Acri, Roger M. Blench, and Alix Landmann, 1–37. Singapore: ISEAS.

Adelaar, K. Alexander. 1992. *Proto-Malayic; The Reconstruction of its Phonology and Parts of its Lexicon and Morphology*. [Pacific Linguistics C-119.] Canberra: Australian National University.

Akamine, Jun. 2003. *A Basic Grammar of Southern Sinama*. (ELPR A3-012, A3-012.) Osaka Gakuin University, Japan: Endangered Languages of the Pacific Rim, Faculty of Informatics.

Allison, Karen J. 1984. *A View from the Islands: The Samal of Tawi-tawi*. International Museum of Cultures Publication, 15. Dallas: International Museum of Cultures.

Anderbeck, Karl. 2012. 'The Malayic-speaking; Orang Laut Dialects and Directions for Research.' *Wacana* 14 (2): 265–312.

Anderson, Eugene Newton. 1972. *Essays on South China's Boat People*. Taipei: Orient Cultural Service.

Anderson, John. 1890. *The Selungs of the Mergui Archipelago*. London: Trübner &Co.

Anonymous. 1862. 'De Orang Lom of Belom op het Eiland Banka.' *Tijdschrift voor Indische Taal-, Land- en Volkenkunde* XI: 388–94.

Astuti, Rita. 1995. *People of the Sea: Identity and Descent Among the Vezo of Madagascar*. Cambridge Studies in Social & Cultural Anthropology. Cambridge: Cambridge University Press.

Bauchot, Marie-Louise and Gabriella Bianchi. 1984. *Guide de Poissons Commerciaux de Madagascar (Espèces Marines et d'eaux Saumâtres)*. Rome: FAO.

Behrens, Dietlinde. 2002. *Yakan-English Dictionary*. Manila: Linguistic Society of the Philippines, Special Monograph Issue, 40.

Bellina, Bérénice and Praon Silapanth. 2006a. 'Khao Sam Kaeo and the Upper Thai-Malay Peninsula: Understanding the Mechanisms of Early Trans-Asiatic Trade and Cultural Exchange.' In *Uncovering Southeast Asia's Past: Selected Papers from the 10th International Conference of the European Association of Southeast Asian Archaeologists*, ed. Elizabeth A. Bacus, Ian C. Glover, and Vincent C. Pigott, 379–92. Singapore: NUS Press.

Bellina-Pryce, Bérénice and Praon Silapanth. 2006b. 'Weaving Cultural Identities on Trans-Asiatic Networks: Upper Thai-Malay Peninsula – An early socio-political landscape.' *Bulletin de l'École Française d'Êxtreme-Orient* 93: 257–93.

Bellina, Bérénice, ed. 2017. *Khao Sam Kaeo: An Early Port-city Between the Indian Ocean and the South China Sea*. Mémoires Archéologiques 28. Paris: Ecole française d'Extrême-Orient.

Blench, Roger M. 2010. 'New Evidence for the Austronesian Impact on the East African Coast.' In *Global Origins and the Development of Seafaring*, ed. Atholl Anderson, John H. Barrett, and Katie V. Boyle, 239–48. Cambridge: Macdonald Institute.

———. 2012. 'Almost Everything you Believed about the Austronesians Isn't True.' In *Crossing Borders: Selected Papers from the 13th International Conference of the European Association of Southeast Asian Archaeologists,* Volume 1, ed. M.L. Tjoa-Bonatz, A. Reinecke, and D. Bonatz, 122–42. Singapore: NUS Press.

———. 2016. 'Splitting Up Proto-Malayopolynesian; New Models of Dispersals from Taiwan.' In *Austronesian Diaspora, A New Perspective*, ed. Bagyo Prasetyo, Titi Surti Nastiti, and Truman Simanjuntak, 77–104. Yogyakarta: Gadjah Mada University Press.

———. 2017a. 'Ethnographic and Archaeological Correlates for an MSEA Linguistic Area.' In *Spirits and Ships: Cultural Exchanges in Monsoon Asia*, ed. Andrea Acri, Roger M. Blench, and Alix Landmann, 207–38. Singapore: ISEAS.

———. 2017b. 'Origins of Ethnolinguistic Identity in Southeast Asia.' In *Handbook of East and Southeast Asian Archaeology*, ed. Junko Habu, Peter Lape, and John Olsen, 733–53. New York: Springer.

———. 2018. 'Interdisciplinary Approaches to Stratifying the Peopling of Madagascar.' In *Proceedings of the Indian Ocean Conference, Madison, Wisconsin*, ed. Akshay Sarathi. Oxford: Archaeopress.

———. In press. 'Restructuring our Understanding of the South China Sea Interaction Sphere: The Evidence from Multiple Disciplines.' In *Taiwan Maritime Landscapes from Neolithic to Early Modern Times: Cross-Regional Perspectives*, ed. Paola Calanca and Frank Muyard. Taiwan: Academica Sinica.

Blust, Robert. 2005. 'The Linguistic Macrohistory of the Philippines.' In *Current Issues in Philippine Linguistics and Anthropology Parangal Kay Lawrence A. Reid*, ed. Hsiu-chuan Liao and Carl R. Galvez Rubino, 31–68. Manila: SIL.

Brainard, Sherri and Dietlinde Behrens. 2002. *A Grammar of Yakan*. Manila: Linguistic Society of the Philippines, No. 40.

Chantanakomes, Veena. 1980. 'A Description of Moken: A Malay-Polynesian Language.' MA thesis. Mahidol University.

Chen, J. Chung-Yu. 2002. 'Sea Nomads in Prehistory on the Southeast Coast of China.' *Indo-Pacific Prehistory Association Bulletin* 22: 51–4.

Chou, Cynthia. 2003. *Indonesian Sea Nomads: Money, Magic, and Fear of the Orang Suku Laut*. Leiden, London and New York: International Institute for Asian Studies and RoutledgeCurzon.

———. 2010. *The Orang Suku Laut of Riau, Indonesia: The Inalienable Gift of Territory*. London: Routledge.

Collins, Millard A. and Virginia R. Collins. 2001. *Mapun-English Dictionary*. Manila: SIL.

Dahl, Otto Christian. 1988. 'Bantu Substratum in Malagasy.' In *Linguistique de Madagascar et des Comores. Etudes Océan Indien* 9: 91–132.

Ecoma Verstege, Ch. M.G.A.M. 1877. 'Bijzonderheden Over de Sekah Bevolking van Billiton.' [Details about the Sekah population of Billiton]. *Tijdschrift voor Indische Taal-, Land- en Volkenkunde* XXIV: 201–11.

Granbom, Ann-Charlotte. 2007. *Urak Lawoi: Sea Nomads in Andaman Sea*. Lund: Sociologiska Institutionen, Lunds Universitet.

Hagen, Bernard. 1908. 'Beitrag zur Kenntnis der Orang Sekka (Sakai) oder Orang Laut, Sowie der Orang Lom oder Mapor, Zweier Nichtmuhamedanischer Volksstämme auf Insel Banka' [Contribution to the knowledge of the Orangutan Sekka (Sakai) or Orang Laut, as well as the Oran Lom or Mapor, Two Non-Muhamedan Tribes on the Island of Banka.]. In *Abhandlungen zur Anthropologie, Ethnologie, und Urgeschichte*, 37–46. Frankfurt am Main: Josef Baer & Co.

Hebert, J.C. 1964. 'Les noms d'animaux à Madagascar.' In *Civilisation Malgache*. Faculté des Lettres et Sciences humaines Tananarive T.1.

Hogan, David. 1972. 'Men of the Sea: Coastal Tribes of South Thailand's West Coast.' *Journal of the Siam Society* 60: 205–35.

Hogan, David W. and Stephen W. Pattemore. 1988. *Urak Lawoi': Basic Structures and a Dictionary*. Pacific Linguistics: Series C, Books, 109. Canberra: Pacific Linguistics.

Ivanoff, Jacques. 1997. *Moken: Sea-gypsies of the Andaman Sea: Post-war Chronicles*. Bangkok, Thailand: White Lotus Press.

Kähler, Hans. 1946a. 'Ethnographische und Linguistische Studien von den Orang Laut auf der Insel Rangsang an der Ostküste von Sumatra.' *Anthropos* 41/44(1/3): 1–31.

———. 1946b. 'Ethnographische und Linguistische Studien von den Orang Laut auf der Insel Rangsang an der Ostküste von Sumatra' [Ethnographic and Linguistic Studies of the Orang Utan Laut on the Island of Rangsang on the East Coast of Sumatra]. *Anthropos* 41/44(4/6): 757–85.

———. 1960. *Ethnographische und Linguistiche Studien über die Orang Darat, Orang Akit, Orang Laut und Orang Utan im Riau-Archipel und auf den Inseln an du Ostküste von Sumatra* [Ethnographic and Linguistic Studies on the *Orang Darat, Orang Akit, Orang Laut und Orang Utan* in the Riau Archipelago and on the Islands on the East Coast of Sumatra]. Berlin: Verlag von Dietrich Reimar.

———. 1966. *Wörterverzeichnis des Omong Jakarta*. Veröffentlichen des Seminars für Indonesische und Südseesprachen der Universität Hamburg, 5. Berlin: Dietrich Reimer.

Koechlin, Bernard. 1975. *Les Vezo du Sud-Ouest de Madagascar. Contribution à l'étude de l'écosystème de Semi-nomades Marins*. Paris/La Haye: Mouton.

Kusuma, Pradiptajati et al. This volume. 'A Genomic Perspective of the Origin and Dispersal of the Bajaw Sea Nomads in Indonesia.' In *Sea Nomads of Southeast Asia: From the Past to the Present*, ed. B. Bellina, R. Blench, and J.-C. Galipaud. Singapore: NUS Press.

Larish, Michael David. 2000. *The Position of Moken and Moklen within the Austronesian Language Family (Thailand)*. Ann Arbor: University Microfilms.

———. 2005. 'Moken and Moklen.' In *The Austronesian Languages of Asia and Madagascar*, ed. Sander Adelaar and Niklaus Himmelmann, 513–33. London: Routledge.

Makboon, Sorat. 1981. 'Survey of Sea Peoples' Dialects along the West Coast of Thailand.' MA thesis, University of Bangkok.

Mead, David and Myung-young Lee. 2007. *Mapping Indonesian Bajau Communities in Sulawesi*. SIL Electronic Survey Reports 2007-019.

Miller, Mark. 2007. 'A Grammar of West Coast Bajau.' PhD dissertation, University of Texas at Arlington.

Nimmo, H. Arlo. 1972. *The Sea People of Sulu*. London: Intertext Books.

Nothofer, Bernd. 1994. 'Bahasa Lom: Dari mana Asalnya?' In *Bahasawan Cendekia: Seuntai Karangan untuk Anton M. Moeliono*, ed. Liberty P. Sihombing, 193–208. Jakarta: PT Intermasa.

Nuraini-Grangé, Chandra. 2008. 'Langue et Production de Récits d'une Communauté Bajo des îles Kangean (Indonésie).' PhD dissertation, University de La Rochelle.

Ono, Rintaro, Santoso Soegondho, and Minoru Yoneda. 2010. 'Changing Marine Exploitation During Late Pleistocene in Northern Wallacea: Shell Remains from Leang Sarru Rockshelter in Talaud Islands.' *Asian Perspectives* 48(2): 318–41.

Pallesen, A. Kemp. 1985. *Culture Contact and Language Convergence*. (Philippine Journal of Linguistics: Special Monograph Issue, 24.) Manila: Linguistic Society of the Philippines.

Poirot, Gérard. 2011. *Dictionnaire Vezo–français Suivi d'un Index Français–vezo*. Published privately and distributed by ShopMyBook [Belgium] [www.unibook.com].

Riedel, J.G.F. 1881. 'Twee Volksverhalen in het Dialekt der Orang Lawoet of Orang Sekah van Belitoeng' [Two Folk Tales in the Dialect of the Orang Lawoet or Orang Sekah van Belitoeng]. *Tijdschrift voor Indische Taal-, Land- en Volkenkunde* 26: 264–73.

Robert, Chongkit Sripun. 2010. 'Changes in Patterns of Communication of the Urak Lawoi.' PhD dissertation, University of Wisconsin.

Ross, Malcolm D., Andrew Pawley, and Meredith Osmond, eds. 2011. *The Lexicon of Proto Oceanic: The Culture and Environment of Ancestral Oceanic Society. Animals*. Canberra: Pacific Linguistics.

Saengmani, Amon. 1979. 'Phonology of the Urak Lawoi' Language: Adang Island.' MA thesis, Mahidol University.

Sandbukt, Af Øyvind. 1983. 'Duano Littoral Fishing: Adaptive Strategies within a Market Economy.' PhD dissertation. University of Cambridge.

Sanders, Eartl Furman. 2005. 'Fombandrazana Vezo: Ethnic Identity and Subsistence Strategies among Coastal Fishers of Western Madagascar.' PhD dissertation, University of Georgia.

Sather, Clifford. 1975. *The Bajau Laut: Adaptation, History, and Fate in a Maritime Fishing Society of Southeastern Sabah*. Kuala Lumpur: Oxford University Press.

Schot, J.G. 1884. 'Het Stroomgebied der Kateman; Bijdrage tot de Kennis von Oost Sumatra' [The Kateman Catchment Area; Contribution to the Knowledge of East Sumatra]. *Tijdschrift voor Indische Taal-, Land- en Volkenkunde* 29: 555–81.

Seidlitz, Eric. 2007. 'Duano: A First Look at its Phonology.' In *Reflections in Southeast Asian seas: Essays in Honour of Professor James T. Collins*, Book II, ed. Chong Shin, Karim Harun, and Yabit Alas, 23–49. Pontianak: STAIN Pontianak Press.

Skeat, Walter William and Charles Otto Blagden. 1906. *Pagan Races of the Malay Peninsula*. London: Macmillan and Co.

Skeat, Walter William and H.N. Ridley. 1900. 'The Orang Laut of Singapore.' *Journal of the Straits Branch of the Royal Asiatic Society* 33–34: 247–50.

Smedal, Olaf H. 1987. *Lom-Indonesian-English and English-Lom Wordlists*. (NUSA, 28/29.) Jakarta: Universitas Atma Jaya.

———. 1989. *Order and Difference: An Ethnographic Study of Orang Lom of Bangka, West Indonesia*. Occasional Papers in Social Anthropology, 19. Oslo: Department of Social Anthropology, University of Oslo.

Smith, Sydney, MacVey Napier, and William Empson. 1814. 'History and Languages of the Indian Islands (Review of Marsden's Grammar and Dictionary of the Malayan Language).' *The Edinburgh Review or Critical Journal* 23 (45): 151–89.

Sopher, David E. 1977. *The Sea Nomads; A Study Based on the Literature of the Maritime Boat People of Southeast Asia*. Singapore: National Museum.

Spriggs, Matthew T.J. 2011. 'Archaeology and the Austronesian Expansion: Where Are We Now?' *Antiquity* 85: 510–28.

Steinhauer, Hein. 2008. 'On the Development of Urak Lawoi' Malay.' *Wacana* 10 (1): 117–43.

Suwardi. 1993. 'Bahasa Melayu Suku Asli di Riau: Satu Tinjauan Linguistik Historis Komparatif.' [Indigenous Malay Tribes in Riau: A Comparative Historical Linguistic Review]. *Dewan Bahasa* 37 (2):128–47.

Verheijen, Jilis A.J. 1986. *The Sama/Bajau Language in the Lesser Sunda Islands*. (Pacific Linguistics: Series D, 70.) Canberra: Research School of Pacific and Asian Studies, Australian National University.

Wheatley, Paul. 1961. *The Golden Khersonese: Studies in the Historical Geography of the Malay Peninsula before AD 1500*. Kuala Lumpur: University of Malaya Press.

White, Walter Grainge. 1922. *The Sea Gypsies of Malaya: An Account of the Nomadic Mawken People of the Mergui Archipelago with a Description of their Ways of Living, Customs, Habits, Boats, Occupations*. London: Seeley, Service & Co.

Wilensky, Julie. 2002. *The Magical Kunlun and 'Devil Slaves': Chinese Perceptions of Dark-skinned People and Africa Before 1500*. Sino-Platonic Papers No. 122. Department of Asian and Middle Eastern Studies, University of Pennsylvania.

Yesner, David R. 1980. 'Maritime Hunter-gatherers: Ecology and Prehistory.' *Current Anthropology* 21: 727–50.

Yusof, Mohhamed Sharifudin. 2006. 'Obsolesensi dan Kenazakan Bahasa Orang Melayu Proto; Kajian Sosiologi Bahasa Terhadap Dialek Duano dan Dialek Kanaq di Johor.' PhD thesis, Universiti Kebangsaan Malaysia.

Zacot, Francois. 1978. 'The Voice of the Bajo People.' In *Proceedings: Second International Conference on Austronesian Linguistics*, Vol. 1: *Western Austronesian*, ed. S.A. Wurm and L. Carrington, 665–78. Pacific Linguistics, Series C, no. 61, Canberra: The Australian National University Research School of Pacific Studies.

7

A Genomic Perspective of the Origin and Dispersal of the Bajau Sea Nomads in Indonesia

Pradiptajati Kusuma, Nicolas Brucato, Murray P. Cox, Chandra Nuraini, Thierry Letellier, Philippe Grangé, Herawati Sudoyo and François-Xavier Ricaut

INTRODUCTION

Since the post-glacial coastline stabilised around 8,000 years ago, south-eastern Sunda and north-western Sahul have developed into a maritime region today called Insular Asia or Island Southeast Asia (ISEA), a region encompassing more than 25,000 islands (Voris 2000). From around 4,000 years before present (BP), the development of long distance seafaring technologies placed ISEA at the heart of new maritime corridors that crossed vast swaths of two oceans: the Indian Ocean to the west and the Pacific Ocean to the east (Beaujard 2012a, 2012b; Fuller et al. 2011; Lawler 2014). As new trade routes linked East Africa, South Asia, the islands of Southeast Asia, Australia, Melanesia and Polynesia, the Indo-Pacific region became one of the first regions where maritime networks connected far distant continents, thus initiating one of the world's earliest proto-globalisation processes (Beaujard 2012a, 2012b). These cultural, trading and population exchanges were, and still are, based on a strong network of maritime interactions (Bulbeck 2008; Nuraini 2008; Solheim et al. 2006; Stacey 2007). At its inception, this network likely stimulated the emergence of sea-oriented peoples, including sea nomads, which played such an important role in the development and structuring of population interactions in the Indo-Pacific region.

Several human groups in ISEA have long maintained a sea-oriented way of life, often based on fishing (maritime hunter-gatherers) and facilitators of inter-regional trade. Most of these groups are still connected to a land-based homeland territory, with the exception of the Sama Bajau (hereafter called the Bajau) (Blust 2007; Nuraini 2008). The main other sea nomad groups include the Moken, an Austronesian-speaking group located in peninsular Burma and southern Thailand, and the Urak Lawoi, a Malay-speaking population based around the islands of southern Thailand. The Bugis, an Austronesian speaking group originating in southern Sulawesi in eastern Indonesia, are still famous seafarers and maritime transporters (Hogan and Pattemore 1988; Larish 1999; Pelras 1997) although they cannot be classified as sea nomads. Unlike the Moken and Urak Lawoi, the Bajau do not have any clear ancestral homeland, and despite several hypotheses, their geographic origin remains unknown (Nuraini 2008; Sopher 1977).

The Bajau currently number approximately 1.1 million people, who live in numerous scattered hamlets and villages along the coasts across the Indonesian archipelago, as well as Sabah (Malaysia) and the southern Philippines (Sulu Archipelago and south-western Mindanao). The largest community, with 350,000 individuals, is located in Sabah. In Indonesia, the Bajau presence extends over a wide geographical area, from Kangean archipelago (near Madura, East Java) as the most western settlement, to coastal Sulawesi, the Maluku Islands and the Lesser Sunda Islands of Lombok, Sumba and Flores to the east. Some villages have even recently been identified on the northern coast of the Indonesian Papua province (Nuraini 2008) (Figure 7.1). The Bajau are the only minority group in ISEA that is so widely dispersed.

Some distant Bajau communities know of each other's existence (for instance, the Bajau from Sabah are aware of Bajau populations in Sulawesi, although they do not have family links), but these connections are not universal (for instance, the Sabah Bajau do not know of Bajau in the Lesser Sunda Islands). Nevertheless, interactions still take place at a regional level (e.g., between Kangean Island and South Sulawesi Bajau, or between East and North Kalimantan and the Sulu Archipelago). Notably, the geographic distribution of Bajau communities overlaps a zone of extraordinary marine biodiversity, and unsurprisingly, Bajau villages were historically situated near coral reefs.

The activities of the Bajau are played out at the 'maritime frontier', defined by Nagatsu (2013) as a socio-ecological space where a minority group can exploit and trade maritime resources, while avoiding pressure from central authorities. The Bajau economy has been based on exploiting marine resources—including fish, tortoise shell and trepang or sea cucumber—at least since the seventeenth century (Nuraini 2008; Stacey 2007). However, the Bajau almost certainly have an older presence in the region. Historically, Bajau fishers and/or seamen were associated with Bugis traders and/or ship owners. They were well known for travelling with their families, even on long distance journeys. Before European sailors began venturing into Southeast Asia, the Bajau were involved in long distance maritime trading networks reaching as far as New Guinea and northern Australia (Nuraini 2008; Stacey 2007). Some scholars have even suggested that the Bajau may have mediated westward dispersals into the Indian Ocean, perhaps

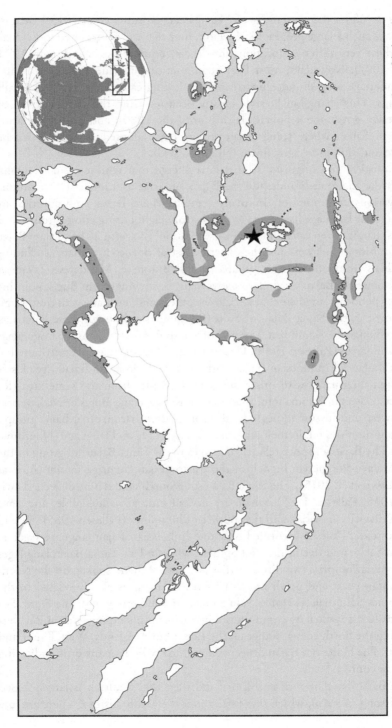

Figure 7.1 Geographic distribution of Bajau communities in Island Southeast Asia (dark grey) and the Kendari population in south-western Sulawesi (black star).

playing a role in the settlement of Madagascar (Kusuma et al. 2015). Because this spans such a large geographical region, they may have integrated individuals from these very different locations into their communities (Macknight 1973; Stacey 2007). Nowadays, most Bajau communities are sedentary, even if they still undertake long distance boat travel for fishing campaigns, trade or family meetings. This change in lifestyle mostly occurred from the 1950s, driven by Indonesian government policies lasting until the 1980s, and probably started earlier in Sabah where some Bajau groups have adopted an entirely inland lifestyle and shifted to agriculture (Nuraini 2008).

Sociological and linguistic studies have shown that remote insular regions, such as the Kangean Islands, use the Bajau language as a lingua franca among their various communities. In many regions where Bajau communities are present, their language has mixed with those of neighbouring ethnic groups, in a process that has been called 'maritime creolisation' (Nagatsu 2013). Many Bajau communities in Sulawesi and the eastern coast of Borneo are mixed, including individuals from other ethnic groups (Bugis, Butonese, Mandarese, Javanese, etc.). Indonesian Bajau vocabulary shows many borrowings from Bugis, pointing to a long period of language contact. On the other hand, no loanwords from Bugis are known in the Sama Bajau of Sulu (Philippines), although these languages have exchanged a significant amount of vocabulary with Tausug, a language from Mindanao (Pallesen 1985). Unsurprisingly, Tausug has not contributed to the vocabulary of Indonesian Bajau. Although the Indonesian Bajau live closely and often intermarry with other indigenous peoples from the same area (for instance, Dayak in Kalimantan, Madurese in Kangean and Bugis or Makassarese in Sulawesi) and are sometimes located at some distance from other Bajau groups, these communities retain their sea-oriented way of life and language (Noorduyn 1991). The Bajau all speak related languages in the Sama Bajau subgroup of the West Malayo-Polynesian branch of the Austronesian language family (Adelaar 2005; Lewis et al. 2015). The Sama Bajau subgroup includes nine dialects (Lewis et al. 2015; Pallesen 1985), which are not all mutually intelligible, and have highest diversity in Sabah and the southern Philippines (Pallesen 1985). Due to a lack of data, Pallesen identified only one Indonesian Bajau language (against three in Sabah and five in the Philippines), while in fact, Sama Bajau languages in Indonesia comprise two different dialects. One of them, spoken on the North Kalimantan coast and north coast of North Sulawesi, is closely related to the Philippines Sulu dialects (Inner Sulu Sama and Southern Sama).The Flores Sea Bajau dialect is spoken by communities in Sulawesi (including Tomini Bay, but excluding the north coast), Kangean, the Lesser Sunda Islands, West Timor and Maluku. The Flores Sea Bajau dialect contains many Bugis loanwords, indicating extensive contact.

The Bajau have no written history and their oral tradition is largely based on epic song (*iko iko*), which says little about their early history. There are rare records from European sailors/explorers from the sixteenth century onwards that connect Bajau with the Makassar and Bugis kingdoms in South Sulawesi (Nuraini 2008). In addition, there is indirect evidence for a presence of Bajau in regions other than southern Sulawesi earlier than the sixteenth century. These mainly rely on linguistic evidence and oral tradition (such as the *iko iko*), and suggest that the Bajau may have settled the Sulu Archipelago in the southern Philippines by the thirteenth century to control the northern spice route to China (Blust 2007). Their earlier movements remain essentially unknown. Nevertheless, five hypotheses have been proposed to explain the different possible origins of the Bajau and their diaspora (Nuraini 2008; Sopher 1977). The hypotheses below describe five different regions—some mentioned in the oral history of the Bajau—and may reflect the locations visited during later trading activities, rather than their actual places of origin (Nuraini 2008). Briefly, the proposed scenarios are:

(i) The Johore princess hypothesis (oral tradition), which locates the origin of the Bajau in the Malay peninsula near the Riau-Lingga Archipelago (Sopher 1977).

(ii) The Sulu Archipelago hypothesis, which places the origin of the Bajau in the southern Philippines. The highest Bajau linguistic diversity is found there, indicating that they settled there centuries ago, although a Philippine origin can now be ruled out (Pallesen 1985).

(iii) The western hypothesis (oral tradition), which suggests an origin in India or Arabia.

(iv) The Pigafetta hypothesis from 1521, which places the origin of the Bajau in northwest Borneo (Brunei) (Nuraini 2008).

(v) The southeast Borneo/Barito origin, based on modern linguistic evidence (Blust 2007).

Of all five hypotheses, the southeast Borneo hypothesis (hypothesis v) seems most well supported by multiple lines of evidence, including linguistic, historical and paleo-environmental data, as summarised by Blust (2007). In this hypothesis, the ancestors of the Bajau once inhabited the coastal regions of south-eastern Borneo where a gulf previously extended 100 kilometres further inland (Van Bemmelen 1949; Hall 2017). The Bajau dispersal may have been stimulated by contact with the Malay kingdom of Śrīvijaya from the seventh century onwards, leading the Bajau to play a key role in the spice trade from eastern Indonesia through the southern Philippines to Borneo. Similar causes may have also triggered the dispersal of southeast Barito language speakers from southeast Borneo, causing them to settle on Madagascar (Brucato et al. 2016; Kusuma et al. 2016a). Building on Blust's hypothesis of a southeast Borneo/Barito origin, Nuraini (2008) suggested that the Bajau may have moved up the east coast of Borneo in the eleventh century before settling in the southern Philippines and northeast Borneo in the thirteenth to fourteenth centuries, later pushing southward to southern Sulawesi before the fall of the Makassar kingdom in 1669 triggered yet another dispersal further south into the Lesser Sunda Islands and up the east coast of Sulawesi. However, this hypothesis has not been tested, as no archaeological or genetic studies have yet been performed.

Genetic studies on sea nomad populations from Southeast Asia are scarce. One study analysed the mitochondrial DNA (mtDNA) of sea nomad Moken from southern Thailand, showing that they mixed with neighbouring indigenous populations (Dancause et al. 2009), a group of traditionally boat-dwelling nomadic foragers, remain speculative despite previous examinations from linguistic, sociocultural and genetic perspectives. Kusuma et al. (2015) conducted a study of the mtDNA and paternal Y chromosomes of Bajau sea nomads from Sulawesi. The only study of autosomal DNA is preliminary, with a discussion restricted to potential implications for the Malagasy settlement (Pierron et al. 2014). Bajau genetic history deserves to be investigated to better understand their origin, admixture with regional groups, and their broader biological influence across ISEA.

Here, we summarise genetic analyses performed on 27 Bajau individuals from the Kendari region of south-eastern Sulawesi, who self-identify and are identified by others as Bajau. We report uniparental (mtDNA and the Y chromosome) markers, together with over 700,000 autosomal markers, which were studied to better understand the origins and genetic structure of the Kendari Bajau. This study specifically aims to:

(i) Investigate the genetic diversity of the Bajau in eastern Sulawesi and thereby place them within the wider genetic diversity of ISEA.
(ii) Determine whether the genetic diversity of the Bajau reflects maritime creolisation, as suggested from socio-ethnological work.
(iii) Help to disentangle the various hypotheses regarding the geographic origin of the Bajau.

MATERIAL AND METHODS

POPULATION SAMPLES

All samples analysed in this study were collected with informed consent from unrelated individuals. Subjects were surveyed for language affiliation, current residence, familial birthplace and a short genealogy of four generations to establish regional ancestry. A total of 27 DNA samples were analysed from the sea nomad Bajau living in Kendari Province of south-eastern Sulawesi, Indonesia. The collection and use of these samples were approved by the Research Ethics Commission of the University of Kendari. Data for additional Indonesian and regional populations were included from published and unpublished sources (see Kusuma et al. 2015 and Kusuma et al. 2016a for a full description). The complete regional dataset comprises 2,841 and 2,095 individuals for mtDNA and Y chromosome analyses, respectively, and 2,183 individuals from 61 populations for analyses of autosomal markers.

DNA EXTRACTION, SEQUENCING AND GENOTYPING

Saliva samples were collected using the Oragene DNA Collection kit (http://dnagenotek.com) and DNA was extracted using the manufacturer's standard protocol. Genetic analyses were conducted on mtDNA, Y chromosome and autosomal markers. The mtDNA hyper-variable region I was sequenced using primers detailed in a previous publication (Kusuma et al. 2015), together with paternal lineages analysed using 96 binary markers on the Y chromosome. Genome-wide autosomal genotypes were screened using the Illumina Human Omni Express-24 v.1.0 Bead Chip (Illumina Inc., San Diego, CA, USA), which surveys 730,525 single nucleotide polymorphism (SNP) markers spaced regularly across the genome (Kusuma et al. 2016a).

STATISTICAL ANALYSIS

Uniparental genetic data were analysed by calculating pairwise F_{ST} distances between Indonesian and other regional populations from haplogroup frequency data using Arlequin v.3.5. Multidimensional scaling (MDS) from F_{ST} values based on mtDNA and Y chromosome haplogroup frequencies was performed to visualise inter-population relationships.

Autosomal data were computed in ADMIXTURE v.1.23 (Alexander et al. 2009) to estimate the profile of individual genomic ancestries using maximum likelihood (components $2 \geq K \leq 20$). Ten replicates were run at each value of K with different random seeds, then merged and assessed for clustering quality using CLUMPP v.1.1.2 (Jakobsson and Rosenberg 2007). A cross-validation value was calculated to determine the optimal number of genomic components (here, K = 15). Gene flow between populations was investigated using two different approaches: (i) SNP frequencies analysed using TreeMix v.1.12 (Pickrell and Pritchard 2012), with blocks of 200 SNPs to account for linkage disequilibrium and migration edges added sequentially until the model explained 99% of the variance (the TreeMix outputs in Newick format were visualised with FigTree v.1.4.2); and (ii) haplotype sharing using the Refined IBD algorithm of Beagle v.4.0 visualised with Cytoscape v.3.2.1 (Shannon et al. 2003) to estimate the total number of shared genetic fragments (logarithm of odds ratio > 3) between each pair of individuals. Reconstructing haplotype information (i.e. determining linkage between different polymorphisms) was performed using SHAPEIT v.2 (Delaneau et al. 2013). The maps were generated with the Global Mapper v.15 software. Networks lines were generated by Cytoscape v.3.2.1.

Haplotype 'painting' with Chromopainter v.2 (Lawson et al. 2012) was performed to define each cluster of populations as either a target or donor/

surrogate, according to the anthropological question addressed. Mutation rate and effective population size parameters were first estimated with an Expectation-Maximization algorithm running Chromopainter on all 22 autosomes for the entire dataset with ten iterations (Lawson et al. 2012). The weighted average of these parameters, according to the SNP coverage of each chromosome and the number of individuals, was then used to compute the chromosomal painting. Once defined, the Bajau cluster was defined as the target, and the other clusters as surrogates. Population structure of the dataset was evaluated using the fineSTRUCTURE v.2.07 package (Lawson et al. 2012) after 100,000 MCMC iterations. The painted chromosomes obtained for each cluster were used in GLOBETROTTER v.1.0 (Hellenthal et al. 2014) to estimate the ratios and dates of potential admixture events. Co-ancestry curves were estimated with and without standardisation via a 'NULL' individual, and consistency between each estimated parameter was checked. Bootstrap re-samplings ($n = 100$) were calculated to estimate the P value of the admixture events (considering the 'NULL' individual), as well as to generate 95% confidence interval for the dates (without the 'NULL' individual). The 'best-guess' admixture scenario given by GLOBETROTTER is reported.

Table 7.1 Frequency of Bajau haplogroups for (left) mtDNA and (right) the Y chromosome.

Haplogroups	Frequency	Geographic origin
B4a	0,0741	MA
B4c1b	0,0741	MA
B5a	0,037	MA
B4a4	0,0741	MA
M73	0,037	MA
R22	0,037	MA
X	0,037	MA
Q1	0,0741	MA
B4a1a1	0,037	Taiw
E1a	0,0741	Taiw
F1a	0,037	Taiw
F1a3	0,0741	Taiw
M7b1a1i	0,1481	Taiw
M7c1a4a	0,0741	Taiw
M7c1a4a	0,1111	Taiw

Note:
MA: Mainland Asian origin; Taiw: Out of Taiwan origin; WE: Western Eurasian origin

Haplogroups		Frequency	Geographic origin
C*	C-RPS4Y*	0,037	SEA
KxLT	K-M526*	0,2222	SEA
O1a	O-M119*	0,037	SEA
O3	O-M122*	0,037	SEA
C1c	C-M38*	0,2222	SEA
O3a2	O-P201*	0,0741	SEA
O3a2b	O-M7	0,037	SEA
M1a	M-186	0,0741	SEA
R*	M-207*	0,1481	WE
T1a	T-M70	0,0741	WE
L1a	L-M76	0,037	WE

Note:
SEA: Southeast Asian origin; WE: Western Eurasian origin

RESULTS AND DISCUSSION

THE KENDARI BAJAW ARE A GENETICALLY DISTINCT POPULATION

Uniparental loci markers (mtDNA and Y chromosome) reveal high genetic diversity in the Kendari Bajau (H_{mtDNA} = 0.954 + 0.020, $H_{Y\,chromosome}$ = 0.855 + 0.043), falling in the upper range of values compared to other ISEA populations (HUGO Pan-Asian SNP Consortium 2009; Karafet et al. 2010; Mörseburg et al. 2016; Tumonggor et al. 2013). This suggests limited effects of genetic drift in this group and hence large effective population sizes, perhaps driven by exogamous marriages. The uniparental lineages include many major Asian haplogroups (Table 7.1), in common with most other populations in ISEA (Karafet et al. 2010; Soares et al. 2016; Tumonggor et al. 2013). For instance, the high frequency of mtDNA haplogroups M7b1a and M7c1a, together with Y chromosome haplogroups C-M38 and K*-M526, are commonly found in many Austronesian-speaking populations. Such a diverse array of haplogroups also hints that the Bajau may have integrated many genetic influences, perhaps reflecting the social process of creolisation suggested by Nagatsu (2013).

Solely from a uniparental lineage perspective, the high maternal and paternal genetic diversity of the Kendari Bajau implies that it may be complex to define the Bajau as a homogeneous population (see Lawson et al. 2012 for details). We therefore turned to autosomal DNA data to test whether Bajau individuals are more similar to each other than to other regional groups, or whether the term Bajau should instead be viewed more as a 'label'; an 'accommodative ethnic identity' of individuals sharing a common culture or language but constituting genetically diverse individuals (Nagatsu 2013). After reconstructing haplotype information (i.e., determining linkages between different polymorphisms), we used fineSTRUCTURE analysis to define the population genetic structure of our regional dataset. Like most Southeast Asian groups, the Bajau do form a distinct genetic unit that differs statistically from other ethnic groups (posterior probability of 100%; Figure 7.2). Therefore, although the Bajau culture tends to assimilate individuals from diverse origins (Nagatsu 2013; Nuraini 2008), this phenomenon must be gradual, taking place over sufficiently long time periods to create a shared genetic Bajau identity. The common culture of the Bajau from Kendari is therefore matched by a common genetic profile.

The diversity of the Kendari Bajau nevertheless falls into the wider ISEA genetic landscape. Genetic distances between Indonesian populations were estimated using F_{ST} for both mtDNA and the Y chromosome. MDS analysis of these genetic distances places the Bajau broadly at the centre of other regional populations (Figure 7.3). Indeed, the Bajau act as a junction between a cluster of populations from western Indonesia and eastern Indonesia, corresponding to the geographical location of this particular Bajau community in Sulawesi, central Indonesia. It is therefore not surprising that the closest populations to

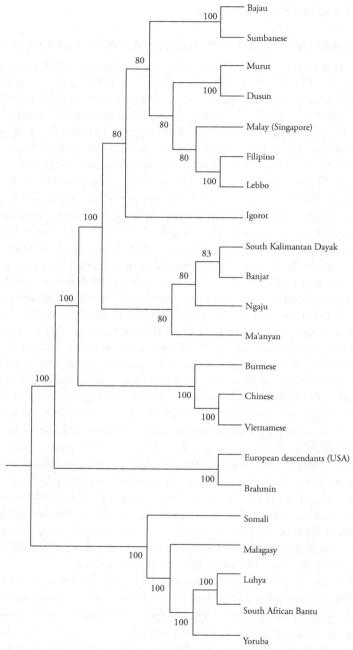

Figure 7.2 Phylogenetic analysis with fineSTRUCTURE showing that the Kendari Bajau (Sulawesi) cluster with populations from Sumba (eastern Indonesia), the Philippines and North Borneo.

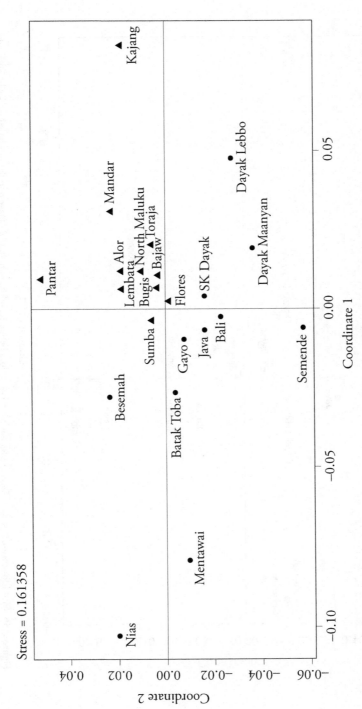

Figure 7.3a Multidimensional scaling (MDS) plot showing F_{ST} values between Indonesian and Malagasy populations based on mtDNA and haplogroup frequencies. Western Indonesian populations are shown by triangles; eastern Indonesian populations are shown by circles.

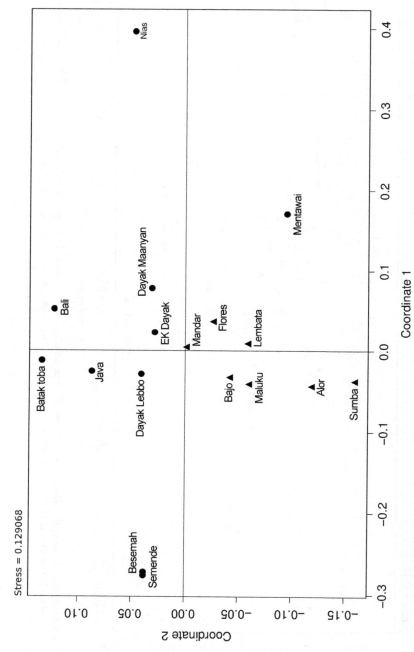

Figure 7.3b Multidimensional scaling (MDS) plot showing F_{ST} values between Indonesian and Malagasy populations based on Y-chromosome haplogroup frequencies. Western Indonesian populations are shown by triangles; eastern Indonesian populations are shown by circles.

this Bajau group from Kendari are other populations from Sulawesi, such as the Bugis and Mandar, followed by populations from the Maluku and Lesser Sunda Islands. The Bajau consequently carry genetic lineages belonging to at least two genetically distinct areas of ISEA, bisected by the Wallace Line (Lipson et al. 2014; Tumonggor et al. 2013; Xu et al. 2012). This theoretical division, represented physically by the Makassar Strait, separates the Indonesian archipelago into two biogeographical areas distinct in their fauna and flora. It also broadly marks a human genetic division, notable for more Papuan-like lineages in eastern Indonesian populations and more Mainland Southeast Asian (MSEA)-like lineages in western Indonesia. The sea nomad culture of the Bajau in south-western Sulawesi places them in contact with regional groups with quite different genomic ancestries, thus breaking the influence of Wallace's line and creating a genetic patrimony that places the Kendari Bajau community at the epicentre of Island Southeast Asian genetic diversity.

MULTIPLE GENETIC ANCESTRIES REFLECT THE HISTORY OF THE BAJAW

Through their mobile maritime way of life, Bajau sea nomad groups acted as a regional link between populations with different genomic backgrounds. This is reflected in a high proportion of Asian uniparental haplogroups (93% of maternal lineages and 74% of paternal lineages), denoting both their probable ancestry, as well as frequent contact with other MSEA and ISEA groups. A substantial proportion of this diversity has Papuan connections, as represented by mtDNA haplogroup Q1 (7.4% of Bajau maternal lineages; Table 7.1). Links to the Indian subcontinent also occur, as noted by the presence of Y chromosome haplogroups L1a, T1a and R* (26% of Bajau paternal lineages; Table 7.1). At least some of these South Asian genetic lineages may have been acquired through intermediary groups, in this case Indianised populations on the western Indonesian islands of Sumatra, Java and Bali. It is striking that, while the Bajau were clearly recipients of gene flow from far distant groups, these genetic inputs appear to be sex-biased. Indeed, no trace of paternal Papuan lineages or maternal South Asian lineages were identified. How strong and widespread this pattern of admixture is among different Bajau communities remains unclear and argues for further investigation.

To further study these diverse contributions, we decomposed the autosomal genomic diversity of the Kendari Bajau, together with regional groups, using the ADMIXTURE software. Bajau population genetic components look relatively similar to other eastern Indonesian populations (e.g., Toraja, Sumba, Kambera and Manggarai). The most probable model assigns Bajau diversity to two main components: Austronesian and Papuan, with two other minor Austronesian components.The Austronesian influence represents the largest part of the Bajau genome (~50%) and traces to three Austronesian ancestries (Kusuma et al. 2016a) currently preserved in the Ma'anyan population of Southeast

Borneo, the Kankanaey, a population from the northern Philippines, and the Mentawai group (Sumatra), which has an Austronesian genetic component that subsequently differentiated due to genetic drift in this small population. These three ancestries are common to many Austronesian-speaking populations and may reflect different dispersal patterns or subsequent genetic drift among expanding Austronesian populations (Kusuma et al. 2016a). A second major genetic influence, already identified from uniparental data, is Papuan ancestry, representing an average of ~15% of the Bajau genome. This Papuan component is typical in eastern Indonesia, such as the Maluku and Lesser Sunda Islands, where it commonly occurs at around 30 per cent frequency. The presence of this component in the Bajau fits with a TreeMix analysis (Figure 7.4), which reveals frequent gene flow of genetic lineages associated with New Guinea and eastern Indonesia. Although traces of South Asian ancestry are more difficult to identify in the ADMIXTURE analysis, TreeMix clearly detects this gene flow, likely from southern India, in addition to the Austronesian and Papuan contributions noted from other methods (Figure 7.4). The South Asian gene flow into the Bajau, driven by men rather than women as shown by uniparental data, is rather small compared to the other components, but nevertheless indicates ultimate contact with India, and perhaps more likely, proximate contact with Indianised kingdoms in western Indonesia (Kusuma et al. 2016b) notably the Near East and South Asia (Indian sub-continent). Trade has flowed between the Indian sub-continent and the Indonesian archipelago since at least the first millennium BCE (Calo 2014; Lawler 2014), later leading to the creation of Indianised kingdoms in Indonesia, such as Śrīvijaya and Majapahit.

These various genetic inputs into the Bajau gene pool were examined using Identity-By-Descent (IBD) information calculated with RefinedIBD. Haplotype sharing between pairs of individuals signals common ancestry, and the length of shared haplotypes reflects recent contact. The average IBD sharing between a Bajau individual and another individual in our dataset can be visualised for different length thresholds (Figure 7.5). A low IBD threshold (20 cM or greater) (Figure 7.5A) identifies all common shared ancestries, both old and recent. At this threshold, Kendari Bajau individuals show clear connections to all ISEA populations, reflecting their common interactions with most regional groups. Links were also identified with MSEA individuals and Malagasy, reflecting the settlement of Madagascar from Indonesia. While Malagasy appear to have originated from the Banjar population of southeast Borneo (Brucato et al. 2016), these wider connections partially implicate a role for the sea nomad Bajau in the settlement of Madagascar (Kusuma et al. 2015). At higher IBD thresholds (Figure 7.5B–D), which reflect more recent connections, these long distance linkages disappear, while connections to the Lesser Sunda Islands, Philippines and southeast Borneo are preserved

(Figure 7.5C–D). Interestingly, at the highest IBD thresholds (Figure 7.5D), before external connections disappear entirely, clear links remain with the two Austronesian speaking populations mentioned above, the Kankanaey of the Philippines and the Ma'anyan of Borneo, but also the Dayak Ngaju of south-eastern Borneo. While the first two groups may simply reflect the strong influence of Austronesian genomic components in ISEA, the connection between the Bajau and the Ngaju has greater implications for Bajau ancestry. Ethno-linguistic studies (Blust 2007) suggest linguistic affinities between the Dayak Ngaju in south-eastern Borneo and Bajau languages, thus potentially supporting an origin of the Bajau in Borneo.

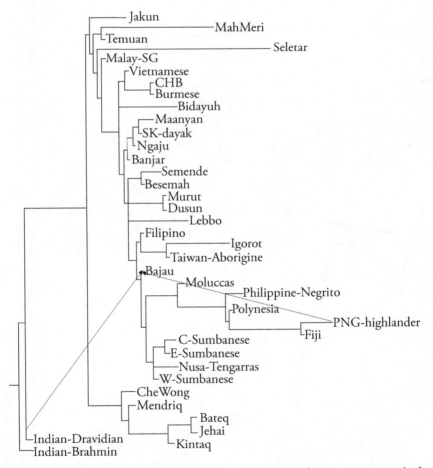

Figure 7.4 TreeMix analysis on autosomal genome-wide SNP data showing migration nodes from Papua New Guinea Highlander and South Asian groups to the Kendari Bajau population, with migration weights of 13% and 9%, respectively.

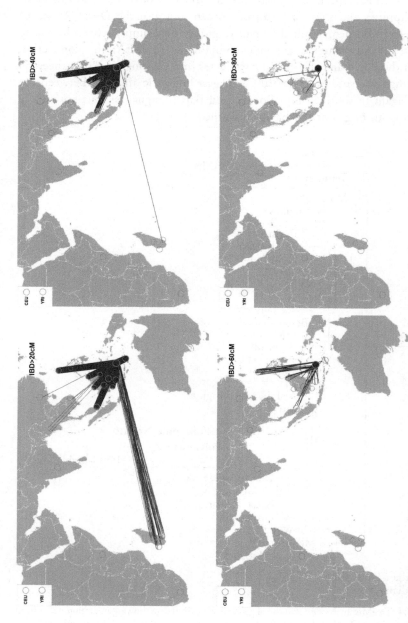

Figure 7.5 Shared Identity-By-Descent (IBD) fragments between pairs of individuals in Southeast Asia, using nine filtering thresholds representing old connections (20 cM) to recent connections (80 cM). Top left: Figure B; Top right: Figure C; Bottom left: Figure A; Bottom right: Figure D.

To disentangle the genetic ancestries of the Kendari Bajau further, we reconstructed admixture using GLOBETROTTER (Table 7.2). The two main contributions already suggested are clearly identified again: South Asia (likely through Indianised kingdoms in western Indonesia) and the Lesser Sunda Islands (Sumbanese) (surrogate 1); and the Philippines, Malaysia and Borneo (Banjar and Ngaju) (surrogate 2) (Figure 7.5D). This again reinforces that the Bajau, as a sea nomad population and participant in the maritime trading network, are the product of interaction with far distant regions and culturally different populations. The admixture between these two components dates to 875 years BP (95% confidence interval: 800–1000 years BP) (Table 7.2), and the link to southern Borneo populations agrees with linguistic and anthropological evidence suggesting an origin of the Bajau in the Barito region of southeast Borneo, from which they dispersed around the end of the first millennium CE as a result of contact with the Malay kingdom of Śrīvijaya (Blust 2007).

The Kendari Bajau comprise a distinct genetic group, albeit one with numerous regional connections. The complexity of their genomic profile is a striking reflection of their past history, summarising major migratory and admixture events that led to the settlement of this particular Bajau group in southern Sulawesi. From the convergence of genetic and anthropological evidence, we postulate that the Bajau originated in south-eastern Borneo from a group close to the current Dayak Ngaju. Like the migration of Banjar ancestors to Madagascar following the arrival of the Malay people, a Malay influence may also have triggered—directly or indirectly—the beginning of the Bajau diaspora. Their sea-oriented way of life, their prime role in the maritime trading network and their location at the maritime frontier, placed the Bajau in contact with diverse populations, whose genomes left secondary traces. Whether this pattern holds for other Bajau communities beyond the Kendari remains to be tested. Nevertheless, we can provide tentative answers to the three research questions:

(i) The Bajau are a genetically distinct group with genetic influences from western and eastern Indonesia, and even beyond (South Asians and Papuans), reflecting sex-biased patterns of cultural interaction and trading that still need to be fully explained.

(ii) Genetic analyses provide support for the argument from socio-ethnological and linguistic studies that the Bajau result from 'maritime creolisation' (i.e., admixture).

(iii) Admixture patterns and molecular dating agree with linguistic and anthropological evidence in proposing an origin for the Bajau diaspora in south-eastern Borneo.

Table 7.2 Admixture sources showing the percentage of admixture for each population of interest with dates in generations and years before present (YBP). Bootstrap 95% confidence intervals are given in parentheses.

Target Group	Analysis	P	R^2	FQ_1	FQ_2	M	Best-guess	1-date (gen.)	1-date (YBP)	1-date Best Surrogate 1	1-date Best Surrogate 2
Bajau	Main	<0.01	0.946	0.882	0.998	0.22	One-date-multiway	35 (32–40)	875 (800–1000)	Sumbanese (23%)	Banjar (25%), Filipino (25%)
										Brahmin (12%)	Malay (23%), Ngaju (6%)
	Main.null	<0.01	0.953	0.96	0.999	0.22	One-date-multiway	47 (43–54)	1175 (1075–1350)	Sumbanese (27%)	Banjar (23%), Filipino (27%), Ngaju (8%)
										Brahmin (15%)	

ACKNOWLEDGEMENTS

The authors acknowledge support from the GenoToul bioinformatics facility of the GenopoleToulouse Midi Pyrénées, France. We also thank Patrice Gerard for his help in making the figures. This research was supported by the French ANR grant ANR-14-CE31-0013-01 (OCEOADAPTO) to François-Xavier Ricaut; the French Ministry of Foreign and European Affairs (French Archaeological Mission in Borneo (MAFBO) to François-Xavier Ricaut; a Rutherford Fellowship from the Royal Society of New Zealand (RDF-10-MAU-001) to Murray P. Cox and the French Embassy in Indonesia through its Cultural and Cooperation Services (Institut Français en Indonésie).

REFERENCES

Adelaar, K. Alexander. 2005. 'The Austronesian Languages of Asia and Madagascar: A Historical Perspective.' In *The Austronesian Languages of Asia and Madagascar*, ed. K.A. Adelaar and N. Himmelmann, 1–42. New York: Routledge.

Alexander, David Henry, John Novembre, and Kenneth Lange. 2009. 'Fast model-based estimation of ancestry in unrelated individuals.' *Genome Research* 19: 1655–64.

Beaujard, Philippe. 2012a. 'Les Mondes de l'Océan Indien.' Vol. 2: *L'océan Indien, au cœur des globalisations de l'Ancien Monde (7e-15e siècles)*. Paris, France: Armand Collin.

———. 2012b. 'Les Mondes de l'Océan Indien.' Vol. 1: *De la formation de l'État au premier système-monde afro-eurasien (4e millénaire av. J.-C.-6e siècle apr. J.-C.)*. Paris, France: Armand Collin.

Blust, Robert. 2007. 'The Linguistic Position of Sama-Bajaw.' *Studies in Philippine Languages and Cultures* 15: 73–114.

Brucato, Nicolas, Pradiptajati Kusuma, Murray P. Cox, Denis Pierron, Gludhug A. Purnomo, K. Alexander Adelaar, Toomas Kivisild, Thierry Letellier, Herawati Sudoyo, and François-Xavier Ricaut. 2016. 'Malagasy Genetic Ancestry Comes from an Historical Malay Trading Post in Southeast Borneo.' *Molecular Biology and Evolution* 33: 2396–400.

Bulbeck, David. 2008. 'An Integrated Perspective on the Austronesian Diaspora: The Switch from Cereal Agriculture to Maritime Foraging in the Colonisation of Island Southeast Asia.' *Australian Archaeology* 67: 31–52.

Calo, Ambra. 2014. 'Ancient trade between India and Indonesia.' *Science* 345: 1255.

Dancause, Kelsey Nidham, C. Wan Chan, Narumon H. Arunotai, and J. Koji Lum. 2009. 'Origins of the Moken Sea Gypsies Inferred from Mitochondrial Hypervariable Region and Whole Genome sequences.' *Journal of Human Genetics* 54: 86–93.

Delaneau, Olivier, Jean-François Zagury, and Jonathan Marchini. 2013. 'Improved Whole-chromosome Phasing for Disease and Population Genetic Studies.' *Nature Methods* 10: 5–6.

Fuller, Dorian Q., Nicole Boivin, Thomas Hoogervorst, and Robert Allaby. 2011. 'Across the Indian Ocean: The Prehistoric Movement of Plants and Animals.' *Antiquity* 85: 544–58.

Hall, Robert. 2017. 'Southeast Asia: New Views of the Geology of the Malay Archipelago.' *Annual Review of Earth and Planetary Sciences* 45: 331–58.

Hellenthal, Garett, George B.J. Busby, Gavin Band, James F. Wilson, Cristian Capelli, Daniel Falush, and Simon Myers. 2014. 'A Genetic Atlas of Human Admixture History.' *Science* 343: 747–51.

Hogan, David W. and Stephen W. Pattemore, 1988. *Urak Lawoi': Basic Structures and a Dictionary*. Department of Linguistics, Research School of Pacific Studies. Canberra: Australian National University.

HUGO Pan-Asian SNP Consortium. 2009. 'Mapping Human Genetic Diversity in Asia.' *Science* 326: 1541–5.

Jakobsson, Mattias and Noah A. Rosenberg. 2007. 'CLUMPP: A Cluster Matching and Permutation Program for Dealing with Label Switching and Multimodality in Analysis of Population Structure.' *Bioinformatics* 23: 1801–6.

Karafet, Tatiana M., Brian Hallmark, Murray P. Cox, Herawati Sudoyo, Sean Downey, John Stephen Lansing, and Michael F. Hammer, 2010. 'Major East–west Division Underlies Y Chromosome Stratification Across Indonesia.' *Molecular Biology and Evolution* 27: 1833–44.

Kusuma, Pradiptajati, Murray P. Cox, Denis Pierron, Harilanto Razafindrazaka, Nicolas Brucato, Laure Tonasso, H.L. Suryadi, Thierry Letellier, Helena Sudoyo, and François-Xavier Ricaut. 2015. 'Mitochondrial DNA and the Y Chromosome Suggest the Settlement of Madagascar by Indonesian Sea Nomad Populations.' *BMC Genomics* 16: 191.

Kusuma, Pradiptajati, Nicolas Brucato, Murray P. Cox, Denis Pierron, Harilanto Razafindrazaka, Alexander Adelaar, Herawati Sudoyo, Thierry Letellier, and François-Xavier Ricaut. 2016a. 'Contrasting Linguistic and Genetic Origins of the Asian Source Populations of Malagasy.' *Scientific Reports* 6: 26066.

Kusuma, Pradiptajati, Murray P. Cox, Nicolas Brucato, Herawati Sudoyo, Thierry Letellier, and François-Xavier Ricaut. 2016b. 'Western Eurasian Genetic Influences in the Indonesian Archipelago.' *Quaternary International* 416: 243–8.

Larish, Michael D. 1999. 'The Position of Moken and Moklen within the Austronesian Language Family.' PhD thesis. University of Hawai'i.

Lawler, Andrew. 2014. 'Sailing Sinbad's Seas.' *Science* 344: 1440–5.

Lawson, Daniel John, Garrett Hellenthal, Simon Myers, and Daniel Falush. 2012. 'Inference of Population Structure Using Dense Haplotype Data.' *PLOS Genetics* 8: e1002453.

Lewis, M. Paul, Gary F. Simons, and Charles D. Fennig, eds. 2015. *Ethnologue: Languages of the World*, 18th ed. Texas: SIL International.

Lipson, Mark, Po-Ru Loh, Nick Patterson, Priya Moorjani, Ying-Chin Ko, Mark Stoneking, Bonnie Berger, and David Reich. 2014. 'Reconstructing Austronesian Population History in Island Southeast Asia.' *Nature Communications* 5: 4689.

Macknight, Charles Campbell. 1973. 'The Nature of Early Maritime Trade: Some Points of Analogy from the Eastern Part of the Indonesian Archipelago.' *World Archaeology* 5: 198–208.

Mörseburg, Alexander, Luca Pagani, François-Xavier Ricaut, Bryndis Yngvadottir, Eadaoin Harney, Cristina Castillo, Tom Hoogervorst, Tiago Antao, Pradiptajati Kusuma, Nicolas Brucato, Alexia Cardona, Denis Pierron, Thierry Letellier, Joseph Wee, Syafiq Abdullah, Mait Metspalu, and Toomas Kivisild. 2016. 'Multi-layered Population Structure in Island Southeast Asians.' *European Journal of Human Genetics* 24 (11): 1605–11.

Nagatsu, Kazufumi. 2013. 'Persisting Maritime Frontiers and Multi-layered Networks in Wallacea.' Presented at the Asian Core Program Seminar, Kyoto, Japan.

Noorduyn, Jane. 1991. *A Critical Survey of Studies on the Languages of Sulawesi.* Leiden: University of Washington Press.

Nuraini, Chandra. 2008. 'Langue et Production de Récits d'une Communauté Bajaw des Îles Kangean (Indonésie).' PhD thesis. Université de La Rochelle, France.

Pallesen, A. Kemp. 1985. *Culture Contact and Language Convergence.* Manila, Philippines: Linguistic Society of the Philippines.

Pelras, Christian. 1997. *The Bugis.* Oxford: Wiley-Blackwell.

Pickrell, Joseph K. and Jonathan Pritchard. 2012. 'Inference of Population Splits and Mixtures from Genome-wide Allele Frequency Data.' *PLOS Genetics* 8: e1002967.

Pierron, Denis, Harilanto Razafindrazaka, Luca Pagani, François-Xavier Ricaut, Tiago Antao, Mélanie Capredon, Clément Sambo, Chantal Radimilahy, Jean-Aimée Rakotoarisoa, Roger M. Blench, Thierry Letellier, and Toomas Kivisild. 2014. 'Genome-wide Evidence of Austronesian–Bantu Admixture and Cultural Reversion in a Hunter-gatherer Group of Madagascar.' *Proceedings of the National Academy of Sciences of the United States of America* 111: 936–41.

Shannon, Paul, Andrew Markiel, Owen Ozier, Nitin S. Baliga, Jonathan T. Wang, Daniel Ramage, Nada Amin, Benno Schwikowski, and Trey Ideker. 2003. 'Cytoscape: A Software Environment for Integrated Models of Biomolecular Interaction Networks.' *Genome Research* 13: 2498–504.

Soares, Pedro A., Jean A.Trejaut, Teresa Rito, Bruno Cavadas, Catherine Hill, Ken Khong Eng, Maru Mormina, Andreia Brandão, Ross M. Fraser, Tse-Yi Wang, Jun-Hun Loo, Christopher Snell, Tsang-Ming Ko, António Amorim, Maria Pala, Vincent Macaulay, David Bulbeck, James F. Wilson, Leonor Gusmão, Luísa Pereira, Stephen Oppenheimer, Marie Lin, and Martin B. Richards. 2016. 'Resolving the Ancestry of Austronesian-speaking Populations.' *Human Genetics* 135: 309–26.

Solheim, Wilhelm G., David Bulbeck, and Amba Flavel. 2006. *Archaeology and Culture in Southeast Asia: Unraveling the Nusantao.* Quezon City, Philippines: University of Philippines Press.

Sopher, David E. 1977. *The Sea Nomads: A Study of the Maritime Boat People of Southeast Asia.* Singapore: National Museum.

Stacey, Natasha. 2007. *Boats to Burn: Bajaw Fishing Activity in the Australian Fishing Zone.* Canberra: ANU E-Press.

Tumonggor, Meryanne K., Tatiana M. Karafet, J. Stephen Lansing, Herawat Sudoyo, Michael F. Hammer, and Murray P. Cox. 2013. 'The Indonesian Archipelago: An Ancient Genetic Highway Linking Asia and the Pacific.' *Journal of Human Genetics* 58: 165–73.

Van Bemmelen, Reinout W. 1949. *The Geology of Indonesia.* Government Printing Office, Martinus Nijhoff, The Hague.

Voris, Harold K. 2000. 'Maps of Pleistocene Sea Levels in Southeast Asia: Shorelines, River Systems and Time Durations.' *Journal of Biogeography* 27: 1153–67.

Xu, Shuhua, Irene Pugach, Mark Stoneking, Manfred Kayser, and Li Jin. 2012. 'Genetic Dating Indicates that the Asian–Papuan Admixture through Eastern Indonesia Corresponds to the Austronesian Expansion.' *Proceedings of the National Academy of Sciences of the United States of America* 109: 4574–79.

8

Ship Construction and Navigation in the Early South China Seas

Roger Blench

INTRODUCTION

History is often about secondary effects; we can see evidence for migration or trade without necessarily understanding the technical means whereby these are achieved. Many more commentators can discuss the effects of social media than can understand the software and hardware by which these are facilitated. The impressive economic and political enterprise of maritime Southeast Asia would not have been possible without significant technical advances both in the construction of ships and the techniques of navigation.

The earliest Portuguese traders to enter Indonesian waters found to their surprise that they were confronted with ships larger than their own. Gaspar de Correia (1858–66), describing a naval battle against a 'junk' in the 1520s, found their opponents so heavy and well-defended that they could not immediately make headway against them. However, Ferrand (1919), in his recension of early Chinese texts concerning shipping, shows that already by the third century CE, the Chinese were encountering extremely large trading ships with as many as four sails, far larger than anything they could construct. It seems Chinese shipwrights learnt from this and by the Sung dynasty had begun to design ships which merged both Chinese and Southeast Asian constructional techniques. By the time of the Yuan (thirteenth century) their ships dominated trade in the South China Seas. All of this evidence points to a remarkable evolution of maritime technology indigenous to Island Southeast Asia (ISEA), which was far ahead of other naval traditions until the appearance of very large European vessels from the end of the sixteenth century.

Similarly with navigation; the techniques of crossing open ocean were evidently known in the Palaeolithic (Bulbeck this volume). A combination of stars, winds and currents must have been at the heart of early navigation. It is known that the Micronesians had a highly sophisticated knowledge of star positions. For ISEA, techniques are less well-documented. It is only by the time Chinese naval manuals and related maps began to be produced that we have a sense of the extent to which cartographic knowledge had advanced.

This chapter discusses the evidence for boat-building in the South China Sea, drawing on a variety of sources, notably archaeology, actual shipwrecks, but also iconography, ethnography and textual sources. The process where the earliest bamboo rafts developed into massive cargo ships is still only very partially known. The growing list of archaeological shipwrecks is gradually adding to our knowledge in this area. As the primary explorers of trade routes in the maritime world, sea nomads benefitted from advances in shipbuilding and navigation, just as they contributed knowledge of coastlines, reefs, winds and hazards to shipping. Without the advances described here, sea nomads such as the Orang Laut could not have existed in their present form.

NAVIGATION AND SHIPS FROM THE PALAEOLITHIC ONWARDS: INDIRECT EVIDENCE

THE DIFFUSION OF TRADE GOODS

The migrations of modern humans across large stretches of water in the Palaeolithic is incontrovertible evidence for the existence of some type of sophisticated water transport (Bednarik 1997). If modern humans could reach Australia by 65,000 BP either via Timor or the Halmahera-Papua route, this implies some open ocean capacity. Evidence for movement between islands in the Ryukyus goes back to 35,000 BP; in the Talaud Islands 20,000 BP (Ono, Soegondho and Yoneda 2010). Obsidian was being transported around Bismarcks as early as 20,000 BP. There is archaeological and genetic evidence for long-distance circulation between the Mainland and Island Southeast Asia in the early Holocene (Bulbeck this volume; O'Connor et al. this volume). Hung (2019) has argued that the South China coast was occupied by 'affluent fisher-foragers' until around 3000 BCE, which implies complex cross-straits movements before farming. Various lines of evidence point to thriving inter-island traffic in the South China Sea well before there is any direct evidence for boats and navigational expertise (Hung et al. 2007). The question therefore is where, when and how did the transition to the sophisticated watercraft recorded in the historic period take place?

Chinese records point clearly to the use of sailing rafts in the Taiwan Strait, but since these were described as used by the indigenous people to raid the mainland this was clearly an unfamiliar technology (Needham and Wang 1971: 393). It is plausible that these rafts developed into outriggers at the point where the Austronesians left the southern tip of Taiwan some 4,000 years ago, since the scope of their oceangoing voyages denote a major advance in boat construction technology. Mahdi (1999: 145) discusses the various hypotheses which have been advanced to model the evolution from rafts to open ocean vessels. At this point the Austronesian boats must have been some version of the outrigger, with both floats and sails, since not only do terms for these reconstruct in Proto-Malayopolynesian, but the Austronesians reached the Marianas shortly after this, requiring oceangoing capacities.

Horridge (1995: 146) summarises the construction of Austronesian boats as using the lashed-lug technique, where projecting perforated lugs are left in the dug-out base of the hull and on the additional planks sewn on to its sides. The descendants of these boats became the giant outriggers which enabled the conquest of the Pacific. However, within ISEA, technology developed in a different direction. Distances were shorter, larger cargo capacities were required, and it was necessary to easily return to the point of departure. A far more ancient technology, sewn planks, used for inland and coast boats, was adapted to much larger vessels and eventually the cargo ships which underwrote the rise of Srivijaya in the sixth century. Sewn planks were also known in the Pacific but never achieved the importance they had in the ISEA area. Horridge (1995: 146) points out that technologies such as the fixed mast, dowelling techniques, the quarter rudder and the trapezoid sail appear to have spread eastwards from the Indian Ocean into ISEA some 2,000 years ago, so it is likely the innovative aspects of ship construction represent the creative merger of two quite different traditions. Mahdi (1999: 153) characterises this as the encounter with 'Semitic shipping', hence the argument that this engendered a revolution in ship construction. These traditions effectively came to an end for large trading ships as soon as European shipbuilding techniques spread widely in the region (Manguin 1993b).

Figure 8.1 schematises the broad outline of the evolution of boat types in the South China Seas from the unknown forms of the Palaeolithic to those encountered by the first European mariners.

There is one curious exception to this model which is yet to be explained. Austronesian speakers on Taiwan today do not have outriggers, even though they must have once possessed them. However, the Yami, ancestral to almost all non-Formosan Austronesians, who live on Lanyu Island southwest of Taiwan proper, have extremely unusual boats (Figure 8.2). Their symmetrical high prows and sterns are made in the sewn plank tradition, and the larger specimens were paddled by up to 20 paddlers. The Yami were experienced pelagic fishers, but they could hardly have reached the Marianas in such vessels. Mahdi (1999: 167) notes that similar boat forms are found in Maluku and the Solomons, as well as being represented in rock art in Timor (Lape, O'Connor and Burningham 2007). So either this style of boat existed before outriggers spread and was displaced in most areas or else it was a parallel development, which spread with the early Austronesian dispersal and has gone out of use in most zones.

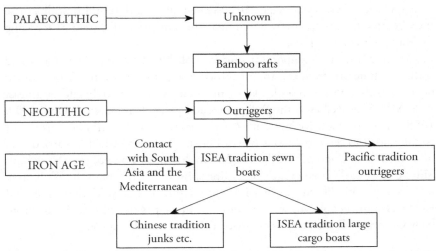

Figure 8.1 Schematic evolution of boat types in the South China Seas.

Figure 8.2 High-keel boats of the Yami on Lanyu Island (Photo credit: R. Blench).

BOAT SYMBOLISM

Another way to characterise the embeddedness of maritime culture in Southeast Asia is the widespread symbolism of boats. Manguin (1986), in a wide-ranging review of ship symbolism, points to the relationship between boat names and those of social units, such as the 'barangay' in the Philippines. Bonnemaison (1994) describes a similar equation on the island of Tanna in Vanuatu. Similarly, the Toraja in Northern Sulawesi were famous for their boat-shaped houses, which mimicked and even exaggerated the high prow and stern. Ironically, these then became transferred onto monuments in cemeteries (Figure 8.3) retracing the route of the log-coffins.

However, the most important link is probably the complex of boats and coffins in funerary contexts. Inhumations in dugout canoes, plank-built small boats or coffins made to look like them, occur widely in Mainland Southeast Asia (MSEA) as well as in the Philippines and parts of Indonesia (Mahdi 1999: 165ff). The common Malay term, *long*, appears both as 'coffin' and as a root compounded to refer to various types of boat, a polysemy which is carried over into Austroasiatic and Sino-Tibetan (Blench 2018). In Borneo, the Dayak built 'ships of the dead', large models of trading ships with a dragon or hornbill prow intended to symbolise the journey into the afterlife. In many Southeast Asia and Pacific islands, people are interred in caves in canoes or old boat hulls. From New Guinea to Tonga, tombs are shaped in the form of a canoe.

EVIDENCE FOR METHODS OF SHIP CONSTRUCTION

TEXTUAL

The most important sources we have for the construction of boats until European contact are Chinese records (Needham and Wang 1971). Unfortunately, most of these are late and much of the earlier history of construction is speculation. Needham and Wang (1971: 392) point out that some of the archaic vocabulary relating to ships does suggest a double-hull construction. If so, then the ultimate inspiration for the junk would have been an outrigger, though none are used on the Chinese coast today. However, indigenous Chinese traditions suggest that the development was from the raft (Needham and Wang 1971: 395).

The key occurrence for Chinese naval engineers was the encounter with the large cargo ships of ISEA, which developed the Chinese tradition by the end of the Song (tenth to eleventh centuries) (Lo 1955; Manguin 1984). By the eighth century, Chinese authors were describing the visits of the *kunlun bo*, or foreign ships, coming from Southeast Asia, carrying pilgrims (Manguin 1993a: 262). Chinese writers noted these ships, which could carry up to 700 passengers, had complex rigging that could be manipulated to increase their speed.

One of the important points of divergence between ISEA ships and the invigorated Chinese tradition was the use of iron nails. All of the ISEA vessels remained of the sewn plank type. According to Chinese records, Southeast Asian captains were afraid of nails, because if they became heated during battle they might set fire to the whole ship. Evidently this technique spread later in the medieval period as Manguin (2012: 613) notes that there are some 15 large shipwrecks recorded in Southeast Asian waters dated to between the fourteenth and seventeenth centuries, and all of these use some type of iron nail or clamp. The compartmentalised hull structure (i.e., bulkheads) ensuring that a vessel was

Figure 8.3 Toraja funerary monument, Waseput (Photo credit: R. Blench).

watertight, characteristic of vessels of Chinese construction, appears from the thirteenth century onwards (Heng 2018).

ARCHAEOLOGICAL

The waters of the South China Seas are rich in shipwrecks and their discovery and excavation has been stimulated by the recovery of their cargoes, often porcelain and other highly saleable goods. By definition, ships are mobile and therefore shipwrecks do not necessarily represent local shipbuilding traditions. Arab, Indian and Mediterranean wrecks have all been recovered from Southeast Asian waters. The ninth-century Phanom Surin shipwreck in Central Thailand is a remarkable example of the penetration of Mediterranean shipping to Southeast Asia during this period (Guy 2017). Manguin (1989, 1993a) reviews all the finds of shipwrecks to the date of the article with accompanying archaeological interpretation. More recent examples of shipwrecks in Southeast Asia include the Bakau wreck of Chinese origin (Flecker 2001) and the thirteenth-century Java Sea Wreck, which was an Indonesian ship carrying Chinese trade goods (Flecker 2003). Kimura (2016) is a monograph of archaeological finds of East Asian shipping, while the most recent conspectus can be found in Heng (2018).

ICONOGRAPHIC

Drawings, engravings and stone-carvings can also provide some information about ship construction techniques. Cave paintings in Eastern Indonesia point to evidence for a maritime culture some 2,000 years ago, although details of construction are obviously unclear (Lape et al. 2007; Ballard et al. 2003). The Dong Son culture bronze drums represent large canoes, although these were probably only for inland and coastal waters. For ISEA, the most widely reproduced images are the friezes at Borobudur on the island of Java, dated to around 850 CE. These illustrate a variety of boats, from a small bamboo raft apparently under threat from whales (Figure 8.4), to an inshore trading vessel (Figure 8.5), to a large oceangoing trader, such as must have been used in the Indian Ocean trade (Figure 8.6). It is very striking that both larger vessels still have outriggers despite their relatively large size, suggesting that stability was still a problem at this period.

Surprisingly, the most informative image Needham and Wang (1971: 404) could discover is very late, the drawing of a junk in the Liu Chhiu Kuo Chih Lüeh of 1757, which actually has a key naming the parts of the ship. By this time, all the features of the classic junk are in place. At about the same time, Japanese mariners were also taking an interest in the shipping of other nations. Figure 8.7 shows an eighteenth-century Japanese scroll painting, the *Tōsen no Zu* (日本語), which illustrates both Chinese junks and a Siamese trading ship with distinctive rigging and stern. This only serves to underline how problematic it still is to reconstruct the evolution of shipping in the South China Seas.

Figure 8.4 Sailing raft, Borobudur (Photo credit: R. Blench).

Figure 8.5 Coastal craft, Borobudur (Photo credit: R. Blench).

Figure 8.6 Large trading ship, Borobudur (Photo credit: R. Blench).

Figure 8.7 Siamese ship in Japanese scroll (Source: Matsura Historical Museum).

NAVIGATION

FAR STARS

As with ship construction, the earliest techniques of navigation are unknown. It is assumed that stars, currents and winds must have been major components and certainly wind names show sound reconstructions in Proto-Malayo-Polynesian (PMP) and in some cases, Proto-Austronesian. As for stars and constellations, at least the Morning Star (*talaq*) and the Pleiades (*buluq*) were known to PMP speakers. However, it is likely that skills in identifying and recording discoveries must have grown rapidly following the exit from Taiwan. By the time European ships reached Micronesia, sophisticated techniques of navigation and replication of existing voyages had developed (Åkerblom 1968; Hutchins 1983), including the remarkable star charts of the Marshall Islands (Figure 8.8).

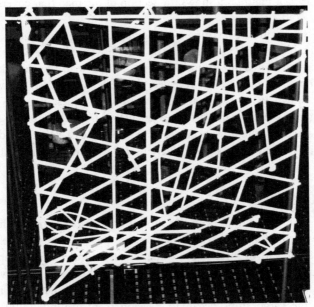

Figure 8.8 Star chart, Marshall Islands (Photo credit: R. Blench).

We know much less about navigational techniques in ISEA. It is assumed that in the earliest phases, sea-captains made far more use of coastal trajectories, hopping between islands, to avoid open oceans. However, this must have all changed in the period of the first encounters with Indian Ocean shipping. South Indian, Graeco-Roman, Sassanian and Arab merchants all made their way to ISEA, drawn by spices and other high-value goods. Suarez (2012) summarises the history of cartography in the Southeast Asian region, right through from Ptolemy, whose fourth-century texts were still in use a millennium later. We can assume there was a transmission of skills, which increasingly employed estimates of fixed distance, rather than the far more indeterminate measures used out of necessity in the Pacific. By the ninth century, when an expedition of a 'thousand ships' was sent from Sumatra to raid the coast of East Africa, mariners must have been very confident in their estimates of time and distance (Blench 2010).

CHINESE NAVAL CHARTS

Cartography in China probably began in the early centuries BCE, with the first unambiguous reference in 227 BCE. However, maps remained focused on the mainland, and only the extensive voyages of Zhèng Hé 鄭和 (who lived from 1371–1433/35) produced significant maritime maps. The most striking of these is the Mao Kun map, Zhèng Hé hánghǎi tú 鄭和航海圖 (ca. 1423) which summarises the voyages of Zhèng Hé in ISEA and the Indian Ocean (Mills 1970; Sun 1992). Figure 8.9 shows the section of the map that covers the South China Sea.

From this date onwards, Chinese cartographic skills grow rapidly. One of the most remarkable testaments of this is the Selden Map (Figure 8.10) apparently drawn for a rich merchant around 1620 CE, and now in the Bodleian Library, Oxford. Conservation in 2008 revealed that this is the first known Chinese map to be drawn using systematic geometric techniques. It uses voyage data from a magnetic compass and distances calculated from the number of watches. Moreover, since it is the most accurate map of Southeast Asia to be drawn until two centuries later, it is considered likely that it was prepared in Southeast Asia rather than on mainland China.

CONCLUSIONS

The South China Seas have been the subject of a series of striking innovations in maritime technology, as befits the largest mosaic of islands in the world and one where some sort of inter-island trade has been under way for approaching 20,000 years. The outrigger, appearing around 4,000 years ago, evolved into the large transoceanic vessels characteristic of Eastern Indonesia and the Pacific. In ISEA, large cargo ships began to develop from around 2,000 years ago, enabling the expansion of the Srivijaya Empire and remarkable enterprises such as the invasion of the coast of East Africa. Despite its engineering capacities in other areas, China initially lagged well behind ISEA, and it was only when the Chinese adopted some of their construction techniques and designs that they began to dominate the sea in the medieval era. Islamic shipping also influenced construction from the medieval era, and when the Portuguese arrived in the sixteenth century, further new techniques were introduced.

Elsewhere in this volume, Blench argues that the culture of sea nomads in its present form could only have evolved in conjunction with the large seaborne

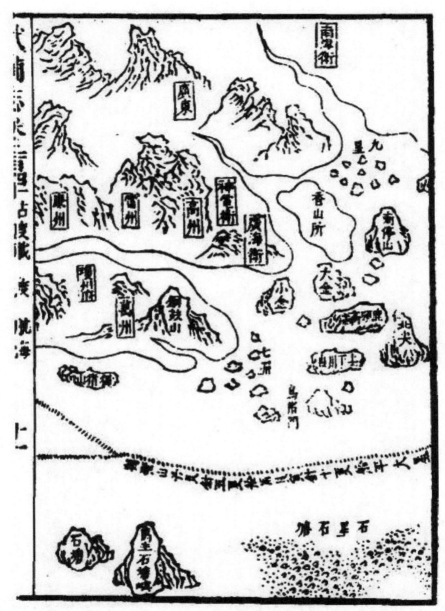

Figure 8.9 Astro-navigation chart of the South China Sea (Source: Creative Commons).

Figure 8.10 The Selden map of China and Southeast Asia, ca. 1620 (Source: Creative Commons).

empires (Chapter 1). The capacity to feed large-scale trade networks from small to medium-sized vessels, depended on the introduction of large cargo ships. At the same time, sea nomads must have been heavily involved in the detailed mapping of the island seascape, and provided awareness of winds, currents and reefs, as well as the capacity to make use of seasonal phenomena. For this reason, sea nomads persist up to the present, albeit much changed. There is still a necessity for small-scale inter-island exchange of goods and services by fishermen and traders who do not have a profound regard for the nuances of the nation-state.

REFERENCES

Åkerblom, Kjell. 1968. *Astronomy and Avigation in Polynesia and Micronesia*. Stockholm: Etnografiska museet.

Ballard, Chris, Richard Bradley, Lise Nordenborg Myhre, and Meredith Wilson. 2003. 'The Ship as Symbol in the Prehistory of Scandinavia and Southeast Asia.' *World Archaeology* 35 (3): 385–403.

Bednarik, Robert G. 1997. 'The Earliest Evidence of Ocean Navigation.' *International Journal of Nautical Archaeology* 26 (3): 183–91.

Blench, Roger M. 2010. 'New Evidence for the Austronesian Impact on the East African Coast.' In *Global Origins and the Development of Seafaring*, ed. A. Anderson, J.H. Barrett, and K.V. Boyle, 239–48. Cambridge: McDonald Institute.

———. 2018. 'Waterworld: Lexical Evidence for Aquatic Subsistence Strategies in Austroasiatic.' *JSEALS*, Special Issue 3, ed. Felix Rau and Hiram Ring, 174–93. Honolulu: University of Hawai'i Press.

Bonnemaison, Joel. 1994. *The Tree and the Canoe: History and Ethnogeography of Tanna*. Mānoa: University of Hawai'i Press.

Bulbeck, David. This volume. 'Late Pleistocene to Mid-Holocene Maritime Exchange Networks in Island Southeast Asia.' In *Sea Nomads of Southeast Asia: From the Past to the Present*, ed. B. Bellina, R. Blench, and J.-C. Galipaud. Singapore: NUS Press.

Correia, Gaspar. 1858–66. *Lendas da India*. 8 volumes. Lisboa: Academia Real das Sciencias de Lisboa.

Ferrand, Gabriel. 1919. 'Le K'ouen-louen et les Anciennes Navigations dans les Mers du Sud.' *Journal Asiatique* 13: 239–333, 431–92; 14: 5–68, 201–42.

Flecker, Michael. 2001. 'The Bakau Wreck: An Early Example of Chinese Shipping in Southeast Asia.' *The International Journal of Nautical Archaeology* 30 (2): 221–30.

———. 2003. 'The Thirteenth-century Java Sea Wreck: A Chinese Cargo in an Indonesian Ship.' *The Mariner's Mirror* 89 (4): 388–404.

Guy, John. 2017. 'The Phanom Surin Shipwreck, a Pahlavi Inscription, and their Significance for the History of Early Lower Central Thailand.' *Journal of the Siam Society* 105: 179–96.

Heng, Derek. 2018. 'Ships, Shipwrecks, and Archaeological Recoveries as Sources of Southeast Asian History.' *Oxford Research Encyclopaedia*. DOI:10.1093/acrefore/9780190277727.013.97.

Horridge, Adrian. 1995. 'The Austronesian Conquest of the Sea—Upwind.' In *The Austronesians: Historical and Comparative Perspectives*, ed. P. Bellwood, J.J. Fox, and D. Tryon, 143–60. Canberra: ANU Press.

Hung, Hsiao-Chun et al. 2007. 'Ancient Jades Map 3,000 Years of Prehistoric Exchange in Southeast Asia.' *Proceedings of the National Academy of Sciences of the United States of America* 104/50 (December):19745–50.

Hung, Hsiao-Chun. 2019. 'Prosperity and Complexity without Farming: The South China Coast, c. 5000–3000 BC.' *Antiquity* 93 (368): 325–41.

Hutchins, Edwin. 1983. 'Understanding Micronesian Navigation.' In *Mental Models*, ed. D. Gentner, and A. Stevens, 191–225. Hillsdale, NJ: Lawrence Erlbaum.

Kimura, Jun. 2016. *Archaeology of East Asian Shipbuilding*. Gainesville: University Press of Florida.

Lape, Peter V., Sue O'Connor, and Nick Burningham. 2007. 'Rock Art: A Potential Source of Information about Past Maritime Technology in the South-East Asia-Pacific Region.' *International Journal of Nautical Archaeology* 36 (2): 238–53.

Lo, Jung Pang. 1955. 'The Emergence of China as a Sea Power During the Late Sung and Early Yüan Periods.' *Far Eastern Quarterly* 14 (4): 489–503.

Mahdi, Waruno. 1999. 'The Dispersal of Austronesian Boat Forms in the Indian Ocean.' In *Archaeology and Language III: Artefacts, Languages and Texts*, ed. R.M. Blench and M. Spriggs, 144–79. London: Routledge.

Manguin, Pierre-Yves. 1984. *Relationships and Cross-influences between Southeast Asian and Chinese Shipbuilding Traditions*. SPAFA final report on maritime shipping and trade networks in Southeast Asia. Cisarua, West Java, Indonesia: SPAFA.

———. 1986. 'Shipshape Societies: Boat Symbolism and Political Systems in Insular Southeast Asia.' In *Southeast Asia in the 9th to 14th Centuries*, ed. D.G. Marr and A.C. Milner, 187–213. Singapore: ANU/ISEAS. Reprinted in *Techniques & Culture. Revue semestrielle d'anthropologie des techniques* 2001 (35–36): 373–400.

———. 1989. 'The Trading Ships of Insular Southeast Asia: New Evidence from Indonesian Archaeological Sites.' *Prosidings Pertemuan Ilmiah Arkeologi* 5: 200–20.

———. 1993a. 'Trading Ships of the South China Sea.' *Journal of the Economic and Social History of the Orient* 36 (3): 253–80.

———. 1993b. 'The Vanishing Jong: Insular Southeast Asian Fleets in Trade and War (Fifteenth to Seventeenth Centuries).' In *Southeast Asia in the Early Modern Era: Trade, Power and Belief*, ed. A. Reid, 197–213. Ithaca, New York: Cornell University Press.

———. 2012. 'Asian Ship-building Traditions in the Indian Ocean at the Dawn of European Expansion.' In *The Trading World of the Indian Ocean, 1500–1800*, ed. O. Prakash, 597–629. Delhi: Pearson Education and Centre for Studies in Civilizations.

Mills, J.V. 1970. *Ma Huan Ying Yai Sheng Lan: The Overall Survey of the Ocean Shores*. Cambridge: Cambridge University Press.

Needham, Joseph and Wang Ling. 1971. *Science in Civilisation in China, Vol IV: Physics and Physical Technology: Part III Civil Engineering and Nautics*. Cambridge: Cambridge University Press.

O'Connor, Sue, Christian Reepmeyer, Mahirta, Michelle C. Langley, and Elena Piotto. This volume. 'Communities of Practice in a Maritime World: Shared Shell Technology and Obsidian Exchange in the Lesser Sunda Islands, Wallacea.' In *Sea Nomads of Southeast*

Asia: From the Past to the Present, ed. B. Bellina, R. Blench, and J.-C. Galipaud. Singapore: NUS Press.

Ono, Rintaro, Santoso Soegondho, and Minoru Yoneda. 2010. 'Changing Marine Exploitation During Late Pleistocene in Northern Wallacea: Shell Remains from Leang Sarru Rockshelter in Talaud Islands.' *Asian Perspectives* 48 (2): 318–41.

Suarez, Thomas. 2012. *Early Mapping of Southeast Asia: The Epic Story of Seafarers, Adventurers, and Cartographers Who First Mapped the Regions between China and India*. Clarendon, Vermont: Tuttle Publishing.

Sun, Guangqi. 1992. 'Zheng He's Expeditions to the Western Ocean and his Navigation Technology.' *The Journal of Navigation* 45 (3): 329–43.

9

'The Muscles and Sinews of the Kingdom': The Sama Bajau in Early Modern Eastern Indonesia

Lance Nolde

INTRODUCTION

The Sama Bajau of eastern Indonesia are one part of the larger Samalan ethnolinguistic group, the members of which are found not only throughout the eastern Indonesian archipelago but also scattered across the littorals of the southern Philippines and the Borneo states of Malaysia. Distributed across an area of roughly 1.25 million square kilometres, it has been suggested that Samalan peoples are 'the most widely dispersed ethnolinguistic group indigenous to Southeast Asia' (Sather 1995: 256–7). In this vast archipelagic world, the Sama Bajau have long filled an important cultural-ecological niche as 'sea peoples' in a region dominated by the sea. They were expert seafarers, the principal components of the navies of landed kingdoms, and primary procurers and traders of sea products. In essence, their value lay in their ability to link the land and sea environment more effectively than any other group.

Because of their unique adaptation to the marine environment and their highly mobile lifestyle, the Sama Bajau came to be called 'sea nomads' or 'sea gypsies' by Europeans and by a variety of names by Southeast Asians, including *'orang laut'* (Indonesian/Malay: sea people), *'Turijeqneq'* (Makassarese: people of the water), and *'wong kambang'* (Javanese/Balinese: floating people). In certain contemporary contexts these names have taken on derogatory connotations based on stereotypes that ignore the dynamic and historically rich Sama Bajau culture. Among the Sama Bajau peoples themselves, the descriptive *dilau* or *madilau* ('of the sea') is commonly added to the autonym Sama, as in *Sama dilau* (meaning 'Sama of the sea'), to emphasise the importance of the sea in their culture and history. Thus, while these exonyms carry unwelcome discursive baggage, they nevertheless clearly demonstrate the centrality of the sea to the Sama Bajau people, much of whose history has been determined by their relationship to the sea.

The unique sea-centred lifestyle of the Sama Bajau has long attracted the attention of outsiders and inspired a fair amount of scholarly inquiry. Some of the most detailed accounts come from nineteenth-century Dutch colonial officials, government employees and traders seeking answers to questions about Sama Bajau origins and political status. These authors relied on the assessments of their predecessors and a handful of local, but non-Sama Bajau informants. Writings from this period were often heavily influenced by earlier seventeenth-century descriptions of Sama Bajau peoples and were coloured by the transformed socio-political status of the Sama Bajau in mid- to late nineteenth-century Indonesia. In the writings of Cornelis Speelman—who led a Dutch-Bugis alliance in defeating the dominant south Sulawesi kingdom of Gowa-Talloq in the 1660s—the Sama Bajau were depicted as nomads of the sea wandering in search of tortoiseshell and other sea products, with no homeland, ruler, nor any political unity. Observers believed that they were slaves of the powerful landed kingdoms of Gowa-Talloq and Bone in south Sulawesi and served them in the capacity of fisherfolk and seaborne couriers. They were described as living a humble existence and were wholly dependent upon sea products, which they brought as tribute to their lords and sold to foreign traders.[1]

While there is some truth in the description, it ignores the major role that the Sama Bajau played in the history of Island Southeast Asia (ISEA). This chapter depicts a community that was essential to the creation, expansion and maintenance of some of the region's most powerful polities and most successful trading networks (Nolde 2014; Nolde 2015: 6–7). Their mastery of the seas also assured them of prestigious and powerful positions within many littoral kingdoms. What is not generally known is that many of the numerous groups of Sama Bajau peoples dispersed throughout the eastern Indonesian seascape in the early modern period were organised in a much more complex manner than previously assumed and some became important territorial powers in their own right.

A diverse body of oral traditions and written sources provide evidence of the existence of two important Sama Bajau entities in eastern Indonesia, which are referred to in this chapter as the Papuq and Lolo Bajau polities. Each was led by a paramount head of noble lineage and consisted of a loose unity of a large number of geographically dispersed communities of Sama Bajau under their own local leaders. These paramount leaders served as the primary links between the scattered Sama Bajau population and the Makassarese kingdom of Gowa-Talloq and its rival, the Bugis kingdom of Bone. Although these two Sama Bajau polities served rival kingdoms, they had a shared history and lineage. The first and oldest polity was headed by the Papuq and was allied with Gowa-Talloq, and the second and more recent polity was headed by the Lolo Bajau, with strong links to Bone.

This chapter will focus on the history of the Papuq Sama Bajau and their relationship to the Makassarese kingdoms of Gowa and Talloq.[2] The principal aim is to bring into sharper focus the importance of the Sama Bajau to the socio-political and commercial networks of eastern Indonesia between the thirteenth and late eighteenth centuries.

EASTERN INDONESIA[3]

The early modern world of eastern Indonesia was one of expansive seas punctuated by numerous large, high islands and small, low-lying coral atolls. This vast area stretched from Bali and eastern Borneo in the west to the Bird's Head peninsula of New Guinea in the east and encompassed a great diversity of languages and cultures. For the Sama Bajau in particular, this 'sea of islands' (Hau'ofa 1994) comprised numerous settlements, fishing grounds and catchment areas, spiritually potent places, navigation routes, anchorages and safe harbours, as well as seaboard markets and port cities. The sea was and still remains the central feature of their world and formed the basis of their mental charting of the region, from tiny outcrops of land only visible at high tide to coral reef complexes, extensive littorals and barely visible entrances to rivers.

Throughout recorded history, the natural resources provided by the seas and islands of eastern Indonesia have served as the foundation of cross-cultural interaction and exchange in the region. The natural riches of the eastern islands impressed early European naturalists like Gerhardus Rumphius and Alfred Lord Wallace, and scientists have since singled out this eastern portion of the Indo-Malay Archipelago as being among the most biodiverse regions in the world, especially in regard to marine life (Hoeksema 2007: 117–78; Majors 2008: 263). The uniformly warm and relatively shallow seas, moderate salinity and strong ocean currents combined to make eastern Indonesia particularly rich in certain marine species, such as neritic phytoplankton, which formed the basic food source for the region's abundant marine fish populations. Located within an area dubbed the 'Coral Triangle', the seas of this part of the archipelago were and still are also home to some of the largest coral reef complexes in the world. These sweeping tracts of coral formations are spread throughout the region and formed a central element in the Sama Bajau world. This importance is reflected in the richness of the Sama Bajau language with regard to the maritime environment, including specific names to describe numerous types of reef formations.

The numerous islands and coral reef formations that peppered the region were also home to large populations of various species of sea turtle, holothurians or trepang, agar-agar, molluscs (like trochus), giant clams, pearl-oysters, amongst many others. These creatures played a vital role in the histories of Sama Bajau peoples in the eastern archipelago. For most Sama Bajau, their daily activity involved the gathering, hunting, fishing and sale of sea turtles, trepang, clams and other molluscs, fish, sharks, rays, cephalopods and large marine mammals like the dugong. This wealth of marine resources in eastern Indonesia served as a primary source of subsistence for local populations and has for centuries attracted traders from the region and beyond. The Sama Bajau were an essential link between sea and shore, coast and hinterland, making the much desired products of the sea available to the landed populations of the archipelago.

Certain land resources found only or predominantly in the islands of eastern Indonesia were also central to the histories of the region and its peoples, including the Sama Bajau. While comparatively poorer than the western archipelago in terms of agricultural production, the inland areas of the islands of eastern Indonesia were blessed with a number of important natural resources that formed the basis of local and regional exchange networks and attracted traders from all over the world. Chief among these are the 'trinity of spices'—clove, nutmeg and mace—found in Maluku, as well as sandalwood, which grew in large quantities on Timor and in lesser amounts on Sumba. Sappanwood, teak, cinnamon, honey, wax, rice, iron, various resins and several other natural products of eastern Indonesia were additional staples of regional and international trade. In the early modern period, enslaved people were another important export of eastern Indonesia, most of whom came to market as war captives, debt slaves or victims of slave raids.

In accordance with the rhythm of the monsoons, these marine and terrestrial goods were traded within a complex web of interlocking local and regional trade networks that linked the numerous islands of eastern Indonesia to important regional emporia, such as Makassar (south Sulawesi), Banjarmasin (east Borneo) and Batavia (Jakarta), and finally to international markets in China, India, the Middle East and Europe. Sama Bajau peoples were among the chief collectors, shippers and traders of sea products in eastern Indonesia. They sailed as captains as well as crewmen and operated vessels of various styles and tonnage (Nolde 2014: 81–96, 122–207). The extensive eastern Indonesian trade networks were at the heart of social and political interaction throughout the region, and the wealth and prestige generated by the flow of goods were vital to the formation, growth and maintenance of local polities, both large and small, across the eastern archipelago.

THE SAMA BAJAU IN SOUTH SULAWESI

The southwestern peninsula of the island of Sulawesi was one such area where participation in these east-west networks of exchange stimulated the development of numerous local polities. The social and political landscape of South Sulawesi was a complex assortment of ethnic groups and political confederations. As traditionally defined, the four major ethnic groups include the Makassar, Bugis, Toraja and Mandar, of which the Bugis and Makassar peoples have historically been the largest and most politically dominant groups. Although important to the region's history, the Sama Bajau traditionally have not been included among the major ethnic groups of South Sulawesi. Most scholars have instead categorised the Sama Bajau as a non-native ethnic community, pointing to their foreign origins and what scholars believed to be a relatively late arrival in the region, sometime in the sixteenth century. More recent archaeological and historical research has provided strong evidence for sustained Sama Bajau settlement and influence in the region from at least the mid-thirteenth century onward (Bulbeck 1992; Bulbeck and Caldwell 2000; Bulbeck and Clune 2003; Nolde 2014: 102–20). Evidence of such a long history of interaction, intermarriage and exchange calls into question the prevailing conception of the Sama Bajau as foreigners in the world of South Sulawesi.

The earliest polities to benefit from south Sulawesi's geographic position amid the natural resource zones of eastern Indonesia were those that formed in the rich agricultural lands on the peninsula or those that had access to the most favourable harbour and riverine sites for trade. It is important to note that each of the polities that once dominated South Sulawesi politics and trade benefitted from Sama Bajau populations living within their realm. Beginning sometime in the thirteenth century, the Bugis polity of Luwuq, with its capital at Wareq in the northern coastal region of the Gulf of Bone, was among the earliest of these trade-based South Sulawesi confederations to exercise its authority and influence beyond its immediate political heartland (Bulbeck and Caldwell 2000). Located on the southern shore of the southwestern peninsula, the Makassarese polity of Bantaeng was another important site of trade in this early period. Drawing on its control of inland agricultural wealth and its strategic location as a coastal entrepôt in the spice trade network that linked Maluku and eastern Java in the fourteenth century, the Bantaeng confederation formed a powerful polity until its incorporation into Gowa in the early sixteenth century (Bougas 1998: 83–123). To the north, the Makassarese port polity of Siang was favourably situated along the west coast of Sulawesi and controlled yet another important site of trade, making it another centre of power between the fourteenth and early sixteenth centuries (Pelras 1973). In each of these early polities, the presence of Sama Bajau peoples was crucial to their success.

Beginning in the sixteenth century, the Makassarese kingdom of Gowa in South Sulawesi rose to become the dominant power in all of eastern Indonesia. Having absorbed several smaller surrounding Sulawesian polities—including the prime seaport of Garassiq, which would become Makassar—and having formed an alliance with the related kingdom of Talloq, Gowa positioned itself to quickly become a primary centre of the eastern Indonesian world. The union of the dual kingdom of Gowa-Talloq in the mid-1500s would prove to be the foundation for the dramatic political expansion and commercial success that would follow. At the time of the alliance, Talloq was a maritime-oriented polity with extensive trade and tributary links to key areas of eastern Indonesia, such as Maluku, Flores and Timor, as well as to the western archipelago. It maintained a strong relationship with local Sama Bajau communities under the authority of their paramount leader, a high-status Sama Bajau who was given the title of Papuq.[4] Gowa, on the other hand, was mostly an inland-oriented polity with access to extensive agrarian populations and resources, but it too had ambitions to control maritime trade. This joining of Gowa's inland-agrarian orientation with the outward-maritime orientation of Talloq proved to be a highly successful combination that enabled the dual kingdom to dominate much of eastern Indonesian trade and politics until the latter half of the seventeenth century.

Gowa-Talloq embarked on a period of expansion in the sixteenth and seventeenth centuries that would firmly secure its position as a dominant power in the archipelago. These major naval expeditions in eastern Indonesia subjugated new lands, which joined others such as Sandao, Solor and Ende conquered earlier by Talloq and its Sama Bajau allies led by the Papuq in the late 1400s and early 1500s.[5] They also expanded Makassarese influence into areas of eastern Borneo, northern and eastern Sulawesi, the islands of Buton, Ternate, Tidore and Lombok, and the Sumbawa kingdoms of Bima, Sumbawa, Dompo and Pekat. After Gowa-Talloq adopted Islam in the reign of Karaeng Matoaya of Talloq (r. 1593–1623) and Sultan Ala'uddin of Gowa (r. 1593–1639), Gowa-Talloq undertook the so-called 'wars of Islamisation', by which all of the major polities of South Sulawesi to the south of the Toraja lands, including Bugis Bone, were forcibly converted to Islam between 1608 and 1611 (Cummings 2002: 32–3; Andaya 1981: 32–5). Islam was introduced to the kingdom of Bima on Sumbawa by similar means beginning in 1618 (Noorduyn 1987: 312–42).

The history of Gowa-Talloq's meteoric rise from small beginnings to a position of nearly unchallenged dominance in Sulawesi and across much of the eastern Indonesian archipelago is impressive. In Anthony Reid's assessment, it is 'one of the most rapid and spectacular success stories which Indonesian history affords' (Reid 1983: 117). In studying this fascinating history, it is important to remember that Gowa-Talloq's increasing expansion and success was highly dependent on regional trade, and that Gowa-Talloq itself was enmeshed in a much larger framework of trade networks and socio-political relations that spanned far beyond the shores of South Sulawesi. Makassar's success was due in large part to the influx of traders who were attracted to the variety of eastern Indonesian goods on offer as well as to the freedom and security enjoyed by foreign merchants. By the first quarter of the seventeenth century, the English, Danes, Dutch, Portuguese and Spanish had all established trading settlements in the growing port city and the first of many Chinese junks began to visit Makassar. Gowa-Talloq's primacy in the trade networks of the eastern Indonesian seas was also crucial to Makassar's attractiveness and prosperity as a regional entrepôt. The presence of Gowa-Talloq's Makassarese subjects and Sama Bajau allies in nearly every corner of the archipelago assured a steady supply of sea products, Malukan spices, enslaved people and other key commodities in Makassar's harbour each season. Through warfare, raiding and intermarriage with local rulers, Gowa-Talloq incorporated numerous areas into its sphere of influence and tied key resource zones to Makassar and its elites through tributary relations. Through these overseas ventures, both violent and peaceful, Gowa-Talloq formed lasting relationships with the ruling lines of Selayar, Buton and Tobungku on the east coast of Sulawesi; Ternate, Tidore and Banda in Maluku; Salaparang in Lombok; Sumbawa, Dompu, Pekat and Bima, all on the island of Sumbawa; Ade, Wehali and Manatuto on Timor; Pasir and Kutei on east Borneo etc. Many of these social bonds were the basis for valuable trade and tribute arrangements which fed Makassar's insatiable demand for commodities from eastern Indonesia (Cummings 2015: 215).

With the conquest of Gowa-Talloq by the Dutch United East India Company (*Vereenigde Oost-Indische Compagnie*, VOC) and its Bugis allies in 1669, the kingdom's control over its peripheries and its domination of eastern Indonesian trade were greatly reduced. The VOC took control of Makassar in order to mostly eliminate what had been the main source of spices outside its control. Gowa-Talloq's defeat also resulted in a permanent Dutch presence in South Sulawesi and the creation of a system of port controls, maritime patrols and sailing passes designed to regulate and restrain the movement of people and goods between Makassar and other areas of the Indo-Malay Archipelago.

While many readers may be familiar with the above history of Makassar's rise to a position of dominance and its subsequent demise at the hands of the VOC and its Bugis allies, the role of the Sama Bajau in the history of south Sulawesi and eastern Indonesia during this formative period is poorly understood. Yet, through a close reading of Dutch archival sources, Sama Bajau oral traditions and manuscripts (*lontaraq*) in Bimanese, Makassarese and Bugis (including the valuable *Lontaraq Bajo Lemobajo*, a history of the Sama Bajau kept in the southeast Sulawesi village of Lemobajo, hereafter, *LB Lemobajo*), a clearer picture of the Sama Bajau's important place in this history begins to emerge.[6] From the thirteenth century until well into the eighteenth century, the Makassarese kingdoms benefited greatly from alliances with Sama Bajau peoples, particularly those united loosely under the leadership of the Papuq. These Sama Bajau communities and their extended networks constituted a vital source of power and wealth for Gowa-Talloq. The alliances formed between Gowa-Talloq and the paramount leaders of the Sama Bajau people ensured a steady flow of valuable trade items from those groups of Sama Bajau linked to the Papuq. These relationships were also central to the expansion and maintenance of territorial control of key areas in the archipelago for the kingdom, as well as the defence of their interests against external threats.

Thus, it would be a mistake to see the Sama Bajau as simply subordinates or enslaved people of the landed kingdoms, as Speelman and later authors believed. Instead, the Sama Bajau formed highly regarded and independent cultural and political entities that operated as a part of—as well as apart from—these larger land-based polities. The highly mobile and polycentric nature of the Sama Bajau peoples and their traditional political systems allowed them to occupy powerful positions within the hierarchies of the landed kingdoms while simultaneously maintaining the relative autonomy of their own polities and networks.

THE PAPUQ SAMA BAJAU POLITY

Despite the comparative dearth of sources regarding those persons who held the title of Papuq, we can formulate a general outline of the history of this office, some of the personalities who once held this esteemed title, the structure and the parameters of the networks under his leadership, as well as the relationship of the Papuq and his people to the landed polities of south Sulawesi, particularly the powerful dual kingdom of Gowa-Talloq.[7] The story thus extends to vast areas of the eastern Indonesian seas far beyond their homeland in the southwest Sulawesi littoral. It reveals the geographic extent of the Papuq polity and the significant role played by the Sama Bajau in the politics and the economy of the region in the early modern period.

Beginning sometime in the mid-thirteenth century, an unknown number of Sama Bajau communities settled in the littoral of southwest Sulawesi and its offshore islands. A great deal about the history of these early settlers remains unknown but we can be certain that they occupied a position of importance and prestige in the region from early on, much earlier than previously assumed.[8] Furthermore, based on the oral and written traditions of the Sama Bajau, as well as a variety of other indigenous and European historical sources, it is clear that among those early Sama Bajau communities there was a common recognition of the paramount cultural and political authority of an individual selected from among their noble ranks. According to these sources, this individual was known by the title of 'Papuq'.

The Papuq appears most prominently in oral and written traditions concerning the advent of the Sama Bajau people in the greater southwest Sulawesi area and remains a recurrent feature of Sama Bajau, Makassarese, Bimanese and Dutch historical records well into the closing years of the eighteenth century. After that point, the title disappears from the record and only traces of its former significance remain in oral tradition. While the origin of the name is unmentioned in the sources, there is no doubt that in both historical and present-day contexts the title was associated with power.[9] With the defeat of the Papuq by the Sultanate of Bima and the loss of two Papuq-ruled settlements on Flores in the late 1700s, the title disappears from the extant written sources.[10] But for Sama Bajau communities in eastern Indonesia today, Papuq has come to serve as the Sama Bajau name for the supreme deity or god, and in certain contexts it is used in lieu of, or in conjunction with Allah (as in, *Papuq Allah Ta'ala*). The title still retains traces of its former connotation in several Sama Bajau communities of the northern Flores coast, where it is remembered as a respectful form of address used in the not so distant past for high status Sama Bajau individuals who owned a large number of enslaved people (Verheijen 1986).[11] Even in those communities where the meaning has changed in contemporary contexts, the memory of the Papuq as a historical ancestor of great power and importance is still strong in oral and written traditions of the Sama Bajau, particularly those pertaining to the formation of the earliest relationships between Sama Bajau and the landed polities of southwest Sulawesi (Liebner 1998: 107–33).

At the most basic level, the oral and written traditions clearly establish the Papuq as the paramount leader of a particularly large group of Sama Bajau people who came to form an alliance with an emergent Makassarese polity identified in the manuscripts as Gowa. Furthermore, in these traditions his daughter is known by the title or name 'I Lolo', which became the primary marker of Sama Bajau noble lineage in the period before and after the Makassar War (1666–69).

Makassarese manuscript sources also clearly identify Papuq as the title of the head of the Sama Bajau, or *Turijeqneq* (Makassarese: 'people of the water'), who were loyal to the kingdoms of Gowa and Talloq. 'Papuq' is first mentioned in Makassarese sources to refer to an individual who formed a close relationship with Karaeng Tunilabu ri Suriwa, the second ruler of Talloq (r. late 1400s to early 1500s).[12] Prior to the mid-nineteenth century the Dutch were apparently unaware of the Papuq's role as leader of the Sama Bajau under Gowa-Talloq and assumed instead that the Papuq must have been a title of Makassarese nobility (Nolde 2014: 208–60; Nolde 2015: 6–7). It is clear, however, that Papuq was not a Makassarese term, title, or position, but rather a title given to the Sama Bajau leader by the Sama Bajau themselves and predated the Sama Bajau's presence in Gowa.

From the first two references to the Papuq that appear in the *lontaraq bilang*—royal court annals—of Gowa-Talloq, we learn that on 12 March 1703 the reigning Papuq, Daeng Numalo, passed away and was replaced by a man named Daeng Makkulle Ahmad less than three months later. The entry regarding his investiture states that Daeng Makkulle Ahmad was 'installed as Papuq by his family' (Cummings 2010: 176). Based on other entries in the annals and information from other manuscripts we know that Daeng Makkulle Ahmad was the grandson of an important and well-respected Sama Bajau woman of noble birth named I Amboq, and that he was either the son or the nephew of the previous Papuq, Daeng Numalo. From this brief but telling passage we know that the Papuq was not appointed by the ruler of Gowa, but by his 'family' (Makassarese: *pamanakanna*). Thus, whereas high-ranking positions within the Gowa court, such as *tumailalang*, *tumakkajannang*, or *sabannaraq*, were always 'appointed' (Makassarese: *nanitannang*) by the ruler, the Papuq was chosen by his kinfolk as lord of the Sama Bajau peoples allied with Gowa-Talloq. The manner of the Papuq's appointment accords with Sama Bajau traditions. In the *LB Lemobajo* and MS 260 manuscripts, as well as in oral traditions, we find that the leadership group is comprised of respected elders, many of whom are of noble birth and part of a widely dispersed extended family. Manuscripts and oral traditions from Sulawesi, Sumbawa and Flores affirm that the individual was selected as leader based on both ascribed and achieved status, in that he or she had the desired qualities and came from noble lineage (Nolde 2015: 208–58).

In Sama Bajau communities the social hierarchy is based on noble status determined by one's link, fictive or real, to the Lolo Bajau bloodline and thus ultimately to the progenitor of that line, the Papuq. This extended family of individuals who claim to belong to this bloodline of early Sama Bajau nobility still forms the upper strata of the Sama Bajau communities throughout the region today. It is said that in the past they emphasised their position of high-status by donning certain clothing, demonstrating wealth through extravagant ceremonies and celebrations, and by amassing an entourage comprised of kin, supporters, clients and enslaved people. In the *LB Lemobajo* manuscript we are given examples of *adat* or customary law that further delineated the many rights, privileges and protections afforded those of high-level status. Such status determined matters of bride price, form or severity of punishment, and tribute. From these and similar records we are given a clear sense that status and hierarchy were pervasive in Sama Bajau society and, just as William Cummings noted for their Makassarese neighbours, served to mark out a 'coherent system of relative statuses and clear political and social relationships within an integrated whole' (Cummings 2002: 29).

In many Sama Bajau communities today, tangible evidence of one's noble lineage is found in the possession of certain regalia, such as *lontaraq* manuscripts (rumoured or real), *keris* and other weapons, clothing, musical instruments, and perhaps most importantly, a uniquely Sama Bajau banner or pennant known as *ula-ula*. Today *ula-ula* are still found scattered about the archipelago, stored with the utmost reverence in the homes of certain Sama Bajau nobility. Some traditions suggest that *ula-ula* were once the pennants flown above the decks of noble Sama Bajau ships and as banners marched into war, but more commonly, and still today, *ula-ula* are only brought out on special occasions such as circumcisions and wedding ceremonies. As objects of the living past that provided a link to the power and authority of the ancestors, these heirlooms were, and often still are, thought to be sources of immense supernatural power.

RELATIONSHIP OF THE PAPUQ SAMA BAJAU POLITY AND GOWA-TALLOQ

The primary role of the Papuq within the social and political world of Gowa-Talloq was to serve as the paramount head of a large number of Sama Bajau communities that operated within the ever-expanding realm of those kingdoms, and perhaps beyond. In the written and oral traditions of the Sama Bajau and Makassarese it is evident that, upon incorporation into the Gowa polity, the Papuq retained his traditional authority and role as lord of his Sama Bajau followers.[13] The available sources unfortunately do not provide enough information for even an approximate count of the Sama Bajau population during the early modern period. However, of the several Sama Bajau communities we do know of in the sixteenth and seventeenth centuries, the manuscript sources clearly indicate that the Papuq was acknowledged as paramount head of the Sama Bajau, including by at least some of those groups who were not reckoned as part of the Papuq's immediate following.[14]

During Gowa-Talloq's sixteenth-century expansion and incorporation of surrounding Sulawesi polities, the rulers of the dual kingdom relied upon the Papuq to oversee matters dealing with the scattered Sama Bajau people. One example of the way in which the Papuq's authority was implemented on behalf of Gowa-Talloq was through the management of corvée by subject Sama Bajau populations. The Gowa chronicle records that Tunipalangga (r.1546–65) was the first ruler to issue frequent summons for corvée labour, and in this period the Papuq served a supervisory role in the process. One manuscript source notes, for instance, that the Papuq managed and oversaw the performance of corvée labour (Makassarese: *pappaqngara*) by those Sama Bajau considered to be subjects of the kingdom.[15] Among those called up were the descendants of the Sama Bajau of Katingang, Barasaq and Kandeaq (all in southwest Sulawesi) who fought against and were defeated by the ruler of Talloq in the mid-sixteenth century.[16] Yet, the sources also indicate that the Papuq's authority was not limited to the Sama Bajau population but also extended to non-Sama Bajau peoples. The sources mention, for example, that the Papuq was also charged with supervising the *corvée* of all those who came to settle in the areas around the region of Bayoa.[17]

There are also references in the Makassarese manuscripts that suggest that the ruler of Talloq may have granted the Papuq authority over the Makassarese of the inland riverine polity of Panaikang in the early 1500s. In a record of the subject domains (*paqrasangang*) of Talloq found in a Makassarese manuscript, for example, it is said that the people of Panaikang belonged to the Sama Bajau, and that the Sama Bajau requested that their authority be extended along the Talloq river as far west as Pateqne.[18] Based on the information given in the text it is possible that this is a description of the territories controlled during the reign of either Tunipasuruq (r.1500s–40/43) or Tumenanga ri Makkoayang (r.1540/43–76). As the paramount leader of the Sama Bajau under Talloq during this period, the Papuq would likely have been in control of the Panaikang people.[19]

The Papuq's authority also extended well beyond the Gowa-Talloq heartland and included many of the Sama Bajau who lived and sailed in other areas of the eastern Indonesian archipelago. As described above, the rich seas of the vast eastern archipelago were an ideal setting in which the Sama Bajau could seek a livelihood. Furthermore, their sea-centred culture and highly mobile lifestyle was conducive to extensive exploration and settlement far beyond their base in Sulawesi. Early on, Sama Bajau sailors and fishers set out from southwest Sulawesi and navigated to distant areas of the archipelago. Yet, even as they dispersed into various areas, the sources show that the Papuq maintained a clear measure of authority and influence over some of these mobile Sama Bajau groups. When, for example, a VOC Company official led an expedition along the northern Sulawesi coast in 1681, he encountered a large fleet of Sama Bajau from 'Manggarai' (West Flores) bearing the flag of their ruler en route to the small polity of Kaidipang. This ruler undoubtedly was the Papuq, who at this time resided primarily in Sama Bajau controlled territories of western Flores, known to the Sama Bajau and Makassarese as Sandao.[20] Throughout the 1680s and 1690s there is frequent mention of mixed Makassarese and Sama Bajau fleets roaming the coasts of Borneo, Sumbawa, Flores and Timor, many of which were involved in local trade and politics as well as what VOC Company officials called 'piracy' and 'smuggling'. At the behest of the VOC administration in Makassar—which was extremely frustrated by the disturbances caused by these roving groups in the overseas territories (Dutch: *overwal*)—on more than one occasion the ruler of Gowa asked the Papuq to order his Sama Bajau constituents to return to Makassar.[21]

In addition to the paramount leadership of the Sama Bajau populations under Gowa-Talloq, Makassarese sources also suggest that the Papuq was an authority in matters of shipping, ship technology and maritime law within Gowa and Talloq. In an early, but undated *rapang* collection, for example, the words of the Papuq are quoted as the chief source of knowledge regarding the laws that applied to ships, their captains and crew.[22] The Papuq's laws not only determined the distribution of profit shares among the ship's owner, the captain and crew, but they also defined the particular financial and legal obligations for these parties in the case of various unfortunate circumstances. Certain statutes also determined the various rates of tax (*sima*) to be paid by incoming ships and the freight price for shipped goods.[23] These same laws appear in another, later manuscript, this time conveyed by a Sama Bajau noble known as the *Lolo Bayo* (Lolo Bajau) of Sanrabone as 'the words of our ancestor the I Papuq'.[24] It is not clear whether these maritime laws and the Papuq's position as arbiter in such matters predated the creation of the separate office of *sabannaraq* (harbourmaster) by the ruler of Gowa Tumapaqrisiq Kallonna (r.1510–1546), but the fact that the words of the Papuq regarding these laws were recorded in the *rapang* for later rulers and officials to consult is noteworthy.

The authority of the Papuq and Sama Bajau nobles in maritime affairs is further attested by the successive appointment of several Sama Bajau nobles as *sabannaraq*, or harbourmaster, of Gowa-Talloq between the late sixteenth and mid-eighteenth centuries. At least two of those men were also chosen to become Papuq by the Sama Bajau people. Some scholars have suggested that the position of *sabannaraq* was a non-hereditary post (Mukhlis 1975: 92; Bulbeck

1992: 105–7). The Makassarese records indicate, however, that many of the Sama Bajau nobles who were appointed as *sabannaraq* were related by blood and the position remained in the Papuq lineage, at least for a time. According to the *lontaraq bilang* (royal annals) of Gowa-Talloq, Daeng Makkulle Ahmad was appointed in 1710 as *sabannaraq*, succeeding the recently deceased I Daeng Makkulle Abdul Wahid, who likely was his father (Cummings 2007: 139; 2010: 22).[25] In 1703, this same Daeng Makkulle Ahmad would be appointed as Papuq by his family. That there was at least a de facto hereditary succession within one family to the position of *sabannaraq* during this period is further suggested by the fact that, after his death in 1724, Daeng Makkulle Ahmad was replaced as *sabannaraq* by his nephew, Daeng Mangewai.[26] Though the *lontaraq bilang* does not state their relationship, we know that in 1733 Daeng Mangewai was replaced as *sabannaraq* by Daeng Manggappa Mommiq, who would also be chosen by his family to become Papuq sometime in the 1730s.[27]

As far as the *lontaraq bilang* is concerned, the history of this important, high-status Sama Bajau family begins with an entry for the birth of I Amboq in 1611, the mother of Papuq Daeng Numalo (d.1703) and the grandmother of Papuq and *sabannaraq* Daeng Makkulle Ahmad (d.1725).[28] The record of her birth in the royal annals is notable, as it was among a select number of events added retrospectively in the 1630s and shares the page with some of the most important events in Makassarese history such as the adoption of Islam, the wars of Islamisation, and the birth of the highest status royals. Between the birth of I Amboq in 1611 and the *lontaraq bilang*'s last entry in 1751, the annals contain 45 entries recording the births, deaths, marriages, divorces and important actions taken by the Sama Bajau nobles in her extended family. It is also noteworthy that one of the known annalists, Karaeng Lempangang Safiyuddin, who would go on to become the ruler of Talloq (r.1739–60), refers to two of these Sama Bajau men as his 'grandparent' (Cummings 2010: 219, 268).[29] The extant genealogical information does not reveal any direct links between these men and Karaeng Lempangang, but the desire of the ruler to create a kin relationship, even a fictive one, to the ruling lineage of the Sama Bajau is noteworthy.

The *lontaraq bilang* entries pertaining to this particular extended family of Sama Bajau nobles allow us a rare insight into the world of Sama Bajau elite in the seventeenth and eighteenth centuries. Indeed, the very fact of their appearance in the royal annals affords historians a clear sense of the status and socio-political importance of the Sama Bajau in the Gowa-Talloq court during this period. As argued by William Cummings, the translator of the most complete and accurate version of the *lontaraq bilang* to date, the '*Lontaraq bilang* map the lives of prominent individuals. The more closely related an individual was to the ruler of Gowa … the greater the chance that the events of his or her life (and even the fact that he or she existed) would be judged significant' (Cummings 2010: 17; Cummings 2005: 40–62). In regard to the extended family of the successive Papuq during this period, the social status and political favour of these individuals must have truly been great.

In addition to the position of *sabannaraq* as an authority of matters of shipping and ship technology, the seafaring prowess of the Papuq and his followers also made them invaluable in any maritime venture. The Makassarese admiration of the Sama Bajau's skills and bravery on the sea is well documented in the oral and written record. Important Makassarese nobles preferred being transported on Sama Bajau ships. When, for instance, in 1646 Sultan Malikussaid of Gowa (r.1639–53) arranged the marriage of his daughter Karaeng Bontojeqneq to the Sultan of Bima, I Ambela Abi'l Khair Sirajuddin, he entrusted her passage across the dangerous Flores Sea to a crew of Sama Bajau (Chambert-Loir and Salahuddin 1999: 119–20). A similar event took place in 1767, when two Sama Bajau vessels were chosen to transport and protect the refugee prince Batara Gowa Amas Madina to Sumbawa, Bali, and ultimately to Bima.[30] In addition to these incidents, Dutch sources also note that Sama Bajau nobleman, sailors and their ships comprised a significant part of the following of the many refugee Makassarese and Bugis princes that roamed the archipelago at the end of the seventeenth century (Nolde 2014). Though he interpreted it as a sign of their bondage, Speelman noted in 1669 that the Sama Bajau were at the ready to sail wherever the ruler asked, further indicating the level of confidence the ruler placed in these communities (Speelman 1669: 27). A famous Makassarese tale, *sinriliq Datu Museng*, captures this sentiment of trust in verse, in which the protagonist declares: 'I am not afraid to sail to distant lands; Behold! I sail on a Bayo [Sama Bajo] ship' (Matthes 1883: 129). Though the references to these voyages in the archives are scattered across two centuries, Makassarese wisdom regarding the sailing skill and fearlessness of the Sama Bajau as recorded in the manuscript sources suggests that these sorts of voyages likely occurred frequently.

Their universally recognised prowess as sailors and navigators made the Sama Bajau the desired means of communication and transport of goods overseas. In addition to the precious cargo of Makassarese princes and princesses, the Sama Bajau were a key means of conveying a wide variety of goods. When, for example, in the beginning of the eighteenth century the rulers of Gowa-Talloq sought to establish a commercial and military alliance with the English at Banjarmasin, the gifts, goods, ammunition and communications exchanged clandestinely between the two parties were entrusted to the Papuq's Sama Bajau. They sailed out from the river of Gowa to east coast Borneo and back without being detected by the VOC post in Makassar.[31] The VOC Company records contain numerous reports of Sama Bajau 'smuggling' on behalf of the Papuq and the rulers of Gowa-Talloq, by which much needed goods and revenue flowed to the rulers despite the Company's best efforts at regulation and monopoly. While some of these sailors were caught and punished, the vast majority succeeded in avoiding capture, leaving the Dutch to only complain about the frequency of such illicit movement in their domain. Indeed, one Dutch official in Makassar reckoned the Sama Bajau were the very source of Gowa-Talloq's power and prestige, referring to them as 'the muscles and sinews' of the kingdom.[32]

While the Sama Bajau played a significant part in the ability of Gowa and Talloq to subdue their rivals in southwest Sulawesi, it was their unrivalled skill and courage at sea which made them so valuable in Gowa-Talloq's overseas expansion between the fifteenth and eighteenth centuries.[33] In the first documented attack on the land known as Sandao (a large area of Flores and East Nusa Tenggara) undertaken by the second ruler of Talloq, Tunilabu ri Suriwa, in the late 1400s, the sources state that it was, 'I Papuq who led Karaeng Tunilabu ri Suriwa across to war in Sandao. Thus the Karaeng crossed together with I Papuq and defeated the land of Sandao.' To reward the Papuq for his role in the conquest of Sandao, Tunilabu ri Suriwa offered him a choice of land in Sandao as his own and appointed him as representative of Talloq in the surrounding lands.[34] That the Papuq was able to 'lead' (*ampicini-ciniki*) the Talloq fleet to Sandao in the late fifteenth century is evidence that he was well acquainted with the Sandao area and that the Sama Bajau were a crucial part of Talloq's early military expansion beyond the southwest Sulawesi peninsula.

The Talloq chronicle mentions that Tunilabu ri Suriwa made extensive voyages to Banda in the east and to Melaka in the west, journeying for three years before returning to Makassar (Cummings 2007: 84). It is likely that the Sama Bajau were also an important part of these Talloq voyages. Tomé Pires' writing in the sixteenth century describes Sama Bajau fleets from South Sulawesi roaming with impunity in the waters of Melaka and the western archipelago (Pires 1944: 326–7). Reference in the *Sejarah Melayu* to Karaeng Semerluki, the war leader from Makassar or Talloq who is cited as having attacked Melaka during the reign of Sultan Mansur Syah (r.1459–77), could also have occurred with the involvement of the Sama Bajau of the Papuq polity (Brown 1970: 90–2; Pelras 1981: 154–5; Abidin 1974: 164).[35]

The Sama Bajau followers of I Papuq were undoubtedly a part of the later Talloq conquests of Sandao, Solor and Ende that took place under Tunilabu ri Suriwa's son and successor, Tunipasuruq (c. 1500s–43), and the recurring expeditions into those areas that took place until the late eighteenth century. The importance of the Papuq in the Talloq and, later, Gowa conquests of Flores and areas of the Solor-Alor archipelago is further underscored by a lengthy list of the *paqrasangang* (subject domains) of Sandao and Ende found in a Makassarese manuscript. In it the Papuq, rather than any other Makassarese ruler or noble, is recorded as the primary source of knowledge regarding these conquered territories.[36]

The Sama Bajau's renown as brave sailors and warriors of the sea during this period is a recurrent feature in oral traditions still remembered by descendants of the Makassarese nobility. As one descendant of the Gowa court said, 'The spirit of the *Turijeqneq* was strong, their virtue was bravery. That is why they were always the warriors at the tip of Gowa's spear. They sailed into war first, and once the *Turijeqneq* flag was raised, then the rest [of the fleet] would follow.'[37] Their strength as paddlers and expertise in the art of sailing and navigation made them a highly valued group within the impressive Makassar armada. Thus it is not hard to imagine, for example, the ships of the Sama Bajau being represented among the 'forest of sails' that comprised Sultan Malikussaid's massive war fleet, as described by one observer in 1640 (Tapala 1975: 159–71).

It is worthwhile to also consider the association of the Sama Bajau with ship types used as war vessels in Makassarese society, namely the *lambere Bayo* and the *pancajaq*. Sopher and Pelras have suggested that the ships on which the Sama Bajau travelled in the Melaka region, which Pires described as '*pangajavas*', were the long and narrow two-masted vessels known to the Makassarese as *pancajaq*. These war vessels could be supplemented by the rowing power of 20 or more men and were often used in war. The similarities between the *pancajaq* or *pangajavas* and the ship-type known as *lambere Bayo*—which was described as being propelled by upwards of 80 rowers and said to be used in Gowa-Talloq's armada—are noteworthy.[38]

Just as in later periods when the Papuq is listed among the war leaders sent to battle overseas, the Papuq and his followers would have been involved in the sixteenth- and seventeenth-century Gowa-Talloq naval expeditions into areas such as Buton, Muna, Banggai, Sula and Tobungku in eastern Sulawesi, as well as Salaparang on Lombok, and Pasir and Kutei in east coast Borneo (Cummings 2007: 41, 42, 84–6, 88–9, 91–2). There are even a few scattered references in the Makassarese manuscripts that suggest that Daeng ri Bulekang, the much lauded Makassarese war captain who led Gowa-Talloq in the conquests of Buton (1639) and Ambon (1652), may have been kin to I Amboq and thus related to Sama Bajau nobility.[39] The presence of Sama Bajau settlements in these lands today may have been a consequence of the involvement of the Sama Bajau in the Makassarese fleets that conquered these areas in earlier centuries.

CONCLUSION

The preceding discussion of the Sama Bajau under the Papuq is perhaps the only well-documented record of the existence of a polity founded and organised by sea people. It explains how the Sama Bajau's special knowledge of the maritime environment, their expertise at sea, and their fearsome reputation as warriors made them valuable allies to ambitious littoral kingdoms. While the role of sea-centred peoples in the emergence and maintenance of powerful kingdoms in the island world of Southeast Asia is comparatively well known, less documented is the intricate workings of the societies of the sea people in this crucial period. By fortunate coincidence, oral traditions and indigenous manuscripts combined with archival documents have revealed the existence of a Sama Bajau polity and its intimate relationship with the Makassarese kingdom of Gowa-Talloq in the early modern period.

The existence of an actual paramount leader of the Sama Bajau is not only mentioned but discussed in detail over an extended historical period. It is thus possible to see how the sea people interacted with coastal kingdoms, and how they organised and conducted their affairs as any other political entity in the early modern period. While previous scholars have written about this relationship often based on very meagre documentation, the story of the Papuq Sama Bajau can be reconstructed more thoroughly with existing records. The constellation of Sama Bajau communities that acknowledged the paramount authority of the Papuq proved to be crucial in the political expansion and economic prosperity of the dual kingdom of Gowa-Talloq and a primary force in the extension of Makassar's influence throughout eastern Indonesia. The perception of sea peoples as lacking a ruler, a social and political hierarchy, and a political unity can now be critically reassessed in light of the new and exciting materials that we now have of the Papuq Sama Bajau polity.

NOTES

[1] Cornelis Speelman, 'Notitie dienende voor eenen corten tijt en tot nader last van de Hooge Regeeringe op Batavia, tot naarrigtinge van de Onderkoopman Jan van den Oppijnen, bij provisie gesteldt tot Opperhoofd en Commandant in't Casteel Rotterdam, op Macasser, en van den Capitain Fransz; als hoofd over de Militie, mitsgaders die van den Raadt, anno 1669', unpublished typescript, KITLV DH 802. Hereafter cited as Speelman, 'Notitie'.

[2] See Lance Nolde 'Changing Tides', for a more detailed account of the histories of the two Sama Bajau polities.

[3] Although anachronistic, this chapter follows the most common scholarly convention of using 'eastern Indonesia' in the geographical sense to refer to a particular region of the Indo-Malay Archipelago, which now falls roughly within the borders of the modern nation-state of Indonesia. This convention also serves to demarcate for the reader the particular space of the Papuq Sama Bajau polity, which, as far as we know, did not regularly extend into areas of what are today the southern Philippines and island Malaysia.

[4] Nederlandsch Bijbel Genootschap (hereafter NBG) 17, f.97-9; NBG 208, f.62-3; Matthes Stichting (hereafter MS) 193, f.12; Koninklijk Instituut voor Taal-, Land- en Volkenkunde (hereafter KITLV) Or.545, no.233, f.3-6.

[5] NBG 208, f.62-3; MS 193, f.12.

[6] I am aware of only a few extant *lontaraq* manuscripts owned by high status Sama Bajau families that form an invaluable source of Sama Bajau history. Written in the Bugis language and in the Bugis script, these extremely rare manuscripts relate the histories of certain Sama Bajau groups in eastern Indonesia from well before the Makassar War (1666–69) to the early twentieth century. The lengthiest of these manuscripts is in the possession of a high status Sama Bajau family living in the small coastal village of Lemobajo, north of Kendari (southeast Sulawesi). *LB Lemobajo* is a codex of around 300 pages and contains a wealth of valuable information on the history of the Sama Bajau in eastern Indonesia.

Jennifer Gaynor (PhD, University of Michigan, 2005) analyses elements of a Sama Bajau etiological tradition told in *LB Lemobajo* and gave it the title, which I use here. The only extensive historical studies of the entire manuscript published to date are Nolde, 'Changing Tides' and Jennifer Gaynor, 'Liquid Territory: Subordination, Memory, and Manuscripts among the Sama People of Sulawesi's Southern Littoral'.

[7] The *LB Lemobajo* manuscript contains a far more detailed description of the Sama Bajau socio-political and economic networks that comprise the Lolo Bajau polity than for those of the Papuq. This is probably because Lolo Bajau and Bone-affiliated Sama Bajau elites appear to have produced this particular Sama Bajau *lontaraq*. See Nolde, 'Changing Tides', 19–27.

[8] The archaeological findings of Bulbeck, Caldwell and others, as well as the historical evidence presented in Nolde, 'Changing Tides', have forced scholars to rethink the accepted theories and chronology regarding Sama Bajau settlement and influence in South Sulawesi prior to the sixteenth century.

[9] As far as I am aware, the term 'Papuq' or any of its variants are not found in Sama speaking communities of the Sulu and northeast Borneo areas. The absence of the term or title in these areas may indicate that 'Papuq' came into use only after the arrival of Sama speakers in the eastern Indonesian archipelago. The first instance of the Papuq in that context is in conjunction with Luwuq in the northwest corner of the Gulf of Bone.

[10] In a forthcoming manuscript, I detail the history of the Papuq polity's establishment of the Sandao settlements and the more than two centuries long struggle to retain territorial and commercial control over those coastal centers of trade. See also Nolde, 'Changing Tides'.

[11] This was also explained to me as the meaning of 'Papuq' in several Sama Bajau villages in the Flores region. Verheijen received the same explanation of the title from Sama Bajau communities in northern Flores.

[12] NBG 17, f.97-9; NBG 208, f.62-3; MS 193, f.12; KITLV Or.545, no.233, f.3-6.

[13] MS 260, f.1-4; MS 250a, f.3; *LB Lemobajo*, f.8-9. See also Nolde, 'Changing Tides', 208–30.

[14] NBG 17, f.97-9; NBG 208, f.63-4; MS 193, f.13-14; KITLV Or.545, no.233, f.3-4; Nolde, 'Changing Tides', 242–47.

[15] KITLV Or.545, no.18.

[16] According to the Makassarese sources these three Sama Bajau groups fought against Talloq in the mid-sixteenth century and were defeated by the ruler of Talloq, Tumamenang ri Makkoayang Karaeng Pattingalloang. The Makassarese manuscripts clearly state that, even after defeat, these Sama Bajau groups acknowledged the Papuq as their lord rather than the ruler of Talloq. They all occupied roles of relatively high status as far as the defeated peoples were concerned. See Nolde, 'Changing Tides', 242–7.

[17] NBG 17, f.97-9; NBG 208, f.63-4; MS 193, f.13-14; KITLV Or.545, no.233, f.3-4. Exactly which of the several South Sulawesi settlements known as Bayoa is meant by this passage is not clear.

[18] Panaikang was located along a branch of the Talloq River roughly four miles to the south-southeast of the Talloq fortress. KITLV Or.545, no.82; see also NBG 17, f.105–6.

[19] Although we cannot be certain of the correlation, the Talloq chronicle records that the earliest identified Talloq ally of the Papuq polity, Tunilabu ri Suriwa, gave the lordship of both Panaikang and Pateqne to children from his marriage to an unknown woman from Garassiq, which was an early and important Sama Bajau settlement. Cummings, *Chain of Kings*, 84.

[20] VOC 1366, f.691-2. Kaidipang came under Gowa-Talloq overlordship in the early sixteenth century but after Gowa-Talloq's defeat by the VOC in 1667 it was listed among those polities that were to be relinquished to Ternate. Leonard Y. Andaya, *The World of Maluku: Eastern Indonesia in the Early Modern Period* (Honolulu: University of Hawai'i Press, 1993), 166.

[21] For example, VOC Makassar 1403, f.254v; VOC Makassar 1414, f.121r.

[22] *Rapang* can be defined as a genre of Makassarese writing that contains the knowledge of renowned and revered ancestors.

[23] MS 159a, f.51.

[24] NBG 23, f.8–9.

[25] Cummings notes that I Daeng Makkulle Ahmad was 'presumably the son and successor to the *sabannaraq* I Daeng Makkulle who died on 7 September 1677'. It is important to note that Bulbeck's analysis of the *sabannaraq* position in his dissertation (p. 25) is based on the transcription and Indonesian translation of the *Lontaraq Bilang* in H.D. Kamaruddin et al., *Lontarak Bilang Raja Gowa dan Tallok (Naskah Makassar)* (Ujung Pandang, 1985–86), which Cummings has shown to be deficient on several matters including, most importantly for this discussion, those pertaining to the identification of the *sabannaraq*. Kamaruddin et al., for instance, incorrectly treat Daeng Makkulle Abdul Wahid and Daeng Makkulle Ahmad as one person.

[26] I Daeng Mangewai was appointed on 27 November 1724 and died on 17 November 1733. We do not know if he was ever appointed as Papuq.

[27] He is listed as *sabannaraq* by 6 November 1735.

[28] This would mean that she was possibly the mother of I Daeng Makkulle Abdul Wahid as well.

[29] Cummings notes that 'Makassarese frequently use kinship terms as honorifics', and the use of 'grandparent' was 'a sign of respect and kinship'. The fictive Sama Bajau grandparents are Daeng Maingaq and Daeng Manggappa.

[30] ANRI Makassar 273cc.29, f.2-4.

[31] VOC Makassar 1663, f.201-3. Their activities were only discovered at a later date, when a local informant was interrogated regarding Makassarese and English activities in Banjarmasin.

[32] VOC Makassar 8201, f.105-6. The value of the Sama Bajau did not go unnoticed by the Dutch, and from their earliest encounters the Dutch considered the idea of paying several Sama Bajau families living in the Buton and Tidore areas to move to Batavia and serve as the Company's couriers. *Batavias Uijtgaande Briefboeck* 1667, f.723rv; F.W. Stapel, *Het Bongaais Verdrag* (Leiden: University of Leiden, 1922), 205. See also Speelman's suggestion in his 'Notitie', f.27.

[33] NBG 17, f.89-91, f.105-6; KITLV Or.545, no.82; MS 193, f.86.

[34] NBG 17, f.97-9; NBG 208, f.62-3; MS 193, f.12; KITLV Or.545, no.233, f.3-6.

[35] Pelras argues that Karaeng Semerluki described in the *Sejarah Melayu* were possibly Sama Bajau sailors from South Sulawesi. He suggests that the commonly used Romanised transliteration of the title, 'Keraing Semerluki', is incorrect and should instead be transliterated as 'Karaeng Samaq ri Luq' (Lord Bajau of Luwuq). Zainal Abidin suggests the proper transliteration and translation is 'Karaeng Samaq ri Liukang' (Lord Bajau of the Islands).

[36] KITLV Or.545, no.233a, f. 3-6.

[37] Interview with Jufri Tenribali, Sombaopu, Makassar, 10-09-2011.

[38] KITLV Or.545, no.82.

[39] NBG 17, f.97-9; NBG 208, f.62-3; MS 193, f.12; Cummings, *Makassar Annals*, 55, 77.

REFERENCES

Archival sources and unpublished manuscripts:

Koninklijk Instituut voor Taal-, Land- en Volkenkunde:

DH 802. Cornelis Speelman, 'Notitie dienende voor eenen corten tijt en tot nader last van de Hooge Regeeringe op Batavia, tot naarrigtinge van de Onderkoopman Jan van den Oppijnen, bij provisie gesteldt tot Opperhooft en Commandant in 't Casteel Rotterdam, op Macasser, en van den Capitain Fransz; als hoofd over de Militie, mitsgaders die van den Raadt, anno 1669,' [Memorandum ... for the guidance of the Junior Merchant Jan van den Oppijnen, provisionally appointed Resident and Commandant in Fort Rotterdam at Macasser, and of Captain Fransz, head of the Militia, as well as for those of the Council, 1669], unpublished typescript.

Or.545, no.18

Or.545, no.82

Or.545, no.233

Universiteits Bibliotheek, Rijks Universiteit, Leiden [University Library, University of Groningen, Leiden]:

Nederlandsch Bijbel Genootschap [Dutch Bible Society] 17

Nederlandsch Bijbel Genootschap [Dutch Bible Society] 23

Nederlandsch Bijbel Genootschap [Dutch Bible Society] 208

Matthes Stichting [Matthes Foundation] 159a

Matthes Stichting [Matthes Foundation] 193

Matthes Stichting [Matthes Foundation] 233a

Matthes Stichting [Matthes Foundation] 250a

Matthes Stichting [Matthes Foundation] 260

Algemeen Rijksarchief, den Haag [National Archives, The Hague]

Verenigde Oost-Indische Compagnie (VOC) Archieven [Dutch East India Company (VOC) Archives]: VOC 1403; VOC 1414; VOC 1663; VOC 8201

Arsip Nasional Republic Indonesia, Jakarta [National Archives of the Republic of Indonesia, Jakarta]

ANRI Makassar 273cc.29

Privately-owned manuscripts:

Lontaraq Bajo Lemobajo

Published sources:

Abidin, Andi Z. 1974. 'The La Galigo Cycle of South Celebes and its Diffusion.' *Indonesia* 17: 161–9.

Andaya, Leonard Y. 1981. *The Heritage of Arung Palakka: A History of South Sulawesi (Celebes) in the Seventeenth Century*. Den Haag: Martinus Nijhoff.

———. 1993. *The World of Maluku: Eastern Indonesia in the Early Modern Period*. Honolulu: University of Hawai'i Press.

Bougas, Wayne. 1998. 'Bantayan: An Early Makassarese Kingdom, 1200–1600 A.D.' *Archipel* 55: 83–123.

Brown, Charles C. 1970. *Sejarah Melayu or Malay Annals: An Annotated Translation*. Kuala Lumpur: Oxford University Press.

Bulbeck, David F. 1992. 'A Tale of Two Kingdoms: The Historical Archaeology of Gowa and Tallok, South Sulawesi, Indonesia.' PhD dissertation. Australian National University.

Bulbeck, David F. and Ian Caldwell. 2000. *The Land of Iron: The Historical Archaeology of Luwu and the Cenrana Valley*. Hull: The Centre for South-East Asian Studies, University of Hull.

Bulbeck, David F. and Genevieve Clune. 2003. 'Macassar Historical Decorated Earthenwares: Preliminary Chronology and Bajau Connections.' In *Earthenware in Southeast Asia: Proceedings of the Singapore Symposium on Premodern Southeast Asian Earthenwares*, ed. J.N. Miksic. Singapore: NUS Press.

Chambert-Loir, Henri and Siti Maryam R. Salahuddin, eds. 1999. *Bo' Sangaji Kai: Catatan Kerajaan Bima* [The Book of Sangaji Kai: Records of the Kingdom of Bima]. Jakarta: Ecole française d'Extrême-Orient and Yayasan Obor Indonesia.

Cummings, William. 2002. *Making Blood White: Historical Transformations in Early Modern Makassar*. Honolulu: University of Hawai'i Press.

———. 2005. 'Historical Texts as Social Maps: *Lontaraq bilang* in Early Modern Makassar.' *Bijdragen tot de Taal-, Land-, en Volkenkunde* 161 (1): 40–62.

———. 2007. *A Chain of Kings: The Makassarese Chronicles of Gowa and Talloq*. Leiden: KITLV Press.

———. 2010. *The Makassar Annals*. Leiden: KITLV Press.

———. 2015. 'Re-evaluating State, Society and the Dynamics of Expansion in Precolonial Gowa.' In *Asian Expansions: The Historical Experiences of Polity Expansion in Asia*, ed. G. Wade. New York: Routledge.

Hagerdal, Hans. 2001. *Hindu Rulers, Muslim Subjects: Lombok and Bali in the Seventeenth and Eighteenth Centuries*. Bangkok: White Lotus Press.

Hau'ofa, Epeli. 1994. 'Our Sea of Islands.' *The Contemporary Pacific* 6 (1): 148–61.

Hoeksema, Bert W. 2007. 'Delineation of the Indo-Malay Centre of Maximum Marine Biodiversity: The Coral Triangle.' *Biogeography, Time, and Place: Distributions, Barriers and Islands, Topics in Geobiology* 29: 117–78.

Kamaruddin, H.D. et al. 1969, 1986. *Lontarak Bilang Raja Gowa dan Tallok (Naskah Makassar)* [Lontarak Bilang of the Kings of Gowa and Tallok]. Ujung Pandang: Proyek Penelitian dan Pengkajian Kebudayaan Sulawesi Selatan La Galigo.

Liebner, Horst. 1998. 'Four Oral Versions of a Story about the Origin of the Bajo People of Southern Selayar.' In *Living through Histories: Culture, History and Social Life in South Sulawesi*, ed. K. Robinson and Mukhlis Paeni. Canberra: Research School of Pacific and Asian Studies, The Australian National University.

Majors, Chris. 2008. 'Seas of Discontent: Conflicting Knowledge Paradigms within Indonesia's Marine Environmental Arena.' In *Biodiversity and Human Livelihoods in Protected Areas: Case Studies from the Malay Archipelago*, ed. G. Acciaioli et al. Cambridge: Cambridge University Press.

Matthes, Benjamin F. 1859. *Makassaarsch-Hollandsch Woordenboek* [Makassarese-Dutch Dictionary]. Amsterdam: Het Nederlandsch Bijbelgenootschap.

———. 1883. *Makassaarsche Chrestomathie: Oorspronkelijke Makassaarsche Geschriften, in Proza en Poezy* [Makassarese Anthology: Original Makassarese Writings, in Prose and Poetry]. Gravenhage: Martinus Nijhoff.

Mukhlis. 1975. *Struktur Birokrasi Kerajaan Gowa Jaman Pemerintah Sultan Hasanuddin (1653–1669)* [Bureaucratic Structure of the Kingdom of Gowa during the Reign of Sultan Hasanuddin (1653–1669)]. Thesis Sarjana, Universitas Gajah Mada.

Nolde, Lance. 2014. 'Changing Tides: A History of Power, Trade, and Transformation among the Sama Bajo Sea Peoples of Eastern Indonesia in the Early Modern Period.' PhD dissertation. University of Hawai'i at Mānoa.

———. 2015. 'Strange Peoples: The Sama Bajo in VOC Perception and Policy.' *IIAS: The Newsletter* 70 (Spring): 6–7.

Noorduyn, Jacobus. 1987. 'Makassar and the Islamization of Bima.' *Bijdragen tot de Taal-, Land-, en Volkenkunde* 143 (2/3): 312–42.

Pelras, Christian. 1973. 'Sumber Kepustakaan Eropah Barat Mengenai Sulawesi Selatan'. [Resources in Western European Libraries on South Sulawesi.] In *Buku Peringatan* [Book of Memories]. Ujung Pandang: Dies Natales ke-XXI, Fakultas Hukum, Universitas Hasanuddin.

———. 1981. 'Célèbes-sud avant l'Islam, selon les premiers témoignages étrangers.' *Archipel* 21: 153–84.

Pires, Tomé. 1944. *Suma Oriental: An Account of the East, from the Red Sea to Japan*. Translated by Armando Cortesão. London: The Hakluyt Society.

Reid, Anthony. 1983. 'The Rise of Makassar.' *Review of Indonesian and Malaysian Affairs* 17: 117–60.

Sather, Clifford. 1995. 'Sea Nomads and Rainforest Hunter-gatherers: Foraging Adaptations in the Indo-Malaysian Archipelago.' In *The Austronesians: Historical and Comparative Perspectives*, ed. P. Bellwood, J.J. Fox, and D. Tryon. Canberra: The Australian National University Press.

Sopher, David E. 1977. *The Sea Nomads: A Study of the Maritime Boat People of Southeast Asia*. Singapore: National Museum of Singapore Publications.

Stapel, Frederik W. 1922. *Het Bongaais Verdrag* [The Bongaya Treaty]. Leiden: University of Leiden.

Tapala, La Side' Daeng. 1975. 'L'expansion du Royaume de Goa et sa Politique Maritime aux XVIe et XVIIe siecles' [The Expansion of the Kingdom of Goa and its Maritime Policy in the Sixteenth and Seventeenth Centuries]. *Archipel* 10: 159–71.

Verheijen, Jilis A.J. 1986. *The Sama/Bajau Language in the Lesser Sunda Islands*. Canberra: Research School of Pacific Studies, The Australian National University.

10

Nomads in the Interstices of History

Jacques Ivanoff

INTRODUCTION

When it comes to exploring the transitions from foraging to farming throughout the history of Maritime Southeast Asia, specifically in regards to the Austronesian dispersal, the differing interpretations advanced thus far have been progressively leading towards a wider acceptance that a single metanarrative cannot in itself account for the region's Holocene archaeological record. As more discoveries are being made and studies undertaken—such as in places like the Niah Caves and the Kuk Swamp—approaches are shifting from a wider scale regional narrative to examining the features and significance of smaller scale continuities and discontinuities affecting communities in their everyday practices and cultural norms.

This chapter is an attempt to share the significance of localised studies as important considerations in shaping wider narratives by examining the trajectories of two Austronesian groups of sea nomads: the Moken and the Moklen. Before delving into the specifics of these movements, it must be explained that the nomadic migratory strategy adopted by these specific communities is related to specific notions of and relations to time (Ivanoff 2004; Scott 2009; Bourdier, Boutry and Ivanoff 2015). This strategy may be motivated by the nomad's desire to remain on the margins of the dominant population's ideological mainstream and to avoid global integration (Benjamin 2002; Scott 2009; Bellina, Favereau and Dussubieux this volume).

This chapter aims to explore the ways in which a society may organise themselves while living in mobility as a response to oppression, demonstrating how they can maintain their cultural features, especially their cultural strengths, in times of crisis. Sea nomads pursue their livelihoods in ways that make them, culturally speaking, permanently resilient to constraints (oppressive or inhospitable environments, disparate resources, dangers inherent to the sea, slavery, war, disease, etc.) that by and large determine their ways of life. Manifestations of this resilience are visible today, specifically in the gradual resurgence of rituals among the Moken, which are resurfacing after these were thought by most to have disappeared together with their traditional boats and the cultural 'value' of hunting. The Moken have been increasingly returning to ancient practices, starting with their rituals, and re-entered the 'interstices' (Winichakul 2003) left by Burmese fishermen, whose population has increased from a few hundred to several tens of thousands on the islands in recent years. They have rebuilt a social space within which they have reconnected the links they previously had between myth, the anthropisation of the territory, the insular environment, gathering, hunting and social organisation. To manage these 800 islands spread over more than 400 kilometres from south to north, the Moken have succeeded in building a global social system that elevates 'mythical' and 'real' facts to an equal level. The links developed by these nomads are governed by cycles, i.e. the tide, the moon, the wind, plant seasons, which create an order to their nomadic lifestyle in how the collection and distribution of resources are shared among the various subgroups.

THE MOKEN NOTION OF 'SPACE-TIME'

The Moken's strategy to survive by migrating towards a better future, a displacement that is only triggered as a reaction to certain phenomena (i.e. famine, wars, slavery), brings with it a latent knowledge that acts as a security belt linking all the groups that may have been fragmented by these migration triggers, enabling them to turn to one another and thus go 'back in time' to revive whatever knowledge is needed to bounce back and ensure their resilience. As a result, the Moken notion of space intersects with time, and is essentially a system linking together diverse coastal communities under one coastal civilisation. These relationships add richness and layers to their volume of knowledge, which is maintained in Moken myths, toponyms and place names (Ivanoff 2004). Figure 10.1 highlights a desire for discovery and learning, revealing a binomial way of life and impacting the crossed environments that can still be found today in some nomadic gatherings (Ivanoff 2018).

Nomads have built an ethnic calendar with groups of dispersed coastal and island populations, linked by languages, practices and myths. The development of their nomadic ideology as being essentially based on egalitarian principles (non-accumulation, non-violence, refusal to attend school) adopted in response to the often oppressive history experienced by the Moken is a significant consideration in explaining how they have maintained their ways of life.

The Moken developed their own notion of time by rejecting the linear calculations of calendars and instead referring to cycles associated with the seasons and with the links they create between the stars and social contracts (including marriage), which are culturally interdependent on one another. One example of this reference to the past can be found in their relationship with the *taukay*,[1] trade intermediaries who have become members of their society through kinship. The *taukay* also represent temporal markers, as they are associated with a type of resource (tin, pearls, edible bird's nests, sea cucumbers, etc.) dominating barter and trade between the Moken and the outside world. These temporal markers are also inscribed in the environment, with places bearing references to the *taukay* or to a significant type of resource (i.e. *luark machong* or 'Machong's canal' and *djelay bidge* or 'the tin mountain'). These references to the anthropic environment allow the Moken to share common references, starting from the story of their 'origins'—the creation of the Ancestors' Mountains, the founding couples of the subgroups which each have their own stories and specificities. These ancestors command legions of spirits and watch the spirit poles at their feet, which are worshipped by the descendants of the original sacred men. This collective memory and practice allows for the origins of certain groups to be traced back over many generations.

Figure 10.1 First photographed encounter between the Moken and British government officers in colonial Burma (Photo credit: L. Lapicque 1894).

Each act in the nomads' life cycle is part of a global whole that includes the myth, the rite and the social fact. Marriage is an example of this amalgamation, as it relates to a myth according to which Venus and Jupiter, the two newly-weds, move away from the former's mother, the Moon, and finally end up going back to live by Her side, resulting in a mother-son proximity that carries with it an ongoing risk of potential incest. This story of exposure to incest—found in other myths that descend from the celestial vault—explains to men that the introduction of the terms of kinship must reflect certain realities. Therefore, the last born boy of a family is called 'dugong' (*duyong*), which also means 'incest' (Ivanoff 2004), as he is considered the most at risk of committing this transgression as a result of a mother's inclination towards doting on the youngest boy. We have here a cycle that links alliance, residential instability, the return to the matrilocality and the risk of incest, which together form the basis of the kinship system that includes references to myths without which this system cannot be understood.

The Moken have built a global system that impacts the environment while simultaneously adding cultural value to it, through the discovery, utilisation and sharing, often in dangerous conditions, of resources, or through the death of an individual in a place that subsequently becomes sacred. The names of the mountains designate the ancestors who protect the subgroups, while the cemeteries, water channels and villages form a whole that should allow for the rebirth of the dead in their families. It is through the environment and their knowledge of it that we find the history of the Moken (Figure 10.2). This Moken history retains in its tales, legends, songs, myths and pieces of history, the links between the nomads and the region. It relates to the exploitation of tin and its impact on the surroundings; it also makes it possible to delimit the landscapes they perceive and to provide information on the successive waves of arrivals of Malays, Siamese, Indians and Westerners. In short, the Moken are the memory of the forgotten archipelago. Presented here are the practices and strategies that the Moken have developed to remember their history as well as to manage the environment and the relationships they maintain with the dominant populations therein. These practices and strategies form the basis of the structure of this nomadic society and, by extension, that of all other related sea nomads.

If the State in which the nomads live wishes to integrate the Moken—or other nomads culturally associated with them such as the Moklen and Urak Lawoi in Thailand or the Orang Kuala in Malaysia—the ways in which this integration process is carried out do vary (Map 10.1). This difference is reflected in the rise or decline of nomadic societies, which have always lived on the periphery of larger systems, while integrating their references by metabolising them into their ecosystems, both cognitively (knowledge transmitted, recognition of traces of history inscribed within the environment) and symbolically (foreigners integrated into the kinship system, the mythology that encompasses and links the Moken sociocultural system together) (Ivanoff 2018). Everything that surrounds the Moken—fauna, flora, celestial vault, seabed, foreign peoples—is integrated into a system of references that is drawn from the technical, ideological and mythological knowledge they have acquired over centuries of nomadism and interaction. This system of references inscribed in their natural and sociocultural environment carries within it the traces of their historical knowledge.

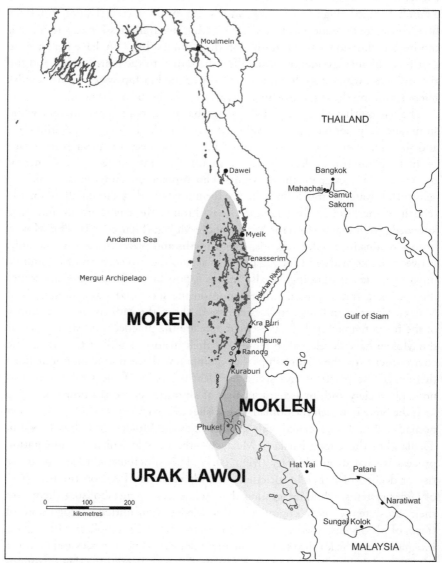

Map 10.1 Distribution of the main Austronesian sea nomad groups of the Malay Peninsula (map by the author).

Figure 10.2 For the Moken, harpooning and eating turtles symbolises harpooning women, an act of cultural anthropophagy, as well as their refusal of literacy, as script is believed to have been written on the shells of turtles, the consumption of which deprived them of this opportunity (Photo credit: E. Bouvet 1992).

All their nomadic knowledge, originating from their know-how and techniques in resource management and mobility, is consolidated by their integration into the cycles of seasons, tides, winds and plants (fruits or yams, the latter of which is known as the 'rice' of the Moken). These cycles which integrate historical episodes (short cycles) and are recorded in their myths (long cycles) are the determining factors in Moken nomadism because they represent an integral part of their environment. As an oral society, the Moken structure their environment through their collective memory of 'reality', what we refer to as 'history', through specific episodes, such as slavery for example (Figure 10.3). Undergoing slavery is still known to the Moklen (nomads of Thailand) and Moken memory, a historical episode that has since been recognised in academic research (Court 1995; Ivanoff 2004; Larish 1992), and is considered as the catalyst factor at the origin of the previously wider group's segmentation into subgroups (i.e. the Moken and Moklen fragmentation). It also helps to understand why nomads have placed themselves under the protection of the *taukay* by accepting unequal exchange in which the Moken are at a disadvantage as the price to pay for their freedom. Threats to their freedom are still very real to them; they remain a reference in their original myths to this day, and make it possible to connect the migrations of the Moken throughout history: as transporters on transisthmian roads; as slaves to a seventeenth-century Siamese temple; as the victims of raids by Malaysian pirates from the sixteenth to eighteenth centuries; as trafficked and imprisoned human beings in the nineteenth and twentieth centuries; as victims of forced labour in tin mines during the Japanese Occupation (Ivanoff 2004). Threats to their freedom and the development of their uneven relationship with the *taukay* thus became part of their ethnic identity. It is therefore not surprising to know that the *taukay* has been integrated into the kinship system—becoming the *biay* ('elder brother-in-law') whose presence in the terms of classificatory kinship is not justified—appearing as the dynamic element of the system. It is this *biay* (the *taukay* who marries a Moken woman) whose existence is recorded in the founding myth of Gaman (Ivanoff 2004). The *taukay* bridges the Moken system of kinship with the outside world, and by extension represents the Moken's door to 'modernity'. In contrast to the modernity inscribed in their kinship system, which is their sociocultural code, marriages follow tradition in how they must follow certain stellar and lunar cycles, immersing their roots in the same myth as the one that introduces the *taukay* (Myth of Gaman, Ivanoff 2004). Sea fauna also forms an integral part of their mythical knowledge and kinship system. Turtles for instance symbolise women—mothers and daughters. Harpooning and devouring turtles is thus a symbolic act of cultural anthropophagy, preventing the Moken from accessing writing (as script is believed to have been written on the shells of turtles, the consumption of which thereby deprived them from learning), therefore preventing them from being assimilated to the outside world.

Figure 10.3 A Moken flotilla of more than 40 boats, representing about 40 nuclear families, hiding from the military underneath foliage (Photo credit: J.-C. Auffret 1998).

Thus, while the *taukay* helps to open Moken society to the modern world (symbolically through kinship and physically through trade), their perception of dugongs and turtles, which they consider as blood relatives in their kinship system, sets the terms for the expansion of the Moken social space, as in through exogamy to avoid incest, all while determining the limits to this space as being the living memory of an oral society existing at the 'margins' of dominant populations (Figure 10.4). It can be understood that the Moken are able to manipulate time, integrating various components of history and external reality, and preserve these in a particular form.

Figure 10.4 Ritually consumed turtles are offered to the ancestors by sacred men. This symbolic act of social anthropophagy (as turtles represent women) enables the Moken to retain their collective memory of and refocus on their relationship with the world and the myths that determine the specificities of their social space (Photo credit: J. Ivanoff 2004).

The social anthropophagy behind the symbolic act of turtle consumption in fact describes how their kinship system is organised, explaining the importance attached to exogamy, their rejection of school, and resource management.[2] The Moken thus impose a demographic and ecological balance in the pursuit of their livelihood that takes into account natural resources, people, and historical references. This balance, the practice of which extends across the entire archipelago, was established when the Mergui Archipelago was discovered, after their people had split as a result of slavery imposed by Siamese temples in the seventeenth century, after which this population segmentation resulted in the Moklen people of the coast (Ivanoff 2004).

Another segmentation occurred while fleeing from Burmese slavery, as subgroups led by founding ancestors arrived in the archipelago and colonised the islands (Ivanoff 2004). In so doing, the Moken have anthropised the environment, built links that form a common reference system, and created a temporality embedded in the landscape. This is how the Moken manage to remember the subgroups from whom they have had to separate, the names of the mountain ancestors, the reference points for all of the Moken mental representations and historical landmarks (i.e. cemeteries, islands where ancestors lived and died). The whole archipelago represents a vast network of culturally and historically significant places that tells us the history of settlement, the discovery of resources, the locations where important events took place, prohibited areas, and the junctions where different peoples meet. Mountains for instance bear the names of ancestors (*kula* for the Indians, *batak* for the Malays, etc.) originating from their past interactions with dominant populations. The Moken acknowledge the influence of all the populations they have encountered in their history—Malay and Thai, Indian, Chinese—who each in their own way have made their mark on the environment utilised by the nomads. Each Moken is therefore the bearer of this knowledge of the environment in its entirety.

This personal and social organisation of space makes it possible to define a Moken territory, of which the cemeteries are the pivot. Moken toponyms connect places to significant events, especially the deaths of ancestors. As a result, there are a considerable number of milestones mapping their history, far exceeding the last few generations governed by their current system of kinship: significant events (whether real or imaginary), prohibited places, locations of plants with miraculous properties, and areas to which access is reserved for specific resources. All of this allows for these places to be considered as having been anthropised in their own terms. By carefully deciphering the stories of these places and the links between history and myth, which are still known to this day thanks to the corpus of oral knowledge accumulated over decades, and by studying toponyms, it is possible to travel with them across the archipelago, and through time to discover its history. All these semantic characteristics in reading the Moken landscape give meaning to the nomads' mobility as being organised according to resources, environmental management practices and the cultural configuration they have developed, in ways for the archipelago to be considered as one and for each to be able to recognise their place within it.

THE REALITY TODAY: THE MOKEN IN MYANMAR

Nowadays, the Moken in Myanmar number approximately 2,000 people distributed among eight subgroups across the Mergui Archipelago in the Andaman Sea. In recent years, the Moken of Myanmar have been facing the incoming migration of thousands of Burmese fishermen to the archipelago, which in turn has seen an unprecedented rise in development through the establishment of fisheries and tourism facilities, new threats to their ways of life that are comparable to the previous historical jolts that have shaped their society. Contemporary threats to the Moken's social and cultural reproduction differ depending on the country where they live. 'Burmanization' (Boutry 2015) or 'Thai-icization' (Ferrari and Hinshiranan Arunotai 2011) of the national territory do not operate in the same ways. The Burmese integrate the nomads by taking Moken wives and settling in their villages (Boutry 2015). Although the Burmese do not force nomads to become Malay or Muslim (*masuk malayu*), separate them in distinct villages or force them to integrate into dominant society (as in Thailand) (Ferrari et al. 2006), Moken ethnicity is being progressively dissolved as a result of these intermarriages with Burmese fishermen. Burmese pagodas, houses, vendors and schools are being built within Moken villages, surrounding their traditional spirit poles and their traditional cycles of time, i.e. comings and goings to the cemetery, and the erection of spirit poles at the foot of the main ancestor-mountain, the village and the cemetery, are more than disturbed by new government-backed projects such as hotels and pearl concessions, all of which are progressively destroying their system (Boutry and Ivanoff 2018). They must therefore reconfigure all of the terms and references inscribed within their mobility as their anthropised environment, which has become the landing point of foreign waves of exploitation, is threatened with destruction and their ecological and economic niche is disappearing. They can no longer live on the margins, under the protection of a more or less benevolent *taukay* in charge of external relations, and instead are now forced to follow the dominant population and their activities. Indeed, resources formerly central to the Moken's trade (pearls, sea-cucumbers, shells, etc.) have been exhausted by the development of Burmese marine fisheries since the 1990s (Boutry 2007). The Moken have therefore little choice but to adapt to the pursuit of new economic niches together with the Burmese (squid fishing for instance). The Moken have however managed to exercise their singularity in ways that are distinctively different from Burmese practices while collecting the same resource as the Burmese. While Burmese fishermen operate with lightning boats and nets, the Moken fish for squid with a hook line, by roaming around islands in their small secondary boats, over rocky beds where larger boats cannot fish. Despite this assertion of ethnic singularity through means of resource collection, fishing for squid is destroying their traditional social organisation by affecting the previous harmony in the gender distribution of activities. Previously, men were responsible for obtaining rice in exchange for shellfish or sea-cucumbers they collected, while women collected foods from the foreshore to accompany the rice. Nowadays, women go fishing, which stands in violation of two customs, not to be confused with prohibitions: keeping a distance between women and the open sea, called 'the outside' (*taao*) and known as the domain of men; and the practice of fishing in itself, a violation that seems to go against the very nature of their culture since the Moken are sea hunters.

In short, the Moken social space as described above (enmeshing the entire archipelago through resources, history, kinship, shamanic journeys, etc.) became a net with holes through it, and the Moken socio-economic organisation prevailing before the massive arrival of Burmese onto the islands of the Myeik (Mergui) Archipelago had to be rethought.

SEGMENTATION OR 'PIVOT' AS THE HISTORICAL STRUCTURE OF NOMADIC ADAPTABILITY

This contemporary crisis lived by the Moken of Myanmar reveals the strategies they implement in order to perpetuate their identity. The logic of being in a nuclear family on a boat, as part of a 'fleet' (the extended family), attached to a subgroup in a shared archipelago, is over. New forms of mobility are being created, with new links and even new Moken emerging. Based notably on the degree of one's interactions with the Burmese, and on the extent of 'integration' into Burmese society, nomads now recognise two kinds of Moken: the 'Sea Moken' (*moken okèn*) and the 'Freshwater Moken' (*moken oèn*). Some go even further by acknowledging only 'real' (i.e. sea) Moken and relatives, who may be their own mixed-blood children. This generational conflict, which calls into question the renewal of Moken culture, divides the new nomads and the old. The 'real' ones find themselves marginalised because their vision of the world is totally incomprehensible to the dominant culture, aid organisations and government officials. The young people, even the sons and daughters of *taukay* who have the ancient knowledge integrated into their minds, do not have the necessary references to make the archipelago a unique place of multiple coordinates that link different levels of reality or culture: myths, ideology and history.

It seems possible that, at this point, their society could split into two, as it does in times of major crisis (creation of the Moken/Moklen segmentation resulting from the threat of slavery for example, Ivanoff 2018). 'Real' Moken may sink into the limbo of a lost history, with their landmarks vanishing (spirit poles, cemeteries, tree wood, sacred and medicinal plants) within a transformed or even a lost environment.

This segmentation process that sees populations getting split apart (Boutry and Ivanoff 2018) can also be applied to other maritime populations of the western coast of the Malay Peninsula. In the course of centuries, many of those who lived as nomads were captured by Malays and kept as slaves within the vicinity of coastal villages. Their descendants intermarried with Malays, Chinese, and even forest nomads. Some of them gave up their own culture, adopted Islam and spoke only Malay. The Malays refer to them as *orang laut*, 'men of the sea', while the Moken call them *orang lonta*. In that respect, the Moken living in the Mergui Archipelago today can be considered as representing the northernmost point of a migration that started in the Riau-Lingga Archipelago, and as the prototype of a truly nomadic sea population, while the others were 'left behind' over the course of the northward migration and were more or less forced into sedentarisation or semi-sedentarisation (Figure 10.5).

Figure 10.5 Despite all the threats that could potentially lead to the disappearance of nomads and their traditions, the Moken are resilient and still know how to build the *kabang*, a marvel of naval technology, and know where to flee if oppression were to become unbearable (Photo credit: J. Ivanoff 2007).

Thus, these nomad populations share, through their segmentation, flight from slavery or movements on transisthmian roads, a common experience: dispersal and dissimilation (Benjamin 2002), all while creating historical places where nomads can regroup, recall their traditions, share their respective discoveries thereby connecting the entire west coast under one cultural umbrella, conduct dealings among one another, and develop an ideology designed for resilience. The known historical places to regroup were the Riau-Lingga Archipelago and the islands of Langkawi and Phuket. Though Langkawi has disappeared as a nomadic landmark territory, Phuket remains a place where the Moken, Moklen and Urak Lawoi gather and regroup. While the author observed that some of the cultural patterns of each community are declining, such as the Moken destroying their *kabang* boat traditions upon settling in Phuket (Rawai Beach), the spirit pole ceremony is still a collective ritual practised to this day. While the Urak

Lawoi do not perform their great ritual in this place, and the Moklen have been living in the interstices left by the two others groups, it is a place where they can think about the future of their ethnicity and assert the connection between nomad populations. The diversity within nomad ethnicity itself is the memento of a long and common history that still connects the whole region.

It is interesting to note that the most important Moklen ritual follows the Moken lunar calendar, and has now become a rice ritual. In becoming sedentary, one of the first pre-Islamic beliefs the Moklen discovered was rice, an ancient Austronesian tradition. Their history highlights the transformation of nomads confronted with the sedentary world (see Illouz and Nuraini this volume). As such, they exemplify some potential evolutions in other Southeast Asian islands (see Galipaud, Guillaud and Crespi this volume for an example of such a potential transformation). Whenever they can, these coastal communities engage in shifting cultivation. This is the main economic activity of the Austronesian groups who came and settled in these regions. The Moklen have become the guardians of these techniques, which are disappearing in the peninsula. They are the symbol of a coastal population who, when they came into contact with more 'developed' peoples, were unable to continue to follow the nomadic way of life. They represent, culturally if not ethnically, a stage in the migratory trajectory of the People of the Sea (Figure 10.6).

Figure 10.6 The Moklen keep traces of past and external influences, illustrated here by an authentic version of the *Manora* (a well-known theatrical performance in Thailand) performed around a shamanic trance intended to invoke the spirits of the earth and to call upon the divinities to 'repair' what has been destroyed (here, the land devastated by tin mines) (Photo credit: J. Ivanoff 1986).

RESEARCH OPPORTUNITIES FOR INTERPRETING PREHISTORICAL AND HISTORICAL LANDSCAPES THROUGH MOKEN AND MOKLEN KNOWLEDGE

The Moklen reject accumulation to avoid competition and violence, and organise their mobility by following slash-and-burn cycles, or by moving between islands and the coast to cultivate dry fields. An example of this is Ko Kloy, an island in the centre of the bigger and flat island of Ko Phra Thong (Phang Nga Province), the last Moklen colony and a meeting point for the Moken and the Moklen. In 1985, the Moklen utilised the land by dividing it into plots according to groups and lineage, thus inscribing kinship rights and history in the environment, marking the territory in a personal and permanent way (Ferrari et al. 2006). There, the myth of the cave and its treasure protected by a naga[3] is shared by each population living near Ko Phra Thong. The Moklen, more specifically, keep a memory of what could possibly be actual historical remains, but to which they add their own singularity entrenched between myth and reality. The Moken and Moklen keep mental records of foreign—including Indian—ships that had been loaded, been discharged or sunk in Ko Phra Thong and its surroundings, and of what could be found in the port warehouse of Ko Ko Khao, located on the commercial route between India and China as described by Jacq-Hergoualc'h (2002). This memory of past human activity was observed firsthand during fieldwork in 1982 when the Moklen would often return with Indian coins or fragments of porcelain, but never with beads. Beads and rock paintings are two of the many 'old' things they avoid, the former because it instils competition to find and sell them, and the latter because they do not want to interfere with previous populations (at least those they do not know of). This knowledge of the landscape could potentially provide opportunities in helping to locate historical and archaeological sites, and could also help the ethnologist to distinguish myth from reality.

Though nomads interacted with other populations whose historical sites they can trace through their oral literature, the Moken, or future Moken, which include the populations living in the estuaries of Malaysia (Orang Kuala), the Urak Lawoi and the Moklen, were nonetheless Austronesian pioneers who avoided pre-existing populations, even though they were not always successful at doing so (especially due to the absence of islands off the coast of the Malay Peninsula).

For them, utilising land or taking possession of something that did not belong to them was out of the question, however symbolic the act. These nomads, since the beginning of their migration from the Riau Archipelago around the sixteenth century, have tried to avoid local populations before attempting to dominate a territory. This is why they can be found in estuaries (Orang Kuala), mangroves (Moklen), and islands (Moken and Urak Lawoi). The Moken consciously avoided areas that presented prehistoric traces that predated their arrival.

The Moken settled in places where the territory had no prior ritual or symbolic power generated by the presence of another population. In short, while they are traditionally inclined to remain distant from prehistoric sites, as they do in Phang Nga Bay or around Mergui, their interactions with other populations and past experiences keep them close to historic sites, such as Ko Ko Khao. They do not acknowledge cave paintings and do not, or will not, nurture awareness of the links between India and where they pursue their existence. They are the guardians of historic places of exchange, and have sometimes even adopted place names defined by others. For instance, the Moklen of Ko Phra Thong also refer to themselves as Olang Kalah, which, according to Rozier and Ivanoff (1986), could mean "men of the Isthmus of Kra", 'Kra' being pronounced 'Kala' in Thai. It is also possible that *kalah* refers to the old name of the ancient town of Takuapa, Kalah (Ferrari 2012). Reversely, the Moken refer to the 'People of Dawei' as a distinct population (*Olang Dawei* in Moken) from the Burmese, who are in turn referred to as *Olang Pugam*, probably after the ancient royal capital Bagan (Myth of Gaman, Ivanoff 2004). While they are often not given too much consideration in the field of archaeology, the study of sea nomad exonyms could provide interesting insights in future research.

CONCLUSION

Understandings of the history of human activity in the region's coasts and seas could indeed benefit from Moken and Moklen knowledge, since it represents one of the few sources on the past of the west coast of the Malay Peninsula. Oral histories should thus be systematically analysed in order to complement the scarce records on this area, paying special attention to references to peoples, landscapes and activities (i.e. tin mining) (Figure 10.7). Should the above suggestion become standard practice, it will be found that there are many similarities between the narratives of material records and the oral literature of the Moken, each of which complement one another. The sea nomads' body of knowledge could help to provide some of the missing pieces to reconstruct a more comprehensive history of the region.

According to the accepted 'out-of-Taiwan' model, the early Austronesians were farmers who migrated around 5500 BP from China to Taiwan and from there to Southeast Asia around 4000 BP (Bellwood et al. 2011). We are not in a position to validate or invalidate the different models proposed for Austronesian expansion, but when it comes to the history and archaeology of sea nomads, ethnography and the study of oral literature may provide valuable hints to examining the past, especially on the western coasts of southern Myanmar and Thailand. In acknowledging the co-existence of multiple temporalities—the linear one, the ethnic one, the one etched in the landscape—we may learn that nomads are landmarks of local history who have created and left behind identity markers that can be found from the coast of Dawei in Myanmar to the Riau

Archipelago south of Singapore. Traces of identity markers drawn from oral literature and languages can be found in the works of some archaeologists, i.e. Bellina, Favereau and Dussubieux (this volume), art historians (Moore 2013, and anthropologists like Chou (2012) and Wee (1985). These evidences point to a set of survival strategies, techniques and rituals common to all Austronesians. They are culturally resilient enough to borrow from or resist external influences and to relaunch their cultural expressions each time they are subjected to, then released from, threats to their freedom. Their social structure depends on warfare and raids, of which they keep a living and collective memory forming part of history. They are more than a people living at the interstices (Winichakul 2003) of nation-states or in a 'Zomia within' (Bourdier, Boutry and Ivanoff 2015).

Figure 10.7 Moken extracting tin from the river in Ko Ra (southern Thailand) (Photo credit: J. Ivanoff 1973).

NOTES

[1] A Hokkien term referring to a commercial intermediary, often Chinese, who manages trade relations between the Moken and the outside world.

[2] Turtles are never traded, and cannot be hunted anywhere or in any way; similarly, trees are only felled at certain times; shellfish and oysters are only collected according to the rhythm of the seasons and according to their regeneration.

[3] The naga is a mythical serpent present in Hinduism and Buddhist cosmology. In most of Southeast Asia, they are associated with autochthonous principles and symbolize legitimate sovereignty (Brac de la Perrière 2002).

REFERENCES

Bellina, Bérénice, Aude Favereau, and Laure Dussubieux. This volume. 'Southeast Asian Early Maritime Silk Road Trading Polities' Hinterland and the Sea Nomads of the Isthmus of Kra.' In *Sea Nomads of Southeast Asia: From the Past to the Present*, ed. B. Bellina, R. Blench, and J.-C. Galipaud. Singapore: NUS Press.

Bellwood, Peter et al., 2011. 'Are 'Cultures' Inherited? Multidisciplinary Perspectives on the Origins and Migrations of Austronesian-Speaking Peoples Prior to 1000.' In *Investigating Archaeological Cultures: Material Culture, Variability, and Transmission*, ed. B.W. Roberts and M. Vander Linden, 321–54. Springer.

Benjamin, Geoffrey. 2002. 'On Being Tribal in the Malay World.' In *Tribal Communities in the Malay World. Historical, Cultural and Social Perspectives*, ed. Geoffrey Benjamin and Cynthia Chou, 7–76. Singapore: Institute of Southeast Asian Studies.

Bourdier, Frédéric, Maxime Boutry, and Jacques Ivanoff. 2015. *From Padi States to Commercial States. Reflections on Identity and the Social Construction Space in the Borderlands of Cambodia, Vietnam, Thailand and Myanmar*. IIAS Leiden: Amsterdam University Press.

Boutry, Maxime. 2007. 'L'appropriation du domaine maritime : des enjeux revisités.' In *Birmanie Contemporaine*, ed. Guillaume Defert. Paris: Eds IRASEC et Les Indes Savantes.

———. 2015. 'How far from national identity? Dealing with the concealed diversity of Myanmar.' In *Metamorphosis: Studies in Social and Political Change in Myanmar*, ed. Francois Robinne and Renaud Egreteau, 103–26. Singapore: NUS Press.

Boutry, Maxime and Jacques Ivanoff. 2018. 'Mastering Territories from the Sea. The Binomial Cultural Way of Resilience of Southeast Asia's Sea Nomads.' In *The Sea Within. Marine Tenure and Cosmopolitical Debates*, ed. Hélène Artaud and Alexandre Surrallés. Copenhagen: IWGIA.

Brac de la Perrière, Bénédicte. 2002. 'Sibling Relationships in the *nat* Stories of the Burmese Cult of the "Thirty-Seven".' *Moussons, Recherche en Sciences Humaines sur l'Asie du Sud-Est* (5): 31–48.

Chou, Cynthia. 2012. 'The Orang Suku Laut of Riau, Indonesia. The Inalienable Gift of Territory.' In *Southeast Asian Perspectives on Power*, ed. Liana Chua, Joanna Cook, Nicholas Long, and Lee Wilson. London: Routledge (The Modern Anthropology of Southeast Asia).

Court, Christopher. 1995. *The Phonology of Patani-Malay. II*. Workshop: Prince of Songkla University, Patani, Thailand.

Ferrari, Olivier. 2012. 'Duean Sip, Théâtre de L'ethnorégionalisme Sud. Les Nomades de La Mer et Le Cycle Rituel Du Dixième Mois Dans La Province de Phang Nga (Sud de La Thaïlande).' *Moussons, Recherche En Sciences Humaines Sur l'Asie Du Sud-Est* (20): 101–20.

Ferrari, Olivier and Narumon Hinshiranan Arunotai. 2011. 'Khwanpenthai ou la pratique de l'idéologie culturelle en Thaïlande.' In *Thaïlande Contemporaine* (2nd Edition), ed. Stéphane Dovert and Jacques Ivanoff. Bangkok/Paris: IRASEC/Les Indes Savantes.

Ferrari, Olivier, Narumon Hinshiranan Arunotai, Jacques Ivanoff, and Kunlasab Utpuay. 2006. *Turbulence on Ko Phra Thong (Phang Nga Province, Thailand)*, coll. Kétos Anthropologie maritime/SDC (Swiss Agency for Cooperation and Development).

Galipaud, Jean-Christophe, Dominique Guillaud, Rebecca Kinaston, and Brunna Crespi. This volume. 'Sea People, Coastal Territories and Cultural Interactions: Tetun Terik and Bunak in the Suai District on the South Coast of Timor-Leste.' In *Sea Nomads of Southeast*

Asia: From the Past to the Present, ed. B. Bellina, R. Blench, and J.-C. Galipaud. Singapore: NUS Press.

Illouz, Charles and Chandra Nuraini. This volume. 'The Bajau Diaspora: Origin and Transformation.' In Sea Nomads of Southeast Asia: From the Past to the Present, ed. B. Bellina, R. Blench, and J.-C. Galipaud. Singapore: NUS Press.

Ivanoff, Jacques. 2004. *Les Naufragés de l'histoire. Les Jalons Épiques de l'Identité Moken.* Paris: Les Indes Savantes.

———. 2018. 'Ethnic Reconstruction and Austronesian Strategies at the Borders. The Moken Social Space in Burma.' In *Routledge Handbook of Asian Borderlands*, ed. A. Horstmann, M. Saxeret, and A. Rippa, 277–88. New York: Routledge.

Jacq-Hergoualc'h, Michel. 2002. *The Malay Peninsula: Crossroads of the Maritime Silk-Road (100 BC–1300 AD).* Leiden: Brill.

Larish, Michael D. 1992. *Who are the Moken and the Moklen on the Islands and Coasts of the Andaman Sea?* Fullbright-Bays, Doctoral Dissertation Research Fellow. Honolulu: University of Hawai'i at Mānoa, Department of Linguistics.

Moore, Elizabeth H. 2015. 'The Inter-Regional Archaeology of Dawei, Lower Myanmar.' In *Advancing Southeast Asian Archaeology*, ed. H. Tan, 162–9. Bangkok, Thailand: SEAMEO SPAFA Regional Centre for Archaeology and Fine Arts.

Rozier, Christine and Jacques Ivanoff. 1986. 'De Mergui à Patani, d'une mer à l'autre, d'une histoire à l'autre.' In *Rôles et Représentations de la mer en Asie du Sud-Est*, Vol. XIV: 69–96, ed. P. Roux and J. Ivanoff. Asie du Sud-Est et Monde Insulaire.

Scott, James C. 2009. *The Art of Not Being Governed: An Anarchist History of Southeast Asia.* Singapore: NUS Press.

Wee, Vivian. 1985. 'Melayu: Hierarchies of being in Riau.' PhD thesis. Canberra: The Australian National University.

Winichakul, Thongchai. 2003. 'Writing at the Interstices: Southeast Asian Historians and Post-national Histories in Southeast Asia.' In *New Terrains in Southeast Asian History*, ed. Abu Talib Ahmad and Tan Like, 3–29. Athens: Ohio University Press; Singapore: Singapore University Press.

11

Ethno-archaeological Evidence of 'Resilience' Underlying the Subsistence Strategy of the Maritime-adapted Inhabitants of the Andaman Sea

Ayesha Pamela Rogers and Richard Engelhardt

INTRODUCTION

In this chapter, the authors utilise concepts of Resilience Theory to analyse and interpret, through time and space, the distribution and patterning of ethno-archaeological evidence of the maritime-adapted populations of the Andaman Sea.

Resilience is 'the capacity of a social-ecological system to absorb or withstand perturbations and other stressors such that the system remains within the same regime, essentially maintaining its structure and functions. It describes the degree to which the system is capable of self-organisation, learning and adaptation' (Holling 1973; Gunderson and Holling 2002; Walker and Meyers 2004). The greater the resilience is in a particular system the more it can resist large or prolonged disturbances. If resilience is low or weakened, then smaller or briefer disturbances can push the system into a different state, where its dynamics change.

For millennia the maritime-adapted populations of island and coastal Southeast Asia have displayed high levels of such resilience in their response to a volatile habitat and constantly changing cultural environment. The Phuket Project has been carrying out ethno-archaeological study of one such group—the 'sea gypsies' of Phuket on the Andaman coast of Thailand—for more than 30 years. This extended time frame from the archaeological past to the ethnographic present has allowed us to identify and document the cultural resilience of this way of life, in longitudinal perspective.

This chapter will focus on aspects of the maritime-adapted resilience of strandloping 'sea gypsies' or Chaw Lay within a framework of Resilience Theory and essential concepts. The aim is to understand the cultural resilience evident in the ethnographic and historical records. We will then address the questions: What does this pattern of cultural resilience look like in the archaeological deposits in sand and mud that characterise insular and coastal sites? What is the archaeologically retrievable evidence of tangible adaptations to ensure resilience and intangible acts which bind the community and pass on knowledge and values in an 'equitable' and sustainable way?

PHUKET PROJECT

BACKGROUND TO THE PROJECT

The Phuket Project is a long-term, multi-disciplinary investigation initiated in the late 1970s and early 1980s as a means to investigate the ways in which adaptive strategies based on the specialisation in marine resources have evolved in the post-Pleistocene tropical island environment of Southeast Asia. These strategies have resulted in a widespread distribution of archaeological deposits throughout the archipelago; a phenomenon which had been widely remarked upon but not explained. To investigate this phenomenon a multi-disciplinary team with a commitment to long-term geographical, ecological, material culture and ethno-archaeological research was constituted, under the framework of the Phuket Project.

The primary approach taken has been ethno-archaeology used to study material culture within an environmental and geographical context. Study has focused on the economic adaptation of sea-based and coastal populations, the visibility of this adaptation in the archaeological record, and the way in which retrievable data is patterned to reflect intra-site structure and their networks across water. To constitute the primary ethnographic database, over a period of 40 years, the material culture transforms of the Chaw Lay or 'sea gypsies' of the Phuket Island Group of the Andaman Sea has been documented. In a series of papers, the insights this work has brought to the interpretation of the archaeological record of the region is presented (Engelhardt 1989; Engelhardt and Rogers 1995, 1997a, 1997b, 1998, 1999, Rogers 1992; Rogers and Engelhardt 1988).

Phuket is the present-day home to three of the existing groups of transhumant sea peoples known collectively in the Thai vernacular as 'Chaw Lay', or 'Sea Gypsies' or 'People of the Sea'. In the mid-1970s, when the Phuket Project was initiated, the Phuket Island Group (Phuket Group), now well known as an international tourist destination, was already poised for rapid economic development and thus inevitable social change for the indigenous inhabitants of the area. For these reasons—the widespread distribution of archaeological remains; the existence of an ethnographically analogous indigenous population; and impending social change—the area was chosen as the laboratory in which to investigate the issues concerning specialisation in maritime resources, in this case resources which are ecologically threatened—issues which have wide relevance throughout insular Southeast Asia. The initial phase of ethnographic documentation and archaeological research continued for a period of three full years from 1978 through 1981, during which a series of nine living communities of Chaw Lay were studied and 15 sites were excavated.

Recognising that much ethno-archaeological research lacks a longitudinal time dimension and thus is open to a critique of speculation, our research has been updated by periodic return visits culminating in a formal project extension in the spring of 1996 in which eight sites were re-excavated and one newly-discovered site investigated. The ethnographic data pertaining to the populations of four Chaw Lay communities was updated and the demographic connections of these population re-mapped in order to determine what, if any, changes in the pattern of movements had taken place over the course of a generation (Engelhardt and Rogers 1997b).

THE CHAW LAY

Figure 11.1 View of Chaw Lay Sea of Phuket, southern Thailand; tying up a boat in the bay (Photo credit: Authors 1980).

The Chaw Lay are an indigenous population living on the west coast of Thailand (Sopher 1977; Ivanoff 1997, 1999, 2001). Traditionally, they live a nomadic existence travelling by boat over an area extending from Myanmar to Singapore. They are reported to be of proto-Malay racial stock, but no genetic mapping has been done, as far as these authors are aware, to confirm this. The Chaw Lay speak

Malayo-Polynesian dialects related to Malay (Hogan 1972; Larish 1999). Their language has three subgroups reflecting regional variation: Moken, spoken from southern Myanmar southwards to Phuket; Moklen, from Phang Nga southward to Phuket; and Urak Lawoi, spoken from Phuket southward along the coast of Malaysia, to the Riau-Lingga Islands south of Singapore. Phuket, at the meeting point of all these dialects, has speakers of all three.

The tribal groups in question all have names for themselves, but refer to themselves as a group in the southern Thai vernacular as 'Chaw Lay'. Although unscientific, use of this term breaks the dangerous misconception that these people are 'nomads' in the true sense of the word, a misconception that the term 'sea gypsies' perpetuates.

In 1981, in the areas studied, there were approximately 4500 Chaw Lay living in more than 40 groups of settlements ranging in size from two to more than 800 people. Of these about 1600 lived on Phuket Island itself and the nearby islands; mostly in the main settlements of Rawai, Tukay, Sapam, Laem La and Laem Tong on Ko Phi Phi. They traveled to and from these base settlements and a wide range of fishing camps by small boat (Figure 11.1).

ETHNO-ARCHAEOLOGICAL APPROACH

The objective of the Phuket Project has been to identify all significant physical attributes of this maritime adaptive strategy in order to model the various activities, and to identify their evolutionary sequence in the archaeological record. 'Ethnoarchaeology' was the approach used: a method of studying how the many behavioural parts of a living human system—that is to a say a *community*—are revealed in the physical by-products of this system, their distribution and patterning (Schiffer 1976). These physical by-products—be they artefacts, depositions or physically-altered ground surfaces—are what persist through time as evidence of the function of the living system. These by-products are what is retrievable through archaeological excavation. The use of these by-products and their inter-relationships in order to reconstruct the components of the past living system is what we understand to be the method and technique of 'ethnoarchaeology'.

In ethno-archaeology, interpretation is not achieved by direct ethnographic analogy, but rather by documenting the transformations of units of archaeological analysis from the ethnographically recorded event to the resulting archaeological deposit. These units of analysis may include: the distribution of sites; alternations of the environment and landscape; artefacts and their relationship to activities in which they are used; the recycling and accumulations of debris; and so forth. The objective of such an analysis is to determine regularities in interpretation over time and space, of activities which create characteristic archaeological deposits.

Ethno-archaeology is, therefore, a tool for developing an explanatory model or framework for interpretation of statistically-relevant archaeological finds and the spatial matrix in which they are found. The usefulness of this technique is in the building of models that explain structural relationships between elements of the system independent of specific locations in time and space and independent of specific finds.

The research strategy used to generate the data to build the model consisted of several main lines of investigation (Engelhardt and Rogers 1995, 1997a, 1997b, 1998). Firstly, a series of environmental studies was undertaken to clarify the geology, geography and resource base characteristic of the region. Much of this work was original field research because of the paucity of available data relevant to the coastal econiche under study. Secondly, a programme of demographic studies was designed to supply data on the sea-based population of the area, their distribution and movements (Figure 11.2). During the course of research more than 1,600 individuals were tracked, which accounts for more than one-third of all known Chaw Lay inhabiting Thai waters. This was followed by aerial, boat and ground survey which identified a series of sites, ranging from long abandoned locations to those still in use. At the latter, detailed mapping was done of all the material, spatial and demographic components of living sites.

Figure 11.2 Cultural mapping of the Chaw Lay living within the Phuket area (Photo credit: Authors 1978).

Studies were undertaken of specific types of material culture and its role in site-based activities. These studies focused on the ethno-archaeological journey of artefacts and materials through use in an activity, re-use, storage, recycling and finally discard, at which point they become part of the depositional record, to be recovered through archaeology. During the course of the multi-year research programme, all Chaw Lay daily, seasonal and specialised activities were analysed and broken down into their component physical and functional parts. Particular emphasis was put on mapping the spatial distribution of these activities and quantifying them. Associated discard and the resulting impact on the activity areas in question were also quantified and recorded over time. The effect these activities had on the soil was recorded photographically, mapped and physically sampled for chemical and microscopic analysis (Figure 11.3).

Figure 11.3 Detailed mapping of the elements of a maritime-adapted settlement, including the contents and location of discard middens (Photo credit: Authors 1980).

In order to evaluate the visibility of these artefacts and activities in the archaeological record and the effectiveness of various methods of retrieval, a series of micro-excavations—or 'dermabrasions'—were carried out using razor blades and calligraphy brushes of both activity areas and depositions (Figure 11.4). The archaeological transforms which were examined in particular included those which have been shown by previous ethno-archaeological study to be those which enter the depositional record and are archaeologically retrievable. These are (a) ground evidence of structures; (b) compacted surfaces with and without inclusions; and (c) debris depositions. Repeated partial erasure of these three variables form the traces we see in the archaeological palimpsest at coastal sites.

Figure 11.4 View of 'dermabrasion' of the area underneath a stilted house at Phap Pha—a base camp abandoned more than 100 years ago—to examine fine vertical and horizontal detail (Photo credit: Authors 1978).

These studies at environmental, community, site, activity area and subsoil levels were disaggregated into a number of predictive models of site use and formation. For purposes of testing at archaeological sites, the resulting ethnographically derived patterns were conceptualised as culturally-identifiable 'type sites' and a predictive model of archaeological expectation was developed. Translated into behavioural predictions, they form the basis of a model of Chaw Lay site formation and use. This was abstracted into a conceptual or archetypal site, suggesting what would be found in the archaeological record, in what frequencies and in what spatial patterning. The interplay of activity areas, secondary depositions and post holes, roof driplines and circumstantial artefactual evidence allowed the identification and reconstruction of a normative Chaw Lay archaeological site, in all its functional detail.

Fundamental to this model-building have been such concepts of 'catastrophe theory' (Postle 1980) and theories borrowed from biogeography such as 'carrying capacity', 'nearest neighbour analysis' and the 'founder effect' (MacArthur and Wilson 1967). Such theories provide tools to explain the ways in which multiple, small niches are selected and developed, linked, abandoned and then re-used.

A final important line of investigation was the critical evaluation of these models. The model was tested by survey and excavation of a number of abandoned Chaw Lay sites which were then compared to the normative 'type site'. This reconstruction was then evaluated for the degree to which it fits expectations based on the ethno-archaeological derived models. After evaluating the accuracy of fit, the ethnographic situations were returned to in an attempt to identify the archaeological findings unexplained by the model. Throughout, native informants were worked with in order to interpret the data. As a result of a follow-up phase of fieldwork in 1996, the models were re-tested, refined and given a longitudinal degree of time depth (Engelhardt and Rogers 1998).

RESILIENCE CONCEPTS APPLICABLE TO MARITIME SUBSISTENCE STRATEGIES

The understanding of resilience adopted for this study is that elaborated by the Resilience Alliance, a research organisation that focuses on resilience in social-ecological systems as a basis for sustainability (http://www.resalliance.org/). A selection of the main concepts of resilience theory is presented here; these elaborate the definition and workings of resilience and will be used to test the relevance and usefulness of Resilience Theory to understanding the Chaw Lay maritime adaptation. This discussion of resilience should be read in conjunction with the previously-cited published work by Engelhardt and Rogers on other aspects of the Chaw Lay and maritime adaptation in Southeast Asia.

ADAPTIVE CAPACITY

Adaptive capacity underlies the concept of resilience; it is the *ability* of a system to cope and respond if the environment where the ecological or social system exists is changing. Systems with high adaptive capacity are more able to re-configure without significant changes in crucial functions or declines in ecosystem services (Folke et al. 2002).

A consideration of the environmental niche which the Chaw Lay have chosen to occupy is crucial to an understanding of their adaptive strategy. The entire coast from the Bay of Bengal to the Riau-Lingga Archipelago and beyond into the Indonesian Islands is characterised by long stretches of sandy beach broken by estuarine areas of mangrove and mud-flat, rocky outcrops and off-shore island groups, closely enough spaced as to be easily visible one from another all along the chain.

The sea is shallow over the narrow continental shelf, with warm temperatures and low salinity resulting in plentiful marine fauna and a great diversity of species. This environment was created by the flooding of the Sunda Shelf at the end of Pleistocene. The resulting Southeast Asian land and seascape is unique in its high ratio of sea to land.

This entire stretch of coast is a vast and homogenous environment in which fish, the highest protein resource, are sparsely but widely distributed and highly mobile. This benign environment provides a year-round supply of fish, shellfish, fruit and vegetables (Figure 11.5).

The climate is always warm, with a monsoon pattern of a mild, sunny period during the northwest winter monsoon and a period of strong winds and rains during the summer monsoon from the southwest. During this summer monsoon the seas are not safely navigable by small craft.

Unlike human groups in temperate continental areas who must adapt to the limitations of food resources availability in an environment with concentrations of these resources in space and time, the inhabitants of Southeast Asia's coastal areas had to develop ways to access the many small, but resource-abundant pockets of resources widely distributed throughout the seas of the region. The Chaw Lay of the area have adopted a subsistence strategy wholly devoted to the exploitation of these deep sea, coastal shelf, reef, intertidal and shoreline resources. There is archaeological evidence suggesting occupation of the area since at least the end of the Pleistocene by people who for the past several millennia have increasingly specialised in exploiting the marine resources of this ecologically diverse area (Anderson 1987). It is this ability to deal with short and long-term change, uncertainty and historical events—in other words the resilience of their adaptation—without loss of cultural identity that constitutes their adaptive capacity.

Resilience theory proposes that adaptive capacity of a group or community is augmented by the following traits (Walker and Salt 2006):

Figure 11.5 The landscape which the Chaw Lay inhabit is characterised by long stretches of sandy beach broken by estuarine areas of mangrove and mud-flat, rocky outcrops and off-shore island groups (Photo credit: Authors 1979).

1. Learning to live with change and uncertainty—which requires *persistence*: the capacity of a system to maintain structure and function when faced with shocks and change.

Throughout the region, the Chaw Lay have adopted a subsistence strategy devoted exclusively to the exploitation of the resources of the sea and the shoreline. The Chaw Lay by strategic preference pursue larger species of fish because of the higher economic value in terms of energy return of large fish as compared to the smaller fish and shellfish of the reefs and intertidal zones. These larger fish tend to be solitary wanderers in the sea and therefore a heavy concentration of fishermen in any one area reduces the economic validity of the expedition. This encourages widespread and sparse but even spacing of Chaw Lay groups throughout the archipelago, and puts limits to the human population which a given area can support from fish alone.

Although ethnographic study has documented that fish are the preferred resource exploited by the Chaw Lay, shellfish form the baseline of their subsistence (Engelhardt and Rogers 1997a, 1998). If the biomass of the preferred resource, fish, is low for one reason or another, the ecological diversity of the coastal niche assures that alternatives are available to buffer the population. While this may at first glance seem to be counter-intuitive, Resilience Theory explains why this would and should be so.

The *persistence* or the buffering effect of easily available shellfish is therefore the most important consideration of the Chaw Lay adaptive strategy. Access to and harvesting of shellfish is the essential feature of their economic adaptation. As a result, bulky and highly visible shell debris is the main archaeological marker of their use of a site (Figure 11.6). The presence and density, or lack thereof, of deposits of shellfish debris are the essential archaeological features which must be examined and explained if we are to understand the evolution and workings of a subsistence strategy based on maritime resources.

2. Nurturing diversity for resilience—which requires *adaptability:* the capacity of people in a social-ecological system to manage resilience through collective action in order to stay within a desired state during periods of change.

Throughout this study of the evolution of maritime adaptation in Southeast Asia, the interchangeability of the coastal econiche coupled with the specialisation of certain communities in the exploitation of this econiche is the basic phenomenon of which modeling, understanding and explanation has been attempted. As a wide range of beach and strand camp sites were examined, and the spaces between these sites were travelled by boat with Chaw Lay informants, it became clear that the catchment area exploited by each Chaw Lay group includes a much larger area than their immediate habitation sites. It is the limit of the extended catchment area that determines the spacing of Chaw Lay throughout the potential econiches at any given time. This has created the pattern of archaeological deposits to be found on so many islands of the archipelago.

Figure 11.6. Access to and harvesting of shellfish is the essential feature of the traditional economic adaptation of all Chaw Lay communities. As a result, bulky and highly visible shell debris is the main archaeological marker of their use of a site (Photo credit: Authors 1978).

Each site in the network has the potential to be used in a continuous but intermittent fashion in both a regular and intermittent manner. This seemingly contradictory situation is a result of the varied patterns of diverse econiche use. A site, or a portion of a site, may be used as a base camp by one Chaw Lay group, while several small and transient groups may use portions of the site for temporary occupation. At the same time space, a boat group may use the econiche for water and vegetable collection, but not for residence, as they stay on their boats and move on. The pattern is further refined by aspects of seasonality and the occasional need for a site to be temporarily, but regularly under-utilised while its resources regenerate.

In the attempt to conceptualise and understand this diversity, a typology—or more precisely phrased, a 'palimpsest'—of archaeological sites and their interlinkages or networks throughout the catchment area has been developed. To develop this palimpsest, the ethnographic and archaeological patterning at four levels of socio-economic organisation were originally identified:

1. temporary seasonal camp sites, forming the basic unit of Chaw Lay colonisation of a site;
2. base settlements of longer-term occupancy, functioning in a sustained manner well within a site's carrying capacity;
3. settlements at the point of ecological collapse; and
4. abandoned occupation areas, past the point of collapse now in a state of environmental regeneration and used only for intermittent scavenging.

The Chaw Lay's conceptual organisation and use of space for social and economic subsistence activities is what determines the spatial patterning of archaeological remains at ground and below-ground levels. The complex patterning creates, on the sandy matrix of the beach sites, a multiple overlay of partly visible lines of archaeological 'text'; each one imperfectly erased but remaining in partial form. The concept of palimpsest is particularly applicable for intermittently occupied coastal sites, where the annual monsoon and the action of the inhabitants through regular maintenance of activity areas and scavenging of abandoned sites partially erases the evidence on the ground.

At each site the Chaw Lay adaptive strategy implies a range of activities for extraction, processing and consumption of the resources from their environment. Those activities which occur on-site have potential impact on the archaeological record of a site. The tools and materials used, associated discard, deposition and impact on the activity loci are the elements which make up each layer of the palimpsest.

The toolkit utilised in this strategy reflects this approach to *adaptability*; tools are few in number and easily movable, as suits a lifestyle where numerous possessions would be a burden. Items are multi-purpose, light and easy to transport, with an emphasis on wood, coconut, bamboo, stone and other material easily available from the local environment (Figure 11.7). The larger the item, the more statistically likely there will be only one shared by a group. The only specialised technology common to all the groups studied were boats, to provide mobility, and fishing gear, to facilitate the capture of mobile sea resources.

Figure 11.7 Tools used by the Chaw Lay are characteristically few in number and easily movable, as they suit a lifestyle where numerous possessions would be a burden. Items are multi-purpose, light and easy to transport, made of wood, coconut, bamboo, stone and other materials easily available from the local environment (Photo credit: Authors 1979).

An important feature of Chaw Lay subsistence is the re-use of materials and tools. All objects are re-used until they disappear, are consumed, or broken into tiny fragments too small to be manipulated. This is less a condition of poverty than that a large number of material possessions are a liability in a mobile society. The richness of the environment and the effectiveness of their adaptation frees them from the need to stockpile against environmental uncertainty. This results in a notion of collective action with each member of the community cooperating in a culturally-specific pattern of learned behavior understood and acted upon by all members of the group. An anecdotal but emotive example of this was observed when a cookie was distributed to each child in Rawai village. The children promptly sat in a circle in the middle of the village, broke their cookies into small pieces and each shared a piece of their identical cookie with all of the other children—a living example of *adaptability*: the capacity of people in a social-ecological system to manage resilience through collective action in order to stay within a desired state during periods of change.

3. Different types of knowledge for learning and creating opportunities for self-combining organisation towards social-ecological sustainability—which requires *transformability*: the capacity of people in a social-ecological system 'to learn, innovate and transform in periods of crisis in order to create a new system when ecological, political, social or economic conditions make the existing

system untenable, with institutions and networks that learn and store knowledge and experience, create flexibility in problem solving and balance power among interest groups' (Walker and Salt 2006).

In the 'sea gypsy' adaptation all essential knowledge is shared by everyone, making them all broad-based generalists. This means that every small boat-based unit can function smoothly without the need of specialists. The only specialists are those few people who have knowledge of spirit matters and can lead ritual activities. They function at ceremonies such as Loy Rua, the biannual gathering with the ancestors immediately before annual dispersal at the end of the monsoon season and regathering when the monsoon returns. This particular ceremony demonstrates both the shared and intergenerational nature of knowledge transfer but also the role of ceremonial specialists in adaptive capacity (Rogers 1992).

Figure 11.8 Among the few functional specialists in a Chaw Lay community are those self-identified individuals who have knowledge of spirit matters and can lead ritual activities. They function at ceremonies such as Loy Rua, the biannual gathering with the ancestors immediately before and after annual dispersal at the end of the monsoon season (Photo credit: Authors 1979).

There is a pre-existing dendritic network of fishing and migratory links which characterises the physical and abstract world of people adapted to a maritime subsistence strategy (Engelhardt and Rogers 1997a; 1997b). Sea people move along these networks, dispersing to small extraction camps, moving on to seasonal processing camps and gathering together at large, year-round base camps for the economic 'down time' of the rainy season. Every group functions self-sufficiently, meeting their own needs; the network does not serve to exchange or redistribute goods, nor does it deal with surplus or storage. The underlying economic relationship between groups and individuals is sharing of resources to ensure their equitable consumption by all members of the community.

At various times boat-based populations have taken their products to market—sometimes in small boat groups, sometimes banding together to form flotillas—calling at one of the established trading centres. We read of this occurring in times and situations of political or social stress and upheaval, when the seas become unsafe for traders to travel to outlying areas. For example, White refers to large groups of Moken (Chaw Lay) journeying to Mergui in the later years of British administration to trade in safety (White 1922). Similarly, in the 1840s under the threat of piracy, 100 to 150 boats of Bajau would come to port to deliver the trepang and tortoiseshell upon which the Sultan of Ternate relied for export to China (Sopher 1977). A modern example is the black-market delivery of mangrove woods to Malaysian lumber traders by Sumatran-based sea peoples. When traders are unable to come to the product source, the maritime adapted peoples can employ their characteristic mobility to take the product to the market. Although this may not be as economically efficient, it functions as a fail-safe mechanism based on flexibility in problem solving and deeply engrained *transformability*.

ADAPTIVE CYCLE

The interaction and function of these traits of resilience can be modelled using the concept of an Adaptive Cycle (http://www.resalliance.org/). This cycle has four distinct phases (Figure 11.9):

1. growth or exploitation (r)
2. conservation (K)
3. collapse or release (Ω)
4. reorganisation (α)

There are two major phases of the Adaptive Cycle: the first, called the foreloop, from r to K, is the slow, incremental phase of growth and accumulation. The second, referred to as the backloop, from Ω to α, is the rapid phase of reorganisation leading to renewal. However, if there is a failure to reorganise, the backloop can also lead to X state, or the potential for the system to undergo a regime shift.

An adaptive cycle that alternates between long periods of aggregation and transformation of resources and shorter periods that create opportunities for innovation, is proposed as a fundamental unit for understanding complex systems from cells to ecosystems to societies (Resilience Alliance website).

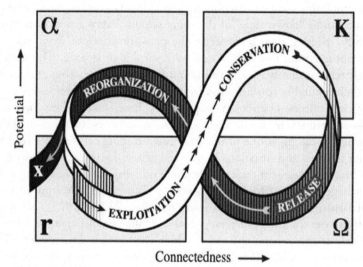

Figure 11.9 Diagram illustrating the Adaptive Cycle, which models the interaction and function of traits of resilience (Source: *Panarchy* by Lance Gunderson and C.S. Holling [Washington, DC: Island Press, 2002]).

Adaptive Cycles generate novel re-combinations that are tested during longer periods of capital accumulation and storage (foreloop). These windows of experimentation open briefly, but the results do not trigger cascading instabilities of the whole because of the stabilising nature of nested hierarchies.

> In essence, larger and slower components of the hierarchy provide the memory of the past and of the distant to allow recovery of smaller and faster adaptive cycles (backloop). A nested hierarchy of adaptive cycles represents a *Panarchy* with multiple scales of space, time and social organization which determine the dynamics of the system (Gunderson and Holling 2002).

This characterises the Adaptive Cycle of the Chaw Lay and allows us to link the intangible ethnographic observations we have observed to the tangible archaeological data we have collected. While the Chaw Lay strategy requires both (a) the nodes of settlement sites to coalesce on an annual basis, and (b) the cyclical dispersal of the population to the small sites, in order to efficiently exploit the resources, neither type of site is dependent upon a specific, fixed geographical location. Because of the interchangeability of sites within the maritime coastal environment, if one site is not available, then another site will provide an equal alternative.

Ethnographic and archaeological evidence both point to a characteristic long-term but intermittent occupation of coastal sites (Engelhardt and Rogers 1997a, 1997b, 1998) reflecting growth or *exploitation phase (r)*. This is the phase in which networks are formed and the palimpsest of settlements reflecting the different levels of socio-economic organisation is formed. As base camps evolve to supply central points and rainy season gathering nodes, the system enters the *conservation phase* (K) for the 'slow accumulation and storage of energy and material' (Resilience Alliance website) (Figure 11.10).

At any one location, the space available for both productive and social activities becomes, over time, increasingly constricted by increasing population and accumulating refuse. Eventually the carrying capacity of a site is reached and a way must be found to enlarge the site, or, to reduce the number of persons relying on the site for their subsistence—*collapse or release phase (Ω)*. The organised pattern of spatial segregation of activities become increasingly disorganised as open communal spaces shrink, more and more space is occupied by deposition and structures are more densely packed. In the archaeological record this is seen in the loss of segregation between depositions, activity areas and habitation space. Within secondary depositions there is evidence of more frequent dumps as more and more time is devoted to maintaining the environment in an attempt to provide recycle space.

In response to these pressures we often see attempts to increase carrying capacity through various means: the artificial enlargement of the site itself as tertiary depositions fill topographic hollows to level land, dyke the front of the site or reclaim land along the back of the site (Engelhardt and Rogers 1997b); the establishment of very close 'suburban' neighbourhoods; the movement of houses into the intertidal by construction on stilts (Figure 11.11); or a combined style of settlement with some people living on boats and others on land. These carrying capacity adjustments or augmentations can be seen in terms of Catastrophe Theory (Postle 1980), where small incremental changes, with adjustments here, there and everywhere keep things ticking along for as long as possible along the same geometric plane, until suddenly the edge (breaking point) is reached and there is a complete fall or jump from one plane to another.

In response to this catastrophic event, the group must abandon the site, splintering and moving on to one or more of the other similar available econiches available within the network's catchment area—*reorganization phase (α)*. When faced with this degree of spatial and economic stress, our model predicts that mobile populations respond in a typically mobile manner, by removing themselves and/or specific activities from the site under pressure (Engelhardt and Rogers 1997a, 1997b, 1998). In this safety-valve strategy we see out-migration of individuals or small splinter groups in an attempt to establish a new equilibrium, and thus postpone the need to abandon a site and move the community's base camp to a new location.

Figure 11.10 View of a base camp evolved to supply central points and rainy season gathering nodes, reflecting the conservation phase (K) of the Adaptive Cycle (Photo credit: Authors 1979).

Figure 11.11 Extending the construction of houses into the intertidal by building on stilts in an attempt to increase carrying capacity at a base camp under stress (Photo credit: Authors 1980).

This is the final phase in the Adaptive Cycle model, an adaptation of strategy to evolving circumstances, but it does not represent a culture or population replacement. The basic socio-economic strategy of reliance on specialised adaptation to maritime resources remains unchanged. Sites continue to be located in the same places or in expanded marine niches; there is no evidence of a population decline reflected in disappearing sites and increased number of cemeteries, or other such phenomena that precede or accompany the first phases of cultural replacement. Most importantly, the subsistence base remains unchanged as reflected in marine by-products and associated technology and continues unchanged in the ethnohistorical records. There are other examples that could be pointed to: for example, diving for pearls, or better still diving to place the hoses for the tin dredges. Both were opportunistic responses to a specific time-bound situation, which now no longer exists. The Chaw Lay used their strategic adaptive fitness to take advantage of the opportunities, while not having to undergo cultural transformation to do so. As pointed out by Folke, "… resilience is not only about being persistent or robust to disturbance. It is also about the opportunities that disturbance opens up in terms of recombination of evolved structures, renewal of the system and new emergence" (2006: 259).

ARCHAEOLOGICAL EVIDENCE OF THE ADAPTIVE CYCLE

The degree to which a site has reached its carrying capacity, and therefore the stage it has attained in the Adaptive Cycle, can be calculated from the excavation and reconstruction of the extent and position of secondary deposition of subsistence refuse (Figure 11.9) (Engelhardt and Rogers 1997b, 1998). Another marker of site carrying capacity stress which typically is visible in the archaeological record is the lack of spatial segregation at a site. Deposits which once occurred as patches in a clean matrix are replaced by a blanketing layer of occupational debris (Engelhardt and Rogers 1997b) (Figure 11.13).

When first studied 15 years ago, Sapam was a coastal settlement already in crisis (Adaptive Cycle Ω *collapse or release phase*). It served as the type site for the next to last stage of the palimpsest: an overpopulated and overexploited econiche at the limits of its carrying capacity. The density of structures had increased to the point where virtually all available space was filled, with a post count of 49 in a 10 metre square site. This is in contrast to an average of two posts or less in sample 10 metre squares at other sites. The quantities of secondarily-deposited refuse had increased until discrete mounds had merged to cover the entire surface of the site. No attempt was being made to maintain the area, nor were there any discernible open, communal spaces or activity areas which were not themselves on top of terminal deposits of shell middens (Figures 11.12 and 11.13).

Figure 11.12 A woman processing fish at Sapam on a village-wide secondary deposition of subsistence refuse (Photo credit: Authors 1980).

Figure 11.13 View of Rawai illustrating the blanketing layer of occupation filling up what were formerly open, clean communal spaces (Photo credit: Authors 1996).

This stress was also reflected in the greater amount of time expended at Sapam on the basic acquisition of food, which during initial research was 65 per cent of time, as compared to 35 per cent of time at a mature and flourishing base camp. This meant that virtually all daylight hours were spent in subsistence activities. Furthermore, in terms of fish versus shellfish, 100 per cent of Sapam residents reported that shellfish was the primary resource on which they relied.

Catastrophe Theory suggested a predictive model of what would happen at Sapam; when such a system becomes unsustainable in the long term a radical or 'catastrophic' change is to be expected which equates with Adaptive Cycle (α) reorganisation phase (Scheffer et al. 2001). The 'catastrophic jump' predicted was called the *Removal Response*. In this problem-solving strategy, when the carrying capacity of a site is reached, it can be expected that out-migration either of individuals or of small splinter groups in an attempt to establish a new equilibrium will precede any final abandonment of the site, in the attempt to re-establish equilibrium. However, if the pressure has already resulted in the decline of the essential shellfish resource base, removal of the group to another site is inevitable and the abandoned site reverts in status to a temporary camp, allowing the site time for the very slow process of regeneration.

At Sapam, displacement has resulted in removal to the fringe of the site and to the splintering and out-migration of population. Only two of the original 32 resident boat groups present during the original research phase at Sapam are still intact. However, Sapam continues to be exploited even under these very adverse conditions. The question this poses is: What has enabled Sapam to be retained in the Chaw Lay network of sites instead of dropping out entirely?

Such episodes of infiltration, displacement, expansion and replacement of one cultural group by another, are frequently presumed to be the cause of complex stratified deposits which archaeology attempts to unravel. Sapam supplies us with a stunning example of just how easily the most mystifying stratigraphy can be created. If we were to look at a schematic presentation of what archaeology might reveal at this site we would see a complex interweaving of Chaw Lay presence in a matrix of midden and mud co-existing beside Thai presence in soil, then in artificial fill over Chaw Lay midden and in landfill over mud. Complicating this picture, we have a spirit area outliving its related settlement; two distinct stages of Chaw Lay habitation of both sides of the channel; a Thai shop in a Chaw Lay matrix; and evidence of the displaced Chaw Lay present in a potentially confusing manner at the site's new periphery.

Sapam provides us with a good example of the tenacity of the survival mechanisms of the maritime adaptation. Their elasticity allows them to absorb a great deal of stress without the necessity for abandonment of the basic adaptation. It also points out that the network itself is constantly in flux with the relative position, function and importance of sites within the network constantly changing, as Sapam has changed its position in the palimpsest and has 'jumped' to near the bottom of the sequence. We saw how over a period of 17 years, the centre of the network switched from Rawai to Tukay (Map 11.1). The central position of Tukay was reinforced by the in-migration of the population of another settlement pushed into a catastrophic response. The shift of the centre to Tukay has also given Sapam an extended lease on life as it has brought Sapam closer to the centre and makes it a viable site for base settlement exploitation on a more casual or temporary basis, with Tukay fulfilling the base camp social and support functions for the Sapam population.

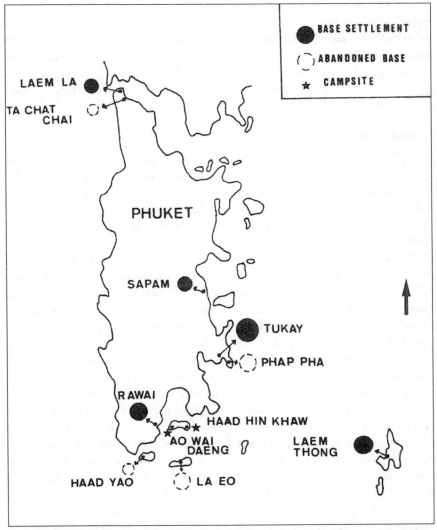

Map 11.1 The main base camps discussed showing their locations in the network, evolving towards entropy through a series of seasonal fluctuations in size and population density (Credit: Authors 1997).

How and why certain sites change their relative importance and drop in and out of the network, depends upon the interplay of a set of factors which include (i) the position and relative isolation of a site along dendritic networks linking satellites with base camps; (ii) the absolute size of the satellite site; (iii) the critical level of population which the buffering resources of the site can support; and (iv) the degree to which the site's carrying capacity has been overreached and its resources exhausted.

The *removal response* that results is a maritime-adapted solution to the problem of how to sustain human population densities and conserve resources over an extended period of time in an environment where the resources themselves are mobile and widely scattered. Because of the population's mobility and the availability of interchangeable econiches, a complex pattern of movement, social splintering and re-grouping has evolved. The advantage of this strategy is that it does not entail a change in the classical cultural transformations of means, forces or in the relations of production—it is, in fact, resilient.

THRESHOLDS

In resilience terms the Chaw Lay at Rawai have reached a *threshold*, a point between acceptable and unacceptable conditions. Thresholds are used to describe 'breakpoints' between two regimes or alternate stable states in a system (Walker and Meyers 2004). In theory, when a threshold level is passed, a regime shift of culture change occurs, and as a result, the nature and extent of feedback in the system changes.

We can see this clearly in the current situation at Rawai base camp—a constricted site under severe stress, where in the past decades site space has been seriously encroached upon along the sea front and along the rear lagoon by alien buildings and associated landfill. A frontage road limits one side of the site and a new perpendicular road now cuts the settlement in half and gives access to the lagoon behind the site which has been filled in by developers. There is no option for expansion by moving the frame outwards. These are all indications that the econiche has been over-populated and over-exploited with the result that we see the blurring or loss of the characteristic Chaw Lay sense of space and grouping.

Archaeological evidence of 'crossing the threshold' can be seen in the form of intrusive material cultural elements and also the use of space by intrusive cultural carpetbaggers—a Chinese coffee shop; a tourism boat dock; fish restaurants; souvenir shops. The Chaw Lay's physical world is being occupied by external entrepreneurs who have expropriated by force shoreline base camp space and dramatically limited the Chaw Lay's access to the water and the marine resources contained therein (Figure 11.14). The privatisation of both land and water—as part of the reconfiguration of the maritime econiche to suit the demands of the new industry of mass tourism—has meant that the Chaw Lay's traditional economic options have been effectively eliminated. This is what Resilience Theory refers to as a forced transformation: an imposed transformation of a social-ecological system that is not introduced deliberately by the actors themselves.

Resilience Theory proposes the dual concepts of *revolt* and *remember* (Abidi-Habib and Lawrence 2007) as part of the cycle of a resilience system and a way of responding to the crossing of such dangerous thresholds. In a period of *revolt* a disturbance occurs, often signaled by an institutional innovation, whose every step triggers a cascade of events that move the disturbance to a larger and slower level of *remember* in the social-ecological system. The period is marked by social learning and institutional innovation. In such times of reorganisation and change, resilient systems rely on remembrance as a cross-scale connection (Resilience Alliance 2007). It is associated with social memory, knowledge-system integration and 'visioning' and helps guide the community back to a resilient status (Folke 2006).

Figure 11.14 Rawai base camp – a constricted settlement under severe stress, where over recent decades site space has become so spatially packed that there is no option for expansion, resulting in the blurring or loss of the characteristic Chaw Lay sense of differentiation of space and functional grouping (Photo credit: Authors 1996).

If we look at the base camp settlement at Rawai, we see this *revolt* and *remember* syndrome vividly enacted as the community is pushed beyond its threshold by imposed, external events—specifically focused attempts by tourism development companies to seize village land, burial grounds and coastal access from the Chaw Lay in order to develop tourism complexes. This seizure brings about *revolt* with its cascading events in the form of sit-ins, physical fights and conflict, site degradation and political and legal interventions.

Remembrance is also occurring. There is united Chaw Lay action, support systems for those being injured or called to court and new activism with a campaign of posters and pamphlets saying things like 'Protect our Culture' and 'Restore our Lands, Livelihoods and Culture'. We see knowledge-system integration as the Chaw Lay are forced into the digital world as part of their survival attempts and fight for resilience. There is also serious 'visioning' taking place as they plan for their longer term future as a community. The use of genetic and archaeological evidence to support their case in court for land and sea access is an example of *tools of remembrance* used to combine social memory and scientific data to maintain resilience and counter the very real threat of a regime shift, resulting in culture loss and an end to their millennia old adaptation and resilience.

REFERENCES

Abidi-Habib, Mehjabeen and Anna Lawrence. 2007. 'Revolt and Remember: How the Shimshal Nature Trust Develops and Sustains Social-Ecological Resilience in Northern Pakistan.' *Ecology and Society* 12 (2): 35.

Anderson, Douglas D. 1987. 'A Pleistocene – Early Holocene Rock Shelter in Peninsular Thailand.' *National Geographic Research* 3 (2): 184–98.

Engelhardt, Richard A. 1989. 'Forest-gatherers and Strandlopers.' *Culture and Environment in Thailand*, 125–41. Bangkok: The Siam Society.

Engelhardt, Richard A. and Pamela R. Rogers. 1995. '"Traits" or "Treats"? Units of Archaeological Study: The Example of Maritime-adapted Cultures in Southeast Asia.' In *Conference Papers on Archaeology in Southeast Asia*, ed. C.T. Yeung and Li W.L., 305–18. Hong Kong: The University of Hong Kong Museum and Art Gallery, University of Hong Kong.

———. 1997a. 'Maritime Adapted Strategies in Post-Pleistocene Southeast Asia.' *Bulletin of the Indo-Pacific Prehistory Association* 16, The Chiang Mai Papers 3: 177–92.

———. 1997b. 'The Phuket Project Revisited: The Ethno-archaeology Through Time of Maritime Adapted Communities in Southeast Asia.' *Journal of the Siam Society* 85: 17–34.

———. 1998. 'The Ethno-archaeology of Southeast Asian Coastal Sites: A Model for the Deposition and Recovery of Archaeological Material.' *Journal of the Siam Society* 86: 131–59.

———. 1999. 'Strandlopers and Interlopers: Identifying the Archaeological Evidence for Intrusive Economic Activity at Subsistence Sites of Maritime Adapted Communities.'

Unpublished paper delivered at 13th International Conference of the European Association of Southeast Asian Archaeologists, Berlin.

Folke, Carl. 2006. 'Resilience: The Emergence of a Perspective for Socio-ecological Analyses.' *Global Environmental Change* 16: 253–67.

Folke, C., S. Carpenter, T. Elmqvist, L. Gunderson, C.S. Holling, and B. Walker. 2002. 'Resilience and sustainable development: building adaptive capacity in a world of transformations.' *Ambio* 31: 437–40.

Gunderson, Lance H. and Crawford S. Holling, eds. 2002. *Panarchy: Understanding Transformations in Systems of Humans and Nature.* Washington DC: Island Press.

Hogan, David H. 1972. 'Men of the Sea: Coastal Tribes of South Thailand's West Coast.' *Journal of the Siam Society* 60: 205–35.

Holling, Crawford S. 1973. 'Resilience and Stability of Ecological Systems.' *Annual Review of Ecology and Systematics* 4: 1–23.

Ivanoff, Jacques. 1997. *Moken: Sea Gypsies of the Andaman Sea, Post-War Chronicles.* Bangkok: White Lotus Press.

———. 1999. *The Moken Boat: Symbolic Technology.* Bangkok: White Lotus Press.

———. 2001. *Rings of Coral: Moken Folktales.* Bangkok: White Lotus Press.

Larish, Michael D. 1999. *The Position of Moken and Moklen within the Austronesian Language Family.* Honolulu: University of Hawai'i at Mānoa, Department of Linguistics.

MacArthur, R.H. and E.O. Wilson. 1967. *The Theory of Island Biogeography.* Princeton: Princeton University Press.

Postle, C. 1980. *Catastrophe Theory.* New York: Harper Collins.

Resilience Alliance at http://www.resalliance.org/

Resilience Alliance. 2007. *Assessing and Managing Resilience in Socio-ecological Systems: A Practitioners Workbook.* Resilience Alliance.

Rogers, Pamela R. 1992. 'Celebrations of the Sea People of Southern Thailand.' *The Hong Kong Anthropologist* 5: 25.

Rogers, Pamela R. and Richard A. Engelhardt. 1998. 'Modeling Prehistoric Maritime Adaptation in the Zhujiang Estuary.' *Journal of the 16th Congress of the Indo-Pacific Prehistory Association*, Melaka, 1998.

Schiffer, Michael B. 1976. *Behavioral Archaeology.* New York: Academic Press.

Scheffer, Marten, Steve Carpenter, Jonathan A. Foley, Carl Folke, and Brian Walker. 2001. 'Catastrophic Shifts in Ecosystems.' *Nature* 413: 591–96.

Sopher, David E. 1977. *The Sea Nomads: A Study of the Maritime People of Southeast Asia.* National Museum of Singapore.

Walker, Brian and Jacqueline A. Meyers. 2004. 'Thresholds in Ecological and Social-ecological Systems: A Developing Database.' *Ecology and Society* 9 (2): 3.

Walker, Brian and David Salt. 2006. *Resilience Thinking: Sustaining Ecosystems and People in a Changing World.* Washington DC: Island Press.

White, Walter G. 1922. *The Sea Gypsies of Malaya.* London: Seeley, Service and Co.

12

Sea People, Coastal Territories and Cultural Interactions: Tetun Terik and Bunaq in the Suai District on the South Coast of Timor-Leste

Jean-Christophe Galipaud, Dominique Guillaud, Rebecca Kinaston and Brunna Crespi

INTRODUCTION

Islands Southeast Asia (ISEA) is a large island world bordered on its western margin by the Asian continent, in the south and southeast by Australia and Papua, once a single landmass called Sahul, but also open to the Pacific east of the Philippines. This unique geographic configuration has facilitated sea travel between islands that were mostly inter-visible, as well as the exploitation of rich sea fauna. It is also a crossroad where diverse cultural influences have fostered the development of strong and extended trade empires with connections to the East and West (Sutherland 2007: 32).

When the climate stabilised 6,000 to 4,000 years before the present (BP), on the coasts of insular Southeast Asia, populations originating in mainland Asia enriched the cultural substrate of more ancient migrations with new languages (the groups of Austro-Asiatic and Austronesian languages; Blench this volume; Blench 2010b) and new techniques that have shaped the current identity of the majority of ISEA cultures. The seemingly fast dominance of Austronesian languages in this largely insular world has fostered debates about the origin and the dynamics of such a rapid movement of goods and people, as well as ideas, during this period (Solheim II 1984; Bellwood and Oxenham 2008; Anderson 2005; Spriggs 2011; Hung et al. 2007). The diffusion of Austronesian languages and the settlement of Remote Oceania and Madagascar are ultimately associated with the mastery of ocean navigation (Blench this volume; Kusuma et al. this volume).

The first part of this chapter will discuss sea nomadism globally from an archaeological perspective. In the second part, with examples from research in East Timor, the potential influences and interactions of mobile groups in the construction and evolution of societies in the Lesser Sunda Islands, in ISEA as a whole and even further into Oceania will be questioned. The place of so called 'sea nomads' (Sopher 1965) in the wider perspective of trade, migration and cultural interaction will also be discussed; all of this in an attempt to highlight some ways of archaeologically acknowledging this sea-people dimension.

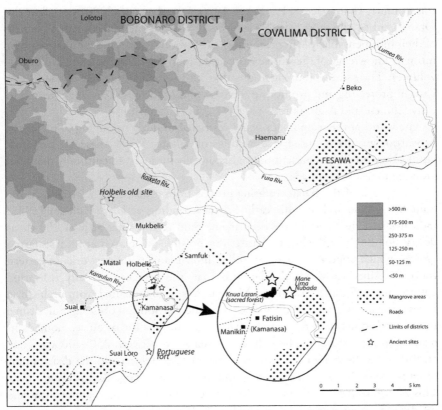

Map 12.1 The area of Suai on the southwest coast of East Timor with localised names cited in the chapter (Copyright: Guillaud/IRD).

ORIGINS OF SEA NOMADS IN THE INDO-PACIFIC REGION

The antiquity of sea nomadism is a key issue for its understanding. Sea nomad populations share origin narratives and preserve stories and myths that give them a historical depth (see Nolde this volume). However, in a fluid and everchanging environment, there is no strict archaeological evidence of their past, although some coastal settlements could relate to sporadic nomadic activities (see Ivanoff this volume; Rogers and Engelhardt this volume). Most attempts at understanding the antiquity of sea nomads rely on third party historical sources which suggest that they were the major actors of last millennium inter-islands trade networks, but do not give a clue as to when they emerged in the distant past. A frequent hypothesis is that the development of sea nomadism followed evolution in maritime technology (Blench 2010a; Ricklefs 1981).

Contemporary sea nomads are said to have appeared around the seventh century CE in association with the rise of the Srivijaya maritime empire (Blench this volume; Calo 2009: 119; Pelras 1996: 75). Andaya (2008) describes the Orang Laut as 'the most valuable subjects or allies of the Malayu rulers because of their indispensable role in promoting international trade' and emphasises their intimate knowledge of the seascape they rule upon (see also Chou and Nolde this volume). The same author mentions that 'this valuable function of the Orang Laut in protecting and promoting Srivijaya and Malayu trade is documented in early Chinese and Arab sources' (Andaya 2008: chapter 6).

The world of the sea nomads is not restricted to those belonging to merchant or warrior groups at the service of kings or sultans. While these are the most visible, they possibly represent only a historically limited and culturally marginal group amongst sea nomads.

The spread of the Bajau seafaring groups from a potential homeland in the Sulu Sea is also linked with early Srivijaya trading activity. Pallesen (1985) indicates that they could have been in the Sulu region since at least 800 CE as does Calo (2009: 113) who emphasises the 'possible role played by local seafaring groups, which appear to have controlled inter-island trade networks in eastern Indonesia since early times'. She adds that 'the presence of early sea-faring cultures in the Sulu, Sulawesi and Maluku Seas is documented from prehistoric times'. Further, Calo (2009: 32) discussing the distribution of Dong Son drums in eastern Indonesia, hints at potentially older origins for Bajau sea nomads in relation to these drums: 'These drums are dated to between 250–400 AD. They arrived by sea from North Vietnam or South-West China and the distribution of finds shows that 7 of them were found in Sangean, a large Bajau community.' This assertion needs to be taken with caution as Bajau nomads are not the sole inhabitants of Sangean (Illouz and Grangé 2013).

Trade, as we will see, is attested much earlier in the region. Could nomadism be a consequence of the development of large-scale trading in a largely insular world?[1]

AN ANCIENT ADAPTATION TO ISLANDS IN ISEA AND OCEANIA?

Central to the question of whether sea-nomadism is an ancient adaptation to islands environments is the evidence of the rapid adoption of new languages belonging to the Austronesian family. Three or four thousand years ago ISEA was already a complex mosaic of cultures and economies sharing pan-regional beliefs (see Sutherland 2007 for a review).

Spriggs (2011) and Blench (2012) both consider what it may have meant to 'become' Austronesian. They argue that the evidence points to a rapid and explosive spread of new people and ideas and suggest that 'powerful ideologies backed by new material symbols and practices' must have underwritten this rapid spread (Spriggs 2011: 524). Blench (2012) develops the idea that Austronesian expansion was driven by a powerful and pervasive ideology and points to the commonality of iconography found across the Austronesian world. These include a 'highly distinctive set of iconographic elements in figurative art ... the linglingo, the jade/nephrite earpieces which occur from Taiwan to New Zealand ...' and the 'bulbul, a seated figure with either the arms crossed or held up to the chin' (Blench 2012: 129). A large-scale adoption of new ideologies regarding the afterlife and the role of ancestors, as seen in the generalisation of urn burials (Galipaud et al. 2016), could also explain the rapid adoption of pottery in ISEA and the spread of urn burials while pointing at earlier influences from the West where similar practices hint at 'symbolic associations between pots, wombs and eggs, facilitating rebirth and transition into the afterlife as early as 6000 BP (Power and Yann 2017).

Trade with India is attested in Bali and elsewhere from the late first millennium BCE (Calo et al. 2015; Favereau and Bellina 2016). Bellwood (1989) hints at 'a strongly maritime-focused economy dating back to 1000 BC' at the site of Bukit Tengkorak in Sabah (see also Bulbeck 2008 and in this volume for a more systematic review of early trade; or Hung et al. 2007 for 3,000-year-old transport of Taiwanese jade). Large exploratory voyages into the Pacific starting even earlier, some 4,000 years ago, also indicate that sophisticated maritime technology and maritime skills were already available.

NAVIGATION AND THE DISCOVERY OF THE PACIFIC ISLANDS

The best example of these early maritime skills is given by the travels from ISEA into the Near and Remote Pacific islands. One of the earliest successful voyages, from northern Philippines to Micronesia, is attested some 3,800 years ago (Carson, Hung and Summerhayes 2013). The transport of pottery as well as results of C14 dates indicate that open sea voyages of more than 2,000 kilometers towards small remote archipelagos were possible. We can thus posit that 4,000 years ago boat technology and life at sea—two important components of sea nomadism—were sufficiently developed to allow any sea voyage in ISEA or even Oceania, the only limit being probably cultural or economical, rather than strictly technical.

These sea travels towards the Mariana Islands can be compared with later movement of goods and people towards islands of Remote Oceania, through the Bismarck Archipelago (the Lapita culture). At the site of Teouma in Vanuatu, the only known large Lapita cemetery, dated to around 2900 BP (Petchey et al.

2014), human remains analysis confirmed a broad-spectrum diet of near shore marine foods and terrestrial protein, including endemic animals and pigs raised by free range methods (Kinaston et al. 2014) and 'high levels of degenerative joint disease, poor dental health, and further evidence of an erosive arthropathy consistent with gout' (Buckley et al. 2008). Gout is a disease often linked with the consumption of marine products and the use of sea water in cooking. Further, a recent study of the genetic affinities of the human remains points to a direct Southeast Asia origin for the first settlers of these Remote Oceanic islands (Skoglund et al. 2016). We can hypothesise from such evidence that the protagonists for the discovery and first settlement (eventually) of these remote islands were sea nomad communities (Noury and Galipaud 2011).

OCEANIC VOYAGES AS A MODEL OF SEA NOMADISM EVOLUTION

If sea nomads have a long antiquity of being influential in coastal or long-distance trading, we could expect to find reminiscences of this nomadic origin in some coastal cultures. The earliest sites in the Remote Pacific islands give us an insight into the ability of mobile sea voyagers to discover or settle remote islands and (where encountered) interact with the inhabitants of already occupied islands on the way. Carson (2014) writes, 'Early-period Marianas sites are shoreline-oriented habitations during the centuries 1500–1000 BC. Only scattered narrow sandy beach fringes were available, while most of the coastal zones were less inviting with rough rocky terrain and steep slopes.' Carson goes on to say that first dwellers in all sites share an 'an almost perfectly homogeneous material signature' (2014: 274). Early Remote Pacific Lapita sites are also coastal and of short duration.

The Tonga islands in the central Pacific offer a precisely dated example of the timing and duration of the initial discovery of these Remote Oceania islands and can thus inform on the process of settlement by sea immigrants. The arrival of Lapita people in Tongatapu is dated to 2863–35 cal BP, the oldest occurrence of Lapita in Tonga (Burley et al. 2015: 7). The Ha'apai and Vava'u colonisation dates are identical, suggesting that both island groups were visited at the same time, some 70 years after Tongatapu. In these later visited islands, the duration of the Lapita phase, characterising the discovery and first settlement, is estimated between 32 to 49 years with a rapid simplification of ceramic decorations towards a non-decorated plain ware. The transition to plain ware ceramics occurred around 2720 BP at the earliest, and this later phase lasted 300 years or a little more (Burley et al. 2015: 10).

This chronology is compatible with a sea-oriented, mobile condition where people moved quickly between islands rather than slowly expanding as the population on a given island reached a threshold. In these remote islands, the transition to plain ware ceramics could have marked the beginning of a permanent settlement, possibly associated with changes in the economy triggered by the arrival of new settlers or isolation. Such evidence supposes that in ISEA at the time of the remote Pacific islands discovery some 3,000 to 4,000 years ago, sea-oriented communities were managing inter-island and long distance maritime resource exploitation and trade.

In the Marianas, a long installation with a rapid change in material culture reflecting isolation is posited. Elsewhere in the Remote Pacific, rapid island discovery by sea nomad merchants of Southeast Asian origin was probably followed by a permanent installation (see also Cochrane 2018 for a theoretical discussion on migrations into the Pacific). A similar model occurred in ISEA in historical times with former sea nomads engaging in inter-island trade, establishing coastal settlements or entrepôts and becoming, over time, coastal farmers.

This summary of archaeological evidence related to the mastery of the sea and the discovery of new lands hints at a potential sea nomad influence in the shaping of ISEA and Oceania societies. We propose now to consider contemporary examples, using evidence from linguistics, archaeology and oral traditions, to understand how interactions between sea nomads and land-based populations can influence the socio-cultural evolution in islands and the potential leading role of ancient trade.

A FIELD-CASE STUDY: THE SOUTH OF TIMOR-LESTE

Timor-Leste was chosen to evaluate the potential influence of former sea nomads on today's cultural configuration. This is because of the occurrence of Austronesian (AN) as well as non-Austronesian (NAN) languages and the long history as a trading destination (for white sandalwood in particular) documented in early accounts and organised during the last millenium through the influence of at least one large trading empire: the Wehali Kingdom.

The Tetun, a coastal AN group on the south coast of the island, is considered here in its relations with the Bunaq, a NAN group living in the mountainous part of central Timor and with a long history of interactions with the Tetun. A quick overview of the linguistic situation in the region is necessary to understand cultural influences and interactions.

LINGUISTIC AND POPULATION ORIGIN IN THE LESSER SUNDA

In ISEA, linguistic has been used to understand the dynamics of ancient migrations. In Timor, Austronesian languages have been traditionally classified into the Central Malayo Polynesian subgroup (CMP) of the Central-Eastern Malayo Polynesian group (CEMP). This subgroup encompasses all AN languages east of Sumbawa, including languages in central and southern Maluku and a few languages along the west coast of Irian Jaya (Blust 1993). Papuan languages belong to the 'Timor-Alor-Pantar' (TAP) family which consists of about 30 languages in eastern and central Timor as well as in Alor and Pantar where they are the dominant languages (Schapper 2015: 106). All these languages, according to Schapper (2015: 101), 'display a distinct set of linguistic features that set them off both from the Southeast Asian Linguistic Area to the West (island Sunda) as well as from the Melanesian Linguistic Area to the East (northern Sahul)'. She proposes to consider this linguistic region, which she refers to as 'Wallacea', a distinct linguistic area.

Similarly, some authors have recently hypothesised that similarities in the CEMP languages observed by Blust come from their evolution in a region at some point dominated by Papuan languages (Donohue and Grimes 2008) rather than from their evolution from a common ancestor. Wallacea AN languages share features that were borrowed from language to language, creating 'a pattern of erratic diffusion' which appears 'to have some antiquity within small, low-level sub-groupings of Austronesian languages' and 'points to early adoption into the Austronesian languages from a Papuan substrate(s) present over the Wallacean area' (Schapper 2015: 140).

Because these adopted features also exist in Wallacean NAN languages, Schapper (2015: 140–1) posits that the breakup of the Papuan language families predates the Austronesian arrival and that such features could be shared among Papuan languages because of the presence of a 'pre-Austronesian maritime culture connecting disparate speaker groups' (see also O'Connor et al. this volume; Bulbeck this volume).

Of further interest is that the contemporary sea nomads in Wallacea speak Austronesian related languages known as Samalic, closely related to the Dayak-Ngaju languages of Southeast Borneo (Blust 2009; Blench this volume). The linguistic situation proposed here contradicts the orthodox model which explains the peopling of these islands by opposing ancient NAN human occupation, associated with foraging, with a more recent AN influx that was thought to have brought modern crops and technology and to have imposed Austronesian languages (Bellwood and Oxenham 2002).

THE BUNAQ, A NON-AUSTRONESIAN SOCIETY ON THE MOVE

The Bunaq people are non-Austronesian agriculturalists living in the mountainous western part of East Timor with an extension over the border into West Timor. They are surrounded by AN speaking groups: the Tetun to the south, the Mambae or Mambai to the east and the Kemak to the north.

According to linguistics, they could be quite ancient settlers and Tetun tradition confirms that Bunaq were already present when they arrived. However ancient they are, the Bunaq are not the first inhabitants of the territory as they state they do not 'master' the land they settled. The so called 'Melus'—the previous inhabitants who were Atoni people (of AN language) pushed back to the west or assimilated by Bunaq[2]—still represent the 'invisible masters of the land' for the Bunaq (Berthe 1972; Françillon 1967).

Schapper (2011: 168) defines the present-day Bunaq's 'homeland' as the region of central-eastern Bobonaro and north-eastern Covalima (see Map 12.1). From this heartland, linguistic evidence suggests several movements at different periods, to the east and west as well as towards the south coastal area. Migration to the west, into what is now West Timor, occurred according to Schapper 'before the beginning of the historical period' (2011: 181) and she explains that 'When they arrived they found either Tetun or Dawan (another term for Melus and Atoni, see note 2) people, with whom they freely mixed. This view of the past is supported by the many village names in Lamaknen and Raihat districts that have at least partial Austronesian etymologies' (Schapper 2011: 171).

The Bunaq of Covalima district consider a specific place on the coast as their ultimate place of origin. This place is Fesawa, today a vast mangrove lagoon south of Beko, which is recalled in several mythical narratives from different groups throughout the region. One such narrative, from the Bunaq village of Holbelis, states that at the beginning Fesawa was a Bunaq village, before the arrival of the Tetun who also founded another village nearby.

Some of the narratives associated with this place describe what appears as the genesis of the Bunaq population, arising from the intermix of people from the coast and people from the hinterland. Berthe (1963) amongst other authors agrees on a mixed Austronesian-Papuan descent of the Bunaq. They mention:

- an original settlement on the coast of a group sometimes described as Bunaq,[3] opposed to the Tetun who came afterwards; and
- the spreading out—from the coast and after Tetun arrivals—of the 'culture of sacred objects' into the hinterland, where there seemed to be another population (speaking a language that was neither Bunaq nor Tetun).

TETUN TERRITORY: MORE RECENT ARRIVALS IN AN ANCIENT BUNAQ LAND?

Ubiquitous in Bunaq narratives, the Tetun form a large group whose territory extends along the fertile south coast plains on both sides of the border. In East Timor, known as South Tetun, they are dispersed across villages around Suai. Tetun's place of reference is Wehali, a plain in West Timor but also the domain of the large polity often referred to as the 'Wehali Kingdom'. In oral literature all over East Timor, references are made to Wehali—'a complex confederation of Timorese political domains which played an important role in sandalwood trade' (McWilliam 2005: 291)—as one of the few centres of power and certainly the only major one that emerged in the early trade with Europeans.

According to Hull (2002: 2), the Tetun language, referred to as the 'language of the plain', spread in the fifteenth century before the arrival of the Portuguese, as a contact language under the influence of the Belunese-speaking kingdom of Wehali. Françillon (1967: 24, 70) writes that this kingdom once exercised supremacy over other polities and that its limits appeared fluctuating—sometimes extending to over almost the entire island, sometimes to the south central coast only—and that this supremacy, rather than real control, was mainly a symbolic and ritual authority over tributaries or allies.

The Tetun retain some mobility in their settlement patterns:

> A little known characteristic, even among most knowledgeable informants of the present time, is that Laran and some of its neighboring villages used to move to and fro between the regions of Fohohun (against the foothills) and of Aintasi (on the seaside) about every 60 to 80 years. Where coconut and palm trees (Borassus, Areca and Corypha) were showing signs of exhaustion, new plantations of these essentials were started at the alternative place and in the next ten years while the plantations grew to maturation the people prepared for a complete removal of their villages to the new places (Françillon 1967: 71).

Interviews about history in the Covalima district confirm this ancient mobility of Tetun groups between the first foothills and the plain nearer to the coast (in locations near riverbeds or near mangroves).

The origin of Tetun speakers in Timor is often said to be Sulawesi but also Savu, Larantuka in Flores or even India. Their origin is closely related to the development of trade; they apparently managed to skilfully handle both the relationships with the Western powers and with the local inhabitants.

> The fact that kingdoms on Sulawesi had an early interest in the Solor-Timor area is also illustrated by the role of Buton, whose sultan formed an alliance with the VOC in order to take control of the Portuguese fort on Solor in 1613. Makassarese, Javanese and other Asian ships are known to have visited Timor and Maluku over the following decades, sometimes being hunted down and captured by the maritime forces of the Dutch East India Company.... All in all, one receives the impression that a lot of trade-related action was going on unbeknownst to the Dutch or the Portuguese (Hägerdal 2012: 83–4).

Historian Peter Spillett's narratives show the role of early Makassarese travellers in the setting up of trade routes:

> One version states that the people of Wewiku-Wehali claim ancestry from Makassar and in particular from Tallo'.... The Makassarese supposedly brought iron technology to Wehali, and taught the locals how to make weapons; intermarrying with local women, they generally remained on peaceful terms with their hosts (Hägerdal 2012: 85, after Spillett 1999: 155–205) (see also Nolde this volume).

Hägerdal mentions a lot of contact between Timor and Makassar by the sixteenth to seventeenth century transition; a time which corresponds to the setting up of 'modern' trade networks in which Europeans were also involved. This does not invalidate the idea of yet more ancient networks but definitely anchors the contemporary Tetun groups in a trade-oriented sphere during the second millennium of our era.

The Tetun mythology can be summed up in a narrative collected in Fatisin (Kamanasa), and concerns again the mangrove site of Fesawa, supposedly the most ancient site in the region for the Tetun as for the Bunaq. Two women of high rank (described as 'princesses'), Rika Lihuwai and Dahu Lihuwai, lived in Lihuwai Wetalas (or Benabuen), a village on the seashore, where they spent their time weaving. The sound of their looms could be heard from far away and two kings from the highlands (a region or place called Hae Manu) heard the noise and came to see what caused it. When they saw the weavers they fell in love and wanted to marry them, but the two women rejected them because they had large feet. Hurt by such rejection, the kings went back home and took their revenge by causing a heavy rain which flooded and destroyed the village on the coast. The weavers carried on working on their looms because they were strong women, but when they realised that their village had been destroyed, they were ashamed for they had not managed to protect it. Therefore, they turned into crocodiles and went into the sea; once in the sea, they sent giant waves to the hills that destroyed the kingdom of Hae Manu. Nobody survived. In Hae Manu one can still see the traces of the waves sent by the crocodiles. On the seashore, the place became a swamp (mangrove) but one can still see the remains of a loom, which is the sacred altar of the people of Fatisin (collected by Guillaud and Crespi from Anacleto Amaral, Fatisin, 26 May 2015).

Another old site mentioned in the narratives of present-day inhabitants concerns Mane Lima Nubada (near Kamanasa). The site is a vast flat area close to the river which holds in some places rather dense concentrations of ceramics, pottery, metal and glass debris, from former habitation; among the remains left on the surface, a very specific stone industry could correspond to the local production of gunflints. This site is very likely related to trade and exchange of goods and could have been an historical entrepôt. Oral traditions about Mane Lima Nubada describe—then in an area 'without a name'—the presence of two warriors (Berek Taran Mauk Taran and Tetifatuk Metan Mauk Lohorai[4]), suggesting again the precedence of Bunaq over Tetun in this coastal region.

Oral traditions further recall the arrival of 'Chinese' setting up a 'kingdom' (possibly a trade post) named Kohobauk Malaka (or Sina Mutin Malaka) in a location near the contemporary Kamanasa, and also mention another village named Kakeu Sikun (near the present village of Samfuk). Versions differ slightly on what happened afterwards, but they mention the arrival of a Liurai (Head, King) from Wehali, who settled in the kingdom of Kamanasa and was allied to the Chinese. This Liurai, Suri Nurak, first arrived by boat in Ta'ro, a rich mangrove lagoon at the estuary, near the village of Fatisin. He came to Kohobauk

Malaka and drove the local population out towards the mountain. Because he was opposed to his settling there, the warrior Berek Taran Mauk Taran launched a war against Liurai Suri Nurak, which the latter won after which he imposed peace. Liurai Suri Nurak settled on the site of Knua Laran (currently a sacred forest) near Kohobauk Malaka, where his subjects were. This place was later renamed Mane Lima Nubada.

From this somewhat sparse oral information emerges a picture of conflicts probably associated with the control of trade by foreign merchants and with the development of a local polity. These traditions refer to a somewhat recent past which is well described in the literature (Hägerdal 2012). At a certain point in history, the Liurai of Kamanasa would also have incited the Bunaq from the hills to come near the coast in order to organise the collection of forest goods for the maritime trade: sandalwood, wax and its by-product, honey (informant: Jorge Alves, Samfuk).

From this diverse information, we can associate the Tetun with:

- an ancient coastal settlement, which is clearly distinct from another inland population (referred to as the kings 'with wide feet'), and, at least at a certain point, a conflictual relationship between both groups;
- several myths with crocodiles: further East, in Waitame, the first king of the Vesoro kingdom arrived from Luca by sea riding a crocodile, whereas his people came by land. Crocodiles stayed and reigned in the sea and the king reigned on the land; today his lineage masters the rituals to control crocodiles (collected by D. Guillaud from Don Maniku Umberto, Waitame, 4–5 December 2013). This version echoes that mentioned by Hägerdal (2012: 84) 'stating that the raja of the Wewiku-Wehali people from Tallo' (Makassar; see above) arrived at the island riding on a crocodile'. It shows the trace of an ancient unified group encompassing petty tribal kingdoms into a unified political system: the Wehali Kingdom;
- the introduction of new skills, techniques and goods: Pigafetta (1922: 177) mentions red cloth, canvas, axes and iron nails as the best barter goods with which to buy sandalwood. The two women in the Tetun myth of origin are also weavers;
- the arrival of new plants, at least via frequent mentions to mortars in the narratives, referring probably to cereals, and via other mythical narratives collected in the region by Brunna Crespi, associating the arrival of 'seeds' with the Fesawa myth of the crocodiles; and
- a specific link with the control of firearms, a good asset in trade (either as a barter product or as a protection).

We have seen that Tetun speakers are strongly linked to the large trading empires that the first Europeans visiting the coast encountered there. Hägerdal, in his title *Lords of the Land, Lord of the Sea* explains:

The exact origin of the immigrants to Belu [Wehali] is a moot point. An early document from 1836 argues that the Belu were descended from Jailolo (Halmahera) in Maluku (Kruseman 1836: 15). This is interesting considering the hypotheses about early Central Malayo-Polynesian migrations from northern Maluku. These hypothetical migrations would have occurred over a very long period of time, and may have left an awareness of their distant origins in the collective memory of the old Indonesian heartland (Granucci 2005: 41). On the other hand, stories recorded in the twentieth century single them out as Sina Mutin Malaka, "the White Chinese of Malacca". This group of people supposedly set off from Malacca on one occasion in order to find new means of earning their livelihood. Bringing sacred items from their homeland, their boats eventually arrived at the fertile plains of South Belu, via Makassar and Larantuka. At that time, the land was inhabited by the Ema Melus, aborigines armed with bows and arrows. These were easily worsted and expelled, and the newcomers expanded their influence over the island (Grijzen 1904: 18–9; Therik 2004: 53) (Hägerdal 2012: 64–5).

This south-Timorese situation might highlight more ancient trends of which only this recent part is visible. The newcomers along these trade routes seem to merge in some way with previous populations: for example, Tetun groups elsewhere in East Timor follow patrilineal transmission and patrilocality, whereas in the region of Suai they follow matrilineal and matrilocal principles (Hicks 1987: 808; 1988), traits they seem to have borrowed from the neighbouring Bunaq. They appear to be part of a multilevel ancient system, even if they have possibly only recently settled (a few hundred years ago) in Suai itself.

Focusing on the recent system can help us understand the more distant past, in particular the way interactions developed between coastal dwellers associated with maritime trading groups/kingdoms and the ancient cultures of the interior. A good way of understanding how sea nomadism may have developed and evolved over time would be to document more of the historically known examples of interactions in the realm of the big trading empires.

A BUNAQ-TETUN OPERATING MODEL

Both the Tetun and Bunaq have a history of mobility, a logical trait in an island world. McWilliam and Traube write, 'On Timor, as throughout the Austronesian world, mobility is culturally constructed as an inevitable feature of social existence and is interwoven with ideas about origins' (2011: 10). Beyond the distant origin of the groups as described in the myths, and the image of an opposition between an inland territory controlled by the Bunaq and a coastal fringe inhabited by the Tetun, there is an intermix of both groups in many localities and a complicated origin of place-names: some Bunaq places have a Tetun name (due to the recent arrivals of Bunaq near the coast) and vice-versa. There seems to be more mixing between the two groups than their very different languages indicate.

For McWilliam and Traube, this situation in Timor is the result of more than two migratory events, as recent NAN influences on an older AN substrate can be discerned: 'Papuan-language speakers are located in central Timor (Bunaq) and in the eastern reaches of the island (including Fataluku, Makassai and Makalero speakers). These groups have interacted with, borrowed from and displaced, as well as been displaced, by Austronesian newcomers' (McWilliam and Traube 2011: 16). There is not one history of interactions between these groups but a series of successful or less successful attempts at expansion and accommodation of newcomers, which eventually, in the last centuries, peaked with the arrival of Dutch and Portuguese traders. This recent history of trade and warfare has often obliterated a more ancient one.

SOME HYPOTHESIS ON THE EMERGENCE OF TRADE NETWORKS

After the journey into the oral and scientific literature, and in field observations, the indicative elements of the operation of sea nomadism can be seen. Some recurring elements in the system are:

(a) transportation/navigation skills;
(b) the importance of mangrove forests in the choice of landing areas (as places providing food resources, refuge, water, wood and places associated with crocodiles);
(c) the setting up and control of trading posts on the coast;
(d) the diffusion of techniques, exchange, trade and the organisation of the collection of local products by inland people (the Bunaq); and
(e) interactions with local society: a new political order imposed,[5] but there is also assimilation, borrowing of local traits (matrilinearity), seemingly in order to merge with local groups.

In Suai, B, C, D and E are observed, but A is still unclear. The ultimate origin of the Tetun in Suai is subject to a prohibition and cannot be revealed. There are no details on any navigation practice as current inhabitants have a limited knowledge of boat building and seafaring, mainly restricted to fishing activities. It seems speculative that the Tetun were seafarers who came from the north-west, settled down on the coast and completely gave up their maritime skills. There appears a gap in understanding of their migration, questioning the intervention of other actors in the process. Alternatively, the same actors could have specialised in different functions, the transportation of people to settle in local outposts and, in the long run, the trade of local goods in a regional and international network. A hypothesis can be drawn from the information provided in Hägerdal (2012) concerning the complementarity between the 'lords of the sea' and the 'lords of the land', which could be seen as a functional specialisation of the same group. Later on, the designation of 'lords of the sea' seems to have been extended to other sea faring groups, such as the Europeans, involved in regional and world trade circuits (Hägerdal 2012: 6).

A complex system is emerging, involving a chain of coordinated actors in the implementation of these trade networks. The interactions observed in this region suggest numerous outside influences and highly mobile groups. Observations also suggest a quite sophisticated work division in the setting up of trade networks involving the implication of previous local groups (also implying alliance). These features, combined with references to the sea in local myths, lead us to propose that the Tetun (and perhaps the Bunaq) have their origin in ancient societies traveling between islands and relying not only on the sea for their subsistence, but also on commerce and exchange of goods. One question remains: that of the antiquity of settlement of the groups concerned on the south coast of Timor.

A MODEL OF INTERACTIONS AND CULTURAL EVOLUTION FOR THE ISLANDS

A model is emerging, the initial impetus of which would be trade rather than agriculture. This initial impetus was followed over time by the emergence of permanent coastal entrepôts which eventually developed into integrated coastal cultures.

The classic model of Austronesian colonisation implies 'population dispersal'. The 'Farming and Language Dispersal Hypothesis' (FLDH) proposed by Bellwood (2005) and Bellwood & Oxenham (2008), attempts to give a suitable answer for what is seen as a massive population dispersal across ISEA and Oceania some 3,000 years ago. It posits that population increase due to higher fecundity in a sedentary/farming environment was the trigger for a steady population dispersal. Instead, we could see the movements of goods and ideas across Southeast Asia and Oceania as the result of an increase in sea traffic between the islands, along already organised sea-lanes whose roots are perhaps as early as the end of the Pleistocene when the first successful sea crossings were achieved. Such an increase could have been facilitated by the emergence of a specific population: the archaeologically nearly invisible sea nomads who could turn out to be, in their capacity to organise trade and change their way of life from sea-farers to farmers, more ubiquitous than is currently recognised.

In the Pacific, the first discovery of islands is now established as a short term episode (Burley et al. 2015), which is linked with decorated Lapita pottery and coastal settlements and was followed, some 200 years after the discovery, by a slow, permanent occupation of islands with evidence of agriculture and husbandry.

Recent analysis (see for instance O'Connor et al. this volume, Bullbeck this volume) indicates a slow process involving maritime trade networks, probably beginning in the Pleistocene, in time favouring language dispersal through the adoption of a trade language, along with the dissemination of new beliefs and technology and, in a later phase, the development of regional trade empires. From the seventh century onwards, the sea nomads' participation in such large trade networks is well documented.

The proposed process is however not a linear one and involves several levels, with sea nomads embracing different roles, from sea life to coastal trading to piracy and also settlement and trade. The example from Timor highlights what we believe has been an ongoing process with sea nomads involved in resource procurement and trade, specialising in coastal dwelling and eventually developing mutually profitable relationships with already established island cultural groups. The example of these two groups can probably be extended to many of the known coastal Austronesian groups like, for instance, the Fataluku NAN language east of East Timor which 'exhibits many cultural ideas and practices suggesting a long period of engagement and accommodation to Austronesian cosmopolitanism' (McWilliam 2007). It highlights a process of mutually beneficial interaction which is well adapted to island cultures. This process over the long term can account, without having to rely on massive population displacement arguments, for the genetic, linguistic and cultural complexity of these island worlds.

NOTES

[1] As is the case with land nomads such as Kubus, who were collecting forest products for the benefit of trade centers such as Srivijaya (Sager 2010).

[2] Schapper, Dawan and Melus are proto-Austronesians and ancestors of today's Atoni.

[3] In Fatisin, whether Bunaq or Tetun, these original inhabitants of the coast belong today to the House Uma Lor, which can be translated from Tetun as 'great house'.

[4] Present-day Bunaq seem unable to translate these names, although they sound Bunaq.

[5] Through the kingdom of Wehali and its local extensions such as the kingdom of Kamanasa, etc., whose social and political organisation can be found in Therik 2004, Françillon 1967, etc.

REFERENCES

Andaya, Leonard Y. 2008. *Leaves of the Same Tree: Trade and Ethnicity in the Straits of Melaka*. Honolulu: University of Hawai'i Press.

Anderson, Atoll. 2005. 'Crossing the Luzon Strait: Archaeological Chronology in the Batanes Islands, Philippines and the Regional Sequence of Neolithic Dispersal.' *Journal of Austronesian Studies* 1 (2): 25–44.

Bellwood, Peter. 1989. 'The Colonisation of the Pacific: Some Current Hypotheses.' In *The Colonisation of the Pacific: A Genetic Trail*, ed. A. Hill and S. Serjeantson, 1–59. Oxford: Clarendon Press.

———. 2005. *First Farmers: The Origins of Agricultural Societies*. UK: Blackwell Publishing.

Bellwood, Peter and Colin Renfrew. 2002. *Examining the Farming/Language Dispersal Hypothesis*. McDonald Institute for Archaeological Research, University of Cambridge.

Bellwood, Peter and Marc Oxenham. 2008. 'The Expansions of Farming Societies and the Role of the Neolithic Demographic Transition.' In *The Neolithic Demographic Transition and its Consequences*, ed. J.-P. Bocquet-Appel, and O. Bar-Yosef, 13–34. Springer Science+Business Media B.V.

Berthe, Louis. 1963. 'Morpho-syntaxe du Bunaq (Timor Central)' [Morpho-syntax of the Bunaq (Central Timor)]. *L'Homme* 3 (1): 106–16.

———. 1972. *Bei Gua, Itinéraire des Ancêtres. Mythes des Bunaq de Timor* [Bei Gua, itinerary of the ancestors. Myths of the Bunaq people in Timor]. Paris: Editions du CNRS.

Blench, Roger. 2010a. 'Evidence for the Austronesian Voyages in the Indian Ocean.' In *The Global Origins and Development of Seafaring*, ed. A. Anderson, J.H. Barrett, and K.V. Boyle, 239–48. Cambridge: McDonald Institute Monographs.

———. 2010b. 'Was There an Austroasiatic Presence in Island Southeast Asia Prior to the Austronesian Expansion?' *Bulletin of the Indo-Pacific Prehistory* 30: 133–44.

———. 2012. 'Almost Everything You Believed about the Austronesians Isn't True.' In *Crossing Borders: Selected Papers from the 13th International Conference of the European Association of Southeast Asian Archaeologists*, Volume 1, ed. M.L. Tjoa-Bonatz, A. Reinecke, and D. Bonatz. Singapore: NUS Press.

———. This volume. 'The Linguistic Background to Southeast Asian Sea Nomadism.' In *Sea Nomads of Southeast Asia: From the Past to the Present*, ed. B. Bellina, R. Blench, and J.-C. Galipaud. Singapore: NUS Press.

Blust, Robert. 1993. 'Central and Central-Eastern Malayo-Polynesian.' *Oceanic Linguistics* (32) 2: 241–93.

———. 2009. *The Austronesian Languages*. Canberra: Pacific Linguistics.

Buckley, Hallie, Nancy Tayles, Matthew Spriggs, and Stuart Bedford. 2008. 'A Preliminary Report on Health and Disease in Early Lapita Skeletons: Possible Biological Costs of Colonization.' *Journal of Island and Coastal Archaeology* 3 (1): 87–114.

Bulbeck, David. 2008. 'An Integrated Perspective on the Austronesian Diaspora: The Switch from Cereal Agriculture to Maritime Foraging in the Colonisation of Island Southeast Asia.' *Australian Archaeology* 67: 31–52.

———. This volume. 'Late Pleistocene to Mid-Holocene Maritime Exchange Networks in Island Southeast Asia.' In *Sea Nomads of Southeast Asia: From the Past to the Present*, ed. B. Bellina, R. Blench, and J.-C. Galipaud. Singapore: NUS Press.

Burley, David et al. 2015. 'Bayesian Modeling and Chronological Precision for Polynesian Settlement of Tonga.' *PloS ONE* 10 (3): 1–14.

Calo, Ambra. 2009. *The Distribution of Bronze Drums in Early Southeast Asia*. Oxford: Archeopress.

Calo, Ambra et al. 2015. 'Sembiran and Pacung on the Northern Coast of Bali: A Strategic Crossroads for Early Trans-Asiatic Exchange.' *Antiquity* 89 (344): 378–96.

Carson, Mike. 2014. 'Paleo-terrain Research: Finding the First Settlement Sites of Remote Oceania.' *Geoarchaeology* 29 (3): 268–75.

Carson, Mike, Hung Hsiao-Chun, and Glenn Summerhayes. 2013. 'The Pottery Trail from Southeast Asia to Remote Oceania.' *The Journal of Island and Coastal Archaeology* 8 (January 2014): 37–41.

Cochrane, Ethan. 2018. 'The Evolution of Migration: The Case of Lapita in the Southwest Pacific.' *Journal of Archaeological Method and Theory* 25 (2): 520–58.

Chou, Cynthia. This volume. 'The Orang Suku Laut: Movement, Maps and Mapping.' In *Sea Nomads of Southeast Asia: From the Past to the Present*, ed. B. Bellina, R. Blench, and J.-C. Galipaud. Singapore: NUS Press.

Donohue, Mark and Charles E. Grimes. 2008. 'Yet More on the Position of the Languages of Eastern Indonesia and East Timor.' *Oceanic Linguistics* 47: 114–58.

Favereau, Aude and Bérénice Bellina. 2016. 'Thai-Malay Peninsula and South China Sea Networks (500 BC–AD 200), Based on a Reappraisal of "Sa Huynh-Kalanay"-related Ceramics.' *Quaternary International*: 1–9.

Françillon, Gérard. 1967. 'Some Matriarchic Aspect of the Social Structure of the Southern Tetun of Middle Timor.' PhD thesis. The Australian National University, Canberra.

Galipaud, Jean-Christophe, Hallie Buckley, Truman Simanjuntak, Sian Halcrow, Rebecca Kinaston, Aimee Foster, and Johnathan Javelle. 2016. 'The Pain Haka Burial Ground in Flores: Indonesian Evidence for a Shared Neolithic Belief System in Southeast Asia.' *Antiquity* 90 (354): 1505–21.

Granucci, Anthony F. 2005. *The Art of the Lesser Sundas*. Singapore: Editions Didier Millet.

Grijzen, H.J. 1904. *Mededeelingen Omtrent Beloe of Midden-Timor*. Verhandelingen van het Bataviaasch Genootschap van Kunsten en Wetenschappen [Some notes on Beloi of Middle Timor. Acts of the Batavian Society of Arts and Sciences] 54. Batavia.

Hägerdal, Hans. 2012. *Lords of the Land, Lords of the Sea. Conflict and Adaptation in Early Colonial Timor, 1600–1800*. Leiden: Koninklijk Instituut voor Taal-, Land- en Volkenkunde.

Hicks, David. 1987. 'Tetum Descent.' *Anthropos* 82 (1–3): 47–61.

———. 1988. 'Literary Masks and Metaphysical Truths: Intimations from Timor.' *American Anthropologist* 90 (4): 807–17. New series.

Hull, Geoffrey. 2002. *The Languages of East Timor – Some Basic Facts*. Working paper. University of Timor Lorosae.

Hung, Hsiao-Chun et al. 2007. 'Ancient Jades Map 3,000 Years of Prehistoric Exchange in Southeast Asia.' *Proceedings of the National Academy of Sciences of the United States of America*, 104 (50): 19745–50.

Illouz, Charles and Philippe Grangé, eds. 2013. *L'archipel Kangean, Sumenep, Java Est, Indonésie. Recherches Appliquées pour le Développement* [The Kangean Archipelago, Sumenep, East Java, Indonesia. Applied Researches for Development]. Paris: Les Indes Savantes.

Ivanoff, Jacques. This volume. 'Nomads in the Interstices of History.' In *Sea Nomads of Southeast Asia: From the Past to the Present*, ed. B. Bellina, R. Blench, and J.-C. Galipaud. Singapore: NUS Press.

Kinaston, R., H. Buckley, F. Valentin, S. Bedford, and M. Spriggs. 2014. "Lapita Diet in Remote Oceania: New Stable Isotope Evidence from the 3000-Year-Old Teouma Site, Efate Island, Vanuatu." *PLoS ONE* 9(3): e90376.

Kusuma, Pradiptajati, Nicolas Brucato, Murray P. Cox, Chandra Nuraini, Thierry Letellier, Philippe Grangé, Herawati Sudoyo, and François-Xavier Ricaut. This volume. 'A Genomic Perspective of the Origin and Dispersal of the Bajaw Sea Nomads in Indonesia.' In *Sea Nomads of Southeast Asia: From the Past to the Present*, ed. B. Bellina, R. Blench, and J.-C. Galipaud. Singapore: NUS Press.

Kruseman, J.D. 1836. 'Beschrijving van Timor en Eenige Naburige Eilanden' [Description of Timor and Some Neighbouring Islands]. *De Oosterling* 2: 1–41.

McWilliam, Andrew. 2005. 'Haumeni, Not Many: Renewed Plunder and Mismanagement in the Timorese Sandalwood Industry.' *Modern Asian Studies* 39 (2): 285–320.

———. 2007. 'Austronesian in Linguistic Disguise: Fataluku Cultural Fusion in East Timor.' *Journal of Southeast Asian Studies* 38 (2): 355–75.

McWilliam, Andrew and Elizabeth G. Traube. 2011. 'Land and Life in Timor-Leste, an Introduction.' In *Land and Life in Timor-Leste: Ethnographic Essays*, ed. A. McWilliam and E.G. Traube. Canberra: ANU E-Press.

Nolde, Lance. This volume. '"The Muscles and Sinews of the Kingdom": The Sama Bajo in Early Modern Eastern Indonesia.' In *Sea Nomads of Southeast Asia: From the Past to the Present*, ed. B. Bellina, R. Blench, and J.-C. Galipaud. Singapore: NUS Press.

Noury, Arnaud and Jean-Christophe Galipaud. 2011. *Les Lapita: Nomades du Pacifique* [The Lapita: Sea Nomads of the Pacific], 127. Marseille: IRD Editions.

O'Connor, Sue, Christian Reepmeyer, Mahirta, Michelle C. Langley and Elena Piotto. This volume. 'Communities of Practice in a Maritime World: Shared Shell Technology and Obsidian Exchange in the Lesser Sunda Islands, Wallacea.' In *Sea Nomads of Southeast Asia: From the Past to the Present*, ed. B. Bellina, R. Blench, and J.-C. Galipaud. Singapore: NUS Press.

Pallesen, Alfred K. 1985. *Culture Contact and Language Convergence*. Manila: Linguistic Society of the Philippines.

Pelras, Christian. 1996. *The Bugis*. Oxford: Blackwell Publishers.

Petchey, Fiona et al. 2014. 'Radiocarbon Dating of Burials from the Teouma Lapita Cemetery, Efate, Vanuatu.' *Journal of Archaeological Science* 50: 227–42.

Pigafetta. 1922. *Primer Viaje en Torno del Globo. Edition del IV entenario* [First Voyage around the World. Edition of the IV centenary]. Madrid: Calpe.

Power, Ronika K. and Tristant Yann. 2017. 'From Refuse to Rebirth: Repositioning the Pot Burial in the Egyptian Archaeological Record.' *Antiquity* 354 (2016): 1474–88.

Ricklefs, Merle C. 1981. *A History of Modern Indonesia, c. 1300 to the Present*. Hong Kong: Macmillan Asian Histories Series.

Rogers, Pamela A. and Richard Engelhardt. This volume. 'Ethno-archaeological Evidence of "Resilience" Underlying the Subsistence Strategy of the Maritime-adapted Inhabitants of the Andaman Sea.' In *Sea Nomads of Southeast Asia: From the Past to the Present*, ed. B. Bellina, R. Blench, and J.-C. Galipaud. Singapore: NUS Press.

Sager, Steven. 2010. 'The Sky is our Roof, the Earth our Floor. Orang Rimba Customs and Religion in the Bukit Duabelas Region of Jambi, Sumatra.' PhD thesis. School of Archaeology & Anthropology, College of Arts and Social Sciences. The Australian National University, Canberra.

Sather, Clifford. 1997. *The Bajau Laut: Adaptation, History, and Fate in a Maritime Fishing Society of South-eastern Sabah*. Kuala Lumpur, New York: Oxford University Press.

Schapper, Antoinette. 2011. 'Finding Bunaq: The Homeland and Expansion of the Bunaq in Central Timor.' In *Land and Life in Timor-Leste: Ethnographic Essays*, ed. A. McWilliam and E.G. Traube. Canberra: ANU E-Press.

———. 2015. 'Wallacea, a linguistic area.' *Archipel* 90 (January): 99–151.

Skoglund, Peter, Cosimo Posth, and Matthew Spriggs et al. 2016. 'Genomic Insights into the Peopling of the Southwest Pacific.' *Nature* 538 (7626): 510–13.

Sopher, David E. 1965. *The Sea Nomads: A Study Based on the Literature of the Maritime Boat People of Southeast Asia.* (*Memoirs of the National Museum, no. 5*). Singapore: National Museum.

Solheim II, Wilhelm G. 1984. 'The Nusantao Hypothesis: The Origin and Spread of Austronesian Speakers.' *Asian Perspectives* XXVI (1): 77–88.

Spillett, Peter. 1999. *The Pre-colonial History of the Island of Timor Together with Some Notes on the Makassan Influence in the Island.* Manuscript, held by the Museum and Art Gallery of the North Territory, Darwin.

Spriggs, Matthew. 2011. 'Archaeology and the Austronesian Expansion: Where Are We Now?' *Antiquity* 85 (328): 510–28.

Sutherland, Heather. 2007. 'Geography as Destiny? The Role of Water in Southeast Asian History.' In *A World of Water, Rain, Rivers and Seas in Southeast Asian Histories*, ed. P. Boomgaard, 27–70. Leiden: KITLV Press.

Therik, Tom. 2004. *Wehali: The Female Land.* Canberra: Pandanus.

13

The Bajau Diaspora: Origin and Transformation

Charles Illouz and Chandra Nuraini

INTRODUCTION

The Sama Bajau, more commonly called the Bajau in Indonesia, are a population dispersed in a diaspora covering a huge area of Southeast Asia. There are other communities that have traditionally emigrated to other islands, such as the Bugis people (South Sulawesi), the Minangkabau (West Sumatra) and others, which maintain family and inheritance ties to their land of origin. Nonetheless, the origin of the Sama Bajau has not been clearly identified yet. Their geographical and historical singularity is not without consequences for the work of linguists and anthropologists. In many communities separated by thousands of nautical miles, languages and dialects have diversified, but cultural systems remain closely connected to a similar mode of production. At the same time, very specific social and cultural features distinguish the Sama Bajau people from other coastal communities.[1]

The ethnography of the 'sea nomads', and the Bajau people in particular, has not prompted extensive studies yet. Research on the Bajau people mainly focuses on the populations living on the Malaysian territory of North Borneo and in the southern Philippines. In an early study, Nimmo discussed the economic and social changes among 'Sea People' of Sulu in southern Philippines (1972); later, this author proposes a monograph about the same Sama of Tawi-Tawi (2001). Geographer David E. Sopher presented a historiographical synthesis of sea populations from various origins (1965). Sather conducted the most important ethno-historical study on the Bajau of Sabah, a Malaysian territory in northern Borneo (1997). Bottignolo carried out an ethnographic study on the religious representations system of Bajau of Tawi-Tawi in the southern Philippines. His monograph explores the cosmological dimension of that society (1995). We should also mention the work of Revel, Martenot and Nimmo et al. which analyses the Sama-Bajau's epic genre also in the southern Philippines (2005). Nuraini's PhD thesis explores a corpus of epic songs from the Bajau of the

Kangean Islands (2008). In Indonesia, there are almost no long-term studies and few articles make recent findings accessible. Regarding history, Lapian organised an international symposium on the Bajau people of the Coral Triangle (1993) followed by a collective publication which included works by Sather, Pelras and Fox (Lapian and Nagatsu 1996). Lapian also published a maritime history of the Celebes in the nineteenth century, dealing with the sea people, pirates and sovereigns of coastal kingdoms (Lapian 2009). Pelras became interested in the South Sulawesi Bajau people alongside his research on the Bugis people and provides guidance to explore the Dutch archives (Pelras 1972). His original lexicological contribution should also be noted (Pelras 1997). Fox presented documentary sources enabling us to understand the past and recent Bajau migrations to the Sunda Islands (Fox 1977). Sutherland (2000) and Tagliacozzo (2004) showed the historical importance of the sea cucumber[2] trade that involved many sea-exploring people of southern Sulawesi and the southern Philippines during the eighteenth and nineteenth centuries. As regards the typical production activities of the Bajau people, but also other sea populations, several recent studies have identified the forms of exploitation suffered by fishermen. Fougeres examines the development of high-value markets; he describes the dynamics of these fishing and aquaculture ventures as a transition to a capitalist mode of production (2008). Ten years earlier, Meereboer addressed the dependence ties connecting fishermen to their patron-clients (Meereboer 1998). On this topic, note the multidisciplinary research conducted on Kangean Islands (Illouz and Grangé 2013).[3]

As for studies on languages, several linguists researched the grammatical and lexical features of the Bajau language (Verheijen 1986; Donohue 1996; Gault 1999, 2002; Hapip et al. 1979; Hinayat 2003; Trick 2006). Unfortunately, except for brief notes in Verheijen (1986), all the publications focus on the Sama Bajau language of the Philippines and Sabah (North Borneo). The language area of the 'Indonesian Bajau' remains largely unexplored. The authors of this chapter believe to have achieved the most comprehensive monographic study involving the Bajau community from the Kangean Islands (Nuraini 2008, 2013, 2021 forthcoming).

Drawing on some of the research currently available and investigations by the chapter authors, this chapter proposes to address three issues that characterise the originality of the Bajau diaspora. First, the reality of this diaspora is based on a linguistic observation: what is the position of the Bajau language among the Malayo-Polynesian languages and thus what can be observed? Next, it will be observed that the dispersion and the geographical location of Bajau groups are consistent with the type of residence imposed on them since the mid twentieth century. It will be shown that this type of residence, the same for most Bajau communities today, is associated with a sedentary mode of production, which contradicts all the elements and production techniques that justified their former nomadic life. Finally, this point will enable the assessment of the relevance of two alternative scenarios of dispersion based on linguistic research about two proto-Bajau homelands.

LINGUISTIC APPROACH

The Sama Bajau is a group of Austronesian languages spoken by a population living mainly on the coast, in areas far removed from each other: Malaysia (Sabah, northern Borneo), the Philippines (Sulu Archipelago, extending between Sabah and southern Philippines) and on many Indonesian shores, mainly Kalimantan (Borneo), Sulawesi (Celebes), Moluccas and the Lesser Sunda Islands. The various Sama Bajau dialects in use in Indonesia have been brought together under the label 'Indonesian Bajau'. Note that a Yakan speaker (Philippines) and a Bajau speaker from the Kangean Islands, for instance (North Bali, Indonesia), do not understand each other any more than a Spanish speaker would understand a French speaker.

The languages of the Sama Bajau subgroup belong to the Western Malayo-Polynesian subgroup. This is the first surprising point, because in the vast area over which the Sama Bajau are scattered, the other vernacular languages tend to belong to the Central Malayo-Polynesian subgroup, like the languages of the Lesser Sunda Islands. This feature seems to indicate a movement of the whole population towards the east.

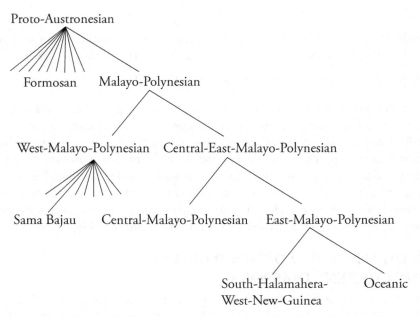

Figure 13.1 Sama Bajau in all Austronesian languages (Adapted from Adelaar 2005: 9).

Linguist Alfred K. Pallesen conducted the first diachronic study of the Sama Bajau people and sketches a reconstruction of Proto Sama Bajau language (1985). Among the languages of the contemporary Sama Bajau group, he identifies nine languages, most of them branching into different dialects:

1. Abaknon
2. Sulu Central (Dilaut Sama, Sama Ubihan South, etc.)
3. Indonesian Bajau (different groups near Sulawesi, Halmahera, Timor and Roti)
4. Territory Bajau North Borneo (Bajau Banggi, Kota Belud Bajau, etc.)
5. North Sulu (sub-dialect Balangingi, Sama Karundung, etc.)
6. South Sulu (Simunul Sama, Sama Pahut, etc.)
7. Sulu West (Pangutaran Sama, Sama North Ubihan)
8. Yakan (Yakan North and South)
9. Zamboanga (Batuan Sama, Sama Sibukuq, etc.)

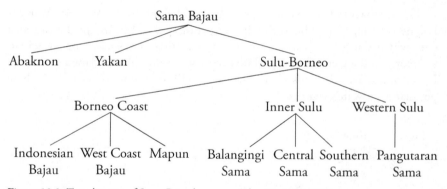

Figure 13.2 Tree diagram of Sama Bajau languages (Akamine 2005: 379).

It is striking that only one branch, Indonesian Bajau, is supposed to represent the entire Sama Bajau group in Indonesia for communities scattered over a vast area, which is five times larger than the area where we find all the other languages of the Sama Bajau group. A glance at the dispersal area of Sama Bajau people (see Map 13.1) enables us to measure the imbalance of such a representation.[4] Pallesen's field of study was the Philippines, and he had very little data on Indonesia. It is very unlikely that the Indonesian Bajau distribution area coincides with the national borders of Indonesia and those of Malaysia and the Philippines.[5]

GEOGRAPHY AND DEMOGRAPHY OF THE CURRENT DIASPORA

The Bajau diaspora covers exactly the 'Coral Triangle' (Melanesia excluded) where ocean biodiversity is one of the richest on the planet. From south of the

Philippines to the north of Borneo (the Sabah Malaysian province) and to many coasts of eastern Indonesia, all the formerly scattered Sama Bajau communities are now sedentarised. Their dispersal area is huge and the Sama Bajau themselves are vaguely aware of the diasporic geography in which they are located. Thus, from the communities of the Sulu Archipelago to those of Flores (Indonesia), it is 1,800 kilometres in a straight line and at least 2,200 kilometres by sea. All Bajau communities live reasonably close to non-Bajau communities. Some Sama Bajau groups, for example, have settled in the hinterland. This is the case particularly in the Sulu Archipelago (Philippines) and especially in the Malaysian province of Sabah in northern Borneo, where several hundred thousand people claim their Sama Bajau origin.

Such dispersion helps explain the difficulty in establishing accurate demographics. According to Gusni Saat, in the year 2000, there was a total of 467,000 people from different Sama Bajau communities present in the Philippines, Malaysia and Indonesia (Saat 2003: 4). Even today, no one knows the exact demographics of the Sama Bajau people. For Indonesia, the data remains very unspecific. It is not only difficult to know what the identity of the 'Bajau' really is, but also to locate and identify their communities. Indeed, Indonesian government census procedures do not take into account the ethnicity of the people[6] and other sources are also problematic. For example, Mead and Lee note that:

> Language atlas compilers have been in a difficult position about where to turn for information on the Bajau. Wurm (1994: 121), for example, [...] relied on the Sulawesi language maps that had been prepared a decade earlier by Sneddon (1983a, 1983b). Sneddon, in turn, followed the location of Bajau communities found in Salzner (1960), who, in turn, had gleaned all his information from the language map in Adriani and Kruyt (1914)! Here the trail ends, as Adriani based his map on personal research and information gathered from his contemporaries. In other words, the "best" language atlases available today have simply been repeating old information from nearly a century ago (2007: 3–4).

Identifying Bajau inhabitants in a village does not prove all the villagers consider themselves as Bajau or that they are native or second-language speakers of the Bajau tongue. Mead and Lee point out an additional obstacle:

> Because the Bajau live in scattered communities without a core language area, language use and overall language vitality are difficult to judge. [...] Even when a community has become so mixed (Bajau, Bugis, Munanese, Butonese, etc.) so that people inside the community no longer identify themselves as Bajau, outsiders may, nonetheless, still refer to the community as "Bajau" (2007: 16).

Thus, in the Kangean archipelago, the island of Sapeken is inhabited mostly by Bajau people, mixed with Bugis, Buton, Mandar, Madurese and a few Javanese. Many marriages take place between people of different communities and nearly everyone speaks the Bajau language, even if husband or wife are not

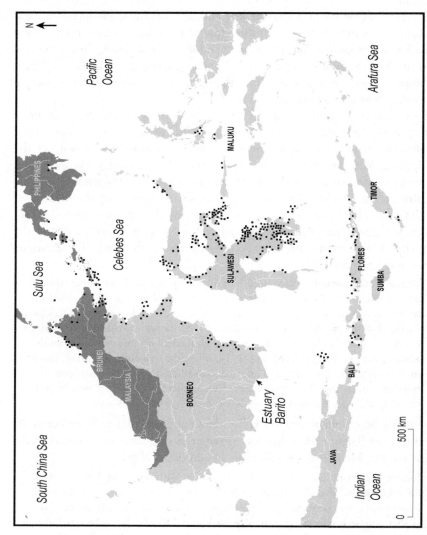

Map 13.1 Overview of locations of Bajau groups over their dispersal area (represented by black squares) (Adapted from Nagatsu 2007).

necessarily Bajau. The Bajau are scattered throughout the Kangean archipelago, which has about 130,000 inhabitants. They live mainly in the eastern part of this small archipelago. On some islands they represent a minority, on others a majority. If it is difficult to define and identify Bajau people in the modest Kangean archipelago; it is more so in hundreds of villages and hamlets of the Bajau diaspora scattered along multiple Indonesian shores.

Mead and Lee rightly state that:

> While it may be hazardous, therefore, to form conclusions about the number of Bajau speakers, nonetheless, the number of ethnic Bajau in Indonesia has heretofore been underestimated. [...] the total Indonesian Bajau population lies perhaps somewhere around 150 000, with the number of actual Bajau speakers yet to be determined (2007: 17).

Beyond the question of numbers, it is difficult to define a 'cultural community'. The original character of the Sama Bajau culture as a whole is the maritime dimension which underlies most of its history. Long ago, many Sama Bajau used to spend most of the year on their boats. Early evidence provided by Western sailors emphasises the nomadic lifestyle of the Bajau people. According to Sather (2004), nomadism virtually ceased in the mid-twentieth century.

THE CURRENT SEDENTARY LIFESTYLE AND THE RESIDENTIAL CONFINEMENT OF THE BAJAU

Maintained on the margins of traditional landholding, the Bajau groups are experiencing an unstable habitat situation and a very insecure condition. In the past, some of them were, sometimes brutally, displaced overnight. Indonesian administrative authorities, with the consent of landowners, set them on narrow strips of soil or sand, or on tiny reefs. They live in simple houses, often built on stilts, and are exposed to all authoritarian displacements that result from regional conflicts or natural disasters (earthquakes and tsunamis). The physical segregation, which has historically affected Bajau groups within social relations involving all the other groups on a given island or archipelago, is shaped by the contours of the residential space assigned to them: the Bajau villages are confinement areas.[7] A satellite view of the village of Wuring, near Maumere in Flores, illustrates such a situation (Map 13.2): actually an encroachment on the sea made by stacking rocks, today with concrete, where some 6,000 people live. This reflects the lack of available land for Bajau people, even though it is they who supply the populations of nearby farmers with products from the sea.

Forced to occupy as little a share of island coastlines as possible, the exploitation of ocean resources is the only option for Bajau people. They excel in all forms of fishing. The fish caught are sold still fresh on the nearest market, or are dried for later sales. Much of the catch is sold to brokers, rarely Bajau themselves, who trade on markets in relatively distant cities. They occasionally fish turtles for the

Map 13.2 Wuring, a Bajau village near Maumere in Flores (Adapted from Google satellite image).

Balinese market, although, they say, Islam prohibits their consumption. It is the same for *tripang* (sea cucumber)—dried, smoked and sold to middlemen—ultimately reaching the Chinese market. This trade has gone on for centuries and Bajau people were not afraid to start on expeditions to fish *tripang*, as far as Papua and Australia.[8] As long as they wandered all over the seas of the East Indies and beyond in Southeast Asia, the Bajau were significant providers and carriers of goods with high added value in international trade. The history of the constitution of their diaspora is strongly related to this commercial context, which for centuries was generally favourable to them.[9]

Today, the residential situation of the Bajau is a reflection of the economic instability in which they are maintained wherever they happen to live. Forced to live on narrow coastal strips or small piers reclaimed from the sea, they do not consider activities other than fishing. No development programme invites them to join in other activities, and if the most resolute sometimes undertake to 'do something else' they usually only manage to be hired on Taiwanese or Japanese trawlers, or to share the exile of many Indonesian people on worksites and plantations in Malaysia (Illouz 2013).

THE CURRENT SEDENTARY LIFESTYLE OF THE BAJAU AND THE PATRON-CLIENT RELATIONSHIP

Indonesian or Malaysian national or regional authorities invariably produce the same paternalistic and discriminatory speech against Bajau people. Regretting their underdevelopment, they point to their inability to fully integrate into urban spaces close to their settlement in order to have access to state public services (administration, police, schools, health clinics). The environmental and economic constraints weighing on the Bajau are completely ignored, so that the only obstacle to development would ultimately be their own resistance to change. The 'refusing change' argument is quickly debunked by an economic analysis. Such talk never addresses the fact that the marginalisation of the Bajau people is based on the logic of a local economic circuit where the fishing market is central (Dervis et al. 1982).

If one can speak of social specificity regarding the Bajau people, it's probably because most Bajau groups, wherever they have settled, are small producers closely connected to a powerful client who appears as the main, and sometimes the only buyer for their catch. This man becomes the patron-client of a merchant activity structured by a debt relationship between a *fisherman-borrower* and a *broker-lender* (Meereboer 1998; Fougères 2008; Illouz 2013). Everywhere today, the Bajau depend on big fishing brokers. The patron-client system for the Bajau, of which Pelras described a much less coercive variant in Bugis territory (Pelras 2000: 399), amounts merely to a dependence relationship for survival, which very few individuals manage to escape.

Whatever the variations of the relationships Bajau people have with a particular local society that has accepted them in its vicinity, the scenario of their unstable life can almost always be derived from a set of factors which can be combined in various degrees, as follows (Illouz 2013: 143–62):[10]

1. Not having the required capital to purchase a fast boat equipped for packing and preserving fragile and perishable products, Bajau fishermen no longer have the opportunity to reach commercial ports where they could sell their catch for a price based on real competition.
2. Short of moving away from their problematic residence, they sell cheaply to a small number of wealthy middlemen who find customers on domestic (Java, Bali, etc.) and international (Hong Kong, Singapore, etc.) markets. These middlemen become patron-clients of Bajau fishermen.
3. Thus Bajau fishermen are bound by a commercial production system holding them away from the free market, which is in turn easily accessible for those intercepting their production.
4. On various occasions involving major events in their life (marriage, birth, death, family projects, buying a boat, motor, fishing equipment, etc.) Bajau fishermen request a loan from their patron-client in exchange for a promise to sell them their fish, the amount of the loan being deducted from the sale, following an unclear payment schedule that can be modified when they need another loan.
5. They are also customers without a choice for non-Bajau shopkeepers who supply basic goods in their village.
6. Purchasing essential household goods immediately depletes their meager incomes, forcing them, in order to maintain their fishing equipment, to borrow money from the brokers again while promising them their next catch.
7. Wherever they are, the Bajau have become a workforce whose earnings depend on buyers who do not actually employ them but keep them as available labor through a debt system that controls all of their existence.
8. Kept away from competitive market practices, fishermen remain poor and helpless when their work is essential to a very profitable operation for others.
9. Forced to accept a game with unfair rules that the administration, local brokers and middlemen have designed, most Bajau fishermen fairly regularly fish with explosives or sodium cyanide.

Fish caught with cyanide is intended for the restaurant market. The consequence of this method is the death of the living coral cover, although the estimated magnitude of this destruction is smaller than the effects of blast fishing or coral bleaching. It provides relatively abundant catch and cuts down on the long and arduous trips for the small amounts of fish left by industrial fishing, which is largely responsible for the collapse of coastal ecosystems (Jackson et al. 2001). Nevertheless, coral reefs will need a very long time to recover from the effects of cyanide fishing (Pet-Soede and Erdmann 1998; Mous et al. 2000).[11] Year after year, the irreparable destruction of coral reefs is making people of all origins more vulnerable. More lucrative for a time, such a strategy of production is a disastrous response to the systematic exploitation the Bajau feel they are subjected to.[12]

THE FORMER NOMADIC LIFESTYLE OF THE BAJAU AND THEIR ACCESS TO MARKETS

What initially drove the Bajau people to start wandering the sea? James Fox consulted the Dutch archives and noted various records of the presence of Bajau groups since the eighteenth century, between Sumbawa, Flores and Timor. Most sources claim they originate from Makassar: 'In summary, [...] Bajau Laut were voyaging as far as Timor by the early part of the eighteenth century. They were largely involved in trepang gathering and were closely associated with 'Makassarese'. Actual settlement probably began in the early nineteenth century' (Fox 1977: 463).

During the presumed period of their settlement in those different places, James Fox finds that in his writings, George Earl mentions small Bajau fleets on the north coast of Australia:

> Earl, [...] documents the presence of Bajau in northen Australia. Among the praus that visited Port Essington in 1840, he notes "a vessel belonging to that singular people the Badju, a tribe without fixed home, living constantly on board their prahus (*sic*), numbers of which congregate among the small islands near the southern coasts of Celebes (Earl 1846: 65)". Five years prior to this, in 1835, Earl had planned to go on a *trepang* gathering expedition with Bajau, setting out from Macassar and going, via the Aru islands, to the coast of Australia (Fox 1977: 461).

The gathering of sea cucumbers was particularly well adapted to the Bajau way of life. For sailors living off exchanges based on sea resources, trading in sea cucumbers offered particularly profitable outlets.[13] In the nineteenth century, that trade boomed in Asia and the Pacific due to demand from China that has remained constant (from Shanghai, Canton, Hong Kong, Singapore, Makassar, etc.). Indeed, the Indonesian language contains the word *tripang*, spelled *trepang* by Fox, borrowed from Chinese, to designate 'sea cucumber'. Sea cucumber could be prepared on site, dried in the sun, preserved and stored for several months before being sold in remote ports. As Fox underlines, the sea cucumber trade is likely to have played a key role, very early on, in the history of the migrations of the maritime peoples of Southeast Asia.[14]

This production activity pre-supposed advanced proficiency with means of communication sometimes over considerable maritime distances. The Bugis and Bajau people also had, on occasion, a solid reputation as pirates.[15] The modes of production and exchange of these 'sea nomads' depended on their capacity to regularly cover long distances at sea.[16] Their voyages, often adventurous, showed that they had direct access to the market and were able to satisfy demand and deal with competition from other traders without a go-between. The social space of Bajau people included the distant places where sea cucumbers were found in profusion, the ports where they traded their goods, the seas they sailed across with wives and children and the uncertain shores where their quest for resources prompted them to stay.

But inside the territorial waters of the colonial States—such as they were defined by the British, Dutch or Portuguese administrations in the eighteenth and nineteenth centuries—and then by the independent States in the second half of the twentieth century, the control of sea routes gradually limited the freedom of movement of sea cucumber fishermen, reputed as sailors of the high seas. Besides, more and more extensive exploitation gradually led sea cucumbers to become rarer at sea levels accessible to snorkelling. Indeed, today, specimens of a size that can viably be sold on the Asian market are only found in much deeper waters.

These historical and economic conditions largely explain why Bajau groups came to attend to the fish-filled reefs they knew so well, where their production activities gradually had to be reorganised. As a result of full sedentarisation and the use of motor boats, whose navigational limits are those imposed by the cost of fuel, the Bajau have lost much more than their practice of long-distance sailing and the freedom of their former 'nomadic' way of life: today, they are denied direct access to the market and have become dependent on 'foreign' middlemen to find buyers for the perishable fruit of their labour. As they have neither the means to package fresh fish nor the possibility to use rapid transport to distant ports where customers await, they have no choice but to deliver the product of their fishing to powerful brokers. Kept out of competitive market practices and unable to profit from its principles, the Bajau fishermen realise they are being exploited but are unable to clearly articulate how.

DISPERSION MODELS

These objective conditions widely contrast with those that enabled their ancestors to reach the distant trading ports where they could negotiate their own shipments of sea cucumbers in person. The commercial momentum that allowed the Bajau groups to sail the seas in the vast space they occupy today has disappeared under the combined pressure of local and global markets.

The political and administrative powers—colonial power or new independent States—exercised their control successively over the exploitation of natural resources—in their transformation and circulation—imposing the new production regimes that their market actors expected and eventually altering social life patterns extensively. The frameworks of social life for Bajau people have changed heavily throughout the twentieth century. Intense commercial activity and their skills as sailors of the high seas, which made them experts in the long transport of high value-added products, had enabled the Bajau to sail the seas since the early times.[17]

No archaeological evidence allows us to say from what region of that vast ocean space they began to disperse.[18] What is known of the history of this people comes from the testimony of sailors and foreign explorers at various times: those are very rare before the nineteenth century. The first Western testimony probably identifying Sama Bajau is that of Pigafetta, Magellan's chronicler, who noticed in 1521 at the southeast tip of the Zamboanga peninsula (Mindanao, Philippines), a population that lives on their boats (Sopher 1977; Sather 1997). However, language elements still provide the most interesting assumptions.

A first argument points to a 'malaisian' origin of Sama Bajau. As mentioned earlier, the Bajau language (*Baun Same*) definitely belongs to the 'Western Malayo-Polynesian' branch, but not to the Philippine language subgroup. One can therefore assume that the Sama Bajau are not from the Philippines, or in any case arrived there much later than other aboriginal people. But the few similarities between Bajau and Malay languages do not prove that the Bajau language is derived from proto-Malay or Malay.

THE 'SULU ARCHIPELAGO' HYPOTHESIS

Pallesen, the American linguist, first discovered that many languages spoken by communities scattered over the south coastal Philippines and North Borneo—except Tausug, which originates from eastern Mindanao—belong to a group of inter-related languages he named Sama Bajau (SB) which also includes the Indonesian Bajau (Pallesen 1985). He assumed that all the currently spoken SB languages, be it elsewhere in the Philippines, in northern Borneo and throughout eastern Indonesia, including Sulawesi, had originated from the southern Philippines. Indeed, according to Pallesen, the Bajau people living in Indonesia probably came from the Sulu Archipelago, where many of them still live.

Almost all Indonesian and Malaysian Bajau are Muslims. They became Muslims before dispersing to the south—to the Lesser Sunda Islands—Flores, Adonara, Timor, etc. where they remained Muslims alongside a Christian majority. The Sama Bajau who have not left the Sulu Archipelago have been acculturated or politically subjugated by the Tausug, hence the numerous words borrowed from Tausug but not found in Sulawesi Bajau language. Blust summarises the scenario proposed by Pallesen:

> In his pathbreaking study of the linguistic consequences of SB-Tausug contact, Pallesen (1985) sketched a scenario for the linguistic history of the Sulu region that includes the following important conclusions:
> 1. Around AD 800 speakers of mutually intelligible PSB [Proto Sama Bajau] dialects lived in the area around the Basilan Strait and included what is now Zamboanga City [...]

2. Initial contact between the Tausug and Sama people probably took place on the north coast of eastern Mindanao, the Tausug homeland.
3. By about AD 1300 the Tausug moved south to Jolo Island in the Sulu group, and during the initial period of contact Tausug began to converge with SB.
4. Soon thereafter Islam was introduced, and in time the Tausug became dominant, with consequent reversal of linguistic convergence affecting SB languages in the Sulu archipelago, but not Abaknon or the SB languages of Indonesia (Blust 2007).

Led to nomadism, Sama Bajau language groups were able to move step-by-step towards the south and east of Indonesia in a few generations. Their great navigation skills and willingness to cross hundreds of miles on small ships enabled them[19] to explore those vast regions fairly quickly, as far as northern Australia in their more distant expeditions. It is impossible to find the timing and routes of their settlements on multiple Indonesian coastlines. However, in view of their diaspora, which now covers a huge maritime area, it becomes clear that their past mobility responded to a powerful momentum.

From a linguistic point of view, the Sama Bajau does not belong to the Philippine language family. Pallesen admits that although he cannot 'say anything about the progress of SB' before Sama Bajau speakers from the Sulu Archipelago started dispersing, 'there is nonetheless important linguistic evidence that this is not a Philippine language' (Pallesen 1985: 117). So the question of the origin of the Bajau people still needs to be asked: the southern Philippine archipelago is probably just a step (lasting several centuries) in the migration and dispersal of Bajau people.

THE 'SOUTHEAST OF BORNEO, BARITO ESTUARY' HYPOTHESIS

Blust notes strong linguistic similarities between the languages of the Sama Bajau group and local languages on the estuary of the Barito, southeast of Kalimantan (Borneo), near the city of Banjarmasin. He observes about two dozen apparent innovations only known in Sama Bajau and in the Barito languages, or only in those languages and one or two others (Blust 2007: 18). This observation, very relevant from a linguistic point of view, allowed him to locate the birthplace of the Sama Bajau people in the Barito region. Languages related to Malay are found not only in Sumatra but also on the western and southern coast of Borneo. According to Blust, the reasons and date of the migration of Sama Bajau ancestors to the southern Philippines are probably linked to the expansion of the Srivijaya empire in the ninth century, a South Sumatran thalassocratic empire that more or less controlled the coasts of the East Indies until the fourteenth century. Blust has this to say about what was happening in about the year 800 CE:

> Malays drew the ancestral Sama Bajau out as partners in a trade network focused on the movement of spices from the Moluccas to the Straits of Malacca. The northern trade route passed through Manado and around Sabah to Brunei and

on to the southern tip of the Malay peninsula. The southern route passed through Kupang at the west end of Timor, and on to Java. The route from Manado to Brunei passed directly through Sulu, and the Sama Bajau came to control this leg of the spice trade, as well as a trade in preserved fish, decorative shells, and other items. In time some groups also moved out to other points along the trade route, closely paralleling the distribution of Malay dialects in eastern Indonesia (2007: 24).

The Sama Bajau would thus put their navigation expertise at the service of powerful kingdoms, much like the Orang Laut in the Malacca-Singapore-Riau area. But we can also imagine that their migration was caused by the threat, even hostility of the Srivijaya empire, which certainly had a powerful fleet already, as the famous bas-reliefs of outrigger vessels on the Buddhist monument of Borobudur in Central Java, built in 800 CE, seem to prove. The 'southeast of Borneo, Barito estuary' hypothesis fits perfectly with the data available, suggesting the Sama Bajau stayed for several centuries in the Sulu Archipelago, south of the Philippines.

CONCLUSION

Numerous oral traditions and linguistic assumptions about the origin of the Bajau people, even archaeological data, fail to provide a definite answer on the proto-Sama Bajau homeland before their settlement in the Sulu Archipelago.[20] It is quite possible that most of the places listed by the Bajau themselves were actually known by their ancestors, even if none is their place of origin. But we can now cautiously attempt to draw some historical lines of the Sama Bajau movements:

- The Sama Bajau are from a coastal region that spoke a language from the same family as the current Malay: east coast of Sumatra, west coast, south and southeast of Borneo. A solid hypothesis would be the estuary of the Barito River in southeast Borneo (Blust 2007).
- Around 800 CE, for some reason probably related to the emergence of the thalassocratic Srivijaya empire, the Sama Bajau leave this region. They settle in the Sulu Archipelago, and probably other coastal areas of Borneo.
- Around 1300 CE, the Tausug from the southern Philippines gradually dominate in the Sulu Archipelago. Bajau culture and language undergo Tausug influences.
- Soon after, Islam was introduced to the Sulu Archipelago. The Sama Bajau not only exploit marine resources for export but are already heavily involved in maritime trade (Bulbeck and Clune 2003).
- From the fifteenth century, some Sama Bajau people emigrate to Borneo and Sulawesi, probably for several reasons: pressure of the Tausug, depletion of some resources and control of the spices trade by the Europeans in the sixteenth century.

- Others remain in the region, move inland and become farmers, such as the Yakan, or the Sama of Sabah (Malaysia).
- Some Sama Bajau groups continue their migration further south and east of the Indonesian archipelago, sometimes moving with families in search of sea species they can trade. If necessary, they recognise a sovereign, such as the Raja of Bone, Southeast Sulawesi (Pelras 1972; Lapian 2009), but often live in small autonomous communities. From southern Sulawesi, they settle on some Lesser Sunda Islands shores and the Kangean archipelago, as many similarities between the dialects of southern Celebes and Flores show.
- In colonial times, the role of the Bajau in commercial shipping is greatly reduced. The Bajau are now only involved in fishing activities. Unfounded accusations of piracy give them a bad reputation that lasts until the early twentieth century.
- After the independence of Indonesia and resolutely since the 1970s, the Indonesian government has encouraged the last Bajau nomads to settle. The economic development of Indonesia has had no positive impact on their daily lives, the Bajau are forgotten by development policies and confined on narrow coastal areas or tiny islands.

NOTES

[1] Populations of 'sea nomads' and speakers of Sama Bajau languages are identified as 'Bajau' in publications relating to coastal South Philippines and North Borneo (Sabah) and as 'Bajo' in those dealing with Indonesia. As the language family is always identified as 'Sama Bajau' we will use 'Bajau' for the sake of consistency, regardless of the origin of the group discussed.

[2] Called *tripang* in Indonesia (*Holothuroidea*).

[3] There are of course other studies dealing with 'seafarers' in Southeast Asia within which the Bajau people cannot be identified: the Bugis people (Pelras 1996), the Suku Laut people of the Riau Archipelago (Chou 2003, 2006), the Moken people (Ivanoff 1985, 1997).

[4] However, defining an 'Indonesia bajau language' in the Indonesian national space is irrelevant. We do not know yet if this language can include the entire Southeast Peninsula of Celebes (Sulawesi Tenggara) or whether it should exclude the dialects of the east coast of Borneo. The inclusion of Timor Leste (East Timor) is coherent because of the presence of Bajau villages in East Point and Leti.

[5] Based on current data, we cannot say that the bajau dialects of North Sulawesi, Maluku and Kangean are close enough to be gathered under the term Indonesian Bajau (bajo language of Indonesia); investigations would be necessary, which is a huge task because of physical barriers and distances.

[6] Nagatsu (2007) and Mead and Lee (2007) worked separately to record an inventory of Bajau communities and draw their own map of the Bajau communities' location. Mead and Lee were limited to Sulawesi, while Nagatsu chartered all the Indonesian locations of Sama Bajau communities that he was aware of. Data from these two authors partially overlap. Nagatsu identifies 67 localities but does not mention 16 locations indicated by Mead et al. Conversely, Mead et al. identify 51 locations but do not mention 19 locations indicated by Nagatsu. These differences can be explained by a difference in methodologies because Nagatsu seems to

identify municipal units (*desa*) where Bajau people are present, while Mead indicates hamlets or villages. Even with compiling both maps, some Bajau villages of Southeast Sulawesi may not appear.

[7] We note, however, that residential situations are relatively more favourable in certain cases: Bajau people of Sapeken, for instance, in the Kangean Islands, came and settled on that small coral island without interest in farming but where fresh water is readily available (Laesanpura and Dahrin 2013: 50).

[8] Sopher (1977: 212 and 245) provides a testimony from the early nineteenth century: Bajau people, together with Southern Celebes Bugis, went on an expedition on 20–30-ton boats, carrying on board small canoes used to fish sea cucumbers off the coast of New Guinea and the north coast of Australia. In the eighteenth century, an English navigator exploring the northern coast of Australia had noticed Bajau sailors. The first contact between Indonesian fishermen (Makassar or Bajau) and Australian Aboriginal people dates back to 1500. In oral traditions of Aboriginals from Arnhem Land, northern Australia, the 'Baijani' visitors are mentioned. See Illouz 2013: 143.

[9] Note that in his contribution to this book, Lance Nolde is interested in the influence of Sama Bajau in some Southern Sulawesi kingdoms. According to him, the Sama Bajau had a major role in the retention of the authority and the power of the kingdoms of Gowa, Talloq and Bone. The Sama Bajau's maritime skill was put to the service of sovereigns who, in exchange, tolerated the autonomy of these polities ruled by recognised leaders in the surrounding area. The titles of *Papuq* or *Lolo* indicated their dominant position among a large number of social groups scattered on the eastern half of the Nusantarian archipelago since ancient times. Some influential Sama Bajau could gather some fleets to accomplish missions for the Makassarese Kingdoms. Such characters could have been privateers mandated by sovereigns, whose power depended on the exploitation of faraway resources, on their commercialisation in harbours very distant from each other, and on their capacity to sustain maritime wars.

[10] These observations are the result of surveys conducted between 2003 and 2014 successively on Kangean islands, Flores and eastern Sulawesi.

[11] The explosives used are homemade bombs consisting of a bottle, potassium nitrate powder and gravel or ammonium nitrate and kerosene. However, these bombs often explode prematurely, causing mutilations and sometimes death. The practice is nonetheless sufficiently profitable to justify the risks.

[12] See Lowe 2000. About the need to integrate the culture and productive practices of the Bajau into ecosystem protection programmes, see Clifton and Majors 2012; Glaser et al. 2010.

[13] If the exploitation of sea cucumbers, the timing of which was defined by the reproductive cycle of this species, structured their itinerant way of life, the economic interest of the Bajau also dealt with the trading of pearls, tortoise shells, spices and all high value-added products available on the islands they visited regularly.

[14] See also Mánez and Ferse 2010.

[15] It is not impossible that at certain times the captains of Bajau fleet, who answered all kinds of market demands, might have also engaged in forms of contraband or trafficking or were appointed by local monarchs to consolidate their political or military projects (Lapian 2009). But the reputation of pirates or slave traders, if not worse, was greatly exaggerated by the European chroniclers. A faulty interpretation that derives the word Bajau from *Bajak* (*laut*): 'pirate' is repeated in different writings. Nagatsu reports the comments of W.B. Pryer who, in 1883, describes the Bajau as 'pirates', 'kidnappers', 'slave traders' and 'practicers of human sacrifice' (Nagatsu 2001).

[16] We cannot deal here with questions relating to navigation, the complex typology of boats, or navigation techniques. On the naval technology of the Sama of the South Sulu Archipelago, see Martenot (2001). The ethno-history of Bajau navigation remains to be written. For an ethnography of fishing as practiced by the Bajau, one can refer to the excellent work of Natasha Stacey about the Bajau of Tukang Besi in Southeast Sulawesi (Stacey 2007).

[17] On shipbuilding and navigation techniques among the Sama of South Sulu in the 1970s, see Martenot, 2001.

[18] According to Bulbeck and Clune, archaeology authorises 'some historical speculations' on the essential role that the Bajau, and doubtless other Orang Laut groups, have played to connect Sulu and Makassar from 1000 CE (2003). The archaeological study of the earthenware in the South Sulawesi area and the archaeological data collected elsewhere between Sulu and Sabah prompt Bulbeck and Clune to hypothesise that 'the Bajau acted as ferriers of motifs between the Makassar and Sulu area, and provide a link between distinct, but related, earthenware traditions' (Bulbeck and Clune 2003: 99). But this research does not make it possible to identify the territorial origin of the Sama Bajau, whatever Bellwood says (1997: 136), whose views are not corroborated by linguistic data.

[19] As mentioned above, starting from the available census data and the arguments developed by Mead and Lee (2007), it is obviously very difficult to conceive an exact superposition between Sama Bajau speakers and populations enrolled in localities where the use of Sama Bajau languages dominates. Among the Sama Bajau language groups undertaking long-distance surveys, there were undoubtedly confirmed sailors from other linguistic and social groups such as the Bugis, Buton, Mandar and others, with whom the Bajau had a long-standing relationship. Unlike those groups, with whom cooperation and exchanges were so varied that they were embarked on the same ships, the Bajau were and always are the only ones who do not have any land of their own in a perennial way.

[20] See recent assumptions of genetic anthropology: Kusuma et al. 2015.

REFERENCES

Adelaar, Alexander and Nikolaus Himmelmann. 2005. *The Austronesian Languages of Asia and Madagascar*. New York: Routledge.

Adriani, N. and A.C. Kruyt. 1914. *De Bare'e-sprekende Toradja's van Midden- Celebes*, vol. 3: *Taal en Letterkunde Schets der Bare'e taal en Overzicht van het Taalgebeid: Celebes–Zuid-Halmahera* [The Bare'e Language of Toradja People from Central Celebes, vol. 3: Language and literature sketch of the Bare'e language and overview of the linguistic area: South Celebes, Halmahera]. Batavia: Landsdrukkerij.

Akamine, Jun. 2005. 'Sama (Bajau).' In *The Austronesian Languages of Asia and Madagascar*, ed. A. Adelaar and N. Himmelmann, 377–96. New York: Routledge.

Bellwood, Peter. 1997. *Prehistory of the Indo-Malaysian Archipelago*. Honolulu: University of Hawai'i Press.

Blust, Robert. 2007. 'The Linguistic Position of Sama-Bajaw.' *Studies in Philippine Languages and Cultures* 15: 73–114.

Bottignolo, Bruno. 1995. *Celebrations with the Sun: An Overview of Religious Phenomena Among the Badjaos*. Manila: Ateneo de Manila University Press.

Bulbeck, David and Genevieve Clune. 2003. 'Macassar Historical Decorated Earthenwares: Preliminary Chronology and Bajau Connections.' In *Earthenware in Southeast Asia*.

Proceeding of the Singapore Symposium on Premodern Southeast Asian Earthenware, ed. J. N. Miksic, 80–102. Singapore: NUS Press.

Chou, Cynthia. 2003. *Indonesian Sea Nomads: Money, Magic, and Fear of the Orang Suku Laut*. London: Routledge/Curzon.

———. 2006. 'Research Trends on Southeast Asia Sea Nomads.' *Kyoto Review of Southeast Asia*. http://kyotoreviewsea.org/images/images/pdffiles/Chou_final.pdf.

Clifton, Julian and Chris Majors. 2012. 'Culture, Conservation, and Conflict: Perspectives on Marine Protection Among the Bajau of Southeast Asia.' *Society & Natural Resources: An International Journal* 25: 716–25.

Dervis, Kemal, Jaime De Melo, and Sherman Robinson. 1982. *General Equilibrium Models for Development Policy*. Washington DC: World Bank Research Publication.

Donohue, Mark. 1996. 'Bajau: A Symmetrical Austronesian Language.' *Language – Journal of the Linguistic Society of America* 72 (4): 782–93.

Earl, George Windsor. 1837. *The Eastern Seas, or Voyages and Adventures in the Indian Archipelago in 1832-33-34*. London: W.H. Allen.

Fougères, Dorian. 2008. *Aquarian Capitalism and Transition in Indonesia*. Saarbrücken: VDM Verlag Dr. Müller.

Fox, James. 1977. 'Notes on the Southern Voyages and Settlements of the Sama-Bajau.' *Bijdragen, Tot de Taal-, Land- en Volkenkunde*, Deel 133, 4ᵉ Aflevering. 's-Gravenhage: Martinus Nijhoff.

Gault, Joan. 2002. 'Some Aspects of "Focus" in Sama Bangingi.' In *The History and Typology of Western Austronesian Voice Systems*, ed. F. Wouk and M. Ross, 367–78. Canberra: Pacific Linguistics.

Glaser, Marion, Irandra Radjawali, Sebastian Ferse, and Bernhard Glaeser. 2010. 'Nested Participation in Hierarchical Societies? Lessons for Social-ecological Research and Management.' *International Journal of Society Systems Science* 2 (4): 390–414.

Grimes, Barbara F. 1999. *Ethnologue – Languages of the World*, 13th ed. Dallas: Summer Institute of Linguistics.

Hapip, Abdul Djebar, Darmansyah, and Noor Basran. 1979. *Bahasa Bajau*. Jakarta: Pusat Bahasa.

Hinayat, Mohamad Said. 2003. *Glosari Bahasa Bajau/Sama – Bahasa Melayu*. Kota Kinabalu: Persatuan Seni Budaya Bajau, Sabah.

Illouz, Charles and Philippe Grangé, eds. 2013. *L'archipel Kangean, Sumenep, Java Est, Indonésie. Recherches Appliquées pour le Développement* [The Kangean Archipelago, Sumenep, East Java, Indonesia. Applied Researches for Development]. Paris: Les Indes Savantes.

Illouz, Charles and Philippe Grangé. 2013. *Kepulauan Kangean. Penelitian Terapan untuk Pembangunan*, Kepustakaan Populer Gramedia (KPG) bekerja sama dengan École Française d'Extrême-Orient (EFEO) [*Kangean Archipelago. Applied Research for Development*, Gramedia Popular Literature (KPG) in collaboration with the École Française d'Extrême-Orient (EFEO)]. Jakarta.

Illouz, Charles. 2013. 'Aperçu d'un mode de vie Difficile : La dette Marchande des Pêcheurs bajos (Sapeken – Kangean)' [Insight into a Difficult Lifestyle : Bajo Fishermen's Market Debt (Sapeken – Kangean)]. *L'Archipel Kangean (Sumenep, Java, Indonésie)*, 143–62. Paris: Les Indes Savantes.

Ivanoff, Jacques. 1985. 'L'épopée de Gaman : Conséquences des Rapports entre Moken/Malais et Moken/Birmans' [The Epic of Gaman : Consequences of the Relationship between Moken/Malays and Moken/Burmese]. *ASEMI* 16: 173–94.

———. 1997. *Moken: Sea Gypsies of the Andaman Sea Post-war Chronicles*. Bangkok: White Lotus.

Jackson, Jeremy et al. 2001. 'Historical Overfishing and the Recent Collapse of Coastal Ecosystems.' *Science* 293: 629–37.

Kusuma, Pradiptajati et al. 2015. 'Mitochondrial DNA and the Y Chromosome Suggest the Settlement of Madagascar by Indonesian Sea Nomad Populations.' *BMC Genomics* 16 (1): 191.

Laesanpura, Agus and Dahrin Darharta Dahrin. 2013. 'Géophysique et Géologie de l'Archipel Kangean' [Geophysics and Geology of the Kangean Archipelago]. *L'Archipel Kangean (Sumenep, Java, Indonésie)*, 37–56. Paris : Les Indes Savantes.

Lapian, Adrian B. et al. 1993. *Studies Bajau Communities*. Jakarta: Lembaga Ilmu Pengetahuan Indonesia.

Lapian, Adrian B. and Kazufumi Nagatsu. 1996. 'Research on Bajau Communities : Maritime People in Southeast Asia.' *Asian Research Trends: A Humanities and Social Science Review* 6: 45–70.

Lapian, Adrian B. 2009. *Orang Laut, Bajak Laut, Raja Laut. Sejarah Kawasan Laut Sulawesi* [Sea People, Pirates, Sea Kings. History of the Sulawesi Sea Area], Abad xix. Jakarta: Komunitas Bambu.

Lowe, Celia. 2000. 'Global Markets, Local Injustice in Southeast Asian Seas: The Live Fish Trade and Local Fishers in the Togean Islands of Sulawesi.' In *People, Plants and Justice: The Politics of Nature Conservation*, ed. C. Zerner. New York: Columbia University Press.

Máñez, Kathleen Schwerdtner and C.A. Sebastian Ferse. 2010. 'The History of Makassan Trepang Fishing and Trade.' *PloS ONE* 5 (6): e11346.

Martenot, Alain. 2001. 'Bateaux sama de Sitangkaï.' *Techniques et Culture* 35–36: 49–83.

Mead, David and Myung-Young Lee. 2007. *Mapping Indonesian Bajau Communities in Sulawesi*, SIL Electronic Survey Report 2007–19: Summer Institute of Linguistics.

Meereboer, M.-T. 1998. 'Fishing for Credit: Patronage and Debt Relations in the Spermonde Archipelago, Indonésia.' In *Living through Histories: Culture, History, and Social Life in South Sulawesi*, ed. K. Robinson and M. Paeni, 249–76. Canberra: Australian National University and the National Archives of Indonesia.

Mous, Peter J. et al. 2000. 'Cyanide Fishing on Indonesian Coral Reefs for the Live Food Fish Market – What is the Problem?' In *Collected Essays on the Economics of Coral Reefs*, ed. HSJ Cesar. Kalmar: Cordio.

Nagatsu, Kazufumi. 2001. 'Pirates, Sea Nomads or Protectors of Islam?: A Note on "Bajau" Identifications in the Malaysian Context.' *Asian and African Area Studies* 1: 212–30.

Nagatsu, Kazufumi, ed. 2007. *The Sama-Bajau in and around Sulawesi: Basic Data on Their Population and Distribution of the Villages*. Sulawesi Area Studies: Kyoto University & Universitas Hasanuddin. http://sulawesi.cseas.kyoto-u.ac.jp/final_reports2007/article/46-nagatsu.pdf.

Nimmo, Arlo. 1972. *The Sea People of Sulu: Studies in Social and Economic Change*. San Francisco: Handler Publishing Company.

———. 2001. *Magosaha, An Ethnography of the Tawi-Tawi Sama Dilaut*. Manila: Ateneo de Manila University Press.

Nuraini, Chandra. 2007. Bajo. *Austronesian Linguistics Database*. http://language.psy.auckland.ac.nz/austronesian/language.php?id=489.

———. 2008. *Langue et Production de Récits d'une Communauté Bajo des Îles Kangean (Indonésie)* [Language and Production of Stories from a Bajo Community in the Kangean Islands (Indonesia)]. Thèse de doctorat. Université de La Rochelle.

———. 2013. 'La Langue Bajo des îles Kangean, Indonésie' [The Bajo Language of the Kangean Islands, Indonesia]. *L'Archipel Kangean (Sumenep, Java, Indonésie)*, 177–210. Paris: Les Indes Savantes.

———. 2016. 'The Intangible Legacy of the Indonesian Bajo.' *Wacana. Jurnal Ilmu Pengetahuan Budaya* 17 (1): 1–18.

———. 2021. *Langue et Chants des Bajos d'Indonésie* [Language and Songs of the Bajo, Indonesia]. *Archipel Kangean*.

Pallesen, Alfred Kemp. 1985. *Culture Contact and Language Convergence*, Special Monograph Issue, 24. Manila: Linguistic Society of the Philippines.

Pelras, Christian. 1972. 'Notes sur Quelques Populations Aquatiques de l'Archipel Nousantarien' [Notes on some Maritime-oriented Populations of the Nusantao Archipelago]. *Archipel* 3: 133–68.

———. 1996. *The Bugis*. Oxford, Cambridge, MA: Blackwell Publication.

———. 1997. 'Langues des Groupes Orang laut et Sama: 67–78; Orang Laut et Sama: Techniques et Culture Matérielle' [Languages of the Orang Laut and Sama Groups: 67–78; Orang Laut and Sama: Techniques and Material Culture]. *Lexique Thématique Plurilingue de Trente Six Langues et Dialectes d'Asie du Sud Est Insulaire* [Thematic Multilingual Lexicon of Thirty Six Languages and Dialects of Insular South East Asia], 648–58 and 466–7. Collectif du Laboratoire Asie du Sud-Est et Monde Austronésien, Paris, l'Harmattan.

———. 2000. 'Patron–client Ties among the Bugis and Makassarese of South Sulawesi.' *Bijdragen tot de Taal-, Land- en Volkenkunde* 156 (3): 393–432.

Pet-Soede, Lida, and Mark Erdmann. 1998. 'An Overview and Comparison of Destructive Fishing Practices in Indonesia.' *SPC Live Reef Fish Information Bulletin* 4.

Revel, Nicole, Alain Martenot, and Harry Arlo Nimmo et al. 2005. *The Voyage to Heaven of a Sama Hero/Le Voyage au ciel d'un héros Sama. Silungan Baltapa*. Paris.

Saat, Gusni. 2003. 'The Identity and Social Mobilty of Sama-Bajau.' *Sari 21* 3–11. http://www.penerbit.ukm.my/sari21-01.pdf.

Salzner, Richard. 1960. *Sprachenatlas des indopazifischen Raumes* [Language Atlas of the Indo-Pacific region]. Wiesbaden: Otto Harrassowitz.

Sather, Clifford A. 1995. 'Sea Nomads and Rainforest Hunter-gatherers: Foraging Adaptations in the Indo-Malaysian Archipelago.' In *The Austronesians: Historical and Comparative Perspectives*, ed. P. Bellwood, J.J. Fox, and D. Tryon, 245–85. Canberra: Department of Anthropology, Research School of Pacific and Asian Studies Publication, Australian National University.

———. 1997. *The Bajau Laut. Adaptation, History, and Fate in a Maritime Fishing Society of South-Eastern Sabah*. Kuala Lumpur, Singapore, New York: Oxford University Press.

Sneddon, James Neil. 1983. 'Northern Celebes (Sulawesi)', map 43. In *Language atlas of the Pacific area, part 2: Japan area, Taiwan (Formosa), Philippines, mainland and insular South-East Asia*, ed. Stephen A. Wurm and Shiro Hattori. Canberra: The Australian Academy of the Humanities, in collaboration with the Japan Academy; PL, C-67.

———. 1996. *Indonesian, a Comprehensive Grammar*. London: Routledge.

Sopher, David E. 1965. *The Sea Nomads. A Study Based on the Literature of the Maritime Boat People of Southeast Asia*. Singapore: Lim Bian Han, Government Printer, Memoirs of the National Museum.

Stacey, Natasha. 2007. *Boats to Burn: Bajo Fishing Activity in the Australian Fishing Zone*. Canberra: ANU E-Press.

Sutherland, Heather. 2000. 'Trepang and Wangkang: The China Trade of Eighteenth-century Makassar, c. 1720s–1840s.' *Bijdragen tot de Taal-, Land- en Volkenkunde* 156 (3): 451–72.

Tagliacozzo, Eric. 2004. 'A necklace of fins: Marine goods trading in maritime Southeast Asia, 1780–1860.' *International Journal of Asian Studies* 1 (1): 23–48.

Trick, Douglas. 2006. 'Ergative Control of Syntactic Processes in Sama Southern.' Paper presented at the 10th International Conference on Austronesian Linguistics. 17–20 January 2006. Puerto Princesa City, Palawan, Philippines.

Verheijen, Jilis A.J. 1986. *The Sama/Bajau Language in the Lesser Sunda Islands*, Pacific Linguistics – Series D – Materials in languages of Indonesia, n° 32. Canberra: The Australian National University.

Wurm, Stephen A. 2007. 'Australasia and the Pacific.' In *Encyclopedia of the World's Endangered Languages*, ed. Christopher Moseley, 425–578. London and New York: Routledge.

14

Maritime Diaspora and Creolisation: A Genealogy of the Sama Bajau in Insular Southeast Asia

Nagatsu Kazufumi

INTRODUCTION

This chapter examines the population dispersal and ethnic formation of the Sama Bajau, who constitute one of the most distinctive 'sea people' in the Southeast Asian maritime world.[1] The Southeast Asian maritime world here is defined as the socio-cultural ecosphere of Southeast Asia, which is tightly bound by the seas. Geographically, it consists of insular Southeast Asia and the adjacent coasts of continental Southeast Asia (Map 14.1). 'Sea people' designates a prototypical group which has been formed on the basis of the ecological environment of this maritime world, an archipelagic terrain predominantly characterised by tropical seas and rainforests.[2]

The settlements of the Sama Bajau are widely spread out from the Sulu Archipelago in the southern Philippines, through Sabah in Malaysia and into eastern Indonesia. With an approximate population of 1,100,000, most of the Sama Bajau inhabit shorelines or islands, and make a living through sea-oriented activities such as fishing, inter-island trade, seafaring, or cultivation of coconut palms. Since some subgroups of the Sama Bajau (e.g. the Sama Dilaut in the Sulu Archipelago) spent their whole lives in houseboats on the sea until the mid-twentieth century, they have often been represented as 'sea nomads' or 'sea gypsies' in European literature [e.g. Taylor 1931; Sopher 1977 (1965)].

Focusing on this sea-oriented people, the study outlined in this chapter aims to:

(1)   demonstrate the population distribution and socio-historical grouping of the Sama Bajau,

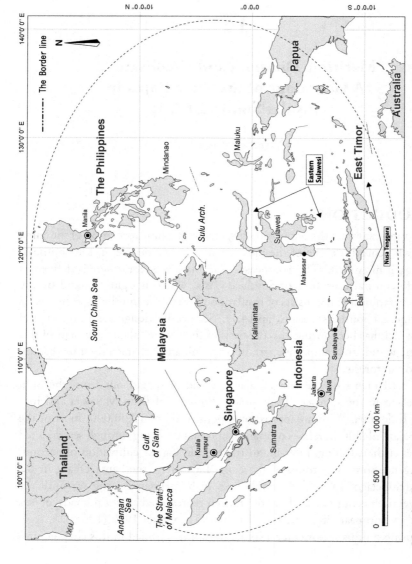

Map 14.1 Southeast Asian Maritime World [Source: The author created this map using digital base maps provided by BPS (2000) and downloaded from GADM (2009) online (http://gadm.org/)]. Hereafter, maps are referred to as "digital base maps".

(2) explore the patterns of their population diaspora and inter-regional social relations to depict some geo-demographic features of the Sama Bajau in eastern Indonesia, and
(3) understand the dynamics of the ethnogenesis of the Sama Bajau as a maritime creole to reconsider the patterns of their geographical expansion.

Although this chapter initially provides an overview of the Sama Bajau in general in the Southeast Asian maritime world, its central focus is directed towards the Sama Bajau in eastern Indonesia, particularly those in the eastern Sulawesi region and the Nusa Tenggara (the Lesser Sunda Islands) region (see Map 14.1).

Intensive and extensive fieldwork for this study has been conducted since 1994 to 2016 in a number of villages of the Sama Bajau and some other groups of sea people in insular Southeast Asia. The research sites are shown in Map 14.2.[3]

The discussion and analysis of this chapter are based on data obtained from the fieldwork, GIS (Geographic Information System) and census data, especially those collected in 2000 in the Philippines, Malaysia and Indonesia (see [Census] in references), historical sources and published literatures.

The first section of this chapter discusses preceding studies on the population distribution of the Sama Bajau, then plots their settlements on maps using the GIS and 2000 censuses, dividing them into several subgroups according to their socio-cultural traits. The second section analyses the geo-demographic features of the Sama Bajau diasporic distribution and population flow in eastern Indonesia based on the data. Finally, the third section explores the process of ethnogenesis of the Sama Bajau in relation to preceding discussions on their distribution and migration. Here the chapter uses ethnographic data collected during intensive fieldwork in Sapeken Island in East Java, Indonesia in 2010 and 2011 for about two months in total.

HABITAT AND DISTRIBUTION OF THE SAMA-BAJAU

THE ETHNIC TERMS AND PREVIOUS STUDIES ON POPULATION MOVEMENTS

Sama Bajau here designates the people who speak the Sama Bajau languages that form a discrete subgroup of the Austronesian language family (Pallesen 1985: 43) and consider themselves as 'Sama', 'Bajau', 'Bajo', or other similar ethnonyms based on a sense of belonging to the larger Sama Bajau group. 'Bajo' is an Indonesian variant of the term Bajau. 'Sama' is an ethnonym by which they identify themselves in their daily life. However, the Sama Bajau have recently tended to use the term 'Bajau' or 'Bajo' to represent themselves since it has become popular domestically as well as internationally.[4] Unlike some other ethnic labels derived from the words of other ethnic groups, the term Bajau itself

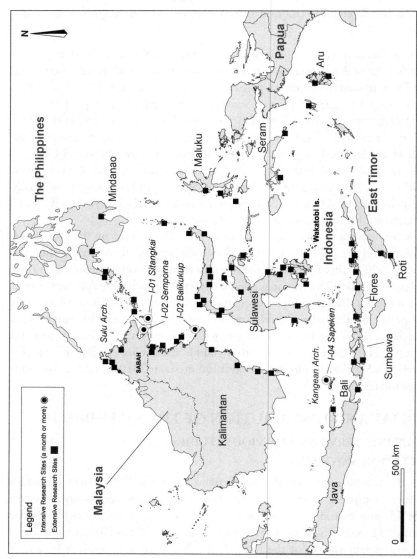

Map 14.2 Selected sites where the author conducted intensive and extensive fieldwork from 1994 to 2016 (Source: Digital base maps, annotations by author).

does not imply any pejorative meaning. With these conditions in mind, the term Bajau shall be adopted in this chapter.

As their homeland or centre of the population is ambiguous, scholars have long discussed the population movements of the Bajau to seek their 'true' historical origin. Research on their origin first appeared in historical geographer D.E. Sopher's pioneering work, *The Sea Nomads* [1977 (1965)]. Sopher comprehensively examined the literature on the cultures and histories of boat-dwelling groups in Southeast Asia, including the Bajau, the Orang Laut and the Mawken. He then advanced a hypothesis that these boat-dwellers originated in the Riau-Lingga Archipelago to the south of the Malay Peninsula. According to his hypothesis, the Bajau gradually emigrated away from the Riau-Lingga Islands from the fourteenth to the seventeenth centuries and voyaged toward the Sulu Islands via the western coast of Borneo, where some of them sailed further southward to the coasts of Sulawesi [1977 (1965): 345–59].

Anders K. Pallesen's linguistic monograph (1985) and H. Arlo Nimmo's ethnography (1968), both of which focus on the Bajau in the Sulu Archipelago, disputed Sopher's hypothesis, and suggested that Bajau belonged to a language group different from those of the other boat dwellers. Furthermore, these studies concluded that the Bajau originated in the southwestern part of Mindanao, the Philippines, and after the tenth century spread southward to the eastern part of insular Southeast Asia. Their works were based on the then latest data obtained through their long-term fieldwork. Therefore, their postulation about the origin of the Bajau is seemingly more convincing than Sopher's assumption (see also Sather 1997).

It seems less significant (if not meaningless) to seek the 'true' origin of the Bajau from the historical essentialist's point of view, as the Bajau and their neighbouring communities are supposed to have constantly switched their ethnic identity from non-Bajau into Bajau, or vice versa. While criticising the conventional view of historians on Island Southeast Asia, who were inclined to regard the ethnicity as a fixed premise, James F. Warren (1981: 255) maintained that Sulu populations—including the Balangingi Samal, a Bajau subgroup—comprised of captives, with diverse ethnic attributes, and their descendants. The 'pirates' brought the captives for sale to the Sulu Archipelago. The Sulu aristocrats organised the pirates from the late eighteenth century through the nineteenth century. The captives were assimilated into Sulu societies in a few generations, and some of them even became a member of the 'pirates'. These captives formed the Balangingi Samal, regardless of their origins. It shall later be confirmed that a similar flexible formation of ethnicity is still evident among the Bajau in eastern Indonesia.

This chapter examines their distribution and its geo-demographic features in order to understand the dynamics of the ethnogenesis of the diasporic population from the constructionist's point of view.

HABITAT AND DISTRIBUTION

Habitats of the Bajau are closely related to certain marine environments, especially coral reefs [Sopher 1977 (1965); Sather 1997]. The Bajau in general have inhabited littorals and islands adjacent to coral reefs for the following reasons:

(1) to take advantage of a commercial fishery-oriented economic life [Sopher 1977 (1965)]; and
(2) to evade interventions by colonial as well as national authorities, who have frequently tried to restrict their sea-going movements (Warren 1971).

In 2000, reliable censuses of population by ethnic group were taken in Indonesia and the Philippines for the first time after the independences of both nation-states. Meanwhile, censuses by ethnic group have been published in Sabah since the early twentieth century. Hence, the Bajau population in insular Southeast Asia as a whole can now be estimated. According to the censuses, their total population is estimated at 1,077,020. Among the total populations, a population of 570,857 was counted in the Philippines, 347,193 in Malaysia (only in Sabah) and 158,970 in Indonesia (Nagatsu 2009).[5]

Map 14.3 shows the distribution of the Bajau in insular Southeast Asia. It tells us that major settlements of the Bajau are scattered over an aquatic area stretching nearly 1,300 kilometres from the Kangean Archipelago, East Java Province in the west to the Kayoa Island, Maluku Province, Indonesia in the east, and 2,000 kilometres from the southwestern tip of Mindanao Island, the Philippines in the north to Roti Island, Nusa Tenggara Timur Province, Indonesia in the south. No other indigenous ethnic groups in insular Southeast Asia are distributed as widely as the Bajau. Here, let us confirm the diasporic formation of their settlements.

SUBGROUPS OF THE BAJAU

The Bajau can be classified into several subgroups according to dialects, proximity of social relations, patterns of historical narratives and other cultural elements as well as social systems (Nagatsu 2009). Although linguistic studies so far have classified the Bajau into nine or more subgroups (e.g. Pallesen 1985; Grimes ed. 2000), this classification is too detailed to take a general view of their socio-historical relations. Since this chapter does address their socio-historical relations, the Bajau are simply classified into four groups: the Abaknon Bajau (abbreviated as ABK), the Bajau of Borneo West Coast (BWC), the Sulu Bajau (SUL), and the Sulawesi Bajau (SLW), as roughly shown in Map 14.4.

The ABK mostly live by fishing and planting coconut trees on Capul Island off the east coast of Samar, the northern Philippines. Since their settlements are separate and distant from those of the other three subgroups, the ABK have rarely been linked with the others socially in modern history. Linguistically, they

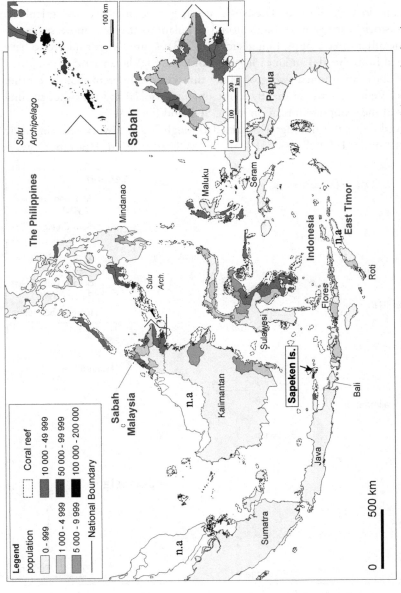

Map 14.3 Distribution of the Bajau population in 2000. The population is projected by province in the Philippines, by *daerah* (district) in Malaysia, and by *kabupaten* (regency) in Indonesia [Source: The author created this map, with modifications, from Nagatsu (2012)].

are considered to have separated from the other three subgroups at a very early stage of history (Pallesen 1985: 16–18).

Meanwhile the settlements of the BWC are located inland on the west coast of Sabah, Malaysia. Although they live close to the SUL, social ties between the two subgroups are fairly limited. The BWC mostly engage in paddy rice agriculture and livestock rearing. As an agricultural population, they are more sedentary than the other three groups. Linguistically, the BWC are also considered to have separated from the SUL at an earlier stage of history (Pallesen 1985: 16–18).

The above-mentioned two groups are thus clearly different from the other groups. We hereafter refer mainly to the linguistic, social and the other cultural aspects of the grouping in relation to the SUL and the SLW.[6]

According to the findings I obtained through my fieldwork and linguistic surveys (Smith 1984; Pallesen 1985), the SUL and the SLW are not always

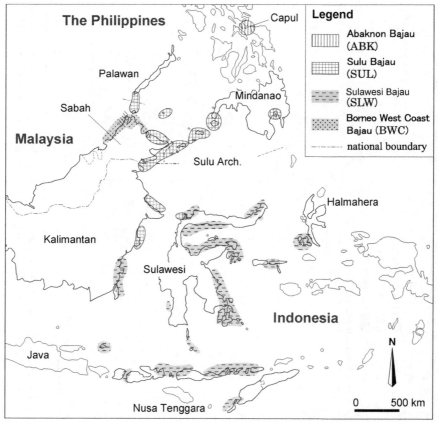

Map 14.4 Distribution of the Bajau subgroups [Source: The author reproduced this map from Grimes ed. (2000) and fieldwork].

mutually intelligible linguistically. For instance, the Bajau in Maratua Island in North Kalimantan (SUL) communicated in Indonesian with the Bajau from Tolitoli in Central Sulawesi (SLW) [see Map 14.5 (A–K) below for the place names in detail]. The former Bajau maintained that the latter's dialects were too 'hard' (*keras*) to understand, though he recognised the latter's tongue as a Bajau dialect. On the contrary, the dialects spoken among the SLW group are relatively uniform. Those spoken among the SUL group are also intelligible to one another, although the dialects are of considerable variation.

Social interactions including intermarriage are also less frequent among the two subgroups except for those who live in the interface between the two subgroups. For example, on Balikukup Island of North Kalimantan the SUL are dominant, but the SLW also frequently visit the island to fish and some of them have migrated here. As a natural consequence, intermarriage relations are now seamlessly confirmed among the members of each subgroup.

Although a basic motif is shared by the two groups, specific patterns of origin myths are different to the extent that one subgroup is totally unfamiliar with the other's historical and geographical setting. The SUL generally have a myth in which drifted ancestors, and Zamboanga in Mindanao Island or Jolo in the Sulu Archipelago, are used as the keywords. For instance, the Bajau in Sitangkai, the Sulu Archipelago said that their ancestors once lived in Johor but later drifted northward to a littoral spot. The spot was named 'Sambuangan' which means in Bajau 'the place where one sticks a pole (into the seabed to moor boats)'. That is, they believe, the etymology of Zamboanga. They continued, 'the ancestors threw a handful of paddies and the paddies turned into islands of the Sulu Archipelago. Thereafter, they began to live there'.

Meanwhile, among the SLW, a lost princess, the place of Johor and the sultanate of Goa or Bone in southern Sulawesi form the central part of their origin myth. According to the story told by the Bajau in the Banggai Islands, the Bajau princess played on a beach in Johor and was drifted to the ocean. Their ancestors were ordered by the sultan to search for the princess but could not find her. They dispersed themselves to the east since they were afraid of being punished by the sultan. One day, a prince of the Goa sultanate found an unidentified beautiful lady and made her his wife. Listening to a song sung by the then princess of Goa, the Bajau followers recognised her as the Bajau princess who had been drifted away and told the prince of Goa that she was the Bajau princess. Thereafter the Bajau began to be treated with respect and were allowed to live on the coasts and islands of Goa.

Thus, the Bajau population can be reasonably classified into four subgroups from the socio-historical point of view. Henceforth specific attention shall be drawn to the Sulawesi Bajau, whose settlements are all located in Indonesian waters.

GEO-DEMOGRAPHIC FEATURES OF THE BAJAU IN EASTERN INDONESIA

SETTLEMENT CLUSTERS IN INDONESIA

As mentioned previously, the Indonesian census counted 158,970 Bajau in 2000. The population is concentrated in the eastern part of the country surrounding Sulawesi. Map 14.5 shows the distribution of the Bajau settlements by *desa*, or administrative village, where their population is more than 50.

Lance Nolde, who conducted anthropological research on the Bajau in Southeast Sulawesi, described the Bajau maritime realm as follows: (it) 'consists of an informal network of historical and contemporary links between families, friends, fishing grounds, trading centres and trade routes, through which knowledge and goods are exchanged' (Nolde 2009: 16).

Here, let us assume a more intensive realm of their socio-historical interplay and call it a 'cluster'. Note that the cluster is not a territorialised space but a flexible zone of social networks and its boundaries are obscured by nature. The Bajau regard a geographical sphere that roughly coincides with the cluster as a spatial unit of dialect, with close social relations and distinct cultural similarities. Since they do not generally have any common geographical name to designate such a spatial unit, the cluster shall be named according to the name of an adjacent city, an administrative region, or an island which is located in or near the cluster. Based on interviews and observations in fieldwork (see Map 14.2), I tentatively delimit, as demonstrated in Map 14.5, 13 clusters of Bajau settlements in Indonesia. Names of the clusters and the Bajau population of all the villages in each cluster are presented in Map 14.5 (A–K). The Bajau in all but the Maratua cluster belong to the SLW group. The Bajau in the Maratua cluster is included in the SLU group.

GEO-DEMOGRAPHIC FEATURES IN EASTERN SULAWESI AND NUSA TENGGARA

Turning to the geo-demographic features of the distribution and flow of the Bajau population, this section will focus on the eastern Sulawesi region and the Nusa Tenggara region (see Map 14.1). The eastern Sulawesi region here covers a chain of littorals and islands situated in Tomini Bay, the Togian Islands, the Banggai Archipelago, Tomori Bay, the Salabangka Archipelago, the Kendari region, Kabaena Island, Muna Island, Buton Island and the Wakatobi Archipelago. The Nusa Tenggara region here includes the islands from the Kangean Archipelago in the west to Timor Island in the east.

The eastern Sulawesi region is divided into four Bajau clusters: Togian, Banggai, Salabangka and Buton. Each cluster consists of numerous Bajau villages of various sizes. Villages where the Bajau population is more than 1,000 will be called 'core Bajau villages'. There the Bajau are usually in the majority and are dominant in the social, cultural or economic arena. The core village often functions as a social, economic and symbolic centre for the Bajau living in the cluster. There are 12 core Bajau villages in eastern Sulawesi: three are in the Togian cluster, three in the Banggai cluster, one in the Salabangka cluster, and five in the Buton cluster. All the core villages are typically built on and around the broad coral reef.

Looking at Map 14.5 E to G which cover eastern Sulawesi, we can confirm that:

(1) the littorals and islands here are densely populated by the Bajau;
(2) several core Bajau villages and a number of villages adjacent to the core villages form each cluster; and
(3) the Bajau settlements extend from north to south, or from Tomini Bay to Buton Island almost seamlessly.

As far as the Bajau are concerned, these are the main geo-demographic characteristics in this region.

The Nusa Tenggara region is divided into four clusters. Map 14.5 H to J provide detailed information about the Bajau in each cluster. Here the villages are situated only on some parts of the north coast of Flores and the Alor Islands, along the Alas Straits and the Sape Straits, in Roti and the western end of West Timor. These villages are apparently established along the sea routes from Sulawesi in the north to Sawu Sea or, more precisely, to the fishing grounds on the border facing Australia in the south. There are also several core Bajau villages in Nusa Tenggara. In this region, however, the core villages and adjacent villages are not contiguous but dispersed.

In the whole insular region including both eastern Sulawesi and Nusa Tenggara, social relations of the Bajau are proximate, extending from the north to south: the clusters are intimately tied through their intermarriages, migrations and mutual visits to relatives and friends. At Kalumbatang, one of the core Bajau villages in the Banggai cluster, the village secretariat maintained that the residents had marital relations with all the clusters in eastern Sulawesi and Nusa Tenggara. He designated specific social ties by individual names with Karumpa in the Bonerate Islands, Bungin in Sumbawa Island, Pasir Putih and Wuring in Flores Islands, Kabir in Pantar Island, Sulamu in West Timor. The Bajau there also voyaged back and forth from the Banggai Archipelago to Flores Island, Roti Island and Australian waters to search for sharks and trochus shell (*Tectus niloticus*), to Bacan Island in Maluku and the Togian Islands in Tomini Bay to seek mother-of-pearl shells, groupers, marine aquarium fish, and a kind of hard coral called '*rotan laut*'.

The Bajau in Roti have close family ties with the Bajau in eastern Sulawesi. The Bajau of Mola villages in the Buton cluster frequently visit Pepela, part of Londalusi village in Roti Island. They use the littoral at Pepela as a port of call

Map 14.5 (A–K) Distribution and cluster of the Bajau in Indonesia, 2000
The map shows administrative villages (*desa*) with more than 50 people of the Bajau population. The village names are listed in Maps A–K. Here the figures in parentheses indicate the population of the Bajau. The author has visited the villages of which names are underlined. Names of the "core Bajau village" are put in italics bold and the numbers are circled on each map [Source: The author created the maps using BPS (2000), referring to BPS (2002) and fieldwork].

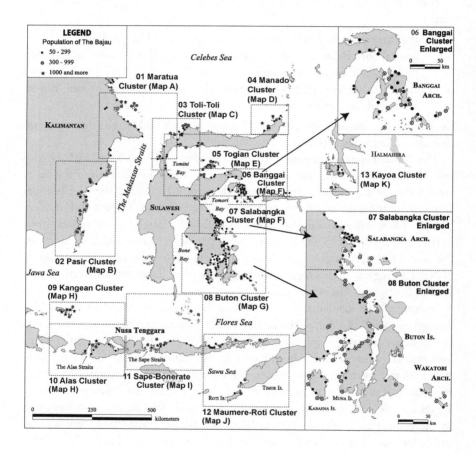

Map A

1 Mangku Padi (169)	13 Batu Putih (238)
2 Tanjung Batu (916)	14 Tanjung Perepat (314)
3 Teluk Semanting (373)	15 Pantai Harapan (650)
4 Tanjung Redeb (241)	16 Biduk-Biduk (253)
5 Bugis (171)	17 Sandaran (66)
6 *Pulau Derawan* (1,171)	18 Simatang
7 Teluk Alulu (497)	Tanjung (444)
8 Teluk Harapan (501)	19 Ogotua (53)
9 Payung-Payung (429)	20 Bontang Baru (69)
10 Bohesilian (773)	21 Bontang Kuala (112)
11 Talisayan (116)	22 Sekambing (51)
12 Tembudan (101)	

Population
- 50 - 99
- 100 - 499
- 500 - 999
- 1000 - 1999
- 2000 - 6000

Map B

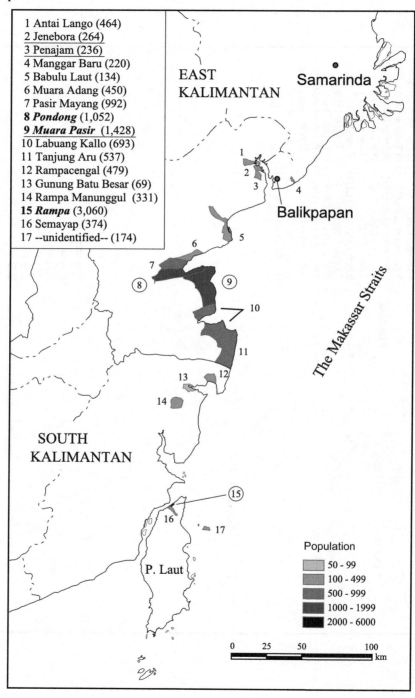

Map C

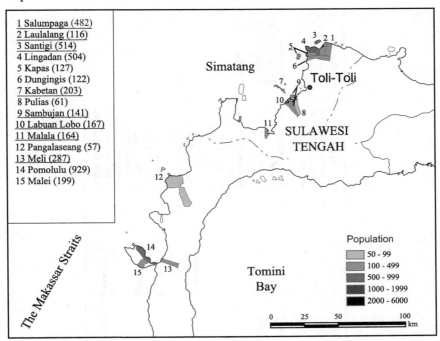

Map D

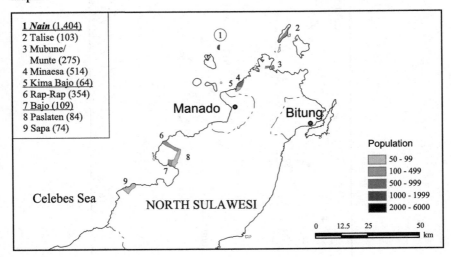

Map E

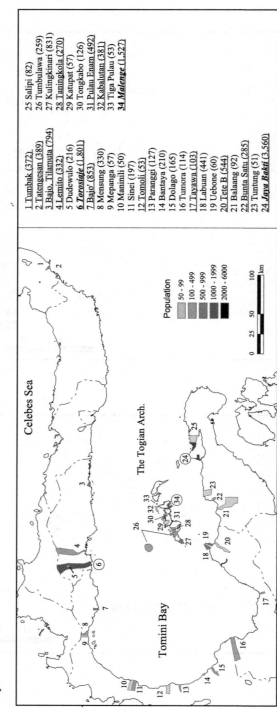

Map F

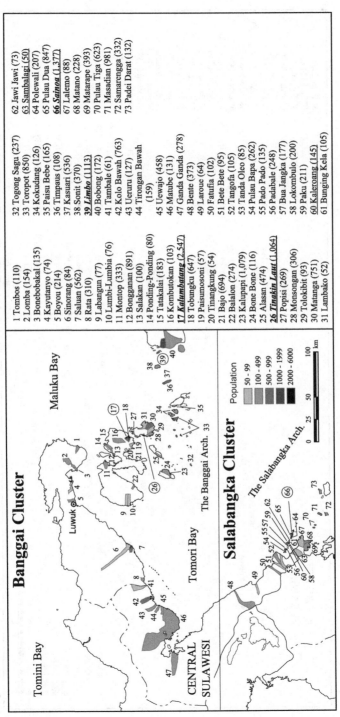

Map G

#	Name (pop)	#	Name (pop)	#	Name (pop)
1	Sulaho (241)	31	Tanomeha (113)	61	Bero (295)
2	Wolo (150)	32	Waturambaha (223)	62	Tasipi (462)
3	Lapao-Pao (59)	33	Boenaga (183)	63	Tiga (178)
4	Lawulo (51)	34	Tapunggaya (124)	64	Santiri (851)
5	Kolakaasih (510)	35	Mandiodo (153)	65	Tondasi (168)
6	Dawi-Dawi (119)	36	Mowundo (125)	66	Lasama (378)
7	Tambea (135)	37	Lemobajo (723)	67	Tanjung Pinang (386)
8	Hakatutobu (213)	38	Kampobunga (573)	68	Napabalano (391)
9	Anaiwoi (138)	39	Laimeo (193)	69	Latawe (410)
10	Boepinang (847)	40	Bajo Indah (536)	70	Pasipadangan (353)
11	Waemputang (195)	41	Mekar (739)	71	Maginti (916)
12	Terapung (223)	42	Bokori (445)	72	Bangko (772)
13	Pulau Tambako (276)	43	Saponda (906)	73	Kawite Wite (156)
14	Lauru (117)	44	Kessilampe (75)	74	*Tapi-Tapi* (1,146)
15	Baliara (659)	45	Upt.Lapulu (201)	75	Pasikuta (331)
16	Sikeli (532)	46	Lapulu (186)	76	Marobo (208)
17	Batuawu (76)	47	Petoaha (284)	77	Laiworu (142)
18	Pongkalaero (73)	48	Labuan Beropa (58)	78	*Lagasa* (1,583)
19	Kokoe (416)	49	Moramo (152)	79	Lakonea (480)
20	Telaga Besar (467)	50	Cempedak (312)	80	Lawata (101)
21	Ulungkura (67)	51	*Langara Laut* (1,506)		
22	Toli-Toli (66)	52	Lalembuu Jaya (330)		
23	Terapung (987)	53	Bungin Permai (804)		
24	Kance Bungi (536)	54	Torokeku (472)		
25	Lawele (108)	55	Puupi (354)		
26	Siomanuru (442)	56	Bangun Jaya (185)		
27	*Mola Selatan* (2,612)	57	Langgapulu (336)		
28	*Mola* (2,417)	58	Wangkolabu (218)		
29	Horuo (857)	59	Lakarama (152)		
30	Samabahari (930)	60	*Bahari* (1,176)		

Population
- 50 - 99
- 100 - 499
- 500 - 999
- 1000 - 1999
- 2000 - 6000

SOUTHEAST SULAWESI
Bone Bay
Kolaka
Kendari
Kabaena
Muna
Buton
Bau Bau
The Wakatobi Arch.
Flores Sea

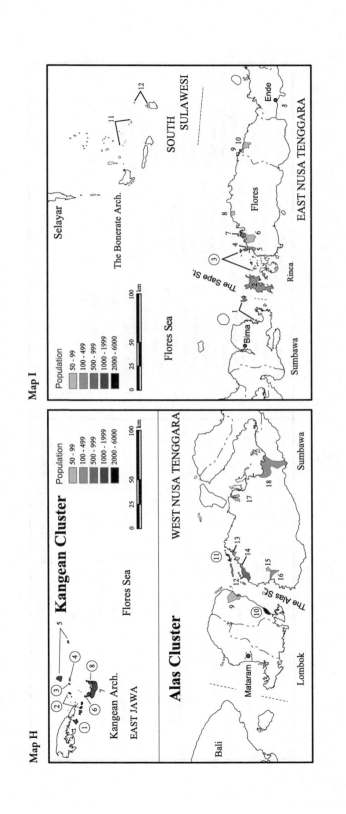

Map J

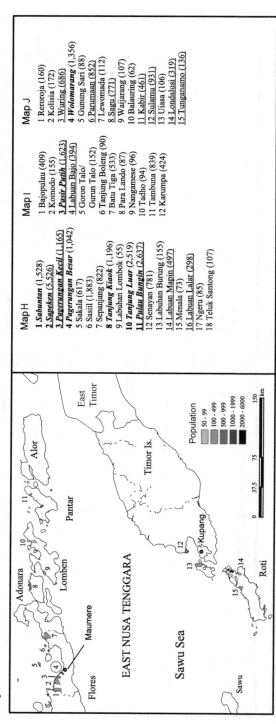

Map H
1 **Sabuntan** (1,528)
2 **Sapeken** (5,526)
3 **Pagerungan Kecil** (1,165)
4 **Pagerungan Besar** (1,042)
5 Sakala (617)
6 Sasiil (1,883)
7 Sepanjang (822)
8 **Tanjung Kiaok** (1,196)
9 Labuhan Lombok (55)
10 **Tanjung Luar** (2,519)
11 **Pulau Bungin** (2,637)
12 Senayan (781)
13 Labuhan Burung (155)
14 Labuan Mapin (497)
15 Menala (73)
16 Labuan Lalar (298)
17 Ngeru (85)
18 Teluk Santong (107)

Map I
1 Bajopulau (409)
2 Komodo (155)
3 **Pasir Putih** (1,623)
4 Labuan Bajo (394)
5 Goron Talo/
  Gurun Talo (152)
6 Tanjung Boleng (90)
7 Batu Tiga (533)
8 Para Lando (87)
9 Nangamese (96)
10 Tadho (94)
11 Tambuna (839)
12 Karumpa (424)

Map J
1 Reroroja (160)
2 Kolisia (172)
3 Wuring (686)
4 **Wolomarang** (1,356)
5 Gunung Sari (88)
6 Parumaan (852)
7 Lewomada (112)
8 Sagu (771)
9 Waijarang (107)
10 Balauring (62)
11 Kabir (461)
12 Sulamu (931)
13 Uiasa (106)
14 Londalusi (319)
15 Tunganamo (136)

Map K

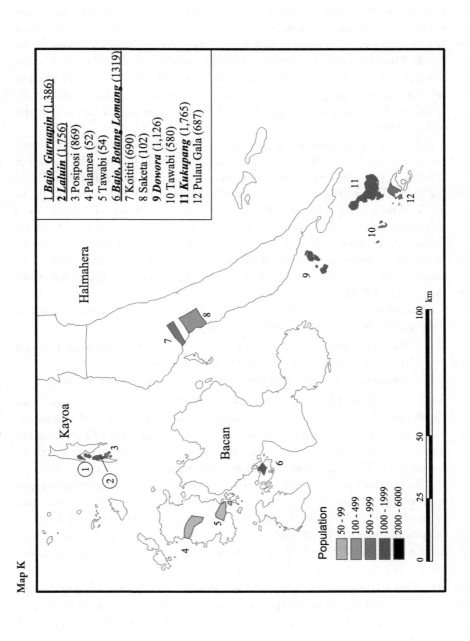

to travel further to the Ashmore Reef in Australian waters, where they fish for sharks with longlines and gather trochus shells. According to Natasha Stacey who comprehensively examined the social history of the Bajau in Southeast Sulawesi, Pepela was originally established by Bajau migrants from the Wakatobi Islands who repeatedly went to seek marine resources in Australian waters in the 1950s. Their migratory movements to Pepela reached its peak in the 1980s when shark fishing in the seas was most active (Stacey 2007: 28–30). The movement still continues, although the Bajau do not go across the boundary as frequently as before due to heightened aggression from Australian border patrol over the past ten years.

The Bajau also sailed from Sulawesi to the southern littorals and islands associated with the trading activities of the Bugis or Makassar. Jilis Verheijen (1986: 23) mentions, based on a Bajau informant's narrative, that around 1820 the Bugis came from southern Sulawesi to Tanjung Luar, Lombok and the Bajau followed them some years later. Voyages to the coasts of northern Australia were also supposedly organised by the Bugis or Makassar traders; people from Sulawesi including the two groups and the Bajau were all regarded as 'Makassan' by the Aboriginal people in northern Australia. The Makassan seasonal voyages to search for trepangs (sea cucumbers) began as late as the early eighteenth century (Macknight 1976).

To summarise, the distribution and flow of the Bajau population in eastern Sulawesi and Nusa Tenggara are characterised by:

(1)   the maritime networks which the Bajau have long maintained through their commercial-oriented fishing activities; and
(2)   intimate social relations extending to all the regions across the seas.

Basic vocabularies of the Bajau at more than 50 Bajau villages in the Sulu Archipelago, Sabah and eastern Indonesia have been collected and compared. The outcomes suggest that the Bajau dialects spoken among the SLU group are significantly varied even though the speakers are mutually intelligible, while those among the SLW group are of little divergence (see in detail Nagatsu 2009a).

The distribution of the SLU settlements around the Sulu Archipelago ranges approximately 1,000 kilometres from east to west and 500 kilometres from north to south. Meanwhile, the distribution of SLW settlements around Sulawesi extends approximately 1,200 kilometres from east to west and 1,500 kilometres from north to south. The SLW speak homogeneous dialects across a vast insular region. This suggests that:

(1)   the Bajau repeated their maritime movements frequently and vigorously;
(2)   their subgroups have maintained social or economic relations intimately and extensively, though the subgroups are geographically separated; and thus
(3)   the Bajau have so far maintained a maritime living zone in the region.

HISTORICAL PERSISTENCE OF THE MARITIME ZONE

The Bajau in eastern Sulawesi were most probably migrants from southern Sulawesi. According to Sopher [1977 (1965)], the dispersion of the Bajau to the east and south occurred in accord with the process in which the Makassar's Goa sultanate or the Bugis's Bone sultanate expanded their spheres of influence in these directions. The former sultanate was centred on the west coast of southern Sulawesi, while the latter was centred on the east coast. The Bajau migrated to eastern Sulawesi or Nusa Tenggara in search of marine products such as tortoise shells since the sixteenth century.

Dutch colonial records tell us that by the mid-nineteenth century the Bajau had established a zone of marine resource exploitation to procure tortoise shells, trepangs, etc. in eastern Sulawesi (Vosmaer 1839; Hart 1853). In the south, they had expanded their fishing zone to the northern coast of Australia by the eighteenth century. There they gathered and processed trepangs or other marine products to be brought back to Sulawesi. All these marine products were exported to China from Makassar or other local ports. In the process of their movements southwards, the Bajau also settled down on the littorals and islands located in Nusa Tenggara. The Bajau villages there are located along the sea routes bridging Sulawesi and the southern seas including Australian waters. Such patterns of their diaspora seem to reflect the historical process of pioneering voyages to seek marine resources from Sulawesi down to the south [Verschuer 1883; Sopher 1977 (1965); Fox 1977].

Summarising the history of the Bajau migrations in Nusa Tenggara, James J. Fox found that most of the Bajau settlements 'have been less stable with populations shifting among various sites. Yet all present-day settlements are in areas frequently visited by Bajau from the time of their early voyages (to search for trepangs, tortoise shells or the other marine resources)'. The pattern of Bajau population movements in the wider region from eastern Sulawesi to Nusa Tenggara can be explained in the same manner. The Bajau have repeatedly created, abandoned and recreated their settlements along certain sea routes in this region. Thus, they have formed and so far maintained a maritime zone for living since as late as the eighteenth century.

THE BAJAU AND CREOLISM: THE CASE OF SAPEKEN, THE KANGEAN ARCHIPELAGO

SAPEKEN

The Bajau established their settlements in a vast maritime zone in eastern Indonesia. The expansion of their settlements has taken place through the process in which they have repeated inter-island migrations in search of marine resources. This explanation is, however, not sufficient to understand their geo-demographic dynamics. In some regions, their populations have increased in number through the process in which the Bajau have emerged as a 'maritime creole', or a hybrid group of sea people with various ethnic origins.

This understanding has come about through the course of fieldwork in several Bajau villages in eastern Indonesia, including in Pasir Putih (to the west of Flores Island, No. 47), Pulau Bungin (western Sumbawa, No. 45), Mola (the Wakatobi Archipelago, No. 39), Lemo Bajo (to the north of Kendari City, No. 36), Kalumbatang (the Banggai Archipelago, No. 34), Pulau Enam (the Togian Archipelago, No. 31), Torosiaje (to the west of Gorontalo City, No. 25), Pulau Nain (to the north of Manado City, No. 21), and Sapeken (No. I-04). (Each number in the parentheses coincides with a number on Map 14.2.) Here let us introduce the case of Sapeken, the Kangean Archipelago, East Java, where the creolisation process of the Bajau was most typically established.

The Kangean Archipelago is located east of Madura Island and on the eastern fringe of the Java Sea. Spots of extensive coral reefs surround the archipelago. The reefs are distinctively rich in marine resources such as trepangs, sea turtles and a variety of edible fish. The Kangean Archipelago is administratively included in the Sumenep Regency, Province of East Java, Indonesia. Centred in the Archipelago is Sapeken Island which belongs to Sapeken Village of Sapeken Sub-district (*Kecamatan*). The total population of Sapeken Village is 11,754, while that of Sumenep Regency is 985,884. As a satellite image of the island in Figure 14.1 shows, Sapeken Island is extremely densely populated given its area of less than one square kilometre.

From a geographical as well as a cultural point of view, Sapeken lies between Java, Bali, Kalimantan and Sulawesi. Although it administratively belongs to Java, its population predominantly consists of migrants from southern Sulawesi. As a migrants' islet, the population of Sapeken is composed of five main ethnic groups: the Mandar, Makassar, Bugis, Bajau and Madura. The first three groups clearly have their origins in southern Sulawesi; the Bajau are also considered to originate in southern Sulawesi. Among the ethnic groups, the Bajau are dominant and *baong Sama* (the Bajau language) is locally spoken as a lingua franca, even though Indonesian is used as the national language and Madura, a lingua franca at the Regency, is widely spoken outside Sapeken and the neighbouring islands. The residents here are mostly Muslim.

Sapeken Island is located at the interface of the seaborne flow of people, goods and information bridging the Java Sea, the Makassar Straits, and the Flores Sea (see Map 14.6). Owing to its location, Sapeken has continuously been thriving as an entrepôt of marine products since as late as the end of the nineteenth century. Van Gennep described Sapeken as follows:

> The trade from Kangean is very insignificant. However, on the island of Sapeken trade is very lively. Each year, five or six large prauw ships sail from there to Singapore, laden with rice, shells, tripang, turtles, *akar bahar*, etc.; from Singapore they bring cloths and trinkets, which in turn are traded on the Lesser

Figure 14.1 An aerial view of Sapeken Island taken by satellite image (Source: A quick bird satellite image owned by BIG (Badan Informasi Geospasial; http://www.bakosurtanal.go.id/). Courtesy of Prof. Aris Poniman and Dr. Suprajaka, BIG.

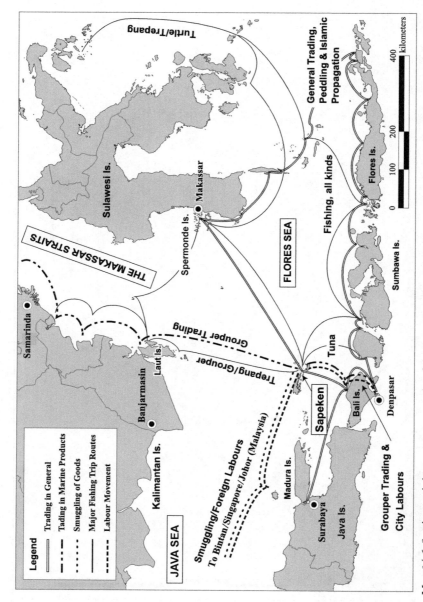

Map 14.6 Sapeken and the maritime networks of the Bajau [Source: The author created this map using digital base maps by BPS (2000), with reference to fieldwork].

Sunda Islands (Nusa Tenggara) and the Maluku. The fish caught in the seas surrounding the small islands are dried and for the most part exported to Bali, rice being brought from Bali in return (1896: 94).

The island was thriving in the business of exporting salted mackerel scads called *layang* (*Decapterus* spp.) to Bali and Java by the 1980s, and in the trade of sea turtle meat to Bali by the 1990s. Since the beginning of the 1990s, the Chinese fish buyers have brought about remarkable increases in catches of grouper all over the Indonesian archipelago. As groupers are abundant in coral seas, the Bajau in most areas rushed to the fishing grounds and benefited from catching or trading. Sapeken is one of the most flourishing islands in trading groupers. Initially the fishers in neighbouring islands were attracted to the business and began gathering at the island. Then the people from Madura and Java followed the fishers and began working as *beca* (rickshaw) drivers or petty vendors in Sapeken. Thus, more and more migrants kept flowing into the island.

ETHNIC SITUATION IN SAPEKEN: BECOMING THE BAJAU

Although the Bajau are dominant in Sapeken, this is a relatively new social phenomenon. In 1906 Sapeken Island had a population of about 6,800. Among the 6,800 individuals, the Mandar were reportedly predominant (Butcher 2004: 105). Table 14.1 summarises the population changes in the Kangean Archipelago and Sapeken, based on Dutch colonial records and the Indonesian census of 2000. It is clear that the Bajau population in Sapeken has rapidly increased in numbers and has become dominant during the period from 1930 to 2000.

The population increase may have occurred, as some Bajau informants claimed, partially due to the influx of Bajau migrants from southern Sulawesi and Nusa Tenggara. After undertaking fieldwork, however, it was found that the drastic increase of their population could more precisely be explained by another social process: the creolisation, or the conversion of the ethnic attributes of various sea people into Bajau. In Sapeken, the non-Bajau migrants from neighbouring islands such as the Mandar, Bugis or even Chinese, have, more often than not, switched their daily language as well as their ethnic identification to the Bajau. Simply speaking, the Bajau population in Sapeken swelled from 1930 through 2000 as the non-Bajau have 'become Bajau'.

During the fieldwork in Sapeken, some "Bajau" were selected as key interviewees because they said, 'if you would like to study the Bajau culture, just ask me. I can explain it (better than others)' (*Kalau kamu mau teliti budaya Bajo, baik tanya pada saya. Saya boleh jelaskan*). As for tracing their life histories, however, uneasiness was sometimes felt, because their genealogies were barely related to the Bajau as their ethnic background. Three cases of 'becoming Bajau', derived from the published data are outlined below (Nagatsu 2015: 130–2).

Table 14.1 Population change in Kangean and Sapeken (1896–2000)

Year	The Kangean Archipelago	Sapeken and Adjacent Islands — Sapeken Island
1896[1]	Total 6,353: Natives 3,997, Chinese 437, Foreign Orientals 1,893 and Others 26	Total 1,237: Only the Madura is referred to.
1917[2]	Total approximately 20,000: Mainly the Madura mixed with the Bugis, Makassar and Bali; Some Kambang (possibly the Bajau), Chinese and Arab.	Total approximately 8,000: The Bugis and Makassar
1930[3]	(Regency of Soemenep) Total 626,715: The Madura 619,084, people from South Sulawesi 5,914, Jawa 487 and Others 1,230	n.a.
2000[4]	[Sapeken & Arjasa Districts (*Kecamatan*)] Total 108264: The Madura 83,100 (76.8%) The Bajau 13,831 (12.8%) The Mandar 7,684 (7.1%) Tha Bugis 1,281 (1.2%) The Jawa 604 (0.6%) The Makassar 323 (0.3%) Others 1,441 (1.3%)	(Sapeken District) Total 37,077: The Bajau 13,825 (37.3%) The Madura 13,569 (36.6%) The Mandar 7,680 (20.7%) The Bugis 826 (2.2%) The Makassar 276 (0.7%) Others 901 (2.4%) (Sapeken Village (*Desa*)) Total 11,755: The Bajau 5,526 (47.0%) The Madura 4,296 (36.5%) The Mandar 1,227 (36.5%) Others 706 (6.1%)

Source: (1) Veth (ed.) (1896: 49, 250); (2) Encyclopædie van Nederlandsch-Indië (1918: 268, 1919: 750); (3) Department van Ekonomische Zaken, Nederlandch-Indie (1930: 151); (4) BPS (2002).

CASE 1. HAJI DILI

Dili was born in 1952 on Barrang Lompo, an island in the Spermonde Archipelago located off the coast of Makassar, the capital of South Sulawesi Province. His father and mother used to live in Makassar, where they ran a grocery store. His father was the son of a Fujianese Chinese man and a Makassar woman, while his mother was the daughter of a Fujianese Chinese man and a Mandar woman. They left Makassar and escaped to Barrang Lompo in 1950 or 1951, after their shop was attacked by insurgents who were supposedly associated with Kahar Muzakkar's armed rebellion against the Jakarta administration in the early 1950s. Dili's mother passed away soon after giving birth to him. In the mid-1950s, his father migrated to Sapeken with Dili since he had heard that the Barrang Lompo villagers, mainly of the Makassar ethnic group, had had *rezeki*, or good fortune and had succeeded in harvesting trepang and fishing for turtles. Dili's father moved to Sapeken and was helped by villagers who had also originally been migrants to Barrang Lompo. After graduating from elementary school in Sapeken, Dili worked with his father as a fisherman for more than a decade. Subsequently, Dili became a broker of marine products such as dried fish and trepang. In 1991, he started working as a middleman for selling grouper and succeeded in the business. By the mid-1990s, he had become the most well-known fish buyer in Sapeken and the neighboring islands. He built an ice factory and constructed a mosque as a donation to the community; he engaged enthusiastically in religious charity activities. Having gained prestige, he was elected a village head in 2001, a role that he fulfilled until he died in 2008.

Dili provided me with a room to sleep when I first visited Sapeken. He often said, 'ask me if you want to know about Bajau culture'. Because he was very busy, we in fact could never find the time. Dili established a business partnership with the Chinese in Bali and Surabaya, through whom he exported grouper to the foreign market. He understood that being of Chinese origin made it easier for him to gain the trust of Chinese merchants outside Sapeken, although he could not speak Chinese. In his daily life, Bajau was his first language; when I asked him what ethnicity he was, he answered that he was Bajau. He passed away in 2008. Now, his second son has taken over the business. The son grew up with Bajau as his first language. He regards himself as 'pure Bajau', (*asli orang Bajo*).

CASE 2. HAJI USTAZ MADINI

Madini was born in Sapeken in 1977. His grandparents on both sides had been born on Pambauan Island off the coast of Majene, the hometown of the Mandar and the capital of West Sulawesi Province. His grandparents migrated to Sapeken looking for rich marine resources. They relied on their relationship with an Islamic leader who had migrated to the island before them. Many residents of Sapeken have ancestors of Pambauan Island origin. His father was born in Sapeken, went to high school and became a teacher of mathematics; he is also an Islamic leader. Influenced by his father, Madini graduated from an Islamic high school in Sapeken and Islamic higher normal school in East Java. In 2001, he entered a master's course at the International Islamic University in Pakistan. He completed the course and graduated with an M.A. in Political Science and International Relations. During his graduate school years, he also made a pilgrimage to Mecca. Now he is a highly respected *ustaz*, or Islamic teacher, in Sapeken and Bali, where he now lives. He runs a souvenir shop in Bali.

Madini is very conscious of his Bajau identity. He is writing 'The History of Sapeken and the *Adat* (custom) of the *Sama* (Bajau)' and is editing the 'Dictionary of the *Sama* (Bajau)'. In speaking with me, he consistently highlighted the significance of 'the Bajau point of view', although he is apparently of Mandar descent: both of his parents are Mandar. Until he finished higher education, he studied many fields in the humanities and social sciences. Based on his knowledge of recent anthropological studies on ethnicity, he said that physical genealogy and ethnic identity are distinct. Furthermore, he emphasised, 'as I speak *baong Sama* (Bajau language) as my first language, I regard myself as *Sama* (the Bajau), and I am knowledgeable about *Sama* culture. Thus, there is no doubt that I am *Sama*, right?'

CASE 3. HAJI HIJAU

Hijau was born in Sapeken in 1974. He grew up on the island and graduated from an Islamic high school, the *Pesantren Persatuan Islam* (PERSIS). He is one of the most successful live grouper dealers in Sapeken. When I first met him, he introduced himself as '*orang Bajo Sulawesi*', meaning Bajau from Sulawesi. I learned later, however, that Hijau was born and grew up in Sapeken. I asked him why he was '*orang Bajo Sulawesi*'. He answered that it was because his father was a Bajau from Sulawesi. When I interviewed his father later, I found out that he in fact was from Sulawesi, but was ethnically Mandar. Hijau is genealogically linked to the Bajau only through his grandmother on his mother's side, who 'was said to be of Bajau descent'. His grandfather on his mother's side is Madura. Nevertheless, he thought it was clear that he was Bajau. His wife was born on Kangean Island to a Chinese father and a Madura mother. She now lives with Hijau; Bajau is the primary language they use to communicate. The couple claims that their two children are 'of course, pure Bajau', though the children are hybrid in their ethnic background.

In Sapeken, many villagers speak Bajau as their first language and identify themselves as Bajau, even though they are not descendants of Bajau, and their lineal tie with the Bajau may be quite slight. These patterns of discourse on genealogy are quite common among the islanders. Consequently, the Bajau here comprise migrants of varied ethnic origins.

ACCOMMODATIVE IDENTITY

Despite these patterns, the immigrant groups have never assimilated uniformly into the Bajau. Although they see themselves as Bajau, they retain mixed daily practices. For instance, these can be found materially in their boat types, fishing techniques, cultural values, religious texts, poetic literature, or the discourses by which they characterise themselves.

In the discourses of self-representation as the Bajau among the Sapeken islanders, for example, the concept of '*dalle*' or 'searching for fortune' (*cari rezeki* in Indonesian) is centered, although '*dalle*' is originally a Makassar term and a key cultural value among them. Furthermore, when they are talking about the characteristics of the Bajau, some informants in Sapeken explained to me that 'we the Bajau do not like to work as an employee, we like to be an independent entrepreneur (*pengusaha mandiri*)'. It is also widely known that the Bugis and Makassar are traditionally fond of this sort of self-representation in their hometown, southern Sulawesi.

These findings are summarised in relation to the identity formation among the Bajau:

(1) The Bajau in Sapeken and some other settlements as mentioned previously constitute '*an emerging society*' as Warren (1981) suggested in relation to the making of the Balangingi Samal (a sub-group of the SLU Bajau) in the Sulu Archipelago from the mid-nineteenth century. The emerging society in the present study can be defined as 'a maritime creole' which comprises a variety of sea people and their descendants. They share a sense of Bajau-ness based on *baong Sama* or Bajau as their lingua franca, but simultaneously have maintained mixed practices in their economic, social as well as cultural lives.

(2) Their way of (re)constructing identity is more 'accommodative' rather than 'assimilative.' In other words, the Bajau in the studied sites share 'an accommodative ethnic identity' and Bajau may better be understood as its label.

Ethnic assimilation has never been rare in the maritime zones in Southeast Asia. In the 1950s–60s, the Samal in the Sulu Archipelago often tended to speak Tausug and sought to identify themselves as Tausug, while the Bajau at Spermonde Archipelago off the coast of Makassar City have supposedly 'become' Makassar since the 1930s (Stone 1962; Nagatsu 2009). Such ethnic conversion, however, usually occurred in the process in which the marginalised were assimilated and absorbed into the majority. What is unique with the cases in Sapeken and some other Bajau settlements is that the majority groups in the neighbouring regions have converted their language and ethnic label to those of the minority: the Bajau.

CONCLUDING REMARKS

The Bajau in the research sites in Indonesia have a maritime ethnic identity which comprises a variety of neighboring sea people and their descendants. Such creolisation has been confirmed widely as well as historically in eastern Indonesia. In 1682, Padbrugge, Governor of VOC (Dutch East India Company) in Ternate, observed that the Bajau were a mixture of Chinese, Java, Makassar, Bali, or Malay (Lapian 2009). This is one of the earliest records about the Bajau. Later in 1908, a colonial inspector of Netherlands East Indies in Banggai region observed:

> The current *Poenggawa* (leader, noted by the author) of the Badjo (Bajau) of Banggaai is ... a man from Mandar; this does not have to be a big surprise, because among the Badjo there appear many outsiders' influences, such as people

from Makassar and Bugis people, etc.; as these people have the same occupation, and are more often than not married to the Badjo girls, they count themselves to the Badjo; they are equally counted to the Badjo by the Banggaai population, and even by the *posthouder*; this being the reason that they, just like the Badjo, also do not pay taxes to the Government (Goedhart 1908: 474).

In 1981, Verheijen in his linguistic study refers to the mixed nature of the Bajau. During his fieldwork, he found that his 'Bajau' informant was Sasak and his wife was of Mandar origin. However, the informant spoke Bajau as his daily tongue. According to him, the Bajau in Bungin and Kaong were partial descendants of the Javanese, Lombok, Makassar, Mandar, Buton, Bugis and Flores. In addition, he also notes that many Bajau in Labuan Bajo were said to come from Manggarai, Maumere, Ende, Solor, Bugis, Bima, Binongko, Selayar and Bonerate (Verheijen 1986: 23).

In this chapter, the pattern of distribution and flow of the Bajau population has been observed. Since as late as the sixteenth century, when they first appeared in the written records, the Bajau have expanded their settlements in search of marine products, initially from southern Sulawesi to the east and south, then from eastern Sulawesi to Nusa Tenggara. Since the eighteenth century they even ventured to voyage to the northern coast of Australia to collect trepang.

It should be noted that the syncretic ethnogenesis of the Bajau and the other sea-oriented people might have been embedded in most of these diasporic processes. The Bajau population has become so widely distributed in eastern Indonesia not merely because they have moved around the seas, but also because they have kept forming maritime creoles in their destinations by accommodating migrants as well as natives of various origins. In this sense it can be understood that Bajau is a more general label shared by sea people in a wider sense in insular Southeast Asia.

NOTES

[1] This chapter is a revised and simplified version of the author's paper, originally published in Osaka Ethnographic Museum's Journal *Senri Ethnological Studies* (Nagatsu 2017).

[2] See Nagatsu (2015) for a detailed definition of 'Southeast Asian maritime world' and 'sea people'. Narifumi-Maeda Tachimoto, a scholar of global area studies, identified three prototypical natures of the sea people in the Southeast Asian maritime world: (1) diasporic settlement, (2) the commoditisation of natural resources, and (3) network-centered social relations. He argued that sea people have played a critical role as the main actors in the formation of the Southeast Asian maritime world (1995: 199).

[3] This research was made possible by the following JSPS Grants-in-Aid for Scientific Research (the names and institutions of the research team leaders are indicated in parentheses): 07041057 (Tanaka Koji, Kyoto University); 14251006 (Tsuyoshi Kato, Kyoto University); 18710210, 21510271, 24651278, and 25300017 (Kazufumi Nagatsu, Toyo University); 19251010 (Haruya Kagami, Kanazawa University); 22310157 and 25283008 (Jun Akamine, Nagoya City University); and 23251004 (Isamu Yamada, Kyoto University). In addition,

library research was supported by a research grant from the Center for Southeast Asian Studies for the International Program of Collaborative Research (Kazufumi Nagatsu, for FY 2009–10 and FY 2016) and research grants from the Inoue Enryo Memorial Foundation for Promoting Sciences, Toyo University (Seiichi Matsumoto, Toyo University for FY 2010–13 and Kazufumi Nagatsu for FY 2014–16). I would like to extend my sincere gratitude to all of the above-mentioned institutions and researchers.

[4] See for instance the local journal titled '*Bajo Bangkit*' which literally means 'The Bajau, Awakening'. The journal is published by some young Bajau leaders in Kendari, Southeast Sulawesi with the financial support of WWF Indonesia. Another example can be found of ethnic representation through the Regatta Lepa, an annual event focusing on the Bajau's traditional boat called '*lepa*' in Semporna, Sabah, Malaysia. The event has been organised as an official event of Sabah State since 1994 (Sabah Tourism Board Official Website 2016).

[5] Note that the 'Bajau' population in the Sumatra region which appeared in the 2000 census of Indonesia is not included in this number, because according to field findings, the 'Bajau' there may have wrongly claimed themselves as 'Bajau', whether intentionally or not. Reliable information could not be found about the Bajau during the author's survey in the Riau Archipelago in 2014.

[6] Pallesen (1985: 113) analysed that the Abaknon Bajau language separated early from the Proto Sama Bajau language in the Philippine islands before a period when active Malay influence spread there.

REFERENCES

Butcher, John G. 2004. *The Closing of the Frontier: A History of the Marine Fisheries of Southeast Asia, c. 1850–2000*. Singapore: Institute of Southeast Asian Studies.

Goedhart, O.H. 1908. 'Drie Landschappen in Celebes (Banggaai, Boengkoe en Mori)' [Three Landscapes in Celebes (Banggaai, Boengkoe and Mori)]. *Tijdschrift voor Indische Taal-, Land- en Volkenkunde* 50: 442–548.

Grimes, Barbara F., ed. 2000. *Ethnologue: Languages of the World*. 14th ed. Dallas: Summer Institute of Linguistics.

Encyclopædie van Nederlandsch-Indië [*Encyclopædia of the Dutch Indies*]. 2nd ed. 1918, vol. 2. 's-Gravenhage: Martinus Nijhoff.

———. 2nd ed. 1919, vol. 3. 's-Gravenhage: Martinus Nijhoff.

Fox, James J. 1977. 'Notes on Southern Voyage and Settlements of the Sama-Bajau.' *Bijdragen tot de Taal-, Land- en Volkenkunde* 133: 459–65.

Hart, C. van der. 1853. *Reize Rondom het Eiland Celebes en naar Eenge der Moluksche Eilanden* [Journeys Around the Island of Celebes and to some of the Moluccan Islands]. 's-Gravenhage, Hague: K. Fuhri.

Lapian, Adrian B. 2009. *Orang Laut, Bajak Laut, Raja Laut: Sejarah Kawasan Laut Sulawesi Abad XIX*. Depok: Komunitas Bambu.

Macknight, Campbell C. 1976. *The Voyage to Marege*. Carlton: Melbourne University Press.

Nagatsu, Kazufumi. 2009. 'Language and Space in Border Zone: Dynamics of Language Use in Malaysia and Indonesia.' In *Indonesia as a Multi-linguistic Society: Changing National Language, Local Languages and Foreign Languages*, ed. M. Moriyama and A. Shiohara, 183–212. Tokyo: Mekon. (In Japanese)

———. 2012. 'A Genealogy of Creolism: An Ethnogenesis of the Bajo and its Context in the Seas surrounding Sulawesi.' In *Indonesia as a Multi-Ethnic Country*, ed. H. Kagami, 249–84. Tokyo: Mokuseisha. (In Japanese)

———. 2015. 'Social Space of the Sea Peoples: A Study on the Arts of Syncretism and Symbiosis in the Southeast Asian Maritime World.' *The Journal of Sophia Asian Studies* 33: 111–40.

———. 2017. 'Maritime Diaspora and Creolization: Genealogy of the Sama-Bajau in Insular Southeast Asia.' *Senri Ethnological Studies* 95: 35–64.

Nimmo, Arlo, H. 1968. 'Reflections on Bajau History.' *Philippine Studies* 16 (1): 32–59.

Nolde, Lance. 2009. 'Great is Our Relationship with the Sea: Charting the Maritime Realm of the Sama of Southeast Sulawesi, Indonesia.' *Explorations: A Graduate Student Journal of Southeast Asian Studies* 9: 15–33.

Pallesen, Anders K. 1985. *Culture Contact and Language Convergence.* Manila: Linguistic Society of the Philippines.

Sather, Clifford. 1997. *The Bajau Laut: Adaptation, History, and Fate in a Maritime Fishing Society of South-eastern Sabah.* Kuala Lumpur: Oxford University Press.

Smith, Kenneth D. 1984. 'The Languages of Sabah: A Tentative Lexicostatistical Classification.' In *Languages of Sabah: A Survey Report*, ed. J.K. King and J.W. King, 1–49. Canberra: The Australian National University.

Sopher, David Edward. 1977 (1965). *The Sea Nomads: A Study of the Maritime Boat People of Southeast Asia.* Singapore: National Museum of Singapore. (Reprinted in 1977 with postscript).

Stacey, Natasha. 2007. *Boats to Burn: Bajo Fishing Activity in the Australian Fishing Zone.* Canberra: ANU E-Press.

Stone, Richard L. 1962. 'Intergroup Relations among the Taosug, Samal and Badjaw of Sulu.' *Philippine Sociological Review* 10: 107–33.

Tachimoto, Narifumi-Maeda. 1996. *Issues and Methodologies of Area Studies: An Approach from Socio-cultural Eco Dynamics.* Kyoto: Kyoto University Press. (In Japanese)

Taylor, Carl N. 1931. 'The Sea Gypsies of Sulu.' *Asia* 31: 476–83, 534–5.

Gennep, J.L. van. 1896. 'Bijdrage tot de Kennis van den Kangéan-archipel' [Contribution to the Knowledge of the Kangéan Archipelago]. *Bijdragen tot de Taal-, Land- en Volkenkunde van Nederlandsch-Indië* 46: 88–108.

Verheijen, Jilis A.J. 1986. *The Sama/Bajau Language in the Lesser Sunda Islands.* Canberra: Department of Linguistics, Research School of Pacific Studies, The Australian National Library.

Verschuer, F.H. van. 1883. 'De Badjo's' [The Bajau]. *Tijdschrift van het Koninklijke Aardrijkskunding Genootschap.* 7: 1–7.

Veth, P. J. 1896. *Aardrijkskundig en Statistisch Woordenboek van Nederlandsch Indie, Bewerkt naar de Jongste en Beste Berigten* [Geography and Statistical Dictionary of the Netherlands Indies, edited with the Newest and Best Information]. Amsterdam: P.N. van Kampen, 2de deel.

Vosmaer, Jan N. 1839. 'Korte Beschrijving van het Zuid-Oostelijk Schiereiland van Celebes, in het Bijzonder van de Vosmaers-Baai of van Kendari; Verrijkt met Eenige Berigten omtrent den Stam der Orang Badjos, en Meer Andere Aanteekeningen' [Brief Description of the

South-Eastern Peninsula of Celebes, Particularly of Vosmaers-Bay or Kendari; Enriched with a Guide to the Orang Bajau people, and Other Information]. *Verhandelingen van het Bataviaasch Genootschap van Kunsten en Wetenschappen* 17(1): 63–184.

Warren, James F. 1971. *The North Borneo Chartered Company's Administration of the Bajau, 1878–1909: The Pacification of Maritime, Nomadic People.* (Papers in International Studies, Southeast Asia Series No. 22). Athens: Center for International Studies, Southeast Asian Program, Ohio University.

———. 1981. *The Sulu Zone 1768–1898: The Dynamics of External Trade, Slavery, and Ethnicity in the Transformation of a Southeast Asian Maritime State.* Singapore: NUS Press.

Website

Sabah Tourism Board Official Website. 2016. '23rd Regatta Lepa Semporna' [accessed 1 September 2016]. <http://sabahtourism.com/events/23rd-regatta-lepa-semporna>.

Census

The Philippines

National Statistics Office, Republic of the Philippines. 2002. *Census 2000, Population and Housing Characteristics* (CD-ROM). Manila: National Statistics Office, Republic of the Philippines (as of each province).

Malaysia

Department of Statistics, Malaysia. 2001. *Population and Housing Census of Malaysia, 2000: Population Distribution by Local Authority Area and Mukims.* Kuala Lumpur: Department of Statistics, Malaysia.

Indonesia/Netherlands East Indies

BPS: Badan Pusat Statistik. 2002. *Raw Data of Digitized Census 2000.* Badan Pusat Statistik (Central Bureau of Statistics), Republik Indonesia (Jl. Dr. Sutomo 6-8, Jakarta) in 2005.

Department van Ekonomische Zaken, Nederlandsch-Indië. 1934. *Volkstelling 1930, vol. 3 Inheemsche Bevolking van Oost-Java.* Batavia: Landsdrukkerij.

———. 1936. *Volkstelling 1930, vol. 5 Inheemsche Bevolking van Borneo, Celebes, de Kleine Soenda Eilanden en de Molukken.* Batavia: Landsdrukkerij.

Map

BPS: Badan Pusat Statistik. 2000. No Title (File Name: Peta 2000, Sensus Penduduk 2000, shape files). Jakarta: BPS: Badan Pusat Statistik. Provided by BPS to the author in 2005.

GADM: Database of Global Administrative Areas. 2009. 'GADM database of Global Administrative Areas, version 1.0.' [Online] [accessed 10 March 2009]. <http://gadm.org/>.

List of Contributors

Bérénice Bellina, archaeologist of South and Southeast Asia, is senior researcher at the National Centre for Scientific Research. Her research focuses on exchange and cultural transfer processes on the Maritime Silk Road and more especially between South and Southeast Asia. In 2005, she created the French-Thai Archaeological Mission in Upper Thai-Malay Peninsula with Silpakorn University (Bangkok). And since 2017, she directs the Myanmar-French Archaeological Mission in Peninsular Thailand-Myanmar with the Department of Archaeology (Ministry of Religious Affairs and Culture of Myanmar). She also has developed an interest in heritage, with a special focus on present-day representations and uses of the past, and in particular of Maritime Silk Road remains in Southeast Asia. This interest has resulted in local communities participating in patrimonialisation projects. Her research combines archaeology, archaeological science, connected history, museology, social anthropology and technology studies.

Roger Blench is a linguist, anthropologist, archaeologist and ethnomusicologist, and is a visiting fellow at the McDonald Institute of Archaeological Research. He has research programmes in West Africa, Northeast India, the Pacific and the Amazon Basin, and has long had a particular interest in the prehistory of seafaring, especially in the Indian Ocean.

Nicolas Brucato (PhD 2010, University of Toulouse, France) is a junior researcher at the National Center for Scientific Research (CNRS) in the Department of Evolution and Biological Diversity at the University of Toulouse, France. He is an expert in human genomics and functional biology. For ten years, he worked on several aspects of human evolution and human demographic history especially in populations from Africa and Island Southeast Asia.

David Bulbeck is a specialist in the archaeology and palaeoanthropology of Peninsular Malaysia and Sulawesi. His MA from the Australian National University (ANU) involved the description and analysis of human burial remains from Gua Cha (Peninsular Malaysia) and Leang Buidane (Talaud Islands, North Sulawesi province). His PhD, also from the ANU, included a survey of thirteenth to seventeenth century CE sites associated with the rise of Makassar as a trading emporium in South Sulawesi province during the sixteenth and seventeenth centuries. Bulbeck's two postdoctoral research projects have respectively focused on the pre-Islamic development of the Bugis kingdoms of South Sulawesi, including the early iron-producing kingdom of Luwuq, and the comparative analysis of human skeletal remains from South Asia and Southeast Asia. Since 2009 he has been a research associate and visiting fellow/visiting senior lecturer at the ANU's Department of Archaeology and Natural History in its School of Culture, History and Languages. He has devoted most of his activities to a project, headed by Sue O'Connor in the same department, on the Holocene prehistory of the lowlands near Lake Towuti in south-eastern Sulawesi.

Cynthia Chou is C. Maxwell and Elizabeth M. Stanley Family Chair of Asian Studies, professor of anthropology, and director of the Center for Asian and Pacific Studies, University of Iowa. Her book publications relevant to the present volume include *Indonesian Sea Nomads: Money, Magic and Fear of the Orang Suku Laut* (2003) and *The Orang Suku Laut of Riau, Indonesia: The Inalienable Gift of Territory* (2010).

Murray Cox is a professor of Computational Biology and deputy head of the School of Fundamental Sciences at Massey University, New Zealand. He has worked extensively with Pacific communities, particularly in Indonesia. With over 125 publications spanning population genetic theory, statistical genetics and computational genomics, he has played a key role in characterizing the genetic diversity of Southeast Asia and the Pacific for over 20 years.

Brunna Crespi is a research associate at UMR 208 Paloc (IRD/MNHN). She obtained a PhD in Cultural Geography at the National Museum of Natural History (France) in 2018. She has a Bachelor's degree in Biology and Ethnoecology from the University of São Paulo, Brazil, and a multi-field Master's Degree in Cultural Geography and Anthropology, specialising in 'Environment, Landscape and Societies' at the National Museum of Natural History and the University Paris 7 – Denis Diderot, Paris. She has worked with Amazon rainforest local communities and her current research focuses on Melanesian communities. She is interested in sacred landscapes, cultural resilience, identity in pluricultural areas and territorial representations.

Laure Dussubieux is a research scientist at the Field Museum where she manages the Elemental Analysis Facility and conducts research on ancient glass and other archaeological materials including ceramic or metals. Her main research focus deals with the reconstruction of trade patterns around the Indian Ocean through the elemental analysis of ancient glass beads.

Richard Engelhardt (BA, Yale; MA, PhD, Harvard) is an archaeologist, anthropologist and heritage expert. Engelhardt joined the United Nations and from this platform has spearheaded cultural heritage conservation efforts throughout Asia for the past four decades. From 1994–2008, Engelhardt was UNESCO Regional Advisor for Culture in Asia and the Pacific, and from 2008–10, UNESCO Senior Advisor for Culture. From 2010–15 he was Visiting Research Professor of Conservation in the Faculty of Architecture of Hong

Kong University. Currently Engelhardt is Honorary Chair Professor in the School of Architecture and Urban Planning at Southeast University (Nanjing); in the World Heritage International Research Institute of Southwest Jiaotong University (Chengdu); and at the UNESCO World Heritage Research and Training Institute for Asia and the Pacific at Tongji University in Shanghai.

Aude Favereau is an assistant professor at the Institute of Archaeology, National Cheng Kung University, in Taiwan. She is also a member of the French-Thai Archaeological Mission/French Archaeological Mission in Peninsular Thailand and Myanmar since 2011. Her research focuses on Southeast Asian Metal Age pottery, late prehistoric exchange networks and interactions between Mainland and Island Southeast Asia.

Jean-Christophe Galipaud is an archaeologist specialising in Southeast Asia and Pacific archaeology at the Institute for Research and Development (IRD). He is a member of the Joint Research Unit PALOC (Local Heritages) at the National Museum of Natural History in Paris (France). He has conducted research in many Pacific islands on the modalities of initial or early settlement, particularly during the Lapita period. Since 2009, he has extended his research in insular Southeast Asia on Austronesian societies that could help to understand the origin of the settlement of the Pacific Islands, marine nomadic societies in particular. He also has participated in the research on the wreckage of the Lapérouse expedition in Vanikoro in 1788.

Philippe Grangé, formerly an associate professor at La Rochelle University (France), works at the Institut Français d'Indonésie (French cultural institute) in Jakarta. Besides modern Indonesian language (syntax, semantics), he studies Lamaholot (Eastern Flores, Indonesia) and Indonesian Bajo (Sama Bajau).

Dominique Guillaud is a geographer, director of research at the Institute for Research and Development (IRD). After taking an interest in the construction of territories in the long term in Oceania and Southeast Asia, she has now shifted her work to the study of local heritages and its valorisation by public policies in East Timor and Indonesia.

Charles Illouz, professor at La Rochelle University (Laboratory CRHIA EA 1163), is an anthropologist of Austronesian societies (Oceania and Indonesia). His fields of research focus on social organisation, mythology and history in anthropology.

Jacques Ivanoff, ethnologist at the CNRS, works on borders, ideological constructions of modern societies and Moken marine nomads in the Mergui Archipelago (Myanmar and Thailand). For more than 30 years he has been working with them, collecting artefacts and oral texts, contributing to the understanding of the local history. He is currently helping to set up a museum (MAM) supported by the Solidarity Fund for French Innovative Projects administered by the French Ministry of Foreign Affairs.

Rebecca Kinaston (PhD) is a research fellow in the Department of Anatomy at the University of Otago and the Director of a bioarchaeology consultancy company, BioArch South. She investigates past human health, diet and migration patterns in the Asia-Pacific region.

Pradiptajati Kusuma is a post-doctoral research fellow at the Eijkman Institute for Molecular Biology, Jakarta, Indonesia, and the Complexity Institute, Nanyang Technological University, Singapore. He received his PhD in Population Genetics/Bioanthropology from the University of Toulouse, France. His current research focuses specifically on the settlement history and genetic adaptation of the indigenous Borneo ethnic groups, especially the hunter-gatherers.

Michelle C. Langley is an Australian Research Council (ARC) Discovery Early Career Researcher Award (DECRA) Research Fellow in the Australian Research Centre for Human Evolution at the Environmental Futures Research Institute of Griffith University, Brisbane, Australia. Her work revolves around investigations of human cognitive evolution, identification of children in the archaeological record, and ancient Australia.

Thierry Letellier is a senior researcher at the French National Institute of Health and Medical Research (INSERM). He is the director of the research unit "EvolSan" (Evolution and Dental Health) at the University of Toulouse, France. With over 100 publications, his research investigates the physiopathology of various diseases from the biochemical to the evolutionary processes. In the last ten years, he develops an evolutionary medicine approach based on the diversity of human populations, using genetic and biological markers. He is also the author of articles on the settlement of Madagascar based on genomic studies.

Mahirta is the head of the Master's study programme in Archaeology, Fakultas Ilmu Budaya at the Universitas Gadjah Mada, Yogyakarta, Indonesia. She specialises in Indonesian prehistoric archaeology with a particular interest in the analysis of stone tools and botanical residues recovered from archaeological excavations.

Nagatsu Kazufumi is professor of Cultural Anthropology and Southeast Asian Studies at the Faculty of Sociology, Toyo University. His recent publications include books on the Sama Dilaut in Sabah (Malaysia) and a book jointly edited with Ono Rintaro on an ethnography of mobile sea people viewed as a cultural history in the western Pacific (in Japanese).

Lance Nolde is assistant professor of history at California State University, Channel Islands. He completed his doctorate in Southeast Asian history at the University of Hawai'i at Mānoa and was a postdoctoral research fellow at the International Institute for Asian Studies in Leiden, The Netherlands in 2014–15. His current book project explores the history of the semi-nomadic Sama Bajau and their important position within the social, political and economic networks that spanned maritime Southeast Asia between the fourteenth and nineteenth centuries.

Chandra Nuraini is associate professor at La Rochelle University (France) who teaches Indonesian language and culture. Her research work in ethno-linguistics focuses on Sama Bajau oral tradition, especially the *iko-iko* epics, which are on the brink of extinction. She has recorded, analysed and translated several of these epic songs in several Bajo (Indonesian Sama Bajau) communities.

Sue O'Connor is a distinguished professor in the Department of Archaeology and Natural History in the School of Culture, History and Language, College of Asia and the Pacific at the Australian National University. She is a member of the Australian Academy of the Humanities. Over the past 40 years, she has undertaken ground-breaking research into the unique maritime adaptations that characterise human dispersal and adaptations in the Asia-Pacific region.

Elena Piotto is a PhD candidate in the Department of Archaeology and Natural History in the School of Culture, History and Language, College of Asia and the Pacific at the Australian National University.

Christian Reepmeyer is a senior lecturer in Archaeology at James Cook University, Cairns. His research focus is the study of prehistoric movement, mobility and exchange from the empirical analysis of igneous rocks with geochemical techniques. This can provide tangible evidence for long-distance connections often over thousands of kilometres of marine terrain. After completing his Master's Degree at the University of Cologne, Germany, he moved to Australia to obtain a PhD at the Australian National University, which was followed by Postdoctoral Fellowships working on the foundations of maritime exchange and interaction in Island Southeast Asia, and the emergence of highly stratified societies in the Pacific.

François-Xavier Ricaut (PhD 2003, School for Advanced Studies in Social Sciences, Paris, France) is a senior researcher at the National Center for Scientific Research (CNRS) in the Department of Evolution and Biological Diversity at the University of Toulouse, France. As a biological anthropologist, his research investigates the ecological, cultural and evolutionary processes that structure the biological diversity of human populations, using archaeological remains and biological markers. He is the author of numerous articles, especially on the population history of the Indo-Pacific region (Madagascar, Indonesia and Papua New Guinea).

Ayesha Pamela Rogers (BA, University of British Columbia; MA, University of Birmingham; PhD, University College London) is an archaeologist and heritage manager with more than 40 years of experience in Asia. Rogers is founding director of two heritage consultancy companies based in Hong Kong and Pakistan. She is visiting professor, Cultural Studies, National College of Arts, Lahore, Pakistan and Expert Advisor in Heritage Impact Assessment, Centre for Global Heritage and Development, Universities of Leiden-Delft-Erasmus, Netherlands. She is co-director with Richard Engelhardt of the long-term Phuket Project on Maritime Adaptation in Coastal Southeast Asia.

Herawati Sudoyo is the deputy for the Fundamental Research of Eijkman Institute. She is also the head of the Forensic DNA Laboratory and principal investigator at the Genome Diversity and Diseases Laboratory. She specialises on mitochondria DNA as a powerful genetic markers for population studies.

Index

aboriginal people, in northern Australia, 313, 317, 344
accommodative ethnic identity, 21, 185, 353
adaptability, concept of, 267
adaptive
    archaeological evidence of, 274–8
    capacity, concept of, 9, 262–9
    concept of, 269–74
    conservation phase of, 271
    exploitation phase of, 271
    removal response, 276
    reorganization phase of, 271
adat (customary law), 223, 351
agriculture
    origins, 54
    production, 217
Agusan River (Mindanao), 5
air pasang belum, 151
Alas Straits, 333
Ala'uddin, Sultan, 219
Alor Islands, 17, 37–41, 333
    shell fish hooks and beads from, 37–40
    Tron Bon Lei (TBL) Pit B, 37, 45, 76
Anak Dalam (Sumatra), 1
anatomically modern humans (AMH)
    bone-tool technology and early osseous artefacts, 53, 66–8
    cultural adaptation of, 53
    exploited resources, 53–4
    in Island Southeast Asia (ISEA), 51
    maritime interconnections, 51
    mortuary practices, 74–6
    Pleistocene rock art, 64–6
    Southeast Asian sites with, 52
    traditions of, 53
Ancestors' Mountains, creation of, 238
ancient adaptation, to islands in ISEA and Oceania, 284–5

Andaman Sea, 158, 244
    languages, 162–5
    maritime-adapted populations of, 254
    'sea gypsies' of the Phuket Island Group of, 255
antiquity of sea nomads, 283
aquaculture, 302
aquatic resources, 6
archaeological invisibility, 2
Aru Islands, 21, 66, 68, 311
Ashmore Reef, 344
Asian uniparental haplogroups, 189
astro-navigation charts 209
Atoni people, 289
Austronesian
    boats, construction of, 200
    Comparative Dictionary (ACD), 163
    cosmopolitanism, 296
    diaspora, 28
    economic activity of, 248
    expansion, 7, 12, 21, 250, 285
    forager-traders, 7
    sea nomads, 8, 240
Austronesian (AN) languages, 158
    Central Malayo Polynesian subgroup (CMP), 287
    dominance of, 282
    Sama-Bajau in, 303
    of Sumbawa, 287
    in Timor-Leste, 287
    Wallacea AN languages, 288

Bajau community, 4, *see also* Bajau diaspora; Sama Bajau community
    of Coral Triangle, 302, 304
    diaspora, 20
    of eastern Indonesia, 4, 11, 15–16
    of Kangean Islands, 302

marginalisation of, 309
migration to the Sulu Archipelago, 20
Papuq Sama Bajau polity, 19
patron-client system for, 309
role in
   rise of Gowa-Talloq, 19
   South Sulawesi, 19
sea nomad community, *see* Bajau Sea nomads, in Indonesia
size and location of, 21
of Tawi-Tawi, 301
Bajau diaspora, 193
   accommodative identity, 352–3
   Coral Triangle, 302, 304
   dispersion models, 312–15
   distribution of, 332
   geo-demographic features in
      Eastern Sulawesi, 332–44
      Nusa Tenggara, 332–44
   geography and demography of, 304–7
   historical persistence of maritime zone, 345
   identity formation, 353
   of Kangean Archipelago, 307, 345–9
   linguistic approach, 303–4
   marginalisation of, 309
   nomadic lifestyle and their access to markets, 311–12
   originality of, 302
   overview of locations of, 306
   and patron-client relationship, 309–11
   residential confinement of, 307–9
   Sama Bajau dialects, 303
   in Sapeken Island, 345–9
   seafaring groups, spread of, 284
   sedentary lifestyle of, 307–11
   settlement clusters, 332–3
   social relations of, 333
   in Southeast Asia, 301
   'southeast of Borneo, Barito estuary' hypothesis, 314–15
   'Sulu Archipelago' hypothesis, 313–14
   zone of marine resource exploitation, 345

Bajau haplogroups, frequency of, 184
Bajau sea nomads, in Indonesia, 18, 177–82
   activities of, 178
   economy based on exploiting marine resources, 178
   ethno-linguistic studies on, 191
   geographic distribution of, 178, 179
   hypotheses on origin of
      Blust's hypothesis, 181
      Johore princess hypothesis, 181
      Pigafetta hypothesis, 181
      southeast Borneo/Barito origin, 181
      Sulu Archipelago hypothesis, 181
      western hypothesis, 181
   maritime frontier of, 178
   material and methods for studying origin of, 182–4
      DNA extraction, sequencing and genotyping, 183
      population samples, 182–3
      statistical analysis, 183–4
   origin of
      geographic, 178
      hypotheses on, 181
      material and methods for studying, 182–4
      results of study on, 185–94
      TreeMix analysis on, 191
   results of study on origin of, 185–94
      Kendari Bajau as genetically distinct population, 185–9
      multiple genetic ancestries, 189–94
   Sama Bajau of Sulu (Philippines), 180
   seafaring technologies, 177
   use of Bajau language as a lingua franca, 180
Bajau villages, 332–3
Balangingi Samal (Bajau sub-group), 327, 353
Bali, 285
Bandung Plateau (West Java), 81–2
Banggai Islands, 331
Banjarmasin, 12, 167, 217, 227, 314
   houseboats in, 14

Ban Khao culture, 105–6
Ban Na Hyan, 113, 120, 122–3, 125
    glass material from, 124
Bantaeng confederation, 218
baong Sama (the Bajau language), 346, 352–3
Barito/Malay ships, 158
Barito River, 20, 315
Basay people, 131
Baun Same (Bajau language), 313
Baxiandong cave (Taiwan), 61, 81
Bay of Bengal, 3, 104, 115, 117, 133, 262
Ba Yue, 14, 169
beads and pendants
    from Alor Island, 37–40
    disc beads, 31
    flat shell beads, 35
    of *Nassarius* spp., 29, 33
    of *Nautilus pompilius*, 31, 33
    of *Oliva* spp., 29, 31, 33–5
    from Timor-Leste, 29–35
    types of, 29–32
Belakang Padang, 150
Benjamin's hypotheses, 128
Bima, kingdom of
    defeat of the Papuq, 221
    Islamisation of, 219
Bismarck Archipelago, 84, 87, 285
blast fishing, 310
boat
    boat-people, 327
        along the coast of China, 167–9
        of Nusantao, 86
    boat-shaped houses, 201
    construction of, 6, 199
        knowledge of, 294
        in the South China Sea, 199
        techniques for, 6, 11, 16
    high-keel boats, of the Yami on Lanyu Island, 201
    nomadism, 4
    symbolism, 201–2
    technology, 285
Bone, kingdom of, 215, 331
bone-tool technology, 53

across Southeast Asia, 66
bone artefacts, 66–8
Holocene appearance of, 67–8
maritime cultural influence related to, 67
morphology of, 68
from North Vietnam, 68
proliferation of, 66
Southeast Asian sites with, 67, 68
Borneo, 12, 14, 18, 20, 67–8, 84, 145, 158–60, 167, 169, 193, 214, 216–17, 220, 305, 313, 361
    Bajau of, 328
    Banjar population of, 190
    connection by land to MSEA, 64
    Dayak Ngaju of, 191, 202, 288
    Holocene cultural transmission from, 75
    languages, 12, 159
    Ma'anyan population of, 189, 191
    Makassarese and Sama Bajau fleets, 225
    Malaysian territory of, 301
    Niah Caves in, 64
    river nomads of, 170
    'southeast of Borneo, Barito estuary' hypothesis, 314–15
    spice trade, 181
broker-lender relationship, 309
bronze axes, 107
bronze industry, 118
    Indian technologies to produce high-tin bronze ingots, 118
Bugis (Austronesian-speaking group), 19, 178, 180–1, 189, 217, 220, 227, 301–2, 305, 311, 346, 354
    Dutch-Bugis alliance, 215
    kingdom of Bone, 215
    polity of Luwuq, 218
    trading activities of, 344
Bugis Bone, 219–20
Bui Ceri Uato Mane (BCUM), 35
Bui Ceri Uato (BCU) rockshelter, Timor-Leste, 29
Bukit Tengkorak (Sabah), 8, 77, 84, 87, 285

Bunaq land
   Bunaq-Tetun operating model, 293–4
   emergence of trade networks, 294–5
   model of interactions and cultural
      evolution, 295–6
   people of, 20, 130, 288–9
      Austronesian-Papuan descent of,
         289
      of Covalima district, 289, 290
      homeland of, 289
      as invisible masters of the land,
         289
      place of origin, 289
      recent arrivals in, 289–93
Burmese fishermen, 237, 244–5
Burmese slavery, 244

capital accumulation, 270
cartography, development of, 6
Catastrophe Theory, 261, 271, 276
cave paintings, 84, 250
   on ship construction techniques, 204
cave sites
   estuarine, coastal and offshore, 125–7
   at Khao Krim, 125
   at Khao Muni, 125
   paintings, 84
cemeteries, 11, 75, 202, 239, 244, 246,
   274
Central-Eastern Malayo Polynesian group
   (CEMP), 287
centralised trading powers, rise of, 103
Central Malayo-Polynesian migrations,
   293
Central Vietnam, Iron Age trading
   polities in, 110
ceramics
   Fine Wares (India), 111
   Han dynasty-related fragments
      (China), 111
   Kalanay-related pottery (Philippines),
      111
   Khao Sam Kaeo (KSK), 111
   'Sa Huynh-Kalanay' style, 111, 121
   SHK-inspired, 111, 119, 126

   Thai-Local-1 products, 119
   Thai-Local-2-SHK-related pottery,
      125–7
ceramic stoves, at Bukit Tengkorak in
   Sabah, 87
Chamic languages, of Vietnam, 163
charcoal kilns, 150
Chaw Lay ('sea gypsies' of Phuket), 20,
   255–6
   adaptive capacity of, 262–74
   behavioural predictions, 261
   catchment area exploited by, 264
   conceptual organisation and use of
      space, 266
   cultural mapping of, 258
   exploitations of sea resources, 264
   genetic mapping of, 256
   knowledge of spirit, 268
   knowledge sharing, 268
   Malayo-Polynesian dialects, 257
   maritime adaptation in Southeast
      Asia, 261
   problem-solving strategy, 276
   Rawai base camp, 279
   resilience system, 279
   re-use of materials and tools, 267
   social-ecological sustainability, 267
   subsistence strategy, 264
   thresholds of, 278–80
   tools of remembrance, 280
   tools used by, 267
Chinese junks, 198, 202, 204, 219
Chinese naval charts
   cartographic skills, 208
   Mao Kun map, 208
   Selden Map, 208, 210
   voyages of Zheng He, 208
Chinese *thau-ke* (bosses), in the Malay,
   149–50
Ch'in-Kuei-Shan (Jinguishan), 8
Christian missionaries, 153
climate change, 310
cloves, trade in, 217
coastal adaptation, 7
coastal caves, 125–7
   links with inland caves, 127–8

coastal communities, 8, 18, 20, 29, 45, 87, 116, 237, 248, 301
  in eastern Indonesia, 20
coastal dwellings, architecture of, 11, 130, 132, 142, 293, 296
coastal fishing, 14–15, 167
coastal shipping, 11
cobble-based industries, 81
colonial States, territorial waters of, 312
coral bleaching, 310
coral reefs, 178, 216, 311, 328, 333, 346
Coral Triangle, 216, 302, 304
cordmarked pottery, 82–3
cornelian, 9
corvée labour, 224
cross-cultural interactions, 8, 216
cross-fertilising exchanges, 8
cross-straits interaction, antiquity of, 172
cross-straits traffic, 15, 169
cultural community, 307
cuttlefish, 150
cyanide fishing 310–11

Da But culture, of North Vietnam, 106
Dalan Serkot Cave (Luzon), 76
  mortuary disposals in jars, 76
dalle, concept of, 352
Dàn, 14, 169
Dayak Ngaju, 191, 193
  languages of Southeast Borneo, 288
Decapterus spp., 349
dermabrasions, 259–60
desa (administrative village), 317, 332
detaching small flakes, technology of, 81
development of sea nomadism, stages of
  early trade, 8–9
  maritime expansion, 7–8
  palaeolithic evidence of movement between islands, 7
dialects of Malay, 12
dilau, 214
Dili, Haji, 350–1
distribution, of sea nomads, 11–12
  in Southeast Asia, 13

domesticated plants, 54
domesticates found in Lapita sites, ISEA dates for, 80
domestication of animals, 78
Dong Son drums, 8, 109, 120, 122–3, 125, 128, 204, 284
Duano language, 162
dugong (*duyong*), 216, 239, 243
Dutch-Bugis alliance, 215
Dutch United East India Company, 19, 290
  conquest of
    Bugis, 220
    Gowa-Talloq, 220
    Makassar, 220
Duyong Cave, Palawan (Philippines), 53, 71–2, 81
  polished stone adze, 81

earthenware burial jars, 116
Eastern Sulawesi
  Bajau clusters in, 332
  core Bajau villages in, 332–3
  distribution and flow of the Bajau population in, 344
  geo-demographic features in, 332–44
East Kalimantan, 65, 67, 84
East Timor, 17, 20, 283, 289, 293
  Bunaq people of, 288–9
  Fataluku NAN language, 296
economic alliance, 129
economically-specialised groups, 103
economic migrations, 105
environmental diversity, 102
estuarine caves, 125–7
  links with inland caves, 127–8
ethnic identity, 1, 21, 185, 242, 327, 352–3
ethno-archaeological project, 10
ethno-archaeology, 255, 257–8
European colonialists
  dominance of, 145
  stance on the seafarers, 145
European mariners, 200

exchange networks involving Neolithic elements
  archaeologically attested maritime interaction axes, 86
  cobble-based industry, 81
  contact between southwest Sulawesi and Java, 81
  cordmarked pottery, 82
  'geometric incised and impressed' pottery of Yunnan origins, 83
  Gua Sireh pottery, 82–3
  Hoabinhian lithics, 81
  during Holocene period, 86
  lithics characterisation of, 82
  mtDNA haplogroup dispersals, 86
  Neolithic material technology, 81
  obsidian arrowheads, 81
  during Pleistocene period, 85
  polished stone tools, 81
  pottery characterisation of sites, 83
  red-slipped pottery, 82, 84
  stone artefacts, 81
existence of sea nomads, 15–16
exploited resources, translocation of, 52, 53–4, 62

Farming and Language Dispersal Hypothesis (FLDH), 295
Fataluku language, 296
faunal translocation, in Holocene period, 77–80
  appearance of wallabies, 77
  civet species, 79–80
  deer species, 79
  domesticated pig
    'Lanyu clade' of, 78
    'Pacific clade' of, 80
  Eurasian wild boar, 78
  inter-island faunal exchange, 77–8
  Java porcupine, 80
  long-tailed macaque, 80
  Macrogalidia musschenbroekii, 80
  Maros karsts, 78–9
  marsupial axis, 77
  in Misool Island, 77
  Nagsabaran *S. scrofa*, 78
  'Pacific clade' of domestic pigs, 80
  placental translocation, 79
  Rattus tanezumi, 80
  Southeast Asian sites with, 78, 79
  Sulawesi warty hog, 78
  'Toalean' inhabitants, 78
  translocated placental axis, 80
feeder trade, 131, 159
fisher-forager systems, 7, 18, 107, 199
fisherman-borrower debt relationship, 309
fish hooks, 28–9
  from Alor Island, 37–40
  circular rotating hooks, 37
  concentric hooks, 44
  J-shaped jabbing hook, 29, 31, 43
  made of *Rochia nilotica*, 29, 44
  profile and position of, 38
  radiocarbon dating, 29
  from Timor-Leste, 29–35
Fix's hypotheses, 128
Flores, 19, 35, 41, 43, 51, 71, 178, 218, 223, 225, 311, 313, 333, 354
  Gowa conquests of, 228
  Larantuka in, 290
  Liang Bua in, 62, 78, 80
  Papuq-ruled settlements on, 221
  Sea Bajau dialect, 180
  translocation of *Sus celebensis* to, 85
Flores Sea, 180, 227, 346
food production, ecological constraints on, 102
forest foragers, role in collecting goods for trading states, 103
forest nomads, 246
  of Batam Island, 16
French-Thai Archaeological Mission, 17, 106, 109, 122, 128

Garassiq seaport, 218
gene flow, 106, 129–30, 189
  of genetic lineages, 190
  between populations, 183
  South Asian, 190

genetic ancestries, of the Kendari Bajau, 189–93
geochemical fingerprinting, 46
Geographic Information System (GIS), 325
'geometric incised and impressed' pottery, of Yunnan origins, 83
glass artefacts, 111–13
    Ban Na Hyan glass waste, 113, 123
    Chinese, 128
    compositions of, 123
    inland transhipment sites, 113
    Lapidary glass beads and bracelets, 117
    later Late Prehistoric South China Sea style, 122
    pattern of distribution of, 117
    at site of Pang Wan, 123
    turquoise blue beads, 128
    in upper Thai-Malay Peninsula, 111
gold panning, 5
Golo Cave, 69, 72
gout, 286
Gowa-Talloq, kingdom of, 215, 221, 230
    adoption of Islam, 219
    conquest by Dutch United East India Company, 220
    dominance in Sulawesi, 219
    expansion and incorporation of surrounding Sulawesi polities, 224
    inland-agrarian orientation, 219
    Karaeng Matoaya of, 219
    lontaraq bilang (royal annals) of, 226
    Makassarese kingdom of, 218
    Makassarese subjects and Sama Bajau allies, 219
    naval expeditions in eastern Indonesia, 219
    overseas expansion, 228
    period of expansion, 219
    relationship with Papuq Sama Bajau polity, 223–9
    social and political hierarchy, 230
    sphere of influence, 219
    status and socio-political importance of the Sama Bajau in, 226
    Sultan Ala'uddin of, 219
    Sultan Malikussaid of, 227
    trade networks and socio-political relations, 219
    wars of Islamisation, 219
Gua Harimau, in South Sumatra, 64, 68
Gua Lawa, Java, 53
Gua Pandan, 81
Gua Sagu (Malay Peninsula), 64
Gua Sireh (Sarawak), 82–3
Gulf of Bone, 218, 231n9
Gulf of Siam, 104, 109

Han
    ceramics, 126–7, 130
    dynasty (206 BCE–220 CE), 14, 111, 169
hawksbill turtle, 145
high-keel boats, of the Yami on Lanyu Island, 201
Hijau, Haji, 352
Hikayat Merong Mahawangsa, 6
'Hoabinhian' industries, 81
Hokkien dialect of Min, 14, 169
Hoklo, 14–15, 167, 169
Holocene, 3, 7, 17, 21, 28, 36–7, 41, 45, 53, 66–8, 72–87, 106, 236, 359
Hominims, 7
honey, trade in, 20, 110, 217, 292
Hooijer, D.A., 79
houseboats, 12, 14–15, 167, 169, 323
human genetics, 84, 189
human translocation, 52
hunter-gatherer lifestyle, 105

Identity-By-Descent (IBD) information, 190–2
Indianised kingdoms, in western Indonesia, 190, 193
Indian Ocean shipping, 204, 207
Indic religious traits, 9
Indo-Malay Archipelago, 216, 220
Indonesia
    Bajau sea nomads in, *see* Bajau Sea nomads, in Indonesia

Gowa-Talloq naval expeditions in, 219
Kayoa Island, 328
marine resources in, 216
Portuguese traders, 198
Riau-Lingga Archipelago of, 142
settlement clusters in, 332
shell beads in, 28
spice trade, 181
Indonesian Bajau, 302–4, 307, 313, 316n5
Indo-Pacific region
    development and structuring of population interactions in, 177
    origins of sea nomads in, 283–4
industrial fishing, 310
infants, burial of, 76
inland caves, 125
    estuarine, costal and offshore caves links with, 127–8
inland-relay stations, 122
inland river boatmen, 158
inland sites
    cave sites, 125
    open-air transhipment, 122
    transhipment places and collecting centres, 122–5
    types of, 122
Insular Asia, 177
inter-ethnic network, 107
inter-island
    exchanges, 3, 8, 16, 130–1, 211
    trade network, 5, 7, 18, 20, 208, 284, 323
    traffic in South China Sea, 199
    translocation, 53
    transport of scarce items, 17
international trade, development of, 145, 148–9, 152, 217, 284, 309
inter-population relationships, 183
inter-regional trade, 132, 177
inter-visible islands, connections between, 51, 66
'invisibility' of sea nomads, 2–3
Irian Jaya, 287
Iron Age, 103, 107, 117
    trading polities in Central Vietnam, 110

Island Southeast Asia (ISEA), 1, 3–4, 7, 12, 45, 157, 177, 282
    adoption of pottery in, 285
    agricultural origins in, 54
    anatomically modern humans (AMH), 51, 70
    ancient adaptation to, 284–5
    Austronesian diaspora, 28
    dispersal of populations during Pleistocene-Holocene transition, 51
    early osseous artefacts, 66–8
    emergence of maritime societies in, 142
    evolution of maritime technology indigenous to, 198
    fish hooks, 28–9
    Holocene connections with Melanesia, 53
    long-distance exchange networks, 17
    maritime exchange in, 53
    mortuary practices, 74–6
    movement of Malayo-Polynesian speakers from Taiwan into, 51
    navigational techniques in, 207
    Neolithic occupants of, 73
    obsidian traffic, 76–7
    'Pacific clade' of domestic pigs, 80
    Pleistocene rock art, 64–6
    practice of sea nomadism in, 157
    pre-Iron Age archaeological sites in, 54
    pre-Neolithic inter-island network, 87
    shell ornaments and tools, 328
Isthmus of Kra, *see* Kra Isthmus

Japanese mariners, 204
Java
    contact with southwest Sulawesi, 81
    Gua Lawa, 53
    Song Gupuh, 68
    Song Terus, 68
Java porcupine (*Hystrix javanica*), 80
Java Sea, 204, 346
Johor, Sultan of, 145

Jolo, trading community of, 5
junk, *see* Chinese junks

kabang, 247
Kalah of Arab, 129
Kalimantan (Borneo), 65, 314
Kallonna, Gowa Tumapaqrisiq, 225
Kangean Archipelago, 178, 305, 307, 328, 345–9
　population change in, 350
Kayoa Island (Indonesia), 328
Kedah Annals, *see* Hikayat Merong Mahawangsa
Kendari Bajau community, 18
　Austronesian influence on, 189
　genetic ancestries of, 193
　genetic diversity in, 185, 189
　origins and genetic structure of, 182
Khao Sam Kaeo (KSK), 111
Khok Phanom Di (Thailand), 104
kin-based territories, 148–9
kinship-infused cultural-economic units, 131, 149–50
kinship system, of nomads, 239, 242–3
knowledge sharing, 268
　intergenerational nature of, 268
Ko Ko Khao, 249–50
Ko Phra Thong (Phang Nga Province), 249–50
Kra Isthmus, 8, 10–11, 17, 22, 103–4, 106, 109, 114, 129, 170, 250
　trans-Isthmian trade, 170
　use of land routes across, 170
Kria Cave, in Western Papua, 68
Kuala Selinsing, 8
Kuk Swamp, 236
kunlun bo, 202

lambere Bayo, 229
land-based
　lifestyle, 132
　trading groups, 133
land nomads, 1, 296n1
Langkawi archipelago, 6

Lang Rongrien, 63, 76
languages of sea nomads, 157–8
　Andaman Sea languages, 162–5
　Austronesian languages, 158
　baong Sama (Bajau language), 346, 353
　Baun Same (Bajau language), 313
　Borneo languages, 159
　Duano language, 162
　linguistic affiliations, 158
　Malayic language, 162
　Malayo-Polynesian languages, 302
　Orang Laut languages, 160–2
　Proto Sama Bajau language, 304
　Sama Bajau of Sulu (Philippines), 180
　Samalic (Bajau) languages, 159–60, 180, 303
　Sekak group of dialects, 162
　Sulawesi Bajau language, 313
Lapita
　cemetery, 285
　dates for domesticates found in, 80
　expansion, 7
　pottery, 71, 295
large-scale trading, development of, 211, 284
laser ablation-inductively coupled plasma-mass spectrometry (LA-ICP-MS), 35, 110
Last Glacial Maximum, 41
Lemo bajo lontaraq manuscript, 19, 223
Lesser Sunda Islands, 30, 182, 193, 313, 316
　construction and evolution of societies in, 282
　linguistic and population origin in, 287–8
　shell decorative items from, 35
Liang Sarru, 51, 63
Lihuwai, Dahu, 291
Lihuwai, Rika, 291
linguistic affiliation, of sea nomad populations, 158
　Austronesian (AN) languages, *see* Austronesian (AN) languages
　in Lesser Sunda, 287–8
　Melanesian Linguistic Area, 288

Papuan languages, 288
  Timor-Alor-Pantar (TAP) family, 288
Liu Chhiu Kuo Chih Lüeh of 1757, 204
log-coffins, 202
Lolo Bajau of Sanrabone, 215, 223, 225, 231n7
long-tailed macaque, 80
Lontaraq Bajo Lemobajo, 220
lontaraq bilang manuscripts, 19, 222, 223, 226, 230n6
lowland trading polities, rise of, 104
Luzon, 51
  Dalan Serkot Cave, 76
  technology of detaching small flakes, 81

mace, trade in, 217
Madagascar, 15, 18, 133, 157–8, 166–7, 170, 282
  colonisation of, 157
madilau, 214
Madini, Haji Ustaz, 351–2
Madura Island, 346
magnetic compass, use of, 208
Mainland Southeast Asia (MSEA), 17, 54, 104, 189
  Austroasiatic substratum of, 84
  mortuary practices in, 76
  'Neolithic I' horizon of, 83
  'Pacific clade' of domestic pigs, 80
  shell ornaments and tools, 28
  Thai-Malay Peninsula, 76
Makassan seasonal voyages, 344
Makassar kingdom, 182
Makassar War (1666–69), 222, 230n6
Malacca, founding of, 6
Malacca Strait, 129, 132
Malagasy language, source of, 158, 170
Malayan ethnography, 16
Malayic language, 160, 162
Malayo-Polynesian
  languages, 20, 302
  speakers from Taiwan, 51, 71, 84, 87
Malay trading empire, 4, 6, 159–60
Mangewai, Daeng, 226

Manora (theatrical performance in Thailand), 248
maps
  cartographic, 146
  cognitive, 146
  definitions of, 146
  process cartography, 147
  updating of, 147
marginalised people, 4, 143
marine nomadic lifestyle, 1
marine shell ornaments, 69–73
  early Holocene marine shell scraper axis, 73
  at Golo Cave in Moluccas, 72
  Hoabinhian shell mounds of northeast Sumatra, 73
  at Pamwak site on Manus, 72
  Southeast Asian sites with, 71, 72
  tradition of, 71
  Tridacna adzes, 71–2
  use in early to mid-Holocene (9–6000 BP), 72
maritime-adapted inhabitants, of the Andaman Sea
  adaptive cycle of, 269–74
  Chaw Lay, *see* Chaw Lay ('sea gypsies' of Phuket)
  cultural resilience, 254–5
  levels of resilience, 254
  mapping of the elements of, 259
  Phuket Project, *see* Phuket Project
  'sea gypsies' of Phuket, 20, 254
maritime archaeology, 5, 18
maritime creolisation, 180, 182, 193
maritime exchange systems, 16
  in ISEA, 53
maritime expansion, 7
maritime-focused economy, 285
maritime forager-traders, 7, 21
maritime hunter-gatherers, 177
maritime lifestyle, 14–15, 132, 169
maritime networks, 21, 46, 53, 87, 127–8, 177, 344
maritime peoples, classification of, 158
maritime resource exploitation and trade, 287

Maritime Silk Road, 5, 17, 21, 103, 128–9, 133
   development of, 104
   trading polities, 109
   transpeninsular routes, 104
maritime Southeast Asia
   development of, 2
   trading polities in, 6
maritime states, rise of, 5
maritime subsistence strategies
   adaptive capacity, 262–9
   resilience concepts applicable to, 261–74
maritime technology, 157, 159, 198, 208, 284–5
maritime trading network, 178, 193
maritime world, movement and mapping of, 146–7
Maros caves, 64
marsupial species, appearance of at North Maluku sites, 53
mastery of the sea, 3–5, 143, 215, 287
masuk malayu, 245
material culture style, in ports-of-trade, 115
materials and methods, to study Southeast Asian archaeological sites, 54
material technology, during Neolithic period, 81
   for detaching small flakes from cores, 81
   polished stone tools, 81
   stone artefacts, 81
Matoaya, Karaeng, 219
matrimonial alliances, 129–30
Melus people, 289
mental mapping, of maritime routes, 4
mercantile innovation, 169–70
mercantile sea-traders, evolution of, 169
Mergui Archipelago, 12, 243, 244, 246, 247
Mergui-Prachuap Khiri Khan route, 132
metal working, 9
micro-excavations, 259
Micronesians, 199

Mien (Yao), 14, 167
Minangkabau (West Sumatra), 301
mitochondrial DNA of sea nomads, 182, 183
mobile intermediaries, 8
mobile sea voyagers, 286
Moken (Austronesian-speaking group), 178, 246
   ethnicity of, 245
   extracting tin from the river in Ko Ra, 251
   flotilla of, 242
   Freshwater Moken (*moken oèn*), 246
   impact of Burmese marine fisheries on, 245
   intermarriages with Burmese fishermen, 245
   of Ko Phra Thong, 250
   languages of, 12
   mitochondrial DNA (mtDNA) of, 182
   in Myanmar, 243, 244–6
   as Olang Kalah, 250
   practice of fishing, 246
   Sea Moken (*moken okèn*), 246
   social space of, 243
   socio-economic organisation, 246
   squid fishing, 245
   strategies to perpetuate their identity, 246
   threats to their ways of life, 244–5
Moklen (Strait of Malacca), 4
Mommiq, Daeng Manggappa, 226
monsoon rains, 150
mortuary practices, in Pleistocene/Holocene transition, 74–6
   burial of infants, 76
   burials in Wallacea, 74
   cremations/fractional burials, 76
   disposal of adults, 76
   disposals in jars, 76
   of early Holocene age, 74
   flexed burials, 76
   flexed inhumations, 76
   fractional burials, 74
   at Niah's West Mouth, 74, 75

pit burials, 75
  at Sa'gung Rockshelter, 75
  Southeast Asian sites with, 75
  Sundaland and Wallacea burials, 74, 76
  at Tabon Caves, 75
mother-of-pearl, 145, 333
multi-ethnic trading polities, 133
multiple genetic ancestries, 189–94
Myanmar, sea nomads of, 103

Nassarius globosus, 33
Nassarius pullus, 33
Nautilus pompilius, 31, 33, 39
Nautilus sp. shells, 17
navigation
  Chinese naval
    charts, 208
    manuals and related maps, 199
  cross-straits movements, 199
  discovery of Pacific Islands, 285–6
  evolution of, 198
  growth of expertise in, 6–7
  knowledge of star positions for, 199, 207–8
    Morning Star, 207
    Pleiades, 207
  magnetic compass, use of, 208
  mastery of, 282
  from the palaeolithic onwards, 199–202
  Proto-Malayo-Polynesian (PMP), 207
  routes for, *see* routes for ship navigation
  star charts of the Marshall Islands, 207
  techniques for
    crossing open ocean, 198
    mastering of, 131
  techniques in ISEA, 207
  voyages of Zheng He, 208
navigation chart
  astro-navigation chart, 209
  Mao Kun map, 208
  Selden Map, 208, 210

'Neolithic I' assemblages, in northern Sumatra, 83
neolithisation, process of, 7
nephrite, 109, 128, 130–1, 285
  circulation of, 8
New Guinea, 21, 72, 81, 84, 178, 190, 202, 216
Niah Caves, Borneo, 64, 66–7, 236
  cobble-based industries at, 81
  flexed inhumations in, 76
  mortuary practices in, 74–5
    mortuary disposals in jars, 76
  paddle-impressed pottery assemblages at, 83
nomadic societies
  act of
    cultural anthropophagy, 242
    social anthropophagy, 243
    turtle consumption, 242–3
  adaptability of, 246–8
  decline of, 239
  foragers, 105–6
  forest nomads, 246
  kinship system in, 239, 242–3
  lifeways of, 102
  myths (long cycles), 241
  nuclear family on a boat, 246
  pastoralism in, 157
  personal and social organisation of space, 244
  resource management and mobility, 241
  risk of incest in, 239
nomadism, concept of, 1
non-Austronesian (NAN) language, 287
  Fataluku language, 296
  Timor-Alor-Pantar (TAP), 288
  Wallacean languages, 288
North Borneo, 186, 302, 313, 316n1
  Malaysian territory of, 301
North Vietnam, 64, 67–8, 284
  Da But culture of, 106
Numalo, Daeng, 222, 226
Number of Identified Specimens (NISP), 37
Nurak, Liurai Suri, 291–2

Nusantao Maritime Trading and
    Communication Network
    (NMTCN), 107
Nusa Tenggara, 325, 349
    Bajau clusters in, 333
    Bajau migrations in, 345
    distribution and flow of the Bajau
        population in, 344
    geo-demographic features in, 332–44
nutmeg, trade in, 217

obsidian arrowheads, 81
obsidian artefacts, from sites in Timor-
    Leste, 17, 35–6
    geochemical characterisation of, 35–6
    geochemical finger-printing of, 35
    from Jerimalai shelter, 36
    from Laili Cave, 36
    obsidian traffic, 76–7
        Southeast Asian sites with, 77
    from TBL site ALOR, 41
    volcanic glass artefacts, 35
oceanic voyages, as a model of sea
    nomadism evolution, 286–7
ocean navigation, see navigation
offshore caves, 125–7
    links with inland caves, 127–8
Olang Pugam, 250
Oliva spp., 17, 33
open sea voyages, 285
Orang Asli (Malaysia), 1, 9, 105–6, 129,
    146
orang darat (land people), 145–6
Orang Laut, see Orang Suku Laut (Tribal
    People of the Sea)
orang lonta, 246
Orang Sawang, 12, 160
Orang Suku Laut, 1, 4–6, 9, 12, 16, 103,
    105, 131, 158, 214, 284, 315
    burial practices, 130
    charcoal kilns owned by, 150
    charcoal producing areas, 150
    as direct descendants of the early
        'oceanic nomads', 143
    ethnography of, 142–3
    existence at sea, 143–6
    identity of, 148
    knowledge and mapping of their
        water spaces, 151
    labelled as criminals by the colonial
        masters, 145
    languages of, 160–2
    lived experiences of, 148
    map of, 144
    marginal status of, 145
    maritime cultural landscape, 142
    matrimonial alliances, 129–30
    movements of the waves, winds, sun,
        moon and stars, 150–2
    navigational skills, 146
    networks of
        inter-related territories, 148–50
        kin-related territories, 149
    process of self-renewal and
        development, 148
    representation of maritime cultural
        space, 18
    seafaring activities of, 143
    as sea nomads, 142
    settlement in Riau, 160
    shipbuilding and navigation, 199
    story of
        Bari, 148
        Buntot, 153
        Ceco, 152–3
        Joya, 148
    Teluk Nipah island group, 149
    world of movements, 152–3

Pacific islands
    navigation and discovery of, 285–6
    Near and Remote Pacific islands, 285
    sea travels towards the Mariana
        Islands, 285
palimpsest, concept of, 105, 259, 266,
    271, 274, 276
palm civet, 79–80
Pambauan Island, 351
Panaikang, inland riverine polity of, 224
pancajaq, 229

pangajavas, 229
Pang Wan, 122–3, 127
Papua New Guinea, 34, 72, 84
  Bismarck Archipelago, 84
Papuq Sama Bajau polity, 19
Parameswara, *see* Sri Tri Buana (Prince of Palembang)
Pasir Panjang Wholesale Centre, Singapore, 150
patron-clients, of Bajau fishermen, 302, 309–10
pengusaha mandiri, 353
personal allegiances and alliances, 5
Phang Nga Bay, 250
Philippines, 5, 8, 12, 18, 21, 28, 43, 67, 76, 78, 80–1, 110–11, 116–19, 122, 125–32, 134, 145, 159, 180, 190, 202, 214, 282
Phuket Island Group of the Andaman Sea
  as international tourist destination, 255
  sea gypsies of, 255
Phuket Project, 254
  background to, 255–6
  ethno-archaeological approach of, 257–61
  objective of, 257
Phu Khao Thong Langsuan cave, 117–19, 126
Pia Hudale Cave, 35
Pinctada maxima, 43
piracy, threat of, 269
Pires, Tomé, 6
pit burials, in China and North Vietnam, 75
Pleistocene, 3, 17, 21, 28–9, 35–6, 41, 43–5, 51, 64–6, 70, 76, 84–5, 87, 143, 255, 295
Pleistocene rock art, 64–6
  AMH habitation deposits in ISEA, 64
  in Maros caves, 64
  Southeast Asian sites with, 65
P. margaritifera, 43
polished stone tools, 81
  of Bandung Plateau, 82
political alliance, 129

port-cities, emergence of, 17
port-entrepôts
  of Kedah region, 6
  leader, 5
  ruler, 5, 131–2
  ruler's navy, 5
port-of-trade leaders, 130
ports-of-trade, 128
  Ban Kluay Nok, 120
  bronze industry, 118
  ceramics artefacts, 116
  cosmopolitan character of, 116
  earthenware burial jars, 116
  immediate hinterland, 118–20
  imports from South and Southeast Asian regions, 116
  in later period, 120–2
  long-distance networks and, 120
  material culture style in, 115
  Phu Khao Thong, 120
  range of services the sea nomads provided to, 131
  as regional economic and cultural centres, 115–18
  Thai-Local-1 products, 119
  upstream-downstream/transpeninsular networks, 125
  workshops for producing stone ornaments, 117
Portuguese traders, in Indonesia, 198
pre-Austronesian maritime culture, 288
prehistorical and historical landscapes, interpretation of, 249–50
process cartography, 147
'proto-Bajau' homelands, 20
proto-globalisation processes, 177
Proto-Malayo-Polynesian (PMP), 163, 200, 207
Proto Sama-Bajau language, 304
Pulau Kelumpang, 8
  non-Indianised maritime groups of, 9
P'upien (Pubian), 8
'pure Bajau' (*asli orang Bajau*), 351–2

radiocarbon dating, 29, 31, 37

raids against passing ships and coastal
    settlements, 5
rapang collection, 225
Rattus tanezumi, 80
red-slipped pottery, 82, 84
    dispersal of, 84
regional exchange networks, 104, 107,
    169, 217
regional ports-of-trade, development of,
    115, 123
Remote Oceania islands, 285, 286
    settlement of, 282, 286
research on sea nomads, overview of, 16
Resilience Alliance, 261, 270–1, 279
Resilience Theory
    applicable to maritime subsistence
        strategies, 261–74
    concept of, 254, 261
    usefulness of, 261
resource collection, 245
revolt, concept of, 279–80
Riau-Lingga Archipelago, 15, 142, 149,
    160, 181, 247, 249, 262, 327
    Orang Laut settlement in, 12, 160
rice cultivation, 104–5
River Bertam (Malacca River), 6
river nomads, 3, 12, 167, 170
river trade, 5
Rochia nilotica, 29, 44
rock crystal, 9
Roman Catholic church, 153
rotan laut, 333
routes for ship navigation, 199
    Halmahera-Papua route, 199
Royal Palace of Gowa (South Sulawesi),
    19
Ryukyus, 3, 7, 199

Sabah community, 16
sabannaraq (harbourmaster), 225–6, 227
safety-valve strategy, 271
Safiyuddin, Karaeng Lempangang, 226
Sahul, 177, 282, 288
Sahulland, colonisation of, 51, 66, 68
sailfish (*Istiophorus* spp.), 164

sailing rafts, use of, 199, 205
sailing technology, 86–7
Sama-Bajau languages, 302, 314, 318,
    325
    tree diagram of, 304
Sama Bajau community, 4, 8, 20, 103,
    305
    adaptation to the marine
        environment, 214
    alliances formed with Gowa-Talloq,
        220, 223–9
    dialects of, 303
        tree diagram of, 304
    diasporic distribution and population
        flow, 325
    distribution of, 325
    in eastern Indonesia, 325
    of eastern Indonesia, 216–17
    ethnic formation of, 323
    followers of I Papuq, 228
    geographically dispersed communities
        of, 215
    habitat and distribution of, 328
        ethnic terms and previous studies
            on population movements,
            325–7
        sub-groups, 328–31
    intermarriage and exchange, 218
    of Katingang, Barasaq and Kandeaq,
        224
    under the leadership of the Papuq,
        220
    Lolo Bayo (Lolo Bajau) of Sanrabone,
        225
    Makassarese admiration of, 227
    Makassar War (1666–69), 222
    'malaisian' origin of, 313
    movements of, 20
    oral traditions and manuscripts
        (*lontaraq*), 220
    Papuq polity, 221–3
    rapang collection, 225
    role in history of Island Southeast
        Asia (ISEA), 215
    Samalan ethnolinguistic group, 214
    sea-centred lifestyle of, 215

as sea peoples, 214
settlements of, 323
skills and bravery on the sea, 227
'smuggling' on behalf of the Papuq, 227
social and cultural features distinguishing, 301
social hierarchy based on noble status, 223
sociopolitical status of, 215
in South Sulawesi, 217–21
of Sulu Archipelago, 305
Talloq voyages, 228
ula-ula, 223
Sama dilau (Sama of the sea), 214
Samalic (Bajau) languages, 12, 18, 132, 159–60, 167, 169, 288
Sama of Tawi-Tawi, 5, 131, 301
sandalwood trade, 9, 20, 130, 132, 217, 287, 289, 292
Sandao, 219, 225, 228
Sapeken Island (East Java), 21, 325
ethnic situation in, 349–52
population of, 349
changes in, 350
Sape Straits, 333
Sawu Sea, 333
scad (*Selar crumenophthalmus*), 164, 349
sea cucumbers, 5, 145, 149, 238, 245, 302, 309, 311, 317, 344
sea exploitation, 4
seafaring technologies, development of, 177
sea for human groups
formation of, 147
as network of inter-related territories, 148–50
sea gypsies, 9, 162
Chaw Lay ('sea gypsies' of Phuket), 20
of Phuket on the Andaman coast of Thailand, 254
Sama Bajau, 214
sea lanes, 2, 5, 131, 145, 295
Sea Moken (*moken okèn*), 246
sea nomadism, 293
antiquity of, 283
archaeology of, 104, 282
emergence of, 21
evolution of, 2
forms of, 6
inter-island exchanges, 8
oceanic voyages as a model of, 286–7
origin of, 16
Southeast Asian, *see* Southeast Asian sea nomadism
sea nomads, 2, 51, 130
activities of, 11
in archaeological assemblages, 2
definition of, 3–9
ethnography of, 301
existing populations related to, 12
historical chronicle relating to, 19
influence on local cultures, 20
invisibility of, 2–3
involved in craft activities, 10
longue-durée historical trajectory, 2
as lower class of Malays, 16
'marginal' groups and, 104
mastery of the sea, 4
material culture of, 10, 104
merchants of Southeast Asian origin, 287
mitochondrial DNA (mtDNA) of, 182
of Myanmar, 103
Orang Laut, 105
origin of, 9
in Indo-Pacific region, 283–4
relations with trading rulers, 6
Sama Bajau, 214
stages of development, 7
of Thailand, 103
upstream–downstream exchanges, 11
'Sea People' of Sulu, 301
sea peoples' languages, 129, 158
sea products for trade, 5
'seascape' for subsistence, 4
sea shells, used as ornaments in funerary deposits, 107
sea travels, towards the Mariana Islands, 282, 285
sedentary communities, 4
Sejarah Melayu, 6, 228

Selden map, of China and Southeast Asia, 18, 208, 210
Semitic shipping, 200
settlement by sea immigrants, process of, 286
sewn plank technology, 200
shell adzes, tradition of, 53, 69, 71–2, 84
shellfish, harvesting of, 37, 245, 262, 264–5, 276
shell ornaments and tools, 45
   beads and pendants, see beads and pendants
   Conus ornaments, 70
   fish hooks, 28–9
      in Timor-Leste, 29–35
   in Indonesia, 28
   Island Southeast Asia (ISEA), 28
   in Lapita assemblages, 28
   from Lesser Sunda Islands, 35
   Mainland Southeast Asia (MSEA), 28
   preceramic tradition of, 70
ship construction
   of Austronesian boats, 200
   boatbuilding, 199
   cargo ships of ISEA, 202
   cave paintings in Eastern Indonesia, 204
   Chinese ships, 198, 202
   divergence between ISEA ships and the Chinese tradition, 202
   double-hull construction, 202
   evidence for methods of
      archaeological, 204
      iconographic, 204–6
      textual, 202–4
   evolution of, 198, 201
   high-keel boats of the Yami on Lanyu Island, 201
   innovative aspects of, 200
   junk, features of, 204
   kunlun bo (foreign ships), 202
   outriggers, 200
   'ships of the dead' models, 202
   in South China Seas, 18, 199, 201
   techniques for, 6, 11
      European, 200
      lashed-lug technique, 200
      sewn planks, 200
   use of
      compartmentalised hull structure, 202–4
      iron nails, 202
ship technology, 225, 227
shipwrecks, 199
   Bakau wreck of Chinese origin, 204
   Java Sea Wreck, 204
   Phanom Surin shipwreck, 204
shuǐshàngrén, 14
Siamese trading ship, 204
Siang, Makassarese port polity of, 218
sima tax, 225
Singapore
   food chain supply, 150
   Pasir Panjang Wholesale Centre, 150
sinriliq Datu Museng (Makassarese tale), 227
slash-and-burn cycles, 249
slavery, threat of, 237, 241, 243–4, 246–7
social anthropophagy, act of, 243
social motivations, for long-distance interactions, 7
social networks, 43, 332
socio-cultural evolution, 287
socio-economically organised groups, 103
socio-political organisation, 4
Solheim's 'Western Lobe', 86
South Asian genetic lineages, 189
South China Sea, 64, 107, 116–17, 119, 133, 142
   evolution of shipping in, 204
   inter-island traffic in, 199
   maritime archaeology of, 5–6
   material culture of coastal groups bordering, 109
   shipbuilding techniques in, 18
   Taiwanese involvement in, 8
   trade-related polities in, 2
South China Sea Interaction Sphere, 157
Southeast Asian Maritime World, 323–5, 354n2
South Kedah entrepôts, 8

South Sulawesi, 301, 302
  ethnic groups of, 217
  inland agricultural wealth, 218
  Makassarese kingdom of Gowa in, 218
  role of the Bajau in, 19, 217–21
  Royal Palace of Gowa, 19
  sea-exploring people of, 302
  social and political landscape of, 217
  spice trade network, 218
  trade-based confederations, 218
  wars of Islamisation, 219
South Tetun, 289
South-West China, 284
space-time, Moken's notion of, 237–44
spice trade, 181, 218, 315
spiritual landscape, 1
squid fishing, 245
Sri Tri Buana (Prince of Palembang), 6
Srivijaya Empire, 20, 315
  construction of cargo ships, 200
  expansion of, 208
  Malay kingdom of, 181, 193
  rise of, 6, 159, 284
  thalassocracy of, 6
star positions, knowledge of, 199, 207–8
  Morning Star (*talaq), 207
  Pleiades (*buluq), 207
  star charts of the Marshall Islands, 207
stone assemblages, 113–15, 123
  chaîne opératoire, 113
  characterisation of, 113
  found in
    funerary deposits, 113
    port-settlements, 118
  Iron Age inhumations, 119
  in Isthmus of Kra, 114
  locally-made hybrid stone ornaments, 119
  pattern of distribution for, 117
Strait of Malacca, 4, 15, 129
Sukajadi Pasar, 73
Sulawesi, 51, 65, 84
  contact with Java, 81
  kingdom of Gowa-Talloq, 215

Sulawesi warty pig (*Sus celebensis*), 62, 85
Sulu Archipelago (Philippines), 12, 181, 305, 313, 315, 327
  Bajau migration to, 20
  introduction of Islam in, 20
  'Sulu Archipelago' hypothesis, 313–14
Sulu Sea, 15, 67, 284
Sulu State of the Philippines, 5
Suma Oriental, 6
  of Tomé Pires, 15
Sumatra, 1, 9, 12, 64, 68, 73, 75–6, 81, 83, 123, 129, 142, 158, 160, 162, 189–90, 208, 314–15, 355
Sumenep Regency, 346
Sunda shelf islands, 17, 87
Suriwa, Tunilabu ri, 222, 228
swidden-farmers, 103, 105
Syah, Mansur, Sultan, 228
symbiotic relationships, 102

Taiwan, 8, 14–15, 17, 29, 41, 43, 51, 71, 76, 78, 80–4, 87, 122, 130–1, 158, 169, 199–200, 207, 250, 285
Talaud Islands, 7, 51, 71, 157, 199
Tanka people, 12, 14, 158, 167
Taran, Berek Taran Mauk, 292
T. argyrostomus, 43
taukay (trade intermediaries), 238, 242, 245
  protection of, 241
Tectus niloticus, 29, 333
Teluk Nipah island group, 149, 151–2
Teouma cemetery, 11
Tetun, 289–93
  mythology, 291
Tetun-Terik linguistic area, 20
Thailand, 6, 10–12, 20, 74, 106–7, 116–18, 126, 131, 178, 182, 204, 239, 241, 245, 250, 254
  sea nomads of, 103
Thai-Malay Peninsula, 8, 82, 105, 126, 129
  arrival of Austroasiatic-speaking farmers, 105, 107

background of, 104–9
Ban Khao culture, 105–6
ceramic assemblages found in, 111
corpus of remains, 111–15
  ceramic assemblages, 111
  glass, 111–13
  stone, 113–15
cultural differentiation, 105
cultural profiles and socio-economic organisation, 115
economic migrations, 105
hunter-gatherer lifestyle, 105
during the late prehistoric period, 104–9
Late Prehistoric South China Sea style, 109
material culture of coastal groups bordering, 109
modes of environmental exploitation, 105
Neolithic lifestyle, 105
regional exchange networks, 104
rice cultivation, 104–5
riverine ports-of-trade, 115–22
social pattern, 105–6
SHK-related pottery from, 126
Tham Chaeng, 111, 115, 127–8
Tham Nam Lot, 107, 122
Tham Tuay, 111, 115, 118, 126–8
thousand ships, expedition of, 208
Tiang Wang Kang island, 150
Timor, 17, 29, 35–6, 41, 43–5, 51, 66, 85, 131–2, 199–200, 217, 225
  origin of Tetun speakers in, 290
Timor-Leste, 17, 65
  archaeological research in, 29
  Bui Ceri Uato (BCU) rockshelter, 29
  early osseous artefacts from, 66
  excavation programme in, 29
  influence of former sea nomads on today's cultural configuration, 287
  obsidian artefacts from, 35–6
  obsidian traffic, 76–7
  shell assemblages of, 44
  shell fish hooks, beads and pendants from, 29–35
tin mines, forced labour in, 242

Tonga islands, 286
tools of remembrance, 280
Toraja funerary monument, Waseput, 203
Tosen no Zu (Japanese scroll painting), 204
trade goods, 4, 6, 12, 14, 18, 167, 204
  diffusion of, 199–201
trade networks, 19, 211, 217–19, 284, 291, 314
  emergence of, 294–5
trade-related polities, in the South China Sea, 2
trading colonies, networks of, 5, 131, 133
trading states, rise of, 6, 9, 103
transhipment places and collecting centres, 122–5
trans-peninsular routes, 6, 104, 107, 122, 125
trepang (sea cucumber), 178, 216, 269, 309, 311, 344–6, 351, 354
'tribal' groups, 104
trinity of spices, 217
Trochus niloticus, 29
T. setosus, 43–4
tukar pasang (change in the tide), 151
Tumenanga ri Makkoayang, King, 224
Tunipalangga, King, 224
Tunipasuruq, King, 224, 228
Turbo marmoratus, 43–4
Turijeqneq (Makassarese: people of the water), 214, 222, 229
turtle consumption, act of, 242–3

Upper Thai-Malay Peninsula, 8, 17, 104, 111
Urak Lawoi (Strait of Malacca), 4, 6, 12, 129, 131, 160, 178, 239, 247, 249, 257
urn burials, spread of, 11, 285

vegeculture, 105
Vereenigde Oost-Indische Compagnie (VOC), *see* Dutch United East India Company

Vesoro kingdom, 292
Vezo hypothesis, 166–7, 168
Vezo of Madagascar, 18
volcanic glass artefacts, 35

Wakatobi Islands, 344
wars of Islamisation, 219, 226
Wat Pathumtaram (Ranong), 122
Wehali Kingdom, 20, 132, 287, 289, 290, 292
western Malayopolynesian (WMP), 162–3
West Timor, 180, 288–9, 333
White Chinese of Malacca, 293
wong kambang (Javanese/Balinese: floating people), 214

Wuring (Bajau village), 307–8, 333

x-ray diffraction (XRD), 32

Yami Island, high-keel boats of, 201

Zamboanga peninsula, 313
Zheng He, voyages of, 208
Zomia, 19, 251
    refuge zone of, 103
zone of marine resource exploitation, 345
zone of occurrence, 53